Intonation in Language Contact

Linguistik Aktuell/Linguistics Today (LA)

ISSN 0166-0829

Linguistik Aktuell/Linguistics Today (LA) publishes original monographs as well as edited collections on synchronic and diachronic linguistics. Studies in LA engage with empirical phenomena and theoretical questions as these are currently discussed in linguistics with the aim to establish robust empirical generalizations within a universalistic perspective.

For an overview of all books published in this series, please see
benjamins.com/catalog/la

General Editor

Elly van Gelderen
Arizona State University

Founding Editor

Werner Abraham
University of Vienna / University of Munich

Advisory Editorial Board

Josef Bayer
University of Konstanz

Cedric Boeckx
ICREA/UB

Guglielmo Cinque
University of Venice

Amy Rose Deal
University of California, Berkeley

Susann Fischer
University of Hamburg

Liliane Haegeman
Ghent University

Heejeong Ko
Seoul National University

William Kruger
Arizona State University

Terje Lohndal
Norwegian University of Science and Technology

Will Oxford
University of Manitoba

Ian Roberts
Cambridge University

Florian Schäfer
Humboldt University

Carola Trips
University of Mannheim

C. Jan-Wouter Zwart
University of Groningen

Volume 286

Intonation in Language Contact. The case of Spanish in Catalonia
by Jonas Grünke

Intonation in Language Contact
The case of Spanish in Catalonia

Jonas Grünke
Johannes-Gutenberg-Universität Mainz

John Benjamins Publishing Company
Amsterdam / Philadelphia

The paper used in this publication meets the minimum requirements of the American National Standard for Information Sciences – Permanence of Paper for Printed Library Materials, ANSI z39.48-1984.

DOI 10.1075/la.286

Cataloging-in-Publication Data available from Library of Congress:
LCCN 2024039295 (PRINT) / 2024039296 (E-BOOK)

ISBN 978 90 272 1816 2 (HB)
ISBN 978 90 272 4634 9 (E-BOOK)

© 2024 – John Benjamins B.V.
No part of this book may be reproduced in any form, by print, photoprint, microfilm, or any other means, without written permission from the publisher.

John Benjamins Publishing Company · https://benjamins.com

Table of contents

CHAPTER 1. Introduction ... 1

CHAPTER 2. Spanish-Catalan language contact and Catalonian Spanish ... 7

2.1 Spanish-Catalan language contact: Historical background and present sociolinguistic situation   7
2.2 Research into Catalan-contact Spanish   17
2.3 Linguistic features of Catalan-contact Spanish   24
    2.3.1 Lexical and grammatical features of CCS   24
    2.3.2 Segmental features of CCS phonetics and phonology   32
    2.3.3 Suprasegmental features of CCS phonetics and phonology   37

CHAPTER 3. Theoretical background and description of Castilian Spanish and Central Catalan intonation ... 42

3.1 Intonation   42
    3.1.1 Models of intonation and annotation systems   42
        3.1.1.1 Autosegmental-Metrical model   45
        3.1.1.2 ToBI   56
    3.1.2 Intonation of Castilian Spanish and Central Catalan in comparison   59
        3.1.2.1 Inventory of pitch accents and boundary tones   63
        3.1.2.2 Intonational tunes in Castilian Spanish and Central Catalan   67
3.2 Language contact   80
    3.2.1 Key terms and approaches   80
    3.2.2 Contact-induced phonological change   99
    3.2.3 Transfer and convergence at the intonational level: Case studies   102
3.3 Bilingualism and language dominance   110

CHAPTER 4. Methodology, speakers, and data ... 126

4.1 Assessing language dominance   126
4.2 Speakers   130
    4.2.1 Language history   136
    4.2.2 Language use   139

4.2.3 Language proficiency   142
4.2.4 Language attitudes   143
4.3 Materials and procedure   144
    4.3.1 Semi-spontaneous data   145
    4.3.2 Read data   147

CHAPTER 5. Results   159

5.1 Intonational analysis   159
    5.1.1 Neutral statements   159
        5.1.1.1 Neutral declarative statements   160
        5.1.1.2 Enumerations   169
        5.1.1.3 Peripheral elements   171
    5.1.2 Biased statements   180
        5.1.2.1 Contrastive-focus statements   180
        5.1.2.2 Exclamative statements   183
        5.1.2.3 Contradiction statements   185
        5.1.2.4 Dubitative statements   188
    5.1.3 Neutral polar questions   189
        5.1.3.1 Information-seeking yes–no questions   189
            5.1.3.1.1 Overview of the analysed neutral yes–no questions   192
            5.1.3.1.2 Intonation of information-seeking yes–no questions without *que*   195
            5.1.3.1.3 Information-seeking yes–no questions headed by *que*   219
            5.1.3.1.4 Peripheral elements in yes–no question of more than one tonal unit   225
            5.1.3.1.5 Effects of speaker origin and language dominance   227
            5.1.3.1.6 Summary: Information-seeking yes–no questions   230
        5.1.3.2 Disjunctive questions   231
    5.1.4 Biased polar questions   235
        5.1.4.1 Exclamative yes–no questions (with counterexpectational meaning)   235
        5.1.4.2 Confirmation-seeking yes–no questions   240
    5.1.5 Neutral wh-questions   243
    5.1.6 Biased wh-questions   254
        5.1.6.1 Exclamative wh-questions   254
        5.1.6.2 Imperative wh-questions   258

5.1.7 Echo questions   262
  5.1.7.1 Echo yes–no questions   262
  5.1.7.2 Echo wh-questions   264
  5.1.7.3 Exclamative echo yes–no questions
   (with counterexpectational meaning)   267
 5.1.8 Imperatives   270
  5.1.8.1 Commands   270
  5.1.8.2 Requests   272
 5.1.9 Vocatives   275
 5.1.10 Supplementary analysis of Girona Spanish read speech   278
  5.1.10.1 Girona Spanish *que*-questions   278
  5.1.10.2 Girona Spanish dislocations   285
5.2 Tonal inventory of Girona Spanish and Girona Catalan   288
 5.2.1 Phonological status of the prenuclear pitch accents in Girona
  Spanish and Girona Catalan   288
 5.2.2 Phonological status of the nuclear configurations of inner ips
  in Girona Spanish and Girona Catalan   292
 5.2.3 Phonological status of the nuclear configurations of IPs
  in Girona Spanish and Girona Catalan   294
 5.2.4 Inventory of pitch accents and boundary tones in Girona
  Spanish and Girona Catalan   305

CHAPTER 6. Discussion   309
6.1 Similarities and differences between the prosodic systems of Girona
 Spanish and Girona Catalan   310
6.2 Variation in Girona Spanish and Girona Catalan   312
6.3 Prosodic distance between Girona Spanish and Castilian Spanish
 and between Girona Catalan and other Central Catalan varieties   317
6.4 How can the similarities and differences between the GS and GC
 intonational systems be explained in terms of language contact?   324
 6.4.1 Neutral statements   324
 6.4.2 Biased statements   325
 6.4.3 Polar questions   329
 6.4.4 Wh-questions   341
 6.4.5 Echo questions   344
 6.4.6 Imperatives   346
 6.4.7 Vocatives   347
 6.4.8 Summary: The prosodic systems of current GS
  and current GC   348

6.5   The status of Girona Spanish (and Catalonian Spanish) as a distinctive variety within the Spanish diasystem   351
6.6   How does contact-induced intonational change work?   353
6.7   Which intonational features are likely to be transferred?   357

CHAPTER 7.   Conclusion   360

Bibliography   364

Appendix   407
1.   Participants' dominance scores and Complementarity Index   408
2.   Language Background Questionnaire (Catalan version)   410
3.   Language Background Questionnaire (Spanish version)   415
4.   Intonation surveys (Spanish and Catalan)   420
5.   Dialogue (with translation)   426

Index   427

Abbreviations

AM	autosegmental-metrical
Cat.	Catalan
CatD	Catalan-dominant
CatS	Spanish spoken in the Autonomous Community of Catalonia, Catalonian Spanish
CC	Central Catalan
CCS	Catalan-contact Spanish, i.e. Spanish spoken in Catalan-speaking regions
CLI	cross-linguistic influence
CR	continuation rise
CS	Castilian Spanish
CYNQ	confirmation-seeking yes–no question(s)
DCT	discourse completion task
F0	fundamental frequency
GC	Girona Catalan
GS	Girona Spanish
ILD	index of language dominance
ip	intermediate phrase
IP	intonation(al) phrase
IYNQ	information-seeking yes–no question(s)
L1	first language
L2	second language
LD	language dominance
Oc.	Occitan
SD	standard deviation
SLA	second-language acquisition
SP	sustained pitch
Sp.	Spanish
SpD	Spanish-dominant
SVO	subject–verb–object
ToBI	Tone and Break Indices

CHAPTER 1

Introduction

The varieties of Catalan and Spanish spoken in present-day Catalonia[1] provide outstanding examples of long-lasting and intense contact between two closely related Romance languages. The historical background helps understand how these two varieties came about: the territories of what is now Catalonia used to constitute the centre of gravity of the Crown of Aragon until 1479, when the dynastic union with the Crown of Castile ensuing the marriage of the Catholic Kings in 1469 and their joint rule marked the *de facto* formation of Spain (see Ferrando 2020). As a consequence thereof, Spanish in a century-long process began to supplant Catalan in virtually all public domains – especially so after the enaction of the *Nueva Planta* decrees (1707–1716), which formally united the kingdoms and made Spanish the sole official language of the state (i.e. banning other languages from use in, e.g., courts, education, or printing). Nonetheless, Catalan never ceased to be the every-day spoken language of all social classes in Catalonia and it is relatively safe to presume that the lion's share of the population was effectively monolingual until well into the 20th century, i.e. in most cases Spanish was only learned as a foreign language at school (see Bernat et al. 2019, 2020; Vila 2020a: 632–636). After various short interludes during which Catalan succeeded to regain a co-official status at the beginning of the 20th century, its repression finally reached its peak under the Francoist regime (1939–1978), when all signs of Catalan identity were severely prohibited from the public sphere and the use of Catalan was relegated to the familial domain. In 1979, after the recovery of democracy, when virtually all Catalan-speakers had become fully bilingual, Catalan anew obtained a co-official status through the Statute of Autonomy of the newly formed Autonomous Community of Catalonia. Since then, it has re-entered all domains of public life in Catalonia, especially the educational and administrative ones, and is even considered a prestige language (Ramallo 2018: 478). Nevertheless, due to the massive and ongoing influx of Spanish-speaking immigrants setting in at the beginning of the 20th century and reaching its peaks between the '50s and '70s and in the first decade of the 21st century, Spanish has

---

1. In this book, I will use the designation Catalonia first and foremost to refer to the present-day Autonomous Community of Catalonia, which is somewhat smaller than the historic Principality of Catalonia that also comprised areas belonging to France today (the so-called *Catalunya del Nord*).

by now become the most widely spoken language and the most common initial language in Catalonia (Vila 2016: 145, 2020a: 634f.). The two languages therefore remain in close contact, and their speakers today are almost invariably bilingual (see, e.g., Boix-Fuster/Sanz 2008). Still, significant differences persist between individual speakers and speaker groups regarding their actual language use and proficiency or, in other words, their language dominance,[2] such that Catalonia's current sociolinguistic situation is characterized by a bilingual continuum with different degrees of competence and use at the individual level (Arnal 2011: 13–15; see also Boix-Fuster 2015).

The results of the secular and ever more intense contact between Catalan and Spanish in Catalonia are said to be mutual influences detected in different linguistic domains, such as phonetics and phonology, morphology, syntax, or the lexicon (for Catalan influence on local Spanish see, e.g., Moll 1961; Badia i Margarit 1979, 1981; Wesch 1992, 1997; Casanovas Català 1995, 2000; Argenter et al. 1998; Sinner 2004, and Section 2.3; for Spanish influence on Catalan see Fabra 1912: IXf., 1925; Payrató 1985; Colón 1993; Veny 2006; Lleó et al. 2009; Cortés et al. 2009; Arnal 2011; Ferrando/Nicolás 2011: 294f., 341, 525–530; Benet et al. 2011, among many others). However, the effects of the close contact on the prosodic properties of the two languages have hardly received any attention to date: while cross-linguistic influence (CLI) has been almost completely neglected in the research on Catalan intonation (flourishing in recent years; see, e.g., Prieto 2002a, 2014; Prieto/Cabré 2007–2012, 2013; Escudero et al. 2012; Prieto et al. 2015, among numerous others), what we know about the intonation of Spanish spoken in present-day Catalonia and other Catalan-speaking areas does not exceed a few impressionistic remarks and some cursory, rather data-poor studies of neutral declaratives and yes–no questions.[3] Likewise, the effects of the almost generalized bilingualism that characterizes the Catalan society today have not sufficiently been taken into account so far: only in very recent years have researchers begun to consider language dominance as an explanatory factor for the variation observed across Catalan–Spanish bilingual speakers (e.g. Simonet 2008, 2011, 2015; Davidson 2012, 2015a, 2020; Amengual 2016; Machuca 2016; Ramírez/Simonet 2017; Amengual/Simonet 2020; Hualde/Nadeu 2020, among others).

The present book, which represents a revised and shortened version of my dissertation (Grünke 2022), attempts to fill this research gap in that it presents a

---

2. For a definition and an extensive discussion of the term *language dominance* see Sections 3.3 and 4.1.

3. Note, however, that the intonation of statements and yes–no questions in the Spanish and Catalan spoken by bilinguals in Majorca has been thoroughly examined by Simonet (2008, 2010, 2011).

thorough investigation into the intonation of both Catalan and Spanish as spoken by bilinguals in Girona.[4] The major goal is thus to offer a detailed description of the intonational patterns of the two contact varieties spoken there, bearing in mind the speakers' language dominance and its effects on their phonetic realizations, so that a more comprehensive understanding of intonational variation in both Romance languages may be achieved. A broad initial approach, enabling principled dialectal comparisons, is pursued to enrich our current knowledge of pan-Hispanic and pan-Catalan intonation and with the secondary aim of opening questions for further research on more specific issues. Given the pioneer character of the enterprise of providing an ample description of its intonational intricacies, a somewhat stronger focus will be allocated to Girona Spanish. In addition to this, the following research questions will be addressed:

1. How similar is the intonation of Girona Spanish and Girona Catalan?
2. How uniform is the intonation of the two contact varieties spoken in Girona across speaker groups and individual speakers? Can variation be linked to bilingualism factors such as language dominance?
3. What are the differences and similarities between Girona Spanish and Castilian Spanish intonation? What are the differences and similarities between Girona Catalan and other Central Catalan varieties on the intonational level?
4. How can the similarities and differences between Girona Catalan and Girona Spanish at the prosodic level be explained in terms of language contact, i.e. how did the current intonational systems emerge?
5. Does the prosodic distance to other Spanish varieties and the level of homogeneity of its intonation across speakers justify that Girona Spanish (or Catalonian Spanish in a wider sense) should be viewed as a distinctive variety or a dialect of Spanish in its own right?[5]
6. How does contact-induced intonational change work? And how is it influenced by the extralinguistic conditions of the contact situation?
7. Which kinds of intonational features can be transferred?

The analysis of the intonation of both varieties is chiefly based on a corpus of semi-spontaneous speech, although some supplementary read data were used

---

4. Girona is a city in the north of Catalonia, located roughly 100 km northeast of Barcelona (for the reasons why this locality was chosen see Section 4.2).

5. It is, of course, very challenging, if not altogether impossible, to establish hard criteria that can serve to assess this issue. Moreover, linguistic varieties are, needless to say, not defined merely by their prosodic characteristics. Nevertheless, it seems worthwhile to discuss this question at least tentatively in the light of the results of the intonational analysis carried out in this study.

as well to endorse the investigation of some interrogative sentence types and of dislocations in Girona Spanish (see Section 4.3.2 for the motivation). The reason for this choice was that in opposition to fully spontaneous data, semi-spontaneous data can be controlled to a certain degree and thus facilitate the comparison of different utterance types across varieties and speakers, while still providing relatively natural and ecologically valid data (see Vanrell et al. 2018 and the discussion in 4.3.1). As in numerous previous studies on Romance intonation, the semi-spontaneous data were elicited by administering a discourse completion task (DCT; see Prieto/Cabré 2007–2012, 2013; Prieto/Roseano 2009–2013, 2010, and Section 4.3.1) and, for the collection of the read data sets, a short dialogue was used (see Section 4.3.2). The intonational analysis was carried out using the *Praat* acoustic analysis software (Boersma/Weenink 2020) and within the theoretical framework provided by the Autosegmental-Metrical (AM) model and the Tone and Break Indices (ToBI) annotation systems for Catalan and Spanish (cf. Pierrehumbert 1980; Beckman/Pierrehumbert 1986; Silverman et al. 1992; Beckman et al. 2005; Ladd 2008; Estebas-Vilaplana/Prieto 2008, 2010; Prieto et al. 2009, 2015, among others). The analysis offers a description of the phonetic realization and the phonological representation of pitch accents and boundary tones in the following sentence types: **neutral statements** (neutral declarative statements with and without peripheral elements such as dislocations, vocatives, and appositions), enumerations, **biased statements** (contrastive-focus statements, exclamative statements, contradiction statements, dubitative statements), **neutral polar questions** (information-seeking yes–no questions with and without peripheral elements and disjunctive questions), **biased polar questions** (exclamative yes–no questions with counterexpectational meaning, confirmation-seeking yes–no questions), **neutral wh-questions** (information-seeking wh-questions), **biased wh-questions** (exclamative and imperative wh-questions), **echo questions** (echo yes–no questions, echo wh-questions, exclamative echo yes–no questions with counterexpectational meaning), **imperatives** (commands and requests), and **vocatives**.

The main findings of the work reveal that Girona Spanish and Girona Catalan share numerous intonational properties and display very few differences. The same tonal inventories underly both varieties and the same combinations of tones are used to mark specific utterance types. Differences can almost exclusively be observed in the frequencies with which some particular tunes occur in a certain context. As a case in point, information-seeking yes–no questions regularly present falling tunes in Girona Catalan, whereas this is rare in Girona Spanish. Typically, such falling tunes co-occur with the use of the interrogative particle *que*, which is customary in Catalan but agrammatical in monolingual or non-contact varieties of Spanish in this context.

The alike prosodic shape of the two contacting varieties allows for the following assumptions: the intonational systems of Girona Spanish and Girona Catalan are an outcome of wholesale convergence between the intonational systems of Spanish and Catalan. Furthermore, both varieties have also been influenced by substratum transfer occurring when monolingual speakers learned the other language as an (early) foreign language (for definitions of the terms convergence and substratum transfer see Section 3.2.1). Yet, these developments have also entailed that the two varieties feature many competing tunes and are characterized by a vast amount of variation, which can often be traced back to the language dominance of their bilingual speakers. For instance, melodical patterns that originally stem from Catalan are more common in the Spanish of Catalan-dominant speakers than in that of Spanish-dominants. Likewise, the Girona Catalan intonation of Spanish-dominant bilinguals is more prone to display 'typically Spanish' features than that of Catalan-dominants. However, the two speaker groups cannot be neatly told apart merely on the grounds of their linguistic behaviour at the intonational level, i.e. clear-cut differences that are likely to have existed at some point in history have become blurred through large-scale convergence processes. As a consequence, the current 'bilingual varieties' of Spanish and Catalan spoken in Girona are not yet completely uniform, as minor differences can be observed between individual bilingual speakers. Yet, unless the external conditions of the language contact situation change (e.g. in the wake of new political or demographic shifts), further convergence can be expected. At the moment, the demolinguistic predominance of Catalan in Girona, i.e. the substantially greater number of Catalan-dominant bilinguals as well as the more widespread use of this language in the public domain, seems to entail that the contact varieties present overall somewhat more 'Catalan' than 'Spanish' features.

The book is structured as follows: in **Chapter 2**, I outline the historical development of the Spanish-Catalan language contact as well as the current sociolinguistic situation of Catalonia. In addition, I provide an overview of previous research into the Spanish spoken in Catalan-speaking regions and, on the basis of these studies, sketch its most important linguistic properties.

Chapter 3 is concerned with the presentation of the theoretical background of this work and with the description of the intonation of the two reference varieties to which Girona Spanish and Girona Catalan will be compared in Chapter 6 (i.e. Castilian Spanish and Central Catalan). The chapter is divided into three sections, with each section devoted to a different theoretical aspect: Section 3.1 deals with intonation, i.e. it focuses on the frameworks applied in the intonational analysis (namely, the AM model and the ToBI annotation system) and presents the inventories of tones and tunes established within these frameworks for various sentence types in Castilian Spanish and Central Catalan. Section 3.2 is dedicated to language contact: it provides definitions of the key terms used to describe language contact and explains the mechanisms underlying contact-induced change which I refer to when interpreting the results of the intonational analysis in Chapter 6. Furthermore, the section discusses the results of numerous case studies on intonation in language contact. Section 3.3, finally, is concerned with the topic of language dominance in bilinguals.

Chapter 4 introduces the methodology applied in the present work. It first discusses the assessment of the bilingual speakers' language dominance (Section 4.1). Then, an extensive overview of the background data for all subjects is given as extralinguistic factors are of particular interest to the present study (Section 4.2). Next, I present the used speech data and specify the criteria adopted for the segmentation and analysis of the linguistic material (Section 4.3).

The aim of **Chapter 5** is to present the results of the intonational analysis of Girona Spanish and Girona Catalan. It includes a detailed description of the phonetic realization of pitch accents and boundary tones in each sentence type (Section 5.1) and the establishment of the phonological categories underlying these surface forms (in Section 5.2).

The purpose of **Chapter 6** is to try and give answers to the research questions formulated above. To begin with, I summarize the similarities and differences between the intonational systems of Girona Spanish and Girona Catalan (Section 6.1). Then, I discuss how uniform the contact varieties are and whether the variation to which they are subject results from bilingualism factors such as language dominance (Section 6.2). In a next step, I depict the distance between Girona Spanish and Castilian Spanish and between Girona Catalan and other Central Catalan varieties on the intonation level (Section 6.3). In Section 6.4, the intonation of the contact varieties will be compared to the respective reference varieties in order to find out which intonational features have resulted from transfer and/or convergence processes during the long-standing contact between Catalan and Spanish in Girona. In Section 6.5, I consider the status of Girona Spanish within the Spanish diasystem and Sections 6.6 and 6.7, eventually, bring the chapter to a close in that they are concerned with intonational change from a more theoretical point of view.

Last, **Chapter 7** recapitulates the main findings of the study, offers some concluding remarks, and puts forth some open questions which remain for further research.

CHAPTER 2

Spanish-Catalan language contact and Catalonian Spanish

This chapter offers a brief description of the Spanish-Catalan language contact and the Spanish varieties that are in contact with Catalan (henceforth referred to as Catalan-contact Spanish, CCS). In Section 2.1, I depict the external historical background of the contact and describe Catalonia's present sociolinguistic situation. In Section 2.2, I provide an overview of previous research into the linguistic features of Spanish spoken in Catalan-speaking territories and identify some major research gaps. In Section 2.3, eventually, I summarize the most important characteristics of CCS based on the outcomes of the few existing studies.

2.1 Spanish-Catalan language contact: Historical background and present sociolinguistic situation

Present-day Catalan and Spanish both developed on the Iberian Peninsula alongside other Romance languages from varieties of the northern Peninsular dialect continuum that came into being after the gradual adoption of the Latin vernacular brought about by the Romans (Penny 2000: 80–104). In the course of the *Reconquista*, i.e. the Christian 'reconquest' of territories controlled by the Moors, the single counties eventually grew into the Crown of Aragon[6] and the Crown of Castile with Catalan and Spanish[7] as their respective 'state languages' (Bossong 2008: 77, 100). However, it was only through the concomitant southward expansion of the respective language areas that the number of their speakers increased considerably and both languages became important languages of culture with a flourishing literature (Ferrando 2020: 472, 478, 480–482; Bossong 2008: 99).[8]

---

6. Despite the name 'Crown of Aragon', the confederation consisted of individual entities, such as the Kingdom of Aragon, the Kingdom of València, or the Principality of Barcelona, and present-day Catalonia was not only an integral part of it but actually its centre of gravity, with Barcelona being the crown's 'capital' (Bossong 2008: 100).
7. When referring to language, I use the terms Spanish and Castilian interchangeably in this chapter.
8. It is interesting to note that the heyday of mediaeval literature begins not in Catalonia but with Ramon Lull (1235–1316) in the Balearic Islands. Also, in the 15th century, it is València

In the 15th century, Spanish for the first time began to sneak in into the Crown of Aragon as language of the royal court when the monarchy fell to the (Castilian) House of Trastámara in consequence of the Compromise of Caspe (1412; Ferrando 2020: 472–473). In 1479, the position of the Spanish language was further expanded through the dynastic union of the Crown of Aragon with the Crown of Castile by the Catholic Monarchs and their subsequent decision "to designate Castilian as the sole national language" (Bochmann 2018: 435), whereby Catalan was hierarchically subordinated to Spanish (Argenter 2020: 600). The 'discovery' of America in 1492 additionally precipitated the decline of Catalan at the end of the Middle Ages in shifting the orientation of the new realm from the Mediterranean to the Atlantic coast, i.e. from Barcelona and València to Cádiz and Seville (Bossong 2008: 101; Nicolás 2020: 486).[9] Especially in the western parts of the former Crown of Aragon, i.e. in the Kingdom of Aragon, where Aragonese dialects were originally spoken, and in the western strip of the Kingdom of València, mainly colonized by Aragonese settlers, the new 'official' language was quickly adopted. In the rest of the territories, Catalan remained the spoken language of all strata of society, even though at least parts of the nobility, clergy, literati, and merchants had already become bilingual by the 15th century.

The following centuries (16th–19th) are commonly referred to as *Decadència* due to the considerable decline of the use of Catalan as a written language in the light of the Spanish Golden Age (Sp. *Siglo de Oro*). However, this term may be misleading, since Catalan always stayed vital as a spoken language: indeed, in Catalonia and the Balearic Islands, it continued to be the every-day spoken (and also written) language of all social classes, and even in València, only the upper classes shifted to Spanish overall (Bossong 2008: 101; see also Vila 2016: 136–141, Escartí 2005; Nicolás 2020: 488–490). Catalan thus "had the status of a tolerated majority language and was [even] used [...] in some areas of public communication" for various centuries (Bochmann 2018: 44).

This was to be changed in the 18th century, when the monarchy began to enforce Castilian in those parts of the kingdom that were not castilophone in the aftermath of the war of the Spanish Succession (1700–1714), in which the Catalan countries had allied themselves with the Habsburgs. Following their military defeat, the new Bourbon king, Philip V — coming from centralist France — took rigorous measures against the defeated: he abolished Catalan institutions, privi-

---

that becomes the centre of the Golden Age of Catalan literature with epic poets such as Ausiàs March (1379-1459) and Joanot Martorell (1410-1468) (Bossong 2008: 100).

9. As a seafaring nation, the Crown of Aragon had been oriented towards the East. Its overseas possessions included, e.g., the Kingdom of Sardinia, the Kingdom of Naples (with Sicily), Malta, and for brief periods even parts of modern-day Greece.

leges, and ancient charters (Cat. *furs*, Sp. *fueros*) and established Castilian as only language in all public areas (e.g. in education, courts, book printing) by enacting the Nueva Planta ('Reform') decrees (Cat. *Decrets de Nova Planta*, Sp. *Decretos de Nueva Planta*; 1707 in València, 1715 in the Balearic Islands, 1716 in Catalonia). A series of additional language decrees followed in the subsequent years (Bochmann 2018: 436f., 440f.; Nicolás 2020: 287f.; for a general overview of the linguistic persecution see Ferrer i Gironés 1985).

Following the centralist trend of most young or arising European national states, this Castilo-centred course was maintained in the succeeding centuries, so that from the 18th until the 20th century Spanish was the only 'official' language of the state (Bernat 2014: 5; Nicolás 2020: 488, 492). "There thus came a point when only Spanish remained ideologically connected to ideas of modernity, progress and reason, forcing the other languages to remain in the realm of traditions and emotions; in other words, considered informal and only useful within the family context" (Ramallo 2018: 464; see Kailuweit 1997 for an extensive analysis of the diglossic situation). Furthermore, the number of Catalans who learned Spanish as a foreign language slowly increased, not least because of the introduction of obligatory Spanish-medium primary education in 1857 by the *Ley Moyano* (see Bernat et al. 2020; Vila 2020a: 633, 2020b: 670).

In the 19th century, however, in spite of the Castilian nationalism and its demand for authority throughout the country, denying other nationalities the right to co-exist within its territory, movements for a national rebirth eventually began to develop in both Catalonia and the Basque Country against the backdrop of their rise as industrial and economic powers (see Kremnitz 2018; Bernat et al. 2020: 100).[10] This process, which is known today under the name of *Renaixença* ('rebirth'), initially began with literary and cultural events in the wake of Romanticism (such as the *Jocs Florals* reviving the mediaeval traditions of the troubadours). At length, it transformed into an ideological and political movement (the so-called *Catalanisme*), which also translated in the programmes of the increasingly strengthened political organizations (Bochmann 2018: 441). The administrative union of the four provinces of Catalonia into the *Mancomunitat de Catalunya* ('Commonwealth of Catalonia') in 1914 under the leadership of Enric Prat de la Riba as well as language policies aiming to reintroduce and promote the use of Catalan in all public domains (see Pla Boix 2005 for an overview) are clearly results of this development. The same holds for the publication of some Catalan-medium newspapers and the foundation of the *Institut d'Estudis Catalans* in 1906, which subsequently initiated a process of standardization (mainly under the aegis of Pompeu Fabra) that had become necessary since Catalan, although it never had

---

10. In València, the process was delayed by local oligarchy (Bochmann 2018: 441).

ceased to be the spoken language of the overwhelming majority of the population, for centuries had been excluded from formal written registers.

This evolution towards the autonomy was interrupted by the dictatorship of Primo de Rivera (1923–1930), restored in 1931 for the short period of the Second Spanish Republic, during which Catalan (and also Basque) gained far-reaching support, "right up to supporting a co-official existence" (Bochmann 2018: 449), and finally disrupted again for more than forty years by the civil war caused by the coup of General Francisco Franco and his dictatorship. Under the Franquist regime, impactful measures for oppressing all hints at Catalan identity (e.g. in public signs, street names, and periodicals) were taken, and Catalan was entirely banned from the public sphere, including the complete prohibition of its use in administration and education at all levels and the enforcement of severe punishments for perpetrators (see Ferrer i Gironés 1985: 177–201; Ferrando/Nicolás 2011: 401–404; Rafanell 2020: 545–548). This relegation of the language to the familial domain, eventually "led to the loss of many text types, the disruption of passing on written norms to the next generation, gradually emerging illiteracy in one's own language, [and] a new dialectal fragmentation of the common language", whose effects continue to the present day (Bochmann 2018: 450; see also Kremnitz 2015). However, during the last years of the dictatorship, i.e. in the period from the 1960s to Franco's death in 1975, sometimes referred to as *dictablanda* 'soft dictatorship', some of the restrictions were relaxed, allowing, for instance, for some publications in Catalan (Rafanell 2020: 551–554).

The advent of democracy in 1978, eventually, entailed the recognition of Catalonia as one of the 'historic nationalities' of the Spanish state in the new Constitution, granting wide-reaching rights for linguistic self-determination. Only one year later, in the Statute of Autonomy of Catalonia of 1979, Catalan was declared co-official language and in 1983, a Normalization Law was passed with the aim of achieving a 'normal' situation for the previously supressed language, i.e. one in which it would be "a fully functional means of communication in the community" (Bochmann 2018: 451) and in which every Catalan can live their whole live – from first-language acquisition to university education – in their own language, without ever having to use another language than the one they speak in daily family life (Bossong 2008: 102). The language policies of the Catalan governments hence focused mainly on adjusting both the public administration and the educational system to the use of Catalan, "rolling back Castilian in public life in a much more decisive and successful way than other communities" (Bochmann 2018: 451).[11] It is mainly therefore that today, at least in Catalonia, Catalan is a lan-

---

11. Within only few years, the Catalan Conjunction Model (CCM) was implemented all over Catalonia (see Vila 2020b for other Catalan-speaking regions). Rejecting the separation of stu-

guage endowed with prestige (Woolard 1989, 2009) and knowing it represents a type of recognized social capital (Ramallo 2018: 478). For instance, knowing it even slightly increases the possibility of employment (Alarcón 2011) and thus may work as "a vehicle of social promotion for working and lower middle-class speakers of non-Catalan origin" (Boix-Fuster/Woolard 2020: 713). Recent studies have even revealed that "the relatively higher status of Catalan appears not only undiminished but even strengthened across the years" (Woolard 2009: 132). However, it must not be forgotten that, in opposition to other regions, the language was never socially ostracized in Catalonia, whose bourgeoisie abandoned it only to a relatively minor degree (Boix-Fuster/Moran 2014). Rather, the Catalan language has always been regarded as a symbol of national identity and independence vis-à-vis Madrid (Bossong 2008: 103; Pujolar 2010: 240, 2020; Boix-Fuster/Woolard 2020).[12] It therefore comes as no surprise that, on the other hand, the Catalan policies (especially those targeting the educational system) have repeatedly engendered resistance of unitary forces, among them the conservative press as well as the Spanish governments led by the post-Franquist *Partido Popular*, who tried to obstruct certain measures of the Catalan *Generalitat* through constitutional acts (Bochmann 2018: 451; Vila 2020b: 671). Namely, this was the case of the new Statute of Autonomy of 2006, which was partly ruled unlawful by the Spanish Constitutional Court in 2010, given that it described Catalonia as a nation and intended to partially repair the shortcoming of the Spanish Constitution of 1978[13]

---

dents according to first language and using Catalan as main language of instruction, this system already by the end of the '90s effectively provided high levels of oral and written proficiency in Catalan and Castilian among pupils, such that it is viewed by many as a means of linguistic and social integration of (Spanish-speaking) immigrants and their descendants (Vila 2020b: 670f.; see also Múñoz 2005 and Pradilla Cardona 2016). In the aftermath of the wave of foreign immigration of the early 2000s, the model was adapted to the increasing diversification of the learners and is now usually referred to as Cat. *immersió lingüística*, i.e. 'language immersion (programme)' (Vila 2020b: 671; see also Pujolar 2010). Furthermore, the Catalan governments – in addition to many private institutions – made considerable efforts to teach Catalan to adult immigrants: for example, until 2019, over two million students had taken a course organized by one of the centres of the Generalitat's Consortium of Language Normalization (CPNL; Generalitat de Catalunya 2021: 71; Vila 2020b: 678–680).

12. Although this was (and is) crucially not the case in other Catalan-speaking areas, such as the Valencian Country, newer studies have reported recent gains in prestige and upgrading of the language status there too (e.g. Casesnoves 2010).

13. The Spanish Constitution of 1978 has (possibly unintendedly) contributed to the minorization of national languages other than Spanish by privileging the latter as only official language of the Spanish state and the only one that all Spaniards are required to know (even in legally bilingual areas), thereby perpetuating a clear hierarchical gulf (Ramallo 2018: 464, 478). Furthermore, this unequal footing has on various occasions been reaffirmed by different judge-

by the means of a 'positive discrimination' of Spanish, i.e. "by giving [Catalan] priority over [Spanish] in Catalonia and creating a more transparent description of the rights and duties that arise from the legislation" (Ramallo 2018: 478; see below and Pons 2013 for the effects of this decision). By the same token, all language laws adopted by the Catalan Parliament to implement the guidelines developed in the Statute of Autonomy (e.g. in areas such as the public media or consumer rights) have equally been challenged by constitutional appeals (Pons 2020: 644).

Today, using the still fitting words of Wesch (1997), Catalonia presents "una realidad lingüística [...] extremadamente compleja", which mainly results from the secular co-existence of and the contact between its two languages.[14] It is "una sociedad oficialmente trilingüe y socialmente plurilingüe" (Vila 2016): trilingual, because in addition to Spanish (official by means of the Spanish Constitution) and Catalan (official through the Statute of Autonomy), in 2006, Aranese, i.e. the variety of Occitan spoken in the Aran valley (Oc. *Val d'Aran*), was declared third official language in all Catalonia; plurilingual, first of all due to the increasing presence of numerous extra-territorial languages spoken by a great many migrants (see below). The Statute of Autonomy of 2006 furthermore defined that Catalan "is the language of normal and preferential[15] use in Public Administration bodies and in the public media of Catalonia, and is also the language of normal use for teaching and learning in the education system" (Parlament de Catalunya 2012: Article 6, paragraph (1)) and that "all persons have the right to use the two official languages and citizens of Catalonia have the right and the duty to know them" (Article 6, paragraph (2)).

Catalan has thus (re-)attained a firm position in Catalonia, being present in all areas of public life: there is no social context in which only one official language would be used (Vila 2016: 145). Although shortcomings continue to persist in certain areas,[16] Catalan is clearly dominant in others, such as the much acclaimed educational system: in primary and secondary education, it is the vehicular lan-

---

ments of the Constitutional Court, emphasizing the supremacy of the official status of Castilian (Pons 2020: 664f.).

14. For a comparison of the demolinguistic and legal situation of Catalan across Catalan-speaking areas see, e.g., Vila (2020a) and Pons (2020).

15. As has been mentioned before, the expression "and preferential" was declared unconstitutional and null and void by the Constitutional Court in 2010 (STC 2010/31), giving rise to a big public polemic in Catalonia, which without doubt fuelled the debate about its independence (see Pons 2013).

16. Especially in the legal system, the use of Catalan is low: e.g. in 2018, the share of sentences in Catalan was of only 7.7% (Generalitat de Catalunya 2019: 49; see also Observatori Català de Justícia 2012). Furthermore, Castilian is overwhelmingly dominant in the mass media and commercial culture (see Woolard 2009: 132f.; Sinner/Wieland 2008).

guage for all non-linguistic subjects, and even in universities, where everyone is free to choose either official language, its use is high (Boix-Fuster/Sanz 2008: 89; Vila 2020b: 676–678; on the linguistic education model in Catalonia see also Fn. 11, above). This exemplary model, which requires everyone to be at least passively bilingual, thus guarantees prestige and vitality for Catalan without preventing full fluency in Spanish (Ramallo 2018: 478): as a matter of fact, in 2018, the percentage of Catalans being able to speak Spanish was almost 100% for all age groups (Generalitat de Catalunya 2019: 13). Essentially bilingual, the Catalan society cannot be conceptualized as a diglossic one today in the sense of Ferguson (1959) or Fishman (1967), since it is not (anymore) one in which there is a social consensus about using one ('high') language or variety in formal situations and another one, the 'low variety', in informal contexts (Vila 2016: 144f.; Pujolar 2011: 366–367; Meisenburg 1999: 32).

Nevertheless, practically everyone being bilingual does not mean that everyone uses both of their languages to the same extent in every-day life, as can easily be seen in the surveys on linguistic uses carried out regularly by the Catalan government. The last reports, referring to 2018 and 2019 (Generalitat de Catalunya 2019, 2021), indicate that the knowledge of Catalan is high and has continually been rising in recent years. Figure 2.1 shows that at present 94.4% of the Catalans can understand it and 81.2% are able to speak it.

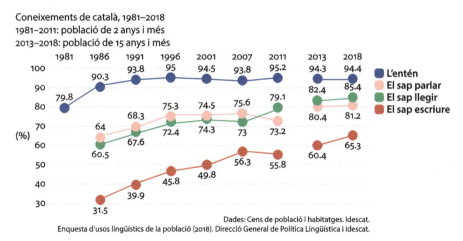

Figure 2.1 Knowledge of Catalan (understanding, speaking, reading, and writing) in Catalonia from 1981 to 2018 (taken from Generalitat de Catalunya 2019: 11)

Interestingly, the percentage of the population who can write Catalan is noticeably lower. This is clearly an aftereffect of the Franco era, during which a great part of today's Catalan adults were alphabetized exclusively in Spanish

(Boix-Fuster/Sanz 2008: 90; Vila 2020a: 638). On the other side, the report also manifests the effectiveness of the contemporary educational system, given that in the age groups under 24 over 90% are able to both speak and write Catalan (Generalitat de Catalunya 2019: 13).

Nonetheless, there is a large gap between the knowledge of Catalan and its day-to-day use. The *Informe de política lingüística 2018* (Generalitat de Catalunya 2019: 19) documents that only 36.1% of the inhabitants of Catalonia make use of Catalan as their habitual language and, indeed, it is known that in the 21st century Spanish has become the most frequently spoken language in Catalonia, being the initial language of 52.7% and the usual language of 48.6% of its population (see also Vila 2016: 145). This fact evinces an enormous change in the course of the 20th century, which finds its explanation in the first place in the massive arrival of Spanish-speaking immigrants and the concomitant changes in the composition of Catalonia's population: whereas until the 1920s the Catalans were largely monolingual and Spanish was only spoken by a very small part of the aristocracy, bourgeoisie, and some immigrants (summing less than 10%), the massive immigrations of workers from other parts of the Spanish state,[17] slowly beginning around the turn of the century and reaching its peaks between 1950–75, entailed that in the 1950s the proportion of initial Spanish-speakers for the first time exceeded the threshold of 10% of the population (Vila 2016: 140; see also Bernat et al. 2020; Vila 2020a: 634f.). However, Spanish only became the most frequent initial language and the socially most used language much later, i.e. after the second big wave of immigration taking place in the first decade of the 21st century (the so-called Cat. *noves immigracions*). Between 2001 and 2012, the Catalan population increased by 1.2 million, mainly due to immigration from other countries, among them many South-American ones, such as Colombia, Ecuador, Argentina, Peru, Venezuela, Honduras, and Bolivia (IDESCAT 2021b; Vila 2016: 141). As a consequence, in 2018, 35.3% of the inhabitants were born outside of Catalonia and many more are part of the second generation of immigrants (Generalitat de Catalunya 2019: 9). It is thus the recent "immigration, much more than language shift, [that] has been the leading cause behind the drop in the percentage of the population whose first language is Catalan" (Comellas 2016: 155) and which, in the words of Vila (2020a: 646), has "shaken" the position of Catalan in Catalonia. Furthermore, migration has noticeably augmented the percentage of speak-

---

17. The lion's share of the immigrants came from the south of the Peninsula, especially from Andalusia. Sinner (2004: 126) gives the following benchmarks: approx. 50% from Andalusia, 20% from Castile, Estremadura, and the province of Albacete, and the rest from other communities such as Galicia (4.5%), the Basque Country, or Aragon (see also Moyer 1991).

ers with other initial languages, such as Arabic or Romanian (approximately 11%, Generalitat de Catalunya 2019: 19).[18]

Still, significant socio-geographic differences can be found in the figures regarding the first language and the language of daily use between urban and rural areas, or sometimes even between different neighbourhoods (Ramallo 2018: 475; Vila 2020a: 638f.), given that immigrants for the most part settled down in the Catalan cities and their metropolitan areas. For example, in the metropolitan area of Barcelona, Catalan is the (exclusive) habitual language of only 27.5% of the population, while it is slightly majoritarian in the region of Girona, attaining a share of 54.1%. Its social use is highest in the Land of the river Ebro (Cat. *Terres de l'Ebre*, 72.2%; Generalitat de Catalunya 2019: 21). Similarly, more people are able to speak Catalan in Girona (87.4%) than in the Metropolitan Area of Barcelona (78.4%), although the composition of the population in terms of immigrants and locals is very similar in both areas (Generalitat de Catalunya 2019: 15).

In sum, Catalan may be characterized today "a vibrant medium-sized language community", "[t]hough always in a context of societal bilingualism or even multilingualism" (Vila 2020a: 645). Before bringing this chapter to a close, the kinds of Catalan and especially of Spanish spoken in Catalonia at present times deserve some mention (for the linguistic characteristics of the latter see Section 2.2). Since the bulk of the Catalans is nowadays (at least) bilingual, these varieties are probably best characterized as "bilingual varieties" (Boix-Fuster and Sanz 2008). This is especially true for younger generations, who typically also have some command of English as a foreign language and quite frequently qualify as speakers of a heritage language.

As for Catalan, the varieties spoken are essentially those of the traditional dialect continuum (Penny 2000: 93–98; Veny/Massanell 2015: 62–63). However, due to growingly intense contact with Spanish for almost half a millennium, no monolingual speakers are left today. While the traditional dialects are on the decline, mainly due to the prescriptive standard norms taught in school and their spread through the media (Ulldemolins-Subirats 2019; Massanell i Messalles 2012; see also Veny/Massanell 2015: 83–85; Camps/Labèrnia 2020: 687f.), a steadily increasing number of initial speakers of Spanish (and/or other languages) have become proficient users of Catalan in recent years to the extent that their number now almost equals that of first-language Catalan speakers (Arnal 2011: 16): "Today, in contrast to the past, the group of [Catalan] speakers whose first language is Spanish includes teachers, politicians, radio and television announcers, actors, and people interviewed in the media". Furthermore, surveys have shown that many of

---

18. In 2020, over 3% of the inhabitants of Catalonia were born in Morocco, and 1% in Romania (IDESCAT 2021b).

them use Catalan at work or with their friends (Arnal 2011: 24; Vila/Sorolla 2019a, 2019b). "As a result, it is now common to hear Catalan spoken with different degrees of competence" and "with a Spanish accent" (Arnal 2011: 16; see also Prats et al. 1990: 36–37). Whereas the Spanish influence was traditionally mainly on the lexicon (see, e.g., Payrató 1985; Colón 1993), it is now increasingly becoming evident in phonology, syntax, and pragmatics (Arnal 2011: 17–19; Ferrando/Nicolás 2011: 527–530; Lleó et al. 2009; Cortés et al. 2009; Benet et al. 2011). As Woolard (1992: 240) points out, this entails that today's young Catalans, especially in urban areas, hear more non-native Catalan spoken than previous generations did, and, in turn, are often no longer able to distinguish between native and non-native speaking styles (Arnal 2011: 16).

Concerning Spanish, we have seen in the historic overview that it clearly was a foreign language for the overwhelming part of Catalonia's inhabitants until the beginning of the 20th century. Before the Civil War (1936–1939), the first contacts with Spanish typically took place at school given that virtually no one actually spoke it in their daily life (Bernat et al. 2020: 105). It was only from the 1950s and in consequence of the massive influx of migrants that a noteworthy part of the Catalan population were initial Spanish-speakers and that initial speakers of Catalan, for their part, had opportunities to speak Spanish in informal situations and to natives (Bernat et al. 2020: 105–108). Still today, however, most of the Spanish spoken in Catalonia is produced by people born outside a Catalan-speaking territory, i.e. "by persons, who with a high degree of certainty, have a variety of Spanish coming from the rest of Spain (32.66%) or from some other hispanophone country (11.79%)" (Vila 2016: 148, translation is mine). Initial Spanish-speakers born in Catalonia account for another 32.49% of the Spanish spoken there, while initial speakers of Catalan contribute only about 10% to this share. This on the one hand shows that the predominance of Spanish at the societal level — however narrow it may be — is mainly a result of the immigration of Spanish-speaking populations. On the other, it raises the question of how uniform the Spanish spoken in Catalonia is at presence and whether there is such a thing as a Catalonian dialect of Spanish (see also Section 2.2, below).

In sum, the linguistic uses show that it would flawed to conceptualize them as springing from the cohabitation of two clear-cut language communities. Rather, between the exclusive users of Spanish and of Catalan, the majority of the Catalans are to be situated somewhere on a bilingual continuum with significant numbers of speakers for all ratios (Vila 2016: 147). In consequence, the Catalan society is characterized by "virtually universalized bilingualism" (Pujolar 2011: 366), but the language-dominance patterns of individual speakers are widely variegated. This aspect of bilingualism will be treated extensively in Section 3.3.

2.2 Research into Catalan-contact Spanish

The aim of this section is to give an overview of the research into the linguistic features of Catalan-contact Spanish (CCS), i.e. Spanish as spoken in Catalonia and other Catalan-speaking areas.[19] Besides, I shall pinpoint the most glaring research gaps and bring up some desiderata for future research at the end of the section.

As outlined in the diachronic synopsis of the intense language contact between Catalan and Spanish in Catalonia in the previous section (2.1), Spanish has passed — mainly in the course of the last century — from being a foreign or second language (L2),[20] acquired only by the societal elites, to being the most frequently spoken language, known by virtually everyone. With respect to the Spanish spoken in Catalonia before the 20th century, little is known about its constitution and few studies have been carried out, possibly owing to the fact that coetaneous written productions and metalinguistic descriptions are the only sources that allow for its analysis. The most important pieces of (later) research are probably Badia i Margarit (1976), Vallverdú (1979), Jorba (1979), Jungbluth (1996), and Kailuweit (1997). Although Spanish in the 19th century had already been the single official language and the only one allowed in public schooling for quite some time, it most likely continued to be an L2 for most Catalans and therefore probably showed typical features of learner varieties (see Lüdtke 1998: 29–30), such as interference (i.e. negative transfer) from the L1 (for definitions and a discussion of the terms 'transfer' and 'interference' see Section 3.2.1). In contemporary sources, such as dictionaries, grammars, or manuals, features of Catalonian Spanish were typically categorized as *catalanismos*, i.e. interferences from Catalan, that 'impoverish' the language and should be avoided. They were also generally attributed to a 'lack of culture'. A compilation of such Catalanisms is provided in Solà (1980). This **puristic view** persisted until wide into the 20th century and the traditional Spanish dialectology largely ignored CCS or else relegated it "to varieties spoken by less cultured sectors of society" (Blas Arroyo 2011: 375).[21] Only in the 1980s and '90s

---

19. The label 'CCS' is used to refer to Spanish spoken in all Catalan-speaking regions (independently of the individual speaker's language dominance or origin) following Davidson (2015a). To refer to 'Catalonian Spanish', i.e. to Spanish as spoken in Catalonia but not in other Catalan-speaking regions such as València or the Balearic Islands, the label 'CatS' is used.

20. Following Montrul (2013b: 168), I understand a second language (L2) as a language that "is acquired after the basic foundations of the first language (L1) are assumed to be in place". The term 'foreign language' is largely used as a synonym, especially when the L2 is acquired through formal instruction. Furthermore, I use 'native' or 'initial language' as synonyms of L1.

21. Most classics of Spanish dialectology either completely ignore CCS (e.g. Zamora Vicente 1960; Alvar 1996) or at best mention it as an "adstrate variety" (Lapesa 1996: 332, see also García Mouton 2007: 44). In more recent years, it is often referred to as "variety in contact with other

would a change of paradigm slowly begin to take place (see Sinner/Wesch 2008: passim and below). Nevertheless, from the negatively tainted remarks in Catalan press texts as well as some other factors, Kailuweit (1996:737) concluded that by the end of the 18th century there was already a relatively clear-cut variety of 'Catalonian Spanish' (CatS), packed with interferences from Catalan, which can be considered a tertiary dialect of Spanish in the sense of Coseriu (1980, 1981; see also Krefeld 2011); a position legitimately questioned by Sinner (2004:22), who takes into consideration the fact that it is completely unknown to which extent the criticized interferences were pervasive in the Catalan society and whether their originators were already L1 speakers of Spanish or simply L2 learners.

In the 20th century, eventually, first research studies on CCS began to appear and Dalmau (1936) was the first author to underpin his critics with extracts from Catalan Spanish-medium press. Moreover, scholars increasingly took into account phonetic features in order to characterize what they typically used to call a Catalan accent (e.g. Navarro Tomás 1935). Later on, in 1961, the Menorcan teacher Francesc de Borja Moll first proposed a classification of the phonetic, lexical, and syntactic characteristics of the Spanish spoken in a Catalan-speaking region, which was followed by many other works (e.g. Moll 1974, 1986; see Sinner/Wesch 2008:14f.). He furthermore drew attention to the fact that schoolteachers of Spanish often transmitted their own language mistakes to their pupils and children, who therefore unconsciously assimilated them in early childhood when learning Spanish as an L2,[22] and he highlighted that Catalanisms were not limited to the uneducated sectors of society (Moll 1961:473; see also Enrique-Arias 2021:199). In such cases of perpetuation of L2 features by intergenerational transmission and subsequent nativization, the respective features should thus rather be viewed as integrated elements of CCS than as interferences in learner varieties (Sinner 2004: passim; for similar cases in Mozambican Portuguese and Argentinian Spanish see Gonçalves 2005; Gabriel/Kireva 2014; Kireva/Gabriel 2015).

The numerous studies by Badia i Margarit (1965, 1979, 1981, among others, see Brumme 1998:39–68 for an overview) provide some simple lists of the most striking linguistic features found in Barcelona Spanish (especially in L1-Catalan speakers educated in the L2 Spanish), such as the velar pronunciation of /l/ or the missing *distinción* of the phonemes /s/ and /θ/ (see Section 2.3). However, the author did not indicate any clear sources and most of his observations were based on intuition and perception. Moreover, he continued to see these char-

---

languages" (e.g. Fernández-Ordóñez 2016; Escobar 2021), but its position within the Spanish diasystem is still to be determined (Sinner/Wesch 2008:11, 20).

22. Please recall that until the 1950s, Spanish was the initial language of less than 10% of the population in Catalonia.

acteristics as "failed productions" vis-à-vis the Castilian norm and accused a "lack of spontaneity" in many L1 Catalan speakers when speaking Spanish (e.g., Badia i Margarit 1981: 28–29, translation is mine), which was in line with the many contemporary "works on applied linguistics, such as grammars, style and pronunciation guides, in which the vernacular variants have traditionally been classed as errors of performance" (Blas Arroyo 2011: 375). On the other hand, he observed that many traits were generalizable to other areas and thus suggested that CCS had common features in all Catalan-speaking regions (Badia i Margarit 1979: 135–136). His work furthermore took note of the massive immigration into Catalonia of monolingual Spanish speakers and thereby retraced the changing sociolinguistic conditions until the beginning of the normalization process of Catalan in the 1980s (Sinner/Wesch 2008: 15). At the latest with Colón (1967: 203), it became apparent that features whose presence can be traced back to contact with Catalan are not only found in the Spanish produced by initial speakers of Catalan but also in the Spanish spoken by the migrants and their descendants. He therefore recommended distinguishing between occasional Catalanisms and "aquellos que arraigan" 'those which take root' (Colón 1967: 238).

While during the '70s many authors had kept compiling and copying stereotyped lists of 'typical errors' from preceding works, it was from the change of perspective in the '80s that the interest in CCS and the number of **empirically based studies** slowly began to grow. Deviations from Castilian Spanish (CS) norms were now increasingly conceived as interferences which came along with (individual and societal) bilingualism rather than as simple speech errors, and the view that 'good' bilinguals should not have an accent in any of their languages was progressively abandoned (Poch Olivé 2016: 316). In this vein, Payrató (1985) provided an extensive classification of the phonetic, morphosyntactic, and lexical interferences that result from Spanish-Catalan language contact from a structuralist and generativist perspective. However, he never considered the existence of CCS as a distinct variety (Poch Olivé 2016: 325). Gómez Molina (1986) analysed the reciprocal influence between the two languages in Sagunt (València), and Marsá (1986: 99) described the typical "marcas del bilingüismo" in Catalan–Spanish bilinguals' behaviour, such as the avoidance of certain forms for fear of making mistakes.

Nevertheless, the "real avalanche of works" (Sinner/Wesch 2008: 26, translation is mine; see also Sinner 2004: 28–36 for an overview) on Spanish in Catalan-speaking areas came only in the **1990s** due to a combination of various boosting factors, such as the profound political and social changes after the advent of democracy that originated an increasing interest in language contact in general and especially in the Catalan educational system, where **didactic issues** of teaching Spanish both as a native and as a foreign language were getting more and more attention in the light of the ongoing bilingualization and the different patterns of language dominance found among students (e.g. Montolío/Vila 1993; Pelegrina 1996; Serrano Vázquez 1996; Hernández García 1998; for a discussion of the term 'language dominance' see Section 3.3). Although initially many works continued to copy more or less extensive, uninspired lists of deviations from the Castilian norm (Sinner/Wesch 2008: 26), the **puristic views** of the past were now eventually abandoned — Vila (2016: 152) speaks of "el *destronamiento* del *castellano acatalanado*" 'the *dethroning* of *Catalanized Spanish*' — and the status of CatS as a distinct regional variety or dialect within the Spanish diasystem was discussed more seriously (Wesch 1992: 94; Kailuweit 1996; see also Sinner 2004: 28). Comprehensive compendia, such as Szigetvári (1994) and Sinner (1996) were created with the aim of compiling, describing, and classifying the greatest possible number of elements that could be considered distinctive features of CCS.

Whereas until the 1990s most studies had relied on existing qualitative descriptions or intuitions and only a minimal part had an **empirical basis**, especially in the second half of the decade, a progressively growing number of corpus- and data-based research studies into more specific and finer-grained aspects of morphosyntax, semantics and pragmatics, and the lexicon were carried out, allowing to draw much more reliable conclusions and hence to both confirm and refute some of the characteristics traditionally ascribed to CCS (see Section 2.3). Although to a lesser extent, this tendency also spread to the domain of phonetics and phonology, in which first quantitative acoustical studies emerged. For instance, Poch Olivé and Harmegnies (1994) studied the phonetic realization of CatS vowels in different speech styles. Wesch (1992, 1994, 1997, 2002, among others), based on recordings of colloquial and formal situations by Catalan L1 speakers and concentrating on lexical and semantic phenomena as well as the differences between spoken and written registers, reached the conclusion that an "influjo mínimo", i.e. a certain number of permanent interferences from Catalan on the CSS system, can be found in all speakers living in bilingual regions (Wesch 1997: 294, 1994: 168). Nevertheless, he also underlined that the characteristics of CatS necessarily need to be studied in a variationist framework, since in many cases only a Labovian perspective allows to explain the facts present in the data (Wesch 1997: 288f., and below). He furthermore introduced the topic of CCS to Hispanistic studies outside of Spain, i.e. in German-speaking countries. Vann (1997, 1998, 2002, among many others) dealt with pragmatic aspects on the basis of corpus studies and thereby addressed questions of language identity and ideology. Also Casanovas Català used corpora to investigate the Spanish variety spoken in Lleida in a series of studies on phonetic, morphosyntactic, and lexical aspects, pointing among other things to the lack of some typical features of habitual vernacular languages in the Spanish produced by Catalan-dominant bilingual subjects, such as missing "relajación fonética" ('phonetic relaxation') or lacking use of phraseology (see, e.g., Casanovas Català 1995:54, 1996a, 2000). For Spanish in València, the numerous works of Blas Arroyo (1991, 1993, 1994, among many others) on interference and convergence resulting from the linguistic contact between Catalan and Spanish ought to be mentioned.

Simultaneously, as the presence of the salient phonetic features (see Section 2.3) that had characterized CCS in previous times notably diminished in view of increasing social bilingualism or was limited to marginal groups of society (Sinner/Wesch 2008: 23, see also Vila 2016: 152), it was, among other things, the documentation of linguistic features of Catalan origin in L1 Spanish speakers that entailed theoretical advances such as the distinction between interferences and integrated elements, and raised the sensitivity for sociolinguistic factors.[23] It became increasingly evident that the nature of Catalan interferences in CCS in large part depends on the **sociolinguistic background** and language history of the analysed subjects: for instance, Moyer (1991) and Báez Aguilar de González (1995, 1997, among others) focused on the Spanish spoken by Andalusian immigrants and their descendants; Blas Arroyo and Porcar (1997) showed the influence of language dominance on speakers' linguistic choices in Castelló; and Hernández García (1998) found that students with the L1 Catalan or grown up with Catalan-medium education primarily exhibit grammatical interferences, whereas those who attended school in Spanish are more likely to display lexical or semantic interferences. She furthermore took into consideration the metalinguistic knowledge of her subjects disclosed in sociolinguistic interviews. In 2004, Sinner, too, used a huge corpus of sociolinguistic interviews to discuss the question of the existence of a regional norm, comparing frequencies and the acceptability of different lexical, morphosyntactic, and pragmatic aspects in CatS and CS. However, Vila (2016:152) recently anew put into doubt whether one can speak at present of a "single variety" of CatS in the view of the "kaleidoscope of varieties imported" in the last decades (translation is mine). A conclusive clarification of the status of CCS within the Spanish dialect system (e.g. as a regional variety or dialect) is thus still pending.

In the first two decades of the third millennium, luckily, most empirical studies have provided at least some information on their subjects' linguistic backgrounds and habits, and works taking into consideration sociolinguistic facets or even directly relating heterogeneity in the data with sociolinguistic factors such as language dominance are progressively becoming more numerous (e.g. Simonet 2008, 2015; Davidson 2012, 2015a, 2020; Torres et al. 2013; Machuca/Poch 2016;

[23.] Note, however, that the term 'interference', just as the term 'accent', usually continued to have a negative connotation at that time, i.e. the presence of 'interferences' was still evaluated as deviation from a systemic norm or from an 'expected' realization (Poch Olivé 2016:317; Blas Arroyo 1991:267).

Machuca 2016; Hualde/Nadeu 2020, among many others). Moreover, there has been an increase in studies devoted to a range of sociolinguistic aspects such as identity, attitudes, language markets, language policies, and related discourses (e.g. Boix-Fuster/Sanz 2008; Pujolar 2008; Woolard 2009, 2013; Pujolar/Gonzàlez 2013; Boix-Fuster 2015; Bochmann 2018, among many others) – possibly also triggered by the rise of Catalan nationalism, independentism, and the ongoing political conflict with the central government.

In synthesis, through the great amount of research carried out in the 1990s and at the beginning of the new millennium, it has become ever more evident that empirical studies essentially need to consider extralinguistic factors such as the participants' sociolinguistic background, language history, and language use when tackling CCS due to the complex sociolinguistic situation that is strongly marked by pervasive bilingualism both at the individual and societal level (see Wesch 1997: 288f.; Blas Arroyo 2011: 391; Poch Olivé 2016: 330). Unfortunately, up to the present time, conducting empirical studies remains difficult because of the persisting lack of (electronic) oral (and also written) corpora (Sinner/Wesch 2008: 28–33)[24] as well as due to the highly complex sociolinguistic situation, resulting first of all from the massive immigration taking place during the last decades (see Section 2.1). Some clear research gaps thus still remain to be filled. Among these, the most outstanding desideratum would probably be to catch the linguistic variation of CCS in a far more systematic way (see Blas Arroyo 2011: 388).

For one thing, the **diastratic variation** would certainly be worth more extensive exploration: in the course of the almost complete bilingualization and diversification of what once used to be a relatively homogeneous Catalan-speaking society, the heavily accented and interfered L2-Spanish of L1 Catalan speakers has become socially secondary or even disappeared completely in the youngest generations (Vila 2016: 152; Arnal 2011: 16) – this is reflected, for instance, in the fact that it is now frequently exploited in humoristic and literary productions (see, e.g., Woolard 1987; Heinemann 1996; Illamola 2003; Igarreta Fernández 2019). Instead,

---

24. Apart from some more or less comprehensive collections of transcribed sociolinguistic interviews (e.g. Vila Pujol 2001; Sinner 2001; Blas Arroyo et al. 2009), there are almost no bigger corpora, since projects with the aim of creating them, such as the one by Grupo de investigación del español de Barcelona (GRIESBA), have "largely failed" as Wesch and Sinner (2008: 29) put it. However, in the meantime, some other corpus projects have been (partly) completed and the respective corpora are available online (e.g. Val.Es.Co for Valencian Spanish (Pons Bordería 2021), the Corpus Mallorca (www.corpusmallorca.es, see also Enrique-Arias 2021) for Majorcan Spanish, or some subcorpora of COSER (Fernández-Ordóñez 2005–) and PRESEEA (2014–), which include various cities and rural areas in Catalan-speaking territories). Besides these, of course some general Spanish corpora also include material from Catalan-speaking territories (e.g. the GADIA corpus; see Garachana 2021: 323f.).

immigration has made Catalonia a melting pot of different languages and cultures, which of course impacts substantially on the varieties of Spanish (and Catalan) spoken there. Besides further taking into consideration the (still understudied) extralinguistic factors that mediate variation in CCS (e.g. ethnolinguistic density, degree of individual bilingualism, patterns of language dominance, ideological factors), future research ought to tap especially into the Spanish varieties spoken by different migrant communities as these have only sporadically been an object of study. This holds true first of all for the Spanish spoken by first-generation migrants (from both Spanish-speaking and alloglottal areas) but equally for their descendants (as well as for the Catalan and the other languages spoken by these social groups). For example, the L1-Spanish produced by Andalusian or Latino communities, which is likely to be affected by the influence of the autochthonous varieties of CCS and Catalan as well as by levelling processes has hardly been addressed yet.[25] The same applies to the L2-Spanish produced, e.g., by Maghribi and Romanian communities, among many others. Furthermore, with respect to the varieties spoken by the Catalonia-born descendants of first-generation migrants, the influence of heritage languages such as Romanian on both Spanish and Catalan and vice versa definitely would require further research (see Schulte 2018). Another interesting question would be which effects political factors such as the normalization of Catalan or the recent rise of nationalism have had on CCS.

Finally, the geographic aspect, i.e. **diatopic variation**, has been widely neglected, as well, most research studies dealing solely with data from Barcelona Spanish (see Section 2.3). Indeed, the Spanish varieties spoken in other Catalan-speaking areas have received little (Lleida, València, Castelló, Majorca) or almost no attention (e.g. the Catalan hinterland and the interior regions, such as Girona, central Catalunya, the Pyrenees, or the Lands of the River Ebro, but also Alacant, Menorca, and the Pityusic Islands Eivissa and Formentera) (see also Sinner/Wesch 2008: 33). The further investigation of the Spanish varieties spoken in such areas would be of particular interest, first and foremost because the Catalan dialects they are in contact with exhibit some major linguistic differences (e.g. with respect to vowel reduction, mid-vowels, or intonation).

Finally, besides variation, there is also an urgent need to address some understudied linguistic areas: for instance, the promising field of prosody – although having often been called an essential characteristic of CCS (see Section 2.3) – has received almost no attention until the present date. However, as will be shown in the following section major research gaps exist in all linguistic domains.

---

25. Some noteworthy exceptions are Moyer (1991), Báez Aguilar de González (1995, 1997) on the Spanish of Andalusian immigrants and, more recently, Corona et al. (2013), Newman et al. (2013), Corona/Block (2020), who focus on adolescents of Latin American descent.

2.3 Linguistic features of Catalan-contact Spanish

Regardless of its complex sociolinguistic situation and the diastratic variation that originates from it (see Section 2.1), Spanish as spoken in Catalonia (CatS) and other Catalan-speaking areas (CCS)[26] presents specific features that evidence long-lasting contact with Catalan at virtually all linguistic levels. In this section, a synthesis of the most important of these characteristics is given, focusing primarily on the phonetic and phonological level. First, a series of lexical, semantic, pragmatic, morphologic, and syntactic examples will be provided (Section 2.3.1), before expanding on segmental phonetic and phonological phenomena (Section 2.3.2). Sections 2.3.3, finally, is dedicated to the less-studied field of suprasegmental phonology.

2.3.1 Lexical and grammatical features of CCS

Doubtlessly, the numerous **lexical** loans represent probably the most apparent manifestation of Catalan influence on CCS. As Bondzio (1980) puts it: "Der Wortschatz ist kontaktbedingten Veränderungen am stärksten ausgesetzt." 'The lexicon is most subjected to contact-induced change'. Cerdà (1984: 297) distinguishes between elements that are borrowed *in praesentia*, i.e. those in which both the phonic form and the meaning are transferred, and borrowings *in absentia*, i.e. when the influence is merely semantic. The first type, i.e. borrowing of whole phonic sequences together with their respective meaning (see Payrató 1985: 88), comprises a range of different items. First, it includes the (virtually inevitable) use of names of unique referents (see Matras 2010: 82), e.g. of institutions (such as *Generalitat*, the Catalan government, *Mossos d'Esquadra*, the Catalan police) or places (*Eixample*, a quarter of Barcelona, *Palau de la Música Catalana*, a concert hall), as well as of culinary and cultural or environment-specific items (*butifarra*, a type of sausage, Cat. *botifarra*; *la Diada de Sant Jordi* 'Saint George's day'). These can sometimes be found in the monolingual Spanish of other regions, too. Second, there is the loan of single Catalan words that are not syntactically integrated into the Spanish sentence, such as interjections (1a) and (b) or fixed expressions (1c), i.e. automatized routines or pragmatic markers which serve the purpose of monitoring and directing the linguistic interaction and escape the speaker's control over selection and inhibition mechanisms (see Matras 2010: 81).

---

26. Given that most of the studies cited in this section draw only on CatS or Barcelona Spanish, the reported examples usually stem from these varieties (if not further specified). However, many or probably most of these are also found in the Spanish varieties spoken in other Catalan-speaking regions (CCS).

Both types can be seen as borrowings of "free-floating", "non-systemic elements" because they are not part of the grammatical structure of a language and do not require integration into the system (Hickey 2013: 11). Finally, there are syntactically more integrated lexical borrowings (such as regular nouns (2a), verbs (2b), or expressions used as attributes (2c)). In some cases, these can be phonetically adapted to the Spanish sound system (3a) and (b).

(1) a. ¡Adéu! 'Bye!' (Sp. ¡Adiós!) (Sinner 1996: 52)
 b. ¡Va! 'Come on!' (Sp. ¡Venga!, ¡Vamos!)
  (Szigetvári 1994 VI; Sinner 2004: 502–505)
 c. ¡No pateixis! 'Nevermind!' (Sp. ¡No te preocupes!) (Wesch 1997: 308)

(2) a. pica 'sink' (Sp. fragadero) (Wesch 1997: 303)
 b. embolicar 'wrap up' (Sp. envolver) (Wesch 1997: 303)
 c. com cal 'as it has to/should be' (Sp. como debe ser, como es debido)
  (Wesch 1992: 10)

(3) a. CCS rachola [ra'tʃola] 'tile' (Cat. rajola [rə'ʒɔlə]; Sp. azulejo, baldosa)
  (Szigetvári 1994: 48)
 b. CCS enchegar [eɲtʃe'ɣaɾ] 'turn on, start' (Cat. engegar [əɲʒə'ɣa]; Sp. poner en marcha, encender) (Wesch 1997: 305)

The second major type of lexical interference, i.e. the already mentioned borrowings *in absentia*, do not entail the integration of originally Catalan morphemes into Spanish but merely concern the **semantic** level. In that case, the meaning of native Spanish words is extended or limited in conformity with a Catalan model (see Payrató 1985: 88; Weinreich 1953: 84). (4a) and (b) offer two examples.

(4) a. CCS faena 'work' vs Sp. 'labor, hard work'
  (Cat. feina 'work', Sp. trabajo 'work')
 b. CCS explicar 'explain, tell' vs Sp. 'explain'
  (Cat. explicar 'explain, tell', Sp. contar 'tell')

A similar case are calques or loan-translations (Weinreich 1953: 51; Payrató 1985: 89), where more or less fixed expressions (5a) and structures (5b), or phraseologisms (5c) are 'literally' translated from Catalan into Spanish:

(5) a. CCS hacer servir 'use, utilize' (Cat. fer servir, Sp. utilizar, emplear)
  (Szigetvári 1994: 29)
 b. CCS a la hora de + infinitive 'when, while' (Cat. a l'hora de, Sp. cuando, al + infinitive) (Sinner 1996: 81)
 c. CCS ¿Quieres decir? 'Do you think so?' (Cat. Vols dir?, Sp. ¿Estás seguro?')
  (Wesch 1997: 308)

Finally, some shifts in meaning also affect the domain of **pragmatics**. Namely, this is the case of the tripartite Spanish deictic system, which generally encompasses proximal, medial, and distal forms (e.g. the demonstratives *este, ese, aquel*). Under the influence of the simpler (Central) Catalan system, this system is often reduced to a bipartite one in CatS by merging the functions of the proximal and medial forms (see Vann 1998; Wesch 1997: 299; Sinner 2004: 549–562).

Also with reference to **morphology**, CCS presents some particularities that set it apart from other Spanish varieties. However, only in very few cases are Catalan morphemes directly transferred to Spanish (e.g. when *ves* is used instead of *ve* as the imperative form of the verb *ir* 'to go'; cf. Cat. *vés*). More recurrently, morphology is affected indirectly. For instance, Catalan lacks a direct equivalent to the Spanish verbal periphrasis '*ir a* + infinitive' to express the immediate or near future. In CCS, both the synthetic future tense as well as the present tense can often be found in contexts where other Spanish varieties would prefer the periphrastic expression: e.g. CCS *Lo haré enseguida* 'I'm going to do it in a moment' (Wesch 1997: 301, see also Sinner 2004: 225–229; Enrique-Arias/Méndez Guerrero 2020; Garachana 2021). Besides that, another phenomenon, which has often been related – for unjustified reasons and without any empirical proof – to a lack of education and culture, is the regularization of certain irregular verb paradigms in CCS via analogy with regular patterns (see Sinner 2008): for example, *andé* instead of *anduve* 'I walked' or *traducí* instead of *traduje* 'I translated'. Such uses are typically regarded as an interlanguage phenomenon resulting from incomplete L2 acquisition. However, even if that were the case, they should sooner be treated today as nativized elements perpetuated as authentic features of CCS via intergenerational transmission considering the fact that they are widely documented in other (monolingual) Spanish varieties, as well (Sinner 2008: 261).

In the field of (morpho-)**syntax**, the presence of the definite article before personal names in colloquial and familiar registers is without doubt one of the most recurrently named characteristics of CCS (see, e.g., Badia i Margarit 1981: 26; Montolío/Vila 1993: 100; Wesch 1997: 299f; Sinner 2004: 233–235, among many others).

(6) a. La Luisa ya lo sabe. (Badia i Margarit 1981: 26)
 'Luisa already knows it.'
 b. Vendrán también la María y el Joaquín. (Wesch: 1997: 300)
 'María and Joaquín will be coming, too.'
 c. La Marina come mandarinas. (example from the present DCT corpus)[27]
 'Marina is eating tangerines.'

---

27. In the semi-spontaneous oral corpus of Girona Spanish utterances recorded for the present study (see Section 4.3.1 for the methodology), examples of personal names preceded by the

Yet, neither this usage is an exclusive feature of CCS, considering that it is well-documented in the history of Spanish (Calderón Campos 2015) and still can be observed in some monolingual varieties of Spanish in both Spain (Andalusia, Extremadura) and Hispano-America (Chile; see Fernández Leborans 1999: 111–113). Due to the massive integration of emigrants from Southern Spain into Catalonia, the use of the definite article before proper names may thus have multiple causes in CatS (Casanovas Català 1996b: 153). Nevertheless, some authors consider its use in Spanish a vulgarism and attribute a derogatory connotation to it (Jordana 1968: 26; Briz 2001). Its relatively common 'neutral' use without any negative connotation might thus indeed be a characteristic of CCS.

A further frequently cited phenomenon is the use of a so-called 'partitive *de*' (see Badia i Margarit 1981: 26; Blas Arroyo 1993: 51, 2007: 85; Szigetvári 1994: 15; Sinner 1996: 44; Fernández-Ordóñez 2016: 400, among others). Although a partitive *de* may be found in monolingual Spanish in some fixed expressions such as *un poco (de agua)*, as signalled by Szigetvári (1994: 15), its usage in CCS is clearly more extended and follows patterns existent in Catalan. For instance, in (7a) it occurs after a numeral and introduces the adjectival complement of a dropped noun. In (7b) and (c), it surfaces in so-called pseudo-partitive constructions, i.e. in conjunction with quantitative quantifiers (see Brucart/Rigau 2002: 1538–1545; Rigau/Pérez Saldanya 2020: 174). The Catalan translations are mine.

(7) a. Hay tres de muy buenos. (Cat. *Hi ha tres de molt bons.*)
        (Badia i Margarit 1981: 26)
    'There are three very good ones'
  b. Tengo muy poca, de paciencia. (Cat. *En tinc molt poca, de paciència.*)
        (Szigetvári 1994: 15)
    'I have very little patience.'
  c. No eran nada, de tontos. (Cat. *No n'eren gens, de ximples.*)
        (Atienza et al. 1998: 8)
    'They weren't stupid at all.'

The examples in (7b) and (c) furthermore show that in CCS *de* may be used following the Catalan model as a "partitive marker" to introduce dislocated elements (Rigau/Pérez Saldanya 2020: 184). This is particularly interesting, as it points towards the possibility that dislocations, which are known to be much more commonplace in Catalan than in other Romance languages (see, e.g., Villalba 2011; Leonetti 2017: 889, 904; Feldhausen/Villalba 2020: 255), could equally appear with a higher frequency in CCS than in CS and emerge even in contexts where Main-

---

definite article were attested in a total of seven speakers, six of whom were Catalan-dominant bilinguals.

stream Spanish[28] prescriptive rules would forbid them. Yet, there exists a crucial difference between the constructions given in (7a) and (b) for the two languages because in Catalan the dislocated quantified element must be resumed by the (partitive) clitic pronoun *en*, inexistent in Spanish. Examples (7b) and (c) therefore illustrate not only that such constructions can be transferred to CCS but also in which way this is achieved, viz. without deploying a resumptive pronoun. Aside from the many single examples presented in the literature, however, 'partitive *de*' is rarely attested in corpus studies: for instance, Sinner (2004: 262) did not find any examples of it in his large oral corpus of CatS. Besides, he underlines that there is a high social awareness among the Catalans about this particular phenomenon being a Catalanism and that many speakers therefore consciously avoid it. Fernández-Ordóñez (2016: 400), too, points out that such pseudo-partitive constructions are less accepted as compared to other characteristics of CCS.[29]

A third phenomenon regularly described as syntactic interference of Catalan in Spanish is the use of *que* in (different types of) yes–no questions. This issue will be dealt with in some more detail as it is going to take on a prominent role in the intonational analysis of Girona Spanish and Girona Catalan presented in Chapter 5. Wesch (1992, 1997) states that in both Catalan and Spanish absolute interrogatives are expressed by means of intonation (he does not specify the shape of the pitch contours). However, according to his account, (Central) Catalan and Barcelona Spanish questions are "for the most part" headed by a "*que* átono" (Wesch 1992: 6) or the occurrence of *que* is at least "very typical" and occurs "very frequently" (Wesch 1997: 301, the translations are mine). For Spanish, he ascribes "a clear diaphasic mark that could be qualified as 'colloquial'" to these questions. Some examples are provided in (8); the Catalan translations are mine.

(8) a. ¿Que te has hecho daño? (Cat. *Que t'has fet mal?*)
            (Moll 1961: 472; Wesch 1997: 301)
      'Have you hurt yourself?'
   b. ¿Que tiene zanahorias? (Cat. *Que té pastanages?*)   (Wesch 1992: 6)
      'Do you have any carrots?' (to a vegetable merchant)
   c. ¿Que me entiendes? (Cat. *Que m'entens?*)   (Wesch 1997: 301)
      'Can you understand me?'

---

28. In accordance with Hualde/Şaul (2011) and Gabriel et al. (2024), I use the term Mainstream Spanish as a generic term to refer to all Peninsular and American non-contact varieties of Spanish, i.e., more precisely, all Spanish varieties that are not considerably influenced by language contact.

29. A series of metalinguistic comments made by the participants of the present study on the dialogue reading task (see Section 4.3.2) confirm this observation (e.g. one participant said *Aquí hay un fallo. Lo sabes, ¿no?* 'There's an error here. You know that, don't you?' when asked to read out the sentence presented in 7b, above).

d. ¿Que te ha gustado? Pues, a mí no. (Cat. *Que t'ha agradat?*)
(Montolío/Vila 1993:100)
'Did you like it? Well, I didn't'
e. ¿Que está Marina, por ahí? (Cat. *Que hi ha la Marina, per aquí?*)
(present corpus)[30]
'Is Marina around?

In other sources, *que* is described as expletive (Payrató 1985: 92; Sinner 2004: 287), particle (Montolío/Vila 1993:100), or atonic introductory element (Szigetvári 1994: 47). Its nature is thus not fully clear yet. In any case, while Briz (2001) points out that it is "not always unstressed", suggesting that it could receive more stress in exclamative than in assertive or confirmatory questions, Sinner (2004: 286) underlines that it is invariably unstressed, penalizing its orthographic rendering as *qué*. He additionally highlights that the phenomenon is apparently quite well known and very easy for the speakers to detect, considering that such questions have a clearly Catalan intonation. As opposed to that, only 20 out of 50 bilingual participants recognized initial *que* in yes–no questions as a non-normative element in Spanish in a test carried out in Barcelona by Hawkey (2014: 407; see also Piqueres Gilabert/Fuss 2018 for similar results in València).

The intonational aspect, on the other hand, was already highlighted by Szigetvári (1994: 47): "[l]a entonación descendente del catalán y el QUE delatan inmediatamente al hablante" ('the descending Catalan intonation and the *que* immediately give away the speaker'). A falling intonational pattern is equally mentioned by Briz (2001) for València, although he remarks that these constructions are less frequent there than in Catalonia. Moreover, Sinner (2004: 288) retraces the intonation of two *que*-questions found in his oral corpus as a high plateau with a fall towards the end, and such an intonation pattern will also be the one described for this question type later on in the first intonational studies on Barcelona Spanish (Romera et al. 2007, 2008, 2009; see below).

Finally, Szigetvári (1994: 47) points out that phrase-initial *que* can also occur in "normative Spanish" when "something is literally repeated in the question", i.e. in so-called echo-questions: e.g. *¿Que viniste antes de ayer, dices?* 'You're saying that you came the-day-before-yesterday, right?' (the translation is mine). These cases thus ought to be distinguished from the ones where *que* is proscribed by Mainstream Spanish prescriptive rules, which is not always done (cf., e.g., Sinner

---

30. In the oral corpus of semi-spontaneous Girona Spanish utterances recorded for this study using a DCT (see methodology in Section 4.3.1), seven information-seeking yes–no questions headed by que were attested, six of which stemmed from clearly Catalan-dominant bilinguals (see Section 5.1.3.1.5). Furthermore, there were also some echo-questions introduced by the complementizer *que*.

1996: 49). Interestingly, none of the existing studies specifies the pragmatic type of question in which *que* may occur in CCS as most authors merely mention that it is the case in yes–no questions. I therefore permit myself a short digression on *que*-questions in the source language Catalan.

According to Prieto/Rigau (2007, 2011), the Catalan dialects present a "substantially rich intra- and interdialectal variation" with reference to this topic. In neutral polar questions, i.e. in information-seeking yes–no questions, the subdialects of Barcelona and Tarragona allow for both (9a) and (b). The presence of the complementizer *que* is thus optional:

(9) a. Plou? (Prieto/Rigau 2007: 33)
    b. Que plou?
       'Is it raining?'

However, different intonational patterns are typically associated with these two questions: a rising pattern with (9a), and a falling one with (9b); see Sections 3.1.2.2 and 5.1.3.1 for a detailed description). While the falling pattern can also occur when *que* is absent, the "presence of the complementizer *que* is incompatible with the rising intonation pattern" (Prieto/Rigau 2007: 34f.; see also Nadeu/Prieto 2011: 845). Furthermore, adopting the view of Payrató (2002: 1203f.), the authors suggest that the use of either intonational pattern is sensitive to the pragmatic cost-benefit scale, on which the cost or benefit of the proposed action to the hearer is estimated (see Leech 1983). In the aforementioned Central Catalan subdialects, the falling intonation pattern (and hence *que*) can thus only be applied when the cost of the proposed action to the hearer is considered low. Asking someone about the weather as in (9a) and (b) is a common situation and rather unlikely to be perceived as imposing a high cost onto the hearer. The same is usually the case, e.g., in offers or invitations (10a) and (10b). Empirical studies such as Nadeu/Prieto (2011) and Astruc et al. (2016) have largely confirmed this.

(10) a. Que vols més cafè? 'Would you like some more coffee?'
                                                          (Prieto/Rigau 2007: 36)
     b. Que vindreu amb mi? 'Are you coming with me?'

These pragmatic associations entail the secondary effect that *que*-questions are generally excluded from formal speech styles (e.g. in courts of law or ceremonial formulas their use would be inappropriate; Prieto/Rigau 2007: 36).

Regarding the Northern Central Catalan subdialect, spoken mainly in the province of Girona, but also Valencian and Rossellonese, the authors state that neutral yes–no questions "cannot begin with the complementizer *que*". In these varieties, the use of *que* is limited to biased questions, i.e. those in which the speaker is biased in favour of one answer over another. For instance, the combination of *que* heading the interrogative and a falling intonation pattern can be found in Northern Central Catalan anti-expectational questions, i.e. when the speaker intends to convey an additional nuance of surprise or astonishment. A similar dialectal distribution of the particle is attested in alternative questions like *(Que) Véns o no (véns)?* 'Are you coming or not?'. In other question types, such as rhetorical or exploratory questions, the use of *que* is considered optional (Prieto/Rigau 2007: 48–51). Confirmation-seeking questions typically use dialect-specific "question markers" such as *oi* or *eh* rather than simple *que*.

Finally, it is worth pointing out that Catalan *que*-questions often present dislocations (Feldhausen/Villalba 2020: 259). This concerns particularly the subject, which, in information-structurally neutral interrogatives (of both the yes–no and wh-type), must usually be dislocated either to the left or the right — and thus be pronounced in a separate intonational phrase (Prieto/Rigau 2007: 54; GEIEC 2018: § 3.3.2, § 30.2.1, § 31.1). This is illustrated in the following examples:

(11) a. En Joan, que viu a Barcelona? (Prieto/Rigau 2007: 54)
     b. Que viu a Barcelona, en Joan?
        'Does John live in Barcelona?'

(12) Que ho ha portat en Joan? (Prieto/Rigau 2007: 54)
     'It was John who brought it?'

Whereas the examples in (11) represent neutral information-seeking yes–no questions, (12) cannot occur in out-of-the-blue contexts and delivers a counterexpectational connotation.

Turning back to Spanish, surprisingly, all authors mentioning the occurrence of yes–no questions headed by *que* in CCS have limited their remarks to the mere existence of the phenomenon, ignoring altogether the huge variation found in the respective Catalan contact varieties as well as the fine-grained pragmatic distinctions between interrogative modalities in Catalan, which are very likely to be present also in CCS unless a generalization, i.e. a semantic extension, has taken place. Moreover, such shortcomings and a general lack of sensitivity in relation to diasystematic variation are a more widespread problem in the research into CCS syntactic properties: also in the aforementioned case of 'partitive *de*', most scholars do not bother to capture its exact use in neither the Catalan contact varieties nor in CCS itself. Instead, they typically present uninspired lists of single and context-less examples without further classifying or categorizing them in any way whatsoever.

2.3.2 Segmental features of CCS phonetics and phonology

The most recurrently named and most iconic feature of CCS pronunciation is probably the velarized realization of /l/. Wesch (1997: 298) calls it "el rasgo clásico", its 'classic feature'. In Catalan, the phoneme /l/ is traditionally described as having two allophones that occur in complementary distribution: 'clear' [l] in the syllabic onset and 'dark', i.e. velarized [ɫ] in the syllabic coda (Wheeler 2005: 34). However, Catalan dialects show some variation in this respect, and some varieties (such as Balearic and Central Catalan) are said to use dark [ɫ]-realizations irrespective of the position of /l/ within the word (Recasens/Espinosa 2005). The transfer of dark [ɫ] to Spanish was thus one of the first phonic characteristics penalized as a "matiz defectuoso", a 'defective hue', of CCS pronunciation (see, e.g., Moll 1961: 470; or Badia i Margarit 1979: 148, who states that it "tant enlletgeix la dicció" 'it so much disfigures the diction'). Yet, authors generally fail to mention how pervasive this transfer is, i.e. whether it occurs throughout or just sporadically. Badia i Margarit (1979: 148) mentions that it is "incorporada per la majoria de catalans a llur pronunciació del castellà" ('integrated by the majority of Catalans into their Spanish pronunciation'), but already Wesch (1997: 298) signals that its use is less strong in younger generations. In fact, recent studies (Simonet 2008; Davidson 2012, 2015a) have revealed that today, i.e. in the light of an on-going bilingualization, the appearance of dark [ɫ] in CCS is by far less pervasive than it was in earlier times when (a) Spanish was still an L2 and (b) the presence of L1 Spanish speakers in Catalan-speaking regions had not yet reached a noteworthy level. Rather than by linguistic factors, the use of this feature seems to be conditioned nowadays by social factors (such as degree of exposure to and usage of Catalan; Davidson 2014, 2015a: 268). In both Simonet's (2008) and Davidson's (2014, 2015a) studies, the degree of velarization was lowest in young and in Spanish-dominant bilinguals (typically descendants of Spanish-speaking immigrants). Simonet (2008: 278–281) furthermore showed that the social stigma connected with dark [ɫ] in Spanish has even led to a decline in its use in Majorcan Catalan because Spanish-dominant speakers as well as Catalan-dominant females habitually use 'clear' allophones of /l/ in both of their languages now (i.e. merely Catalan-dominant males continue to use 'dark' realizations in Catalan). The current social meaning of dark laterals in Majorcan Catalan is thus that of a gender mark. Blas Arroyo (2019), finally, demonstrates that the use of the velarized [ɫ] in CatS can be a sign of identity and (nationalistic) ideology, as is the case in many politicians.

A further characteristic of CCS, mentioned almost with the same frequency, is the sonorization of word-final /s/ to [z]. Whereas in Mainstream Spanish, voiced [z] can only appear as an allophone of /s/ before voiced consonants through assimilation (e.g. in Sp. *mismo* ['mizmo] 'same'; see Gabriel et al. 2013: 64; Hualde 2014: 154–155; Hualde et al. 2010: 74), in Catalan, word-final /s/ and other sibilants become voiced before vowels as a rule (see Palmada 2002: 259–260; Wheeler 2005: 162). This also holds for /s/ at the end of some prefixes, such as {des-} or {trans-}. The transfer of this rule yields examples such as:

(13) a. CCS *los hombres* [loˈzombɾes] 'the men' (Badia i Margarit 1979: 149)
 b. CCS *seis años* [sejˈzaɲɔs] 'six years' (Wesch 1997: 296)
 c. CCS *deshacer* [dezaˈθeɾ] (Badia i Margarit 1979: 149)

The phenomenon is sometimes infelicitously called *liaison* due to a distant resemblance with a phonologic process in French whereby underlying (or latent) word-final consonants surface only in the context before a vowel (e.g. in Moll 1961: 469; Colón 1967: 203; Sinner 1996: 17f.). It has often been condemned as a distinctive feature of a Catalan accent, with Marsá (1986: 101) calling it a "pecado fonético capital", i.e. a 'capital phonetic sin', that needs to be fought (see also Casanovas Català 1995: 56–57). All the same, word-final intervocalic [z], as opposed to the velarized [ɫ], is a linguistic marker of CCS that has no salient social stigma attached to it and generally passes below the level of overt awareness (Davidson 2015a: 257). Traditionally, scholars did not make any reference to its pervasiveness across different groups of society, but recently empirical studies have revealed that it is mediated not only by linguistic factors (e.g. speech style) but crucially also by extralinguistic parameters such as language dominance and gender (Davidson 2012, 2015a, 2020; McKinnon 2012; Grünke 2022). Regarding language dominance, the results of Davidson (2014, 2015a, 2015b) and Grünke (2022) suggest that voicing of intervocalic word-final /s/ — albeit more common in the speech of Catalan-dominant bilinguals — is also being adopted by many Spanish-dominant bilinguals. A possible reason for this might be that its non-stigmatized status makes it "more conducive (or more permissive) to the selection and diffusion" from Catalan- to Spanish-dominant bilinguals (Davidson 2015a: 257f.).

A slightly different case is the word-internal sonorization of Sp. /s/ between vowels that has occasionally been reported too for CCS (Davidson 2015a: 71; McKinnon 2012: 24). Although Catalan can have both /s/ and /z/ in such positions, many cognate words, such as Sp./Cat. *presentar*, display /z/ in Catalan and /s/ in Spanish. The voiced pronunciation in Spanish is thus often interpreted as an interference of the voiced Catalan phoneme /z/.

Another typical phenomenon concerns the pronunciation of the voiced stops /b d g/ in the syllabic coda (both word-internally and word-finally). In monolingual varieties of Spanish, the phonemic contrast with the voiceless counterparts /p t k/[31] is neutralized in these contexts and surface realizations range from voiced

---

31. Note that only /d/ can occur word-finally in the "patrimonial" Spanish lexicon, while the remaining plosives are limited to "more recent loan words". In Catalan, word-final plosives are frequent (Hualde/Nadeu 2020: 22, 23).

plosives ([b d g]) over voiced fricatives or approximants ([β ð ɣ])³² to elision (see Hualde 2005; Gabriel et al. 2013:60; Hualde/Eager 2016). In Catalan, on the other hand, devoicing rules applying to all non-sonorant coda consonants require a voiceless realization of the voiced stop phonemes /b d g/ as [p t k] when no voiced consonant is following (Cat. *ensordiment final*; Wheeler 2005:145–165; Recasens 2014:325). Even though such pronunciations are not considered incorrect in Spanish, they are rare in monolingual varieties and probably perceived as hyperarticulated by most natives, i.e. distinctive of an emphatic speech style (Gabriel et al. 2013:60). Their comparably frequent use in CCS therefore sticks out as a typical feature of these varieties (Hualde/Nadeu 2020:35). This is particularly evident in the case of word-final /d/ pronounced as [t] by bilingual speakers (although it may also be heard in some monolingual Spanish varieties): e.g. *usted* [usˈtet] 'you (formal)', *popularidad* [populariˈðat] 'popularity' (see Moll 1961:469; Wesch 1997:297; Casanovas Català 1995; Radatz 2008:116f.; Blas Arroyo 2020). To my knowledge, the first experimental study on this phenomenon in CCS was carried out by Machuca (2016), who demonstrates that Catalan-dominant bilinguals produce less elisions of coda-consonants when speaking Spanish than bilinguals who speak this language predominantly. The author attributes this to the fact that Catalan-dominants "are used to realizing a greater articulatory effort in this position". Igarreta Fernández (2019) points towards register-specific differences in some L1 Catalan speakers in the sense that they use more voiceless plosives in spontaneous speech than in more controlled and planned registers. Hualde/Nadeu (2020), finally, show that over 90% of word-final plosives are pronounced as voiceless plosives by Catalan–Spanish bilinguals in both Catalan and CatS. Still and all, they observe some more variation in CatS than in Catalan, which is mainly attributable to the elision of /d/ or its realization as a voiceless fricative ([θ]) or voiced fricative or approximant ([ð]) in the speech of Spanish-dominant bilinguals.

Further consonantal features frequently ascribed to CCS are the following:

– Non-elision of the voiced plosive /d/ in intervocalic position: many speakers of monolingual Spanish varieties tend to drop this segment in colloquial speech instead of realizing it as an interdental fricative or approximant ([ð]), especially in participles ending in *-ado(s)* (NGRAE 2011:146–148). Its presence is thus often seen as a typical feature of the Spanish spoken by L1-Catalan

---

32. Following, among others, Wheeler (2005:23, 312–313), I transcribe these sounds as fricatives in the present work (in both Catalan and Spanish). Even though they do not usually display the turbulence characteristic of typical fricatives such as sibilants and hence may be characterized as approximants, the main reason for this is that they behave phonologically like obstruents, i.e. like fricatives, and not like sonorants.

speakers (Casanovas Català 1995; Briz 2001; Blas Arroyo 2007:86; Igarreta Fernández 2019) because it represents a "pronunciación ultracorrecta" 'a hypercorrect pronunciation' as Briz (2001) puts it.

- Presence or retention of *lleísmo*, or rather the absence of *yeísmo*: since the loss of the phonemic contrast between /ʎ/ and /j/ in favour of the latter is characteristic of most contemporary varieties of Mainstream Spanish (see Hualde 2014:42; NGRAE 2011:213–214; Gabriel et al. 2013:66; Rost Bagudanch 2017, 2019), its retention is often seen as a Catalan interference as /ʎ/ continues to be a fully-fledged phoneme in most Catalan varieties (see Navarro Tomás 1971:135; Payrató 1985:105; Marsá 1986:101; Sinner 1996:19f.).[33] However, recent empirical studies show that at least in Barcelona Spanish the "advance of *yeísmo* has been intense in recent years" and the distinction between /ʎ/ and /j/ is no longer systematic (Torres et al. 2013:34, translation is mine). The same holds largely for Spanish in Majorca (Romera 2003; Ramírez/Simonet 2017; Rost Bagudanch/Blecua 2017; Rost Bagudanch 2019). On the other hand, perceptive studies show that in Girona, Catalan-dominant bilinguals are able to discriminate /ʎ/ and /j/ in both Catalan and Spanish, although the phonetic distance of the contrast is significantly smaller in the Spanish pair (Rost Bagudanch 2016). In Majorca, this is true for Catalan-dominant bilinguals, too (although to a lesser extent than in Girona), but not so for Spanish-dominants, who do not identify the segments above chance level (Rost Bagudanch 2020).

- Use of *seseo*: in spite of the fact that *distinción* (i.e. the distinction of /s/ and /θ/) is clearly the norm of (present-day) CCS, some authors maintain that merger of these phonemes in favour of /s/, called *seseo* (see Hualde 2014:42; NGRAE 2011:167–168; Gabriel et al. 2013:63f.), may sometimes still occur in CCS (e.g. Badia i Margarit 1979:148; Payrató 1985:82; Sinner 1996:18f.). Historically, it was certainly one of the most typical features of the L2-Spanish spoken by Catalans before the bilingualization of Catalan society and it is documented as early as in the 16th century (Blas Arroyo 2011:283f.). It is usually explained as a phenomenon of incomplete L2 acquisition by L1 Catalan speakers given that Catalan lacks /θ/. The same holds for the substitution of Sp. /x/ by [k] (Cerdá Massó 1967; Veny 2006:33–60). However, Wesch (1997:297f.) remarks that he did not find any interferences with /θ/ or /x/ in

---

[33]. Note that the phenomenon known as *iodització* or *ieisme històric*, whereby the Latin groups -C'L-, -G'L-, -T'L-, and -L'Y- developed to [j] instead of [ʎ] in some Central and Balearic varieties of Catalan (Veny/Massanell 2015:144–146, 190, 395; Wheeler 2005:35), does not represent a case of phoneme merger (as *yeísmo* in Spanish), since it does not affect the phonemic status of /ʎ/.

Barcelona Spanish. To my knowledge no empirical studies exist on the topic. At present, especially the (competing) use of *seseo* and the *distinción* system in migrants from Latin America and their descendants is a topic that would deserve further study.
- Other phenomena: the sporadic sonorization of word-final /θ/ before following vowels (*diez años* [djeˈðaɲos]; Wesch 1997: 298) and, especially in Majorca, the pronunciation of /tʃ/ as [ʃ], gemination and assimilations of some consonants (e.g. *colegio* as [koˈlːexjo], *amable* as [aˈmabːɫe]), dissimilation of /s/ before sibilants, and the differentiation of <v> /v/ and <b> /b/ (see Moll 1961: 469f.; Badia i Margarit 1979; Payrató 1985; Sinner 1996).

In the vocalic domain, the characteristics of CCS in terms of both stressed and unstressed vowels are traditionally traced back to two fundamental differences between the Spanish and Catalan vowel system. Whereas Mainstream Spanish has only the five vowel phonemes /a e i o u/ (Hualde 2014: 41, 113–114; Gabriel et al. 2013: 78f.), most Catalan varieties exhibit seven, since they distinguish open and close mid-vowels (/e o/ vs /ɛ ɔ/, respectively). In Mainstream Spanish, on the other hand, [ɛ ɔ] can at best be allophones of /e o/ (see Hualde 2014: 78; Gabriel et al. 2013: 79).[34] In addition, Eastern Catalan varieties present regular vowel reduction, i.e. raising and/or centralization of (most) unstressed vowels (Wheeler 2005: 52–61, for exceptions see Wheeler 2005: 61–77). Figure 2.2 illustrates how this process works in Central Catalan, where most phonemic distinctions are neutralized in unstressed position such that only three vowel qualities occur, viz. [i ə u].

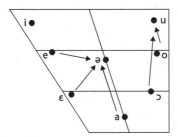

Figure 2.2 The Catalan vowel system (adapted from Carbonell/Llisterri 1999: 62). The arrows represent the vowel reduction of unstressed vowels as it operates in Central Catalan. [ə] only occurs in unstressed positions

---

34. Some Eastern Andalusian varieties constitute an exception to this (see Penny 2000: 125f.; Gabriel et al. 2013: 101; Hualde 2014: 124–125).

Regarding CCS, impressionistic studies typically criticize the use of [ɛ] and [ɔ] as well as the reduction of unstressed vowels according to the Catalan pattern (e.g. Badia i Margarit 1979:150, 1981:25; Marsá 1986:101; Royo 1991:123; Casanovas 1995:55; Sinner 1996:14; Blas Arroyo 2007:84). However, while they typically accuse the Catalans of using too open mid-vowels, already Wesch (1997:298) observed that, in fact, the contrary seems to be the case: speakers of CatS with the L1 Catalan use a very close [e] even in positions where most Mainstream Spanish varieties would recur to the open allophone [ɛ]. This observation was confirmed in acoustic studies on CatS vowels, which showed that the realizations of the mid-vowels /e/ and /o/ in CatS do not occupy the centre of the space between /i/ and /a/ and /u/ and /a/, i.e. mid-positions, but are much closer to the high vowels (Balari et al. 1988; Poch Olivé/Harmegnies 1994; Machuca/Poch 2016). Poch Olivé and Harmegnies (1994:23) therefore conclude that Catalan-dominant bilinguals are conscient of interlinguistic differences and, rather than restructuring their vowel system, they simply deactivate the segments inexistent in Spanish; that is, they use a subsystem of their Catalan vowel system when speaking Spanish. Spanish-dominant bilinguals, on the contrary, performed like Spanish monolinguals in Machuca and Poch (2016). Helms (2021), finally, confirmed that productions of Barcelona Spanish /e/ are closer to Cat. /e/ than to Cat. /ɛ/ in Catalan-dominants, although there still is a phonetic contrast between the /e/ productions in the two languages. She furthermore found that productions of Spanish /e/ are becoming increasingly diffuse, as the corresponding F1 values present more variability in younger than in older speakers. Helms interprets this as an influence from their Catalan, which has lost the mid-vowel contrast.

With respect to unstressed vowels, Wesch (1997:297) indicates that, in Barcelona Spanish, there is a tendency to pronounce unstressed /e/ and /a/ (the latter especially in word-final position) as [ə]: e.g. CatS. *dinámica* [diˈnamikə]. Concerning unstressed /o/, he underlines that its raising to [u] is inexistent in Barcelona Spanish but can be found in rural varieties of CatS. Unfortunately, no acoustic studies have been carried out yet on the quality of CCS unstressed vowels to my knowledge.

2.3.3 Suprasegmental features of CCS phonetics and phonology

At the suprasegmental level, surprisingly little research has been dedicated to CCS to date, even though already the earliest descriptions highlight the strong influence of Catalan on its speech rhythm and intonation: for instance, Navarro Tomás (1935:32) remarks the "ímpetu de su entonación" ('the boost of its intonation'), Badia i Margarit (1979:153) comments on a "dilació sorprenent en el compàs de l'expressió" ('surprising delay in the speech rhythm') in L1 Catalan speakers, which he attributes to a general lack of naturalness of their Spanish. According to Briz (2001), intonation is one of the most distinctive characteristics of Spanish spoken in València, and Poch Olivé (2016: 336) underlines that the investigation of intonation is essential to give a proper account of CCS phonic characteristics: as it "doubtlessly will be very different in the whole of the bilingual geography", it deserves "extraordinary attention" (translation is mine). Besides, it is known that prosodic features are particularly susceptible to be transferred from one language to another, since they are hard to control by the speaker even if one is conscious of them (see, e.g., Weinreich 1953: 24; Baetens Beardsmore 1986: 73–74; Matras 2009: 232–233; and Section 3.2.2), which is not always the case (Bernhard 1998: 10). The neglect of the study of CCS prosody (Poch Olivé 2016: 336) might be linked with the fact that domains such as intonation have traditionally been given little attention by linguists (Font Rotchés 2007: 21) and the interest in studying and describing it – both from an experimental and theoretical perspective – has grown only in recent decades (see Section 3.1.1).

Concerning the intonation of CCS, the aforementioned *que*-questions, to some extent, represent an exception, since they have been attributed a falling intonation pattern in some auditive descriptions (e.g. Szigetvári 1994; Briz 2001; Sinner 2004). The first experimental study of Spanish intonation including CCS varieties is by Sosa (1999: 193f., 210). He observed that declaratives have very similar contours in Barcelona and in Madrid and that Barcelona Spanish follows the model of the canonical Castilian intonation for yes–no questions in using a rising toneme. Later on, Romera et al. (2007, 2008) studied the intonation of declarative and yes–no interrogatives with and without *que* on the basis of read speech from one L1 Spanish speaker from Barcelona within the framework of the AMPER project (Contini 2005; Fernández Planas 2005, 2009; Martínez Celdrán et al. 2003–2020). In synthesis, they found strong similarities with the intonation of Barcelona Catalan but also with other Spanish varieties of the Iberian Peninsula (Valladolid, Salamanca), for both statements and questions. However, it is striking that in (neutral) yes–no interrogatives introduced by the particle *que*, which do not exist in other Spanish varieties, there is an overall coincidence between the Barcelona Spanish and Barcelona Catalan patterns, which the authors describe as H% H* H+L* H+L* L%[35] using the Autosegmental-Metrical (AM) framework

---

[35]. The recorded sentences present a 'verb–object, subject' structure realized with a high initial boundary tone, a high pitch accent on the verb, a steeply falling accent on the complement, and a low plateau until the last stressed syllable of the subject, where another gentle fall is observed before the low final boundary tone. Note that the transcription of the initial boundary tone as 'H%' (instead of '%H') follows Pierrehumbert's (1980) original AM conventions and does not imply a prosodic boundary (see also Section 3.1.1.1).

(see 3.1.1.1). In Romera et al. (2009), a perception experiment was conducted showing that the participating judges were not able to tell apart Barcelona Spanish and Barcelona Catalan merely by intonational cues (i.e. when lexical and segmental information was concealed). The participants generally managed to recognize the sentence modality of statements and questions without *que*, but there were noticeably more confusions with statements in the case of questions headed by *que*. A similar experiment (including Barcelona-Catalan stimuli but no Spanish *que*-questions) had been carried out by Van Oosterzee (2005), who equally found that the two languages can hardly be distinguished by their intonation. However, in his study, monolingual speakers of Spanish had more difficulties than Catalan–Spanish bilinguals to recognize Catalan *que*-questions. Furthermore, important similarities were also found by Martínez Celdrán et al. (2011: 37) in the intonation of declaratives and absolute interrogatives between Spanish and Catalan spoken in Lleida, although the authors show that the contours are not identical in the two languages. Still within the AMPER project, Romera et al. (2015) compared information- and confirmation-seeking interrogatives in different Catalan and CCS varieties (Barcelona, Palma, Tortosa): they found that information-seeking yes–no questions most frequently end with rising nuclear configurations (viz. L* H%, L+H* H%) in all varieties. As for confirmation-seeking yes–no questions, L+H* H% was used in Barcelona Spanish (whereas Barcelona Catalan preferred falling H* L%). However, the number of items in this study was rather small. The same is true for Romera (2014), who studied the realization of different types of interrogatives in Barcelona Spanish spontaneous speech recorded from two speakers. Only partially confirming the findings made for scripted speech, her major conclusion is that confirmation-seeking yes–no questions and wh-questions tend to end in a low boundary tone, while information-seeking yes–no questions usually present a final rise.

Simonet (2008, 2011) investigated sentence-final pitch accents in declaratives and yes–no interrogatives in Majorcan Spanish and Catalan. In declaratives, all of his subjects transferred melodic patterns from their dominant to their non-dominant language ('substratum interference') with the exception of Spanish-dominant young females, who were using configurations that resembled Catalan in both of their languages. Simonet (2008: 274) interpreted this finding as pointing towards an ongoing process of convergence of Majorcan Spanish intonation patterns towards Catalan, led by young females. His analysis of absolute interrogatives confirms this idea, as all speaker groups, independently of their language dominance, show a tendency to use typically Catalan F0 contours when speaking Spanish. While this once more can be interpreted in terms of 'substratum interference' for Catalan-dominant speakers, with Spanish-dominant speakers, it rather represents an instance of 'adstratum interference' or 'borrowing' from Catalan

(Simonet 2008: 278). Again, young Spanish-dominant speakers seem to be the drivers of the convergence process. Simonet concludes that (especially the young) bilinguals seem to collapse the two languages' intonational systems into only one.

Similar observations were made by Romera/Elordieta (2013). In a study into the intonation of four monolingual speakers of Castilian Spanish who had moved to Majorca as adults, the authors found that final falls, i.e. a prosodic feature of L2 Majorcan Spanish, were consistently adopted by the migrants in their interrogatives.

Finally, Alfano (2016) used the INTSINT method (see Hirst et al. 2000 and Section 3.1.1) to analyse the interface between intonation and information structure in Barcelona Spanish yes–no questions. She found that this question type presents a melodic pattern that is stationary-descending or ascending until the first peak (located on the first post-tonic syllable), then globally descending up to the last tonic syllable of the utterance, and, at its termination, decidedly ascending (i.e. essentially the same pattern as Castilian Spanish, see Section 3.1.2.2). Topics within such questions exhibit a significant rise at their right boundary.

Regarding other areas of prosody, such as phrasing, Rao (2007, 2008a) showed that in Barcelona Spanish (as spoken by Spanish-dominant speakers) it is possible to explain the distribution of prosodic words in phonological phrases[36] solely by prosodic factors, while previous proposals (made on the basis of other Spanish and Romance varieties) had placed more emphasis on phrase boundaries being determined mainly by syntactic cues. He found that the ideal length of a phonological phrase in Barcelona Spanish is two prosodic words and that balanced length, symmetry, and a rightward increase in length are other crucial factors influencing phrasing decisions. Concerning the deaccenting of lexically stressed words in spontaneous speech, Rao (2008b, 2009) observed, again for Barcelona Spanish, that the following characteristics increase the odds of stressed words to be deaccented: having few syllables; being globally frequent; being adverbs or verbs; being recently repeated in discourse; and located in an initial or medial position of the phonological phrase. As for the acoustic correlates of stress and accent, Ortega-Llebaria and Prieto (2007) discovered, equally for Barcelona Spanish, that in the absence of a pitch accent, stress is conveyed mainly by duration and to a lesser extent by intensity and vowel quality.

Finally, some works studying the voice quality of CCS speakers on the basis of long-term average spectra are worth mentioning, as they reveal that Spanish–Catalan bilinguals tend to behave differently in their two languages as a func-

---

36. Rao considers phonological or minor phrases to be inferior to the so-called major or intonational phrases (IPs). They thus correspond to the intermediate phrases (ips) suggested in other pieces of research (see Section 3.1.1.1).

tion of their language dominance (Harmegnies et al. 1989; Bruyninckx et al. 1990, 1994; Llisterri et al. 1992). For instance, they exhibit greater voice coherence and their speech is generally more restrained in the non-dominant language due to a "global insecurity", while the dominant one seems to allow for more variability as speakers are more confident.

CHAPTER 3

Theoretical background and description of Castilian Spanish and Central Catalan intonation

Chapter 3 provides the necessary prerequisites to the data analysis and discussion presented later in this book. First, subchapter 3.1 deals with intonation: Section 3.1.1 offers a description of the framework applied in the analyses, the Autosegmental-Metrical (AM) model and the ToBI annotation system. In Section 3.1.2, a comparison Central Catalan (CC) and Castilian Spanish (CS) will be made, focusing on the respective inventories of pitch accents and boundary tones and the tonal realization of various sentence types. Section 3.2 is devoted to the terms and phenomena which will be referred to in Chapter 6 when discussing the results of the intonational analysis of Girona Catalan and Girona Spanish in terms of language contact (e.g. borrowing, transfer, convergence, language attrition, etc.). It also summarizes and discusses the findings of various studies on contact-induced prosodic change. Section 3.3, finally, is dedicated to language dominance.

3.1 Intonation

3.1.1 Models of intonation and annotation systems

Research on intonation has long been a marginal field within linguistics — first and foremost due to a series of unresolved issues regarding its representation and meaning as well as to the lack of a generally accepted model in the face of fundamentally different approaches (see Wakefield 2020; Ladd 2008; Prieto 2003; Navarro Tomás 1974; Stockwell 1972). This is already evident from the difficulty of defining the term *intonation*. Ladd (2008: 4) puts it as follows: "Intonation [...] refers to the use of *suprasegmental* phonetic features to convey 'postlexical' or *sentence-level* pragmatic meanings in a *linguistically structured* way" (emphasis is his). By suprasegmental features he first of all refers to the phonetic properties of fundamental frequency (F0), intensity, and duration, although he remarks that it is often unclear whether these or their psychophysical correlates (i.e. pitch, loudness, and quantity) are most appropriately used as terms of reference when talking about suprasegmental phenomena, which is why they are often used interchangeably (p. 5). Regarding pragmatics, it is said that intonation conveys meanings such as information structure and sentence type (e.g. the difference between neutral and contrastive focus or between declaratives and interrogatives). Such meanings apply to phrases or utterances as a whole (Ladd 2008: 6; for a critical view see Wakefield 2020: 13). Furthermore, Ladd's definition excludes features of stress, accent, and tone that are determined in the lexicon. Finally, he assumes that intonational features are organized "in terms of categorically distinct entities [...] and relations" and that paralinguistic features such as tempo and loudness that signal continuously variable states of the speaker (e.g. arousal) are not part of them.

Taking into consideration this definition of intonation, which will be adopted here, it can be suggested that studies on intonation ought to concentrate on the concrete phonetic realization first before establishing an inventory of contrastive entities and defining the relation between prosodic units relevant for the intonational description of the languages under consideration. Some of the fundamental questions that arise regarding the analysis of intonation are:

1. How can we best describe the intonation of a particular language?
2. Which kinds of prosodic units should be taken into account in order to establish a universal model of intonation?
3. How do languages differ with respect to their intonational properties?

During recent decades, the interest in describing and modelling intonation has steadily grown both from an experimental and theoretical perspective. As a result of this boom, a large array of methodologies and models have been put forth for its analysis. In the aim of describing English prosody to aid foreign-language learning and teaching, the first linguistic frameworks emerged from the important conceptual work of the British (Jones 1918; Palmer 1922; Armstrong/Ward 1926; O'Connor/Arnold 1973 [¹1961]; Crystal 1969; see García-Lecumberri 2003 for an overview) and American Schools (Trager/Smith 1975 [¹1951]; see Martínez-Celdrán 2003 for an overview). While the former analyses the melodic contours as 'configurations' of tonal movements, the primitives of the latter are combinations of static tonal levels — an idea that dates back to Pike (1945) and Wells (1945). Both models have been applied to Spanish in the influential works of Navarro Tomás (1974) and Quilis (1981, 1993), respectively, and have also clearly inspired later frameworks such as, e.g., the IPO model of the Dutch School (Cohen/'t Hart 1967; 't Hart/Collier 1975; De Pijper 1983; see Garrido 2003 for an overview), which takes up tonal movements and configurations as minimal units from the British School but subjects pitch curves to a stylization process prior to the linguistic analysis. This phonetic approach, including resynthesis of the speech signal, is also central in the level-based model of intonation developed by Hirst, Di Cristo, and Espesser in Aix-en-Provence at the *Laboratoire Parole et Lan-*

gage (Hirst/Di Cristo 1998; Hirst et al. 2000; see Baqué/Estruch 2003 for an overview), in the Kiel intonation model (Kohler 1991, 1997) as well as in the many studies elaborated within the AMPER project (*Atlas Multimédia Prosodique de L'Espace Roman*), originated by Michel Contini and Antonio Romano at the *Centre de Dialectologie de Grenoble* (Université Stendhal de Grenoble) (Contini 2005; Fernández Planas 2005; Romano et al. 2005; Martínez Celdrán et al. 2003–2020; among many others). Undoubtedly, the Autosegmental-Metrical (AM) model (Pierrehumbert 1980; Beckman/Pierrehumbert 1986; Pierrehumbert/Beckman 1988; see Hualde 2003a and Section 3.1.2, for an overview), which was originally developed for the analysis of English intonation by Pierrehumbert (1980) in her seminal dissertation and consequently adapted to describe a large variety of Romance and other languages (see Frota/Prieto 2015; Jun 2005, 2014), has had the largest impact on the field and is still dominant today (Martin 2015: 46).

In conjunction with these models of intonation, a variety of annotation systems have been proposed, including, among many others, the transcription systems INTSINT (*INTernational Transcription System of INTonation*; Hirst et al. 2000), OXIGEN (*OXford Intonation GENerator*; Grabe et al. 2003), PENTA (*Parallel Encoding and Pitch Target Approximation*; e.g. Xu 2005), and the ToBI (*Tones and Break Indices*) labelling system, which is based on the AM model (Silverman et al. 1992; Beckman et al. 2005, among others). Especially for German, DIMA (*Deutsche Intonation — Modellierung und Annotation*) was proposed as a consensual system that allows for a phonetically informed phonological annotation and is easily translatable to other AM frameworks (Kügler/Baumann 2020). In recent years, work on an International Prosodic Alphabet (IPrA), similar to the transcription system IPA (*International Phonetic Alphabet*) for speech sounds, has been initiated with the aim of developing a set of cross-linguistically transparent and consistent labels building on the AM framework and the ToBI notation (Hualde/Prieto 2016).[37]

Considering the array of co-existing models of intonation and labelling systems, researchers need to carefully choose the model and the annotation system which best serve the purposes of their investigation. For the intonational analysis of the two contact varieties Girona Spanish and Girona Catalan carried out in the present work this is doubtlessly the AM framework and the ToBI system: first, both are demonstrably adequate tools to describe the intonation of a given language,

---

37. The most important difference between the ToBI and the IPrA annotation systems consists in the fact that ToBI systems are language-specific, whereas the IPrA attempts to offer a cross-linguistic annotation. Furthermore, as opposed to ToBI, the IPrA uses two levels of prosodic representation, a broad phonetic and a phonological one — an idea already put forth by Armstrong/Cruz (2014). However, IPrA is a very new proposal and has not yet been applied to any language.

since they can be used to establish inventories of contrastive pitch contours and to define how the relevant prosodic entities are organized while abstracting irrelevant aspects such as the number or syllables or words of each utterance (Hualde 2003a: 180). Second, as shown in Chapter 5, the ToBI labelling systems proposed for Spanish and Catalan (Sp_ToBI: Estebas-Vilaplana/Prieto 2008, 2010; Hualde/Prieto 2015; Prieto/Roseano 2018, among others; Cat_ToBI: Prieto et al. 2009; Prieto et al. 2015, among others) enable both phonetic and phonological descriptions of the F0 contour. In this, they resemble the IPA, whose symbols are used in both transcriptions of physically realized phones and representations of the corresponding underlying phonemes. Third, the AM model and the ToBI annotation system are nowadays two of the most widespread frameworks (Hualde 2003a; Hualde/Prieto 2016, among others). The fact that they have been applied to several dozen (typologically distinct) languages with very different prosodic systems as well as to a large variety of sentence types, facilitates cross-linguistic comparison of different intonational systems. Fourth and most importantly, the major part of research studies on the intonation of CS and CC, i.e. the two varieties to which I compare Girona Spanish in Chapter 6, were conducted within these two approaches — especially when it comes to the analysis of diatopic and diastratic variation within these varieties as well as of the pitch contours used in different pragmatic situations, there is no comparable amount of studies in any other theoretical framework. In the next sections, I will therefore introduce the AM model and the ToBI annotation system adopted in the present work.

3.1.1.1 *Autosegmental-Metrical model*

The Autosegmental-Metrical model (AM model) has its starting point in the intonational analysis of American English proposed by Pierrehumbert (1980) in her seminal dissertation. However, some of its fundamental aspects are clearly inspired by the ideas of Leben (1973) and Goldsmith (1976) for the analysis of tone languages and other preceding work on the intonation of English (Leben 1976; Liberman 1975) and the tone-accent language Swedish (Bruce 1977) (see Hualde 2003a; Ladd 2008: 43; Beckman/Venditti 2010; Arvaniti 2011, among others).[38] The central aim of the AM model is to neatly distinguish between the phonological structure, which consists of underlying tonal targets represented as strings of (level) tones on a separate tonal tier, and the surface F0 contour produced by

---

[38]. To give some examples, Leben (1973) first conceptualized tones as distinct tonal segments rather than features of particular tone-bearing units, such as syllables. Goldsmith (1976) represented them as *autosegments* on a separate tier and analysed English tunes as sequences of H and L level tones. Bruce (1977), finally, demonstrated the importance of *turning points*, i.e. F0 minima and maxima that temporally align with particular elements of the segmental string (see Arvaniti 2011).

a speaker as a result of phonetic interpolation between phonologically specified underlying tonal units, i.e. it builds on a formal separation between phonetics and phonology. As a phonological model of intonation, it intends to capture and represent exclusively "the linguistically significant parts of the melody" (Arvaniti 2011: 769), instead of providing a merely phonetic description or transcription of the course of the F0 contour. As opposed to most other models, which have focused solely on faithful representations of entire F0 curves, it thus tackles the question of what should be represented phonologically when it comes to annotating intonation in a parsimonious and elegant way (Arvaniti 2011). The term *Autosegmental-Metrical* was coined by Ladd (2008 [¹1996]) (Hualde 2003a: 155; Gussenhoven 2004: 123). It makes reference to the central assumption of Autosegmental Phonology (Goldsmith 1976) that the melody or tonal modulation of an utterance constitutes an independent level, i.e. an apart *tonal tier* containing its *tone-bearing units* ('autosegments'), in addition to the segmental level. Furthermore, it refers to Liberman's (1975) observation that, at least in English, the way in which these tones associate with specific syllables is determined by the prominence relations between the syllables of each word and those between the words of each utterance, i.e. by metrical structure (Hualde 2003a: 156f.). Through a sparse tonal specification of the contour, the model captures the similarities between superficially different melodies that arise from the properties of the metrical structure with which the melodies associate and, in this way, accounts for both local phonetic detail and abstract phonological form, something that configurational and full specification models cannot do (for extensive discussions of this point see Pierrehumbert/Beckman 1988; Arvaniti/Ladd 2009).

As already mentioned, the AM approach is established on the premise that intonational tunes can be characterized adequately as string of categorically distinct tonal events which can be mapped to continuous acoustic parameters by associating them with certain points in the segmental string (Ladd 2008: 43f.). In languages like English, Spanish, or Catalan, the most important events of the tonal string, i.e. the basic components of the model, are *pitch accents*, which are aligned with prominent syllables in the segmental string,[39] and *edge tones*, which are associated with the edges of intonational contours. In Pierrehumbert's (1980) and many following proposals, the latter encompass *phrase accents* and *boundary*

---

39. In languages such as English, Spanish or Catalan, prominent or metrically strong syllables are those which have lexically (or morphologically) defined stress. In consequence, almost all words may bear a tonal accent as a concrete perceptual cue expressing stress of the respective metrically strong syllable (exceptions are mainly the definite articles as well as some (generally monosyllabic) prepositions and functional words; see Hualde 2003a: 157; Ladd 2008: 44). However, it is an asset of the AM model to formally separate stress from intonation and to provide a mechanism for their interaction (Arvaniti 2011).

tones. Whereas boundary tones are anchored at the very end of the intonation phrase (IP),[40] phrase accents follow the last pitch accent and are realized as freestanding tones occupying an intermediate position between the last pitch accent and the boundary tone of the IP (Pierrehumbert 1980: 19–29; see also Hualde 2003a; Gussenhoven 2004: 123f.; Ladd 2008: 87f.; Arvaniti 2011).[41] Both pitch accents and edge tones can be analysed as consisting of the two primitive level tones or pitch targets High (H) and Low (L). In Pierhumbert's (1980) analysis of English, pitch accents encompass a single tone or a combination of two tones, and are indicated with an asterisk or 'star'. While the phonetic description of the H* pitch accent as a local peak and of the L* as a local valley are "fairly straightforward" (Ladd 2008: 92), bitonal pitch accents are used when the F0 is characterized by rapid local movement rather than just a local minimum or maximum. In this case, one tone is assumed to be central in some way and its alignment with the metrically strong syllable is indicated by the asterisk, whereas the other one is considered a leading or a trailing tone depending on its position before or after the starred tone (Pierrehumbert 1980: 25–26; see also Gussenhoven 2004: 128; Ladd 2008: 87–100; Arvaniti 2011).[42] As mentioned above, Pierrehumbert (1980: 22f.) distinguishes two types of edge tones: phrase accents or phrase tones (notated H- and L-) and boundary tones (notated H% and L%).[43] Unlike pitch accents, which can be monotonal or bitonal, these are single tones, i.e. either high or low, in the original proposal (Ladd 2008: 88). When an IP contains more than one pitch accent, the last one is referred to as *nuclear pitch accent*, whereas all preceding pitch accents are called *prenuclear* (Pierrehumbert 1980: 37–40; Ladd 2008: 89–90, 131–134). However, this did not imply an internal constituent structure in the earliest approach, such that Pierrehumbert (1980: 93) proposed the same tonal inventory for both the prenuclear and the nuclear position.

In her original analysis, she suggests two monotonal and five bitonal pitch accents for English and, in addition, two phrase accents and two boundary tones. Given that every intonation phrase is made up of one or more pitch accents the

---

40. The intonational or intonation phrase, IP, is usually considered to be the largest phonological unit in which an utterance can be divided (see also below).

41. Boundary tones have also been associated with the beginning of the IP in some cases, but they are usually considered optional in that position (see Hualde 2003a: 169f.; Ladd 2008: 88).

42. In the original notation, trailing and leading tones were written with a following raised hyphen (H⁻) or (L⁻), dispensed with in subsequent work and used instead as ordinary hyphen to indicate phrase accents. Furthermore, the two tones of a bitonal pitch accent are joined with a plus sign (e.g. L*+H), omitted in some early work based on Pierrehumbert but usually part of the notation today (Ladd 2008: 88).

43. Initial boundary tones are now usually annotated as '%H' and '%L' to avoid ambiguity regarding the position of the boundary.

last one of which must be followed by a phrase accent and a boundary tone, there are actually 28 logically possible combinations for the obligatory phrase-final sequence of pitch accent, phrase accent, and boundary tone. The schematic representation in Figure 3.1 gives all sequences of tonal events theoretically allowed within an English intonational phrase by Pierrehumbert's (1980: 29) finite-state grammar.

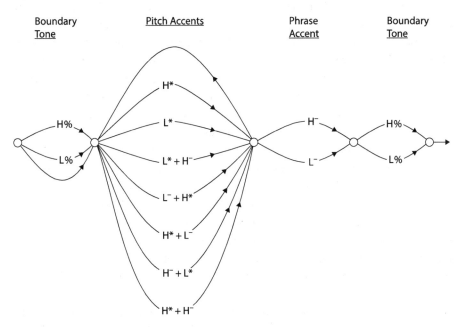

Figure 3.1 Finite-state grammar to generate English tunes according to Pierrehumbert (1980: 29)

However, as she deems six sequences to be indistinguishable from others, Pierrehumbert (1980: 390–401) assumes that only 22 combinations of nuclear pitch accents, phrase accents, and boundary tones are actually possible in English. Many of the problematic sequences involve the H*+H pitch accent, which — after some controversy — is eventually dispensed with in later versions of the model, leaving only six pitch accents (Beckman/Pierrehumbert 1986; see also Ladd 2008: 92, 208f. for a detailed discussion). The same is true of the low initial boundary tone, L% (Silverman et al. 1992).

The major modification of the revised version in Beckman/Pierrehumbert (1986) consists in the introduction of an additional layer of structure, the *intermediate phrase* ('little' or 'minor' ip), such that two levels of phrasing can be distinguished instead of only one (i.e. the intonation phrase, 'big' or 'major' IP). In this reanalysis, each IP may consist of one or more ips. Furthermore, phrase accents are reinterpreted as edge tones for the intermediate phrase.[44] Figure 3.2 illustrates tonal association in the revised model.

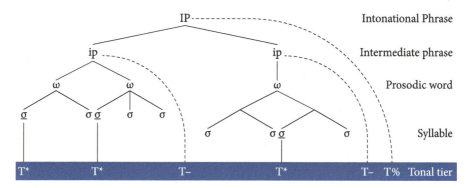

Figure 3.2 Association of tonal targets with different levels of the prosodic hierarchy (adopted from Pešková et al. 2012: 370)

As can be seen, pitch accents (T*)[45] associate with the stressed (i.e. metrically strong) syllables (σ̱) of each ip (or IP)[46] and each ip, be it final or not, ends in an ip boundary tone (T-, the former *phrase accent*). Additionally, each IP ends in an IP boundary tone (T%). According to this revised understanding, nuclear accents can be defined as the last accent of each *intermediate* phrase (Ladd 2008: 90). IPs thus end in a T* T-T% sequence, where T* is the nuclear pitch accent of the (last) ip, T- is the boundary tone of that ip, and T% is the boundary tone of the IP. This sequence is often referred to as nuclear contour or configuration (see Estebas-Vilaplana/Prieto 2008, 2010; Hualde/Prieto 2015 for Spanish; Prieto et al. 2009, 2015; Benet et al. 2011; Prieto 2014 for Catalan, among many others). Optionally, an initial boundary tone (%T) may be produced at the beginning of the IP in

---

44. There seems to be no consensus about which term should be used to refer to the tonal targets signalling a prosodic boundary at the end of an ip. While Beckman/Pierrehumbert (1986) continue to use *phrase accent*, later descriptions adopt the term *intermediate boundary tone* (e.g. Pierrehumbert 2000: 21), as I will do here. Note that the presence of IP-internal intermediate phrases may also be indicated by other than tonal cues such as pauses or phrase-final lengthening (Beckman/Pierrehumbert 1986; Pierrehumbert/Hirschberg 1990; Beckman et al. 2005, among others).

45. 'T' is a placeholder for different pitch (monotonal or bitonal) accents and boundary tones.

46. According to Beckman (1996: 34), "[...] every intermediate phrase must have at least one (nuclear) pitch accent [...]." As opposed to Pierrehumbert's original proposal, in which the nuclear pitch accent was merely the last of the intonational phrase, it should now be thought of as more prominent than prenuclear accents (Ladd 2008: 90) and can be seen as the head of the ip (Terken/Hermes 2000).

some languages. Furthermore, an ip can contain one or several prenuclear pitch accents (T*) in addition to its nuclear configuration. If an IP comprises more than one ip, each of these ips has at least one (i.e. a nuclear) pitch accent (T*) and an ip boundary tone (T-) (Beckman/Pierrehumbert 1986; Beckman 1996; Pierrehumbert 2000; Gussenhoven 2004: 130–141; Ladd 2008: 87–107; Frota 2012, among others). However, it is worth mentioning that these two levels of phrasing have not been retained in all of the intonational analyses proposed for other languages the AM model has been applied to. For instance, intermediate phrases (ips) are usually considered necessary in languages such as Spanish or Catalan (see Sosa 1999; Estebas-Vilaplana/Prieto 2008, 2010; Hualde/Prieto 2015 for Spanish; Prieto et al. 2009, 2015; Benet et al. 2011; Prieto 2014 for Catalan, among many others), but they can be forgone in Portuguese (Frota 2000; Cruz 2013; Frota 2014; Frota et al. 2015). Furthermore, the nuclear configuration of the IP is assumed to consist merely of a nuclear pitch accent and an IP boundary tone in some languages, i.e. the ip boundary tone (or 'phrase accent') of the last and IP-final ip is dropped or merged with the IP boundary tone. Namely, this is the case of the systems proposed for Spanish and Catalan (see Section 3.1.2 for more details).

While the AM model was originally motivated mainly by phonetic and phonological considerations, any model of intonation can only be comprehensive if it can capture and explain the connection between the established tunes and **meaning**, i.e. if it succeeds to provide a semantic or pragmatic interpretation of F0 movements (Pierrehumbert/Hirschberg 1990: 8). To date, research on intonational meaning has not been very extensive (Arvaniti 2011; Prieto 2015). Concerning the AM framework, Büring (2016: 260) recalls that, while its autosegmental analysis has "proven extremely useful", the phonemic status, i.e. the categorical meaning, "of the tones and distinctions it assumes is very much in need of confirmation". However, analogously to the segmental level, where linguistic categories are expected to relate to both differences in sounds and differences in semantic interpretation, several proposals have been made concerning the meaning of the tonal elements posited in the AM model (see Arvaniti 2011; Prieto 2015; Büring 2016: 219–260 for an overview).

While traditional analyses of the meaning of F0 contours have taken a holistic approach, treating F0 contours as gestalts or configurations and confining the domain of interpretation to the entire clause or utterance (see Bolinger 1958, 1982; Delattre 1966; O'Connor/Arnold 1973; Ladd 1980; Truckenbrodt 2012, among others),[47] Pierrehumbert and Hirschberg (1990: 308) defend in their seminal work on English that tune meaning is compositional in the same way as the tone sequences in

---

47. One more recent approach of this type is the 'melodic construction' proposed by Torreira and Grice (2018), who build on Ladd's (2008) ideas to represent tunes as sequences of abstract tones.

the tonal tier are composed of tonal primitives. In their hierarchical model, speakers chose intonational contours to convey, (a), how the hearer should interpret the relationships between (the propositional content of) an utterance and preceding or following ones, and (b), how the hearer should interpret the utterance with respect to the shared mutual beliefs of the conversational participants, the so-called common ground (Büring 2016: 220, 224; Féry 2016: 157f.). The scope of interpretation of tones is the node to which they are attached. Pitch accents and boundary tones are thus interpreted with respect to different phonological domains (Pierrehumbert/Hirschberg 1990: 286). Edge tones, for instance, have scope over the phrase with whose edge they associate, i.e. over the ip or over the whole IP, respectively. Büring (2016: 231) remarks that this tacitly includes the basic "assumption that ips and IPs map one-to-one on syntactic clauses or at least something that has propositional content" (for a critique of this view see Martin 2015: 50, 57).

First, Pierrehumbert and Hirschberg (1990) assume pitch accents to render salient the material with which they are associated and to convey information about its status in discourse. For instance, in English, the H* pitch accent generally signals that the element it is associated with is 'new' in discourse (p. 289) and should be added to the common ground (Féry 2016: 158), while low pitch accents tend to convey 'oldness' (Büring 2016: 233). Pierrehumbert and Hirschberg often phrase these meanings in terms of instructions to the addressee of the utterance or intentions of the speaker, as was noted by Büring (2016: 232). He furthermore objects that informationstructural meanings actually refer to the meaning of the entire clause and operate on its propositional content (p. 235f.). Additionally, Pierrehumbert and Hirschberg (1990: 286, 289) assume that pitch accents can specify the relationship between accented lexical items and modifiers or predicates. Second, phrase accents (i.e. ip boundary tones; Pierrehumbert/Hirschberg 1990: 227) are assumed to convey information about the relatedness of an ip with previous and subsequent ips and, third, boundary tones convey "the directionality of interpretation for the current intonational phrase", i.e. "whether it is 'forward-looking' or not" (Pierrehumbert/Hirschberg 1990: 308). Edge tones are thus supposed to have a mainly structuring function. For instance, phrases that end in a high boundary tone are more likely to be interpreted as units with a phrase that follows (p. 287), whereas low phrasal tones emphasize the separation of a current phrase from a subsequent phrase (p. 302). In consequence, boundary tones play a considerable role in discourse segmentation. In sum, pitch accents, phrase accents, and boundary tones can be seen as tonal morphemes which have their own pragmatic meaning, and, vice versa, the pragmatic meaning of each IP can be defined as the sum of meanings of its pitch accents, phrase accents, and boundary tones (Arvaniti 2011; Büring 2016: 222; see also Ladd 2008: 41 as well as Wakefield 2020, who makes a strong case for the morphemic nature of intonation).[48]

"The bulk of subsequent literature", as Büring (2016: 223) points out, "has been content with repeating Pierrehumbert and Hirschberg's (1990)" assumptions and very little has been done to make their ideas more precise in other compositional approaches (e.g. Steedman 2014 and Portes/Beyssade 2015 for English and French intonation, respectively). However, as mentioned before, there are also more holistic views according to which intonational meaning may depend on strings of intonational primitives rather than being strictly compositional. As Féry (2016: 157) puts it, "even the strictest tone-sequence approach, like the one of Pierrehumbert and Hirschberg, which assigns meanings to every individual tone, needs sequences of tones (and appropriate texts) to illustrate […] meanings". The partly holistic approaches (such as Bolinger 1958 or Gussenhoven 1984; see also Ladd 2008: 286) typically suggest that the nuclear pitch accent or nuclear tunes (i.e. the nuclear pitch accent and the subsequent edge tone) play a crucial role in the interpretation of the meaning of tunes. In contrast, prenuclear pitch accents do not seem to contribute to information structure and thus to meaning (Ladd 2008: 147–156; Arvaniti 2011). In such proposals, it is assumed that an 'abstract tune' containing a meaningful 'intonational morpheme' is linked to prosodic structure in an autosegmental way: the pitch accent associates with the head of the intermediate phrase, i.e. its nuclear syllable, and the boundary tones are linked to the edges of the respective phrases (Büring 2016: 220). Prenuclear accents, on the other hand, can be reiterated as many times as necessary depending on how much prenuclear material there is (Büring 2016: 221). Although approaches of this type have enjoyed great popularity in recent years, and especially in Romance languages (see Frota/Prieto 2015), the special status of the nuclear accent or contour has recently been questioned by Torreira/Grice (2018). In sum, although a series of proposals have been made representing different degrees of the "holistic–compositional" opposition, it remains unclear or at least a subject of controversial debate which the smallest meaning-bearing (prosodic) units are.

Before closing the overview of the AM model presented in this section, some further important terms related with the phonological interpretation of global F0 trends that warrant consideration are *declination, downstep, final lowering, upstep,* and *deaccenting* or *deaccentuation.* Already since Pike (1945), it is known that the F0 tends to decline over the course of phrases and utterances in many languages, although this *declination* is sometimes suspended or can even be reversed

---

48. Note however that such an approach neglects the meanings conveyed through duration-based aspects of the IPs such as speech rate and lengthenings or through intensity (see also below and Martin 2015: 57).

in questions (Ladd 2008:75; Gussenhoven 2004:100). Pierrehumbert (1980:116) defines the term as "a gradual downdrift and narrowing of the pitch range, which occurs within the body of the intonation phrase" (Pierrehumbert 1980:116). It has sometimes been viewed as a merely phonetic and therefore universal effect resulting from the falling subglottal pressure as one speaks (Bolinger 1978; Connell 2002; Pompino-Marschall 2003 246f.). Within the AM framework, declination has generally been interpreted as an effect of *downstep*, i.e. "the stepwise lowering of pitch (or of the tonal space) at specific pitch accents" (Ladd 2008:76), which entails that "each successive F0 peak is lower than the preceding peak" (Face 2003:118). Inspired by many African tone languages, in which the second High in High–Low–High sequences is realized at a lower level than the first one, and then, in turn, sets a new ceiling for the realization of further high targets, Beckman and Pierrehumbert (1986:280) suggest that this "catathesis" (i.e. 'downstep') of following tones (both pitch accents and edge tones) is automatically triggered by bitonal pitch accents (Ladd 2008:97). Due to the local interpretation of pitch events relative to preceding events in the AM model, this kind of downstep does not need to be marked explicitly in the tonal transcription. However, downstepped pitch accents (and boundary tones) can be indicated with an exclamation mark, e.g. !H* (see Silverman et al. 1992; Beckman et al. 2002, among many others). This is necessary, if, on the other hand, they are interpreted as a phonological feature [± downstep] that can be selected independently and applied to essentially any accent in any sequence of tones (Ladd 1980; 2008:97). The effects of downstep disappear at the intermediate phrase boundary, i.e. pitch is reset for each new intermediate phrase (Pierrehumbert/Hirschberg 1990:280). Both the overall downward trend of the F0 contour (gradual declination) and the downstep at specific points in the IP, whose result is a 'terraced' tonal space, are illustrated in the representations in Figure 3.3.

A phenomenon that is usually distinguished from downstep is *final lowering*: as the analysis of production data has shown that the final accent within a prosodic phrase is often lower than would have been predicted by the constant proportion in the phonetic model of downstep, a lowering process is assumed to operate on the last accent in a sequence (Ladd 2008:79–80; see also Liberman/Pierrehumbert 1984; Arvaniti/Godjevac 2003; Face 2003:118). This process is illustrated in Figure 3.4, where the left panel shows common downstep (of the second and third peak) and the right panel downstep (of the second) and final lowering (of the third peak).

Furthermore, the opposite of downstep, i.e. *upstep*, has been proposed for in some languages. Today, it is habitually indicated by an inverted exclamation mark: e.g. ¡H*. Although originally applied solely to boundary tones in the analysis of English and German (Pierrehumbert 1980:144; Grice et al. 2005), many

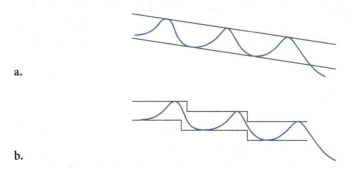

a.

b.

Figure 3.3 Illustration of the overall downward trend as the consequence of (a) gradual declination and (b) downstep at specific points in the utterance (adopted from Ladd 2008: 76)

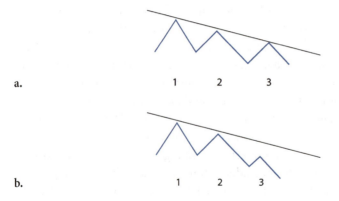

a.

b.

Figure 3.4 Schematic representation of downstep (in both panels) and final lowering (only in the right panel) (adopted from Benet et al. 2011: 109)

analyses of Romance languages assume that upstep can also affect pitch accents (e.g. Hualde 2002; Beckman et al. 2002; Prieto/Roseano 2010, among many others). Unfortunately, however, there is no single definition on how it ought to be employed in intonation labelling practices and its phonological status oftentimes remains unclear (see the discussion in Henriksen/García-Amaya 2012: 148–149). While some researchers simply use the diacritic phonetically to indicate that a peak was higher than a previous one or than all other tonal gestures of the same melody (Estebas-Vilaplana/Prieto 2008, 2010: 23, 28; Willis 2010: 125), others seem to use it on paradigmatic terms, viz. to indicate that a peak is higher than otherwise typical occurrences of the accent in question (e.g. Gabriel et al. 2010: 289,

313; Hualde/Prieto 2015: 362). In the latter case, the upstepped pitch accent is thus not characterized relative to previous peaks but considered an allotonic variant of a given pitch accent. In some cases, scholars have understood the higher scaling of a pitch accent as the manifestation of independent phonological entities basic to the underlying tonal inventory, i.e. they posit contrastive 'upstepped' tones and, hence, assume an additional level of phonological pitch scaling (e.g. Borràs-Comes et al. 2010; Vanrell 2011; Vanrell et al. 2013; Prieto et al. 2015: 29, 49).

In addition, it is worth mentioning that in lexical-stress languages such as English, Spanish, or Catalan, it is sometimes possible for metrically strong syllables not to receive a tonal marking by a pitch accent, i.e. underlyingly stressed syllables may remain pitch *deaccented*.[49] The extent to which this is 'normal' differs widely between languages: whereas *deaccenting* or *deaccentuation* rates have been shown to be high in English or Portuguese (see, e.g., García-Lecumberri 1995; Vigário/Frota 2003: 16; Frota et al. 2015: 281), Catalan and Spanish present higher 'tonal density' (see Hualde 2003a: 164; Rao 2009; Prieto et al. 2015: 11, and Section 3.1.2). The opposite phenomenon, i.e. tonal marking of unstressed syllables, can also be observed in some cases. Especially in French but also in Spanish and Catalan, this often affects the word-initial syllable (see Delais-Roussarie et al. 2015; Hualde 2007, 2009; Nadeu/Hualde 2012; Hualde/Nadeu 2014). Furthermore, enclitics may receive optional or obligatory stress in some Spanish and Catalan varieties (see Moyna 1999; NGRAE 2011: 413; Colantoni/Cuervo 2013; Hualde/Prieto 2015: 384; and Colomina i Castanyer 2002: 578–579; Veny/Massanell 2015: 179, 197, 366). Both pitch deaccenting and the association of pitch movements to unstressed syllables are generally interpreted as conveying pragmatic meanings such as emphasis, focus, or speaker involvement (Bolinger 1972; Hualde 2003a: 173f.; Hualde/Prieto 2015: 358).

Finally, some issues put forth by the critics of the AM model are worthy of mention. For instance, Martin (2015: 57) rightfully points out that the model does not take into account duration parameters although "prosodic events appear in reality in a timely fashion, one after the other in a time sequence". The same is true for intensity. Furthermore, he criticizes the quasi-exclusive use of laboratory speech, which generally involves (very) short sentences. As a result, especially the earlier versions of the AM framework assumed that (a) prosodic structure must be congruent with the syntactic structure of the sentence (i.e. that boundary tones align on syntactic boundaries; see, e.g., Selkirk 1986; Nespor/Vogel 2007; Truckenbrodt 2007) and (b) that only one prosodic structure can be associated with a given sentence (except for syntactically ambiguous sentences) (Martin 2015: 50, 57; see also

---

49. Note that this does not necessarily imply that the respective metrically strong syllable also loses other correlates of stress such as durational or intensity cues (see Torreira et al. 2014).

Ladd 2008: 290). If one looks at spontaneous speech, however, it can be seen that "IPs can float and not maintain any dependency relation with another IP when prosodic parentheses are embedded in the sentence" (p. 50). Hence, "descriptions of the prosodic structure should be strictly separated from other structures organizing the language, and especially the syntactic structure" (p. 57).[50]

3.1.1.2 ToBI

The ToBI ('<u>T</u>ones and <u>B</u>reak <u>I</u>ndices') prosodic labelling system was originally developed by Silverman et al. (1992) for the analysis of corpora of spoken (American) English with the aim of marking phonologically contrastive intonational events based on the Autosegmental-Metrical model (Sosa 2003a: 187; Hualde/Prieto 2016: 1). This original system became known under the term 'Mainstream American English ToBI' (MAE_ToBI). Since then, it has been adapted for a wide range of (typologically diverse) languages and become a general framework for the development of prosodic annotation systems (Beckman et al. 2005: 9; for adaptions to other languages such as Arabic, Basque, Bengali, Catalan, Chinese, Dutch, Georgian, German, Japanese, Papiamentu, Portuguese, or Swedish see Jun 2004, 2015). Essentially phonological in their conception, the ToBI annotation systems proposed are supposed to reflect the current state of knowledge of the intonational phonology of a given language. However, even though there is an ample consensus among researchers on the basic tenets of the AM framework, the phonological labels and phonetic implementation rules of the different ToBI systems are language-specific and cannot always be compared cross-linguistically (see Hualde/Prieto 2016 for a discussion of this problem). In recent years, some efforts have been made to increase ToBI portability (see Prieto/Roseano 2010 for the development of a Sp_ToBI proposal suitable for nine dialects of Spanish and Frota/Prieto 2015 for analyses of nine Romance languages and their geographic varieties).[51]

The ToBI systems comprise a number of so-called 'tiers' or 'annotation levels' which contain segmental and prosodic information that is aligned with the wave-

---

50. Another argument of Martin's (2015: 57) is that the generation of a sentence's syntactic structure depends on the presence of a simultaneously generated prosodic structure in both spontaneous speech and read speech: "One can pronounce a prosodic structure without text, and thus without syntax, but the opposite (i.e. to pronounce a sentence without intonation, without a prosodic structure) is not actually possible, even in silent reading".

51. Moreover, strong arguments in favour of developing an International Prosodic Alphabet (IPrA), i.e., "a set of cross-linguistically transparent and consistent labels", have been recently adduced by Hualde/Prieto (2016: 1). They furthermore advocate a transition from the conceptually phonological ToBI labelling systems to transcriptions using two levels of prosodic representation, i.e. a broad phonetic and a phonological one.

form (or oscillogram) and the pitch curve of the respective utterance. Among these, the *tonal tier*, where pitch accents and edge tones are transcribed applying the AM model, and the *break-index tier*, which reflects the (perceived) strength of the junctures between different prosodic units (such as words or phrases), are the most important and name-giving ones. The inclusion of perceived junctures in the descriptions is one of the main assets of the ToBI model. The original system of break indices proposed by Silverman et al. (1992: 869), represented in Table 3.1, is based on the seven-point scale proposed by Price et al. (1991) and has largely been adopted in subsequent ToBI systems. However, for example, the Catalan and Spanish ToBIs do not recur to break index 2 (see Section 3.1.2), whereas it is used in other languages to indicate the boundary of word groups minor to the intermediate phrase (e.g. in French ToBI, it denotes the right edge of Accentual Phrases (APs); Delais-Roussarie et al. 2015: 68).

Table 3.1 The inventory of MAE_ToBI Break-Indices tier labels (adapted from Beckman et al. 2005: 23)

Basic break-index values	
0	very close inter-word juncture (i.e. a 'zero boundary' or rather the absence of a boundary)[52]
1	ordinary phrase-internal word end
3	intermediate phrase end, with phrase accent (i.e. with ip boundary tone)
4	intonational phrase end, with IP boundary tone
Diacritics	
- uncertainty, e.g. 4- (i.e. intermediate between BI 3 and 4)	
p perceived hesitation: 1p 'cut-off', 2p and 3p for 'prolongation'	
Tones-breaks mismatch	
2 (perceived 1 with unexpected tonal marker, or lengthening, etc., suitable for break index 3 or 4 without an edge tone)	

Regarding the tonal tier, the original ToBI system also proposed a series of labels and diacritics that can be used to indicate phonetic ambiguity or uncertainty of the describer about the presence or absence of a "tonal morpheme" (i.e. *?, -?, %?) or the nature of a tone (i.e. X*?, X-?, X%?), which clearly reflects the practically applied use it had in the beginning (Beckman et al. 2005: 23).

Furthermore, ToBI systems generally include a *word tier* with an orthographic transcription and/or a *syllable tier* (typically providing an IPA or SAMPA

---

52. The use of this break index value is typically motivated orthographically (Beckman et al. 2005: 25). For example, it may indicate the 'boundary' between a clitic and its host (Gabriel et al. 2013: 194).

transcription of the segments comprised in each syllable). Finally, a *miscellaneous tier* may be added, including annotations of hesitations, disfluencies, breaths, coughs, laughs, false starts, or pauses (Silverman et al. 1992).

Figure 3.5 provides an illustration of a Spanish declarative statement annotated following Spanish ToBI (Sp_ToBI; see Section 3.1.2.1). Alongside the waveform of the audio signal, a representation of the F0, and the spectrogram, there are four annotation tiers: the uppermost is the tonal tier, providing a transcription of the intonation contour based on the AM framework and the labels provided by Sp_ToBI; the tier below the tonal tier is a syllable tier, including a broad phonetic IPA transcription; the next one is a word tier encompassing an orthographic transcription of each word, and, finally, the last tier contains the break indices that indicate the degree of boundary strength.

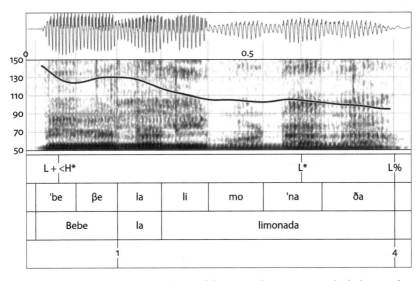

Figure 3.5 Exemplary ToBI-style analysis of the Spanish statement *Bebe la limonada* 'S/he is drinking lemonade' (taken from Hualde/Prieto 2015: 364)

Despite its remarkable success, the ToBI transcription system has also been subject to some criticism: as pointed out by Martin (2015: 56), the quasi-exclusive use of this system involves an oversimplification of the description of melodic events. As a case in point, it provides no explicit means for describing temporal aspects of intonation other than the perceived break durations. Furthermore, transcriptions are often impressionistic and combine both phonetic and phonological elements, which can entail that "the link with the actual data of some specific ToBI sequences seems rather inspired by a theoretical necessity than by the actual reality of facts" (p. 56). Likewise, Torreira and Grice (2018: 23) criticize that ToBI-style transcriptions — while able to encode many important phonetic aspects and hence to provide useful approximations of the phonetic form of a specific utterance — cannot be used to generate new utterances of varying length, i.e. ToBI labels ultimately fail to represent the phonological structure of a tune.

3.1.2 Castilian Spanish and Central Catalan intonation in comparison

CS and CC display numerous similarities concerning their stress patterns, phrasing and intonational systems. Indeed, there might be actually more similarities than differences — which comes as no surprise given that Catalan and Spanish are closely related within the Romance language family. The compilation presented in this section aims to summarize both types of features. Before comparing the typical tunes of the two Iberian standard varieties, I will briefly address their stress systems, tone-bearing units, prosodic phrasing, and tonal density.

Concerning **stress**, both Spanish and Catalan in principle exhibit free stress placement on any of the last three syllables of each stressable word.[53] However, penultimate stress is by far most frequent and rules based on syllable weight and, in the case of verbs, also on morphological factors can account for stress placement in over 95% of the time (see NGRAE 2011:358f.; Gabriel et al. 2013:154–155; Hualde 2014:224–258; Hualde/Prieto 2015:357–358 for Spanish and Oliva/Serra 2002:345–359; Wheeler 2005:276–306; Prieto 2006a; Prieto et al. 2015:11 for Catalan). In non-verbs, stress usually falls on the last syllable if this syllable is heavy, i.e. when its nucleus is complex or when it has a coda. Otherwise, the penultimate bears the stress (for exceptions see Hualde 2005:223–228; Kubarth 2009:180–182; NGRAE 2011:376–378 and Oliva/Serra 2002:352–359; Wheeler

---

53. Some authors, such as Kager (1995:368), therefore describe such systems as "bounded" rather than 'free'. Furthermore, accounts of stress in Spanish and Catalan generally distinguish between 'stressable' and 'unstressable' words (Sp. *palabras tónicas* and *átonas*, Cat. *mots tònics* and *àtons*; see NGRAE 2011:370–376; GEIEC 2018:§3.2; GIEC 2016:96–97). The latter group encompasses mainly clitics such as definite articles, object pronouns, and some prepositions (see Hualde 2007:64–66; Wheeler 2005:278 for an overview), which form clitic groups or 'prosodic words' with a stressable elements of the former group. This cliticization process can sometimes yield prosodic words stressed on the fourth-to-last syllable, such as Sp. *cuéntaselo* 'tell him about it' or Cat. *porta-me-la* 'bring it to me', or even further ahead (e.g. Sp. *comiéndosemelas* 'eating them on me' (Hualde/Prieto 2015:357); *Quedi-se-me-la* 'Keep it to yourself for me' (Wheeler 2005:345)). Nevertheless, these cases are usually not considered to contradict the general rule that Spanish and Catalan words can only be stressed on the last three syllables (known as the 'three-syllable window'), since clitics are not counted within this window. Note, however, that in some dialects not considered here clitics may receive primary or secondary stress in some cases (see Colomina i Castanyer 2002:578–579, Veny/Massanell 2015:366 and passim for Menorcan, Majorcan, Valencian, and Roussillon Catalan; and Moyna 1999; NGRAE 2011:413; Colantoni/Cuervo 2013 for Argentinian Spanish).

2005: 288–297; GEIEC 2018: § 3.2.1). In regular verbs, stress falls on the penultimate or ultimate (in the present tense and imperative)[54] or else it affects the syllable containing either the theme vowel (in the past tenses, participles, infinitives,[55] and gerunds) or the tense/mood marker (in the future tense and conditional)[56] (for more detailed descriptions see Hualde 2005: 222–233; Kubarth 2009: 180–185; Gabriel et al. 2013: 155–160 for CS, and Perea 2002; Wheeler 2005: 284–288; GEIEC 2018: § 3.2.1 for Catalan). This can sometimes yield forms stressed on the third-to-last syllable in Spanish but not in Catalan (e.g. Sp. *hablábamos* vs Cat. *parlàvem* 'we spoke').

The two languages under concern also correspond to the same typological **type with regard to intonation**: in Gussenhoven's (2004: 12) terminology, CS and CC can be classified as intonation-only languages, since both are varieties without lexical tone. Studies couched within the AM model generally assume stressed syllables and phrase edges to be the relevant **tone-bearing units** in both languages. Tones thus associate with stressed syllables in the form of pitch accents and with phrase edges in the form of boundary tones. Concerning **phrasing**, most recent studies on Spanish and Catalan posit two levels: intonational (IPs) and intermediate phrases (ips).[57] However, there still is some controversy about whether there could be a third, inferior level (the phonological phrase). This is "an unresolved issue", as Prieto (2014: 48–49) puts it, since "no conclusive evidence" has been found that would proof the need of such a level, e.g. as the domain of application of phonological processes. Whereas the AM model generally posits separate edge tones for each layer of prosodic constituency, i.e. an (IP) boundary tone for each 'major' IP and an intermediate boundary tone corresponding to each 'minor' ip (see Section 3.1.1.1), recent studies on Catalan and Spanish suggest that no phrase

---

54. In the present tense stress usually falls on the penultimate. Exceptions are: the Spanish 2PL, stressed on the ultimate (e.g. *vosotros habláis* 'you speak') as well as the 2SG in the varieties with verbal *voseo* (e.g. *vos hablás*); and, in Catalan, the 1PL and 2PL (e.g. *nosaltres parlem* 'we speak', *vosaltres parleu* 'you speak') as well as the (often monosyllabic) 2SG and 3SG of many 2nd and 3rd group verbs (e.g. *perd* 's/he loses'). The same holds true for some imperative forms: the Spanish (positive and negative) 2PL (*hablad* 'speak', *no habléis* 'don't speak') and the (positive) 2SG in *voseo* varieties (*hablá* 'speak'); the Catalan (positive and negative) 1PL and 2PL (e.g. *(no) parlem* 'let's (not) speak' and *(no) parleu* '(don't) speak'), as well as the 2SG positive imperatives in most 2nd and 3rd group verbs (*serveix* 'serve') (see Perea 2002).

55. Some (irregular) Catalan 2nd group infinitives, such as *conéixer* 'to know', *batre* 'to beat', are stressed on the penultimate.

56. In the Spanish *indefinido*, theme vowel and personal ending are not always clearly separable. In those cases, it is the compound morpheme that bears the stress, e.g. *hablé* 'I spoke'. The same holds true for the Catalan *passat simple*.

57. An exception is Sosa (1999: 93–95), who assumes only one level of prosodic constituency for Spanish, namely the IP.

accents are needed to describe the intonation of these two Iberian varieties, given that pitch movements at the end of intermediate phrases can be accounted for by combinations of boundary tones (Estebas-Vilaplana/Prieto 2008, 2010 for CS and Prieto et al. 2009; Prieto 2014 for Catalan). It is thus assumed that the same inventory of boundary tones can associate with both ip and IP edges. Although never mentioned explicitly, this entails that the pitch movements at right edge of IP-final ips are (almost invariably) conceived as realizations of IP boundary tones only, not as combinations of ip and IP boundary tones (see also Fn. 161 in Section 4.3.3). Note also, in this context, that Sp_ToBI and Cat_ToBI distinguish between the break indices 3 and 4 (corresponding to the ip and IP, respectively) solely on perceptual grounds (see Aguilar et al. 2009 and Section 3.1.1.2), which automatically entails that the same phrases (e.g. vocatives or the phrases constituting disjunctive questions, etc.) can be analysed as either ips or IPs depending on the degree of perceived disjuncture (Kireva 2016a: 44).

With regard to their **phrasing patterns**, empirical studies again show that the two languages under concern are very similar (Prieto 1997, 2005b, 2006b; Nibert 2000; Elordieta et al. 2003, 2005; Astruc 2005; D'Imperio et al. 2005; Frota et al. 2007; Feldhausen 2010; Benet 2011; Benet et al. 2011, among others). Broad-focus declaratives containing a subject, a verb, and an object (i.e. SVO) most commonly exhibit an (S)(VO) phrasing pattern (Elordieta et al. 2003, 2005; D'Imperio et al. 2005; Frota et al. 2007). Especially in Spanish, this pattern is pervasive across different conditions of length and syntactic complexity of the subject and object phrase, although others such as (S)(V)(O), (SVO), and (SV)(O) are possible when "the weight conditions are 'favourable'", e.g. with prosodically branching objects (Prieto 2006b: 55). In contrast, CC displays a much stronger propensity to divide utterances in phrases of similar length in terms of number of syllables, stresses, and/or prosodic words, often producing (SV)(O) patterns (Elordieta et al. 2003; D'Imperio et al. 2005: 71). The two languages also behave similarly with respect to the phonetic cues used to mark such IP-internal boundaries, i.e both clearly prefer high boundary tones realized as continuation rises[58] (Frota et al. 2007; see also Prieto 2006b; D'Imperio et al. 2005; Elordieta et al. 2005). Only in Spanish, Frota et al. (2007) also found sustained pitches[59] to a minor extent (but see Feldhausen 2010 and Benet et al. 2011 for sustained pitches in Catalan). Pitch

---

[58]. A continuation rise (CR) is "a rise from/on the last stressed syllable into the boundary syllable" (Frota et al. 2007: 134). Within the AM model and the ToBI framework for Spanish and Catalan, the CR is usually labelled as a high boundary tone, H-.

[59]. A sustained pitch (SP) is "a rise on the last stressed syllable followed by a high plateau up to the boundary" (Frota et al. 2007: 134). Different labels have been suggested for SP, such as 'HL-' (Pierrehumbert 1980), 'M-' (Estebas-Vilaplana/Prieto 2008), and '!H-' (Frota et al. 2007, among others). In the present work, '!H-' will be used.

reset was more frequent in CS (76% vs 28% in CC) and pre-boundary lengthening was pervasive in CC but only attained a share of 40.2% in CS. Finally, 28.2% of the IP-internal boundaries were accompanied by a pause in CS, but only 10.5% in CC.

Regarding the frequency of tones, i.e. **tonal density**, CS and CC are characterized by similar distributions of pitch accents and boundary tones. Classically, tonal density is said to be high in both Iberian standard varieties, as all words bearing primary stress tend to be accented unless they occur in a stress-clash situation, where pitch deaccenting (see Section 3.1.1.1) of the first stressed syllable involved (also called 'stress deletion') is the preferred strategy (Hualde 2007, 2009; Ortega-Llebaria/Prieto 2007, 2010; Prieto 2014: 45–46, Prieto/Roseano 2018: 214–216; for the resolution of stress clashes see Oliva 1992; Prieto et al. 2001; Hualde 2010; Prieto 2005a, 2011; Martínez Celdrán/Roseano 2019). Nevertheless, recent studies have shown that the common one-to-one association between stress and pitch accentuation sometimes breaks down in other cases, too, and that speech style, frequency of the respective word, and its position within the phrase crucially determine the presence (or absence) of pitch accents. For instance, formality is assumed to be correlated positively with high tonal density in declaratives, whereas phrase-initial and medial positions as well as a high over-all frequency of the word rather seem to favour pitch deaccenting (see Face 2003; Rao 2007, 2009). Moreover, Torreira et al. (2014) focused on deaccenting of phrase-medial positions in wh-questions and Kimura (2006: 144) presented examples of Spanish wh-questions in which none of the non-final stressed syllables carries any pitch-movement (for sentence-medial deaccenting in Catalan interrogatives see Prieto 2002a: 423f.; Prieto et al. 2015: 11). Deaccentuation of utterance-medial words has furthermore been observed in (Spanish) exclamatives (Hualde 2007: 77f.), in Barcelona Spanish parenthetical and reportative clauses (Ortega-Llebaria/Prieto 2007, 2010), and in CC extra-sentential elements (Astruc 2005; Astruc/Nolan 2007) and post-focal material (Estebas-Vilaplana 2003a). The opposite phenomenon, i.e. the accentuation of unstressed syllables owing to emphasis or focus, which typically though not exclusively affects word-initial syllables or clitics, was already mentioned in Section 3.1.1.1 (see also Hualde 2007, 2009; Nadeu/Hualde 2012; Hualde/Nadeu 2014). In sum, Hualde/Prieto (2015: 389) conclude (for Spanish) that "[i]n careful speech, such as reading, speaking to an audience, or giving instructions, every content word will tend to carry a pitch-accent [...]. [T]he few studies of more casual speech that have been undertaken have noticed that about 30% of content words fail to show evidence of tonal prominence. In even more casual styles, such as conversations between friends, the rate of de-accentuation is likely to be much higher." This is probably true for Catalan, as well.

3.1.2.1 *Inventory of pitch accents and boundary tones*

The Autosegmental-Metrical framework and the ToBI annotation system have been used in recent years to describe and transcribe the intonation of numerous Catalan and Spanish varieties (see Sosa 1991, 1999, 2003a; Face 2002a, 2002b, 2002c; Beckman et al. 2002; Hualde 2002; Ramírez Verdugo 2005; Estebas-Vilaplana 2006, 2009; Face/Prieto 2007; Estebas-Vilaplana/Prieto 2008, 2010; Prieto et al. 2010; Hualde/Prieto 2015; Prieto/Roseano 2018, among others for CS; Gabriel et al. 2010 for Argentinian Spanish, López Bobo/Cuevas Alonso 2010 for Cantabrian Spanish, Cabrera Abreu/Vizcaíno Ortega 2010 for Canarian Spanish, Willis 2010 for Dominican Spanish, Armstrong 2010 for Puerto Rican Spanish, Astruc et al. 2010 for Venezuelan Andean Spanish, O'Rourke 2010 for Ecuadorian Andean Spanish, Ortiz et al. 2010 for Chilean Spanish, and De-la-Mota et al. 2010 for Mexican Spanish; Henriksen/García-Amaya 2012 for Andalusian Jerezano Spanish, Pérez Castillejo/De la Fuente Iglesias 2024 for Galician Spanish, among others; for CC see Estebas-Vilaplana 2000, 2003b; Prieto 2002b, 2009, 2014; Astruc 2005; Prieto et al. 2006, 2009, 2015; Aguilar et al. 2009–2011; Escudero et al. 2012; Roseano et al. 2016a, 2016b among many others; for Valencian see Crespo-Sendra 2011; for Balearic Catalan see Vanrell 2007, 2011, 2013; Roseano et al. 2019; Mascaró/Roseano 2020). Since the AM model and the ToBI annotation systems can be "considered to be the *de facto* standard of prosodic representation" (Kimura 2006: 141; see also Section 3.1.1), this is hardly surprising.

However, as shown in Section 2.2, the intonation of Spanish as spoken in Catalan-speaking territories is still seriously understudied and the few existing studies only cover some minor and very restricted aspects of it. Regarding Catalan intonation, most dialectal varieties have been explored more or less extensively (mainly within Prieto and Cabré's 2007–2012 large-scale intonation-atlas project), but the effects of Catalan-speakers' bilingualism on prosodic realization have basically been disregarded. With the aim of filling these research gaps, the study presented in this book is chiefly concerned with the varieties of Spanish and of Catalan spoken by bilinguals in Girona. To provide a basis for the comparison of the present study's results with what is already known about Spanish and Catalan intonation, the following paragraphs and sections will offer an overview of the inventories of pitch accents and boundary tones proposed for the two 'standard' or 'reference' varieties of Catalan and Peninsular Spanish, which are also the best-described ones: CS, the (geographically) closest variety of monolingual Spanish for whose intonation in-depth descriptions are available, and CC, of which Girona Catalan is a subdialect. Moreover, both are important contact varieties for Girona Spanish and Catalan (for further arguments for these choices see Section 6.3).

With regard to **(Castilian) Spanish**, the first Spanish ToBI (Sp_ToBI) was proposed by Beckman et al. (2002). Refined by Sosa (2003a) and Face/Prieto (2007), the latest 'official' proposal was Estebas-Vilaplana/Prieto (2008). Subsequently, the system was applied to numerous Spanish varieties (see above). The following account of CS intonation mainly relates to Estebas-Vilaplana/Prieto (2010), where an extensive description within the framework of Sp_ToBI is provided. According to that paper, the variety under concern shows two monotonal pitch accents (L* and H*)[60] and five bitonal pitch accents (L*+H, L+H*, L+¡H*, L+<H*, and H+L*).[61] While most of these (L*, L+H*, L+¡H*, (¡)H*) typically occur in nuclear position, where the variety of tonal movements is richer, L+<H*, and L*+H are restricted to prenuclear positions. CS makes use of four monotonal boundary tones (L- %, !H- %, H- %, and ¡H- %)[62] and three bitonal boundary tones (LH- %, HL- %, and L!H- %), all of which can associate with the edges of 'major' intonational (IPs) and 'minor' intermediate phrases (ips). The authors claim that, "in principle, the same inventory of boundary tones can appear at the end" of both types of units. Table 3.2 gives a schematic representation of these tonal movements.

How these pitch accents and boundary tones combine and how the resulting tunes are used will be the matter of the next section (3.1.2.2).

With respect to **Catalan**, the first Cat_ToBI proposal is Prieto et al. (2009), based on CC. It was further diffused in Aguilar et al. (2009–2011) and tested in Escudero et al. (2012), where some minor changes were proposed (mainly concerning the labels used). Prieto (2014), who aimed to give a "full-fledged ToBI annotation proposal for Catalan" (p. 45), can be considered the last version of Cat_ToBI. Accordingly, Catalan has only six basic pitch accents: two monotonal (L*, H*) and four bitonal ones (L*+H, L+H*, L+<H*, and H+L*). As opposed to

---

60. All high pitch accents have "the option of being realized with either downstep or upstep", i.e. as ¡H* or !H* (Estebas-Vilaplana/Prieto 2010: 18).

61. Some of the original labels proposed by Estebas-Vilaplana/Prieto (2010) were slightly adapted to match later applications of Sp_ToBI such as Hualde/Prieto (2015) and Prieto/Roseano (2018) as well as Catalan (and other Romance) ToBIs. This is the case of 'L+<H*' (instead of 'L+>H*') and of the '!H' target (instead of 'M') in boundary tones. Furthermore, original 'HH' is rendered as '¡H', which implies considering this boundary tone underlyingly as monotonal rather than bitonal. As Armstrong/Cruz (2014) point out "HH% has always been treated as a monotonal category, which is perhaps counterintuitive based on the two H characters used in the label". This practice is also in line with the use of '¡H' for the comparable surface contours in Catalan and other Romance varieties (see Prieto 2014).

62. The use of two diacritics — namely, the hyphen (-), marking ip boundaries, and the percent sign (%), marking IP boundaries — indicates that these boundary tones can associate with either of these two levels of prosodic constituency (see also Section 3.2, below).

Table 3.2 Schematic representation of the inventory of pitch accents and boundary tones proposed for Castilian Spanish (adopted from Estebas-Vilaplana/Prieto 2010)

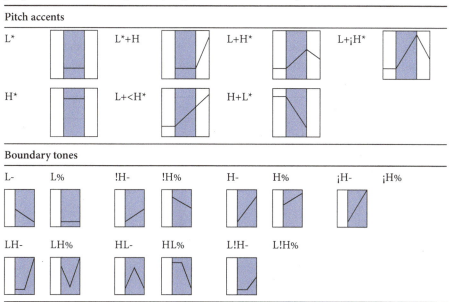

Spanish, L+¡H* is not considered a basic pitch accent of Catalan. Nevertheless, this pitch accent can occur in Catalan as well, given that some of the pitch accents containing a high tonal target can be up- or downstepped: ¡H*, !H*, L+¡H*, L+!H*, and !H+L* (Prieto 2014: 51). As in Spanish, L+<H* and L*+H are restricted to prenuclear positions, whereas the other pitch accents preferably surface in nuclear positions. A further difference to Spanish is that Catalan does not use the same inventory of boundary tones at intermediate and intonational phrase boundaries. Eight boundary tones have been attested at the IP level: four monotonal (L%, H%, !H%, and ¡H%),[63] three bitonal (LH%, L!H%, HL%), and one tritonal one (LHL%). At the ip level, the number of boundary tones is more reduced and apart from four monotonal boundary tones (L-, H-, ¡H-, !H-) there is only bitonal one (LH-). Finally, the high initial boundary tone, %H, proposed in Aguilar et al. (2009–2011) and Escudero et al. (2012), seems to be abandoned by Prieto (2014)[64]

---

63. Although Prieto (2014) posits eight IP boundary tones, her list of boundary tones comprises only seven. Since Escudero et al. (2012) equally suggest eight boundary tones, I assume that ¡H% is the missing one in Prieto's (2014) list. Note furthermore that, similar to Sp_ToBI, and in opposition to Prieto (2014), the first Cat_ToBI proposals still made use of the labels 'M' and 'HH' (see also Fn. 61).

64. Although Prieto (2014) never mentions %H, it is still annotated in some examples.

and Prieto et al. (2015). A schematic representation of the Catalan inventory of pitch accents and boundary tones is given in Table 3.3. Their use will be explained in the following section.

Table 3.3 Schematic representation of the inventory of pitch accents and boundary tones proposed for (Central) Catalan (compiled from Prieto 2014, Aguilar et al. 2009–2011, and Prieto et al. 2009)

Pitch accents

L*		L*+H		L+H*	
H*		L+<H*		H+L*	

Boundary tones

L-	L%	!H-	!H%[65]	H-	H%	¡H-[66]	¡H%

LH-	LH%	HL%		L!H%		LHL%[67]	

%H

---

65. The representation given in Prieto (2014) is the rightmost one, whereas previous proposals use either one or both of the other two. Interestingly, in Prieto et al. (2009), the rightmost representation illustrates an MM% boundary tone, which was abandoned in later proposals.

66. No representation of this boundary tone is given in Prieto (2014). The representation is therefore based on Aguilar et al. (2009–2011).

67. The left-hand representation is the one given in Prieto (2014). Interestingly, the same representation is used in Sp_ToBI to illustrate HL boundary tones. The right-hand representation, on the other hand, was used in previous Cat_ToBi proposals.

3.1.2.2 *Intonational tunes in Castilian Spanish and Central Catalan*

The account of the prenuclear pitch accents and nuclear configurations[68] provided in this section is based primarily on the works of Estebas-Vilaplana/Prieto (2010) and Prieto (2014). It includes all sentence types described in each of these sources, which is why the inventories presented for the two languages in Table 3.4 are not exactly identical. In some cases, further sources, such as, e.g., Hualde/Prieto (2015), were consulted to complete the inventories. Furthermore, it warrants comment that the authors do not always explicitly state that a given nuclear configuration is to be considered the only possible underlying tune in a specific pragmatic context. However, the fact that they appear in the examples used to illustrate the respective accounts very much suggest this. The same holds true for prenuclear pitch accents, which are only described explicitly for a minor number of utterance types in Estebas-Vilaplana/Prieto (2010) and Prieto (2014). With respect to the remaining pragmatic contexts, the nature of the underlying prenuclear pitch accents thus often needs to be inferred from the concrete analyses presented in the examples. Since such a way of proceeding can be problematic because the phonetic surface realization of an underlying tonal target may vary according to the phonetic context, such cases are presented in square brackets in Table 3.4. Finally, some of the original labels were slightly adapted for the sake of uniformity and to increase comparability across the two languages considered (see Fn. 61, above, for details on the adaptations made).

Table 3.4 Intonational tunes in Castilian Spanish and Central Catalan (based on Estebas-Vilaplana/Prieto 2010 and Prieto 2014 unless indicated otherwise)

Sentence type	Castilian Spanish		Central Catalan	
	Prenuclear accents[*]	Nuclear configurations	Prenuclear accents	Nuclear configurations
Statements				
Broad-focus statements	L+<H*	L* L%[69]	L+<H*	L* L%[70]
Continuations		L+H* H-		L+H* H-
				L+H* !H-

---

68. The term 'nuclear configuration' or 'nuclear contour' is refers to the combination of a nuclear pitch accent and a subsequent boundary tone (Estebas-Vilaplana/Prieto 2010; Prieto 2014: 51).

69. Robles-Puente (2011b) also found L+!H* L% in different varieties of Peninsular Spanish (Bilbao, Alacant, Jaén, Pamplona, and Madrid). Accordingly, Hualde/Prieto (2015) present L+H* L% (sic) as an alternative contour to L* L%. They suggest that it simply might indicate more emphasis on the prosodic word on which it is realized, since L+H* expresses narrow focus

Table 3.4 *(continued)*

Sentence type	Castilian Spanish		Central Catalan	
	Prenuclear accents*	Nuclear configurations	Prenuclear accents	Nuclear configurations
Narrow-focus and contrastive-focus statements[71]	[L+<H*]	L+H* L%[72]		L+H* L%[73]
		L* HL%[74]		
Exclamative statements	[L+H*]	L+(¡)H* L%		
Statements of the obvious		L+H* L!H%		L* HL%
		L+H* L[75]		L+H* L!H%[76]
Disapproval statements				L* !H%
Uncertainty or dubitative statements	[L+<!H*, H*]	L+H* !H%		L+H* !H%[77]

(and emphasis) across varieties (see Fn. 72 and Hualde/Prieto 2015: 364, 369). Moreover, they mention H+L* L% for insistent explanations.

70. Prieto et al. (2015: 17) also mention L+H* L% but say that it adds an emphatic meaning (cf. narrow-focus statements).

71. Unfortunately, the accounts do not distinguish clearly between narrow- and contrastive-focus (or contradiction/categoric) statements.

72. This nuclear configuration conveys exclamatory force (i.e. focus) on words in phrase-final position in all Spanish varieties (Estebas-Vilaplana/Prieto 2010: 22). If the given word is not in intonational phrase-final position, an L- intermedial boundary tone may occur at the word edge and all post-focal material is deaccented or pitch-compressed (Hualde/Prieto 2015: 368). Also, the topic or given information may be separated prosodically from the rest of the utterance in an apart intermedial phrase marked with a final rise (Hualde/Prieto 2015: 369).

73. This geographically more restricted contour carries a greater emphatic, contradictory force (see also Hualde/Prieto 2015: 369).

74. This contour expresses contrastive focus in most Catalan varieties (Prieto et al. 2015: 19f.). Usually, the focus is shifted to sentence-initial position and post-focal phrases display a very compressed pitch range. Prieto (2002a: 415 f.) furthermore indicates a 'H+L* L%'-like contour for categorical statements. In Prieto et al. (2015: 21), H+L* HL% is mentioned for contradiction statements.

75. Both patterns can occur across dialects, but the first one is more frequent in Castilian Spanish (Estebas-Vilaplana/Prieto 2010: 23).

76. The second contour is more emphatic. In Prieto et al. (2015), it is the only contour mentioned for Central Catalan.

77. This contour is given by Prieto (2014) for "hesitation statements".

Table 3.4 *(continued)*

Sentence type	Castilian Spanish		Central Catalan	
	Prenuclear accents*	Nuclear configurations	Prenuclear accents	Nuclear configurations
Yes–no questions				
Information-seeking yes–no questions	L*+H[78]	L* ¡H%[79]	(%H) H*[80]	H+L* L%[81]
			L*+H	L* H%
Disjunctive questions	[L+<H*]	L+H* ¡H- L* L%		L+H* ¡H- L* L%[82]
Echo yes–no questions	[L+<H*]	L+¡H* L%[83]	[H*][84]	L+¡H* L%[85]

---

78. Hualde and Prieto (2015: 377) mention sentence-medial deaccentuation as a frequent feature of questions across varieties.

79. This contour is transcribed as L* H% in Hualde/Prieto (2015: 372) and in Prieto/Roseano (2018: 226–227), who tag it as 'low rise'. They also propose a 'circumflex contour' (L+¡H* L%) in this context but add that it is pragmatically marked and imbued with an 'echoic' meaning in Peninsular (Madrid) Spanish, even if it appears to be by far more frequent in casual conversation (p. 374). It is unmarked in northern peninsular varieties (López Bobo/Cuevas Alonso 2010, Robles-Puente 2011a). Finally, Hualde and Prieto (2015: 372) mention a 'high rise' contour, transcribed as (L+)H* H%, used when the speaker knows the answer and is ready to provide it ('quiz question'). Importantly, Estebas-Vilaplana and Prieto (2010: 29) propose a phonological scaling difference between information-seeking (¡H%) and confirmation-seeking yes–no questions (H%), whereas Hualde/Prieto (2015) and some other authors treat both realizations as the same category (see also Armstrong/Cruz 2014).

80. The use of the first pattern is commonly associated with yes–no questions headed by the particle *que*. Prieto (2014: 62) describes its prenuclear part as a high plateau. According to Prieto (2002b: 181), "[p]erceptual impressions of the contour clearly indicate that the contour contains only one accented syllable (a specially prominent syllable) which always falls on the last stressed syllable of the utterance". Consequently, in that paper, the only prenuclear element is a %H initial boundary tone on the particle *que*.

81. Prieto (2014: 63) states that in some areas of Central and Northwestern Catalan, as well as in Majorcan Catalan, "the pretonic syllable is significantly higher", yielding ¡H+L* instead of H+L*. For Majorcan Catalan, Vanrell (2007) and Vanrell et al. (2013) found a phonological contrast between ¡H+L* (information-seeking questions) and H+L* (confirmation-seeking questions).

82. Prieto (2002a: 427) describes a "final falling cadence", i.e. 'H+L* L%'-like contours.

83. Estebas-Vilaplana/Prieto (2010: 22) also found L+H* in their corpus. According to Hualde/Prieto (2015: 380), L* H% can be used in Madrid Spanish and "if the question is not preceded by *(que) si*, the echoic character may be conveyed by a phonetically expanded range including a higher final boundary".

Table 3.4 *(continued)*

Sentence type	Castilian Spanish		Central Catalan	
	Prenuclear accents*	Nuclear configurations	Prenuclear accents	Nuclear configurations
Counterexpectational echo yes–no questions[86]	[H*]	L+H* LH%	[H*]	L+H* LH%[87]
		L+H* ¡H%	[L*+H]	L+H* LHL%[88]
				L* (¡)H%[89],
				L+¡H* L%[90]
Imperative yes–no questions	[L+<H*]	H+L* L%		H+L* L%,
				L* H%[91]
Invitation yes–no questions (offers)			[L+H*]	L+H* H%
Confirmation-seeking yes–no questions	[L*+H]	H+L* L%	[(%H) H*]	H+L* L%[92]
		L* H%		
		L+(¡)H* L%[93]		

---

84. Prieto (2014: 68) states that this utterance type typically starts with a low pitch that continues until the last stressed syllable, but in her examples prenuclear syllables are marked with an H* pitch accent.

85. Prieto et al. (2015) add L* H% as the most typical configuration for Central Catalan.

86. There are no AM analyses of counterexpectational yes–no questions without an echo meaning (also called 'exclamative' or 'incredulity' questions). To my best knowledge, merely Crespo-Sendra et al. (2010) annotate L* HH% (i.e. L* ¡H%) in an example of an incredulity question.

87. This contour conveys a strong meaning of surprise and insistence (Prieto 2014: 68).

88. The complex boundary tone conveys a higher degree of insistence (Prieto 2014: 70).

89. Prieto et al. (2015: 26) note that surprise or incredulity echo questions are produced with a wider pitch range and sometimes with a creaky or whispery voice in opposition to echo questions about understanding. This is also shown by Crespo-Sendra (2011).

90. This nuclear configuration is indicated by Prieto et al. (2015: 54) for Santa Coloma de Farners, a neighbouring municipality of Girona.

91. As no AM accounts are available for this utterance type, these two nuclear configurations were deduced from the descriptions provided in Prieto (2002a, 2013).

92. The circumflex contour is mentioned by Hualde/Prieto (2015: 372–377) and Escandell-Vidal (1999, 2002, 2017), among others.

93. For Girona and its surroundings (Banyoles, Santa Coloma de Farners), Prieto et al. (2015: 55) indicate nuclear L* H%.

Table 3.4 *(continued)*

Sentence type	Castilian Spanish		Central Catalan	
	Prenuclear accents*	Nuclear configurations	Prenuclear accents	Nuclear configurations
Wh-questions				
Information-seeking wh-questions	H*[94]	L* L%[95] L* ¡H%[98]	H*[96]	H* L%[97] (L* L%[99])
Focused wh-question			[H*][100]	L+¡H* L%
Echo wh-questions	L+<H*	L+¡H* L%[101]	[H*]	L* H%[102]

---

94. Emphasis on the question word (see Escandell-Vidal 1999: 3934f.) "may produce de-accentuation of following words with drastic drop in pitch after the stressed syllable of the question word" (Hualde/Prieto 2015: 381f., see also Torreira et al. 2014 on phrase-medial deaccentuation).

95. A rising 'quiz question intonation' (i.e. H* H%) is possible, too (Escandell-Vidal 2011). For Manchego Spanish, Henriksen (2010, 2014) describes two different kinds of falling contours in which the pitch rises on the question-word and stays high either until the last pretonic syllable, falling in the tonic (H+L*), or until the last tonic (¡L+H*), falling on the post-tonic.

96. This contour expresses a nuance of interest and greater speaker involvement in the speech act (Estebas-Vilaplana/Prieto 2010: 35). According to Sosa (2003b), it has a confirmation or reprise function. Henriksen (2010) confirms the more formal character of final rises in a study on Manchego Spanish.

97. Typically, the sentence-initial wh-word is accented with a high tone (H*), followed by a descending pattern until the last pitch accent in the utterance (Prieto 2014: 65).

98. According to Prieto (2014: 67), this pattern is more marked in the sense that it "serves as a way of reactivating an idea that is already part of the listener's background so that it is part of the listener's awareness". In Prieto et al. (2015: 31f.), H* L% is the only contour for Central Catalan. In Roseano et al. (2016b), it is clearly the predominant.

99. This contour is presented in Prieto (2014: 65) in a somewhat contradictory way: she first mentions it as "!H+L* L%" but then describes it as L* L%, which is also the label used in the example she provides. In Prieto and al. (2015), L* L% was observed in some isolated Western Catalan varieties.

100. Prieto (2014: 67) describes the prenuclear part in this type of questions as being produced with compressed pitch range.

101. The nuclear pitch accent attested in Estebas-Vilaplana/Prieto's (2010) data is ¡H*, but they analyse it as a truncated version of L+¡H*, attested in Escandell-Vidal (1999, 2002). They also found L+H* in their corpus (p. 22). In Hualde/Prieto (2015: 382), a "low rise contour" L* H% contour is added to the "circumflex contour" L+¡H* L%, but it is said to imply nuances such as surprise or incredulity.

Table 3.4 *(continued)*

Sentence type	Castilian Spanish		Central Catalan	
	Prenuclear accents*	Nuclear configurations	Prenuclear accents	Nuclear configurations
Counterexpectational echo wh-questions[103]	[H*]	L+(¡)H* ¡H%[104]		
Imperative wh-questions (commands)	L+<H*	H+L* L%		
Invitation wh-questions (offers)		L+¡H* HL%		
Rhetorical wh-questions		H* (!H) !H%[105]		
Imperatives and vocatives				
Imperatives: Commands		L+H* !H%[106]	[H*]	L+(¡)H* L%[107]

102. This sentence type is not mentioned by Prieto (2014), but according to Prieto et al. (2015: 32f.) it is predominantly produced with the rising pattern L* H% in Central Catalan. Nevertheless, two circumflex contours (L+¡H* L% and L+H* LH%) can be found sporadically in some Central Catalan localities, among them Girona (second contour).

103. This question type is also sometimes referred to as 'exclamative' or 'incredulity echo wh-question'.

104. The nuclear pitch accent is upstepped in Estebas-Vilaplana/Prieto's (2010: 35, 37) example and its description but not in their general overview (p. 45).

105. In Estebas-Vilaplana/Prieto's (2010: 38) example, the nuclear accent H* is not on the last word but on the verb of the sentence. It is followed by a dislocated constituent pronounced with a !H* tone, followed by a !H% boundary tone.

106. According to Robles-Puente (2011b), L+<H* L+!H* L% is the most commonly found contour in declaratives and commands in the varieties spoken in Bilbao, Alicante, Jaén, Pamplona, and Madrid (the nuclear pitch may also occur without downstep or even with upstep). These varieties can make use of different strategies to mark imperativity, but this is not always done, as is confirmed in Hualde/Prieto (2015: 384). However, Robles-Puente (2012b: 154) uses sentences containing a verb and another preceding content word, whereas Estebas-Vilaplana and Prieto (2010) base their analyses on simple verb phrases (e.g. ¡Venga! 'Come on', ¡Cállate! 'Be quiet, ¡Ven aquí! 'Come here!'). Hualde and Prieto (2015: 384) add that in such one-word imperatives and exhortatives it is possible to shift the rise to the (otherwise unstressed) final syllable to express greater emphasis, whereas "[i]n phrasal commands, the same pragmatic effect appears to be obtained by de-accenting of non-final words".

107. This contour is used in strong commands. Prieto (2014: 72) distinguishes between early-focus (i.e. focus on the verb) and late-focus commands. In early-focus commands (such as

Table 3.4 (continued)

Sentence type	Castilian Spanish		Central Catalan	
	Prenuclear accents*	Nuclear configurations	Prenuclear accents	Nuclear configurations
Imperatives: Requests		L* HL%		L+H* L!H%[108]
		L+H* L%[109]		L+H* LHL%[110]
Vocatives		L+H* !H%		L+H* !H%
		L+H* HL%[111]		L+H* HL%[112]

* Where prenuclear pitch accents are not described explicitly by Estebas-Vilaplana (2010) and Prieto (2014) but inferred from their examples, they are given in square brackets.

Demana-ho a la Maria! 'Ask Mary about it!'), she posits a post-nuclear L* pitch accent. For soft commands, she suggests an L*+H L* L% contour. For commands consisting only of a verb, Prieto et al. (2015) give L+H* L% and L+H* HL%. The second one is described as soft command on p. 35 but illustrated as insistent command on p. 36. The authors furthermore report L* L% as an alternative in sentences longer than one word for some Central Catalan varieties.

108. This contour is used in non-sentence-final position in Estebas-Vilaplana/Prieto's (2010: 41) example *Va, vente al CIne, hombre* 'Come on, man, come (with us) to the cinema'. Hualde/Prieto (2015: 385) add H+L* L% as an alternative contour for Peninsular Spanish, used in *¡(Venga,) bebe la limoNAda!* '(Come on,) drink the lemonade'.

109. Both contours are illustrated in the verb-only utterance *Vine!* 'Come!'. The first one does not appear in Prieto et al. (2015). Instead, they describe requests as being generally produced with an L* HL% contour in Central Catalan, which is also mentioned by Prieto (2014: 72) later on in the respective section of her paper, when she – in contradiction to her earlier explanations – presents L* HL% (used in requests) as being opposed to L+H* L%, used in commands.

110. This contour is used in insistent requests. Prieto (2014: 72) notes that there is a large variety of boundary tones to express different degrees of insistence. Additionally, other prosodic features such as duration can render subtle pragmatic differences.

111. This contour conveys greater insistence than the typical 'vocative chant' (first contour). All vocatives come along with an extraordinary lengthening of the final syllable (Hualde/Prieto 2015: 386).

112. According to Prieto et al. (2015: 39), the first contour is used in more insistent (second) calls, while the second one represents 'greeting calls'. This is in accordance with Borràs-Comes et al. (2015), but in Prieto (2014: 74) things are described the other way round, matching with the distribution in Spanish. Furthermore, a "rising interrogative contour" L* H% is documented for Catalan (Borràs-Comes et al. 2015: 78; Prieto et al. 2015: 41). It connotes questions such as 'Can you hear me?', 'Are you paying attention to me?'.

As can be seen from Table 3.4, CS and CC display many similarities concerning the intonational realization of the sentence types presented, but there are also some differences. In what follows, both will be briefly described.

Concerning **prenuclear accents**, the literature on neither of the two languages under concern here offers clear descriptions for all sentence types. Nevertheless, it is known that a delayed peak (L+<H*) is generally used in broad-focus statements in both languages. It clearly contrasts with L*+H, which is the typical prenuclear pitch accent in CS yes–no questions and can be used in Catalan as well, if the rising pattern for yes–no questions is chosen. In this case, there is a phonological contrast between the two pitch accents (Prieto et al. 2015: 23; Roseano et al. 2016a: 14). In wh-questions, an H* pitch accent on the initial question word is most frequent in both languages. It is usually followed by deaccentuation, typically yielding a high plateau in Catalan and a "drastic drop" in Spanish (Hualde/Prieto 2015: 381f.). However, contrary to Spanish, H* seems to be used in some other Catalan question types, such as echo questions, too, whereas Spanish frequently resorts to delayed peaks in these contexts. It is worth highlighting that, to date, research has focused primarily on nuclear pitch accents and little efforts have been made to systematically investigate prenuclear pitch accents in sentences other than broad-focus statements and information-seeking questions (see Estebas-Vilaplana 2003b, 2006; Gabriel/Kireva 2014; Roseano et al. 2016a and sources therein).

As for the realization of nuclear pitch accents and boundary tones, there has been much more in-depth research as **nuclear contours** were analysed in a wide range of utterance types. Yet, for some pragmatically biased statement and wh-question types, descriptions are only available for either of the two languages considered here. Regarding the utterance types whose nuclear configurations can be compared on the basis of the existing literature, Peninsular Spanish and CC often pattern alike, i.e. they use the same or fairly similar nuclear contours. Nevertheless, some important differences remain. Both differences and similarities will be addressed in the following:

1. **Statements**: In both languages, the most frequently presented contour consists of prenuclear L+<H* pitch accents followed by an L* L% nuclear contour. Nevertheless, there has been quite a bit of discussion about the nuclear contour, especially for Spanish. Whereas some authors interpret the low end of this sentence type that does not show any pitch excursion as part of a falling contour (i.e. H+L*, !H+L*, or truncated (H+)L*; see Hualde 2005: 257), others note that it may be better described as a simple case of deaccentuation (i.e. *; Hualde/Prieto 2015: 364). The other possibility is a nuclear circumflex contour, i.e. a rising pitch accent and a low boundary tone, noted as L+H* L% or L+!H* L%. According to Robles-Puente 2011b, this is by far the most

frequent pitch accent for broad-focus statements in Peninsular Spanish. It has also been observed in CC (Prieto et al. 2015:17). However, a rising pitch accent in this context is often associated with focus and emphasis.

Concerning narrow-focus statements, L+H* L% is the most common nuclear configuration in both languages. A small difference arises concerning contrastive-focus or contradiction statements, which have a greater emphatic, contradictory force: whereas Catalan still displays L+H* L% or uses a falling H+L* L% or falling–rising–falling H+L* HL% contour, in Spanish, a low L* accent followed by a HL% boundary tone can be found.

In statements of the obvious, L+H* L!H% is used in both languages. For CS, it is said to be most frequent in this sentence type and the alternative contour given (L+H* L%) may simply represent a phonetic variant of the first one. In Catalan, on the other hand, it is assumed to convey a "more emphatic obviousness meaning" than the alternative contour L* HL% (Prieto 2014:59). In uncertainty or dubitative statements, both languages use L+H* !H%.

2. **Yes–no questions**: "Information-seeking yes–no questions is one of the main respects where we find clear differences in intonation among Spanish varieties" (Hualde/Prieto 2015:371) and, without any doubt, Catalan also presents a rich variety of different dialectal contours in this utterance type. This makes it one of the most interesting areas for cross-linguistic comparisons.

The dialects under concern here share one intonational pattern used in this context, which is usually called 'low rise' (see Hualde/Prieto 2015:372). The respective sentences phonologically differ from statements already in their beginning because of the use of an L*+H prenuclear accent instead of the delayed peak. The respective nuclear contour is described as either L* HH% (i.e. L* ¡H%; in Estebas-Vilaplana/Prieto 2010) or L* H% (in Hualde/Prieto 2015 and Prieto/Roseano 2018) for Spanish and as L* H% for Catalan. The confusion of different boundary tones in Spanish can be put down to distinct notational conventions and the wish to express a phonological contrast in the scaling of the high boundary tone between information-seeking (HH%) and confirmation-seeking yes–no questions (H%) by Estebas-Vilaplana/Prieto (2010:29). However, it appears that this contrast has been given up in later work (see also Fn. 79). In Catalan, there is no need to make such a difference as confirmation-seeking yes–no questions usually display a falling contour (for exceptions see Fn. 93). However, even though the low rise can be used in CC information-seeking yes–no questions, it is usually not presented as the most common contour in this language and there is some debate about pragmatic implications/differences between this contour and the seemingly more common falling contour (see Payrató 2002).

The 'iconic' Catalan 'high-falling' question contour, on the other hand, is said to co-occur usually (but not obligatorily) with the interrogative particle *que*. Intonationally, such questions differ from statements in presenting a high plateau in the prenuclear part of the contour, which may be described in different ways, e.g., using an initial high boundary %H and subsequent phrase-medial deaccentuation (*) or high prenuclear pitch accents (H*). In the last stressed syllable, the pitch falls down to the bottom of the speaker's range and this pitch fall is followed by a low boundary tone (L%). There is some dialectal variation in the phonetic implementation of the falling movement, which allows it to be described as H+L* or ¡H+L* (see Prieto et al. 2015: 25; Vanrell 2011, 2013). In CC, the selection of the two extant intonation patterns for information-seeking yes–no questions has been proposed to be sensitive to the pragmatic cost-benefit scale on which the cost or benefit of the proposed action to the hearer is estimated, and which is related to politeness (see Prieto 2014: 64; Nadeu/Prieto 2011; Astruc et al. 2016). As neither *que* nor the same type of falling contour occur in CS information-seeking yes–no questions, this is clearly an area where the intonational systems of the two languages differ fundamentally.

Disjunctive questions and echo yes–no questions, on the other hand, generally display the same intonational patterns in both languages: i.e. L+¡H* L% and L+H* ¡H-/L* L%. In the case of echo yes–no questions, no clear information about prenuclear pitch accents is available in either of the languages, the variation in the given examples reaching from L* over L*+H and L+<H* to H*. In Spanish, L+H* L% and L* H% are also possible in this context (Estebas-Vilaplana/Prieto 2010: 22 and Hualde/Prieto 2015: 380). Similarly, Prieto et al. (2015) report L* H% as an alternative contour for Catalan.

With regard to counterexpectational (also 'exclamative' or 'incredulity') echo yes–no questions, akin contours can be found in both languages. They usually display H* in prenuclear positions and L+H* LH% in nuclear position. Consequently, this question type differs from common echo yes–no questions mainly through the use of a complex boundary tone. Nevertheless, the low–rise contour, L* (¡)H%, is another contour attested in Catalan according to Prieto et al. (2015: 26), even though the authors note that in surprise or incredulity echo questions a wider pitch excursion tends to be used (see Fn. 89). This label might thus refer to the same surface contours as the CS alternative contour L+H* ¡H%. As opposed to Spanish, a third nuclear contour can be found in Catalan (L+H* LHL%), which includes a boundary tone with three tonal targets. It conveys an even higher degree of insistence (Prieto 2014: 70). In sum, the range of different tunes used in this context seems to be greater in Catalan.

In confirmation-seeking yes–no questions both languages prefer falling nuclear contours (H+L* L%). Yet, the general patterns differ in that Spanish seems to use L*+H prenuclear accents as in information-seeking questions, whereas Catalan resorts to the 'high plateau' contour and usually introduces this type of questions with the particle *que*. Alternatively, the 'low rise' contour (L* H%) may be used in CS, too. In CC, it was sporadically found in some localities (see Fn. 93).

3. **Wh-questions**: In both languages, information-seeking wh-questions typically exhibit a high pitch level on the initial question word (i.e. H*) and end with a low boundary tone. Also, sentence-medial stressed syllables are generally unaccented, which comes as no surprise given that the focus of the sentence falls on the wh-word (Escandell-Vidal 1999: 3934; Prieto et al. 2015: 29). However, in Spanish, there is a drop in pitch immediately after the question word and the descending pattern continues until the nuclear L* pitch accent. In CC, on the other hand, the pitch contour remains high after the initial question-word, forming a high plateau, and falls only after the nuclear syllable, which bears an H* pitch accent. In other Catalan varieties, pitch may fall somewhat earlier, i.e. in the nuclear syllable, which bears an H+L* pitch accent in that case (Valencian, Balearic Catalan, among others, see Prieto et al. 2015: 32). In CC, the falling tune thus resembles the contour used in the yes–no questions headed by *que* but it is not identical due to differences in the alignment of the final fall. In yes–no questions, the syllable immeadiately preceeding the nuclear one is the last high one and pitch falls during the nuclear syllable. In wh-questions, on the other hand, the nuclear syllable is still high and pitch falls only after it in the post-nuclear strech.

Interestingly, similar tunes to the Catalan ones were observed in Manchego Spanish wh-questions by Henriksen (2010, 2014). However, their exact alignment patterns seem to be different from Catalan H* L%. Furthermore, CS may also present rising patterns in wh-questions, namely L* H%, which are said to be more formal and to express a nuance of interest and greater speaker involvement (Estebas-Vilaplana/Prieto 2010: 35; Hualde/Prieto 2015: 381). In Catalan, the only rising pattern found is H+L* H%, which occurs in some Balearic and Southern Valencian varieties. It is equally said to function as a politeness-marker (Prieto et al. 2015: 32). So, in sum, information-seeking wh-questions do present some similarities across both languages, but their intonation is essentially distinct.

As for echo wh-questions, a comparison of the different sources they are described in yields that the same nuclear contours may occur in both languages: i.e. the 'circumflex' contour, L+¡H L%, and the 'low rise', L* H%. However, in CC, the low rise seems to be more widespread, while, in CS, it implies nuances such as incredulity and the circumflex contour is more neutral. Furthermore, a third contour is possible in CC, which has not been documented in Spanish: L+H* LH%. This one has also been observed in counterexpectational echo yes–no questions in both languages.

4. **Imperatives**: Many different intonational contours have been described for commands in both languages. Unfortunately, not all available accounts are comparable as they are based on imperatives of different length and constitution (e.g. verb-only imperatives or phrasal imperatives containing objects or adverbs). If we assume that sentences such as ¡*Abre el armario!* 'Open the cupboard!' in Robles-Puente (2011b) and *Demana-ho a la Maria!* 'Ask Mary about it' (with an "early focus") in Prieto (2014: 72) are comparable, we can conclude that the two languages under concern here use similar imperative patterns, i.e. L+H* L* L% in Catalan and the L+<H* L* L%[113] in Spanish (see Hualde/Prieto 2015: 384). If this were right, the two languages would differ concerning the alignment of the prenuclear peak. Nevertheless, Robles-Puente (2011b: 157) also found cases of prenuclear L+H* when the nuance of imperativity should be reinforced (as opposed to declarative intonation). Those cases probably better correspond to what Prieto (2014: 72) calls "commands with early focus".

As for shorter commands (such as verb-only *Vine!* 'Come!' or verb + adverb ¡*Ven aquí!* 'Come here!'), alike though not identical tunes were documented for the two languages: i.e. L+H* !H%, for Spanish, and L+H* L%, for Catalan, with a different scaling of the final boundary tone. However, the intonation of commands seems to be an area that wants further exploration in both languages before we can eventually decide whether there are clear interlingual differences or not.

In the case of requests, too, the descriptions given for the respective intonational contours are challenging to compare because they at least partially refer to different sentential configurations. In one-word requests, consisting only of a verb in the imperative mood (e.g. Sp. ¡*Va!* or Cat. *Vine!* 'Come on!'), L* HL% is possible in both languages (see Estebas-Vilaplana/Prieto 2010: 41; Prieto et al. 2015: 37). In Catalan, L+H* LHL% is an alternative tune for more insistent verb-only requests in different sources (Prieto 2014: 72; Prieto et al. 2015: 37). The compression of the whole tonal sequence of the complex boundary tone conveying the "insistence tune" (see also Prieto 2001) onto the verb clearly shows that Catalan is not a truncation language. No such boundary tone has been documented for Spanish, to my knowledge. Furthermore, Prieto (2014: 72) mentions L+H* L!H% for Catalan soft requests.

---

113. Robles-Puente (2011b) generally uses the label 'L+!H* L%' for the Spanish nuclear configuration.

5. **Vocatives**: As for vocatives, both languages present the cross-linguistically typical 'vocative chant' L+H* !H%, where the last syllable is durationally prolonged and receives a sustained mid boundary tone. Additionally, both languages display L+H* HL% as an alternative contour, with a more drastic final fall and rise, which probably conveys greater insistence. However, it appears that there is some confusion in the literature on Catalan about which of the two tunes serves as greeting call and which as insistent call (see Fn. 112).

To conclude, we can say that CC and CS present quite a lot of similarities in their choices of pitch accents and boundary tones, which comes as no surprise, given that the two languages are closely related within the Romance language family. Yet, there are also some clear differences, especially as concerns the intonation of information-seeking yes–no questions, confirmation-seeking yes–no questions, information-seeking wh-questions, and (possibly) commands. Moreover, there are some minor differences to be found in contradiction statements, in the distribution of tunes used in obviousness statements and in counterexpectational echo yes–no questions, in echo wh-questions, and probably in requests.

To cut a long story short, this section has shown that sentence type and pragmatic meaning can be conveyed by both pitch accents and boundary tones in CS and in CC. For instance, the difference between all-new statements and narrow-focus statements is conveyed by means of pitch accents, rather than by boundary tones: while the same boundary tone occurs in both statement types (viz. L%), two different nuclear pitch accents are utilized (i.e. L* in broad focus statements and L+H* in narrow focus statements). In the same way, H+L* L% can be employed to distinguish confirmation-seeking yes–no questions from the two sentence types just mentioned. Boundary tones, on the other hand, can – but need not – be used to express, for instance, the difference between neutral statements and yes–no questions (L* L% in broad-focus statements vs L* (¡)H% in information-seeking yes–no questions). In addition, the accounts of the intonation of the two languages suggest that distinctive meaning can also be communicated by upsteps (L+H* L% for narrow-focus statements vs L+¡H* L% for echo yes–no questions), i.e. that the upstep is used in a paradigmatic way (see also the discussion in 3.1.1.1, above.). In some cases, pragmatic differences may be rendered either through pitch accents or boundary tones or through entirely different nuclear contours (L* ¡H% for information-seeking yes–no questions vs L+H* ¡H% and L+H* LH% in counterexpectational echo yes–no questions in CS, and L* H% for information-seeking yes–no questions vs L* ¡H% and L+H* LH% in counterexpectational echo yes–no questions in CC). Finally, some utterance types may exhibit the same nuclear contours (e.g. L+H* !H% for both uncertainty statements and vocatives). Since there seems to be no particular intonational marking in such cases, other linguistic means, such as verbal morphology or the lexicon, are used to convey the respective meaning in these cases.

3.2 Language contact

This subchapter deals with language contact. Section 3.2.1 provides a general introduction to the topic and explains the key terms of the field. The ensuing section (3.2.2) addresses phonology in language contact, and, in Section 3.2.1, I summarize the findings of various studies on cross-linguistic influence at the intonational level.

3.2.1 Key terms and approaches

The present section is concerned with what happens when two (or more) languages enter in contact with each other as well as with the linguistic outcomes of such contact, i.e. with linguistic change originated by language-external factors. After a quick overview of the history of research on language contact, the central terms of the field will be discussed, before touching upon several of the more sociolinguistic aspects of the topic, namely, contact situations, sociolinguistic motivations for contact-induced change, and speakers' attitudes.

Since the beginning of the scientific study of language, "language contact has been a focal point of interest to linguists" (Winford 2003: 6). Already in the 19th century, during the heyday of historical linguistic scholarship, it became an integral part of the field (e.g. Müller 1875; Schuchardt 1884, among many others). However, given that the primary interests of the time were language classification in terms of establishing family-tree models of genetic relationships between languages and analysing language change by comparative methods, disagreement arose among historical linguists about the part played by elements from different source languages (such as borrowings), which could make classification decisions difficult. The assumption that every language has only a 'single-parent source', eventually led to the belief — especially common among Neogrammarians and Structuralists — that language change can solely result from language-internal factors like, for instance, regular sound change instigated by universal markedness constraints, or analogy due to pattern pressure (see Odlin 1989: 6–10; Winford 2003: 7). Nevertheless, scholarship on language contact increased and especially the study of linguistic areas and mixed languages, among other topics, brought considerable evidence for the importance of cross-linguistic influences (CLI; Odlin 1989: 12).

In 1953, the pioneer works of Weinreich and Haugen set the foundations for modern contact linguistics by showing that change can result from bilingualism in contact situations and thereby identifying the bilingual individual as the true *locus* of CLI (Matras 2010: 66; Weinreich 1953: 1). Their assumption that second-language learners have more difficulties and display more 'interference' (see below for a definition), the greater the differences between the native and the target language are, further boosted the development of contrastive analyses carried out for the purpose of language teaching (Odlin 1989: 15).

In the 1970s, this so-called Contrastive Analysis Hypothesis (CAH) was heavily attacked and the assumption of L1 transfer in second-language acquisition (henceforth SLA) came into disrepute for the benefit of the so-called identity or 'L1 = L2' hypothesis, which claims that all language acquisition, be it of a first or a second language, proceeds in terms of a fixed set of developmental sequences conditioned by universal cognitive mechanisms (see Appel/Muysken 1987: 82–87; Odlin 1989: 17–23; prominent examples of such studies are Dulay/Burt 1974a, 1974b; Hatch 1977). However, as empirical research led to new and ever more persuasive evidence for acquisitional differences between learners with different native languages attributable to CLI, at the beginning of the 1980s, "interference (or negative transfer) was recognized again as a major component of second-language acquisition" (Appel/Muysken 1987: 87; Odlin 1989: 24; for definitions of the terms 'interference' and 'negative transfer' see below).

In 1988, eventually, Thomason and Kaufman presented their seminal large-scale study on a wide variety of contact scenarios and thereby laid "the foundations for both a typology of contact outcomes and an empirical/theoretical framework for analyzing such outcomes" (Winford 2003: 9; see also Hickey 2013: 1–3). Their book clearly inspired numerous case studies carried out in the 1990s and 2000s, which, focusing on different contact scenarios, linguistic families and areas (e.g. Gilbers et al. 2000 or Clyne 2003) as well as on bi- and multilingualism in a broader sense (e.g. Myers-Scotton 2002), provided the empirical background for more general reflections on the nature of language contact and, in this way, contributed to the maturity of the field (Hickey 2013: 6).

Today, contact-induced language change is viewed as a serious option (Hickey 2013: 21), as "multilingualism by far outweighs monolingualism on a historical and global scale" (Kühl/Braunmüller 2014: 16) and language contact is rather the "rule than exception" (see also Lüdi 1996; Matras 2009). There is a broad consensus that contact always induces change — to varying degree, needless to say — and that foreign influence must have occurred in the history of most, if not all, languages (Hickey 2013: 7; Thomason/Kaufman 1988: 3). Indeed, it is hard to imagine that this could not be the case since "no culture [...] has developed entirely from scratch" (Appel and Muysken 1987: 164). Returning to the beginnings of contact linguistics, we can thus state with Schuchardt (1884:5): "Es gibt keine völlig ungemischte Sprache" 'There is no entirely unmixed language'.

In order to describe language contact and its outcomes, scholars have introduced a plethora of different terms to the extent that "the field is riddled [...] with confusing terminology" (Appel/Muysken 1987:154). The most neutral labels used to cover all kinds of influence are probably **contact-induced change** (Odlin 1989:12) and **cross-linguistic influence** (CLI; Sharwood-Smith/Kellermann 1986). They need no further explanation. Further very general terms are (language) transmission and (language) **transfer** (see, e.g., Van Coetsem 2000:49). However, transfer is used by some to cover all types of contact-induced changes, whereas others, mostly SLA researchers, restrict it to "L1 influence on an L2" (Winford 2003:16, for positive vs negative transfer see below).

This is also true for another central and wide-spread term, **interference**, which has been applied in different frameworks and used in several conflicting senses (Winford 2003:16). Weinreich (1953:1) defines 'interference phenomena' as "those instances of deviation from the norms of either language which occur in the speech of bilinguals as a result of their familiarity with more than one language, i.e. as a result of language contact". He thus employs it as a cover term for both CLI from an L1 to an L2 and vice versa (Odlin 1989:12; Winford 2003:209). Similarly, Mackey (2000:36) states: "Interference is the use of features belonging to one language while speaking or writing another". Thomason (2001:267) defines interference as "[c]ontact-induced change that involves the importation of material and/or structures from one language to another [...]". Yet, many authors distinguish more thoroughly between the directions CLI can take. For instance, Thomason and Kaufman (1988) preferably apply it when referring to the effects an L1 can have on an L2, which they call "(substratum) interference" (Thomason/ Kaufman 1988:37–46 and below).

A somewhat different approach is taken by Müller et al. (2011:18), who propose the following definition: "Die Interferenz wird in der Literatur als ein Performanzphänomen bezeichnet und oft von der Entlehnung („borrowing") abgegrenzt, welche als Kompetenzphänomen beschrieben wird. Als Konsequenz ergibt sich, dass die Interferenz eher individueller Natur ist, die Entlehnung dagegen als kollektiv, also eine Sprachgemeinschaft oder eine Gruppe innerhalb einer Sprachgemeinschaft betreffend, charakterisiert wird. Der Systematik und Stabilität der Entlehnung steht die Variabilität der Interferenz gegenüber."[114] As op-

---

114. Translation: In the literature, interference is referred to as a performance phenomenon and it is often distinguished from borrowing, which, in turn, is described as a competence phenomenon. In consequence, interference is an individual process, while borrowing occurs in speech communities (or in groups within a speech community). The systemic nature and stability of borrowing is contrasted by the variability of interference.

posed to the more or less ephemerous phenomenon of interference, Müller et al. (2011:21) use the term 'transfer' or 'transference' to refer to CLI on the competence level, especially, when L2 learners take over elements or rules from an L1 (see also Clyne 1967 on 'transference').

Convergence is a further term frequently encountered in research dealing with contact-induced language change. The "label has been applied to a whole series of phenomena" (Berruto 2005:81) and the definitions given, if any, vary widely (Höder 2014:39). While some scholars use it with the very general meaning of 'interference', 'transfer' or 'interlingual element', in most cases it refers to a process "making languages more similar" (Clyne 2003:79, see also Kühl/Braunmüller 2014:14; Höder 2014:41). Thomason (2001:262) defines it as "[a] process through which two or more languages in contact change to become more like each other — especially when both or all of the languages change". In a similar vein, Winford (2003:63) states that "two languages can be said to have converged structurally when previous differences in grammar between them are reduced or eliminated either because one adopts structural features from the other as a replacement for its own, or because both adopt an identical compromise between their conflicting structures". He thus emphasizes that convergence can comprise both 'bidirectional' or 'bilateral' convergence in a strict sense, implying a certain degree of reciprocity, i.e. the mutual approximation of two language varieties (Berruto 2005:82), and, in a broader sense, 'unidirectional advergence' (Mattheier 1996:34; see Höder 2014:41 for further logically possible types of convergence). Thomason (2001:262) points out that "the term is not usually used to designate unidirectional changes", such as "ordinary borrowing" (see below), "except (sometimes) when one language changes very extensively to become more like another" (see also Winford 2003:100). Instead, it is frequently applied to changes in (or changes that create) linguistic areas or *Sprachbünde*, which are therefore sometimes also called 'convergence areas' (see Winford 2003:70–71; Matras 2011).

According to Appel/Muysken (1987:154), convergence may occur in situations in which several varieties are spoken in the same geographical area and by the same groups of speakers for a long period of time, i.e. it usually involves (intense) bilingualism (see also Matras 2011). They claim that it is most apparent at the phonetic level, although other linguistic domains can equally be affected (Matras 2009:243–265, 2010:68–76, among others). Typically, the sound systems of the contact languages become progressively more similar through the development of intermediate sounds (Flege 1987:47, 55), i.e. no clear direction of the influence can be determined. Moreover, Matras (2011:153–154) highlights that pragmatic devices are particularly prone to converge as speakers tend to treat pragmatic organization procedures as universal rather than language-specific, i.e. they may easily be generalized across a bilingual's repertoire. Schmid (2011:31) defines the notion as follows: "convergence involves items from both systems, merging or integrating them to create something new that is distinct from both original languages". This is illustrated in Figure 3.7.

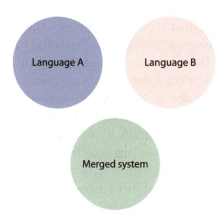

Figure 3.7 A schematic representation of convergence (adopted from Schmid 2011: 32)

As the exact nature of the phenomena referred to as 'convergence' in contact linguistics varies widely, no global motivation or reason for its occurrence can be given, but distinct grounds underly the various cases (for a framework explaining structural convergence see Matras 2011). However, an aspect worth mentioning is the idea that the convergence, i.e. the collapsing of linguistic features in the multilingual repertoire of a bilingual speaker, which originally belonged to different languages or varieties, may cognitively represent a simplification because it eases the bilingual speaker's "linguistic burden" of having to select context-appropriate, i.e. language-specific, structures (Weinreich 1953: 8; Matras 2009: 151, 235; Kühl/Braunmüller 2014: 18–20; Höder 2014; Bullock/Gerfen 2004).

Other uses of the term 'convergence' can be easily found in contact linguistics. For instance, it can point to a setting in which language change has both internal and external sources simultaneously (Hickey 2013: 19). In Communication Accommodation Theory (CAT, Giles et al. 1991), the terms 'convergence' and 'convergent accommodation' refer to the situational language behaviour of individual persons in verbal interaction, i.e., they designate a strategy by which interlocutors accommodate to each other's speech in different ways to achieve the desired social distance, e.g. by adjusting their pronunciation or other linguistic features (Winford 2003: 119; Appel/Muysken 1987: 28; Romera/Elordieta 2013: 132–133). Finally, it can also be applied with more restricted meanings for particular subtypes of transfer phenomena (Myers-Scotton 2002: 101f.).

Divergence is typically regarded as the "other side of the coin", i.e. the opposite concept to the notion of 'convergence' (Hinskens et al. 2005: 2). In Höder's

(2014: 41) terms "convergence and divergence can be said to be types of relational diachronic language change – as opposed to diachronic stability – in which two or more given languages become structurally more similar or dissimilar". Traditionally, divergence has been taken to be rather a "rare element" in language contact (Kaufmann 2010: 481). However, recent research has shown that it is indeed "far more common than normally assumed" (Kühl/Braunmüller 2014: 14). It may occur "sequentially, intertwined or even simultaneously" with convergence within the same variety and is generally assumed to be caused primarily by extra-linguistic factors, owing to the fact that "keep[ing] up the divergence and stability of idiosyncratic [i.e. language specific] features" in settings characterized by intense language contact and bilingualism is a cognitively demanding task (Kühl/Braunmüller 2014: 20; see also Matras 2009: 151, 235). For instance, speakers can actively enlarge salient differences or reject foreign elements with the aim of marking societal independence. A frequently cited example in this context is the revival and codification of Catalan (see Kühl/Braunmüller 2014: 24; Bossong 2008: 102f.).

As already mentioned, recent studies usually distinguish two basic types of CLI, both of which have been given a wide range of different names. Essentially, this distinction refers to whether the influenced language is an already acquired native language (L1), which comes into contact with another language (e.g. an L2), or whether the direction of the influence is from such an already acquired native language (L1) to a language that is learned after the first one, i.e. a target or second language (TL or L2, respectively). Frequently, this distinction is expressed indirectly by referring to contact scenarios in which the influenced language is **maintained** (language **maintenance**, L2 → L1) or not (language **shift**, SLA, L1 → L2). In the latter case, speakers of an L1 'shift to' or 'acquire' another language which is influenced by their L1 (see, e.g., Thomason/Kaufman 1988; Appel/Muysken 1987; Winford 2003). Finally, in settings of complete shift, the original L1 can eventually be lost (**language loss**). In the following, we will take a look at these two major types of CLI based on the distinction between "borrowing" (in situations of language maintenance) and "substratum interference" (in situations of language shift) proposed by Thomason and Kaufman (1988), before briefly addressing the topic of language loss.

Borrowing (or borrowing transfer, borrowing interference)[115] is defined as "the incorporation of foreign elements into the speakers' native language" (Thomason/

---

115. Though well-established in the field, the term 'borrowing' has been criticized for various reasons. First, it lacks accuracy, as Hickey (2013: 20) points out, since "nothing is [actually] 'borrowed from A to B'", which would imply "that the donor language is being 'robbed' of an element that belongs to it" (Matras 2009: 146). Second, it "typically leads to the long-term incorporation of an item into the inventory of the recipient language". Although in some cases,

Kaufman 1988: 21). The respective speaker group maintains its native language (L1), often referred to as recipient language in this context (Weinreich 1953: 31 and passim; Van Coetsem 2000: 49), but it is changed by the addition of elements from an external source or donor language with which it is in contact, i.e. the foreign language or L2 (Thomason/Kaufman 1988: 37; Winford 2003: 11f.). The agents of the change are thus the native speakers of the borrowing language, who perform a transfer that affects their own, linguistically dominant language (Van Coetsem 2000: 53). For this reason, Van Coetsem (1988: 37, 2000: 49–73) in his theoretical model of "transmission or transfer in connection with language contact" refers to the respective process as "recipient language agentivity".

Yet, many authors distinguish more thoroughly and apply the term 'borrowing' only or primarily to **lexical borrowings**, i.e. when a word is borrowed as a whole, including its sound and meaning (Appel/Muysken 1987: 164). In such cases, we deal with the incorporation of phonetic substance (Heine/Kuteva 2013: 86) or linguistic matter in the sense of identifiable sound-shapes of words and morphs (Matras 2009: 148; 2013: 68) from a source language into the borrowing language. This type of borrowing is an extremely common form of CLI and "few, if any, languages are impervious to it" (Winford 2003: 29). The process is illustrated by Schmid (2011: 27) in the following way:

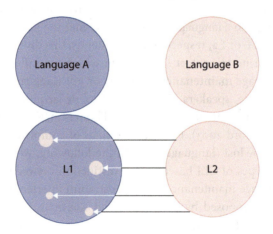

Figure 3.8 A schematic representation of borrowing involving linguistic matter (e.g. words) (adopted from Schmid 2011: 27)

---

bilinguals may well be aware of the origin of an element in a particular donor language, this awareness may be blurred over time. There is thus not only "no intention to return the 'borrowed' item to its rightful 'owner', but for most speakers its original 'ownership' may not always be traceable". A more accurate term could be "copying" (Johanson 2002: 8) but sticking with 'borrowing' ensures continuity with existent literature.

In contrast, CLI from an L2 to an L1 that does not involve the incorporation of new phonetic elements of any kind but instead changes the use of existing elements in the L1 according to patterns present in an L2 (Schmid 2011: 26f.) has been referred to with terms such as **structural or grammatical borrowing** (e.g. by Appel/Muysken 1987: 162), structural convergence, pattern transfer (both Heath 1984: 367), (grammatical) calque or calquing (Heine/Kuteva 2013: 86), (pattern) replication (e.g. Matras 2010; Heine/Kuteva 2013), pattern/category extension (Heine/Kuteva 2013), metatypy (Ross 2001), restructuring, and re-analysis (both Schmid 2011: 27).[116] Accordingly, the borrowing L1, i.e. the recipient language, is sometimes called 'replica language' as opposed to the source or donor language, referred to as 'model language' (Heine/Kuteva 2013: 86). The graph in Figure 3.9 provides a schematic representation.

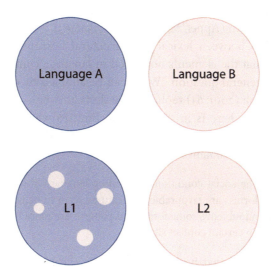

Figure 3.9 A schematic representation of structural borrowing (or restructuring) (adopted from Schmid 2011: 27)

It is usually assumed that linguistic change ensuing from both lexical and structural borrowing starts out with an individual speaker's behaviour in bilingual interaction through which they consciously or unconsciously propagate novel features in the L1 (Heine/Kuteva 2013: 88; Appel/Muysken 1987: 163). Oftentimes

---

116. Some subtypes of structural borrowing are sometimes referred to as 'loan translation' or 'polysemy copying' (Heine/Kuteva 2013: 91). Furthermore, 'grammatical' or 'structural' subtypes are often opposed to those involving lexical changes, e.g. through notions such as 'grammatical' vs 'lexical' replication or calquing. In the present work, I will follow Thomason/Kaufman (1988) in using 'borrowing' for incorporations of both phonetic matter and structure.

such "speaker innovations" (Milroy/Milroy 1985: 15) may be simple *ad hoc* borrowings or "speech errors" and will have no effect on the language concerned; but sometimes, they are accepted by the interlocutor and catch on. They may remain sporadic linguistic acts, occasionally produced by some individuals, but provided that enough speakers ('early adopters') take them up and start using them routinely, they can gradually become established features within the relevant speech community and acquire stability via habitualization and conventionalization (Matras 2009: 147; Kühl/Braunmüller 2014: 18; Höder 2014: 44). When used on a structural basis, e.g. when they are adopted by monolingual speakers, they have become part of the L1 system, and language change has occurred (Matras 2010: 72; Heine/Kuteva 2013: 88f.; Schmid 2011: 21, 26). However, the degree of integration the foreign item or structure attains is a crucial point, since it is possible that such elements keep a special status and are rejected by the language's speakers in the long run (Appel/Muysken 1989: 159, 163).

The distinction between lexical and structural borrowing just mentioned already indicates that the elements borrowed in language contact can be diverse in nature. To the general question "What can be adopted by one language from another?", Thomason (2001: 63) replies: "The short answer is, anything". Winford (2003: 63) specifies "There is in principle no limit to what can be transferred across languages, given the right circumstances", to which Kühl/Braunmüller (2014: 17) add (see also Aikhenvald 2007: 2f.):

> As long as the social conditions (including language attitudes and receptivity to 'foreign' forms) are favourable, no features seem to be impossible to borrow, although, undoubtedly, some forms and patterns are more likely to be borrowed than others in certain contact situations.

It is generally assumed that borrowing begins at the lexical level (Thomason/ Kaufman 1988: 37; Odlin 1989: 13; Van Coetsem 2000: 58f.), considering that the mental lexicon as an open-class system is unstable and able to change rapidly.[117] Foreign words can easily be added to it (Schmid 2011: 18f.) even in settings of 'casual' or 'distant' contact with the external language (Loveday 1996), like, e.g., in the case of 'cultural' borrowings from Latin or Greek in European languages, as "it is quite possible to borrow few words from a language you do not speak at all well" (Thomason 2001: 78). Structural elements, on the other hand, are less likely to be borrowed and higher requirements need to be fulfilled. For instance, Hickey (2013: 8) suggests that "the borrowing of more 'systemic' material — inflections,

---

117. Note, however, that lexical borrowing may also affect the phonological level, as loanwords usually come together with a phonic form (for an overview of loanword phonology in Romance see, e.g., Pustka 2021).

grammatical forms or sentence structures — can only occur via bilinguals" (see also Thomason/Kaufman 1988:37; Thomason 2001:78). A large array of predictors for contact-induced linguistic change have been proposed in the literature, including both social and linguistic factors, such as the intensity of the contact and speakers' attitudes, or typological distance between the languages involved, universal markedness constraints, and the degree of integration of the affected linguistic subsystem, respectively (see, e.g., Thomason 2001; Matras 2011). As a case in point, it is assumed that words are more easily borrowed than, say, inflectional morphology, owing to the tighter integration of the latter in the language system. Furthermore, different hierarchically ordered 'borrowing scales' representing the 'ease' or susceptibility to borrowing of a particular structure, i.e. its likelihood to be borrowed, have been established based on different measures: (a), the intensity of the language contact, (b), the frequency with which structures or categories are found to be borrowed in a sample of case studies, or, (c), structural factors that facilitate borrowing, such as semantic transparency, a consistent form — meaning relationship, or the aforementioned integration in the system (see Matras 2009:153–165, 2013, for an overview; see Appel/Muysken 1987:170–172 for different frequency-based hierarchies). In the following, I outline the borrowing scale proposed by Thomason (2001:70–71), which itself is built on the much renowned scale proposed in the seminal work of Thomason and Kaufman (1988:74–75). It represents a "continuum ranging from relatively slight lexical borrowing under casual contact to extreme structural borrowing under very intense contact" (Winford 2003:28).

Although this and other scales aim to tell us what is likely to be borrowed in different contact situations, a question they leave unanswered is what motivates borrowing in the first place, as they generally take for granted that this motivation must be extra-linguistic (Matras 2010:78).[118] Nevertheless, scholars have suggested various explanations as to why borrowing may occur, adducing different types of factors.

Especially lexical borrowing is often assumed to occur out of 'need', i.e. to fill gaps in the lexicon (Winford 2003:37–38): for example, when "a community is exposed to new areas of cultural knowledge and experience through contact with others" and lacks terms to refer to new or culture-specific items, or when a variety

---

118. For further critique, see Winford (2003:28–29), who — probably justifiably — questions the claim that "there is a clear correspondence between degrees of contact and cultural pressure on the one hand, and degrees of structural borrowing on the other". For instance, Catalonia is characterized by extensive bilingualism of its population in a situation of intense contact between Spanish and Catalan and yet, the L1 speakers of the two languages seem to borrow considerably less than proposed for level 4 contacts in Thomason's (2001) borrowing scale (see Chapter 2).

Table 3.5 Lexical and structural borrowings in different language contact situations (based on the borrowing scale presented in Thomason 2001: 70–71)

Contact-situation	Lexicon	Structure
1. Casual contact: few bilinguals and/or borrowers, need not be fluent in source language	only non-basic content words	none
2. Slightly more intense contact: borrowers are fluent bilinguals but can be a minority among borrowing-language speakers	also function words (conjunctions and adverbial particles)	only minor structural borrowing Phonology: new phonemes and phones only in loanwords Syntax: only different uses or frequencies of previously existing structures
3. More intense contact: more bilinguals, social factors favouring borrowing	also basic vocabulary including closed-class items (pronouns, numerals)	moderate structural borrowing; Phonology: addition and loss of phonemes also in native vocabulary, prosodic features and morphophonemic rules Syntax: beginning changes in word order and subordination patterns (not yet categorical) Morphology: derivational and inflectional affixes and categories
4. Intense contact: extensive bilingualism and strong cultural pressure	heavy lexical borrowing in all sections of the lexicon	heavy structural borrowing, major typological changes, "anything goes"

requires elaboration to meet new demands placed on it, e.g. after declaring its officiality. Whereas lexical borrowing may also occur in situations of 'distant' contact, it has been suggested that borrowing (also of the structural type) in settings of more or less extensive bilingualism is additionally determined by further, social factors, such as "cultural pressure from source-language speakers on the borrowing-language speaker group" (Thomason and Kaufman 1988: 37), arising from some kind of dominance of the group exerting the influence, e.g., in terms of "larger numbers, greater prestige, and more political power" (Odlin 1989: 13).[119]

---

119. Prestige can be overt or covert. "In covert prestige, forms belonging to vernacular dialects are positively valued, emphasizing group solidarity and local identity", whereas in the case of overt prestige, "the forms to be valued are publicly recommended by powerful social institutions" (Crystal 2003: 115, see also Kühl/Braunmüller 2014: 20).

Likewise, the degree of bilingualism *per se* is an often-cited factor, considering that bilinguals can borrow both intentionally and unintentionally (Schmid 2011: 18–37). Borrowing may thus be a more or less conscious choice: it can allow for finer distinctions of meaning or provide the speaker with stylistic choices (Winford 2003: 38–39). Additionally, the use of an L2 element may sometimes carry a personal or emotional component (Schmid 2011: 25–26), or the speaker simply wishes to maintain consistent labelling for unique referents such as institutions (Matras 2009: 148). In other cases, the reasons for borrowing may be rather unconscious and associated with the cognitive condition of the bilingual. As Schmid (2011: 19) hypothesizes, "bilingual speakers have to co-ordinate the lexicon of two languages", i.e. two vast repertoires of knowledge, often with substantial overlap in meaning and sometimes in form. It may thus be cognitively challenging to select context-appropriate structures, while inhibiting features that are not appropriate (Kühl/Braunmüller 2014: 18), and it is "almost inevitable that one will sometimes influence the other in various ways" (Schmid 2011: 19). For instance, this may be the case of "automatized routines" such as discourse markers, fillers, tags, hesitation markers, interjections or focus particles, which are often freely borrowed by bilinguals (Matras 2009: 136–145, 193–198), or when the selection or inhibition mechanisms controlling the retrieval of "language-correct" items from the bilingual repertoire are interfered by external factors that put a strain on the speaker's processing of language: e.g. when talking about "activities that are more likely to be performed in the donor language" (Matras 2010: 80–82). It is generally assumed that this type of convergence through borrowing serves to keep the cognitive cost in language processing low by means of interlingual identifications: bilinguals prefer inter-systematically equivalent forms or patterns to 'ease their linguistic burden' (Weinreich 1953: 8), i.e. the cognitive cost of maintaining two separate language systems (Höder 2014: 46). It therefore represents a 'natural' simplification of the bilinguals' linguistic knowledge (Kühl/Braunmüller 2014: 18–19).

The second major type of CLI is **substratum interference** or **transfer**.[120] According to Odlin (1989: 12), "*substratum transfer* is the type of cross-linguistic influence investigated in most studies of second language acquisition". It "involves

---

120. Also in this case, a large array of terms and labels has been used to refer to the same (or fairly similar) phenomena. For instance, many scholars drop *substratum* and use simply *transfer* (Odlin 1989) or *interference* (Thomason/Kaufman 1988), or both interchangeably (Matras 2009) in opposition to *borrowing*. Thomason (2001: 277) remarks that *substratum interference* is actually "flawed as a general label" because it implies that a shifting group is "socially, economically, and/or politically subordinate to the people whose language they are shifting to", which is not the case in all shifting groups. She therefore suggests using the more appropriate term "shift-induced interference".

the influence of a source language (typically, the native language of a learner [= L1]) on the acquisition of a target language [(TL)], the 'second' language [(L2)] regardless of how many languages the learner already knows", i.e. the agents of the process are source language speakers, who transfer (or impose) features from their dominant language upon the recipient language, in which they are less proficient (Van Coetsem 2000: 60f). Van Coetsem's (1988, 2000) model propagates the terms imposition and "source language agentivity" to refer to this type of linguistic "transmission" and underscores its aggressive and penetrating character (p. 59). Thomason and Kaufman (1988: 38) define substratum interference more specifically as a "subtype of interference that results from imperfect group learning", occurring when a community of speakers acquires or "shifts to" an L2 but fails to learn this target language (TL) perfectly. Since such learning difficulties are most likely to arise with regard to marked features of the TL, the view is commonly held "that substratum interference is largely simplificatory" (Thomason/Kaufman 1988: 51). The elements transferred from the L1 ("errors") may then "survive" and spread to the TL as a whole when they are "imitated" by original speakers of the language (Thomason/Kaufman 1988: 39). Odlin (1989: 27), on the other hand, offers a broader interpretation of (substratum) transfer: "the influence resulting from similarities and differences between the target language and any other language that has been previously (and perhaps imperfectly) acquired". He thus does not restrict the notion to "negative transfer" in the sense of "errors" resulting from imperfect learning (Winford 2003: 210) but equally includes "positive transfer", i.e. the facilitating influence of cognate vocabulary and any other similarities between the L1 and TL (Odlin 1989: 26), also described as match between L1 (retentions) and L2 (elements or structures) (Winford 2003: 210). Furthermore, some scholars mainly employ the term 'transfer' to refer to the psycholinguistic processes involved in SLA, whereas the results of these processes, i.e. the actual manifestations, are called "L1 influence" or "L1 retentions" (Winford 2003: 210).

A distinction should be made between substratum interference in early consecutive bilingual speakers and in adult second-language learners due to different age of learning as well as the different settings in which SLA takes place, respectively (Matras 2009: 72). For instance, when immigrants need to acquire the dominant language of a host community in 'natural' or real-life situations, i.e. without formal instruction, the primary aim may be communication rather than the acquisition of an optimal TL knowledge, whereas foreign-language acquisition in non-migrants typically involves formal instruction at school (Matras 2009: 69f, 72–74; Winford 2003: 208–209; Van Coetsem 1988: 19; Mennen 2015).

As opposed to borrowing (transfer), it is widely agreed that substratum transfer (or interference) does not begin at the lexical level but will be most evident in pronunciation (Thomason/Kaufman 1988: 39; Odlin 1989: 14; Van Coetsem

2000: 58f.). Appel/Muysken (1987: 89–90) suggest that "phonic transfer probably occurs more often than on other levels, because it has neurological and physiological causes: it seems difficult to learn new pronunciation habits". Many researchers even assume that "achieving a native-like pronunciation is the hardest component of second language acquisition (SLA) for most L2 learners" (Schmid 2011: 49). In consequence, hearing someone for 30 milliseconds can be enough to determine whether or not they are native speakers, given that L2 speakers usually exhibit a 'foreign accent' (Flege 1984, 1995). Nevertheless, like borrowing transfer, substratum transfer may affect (and has been attested in) all linguistic domains and subsystems (Odlin 1989: 23; Schmid 2011: 4). This is illustrated in the following graph (where grammar refers to morphology and syntax).

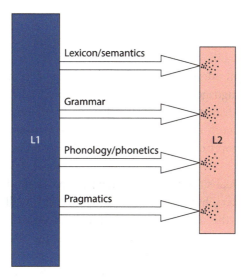

Figure 3.10 A schematic representation of L1 influence on L2 in SLA (adopted from Schmid 2011: 4, based on Schmid/Köpke 2007: 2)

To the question as to why substratum transfer occurs and how L1 influence on an L2 can be modelled, different answers have been given in a wide range of theoretical approaches, often depending on the goals of the respective studies (Muysken 2013 for an overview. Many times, a behaviourist view is adopted: i.e. the idea that an old set of habits (from the L1) influences the acquisition of the L2 (e.g. articulatory or motoric habits; Odlin 1989: 15; Van Coetsem 2000: 75–77, 176–178). Other approaches assume that "by a gradual process of trial and error and by hypothesis testing, the learner slowly and tediously succeeds in establishing closer and closer approximations to the system used by native speakers" (Brown 1980: 163; see also Winford 2003: 220).

A further concept, frequently made reference to in SLA studies, is **interlanguage** (IL, Selinker 1972). Taking the view that SLA constitutes a linear learning process reaching from the L1 as a starting point to the acquisition of full proficiency in the TL or L2, researchers have made use of the term *interlanguage* to refer to points on this continuum. In traditional terms, it thus designates an individual learner's idiosyncratic use of TL structures and can be considered "an incomplete or deficient version of the target language" (Matras 2009:74) or "an intermediate system characterized by features resulting from language-learning strategies" (Appel/Muysken 1987:83).[121] However, learners mostly fail to achieve the goal of full proficiency in the TL and get stuck in one of the intermediate stages (Appel/Muysken 1987:92; Matras 2009:75). This typically happens when they are 'older', have limited contact to the TL, or are satisfied with their own ability to sustain successful and effective communication in it (see Long 2003 for further causes). It is commonly referred to as **fossilization** (Selinker 1972:215f.) or, less frequently, as stabilisation (Matras 2009:75f.) and "capture[s] the phenomenon of a permanent adoption (regardless of age or amount of instruction) of idiosyncratic interlanguage features in a learner's L2" (Matras 2009:75). When a certain structure or feature of the IL fossilizes at the same non-target-like end-state in an entire speech community (or at least in a subgroup), a new variety of the TL may develop from the collective IL (Matras 2009:76, Appel/Muysken 1987:92).[122]

Finally, the gradual shift from one language (L1) to another (TL or L2) in a community of speakers, but also in individuals, can eventually lead to the abandonment or loss of the original L1, sometimes called ancestral language (AL, Winford 2003:256). As the term **language loss** is "somewhat unspecific", Schmid (2011:3) suggests distinguishing between the subtypes shown in Figure 3.11.

Language loss can thus refer to either language **shift** from one language to another over several generations, i.e. gradual abandonment of the AL, or to the overall extinction of a particular language, i.e. 'language **death**' (see also Thomason 2001:223–239). Of course, language death is in the vast majority of cases a sequel of

---

121. A slightly different approach is adopted by scholars such as Myers-Scotton and Jake (2000), who define 'interlanguage' as combination of three systems: the learner's previously acquired languages, a variety of the target language, and the developing learner variety ("composite matrix language", Matras 2009:74). Furthermore, uses of the term interlanguage in the sense of intermediate variety or 'interdialect' (Trudgill 1988) as an outcome of dialect levelling can also be encountered in contact linguistics (Kristensen/Thelander 1984; Auer/Hinskens 1996:6–10).

122. Such 'collective interlanguages' or 'ethnolects' may become markers of identity in the respective speech community (Matras 2009:76). If the speaker group subsequently shifts to the L2 overall, the respective variety may become a native language (L1) in following generations (see Thomason and Kaufman 1988:38).

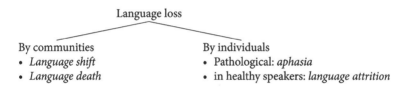

Figure 3.11 The terminology of language loss (adapted from Schmid 2011:3)

the (more or less deliberate) gradual abandonment of an AL by its speakers. However, in some cases languages become extinct because all their speakers die, are killed quickly, or are subjected to extreme repression (Winford 2003: 257). As Winford (2003: 258, 266) informs us, language loss by communities usually occurs in several stages, which overlap to varying degrees: beginning with a period of bilingualism during which the L2 assumes dominance, the AL progressively ceases to be learned by new speakers "in the normal way", which then leads to a gradual demise of competence and production of the AL in the speaker community. The final state is attained when the L2 has completely replaced the AL.

With reference to language loss in individuals, on the other hand, Schmid (2011:3) discriminates between **aphasia**, i.e. loss caused by brain injury or some pathological condition (e.g. dementia), and loss of a language by a healthy person ('**language attrition**'). The latter term, attrition, "refers to the (total or partial) forgetting of a language by a healthy speaker" and thus allows for "a more flexible and gradual interpretation of the forgetting process than the starkly dichotomous [term] language loss" (Schmid 2011:3).[123] Attrition takes place in settings where an L2 has become a speaker's predominant medium of communication in everyday life and the L1 is used only rarely or not at all anymore, e.g. in the case of immigrants who live in a country where only the L2 is spoken (Schmid 2011:4). Although to varying degrees, such a change in the overall circumstances and the consequent lack of exposure to the L1 can entail that the L1 system is "restructured and shrunk to some degree, and that it will show evidence of traffic from L2 on many linguistic levels" (Schmid 2011:5). This is illustrated in Figure 3.12.

Concerning the phenomena involved in language attrition or its linguistic outcomes, many parallels with other types of CLI have been found, such as lexical or structural borrowing (Winford 2003: 256, 260; see Schmid 2011: 38–68 for an overview). In the framework of the *Activation Threshold Hypothesis* (ATH, Paradis 2007:125), their occurrence is explained by the assumption that "attrition is the result of long-term lack of stimulation" (Schmid 2011:16): i.e. the less frequently an item stored in memory (i.e. in the human brain) is accessed, the less

---

[123]. Note that Winford (2003: 258) applies the label 'attrition' to processes of gradual abandonment (i.e. language shift) and subsequent death of the ancestral language.

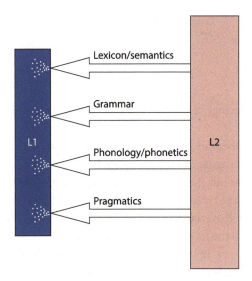

Figure 3.12 A schematic representation of L2 influence on L1 in L1 attrition (adopted from Schmid 2011: 5, based on Schmid/Köpke 2007: 2)

'activated' it is and the more effort is necessary to retrieve it.[124] "A bilingual who speaks his or her second language every day, but has not used the first for a long time, therefore has words and structures that belong to the L2 which are highly active and easy to access, but the corresponding bits of the L1 may have a very high Activation Threshold. This is why the L2 can often get in the way when a speaker attempts to use the L1" (Schmid 2011: 16).

We have discussed the most important key terms of the field of contact linguistics. Couched within different theoretical frameworks and approaches, they typically refer to linguistic processes and their outcomes. However, language contact is obviously based "on the social interaction among speakers (or writers) using more than one language (or dialect)" (Heine/Kuteva 2013: 100), i.e. language contact and contact-induced change have both a cognitive and a social dimension as both individual speakers and speaker groups are involved (Höder 2014: 44). In consequence, the history of a language, and thus the contact-induced change it underwent, cannot be "thoroughly studied without reference to the social context in which it is embedded" (Thomason/Kaufman 1988: 4). Indeed, already Weinreich highlighted the importance of tackling language contact from both a linguistic and sociocultural perspective and taking an interdisci-

---

124. An example frequently adduced to illustrate this 'lack of activation' is the so-called 'tip-of-the-tongue state', i.e. "when we simply cannot recall a name or a word, even though we know that we know it" (Schmid 2011: 16).

plinary approach (Odlin 1989:12; Winford 2003:8). What is more, "his survey of bilingualism shows that the effects of cross-linguistic influence are not monolithic but instead vary considerably according to the social context of the language contact situation" (Odlin 1989:12).

Such **contact situations** arise whenever there is a meeting of speakers who do not share the same language and who need to communicate (Odlin 1989:6). Most often, it involves face-to-face interactions among groups of speakers, at least some of whom have at least some knowledge of more than one of the languages present in the particular geographical locality the contact takes place in (Thomason 2001:3). Such speaker groups can either be neighbours, who may — but need not — be on friendly terms with each other, or live together in a single community. In the latter case, there may be mutual or asymmetrical bilingualism (or multilingualism) (Thomason 2001:4). Both kinds of situations can be stable or not, and, in consequence, the languages involved may be maintained or one group (or several) may shift from their language to another (which can ultimately result in language loss). As Thomason (2001:21) underlines, this solely depends on social factors, while linguistic factors "seem to be totally irrelevant". Giles et al. (1977) subsume these social predictors under the cover term 'ethnolinguistic vitality': high vitality of a variety will lead to maintenance; low vitality will result in shift (Appel/Muysken 1987:33). The factors contributing to a variety's vitality include status, demographics and institutional support (Appel/Muysken 1987:33–38; Thomason 2001:21–25). Concerning status, various subtypes can be distinguished: (1) socioeconomic and political status: speakers of subordinate groups tend to adopt the language of dominant groups, i.e. those with high socioeconomic status, in the hope of thereby raising their own status; (2) sociohistorical status: the remembrance of events in a ethnolinguistic group's history such as a fight for ethnic identity or independence may favour language loyalty; (3) language status: speakers of low status varieties tend to shift to varieties or languages that have a high language status within the community.[125] Furthermore, demographic factors, such as the number and geographical distribution of its speakers can go hand in hand with the respective language's 'usefulness'.[126] For instance, a decrease in numbers of speakers (e.g. through emigration and immigration or mixed and inter-ethnic marriages) can tip the balance against a minority language and this in turn may motivate its speakers

---

125. The reasons for the high or low status of a particular language or variety within a multilingual community can vary widely, depending on the respective situation. Typically, a correlation with the degree of standardization and elaboration, i.e. with its *Ausbau* (see Kloss 1978), can be observed.

126. Note, however, that there is no general correspondence between numerical strength of a speaker community and language maintenance (see Clyne 2003).

to shift to the majority language. Similarly, minority languages tend to be preserved longer in areas where their speakers live concentrated and represent a (geographically restricted) majority, i.e. typically in rural areas (Appel/Muysken 1987:36). Finally, institutional support factors may influence language maintenance: the use of the minority language in governmental or administrative services, education, religious institutions, and mass media stimulates its maintenance and prevents its loss (Appel/Muysken 1987:37–38).[127]

Most of the factors for stability or change in contact situations just mentioned involve relationships of dominance and subordination between two groups of speakers. These are doubtlessly a powerful predictor of contact-induced change, but not its most potent driving force, as "speakers' attitudes can and [...] do produce exceptions to most of the generalizations we have already drawn" (Thomason 2001:77). Crucially, people's attitudes towards the languages they speak cannot be predicted with absolute confidence and thus as all language-change, including contact-induced change, is ultimately unpredictable (Thomason 2001:22). As a case in point, people oftentimes show awareness of CLI and can take different attitudes or stances to it, such that there is, on the one hand, a historical record of people associating language contact and mixing with "contamination" or "corruption" (Odlin 1989:7), whereas, on the other hand, in some communities it may even "carry a certain cachet" (Schmid 2011:19; see Appel/Muysken 1987:11–21; Thomason 2007, 2013: passim, for social aspects of language contact such as attitudes or evaluation). Yet, it is likewise possible that speakers are unaware of "the attitudinal factors that help to shape their linguistic choices" (Thomason 2013:38). Stating constraints on contact-induced change seems thus a "more promising enterprise" than trying to predict that any particular change will occur, considering that speakers' attitudes can trump expectations built on sociolinguistic factors (Thomason 2001:78). But ultimately, this is just as elusive, considering that "speakers' attitudes seem to be able to outdo any linguistic constraint" (Kühl/Braunmüller 2014:21).

---

127. For instance, in Catalonia, there seems to be, at present, a more or less stable situation of extensive societal bilingualism within a single community, and hence, of intense contact between Spanish and Catalan (see Chapter 2), in which both languages display high vitality. The high socioeconomic and (regained) sociocultural status of Catalan as well as the strong institutional support benefit its maintenance in views of the demographic factors, which in many, especially urban areas, tip the balance in favour of Spanish. Also regarding the *Ausbau* of the two languages, Spanish is still in a better position.

3.2.2 Contact-induced phonological change

As shown in the previous section, scholars usually distinguish between borrowings of matter (i.e. typically words and their meaning) and patterns or structure, when analysing contact-induced language change (Matras 2009:146–149; Matras 2010:68). Phonology has a somewhat ambiguous position in between these two types of borrowing as phones and suprasegmental phenomena "can be produced and perceived", which "gives us the impression that they constitute concrete shapes, or linguistic matter" (Matras 2009:221). However, sounds (or phonemes) have no meaning of their own and, in a similar vein, prosodic features (e.g. intonation) take a "peripheral role" in conveying meaning, given that they prototypically operate at the utterance or speech-act level and express, e.g., emotive modes (Matras 2009:233; Odlin 1989:118–119; see Section 3.1.1.1 for the meaning of intonation).

Evidence from a series of case studies shows that virtually every phonological level can be affected by borrowing: "the articulation of individual phones or phonemes within words, length and gemination, stress and tone, prosody and intonation" (Matras 2009:222). Yet, some sub-components of phonology appear to be more susceptible to borrowing, as revealed in various sampling studies (e.g. Matras 2002:205 and the studies in Matras and Sakel 2007). Whereas "prosody [i.e. intonation] is at the top of the hierarchy of adopted features", stress appears as the next step of the scale and segmental phonology seems to be replicated less frequently in contact situations (Matras 2009:231–233; see also Mackey 2000:44; Burridge 2006:192; for the diffusability of (lexical) tones see Matisoff 2001; for contact-induced change in word prominence see Van der Hulst et al. 2015).[128] Indeed, the tendency towards wholesale convergence of the phonological systems of two contact languages seems to be strongest in the prosodic domain (see Bullock 2009:166–170 for a more critical view). Matras (2009:232–233) adduces two interconnected factors for the "volatility of prosody": first, the fact that the function and meaning of prosody (and especially of intonation) relates to units above word-level (e.g. to discourse-related phenomena) "allows speakers to mentally disconnect it from the matter or shape or words associated with a particular language, making it prone to change and modification in contact situations".[129]

---

128. Interestingly, Bullock (2009:166) takes a slightly different view. Namely, she assumes phonological change proceeds linearly following "a path of allophonic change > phonemic change > prosodic change, [which] implies that when prosodic changes are present in a contact variety then, by implication, allophonic and phonemic interference are equally present." However, she also questions whether "prosodic innovations are in any way linked to segmental ones since the two have rarely been examined in tandem".

Second, Matras refers to a series of studies which have demonstrated that prosody is more difficult to control, given that it is neurophysiologically separated from "other aspects of speech production". Interestingly enough, intonation seems to be the first linguistic feature that babies acquire from the language surrounding them (Matisoff 2001: 320–323). In addition, the domain of sound production is known to be generally more "vulnerable to 'interference' phenomena than other areas of structure": as a case in point, it is more difficult to exercise control over the sound-producing apparatus in adulthood than in earlier years and hence to master new sound forms when learning a new language (Matras 2009: 222).

Concerning the segmental domain, there is no reason to assume that some phonemes could be more susceptible to be borrowed than others. However,

> [s]ince the inventory of consonants in any given phonological system is usually larger than the inventory of vowels, two languages in contact are more likely to differ in their consonant systems than in their vowel systems. Loanwords are therefore more likely to introduce more new consonants than new vowels.
>
> (Matras 2009: 232)

Furthermore, some authors, such as Weinreich (1953: 22) and Winford (2003: 55–56), suggest that phonological borrowing may represent a strategy to fill structural 'gaps' or "holes in the pattern" in the recipient system and may be facilitated under conditions of close typological fit (Thomason/Kaufman 1988: 97). Yet, it

---

129. This might become clearer if we conceive intonational patterns as 'constructions' in the sense of Matras (2011: 151f.), i.e. as "viable entities in their own right within a speaker's repertoire of linguistic structures" that present a conventionalized form–meaning mapping (i.e. if we treat them similar to word-forms). Although Matras (2011) refers to exclusively syntactic constructions and explicitly not to "the level of phonology and articulation", there would be strong parallels between such 'melodic' and 'syntactic' constructions. First, "[syntactic] constructions offer [...] derived meanings that are inferred from a particular configuration of word-forms, rather than simply the sum or combination of fixed meanings that are tightly associated with concrete word-forms", i.e. constructions are configurations whose specialized meanings are contextually (i.e. pragmatically) inferred (p. 153). Similarly, the meaning of 'melodic constructions' derives from configurations of tones used in a particular pragmatic context. Second, both types of constructions are volatile in situations of language contact because of the tendency to treat the pragmatic organization of discourse as universal or global rather than language-specific, i.e. bilinguals are prone to generalize constructions over their bilingual repertoire and hence to transfer them from the source language to the target language in that they map the pivotal features of the construction onto word-forms of the latter. Interestingly, Torreira and Grice (2018: 28) have recently proposed that 'melodic constructions', whose meanings may include links to syntax and/or discourse, "are stored as intonational elements in a unified lexicon-grammar [...] [alongside] syntactic structures, words, morphemes, idioms, and phonemes."

appears to occur more easily with patterns of allophonic distribution, i.e. when it does not affect the basic phonemic inventory (Winford 2003: 56).

Regarding the occurrence of substratum interference in SLA, "there is little doubt that native language phonetics and phonology are powerful influences on second language pronunciation" (Odlin 1989: 112). Given the difficulty to master new sounds in adulthood, differences between the L1 and the L2 phonological systems (including allophonic rules) are frequently adduced predictors of production difficulties or errors in the L2 speech, in line with the idea that typological distance between the two languages may have a facilitating or hampering effect on the acquisition of the TL pronunciation, respectively (Odlin 1989: 112–128; see also Winford 2003: 212f.).[130] In the segmental domain, four types of errors can be recognized according to Moulton's (1962) taxonomy: (1) phonemic errors; (2) phonetic errors; (3) allophonic errors; and (4) distributional errors (see Odlin 1989: 115–117 for descriptions of each type). Additionally, substratum interference is also "frequently evident in suprasegmental contrasts involving stress, tone, rhythm, and other factors", so that the ensemble of suprasegmental characteristics certainly figures among "the surest clues to the specific 'foreign accent' of an individual" (Odlin 1989: 117, 119; Jilka 2000; see also Ramus 2002) and L1 prosodic influences can remain present even after many years of learning (Mennen/de Leeuw 2014: 183). Besides, the negative transfer of suprasegmental rules from the L1 to an L2 (e.g. of stress-assignment rules) appears to be much more critical in terms of intelligibility than segmental transfer (Odlin 1989: 117–119; Mennen/de Leeuw 2014: 183–184, 188–189; Levis 2018: 150–182 and sources cited therein). Despite important individual differences between L2 learners, the view is generally held that "only individuals with especially high phonetic sensitivity will be able to overcome most of the inhibiting influence of phonological patterns in the native language" when learning an L2 (in adulthood) and few succeed in sounding like a native (Odlin 1989: 115, 130–136; Selinker 1972: 212f.; Mennen/de Leeuw 2014: 183; Levis 2018: 11).

To summarize the diverse processes leading to contact-induced phonological change, Matras (2009: 224–226) proposes the following classification based on typical linguistic processes in situations of borrowing and substratum interference, as well as on the profiles and attitudes of the speakers involved:

---

130. This assumption is the basis, e.g., of Eckman's (1977) Markedness Differential Hypothesis and Flege's (1987) Speech Learning Model. For an overview of different models focusing on phonology in SLA see Muysken (2013: 721); for a model of L2 acquisition of intonation see Mennen (2015).

Table 3.6 Different types of processes leading to contact-induced phonological change (adapted from Matras 2009: 225)

Type	Description of the process	Speakers/Bilingualism	Language attitudes
A	Borrowed word-forms are adapted to the sound patterns of the recipient language	Semi-bilinguals or monolinguals; superficial contact	Strong loyalty towards, and stability of the recipient language
B	Borrowed and inserted word-forms maintain (fully or partly) the original phonological features of the donor language ('authentication')	Fairly widespread bilingualism	Flexibility in the use of the recipient language, prestigious bilingualism
C	Convergence of systems during second-language acquisition: TL forms are systematically adjusted to match the sound patterns of the native language	Emerging bilingualism; stable minority bilingualism; emergence of ethnolect or language shift	Strong group identity coupled with a need (pressure) to acquire the TL
D	Convergence of systems in stable bilingualism: sound patterns of the native language are adjusted to match those of the second language	Intensive and widespread bilingualism	Second language is 'prestige' language

Whereas type A involves no change to the phonological system but only a change to individual words, types B to D all involve some degree of modification to the system of the recipient language. Furthermore, types A and B revolve 'only' around lexical borrowings, while C and D include the generalization of one set of sounds and patterns to both languages of a bilingual, e.g. convergence of the intonational systems (Matras 2009: 224; for an example of such wholesale convergence see the description of Bulgarian Judaeo-Spanish in the following section).[131]

3.2.3 Transfer and convergence at the intonational level: Case studies

The following tables give a synopsis of some recent case studies on intonation in language contact. Most of them address Romance varieties and particularly Spanish and Catalan, as these are the two languages under concern in this book (for an overview of intonation in Romance contact varieties see also Gabriel/Reich 2022: 485–490). The main goal of this section is to show the wide range of intona-

---

131. The contact situation in Catalonia (see Chapter 2) is characterized by almost generalized bilingualism today, i.e. like in scenarios B and D, while scenarios A and C may be adequate descriptions of past stages of the language contact. It will be the aim of the present study to determine to what extent the current varieties of Catalan and Spanish spoken in Catalonia have converged at the intonational level.

tional (and other prosodic) characteristics that can be interpreted as the results of borrowing, substratum interference or transfer, convergence, and/or attrition (see Section 3.2.1 for definitions of these terms). For a better overview, research into the prosodic characteristics of L1 and L2 varieties will be presented separately — although this distinction might be somewhat artificial in some cases. Table 3.7 offers a selection of some L1 varieties, whose intonation (or at least features of it) has been interpreted as an outcome of linguistic change induced by contact with other languages or varieties.

Table 3.7 Selected case studies on intonation in language contact: L1 varieties[a]

Description of the contact situation and intonation of the languages involved	Linguistic outcomes (in the intonational domain)	References
Cuzco Spanish and Quechua contact between Spanish and Quechua in Cuzco intonation of the Spanish spoken by bilinguals is assumed to be influenced by Quechua (prosodic convergence)	i. Cuzco Spanish and Quechua display early peak alignment of prenuclear pitch accents in broad-focus statements (although there seems to be more variability in Spanish) → early peak alignment is transferred from Quechua to Spanish ii. the contact varieties do not use peak alignment (peak location in the stressed vs in the post-tonic syllable) to distinguish between broad and contrastive focus (although there might be (relics of) alignment differences within the stressed syllable) → prosodic convergence	O'Rourke (2004, 2005); Muntendam (2012); Van Rijswijk/ Muntendam (2014)
Porteño Spanish and Italian intense contact between Spanish and Italian in Buenos Aires due to massive Italian immigration (almost 3 million) between the 1860s and the beginning of the 20th century Porteño Spanish intonation: result of direct and/or indirect transfer from Italian, i.e. convergence of the prosodic system of Spanish with Italian through direct borrowing and/ or (i) transfer from Italian to L2	Porteño Spanish and different Italian varieties share: i. early peak alignment in prenuclear pitch accents (L+H*) ii. realization of nuclear pitch accents in broad-focus statements as H+L* iii. use of a tritonal pitch accent to mark emphasis and contrastive focus (L+H*+L) iv. realization of nuclear contours in information-seeking yes–no questions (L+¡H* HL%)	Colantoni/ Gurlekian (2004); McMahon (2004); Gabriel (2006, 2007); Gabriel et al. (2010); Gabriel et al. (2011); Colantoni (2011); Feldhausen et al. (2011); Gabriel/ Kireva (2012, 2014); Pešková et al. (2012)

Table 3.7 *(continued)*

Description of the contact situation and intonation of the languages involved	Linguistic outcomes (in the intonational domain)	References
Spanish in SLA by Italian immigrants, and (ii) subsequent convergence of L1 Spanish with this L2 variety	v. balanced frequency in use of both CR (H-) and SP (!H-) to mark inner ips in neutral SVO declaratives	
Olivenza Spanish and Portuguese long-lasting contact in Olivenza (Extremadura) due to the incorporation of the Portuguese-speaking city into Spain in 1801 Olivenza Spanish intonation: result of (i) transfer from L1 Portuguese to L2 Spanish in SLA by the inhabitants of the city ('fossilized interlanguage') and (ii) convergence with (Standard) Castilian Spanish	i. (monolingual) Olivenza Spanish and Olivenza Portuguese share the same nuclear configuration in neutral yes–no questions, i.e., (H+)L* !HL%, accompanied by considerable lengthening of the phrase-final syllable ii. Olivenza Spanish and Castilian Spanish share the same prenuclear pitch accents (i.e. L*+H) and nuclear configuration in yes–no questions, i.e. L* H% (without particularly strong final lengthening)	Kireva (2016a, 2016b); Kireva/ Gabriel (2016); Gabriel et al. (2020)
Judaeo-Spanish and Bulgarian secular contact after the expulsion of the Sephardic Jews from Spain in 1492, no monolingual speakers (today) (Bulgarian) Judaeo-Spanish intonation: outcome of convergence with the surrounding language (Bulgarian), which is also the dominant language of the bilinguals (possibly L1 attrition)	(Bulgarian) Judaeo-Spanish and Bulgarian (spoken by both monolinguals and bilinguals) display: i. the same inventory of pitch accents and boundary tones ii. (almost) identical use of this inventory iii. the same stress patterns in comparative structures (i.e. primary stress on the comparative particle instead of the adjective or adverb)	Andreeva et al. (2017, 2019, 2021); Grünke et al. (2023)
Majorcan Spanish and Catalan long-lasting language contact between Spanish and Catalan in Majorca intonation of Majorcan Spanish: result of asymmetric convergence between Spanish and Catalan through (i) substratum transfer from	i. Majorca Spanish (spoken by Catalan-dominant bilinguals and Spanish-dominant young females) and Majorca Catalan share: concave-falling utterance final contours in declaratives (i.e. (H+)L* L%) and falling contours in yes–no questions (i.e. (¡)H+L* L%)	Simonet (2008, 2010, 2011); Romera/Elordieta (2013)

Table 3.7 *(continued)*

Description of the contact situation and intonation of the languages involved	Linguistic outcomes (in the intonational domain)	References
Catalan to Spanish (in Catalan-dominant bilinguals) and (ii) borrowing from Catalan ('direct borrowing') or (perhaps more likely) from the Spanish variety spoken by Catalan-dominants ('indirect borrowing' or accommodation) (by Spanish-dominant bilinguals)	ii. Majorca Spanish (predominantly of older and male Spanish-dominants) and Catalan (spoken by Spanish-dominant males) share: convex-falling utterance-final contours in declaratives ((L+)H* L%) → ongoing process of asymmetrical intonational convergence lead by Spanish-dominant females, mostly unidirectional transfer from Catalan to Spanish iii. Majorca Spanish (predominantly of older and male Spanish-dominants) and Catalan (spoken by Catalan-dominant older females) share: rising contours in yes–no questions (i.e. L* H%) → borrowing from Spanish to Catalan (although this occurs not very frequently)	
Algherese Catalan and Sardinian Italian over 600 years of contact between Sardinian and Catalan in Alghero, more recent contact with Italian Algherese Catalan intonation: result of (i) substratum transfer from (Logudorese) Sardinian that occurred when L1 speakers of Sardinian massively immigrated into Alghero and imperfectly learned Catalan as an L2, and (ii) subsequent convergence of the Catalan varieties spoken by immigrants and natives; Intonation of the Italian variety of Sardinia: result of substratum transfer from Sardinian that	i. Algherese Catalan, Logudorese Sardinian, and Sardinian Italian use the same prenuclear pitch accents and nuclear configurations for broad-focus SVO declaratives (L+H* L+H* H+L* L% and H*+L L+H* H+L* L%) ii. the three contact varieties share the same nuclear configurations for information-seeking yes–no questions (¡H+L* L% and H*+L L%) iii. Algherese Catalan and Sardinian display the same nuclear configurations in orders, contrastive-focus statements, exclamative statements, and (truncated) vocatives	Roseano et al. (2015); Vanrell et al. (2020)

Table 3.7 *(continued)*

Description of the contact situation and intonation of the languages involved	Linguistic outcomes (in the intonational domain)	References
occurred when Sardinians learned Italian as an L2 (imperfect learning)		
Northern Catalan and French over 300 years of intense contact between Catalan and French (and, in part, Occitan) Northern Catalan is seen as a 'transitional dialect' to Occitan	Northern Catalan and French and/or Occitan exhibit: i. use of the phrase-initial accent (L)Hi ii. early rising prenuclear accents L+H* iii. use of L+H* H% in information-seeking yes–no questions → interferences between the prosody of the languages	Sichel-Bazin/Roseano (2013); Prieto et al. (2015)
Occitan and (Southern) French long-lasting contact in Southern France Occitan intonation: result of prosodic interference from French and of first-language attrition; Southern French intonation: result of transfer from Occitan occurring through SLA of French by Occitanophones; innovative/urban Southern French: gradual convergence with Northern (Standard) French.	i. basic prosodic unit for accentuation in both languages: accentual phrase (AP), containing an obligatory pitch accent at its right edge and an optional initial rise (as opposed to Northern (Standard) French, lexically stressed syllables still may show reduced prominence/relics of lexical accents) → adaption of AP in Occitan due to French influence → relics of lexical accents due to Occitan interference ii. Occitan and conservative Southern French exhibit the same nuclear configuration for statements of the obvious (H*+L L%); innovative (urban) Southern French largely patterns with Northern (Standard) French (H* !H%, H*+L !H%) iii. Occitan and conservative Southern French show fewer rising contours than innovative Southern French and Northern French in yes–no and wh-questions (partly owing to the use of more conservative syntactic structures which allow for falling contours)	Meisenburg (2011); Sichel-Bazin et al. (2012a, b, 2015); see also Hualde (2003b)

Table 3.7 *(continued)*

Description of the contact situation and intonation of the languages involved	Linguistic outcomes (in the intonational domain)	References
	→ substrate of Occitan in (conservative) Southern French	
	→ gradual convergence of (innovative) Southern French with the standard	

a. The terminology and the assumptions made with regard to the emergence of the contact-induced linguistic features are those of the authors of the cited studies. Minor adaptions were made regarding the annotation of some pitch accents and boundary tones.

Some further studies worth mentioning are Elordieta (2003), Elordieta/Calleja (2005), Robles-Puente (2012), Elordieta/Romera (2020), and Romera/Elordieta (2020) on intonation in Spanish-Basque contact (finding, among other things, L+H* prenuclear pitch accents in Basque Spanish statements and rising–falling circumflex contours in information-seeking yes–no questions) as well as a series of studies on the Spanish (and English) spoken by heritage speakers in the US. For instance, Alvord (2010) focuses on (Cuban) Spanish in Miami and evinces convergence with English for at least some bilinguals (e.g. in the use of rising patterns in yes–no interrogatives instead of the otherwise typical Cuban-style falling patterns) and, similarly, Robles-Puente (2014) investigates (Mexican) Spanish spoken by heritage speakers and immigrants in Los Angeles, showing, among other things, that early bilinguals exhibit prenuclear and nuclear pitch accents similar to the surrounding language English. Especially the latter case can be seen as an instance of L1 attrition (i.e. as gradual loss of L1 Spanish features in favour of English ones). Finally, contact-influenced prosodic innovations in heritage speakers were also documented by Queen (2001) and Kühn (2016) for Turkish in Germany and by Bullock (2009) for French in Pennsylvania.

Table 3.8 presents some selected studies on intonation in SLA, which suggest that adults learning an L2 tend to transfer some of the intonational characteristics of their L1 to that language (for a more general overview of intonation in SLA see Chun 2002; Rasier/Hiligsmann 2007; Trouvain/Gut 2007 and therein especially Mennen 2007).

Table 3.8 Selected case studies on intonation in language contact: L2 varieties[a]

Description of the context of SLA and the varieties involved	Linguistic outcomes (in the intonational domain)	References
L2 Greek produced by Dutch natives L1 Dutch speakers highly proficient in the L2 (12–35 years of experience); formal instruction (university), age at onset of formal exposure: between 18 and 25	L1 features used by learners in the L2: i. early alignment of prenuclear rising pitch accents (as opposed delayed peaks in L1 Greek) → transfer of L1 alignment patterns to L2 (intonational interference)	Mennen (2004)
L2 Spanish produced by Italian natives L1 speakers of Italian (from different regions of Italy) living in Madrid (for 1–2 years), level of L2 Spanish: middle-advanced or advanced; formal instruction (school or university)	L1 features used by learners in L2 yes–no questions: i. early-aligned prenuclear pitch accents (i.e. L+H*) ii. nuclear configurations (e.g. H+L* LH% and H+L* L%) iii. the tritonal pitch accent L+H*+L (assumed to convey emphasis/focus) → transfer from L1 Italian	Gabriel/Kireva (2014)
L2 Spanish produced by Germans and Czechs L1 speakers for German and Czech, level of L2 Spanish: middle-advanced or advanced; formal instruction (school or university)	Selection of L1 features used by learners in the L2: i. prenuclear pitch accents (e.g. L*+H) on wh-word in wh-questions ii. nuclear pitch accents (e.g. L+H*) in neutral statements and imperative wh-questions iii. boundary tones (L%) in vocatives → negative transfer from L1 German/Czech (besides many cases of positive transfer)	Pešková (2019, 2021, 2023)
L2 French produced by Mexican Spanish natives L1 speakers of Mexican Spanish, intermediate level (A2 – B1), formal instruction (university), onset of learning: after 17 years old	L1 features used by learners in L2 yes–no questions: i. overuse, i.e. exclusive use, of rising final contours ii. lack of tonal (or durational) marking of phrase-internal prosodic words (i.e. French accentual phrases)	Santiago/ Delais-Roussarie (2012, 2015)

Table 3.8 *(continued)*

Description of the context of SLA and the varieties involved	Linguistic outcomes (in the intonational domain)	References
	→ transfer of L1 contours and (lack of marking of phrase-internal) prosodic structure	
L2 French produced by German monolinguals and German–Turkish bilinguals L1 speakers of German (monolinguals) and German and Turkish (bilinguals), beginner level, 3 years of formal instruction (grammar school), onset of learning: 12–14 years old	L1 features used by learners in the L2: word-based intonation, i.e consistent tonal marking of final syllables in lexical words → both learner groups misinterpret French AP-final rise as word-final stress	Gabriel et al. (2022a, b); Gabriel/Grünke (2021, 2022)

a. The terminology and the assumptions made with regard to the emergence of the contact-induced linguistic features are those of the authors of the cited studies. Minor adaptions were made regarding the annotation of some pitch accents and boundary tones.

The studies listed in the two preceding tables show that there are many varieties, whose current intonation is considered a result of CLI. This occurs, for the most part, by means of substratum interference or transfer when speakers of an L1 acquire an L2. We have seen several examples of current L2 varieties influenced by the native language of the learners (e.g. L2 Spanish and L2 French; see Table 3.8) but also cases in which historic L2 varieties have become native varieties (e.g. Porteño, Olivenza, Cuzco, and Majorcan Spanish; Southern French; Sardinian Italian; and, in part, Algherese Catalan; see Table 3.7). Yet, there are also some cases of CLI belonging to the 'borrowing' type, i.e. those involving the integration of intonational features of a foreign language into a native variety or L1 (e.g. Occitan, Northern Catalan, Bulgarian Judaeo-Spanish, or Spanish in the US). Sometimes such cases of 'borrowing' have been attributed to L1 attrition under the pressure of the dominant surrounding language.

The intonational features transferred in the examples include both prenuclear pitch accents (e.g. in Porteño, Cuzco, and Olivenza Spanish; Algherese and Northern Catalan; Occitan and Southern French; L2 Greek and L2 Spanish) and nuclear pitch accents or entire nuclear configurations (e.g. in Porteño, Olivenza, and Majorca Spanish; Northern, Algherese, and Majorca Catalan; Occitan; Southern French; L2 Spanish). Furthermore, CLI can touch upon alignment properties of pitch-accents (see Cuzco Spanish and L2 Greek) or phrasing and prominence patterns (e.g. in the case of APs and phrase-initial accents in Occitan and Northern

Catalan; relics of lexical stress in Southern French; the adaption of stress patterns in Bulgarian Judaeo-Spanish; the use of CR and SP in Porteño Spanish; the signalling of focus in Cuzco Spanish, or the lack vs excess of marking of prosodic structure in L2 French by Mexican vs German and German–Turkish learners). From this large gamut of features, we may thus not only conclude that it is possible – and likely – for intonational and other prosodic features to be transferred in language contact but also that probably any feature of prosody can be transferred given the right circumstances.

3.3 Bilingualism and language dominance

The idea that most frequently comes to (lay)people's mind when thinking of a bilingual is probably that of a person who grew up with two languages from birth and whose mastery of these languages is roughly equivalent (Silva-Corvalán/Treffers-Daller 2016: 1). The view that 'true' bilinguals are exclusively persons with high or native-like linguistic competence has also been held by some scholars, such as Bloomfield (1933: 56) or Macnamara (1967), who, in a nutshell, suggested that bilinguals are two monolinguals in one person. And indeed, if we pretend "to get a better understanding of what makes the bilingual experience unique", it can sometimes be useful to compare bilinguals against monolinguals, and it is a common praxis to do so (Silva-Corvalán/Treffers-Daller 2016: 2). Nevertheless, the compound state of mind with more than one language is a multicompetence (Cook 1991) and setting monolingual norms or benchmarks is often inappropriate when describing bilingual behaviour, processing, or proficiency.[132] Conclusions such as that a bilingual's proficiency is 'deficient' or 'incomplete' or that bilinguals have 'failed to reach monolingual norms' or only partially succeeded in acquiring them should be avoided (see also Meisel 2007). In other words, the conception – prevailing during much of the 20th century – that a 'good' bilingual should not speak with an accent in any of their languages (see Poch Olivé 2016) is clearly outdated, as we now know that there is not necessarily a connection between the knowledge of a language and having an accent in the pronunciation of sounds and in prosody (Grosjean 2015: 38–39).[133] This is, after several decades of research, it has

---

[132]. For instance, while some bilingual learners manage to separate their phonological systems, for many "keeping the two systems separate is too tall an order". Instead, they use (converged) systems that differ from the ones of monolingual speakers of either language (see Treffers-Daller 2016: 246 and studies therein). For example, bilinguals often use compromise VOT values (Goldrick et al. 2014). It is for this reason that they sometimes have an accent in either or both of their languages (Grosjean 2010: 77–84).

become plainly clear that the assumption that bilinguals consist of two monolinguals is a misconception and myth (Montrul 2016: 15): completely balanced bilinguals are very rare, if they exist at all, and even the number of individuals who might be considered fully competent or highly proficient in two languages in one or more dimensions is probably quite low (see Mackey 2000 [1962]; Grosjean 2008; Montrul 2016; Silva-Corvalán/Treffers-Daller 2016: 2).

As a matter of fact, bilinguals differ widely and it is much more common for them to be dominant in one of their languages (Grosjean 1998, 2008; Treffers-Daller 2016: 235). Grosjean (1997: 165) attributes this to what he calls the **Complementarity Principle**, defined as follows: "Bilinguals usually acquire and use their languages for different purposes, in different domains of life, with different people. Different aspects of life require different languages" (see Grosjean 2010, 2016 for an extensive discussion). The origins of this principle go back to observations made by sociolinguists who noted that languages tend to have distinct functions in bilingual communities (e.g. Weinreich 1953; Hoffman 1971; Heye 1979). In consequence, the respective languages must also be distributed (in a complementary way) across the domains of life of the individuals living within these societies. In recent years, as more data and studies have started to appear, it is becoming ever more evident that the Complementarity Principle is pervasive in the life of bilinguals and has major impacts on bilingual language processing, memory, language acquisition, fluency, and language dominance, all of which differ fundamentally from their monolingual counterparts (Grosjean 2016: 67–70; Silva-Corvalán/Treffers-Daller 2016: 2). To give an example, the level of fluency attained by a bilingual in a language (or, more precisely, in a particular language skill) will depend on their need for that language: "If reading and writing skills are not needed in a language, they will not be developed" and if "a language is never used for a particular purpose, it will not develop the linguistic properties needed for that purpose (specialized vocabulary, stylistic variety, some linguistic rules, etc.)" (Grosjean 2016: 68).[134] This entails that the knowledge bilinguals develop of their languages is tightly linked to the use they make of each (Silva-Corvalán/Treffers-Daller 2016: 1), which, in turn, depends on their or their environment's needs and requirements for that language. Moreover, it is self-evident that not all facets of a bilingual's life require the same language — otherwise they would not be bilin-

---

133. Rather, the existence of an 'accent' in bilingual speech might be related with factors such as language use (see, e.g., Guion et al. 2000 for Spanish–Quechua bilinguals).

134. Monolinguals, too, can differ widely from each other in certain respects. For instance, all language users, i.e. both monolinguals and bilinguals, merely have partial knowledge of words, since "mastering the vocabulary of a language is a mammoth task" and the respective knowledge of an individual is linked to their specific language experience (Treffers-Daller 2016: 245).

gual. Similarly, no society needs two languages for the exact same set of functions (Fishman 1971: 560).

As linguistic knowledge is multidimensional at both the structural and psycholinguistic (i.e. processing and use) levels (Montrul 2016: 15), bilinguals are rarely equally or completely fluent in their two languages, but the levels of fluency will be domain-specific (Grosjean 2016: 84; Mackey 2000).[135] For this reason, most researchers nowadays simply define bilinguals as "those who use two or more languages (or dialects) in their everyday lives" shifting the emphasis from competence or proficiency to communication in or use of two (or more) languages (Grosjean 2010: 4; Silva-Corvalán 2014: 1; see also Haugen 1953; Weinreich 1953; Mackey 1976; Treffers-Daller 2016). Indeed, many phenomena are understood better if bilinguals are studied in terms of their total language repertoire with the respective domains of use and functions of their languages, i.e. when the Complementarity Principle is taken into account (Grosjean 2016: 68–69).

A central goal in the study of bilingualism is to get a better grip of the bilinguals that there are in the world and to capture the differences that exist between them. Many researchers seek to achieve this by using notions like language dominance or language proficiency and by distinguishing, for example, *balanced* and *dominant* bilinguals (see below). However, since they do not always provide clear definitions of these terms, there is a considerable amount of terminological confusion (see Meisel 2007; Silva-Corvalán/Treffers-Daller 2016), and studies on bilinguals have sometimes yielded conflicting results which "could have been lessened, if not avoided, had close attention been paid to methodological and conceptual issues" (Grosjean 1998: 132). In what follows, I will first give an overview of the construct of language dominance as well as of other key terms. In the second part, I will address the question of how language dominance in a bilingual can be operationalized or measured.

3.3.1 The construct of language dominance

The term **language dominance** (henceforth abbreviated as LD) can be used in a variety of ways (see Treffers-Daller 2016: 236f.). First, *societal language dominance* refers to multilingual societies (or smaller social groups) in which one language is predominant over the other in that it is most frequently employed for official matters outside the home, such as administration or education, and is most likely to be learned as a second language by L1 speakers of other languages. In such

---

135. Note that such contrasts reflect rather quantitative differences than the actual nature of a bilingual speaker's underlying knowledge (see Meisel 2007; Silva-Corvalán/Treffers-Daller 2016: 3).

'diglossic' situations, the two languages have dissimilar functions in society and often also different status (see Ferguson 1959, 1993 on diglossia), but a predominant language can also simply be the "'main language' in country X, community Y, or family Z" or the 'ambient', 'surrounding', or 'majority' language (Silva-Corvalán/Treffers-Daller 2016: 4). Second, it has been shown that the left hemisphere of the brain is generally more involved in language processing than the right hemisphere (Springer et al. 1999). This phenomenon is sometimes referred to as *hemispheric language dominance*. Finally, *language dominance in the (bilingual) individual* is what the remainder of this chapter is about. As we shall see, it mainly refers to the differences in proficiency and use of two (or more) languages by individual bilinguals.

In the same way as bilingualism *per se*, also the construct of LD is a complex and inherently multidimensional one (Luk/Bialystok 2013; Silva-Corvalán/Treffers-Daller 2016: 5). According to Montrul (2016: 16), it refers to the relative weight and the relative relationship of control and influence between the two languages in a bilingual. Definitions given in the literature usually make reference to either or both of the two key dimensions of the bilingual experience: language competence or proficiency, and communication or use. Fishman, Cooper, and Ma (1971: 484) describe these in a very succinct manner as "what a person *can* do" (language proficiency) and "what a person *typically* does" (language use).

However, LD is oftentimes defined only in relation to **proficiency** (or competence, grammatical ability,[136] fluency) in a language or the two concepts are treated as synonyms (Treffers-Daller 2016: 239; Montrul 2016: 15–16; Silva-Corvalán 2014: 21), i.e. to some the dominant language is simply the one in which the bilingual is more proficient (e.g. Van Coetsem 2000: 66; Deuchar/Muntz 2003). As a case in point, bilinguals often "have words in one of their languages for concepts about which they talk in that language, while they may not have translation equivalents for those words in the other language" (Treffers-Daller 2016: 239).[137] In such a scenario, they would thus be considered dominant in the language in which their vocabulary size is bigger. Yet, given the fact that most

---

136. For some scholars, such as Bachman/Palmer 2010, language ability is a wider concept than language proficiency: whereas proficiency relates solely to grammatical knowledge, language ability builds on the key notion of communicative competence and also includes pragmatic and sociologic components (e.g. the understanding and use of dialects and language varieties). However, to date such aspects have hardly been taken into account in research on LD (see Treffers-Daller 2016: 241–242).

137. According to the studies cited in Grosjean (2016: 81), bilingual children have translation equivalents for only 30–37 per cent of their words, i.e. their lexicon is language-specific to a major extent and the number of words they know in each language is related to the domains in which they use that language.

studies focus on only one language level, we often do not know whether the investigated bilinguals would show the same dominance patterns in other areas of grammar. According to Romaine (1989:13), there is no "necessary connection between ability in one level and another," although she notes that in practice there can be some interdependencies. That being the case, some authors distinguish more closely between (global) linguistic competence or proficiency, on the one hand, and basic aptitudes or skills (namely, reading, writing, listening, and speaking), on the other (see Carroll 1972; Mackey 1976; Romaine 1989; Treffers-Daller 2016: 240–241). Moreover, the view that LD equals proficiency has been strongly criticized by Montrul (2016:16), who points out that "bilinguals may exhibit similar patterns of language dominance but may differ on the levels of proficiency in each language when compared to each other." For instance, adult heritage speakers of minority languages (early bilinguals) and adult second-language learners (late bilinguals) may share the same dominant (e.g. English) and weaker language (e.g. Spanish), but typically heritage speakers will be more proficient in the weaker language than second-language learners (Montrul 2016: 25–34).

Therefore, many researchers defend that LD cannot be understood without involving further dimensions besides proficiency, in particular, language use.[138] For example, Wang (2013:739), defines LD as "a global measure of relative frequency of use and proficiency in each language" and thus closely relies on the two aforementioned key dimensions of the bilingual experience, which any description of bilinguals should minimally involve (see Fishman et al. 1971; Grosjean 2010; Luk/Bialystok 2013; Treffers-Daller 2016, among others). In this respect, LD has occasionally been compared to handedness or manual dominance: humans (and animals having two hands) differ from one another with respect to both the frequency with which they use each of their hands for a given action (e.g. writing or using scissors) and the manual skill with which they perform tasks with each hand (see Birdsong 2016; Treffers-Daller 2016: 239).

Nevertheless, several **other factors** have been claimed, too, to have an impact on a bilingual's LD. For instance, Montrul's model (2016) advocates a wider conceptualization of LD, including (quality and quantity of the) input bilinguals receive in each language as a third, external component besides ability and fluency (i.e. proficiency components) and use or context (i.e functional components). Clearly, input is a further key factor for the emergence of individual LD patterns (see also Silva-Corvalán 2014; Yip/Matthews 2006). Nevertheless, "[h]uman beings are not passive recipients of input but active participants in social situations in which they use language for communicative purposes"

---

138. The term language use is typically used as an umbrella term covering reading, writing, listening, and speaking (i.e. all four basic aptitudes or skills; see Treffers-Daller 2016: 240–241).

(Treffers-Daller 2016: 251). Although the Complementarity Principle (CP) lucidly reflects this, how bilinguals distribute their languages over different domains and functions largely depends on micro and macro sociolinguistic, rather than personal factors: i.e. on language predominance within their direct environment and the wider society (see, e.g., Meisel 2007; Kupisch/Van de Weijer 2016; La Morgia 2016; Schmeißer et al. 2016; Silva-Corvalán 2014). Montrul (2016: 16–17) for this reason underscores that the type and amount of input is determined among other things by "biographical variables like age of acquisition, place of birth and languages of the environment, place of previous and current residence and languages of the environment". Other authors point to further, often psycholinguistic factors such as overall fluency, levels of language activation (Pavlenko 2014), or speed, automaticity, and efficiency (or accuracy) in language processing (Birdsong 2006; Favreau/Segalowitz 1982). In sum, LD is "essentially a psycholinguistic phenomenon closely intermeshed with sociolinguistic parameters" (Lanza 2004: 237).

As we have already seen, the construct of LD is commonly employed to account for differences in the linguistic behaviour of bilinguals by classifying them as belonging to certain groups — most frequently, *balanced* bilinguals and those who are *dominant* in one of their languages, which can be considered the two "traditionally acknowledged" types of bilinguals (Silva-Corvalán/Treffers-Daller 2016: 1). However, besides being used in various ways by the researchers in the field, these notions, and particularly the notion of **balance** implies a series of problematic issues (see Treffers-Daller 2016: 242–248 for an extensive discussion).

In terms of proficiency, a "balanced bilingual would be one who displays equal proficiency in both languages across a range of different variables (grammar, vocabulary, etc.) or across the four skills (reading, writing, listening, speaking)" (Treffers-Daller 2016: 242–243). In this sense, Li (2000: 4–5) defines a balanced bilingual as "someone whose mastery of two languages is roughly equivalent". However, in his definition of the counterpart, i.e. the "dominant bilingual", he also includes the dimension of language use: "someone with greater proficiency in one of his or her languages and [who] uses it significantly more than the other language(s)." Hence, if LD is understood as a global phenomenon, affecting the individual as a whole, a balanced bilingual should be one who displays an equilibrium between both of their languages across all aspects of knowledge, skill, preference, and/or use (see Birdsong 2016: 95). Yet, at least in a strict sense, this is difficult to conceptionalize and would be at odds with Grosjean's (1997, 2016) Complementarity Principle (see Treffers-Daller 2016: 242–243; De Houwer/Bornstein 2016). It is true that most bilinguals have intuitions as to which language is their overall or 'globally' stronger one and only few state to be 'balanced' (Harris et al. 2006). However, upon closer scrutiny, it generally turns out for both groups that their "dominance varies according to the domains and the functions for which the languages are used" or as a function of the specific instruments used to measure it (Treffers-Daller 2016: 243; Bahrick et al. 1994). That is, even if there is an overall state of equilibrium between the two languages in a bilingual and he or she can be considered as globally balanced, this does not necessarily imply that they are able to use both languages for all functions and all domains in the same way. Instead, which one is their dominant language simply differs across domains (Hamers/Blanc 2000; Treffers-Daller 2011; 2016). In these terms, Birdsong (2016: 102) proposes a distinction between two types of consistency in language use based on Bishop et al.'s (1996) observations on handedness: across-domain consistency or preferential use and within-domain consistency. According to the across-domain approach, a balanced bilingual could be defined as someone who uses one language for half of the domains and the other language for the remaining half, whereas in the within-domain approach the bilingual would use both of his or her languages with equal frequency, i.e. to an extent of 50%, within each single domain (Treffers-Daller 2016: 244). Further elaborating this line of thought, an across-domain balanced bilingual would exhibit an exactly complementary distribution of their languages across domains and without any overlap between them, whereas a within-domain balanced bilingual would use their languages to the same extent in all domains of their life. As we have already seen, the latter case is most probably inexistent ('Why would they? — No one needs two languages for the same purpose', see Fishman 1971: 560 and above), while the first may be seen as an idealized description of what a balanced bilingual could look like. In reality, though, we know by now that the distribution of languages in the everyday life of bilinguals is usually much more complex than this. As expanded on above (see Complementarity Principle), different aspects of life require different languages, which automatically entails that LD is domain-specific. In consequence, bilinguals will be dominant in one language for some domains, dominant in the other language for others, and balanced for some others still (Grosjean 2016: 83).

Besides that, the notion of balance is problematic in that it to a certain extent suggests that being balanced — as opposed to unbalanced or non-balanced — is something positive or normal, i.e. that balanced bilingualism would be the default outcome of bilingual development or at least the most desirable state for a bilingual to achieve (see Treffers-Daller 2016: 247–248). Such a preference for symmetry over asymmetry is known from a large variety of fields — however, with reference to the bilingual experience, it is quite unrealistic. A comparison with handedness might be once more illuminating: while only about 1 percent of the population is truly ambidextrous, i.e. able to do any task to the same level of skill with either hand, no one sees ambidexterity as a goal. Instead, the distribution of labour between both hands works very well for most people and consistent right-

or left-handers are not described as 'unbalanced' (see Birdsong 2016; Treffers-Daller 2016: 248).

Another aspect worth mentioning is that the notion of balance needs to be kept separate from proficiency, considering that being balanced does not necessarily imply a high level of competence in both languages (see Hamers/Blanc 2000; Birdsong 2016; Treffers-Daller 2016: 244). This is all the more important as some authors assume that the cognitive advantages of bilingualism are only found among balanced bilinguals with a high proficiency in both languages (see Treffers-Daller 2016: 242; Cummins 1976; Costa et al. 2009; Bialystok 2009; see Antoniou 2019 for an overview of research into the 'bilingual advantage').

A more practical issue concerns the difficulty to establish when an equilibrium or, at least, a 'relative similarity' between the two languages is achieved. As LD is clearly not a categorical variable (Luk/Bialystok 2013; Treffers-Daller 2016: 265), most ways to operationalize it involve gradient scales. In order to draw a line between groups of dominant and balanced bilingual informants, an artificial **cut-off point** needs thus to be chosen. However, there is not yet a consensus as to how this point should best be selected (see below).

In sum, it is certainly possible for bilinguals to be more or less balanced with respect to a specific criterion. Nevertheless, overall balance with regard to both use and proficiency in two languages is an idealized construct and a "fiction that obscures the normal situation" (Treffers-Daller 2016: 248). In this sense, Romaine (1989: 18) concludes: "The search for the true balanced bilingual depicted in some of the literature on bilingualism is elusive. The notion of balanced bilingualism is an ideal one, which is largely an artifact of a theoretical perspective which takes the monolingual as its point of reference".

Concerning the **stability** of LD, there is general agreement that a bilingual's LD may vary over time. In particular in children, there is much evidence that dominance patterns develop relatively dynamically (Lanza 2004; Ronjat 1913; De Houwer 2011; De Houwer/Bornstein 2016; Schmeißer et al. 2016; Grosjean 2019). In adult bilinguals, on the other hand, language dominance is rather unlikely to shift according to Kupisch/Van de Weijer (2016), who found that childhood environment was the main predictor of language proficiency in the highly proficient German–French bilinguals they studied, even upon changing the place of residence. However, it is possible for language dominance to undergo changes during adulthood, too. To take one example, in their large-scale study of Cuban and Mexican immigrants in the US, Bahrick et al. (1994) observed that long-term residence in a country where the environmental language is the L2 can affect language dominance in such a way that the L2 becomes the bilingual's dominant language for certain tasks or domains. Besides, the notion of heritage speakers also often implies a dominance shift from an L1 to an L2 that is acquired later in childhood and which is typically the language of the wider society the speaker lives in (see Treffers-Daller 2016: 205–251; Benmamoun et al. 2013).

3.3.2 The operationalization of language dominance

In research, LD is typically invoked as an explanatory variable to account for dissimilarities between different categories of bilinguals, such as balanced and dominant ones. Unfortunately, it is not always made clear how such classifications are established, and notions as LD or proficiency are often taken for granted (Hulsteijn 2012: 423). In quite some cases, LD is simply assumed, and classifications are founded on the subjective judgements of the experimenters, who purport to know their informants well enough to be able to simply estimate their LD (Treffers-Daller 2016: 236; Montrul 2016: 21). In other studies, the informants' LD is estimated from one or more of its components (Montrul: 2016: 17). However, if we are to advance our understanding of what it means to be bilingual, we need to find consistent ways to **operationalize** LD (Silva-Corvalán/Treffers-Daller 2016: 1). Reliable measures are crucial to level the "playing field when comparing two populations" or (possibly conflicting) results from different studies (Montrul 2016: 35). Only then can we determine how e.g. experience-related variables such as age of acquisition impinge on LD and use it as an independent predictor variable to explain other phenomena (Treffers-Daller 2016: 237).

Regrettably, there are not yet any commonly agreed standardized methods to assess LD, let alone a gold standard (Montrul 2016: 18). Instead, a wide range of instruments are being used and lots of different measures and indices have been proposed in research on bilingualism (Treffers-Daller 2016: 264). One main difficulty departs from the fact that "there is no such thing as global language dominance" (Treffers-Daller 2016: 252): which one of a bilingual's languages is structurally stronger than the other usually varies across functions and domains (see above), and, in consequence, the attempt to devise a measure of 'global' LD is problematic, as well.

As argued in Section 3.3.1, LD has two key dimensions, i.e. language proficiency and use, which should thus both be taken into account in any index of language dominance (ILD). Yet, there is great inconsistency in operationalizing these two key variables. Very often LD is determined indirectly via biographical or background variables (such as age of acquisition, amount of input or language use, place of residence) elicited from background questionnaires, in which subjects are asked to self-report their language use and to self-rate their abilities (e.g. reading or speaking). Such background variables tend to correlate positively with proficiency measures and are for this reason often taken as good indicators in the absence of concrete measures (Montrul 2016: 25). Nevertheless, it is of course more reliable to actually measure proficiency in the two languages (e.g. by using oral or written production and comprehension measures). A problem this involves is that the construct of language proficiency (or ability) itself is highly multidimensional and cannot be captured by a single test covering all its dimensions (Bachman/Palmer 2010). Likewise, it is extremely challenging to develop comparable proficiency measures across languages (see discussion below).

In any case should measures of LD preferably be gradient as it is not a categorical variable (see Dunn/Fox Tree 2009; Luk/Bialystok 2013; and above). The representation of LD on a continuous interval scale furthermore entails the advantage that it can be used this way as a predictor variable in regression analysis (Birdsong 2016; Treffers-Daller/Korybski 2016), which may, in turn, demonstrate the validity of the respective ILD. Most importantly, any ILD can only perform a meaningful task if it explains more variance in the researcher's chosen dependent variable than other predictor variables, such as age of acquisition or length of residence. Moreover, gradient variables avoid the undesirable need to stipulate an arbitrary cut point that separates 'balanced' from 'dominant' bilinguals (Treffers-Daller 2016: 253, 265). At the same time, the use of continuous scale does not impede group classifications should the respective piece of research require them.

The methods used to assess a speaker's LD can generally be classified as belonging to either a generic and subjective (self-ratings and questionnaires) or a specific and objective type (tests of different sorts) (Treffers-Daller 2016). Both types encompass a series of advantages but are also problematic, as we shall see in what follows.

Bilinguals' **subjective evaluations** are a popular instrument to obtain **generic** information about their LD. In most cases, subjects are asked to self-rate their language abilities and skills (speaking, writing, listening, and reading) for both of their languages, and the language they feel they know better is considered the dominant one. Such minimum self-ratings thus solely rely on the informants' intuitive judgements on their own proficiency. However, most of the time, self-assessments of language skills are part of a more detailed **questionnaire**, containing also questions on other dimensions of LD such as language use. Subjects are then asked to provide quantifying information on the degree of use of their languages in different contexts as well as to self-report, e.g., their language history, so that scores can be calculated and compared afterwards.

The most outstanding advantages of subjective evaluations are certainly that they are easy to administer and permit to calculate scores that provide an overall idea of a bilingual's LD based on a relatively wide range of skills and domains of use. However, as they rely on estimations instead of actual measures such assessments must be treated with caution and their validity has been questioned (see Ross 2006). First, self-ratings usually evaluate language competence at a very generic level and are often based on only four skills. They are thus not differentiated enough to capture the complexity of language use and proficiency across a range of tasks (Treffers-Daller 2016: 254). Besides the fact that at least the dimension of language use should be tapped as well, there are also large differences between e.g. written tasks such as an e-mail and an academic essay (Bachman/ Palmer 2010). Moreover, many tasks involve various skills at the same time: for example, speaking in a communicative situation also involves listening. On the other hand, too fine-grained self-ratings are not possible either because it is very challenging for non-experts to assess their own language ability in, say, pronunciation, vocabulary, or grammar (Hulstijn 2012).

A further point of criticism concerns the fact that even relatively detailed questionnaires that pretend to tap into the construct of LD itself by enquiring into both proficiency and frequency of use with different people and in different social situations usually fail to demonstrate the complex distribution of labour between the bilinguals' languages in general as well as the overlap of language use within domains. They thus remain rather coarse instruments (Treffers-Daller 2016: 254–255). Nevertheless, to describe actual language use at higher level of granularity, Grosjean (2016) has recently proposed a Complementarity Index (CI) that indicates to what extent the topics or activities of a bilingual speaker are language-specific or covered by both languages (see below).

In addition, it needs to be pointed out that many questionnaires do not "separate questions that tap into the construct itself from questions that tap into the causes of language dominance" (Treffers-Daller 2016: 254). For instance, this may be the case of questions about the informants' language history or their attitudes to different languages, which probably relate rather to the constructs of language loyalty or identity. It is thus problematic to compute a general dominance score based on questionnaire items that may measure different constructs. Finally, another drawback of self-ratings and self-reports is that they are only possible in research on adult bilinguals and different methods need to be applied in bilingual children. Yet, in some studies, parents have been asked to complete questionnaires as substitutes for their children.

Examples of (standardized) questionnaires that have recently gained some popularity are the Language Experience and Proficiency Questionnaire (LEAP-Q, Marian et al. 2007), the Bilingual Dominance Scale (BDS, Dunn/Fox Tree 2009), the Bilingual Language Profile (BLP, Birdsong et al. 2012; Gertken et al. 2014), and the Language History Questionnaire (LHQ, Li et al. 2014). All of these combine questions covering different dimensions of LD. However, the LEAP-Q is not a dominance assessment per se as it rather elicits descriptive data and can also be used with monolinguals. It furthermore lacks a scoring procedure and is rather lengthy and complex to complete. The same is true of the LHQ, which consists of 22 of the most commonly asked questions in LD assessment questionnaires compiled from 41 studies. The BDS, on the other hand, can be filled in very quickly as it comprises only 12 items. However, avoiding scalar responses, it features some open-ended questions and the assessment is mainly based on biographical and external variables (see Montrul 2016: 22). Additionally, the single items are weighed unequally in the scoring procedure, which entails the risk of inflating the significance of any one factor. The BLP, finally, draws on elements from both of these tools (see the feature comparison in Birdsong et al. 2012). Enquiring on the four equally weighted dimensions language history, use, proficiency, and attitudes, it is easy to administer, concise, and comprehensive. Increasingly popular in recent years (see "Publications" in Birdsong et al. 2012), it is also used as the basis for LD assessment in the current study (see Section 4.1).

As opposed to subjective and generic estimations of LD via self-ratings, operationalizations that rely on performance tests or samples of actual linguistic behaviour have the advantage of being much more **specific and objective**. As independent measures in experimental research, they can facilitate comparability across studies (Montrul 2016: 19). Yet, they also present some disadvantages (see below). In most cases, performance tests, tasks, or tools are developed to measure specific components of language ability or specific skills in both of the bilingual's languages separately, so as to allow that the respective scores can be compared afterwards. As a rule, the operationalization of LD via specific tests relies primarily on measures or quantifications of language proficiency. Sometimes solely one specific ability is considered but frequently tests use different components in order to cover various skills at the same time. In what follows, I shall present an (non-exhaustive) overview of methods recently used in research to gauge LD in bilingual speakers in a specific-objective way.

For a range of languages, there exist some standardized written **tests** of language proficiency, which were for the most part developed and used to evaluate the target language in adult SLA, e.g. the DELE (Sp. *Diploma de español como lengua extranjera*) for Spanish or the TOEFL (*Test of English as a foreign language*) for English. Similarly, cloze or C-tests are another fast, efficient, and reliable tool to measure morphosyntactic proficiency (Tremblay 2011), and the Vocabulary Size Test (VST), devised by Nation and Beglar (2007), is widely used to gauge bilinguals' vocabulary knowledge in English (see Bachman/Palmer 2010). Yet, there are also some tests based on oral production and aural comprehension that can be used with preliterate children and illiterate or low literacy adults (see Montrul 2016: 19). These were often conceived to assess the progress in the development of the target language in L1 acquisition by infants, and typically consist in picture-naming tasks (PNTs) or assess receptive vocabulary via word–picture matching (e.g. the *Peabody Picture Vocabulary Test–Revised*, PPVT–IV; Dunn/Dunn 2007).

Oral translation tasks of words or sentences are equally possible ways of assessment, as is the measurement of reaction times in such tasks (Dunn/Fox Tree 2009). Moreover, oral proficiency interviews (OPIs) can be conducted and evaluated according to pre-established criteria (e.g. following the lines of the ACTFL).

Nevertheless, as the number of languages for which such standardized tasks are available is quite limited, researchers are often bound to rely on the analysis of **speech samples** – particularly when working on less studied languages. Likewise, this is mostly done in studies on bilingual language acquisition because formally testing (small) children is very difficult (Treffers-Daller 2016: 258). Most typically, such extracts involve recordings or transcriptions of spontaneous speech, but written samples (e.g. compositions or written discourse) can equally be evaluated when subjects are literate. In studies on young children, mean utterance length (MLU, usually counted in words or morphemes (see Yip/Matthews 2006; Schmeißer et al. 2016, among many others) is a popular measure for global morphosyntactic development, and so are upper bound or longest utterance (UB), average sentence duration (Flege et al. 2002), and percentage of multimorphemic utterances (MMUs, see Treffers-Daller 2016: 258). However, these measures are no longer able to reliably discriminate linguistic proficiency beyond a certain age, since older children's and adults' language is more complex than that of infants (Montrul 2016: 19). Furthermore, number of unique words and verb types out of 100 utterances can be operationalized as an indicator of vocabulary size (see Montrul 2016: 21), and methods to extract lexical diversity from speech samples have been proposed by Treffers-Daller (2011), Treffers-Daller/Korybski (2016), and Klinger et al. (2019), among others. Schwartz (2005) calculates words per minute and number of error-free units as markers of fluency, and several methods of assessing reading skills are proposed by Schneider et al. (2017). Especially in SLA, accent ratings are a popular measure and phonetic measurements (e.g. of VOT) can be used to assess pronunciation. Finally, some studies have used the direction and quantifications of interference or code-switching in bilinguals' speech to determine LD (e.g. Lanza 2004; Paradis/Nicoladis 2007; Montrul/Ionin 2010; see also Arnal 2011).

In summary, there are many written and oral tests and tasks available to gauge LD in both children and adults. Still, a **problem** of these measures is certainly that they tend to operationalize LD only along its proficiency dimension tapping merely into rather specific aspects of it. It is thus problematic when informants are divided into groups of (globally) dominant and balanced bilinguals solely on the basis of their performance with regard to a specific criterion (see Treffers-Daller 2016: 260). Language proficiency and dominance are task-specific and dynamic, and subjects can perform incongruously across different tests (see above). Besides, LD is broader than only language proficiency, which is merely one of its dimensions (see Montrul 2016: 17 and above). When choosing a particular measure of dominance, scholars should thus carefully motivate their choice and ideally include a variety of different (linguistic and non-linguistic) measures (Treffers-Daller 2016: 240; Montrul 2016: 34; La Morgia 2016).

The two major issues that arise when researchers aim to compare bilinguals' languages on the basis of some proficiency test concern the difficulties (a) to find equivalent measures across languages and (b) to establish an appropriate cut-off point between different groups of bilinguals. As regards the first aspect, proficiency tests usually assess only one language, while LD implies a relationship between the two languages of a bilingual (Montrul 2016: 16). That said, it is extremely difficult to conceive parallel and **equally difficult versions** of the same test for two languages. Mainly owing to morphological and syntactic differences between languages, it is practically impossible, or at least very challenging to assure that exactly the same kind of linguistic ability is measured in both languages (Montrul 2016: 21; Treffers-Daller 2016: 257; 260). Additionally, pragmatic contrasts between languages, or cultural and conceptual disparities may hamper such enterprises, as well, e.g. even in the simple translation of vocabulary items (see Pavlenko 2014). It thus comes as no surprise that only very few such tests exist at all (Treffers-Daller 2016: 245, 264). Likewise, when assessing speech samples, differences in typological complexity can easily be an issue, too. For example, in agglutinative languages, such as Turkish, words typically comprise multiple morphemes and MLU values will thus be notably higher at a comparable level of development than, e.g., in isolating languages, such as Chinese, where words tend to be monomorphemic (see Yip/Matthews 2006). Following Jakobovits' (1969) assumptions, even comparing reaction times in two languages may be problematic because a range of non-linguistic factors might influence how fast a person responds (see also Romaine 1989). Similarly, measures of frequency of CLI or code-switching have been severely criticized in consideration of the fact that the occurrence of such phenomena strongly depends on the norms of a given bilingual community, which can be different from monolingual norms for the use of either language. For example, in many contact situations on the African continent, language mixing is an unmarked choice and also among Hispanic communities in the US it may be considered the norm (see the studies cited in Treffers-Daller 2016: 252, 259–260).

As regards the selection of **dividing points**, it is quite demanding to motivate the division of a sample of bilinguals into different categories in a principled manner. While most scholars concur in that the notion of 'balanced bilingual', and hence the operationalization of 'balance', does not imply a zero difference, i.e. that the bilingual obtains a fully identical score for both languages, in one or several tests (which is virtually impossible and ignores the possibility of measurement errors), it is still pretty unclear how a suitable alternative could look like (Treffers-Daller 2016: 258; Birdsong 2016).

Several ways of operationalization have been suggested and tried out in the research literature (see Treffers-Daller 2016: 256 for an overview). Among these, most compare the scores bilinguals attain in each of their language and define those subjects as 'balanced bilinguals' whose difference in scores does not exceed a certain margin or a maximum difference, typically a specific percentage value (e.g. 6% and 10% in De Houwer/Bornstein 2016 or 10% in Favreau/Segalowitz 1982). As an alternative, the use of z-scores between ±1 and ±0.5 has been tested among others by Treffers-Daller/Korybski (2016), but, as this led to a majority of their informants being classified as balanced, the authors concluded that they were no a suitable measure for their data. The choice of artificial and arbitrary cut-off points thus entails that the proportions of bilinguals classified as balanced vary widely from study to study (i.e. from 0% in Cutler et al. 1989: 229 to over 70 in Treffers-Daller/Korybski 2016). However, this is not surprising as long as it is unclear what 'balanced' actually means (see the discussion above).

Finally, it is worth mentioning that in the calculus of ILD, the straightforward method of subtracting the scores for one language from scores for the other language is not the only possibility to determine the direction and/or the degree of LD. An alternative procedure (applied among others by Flege et al. 2002) calculates between-languages ratios by dividing the smaller of the two raw dominance scores by the larger. In this way, the resulting ILD represents the degree of dominance in terms of a "proportional relationship of the non-dominant language to the dominant", uncaptured by subtraction methods (Birdsong 2016: 87). The more the index approaches 1, the closer the bilingual is to balanced bilingualism. In order to "represent ratio-based indices along a conventional scale, the ratio can be multiplied by 100 to move the decimal point two places to the right" (Birdsong 2016: 88). A clear advantage of ILDs calculated as ratios is that they are interpretable across studies, no matter what measure was originally used (see Birdsong 2016: 90).

Lastly, Birdsong (2016) also proposes to apply a method adapted from the assessment of dominance in handedness: the so-called Edinburgh index. The formula combines both subtraction and division: (scores for language X − scores for language Y) / (scores for language X + scores for language Y) × 100. With this method, results approaching 0 indicate balance, whereas extreme dominance is represented by indices approaching 100 in absolute value. An advantage is that Edinburgh-style indices, as opposed to simple ratios, do not obscure the directionality of increased dominance.

However, independently of the formula used (subtracting, ratio, or Edinburgh), a common issue of composite and global ILDs is the irretrievability of the raw values that are input to the index, which also implies that qualitative differences between bilinguals with the same or very similar overall dominance indices can no longer be recognized (Birdsong 2016: 99–100, 105). For instance, two bilinguals who are substantially different at the local levels of assessment (i.e. dimension-by-dimension, domain-by-domain, item-by-item) and thus quite dissimilar in their underlying performance can obtain similar indices or even be indistinguishable at the global level of dominance. To a certain extent, global measures thus ignore the fact that LD is domain-specific (see Treffers-Daller 2016: 252; Grosjean 2016: 83 and above).

In order to somewhat mitigate this problem, Birdsong (2016: 102–104) suggests separating "dimension-based" (i.e. performance- or skill-related) and "domain-based" (i.e. preference- or use-related) results. He furthermore considers the possibility of exploring distinct indices for domain-related dominance: one for across-domain language use (i.e. how many domains the LX versus the LY is used for) and one for within-domain language use (i.e. how often LX versus LY is used in each of the identified domains; see also above). Similarly, Grosjean (2016: 83) underscores that domain-specific approaches to LD are "crucial to obtain a better description of the bilingual but also to help understand the data that is obtained in linguistic and psycholinguistic studies". His Complementarity Index, which is calculated by summing up the numbers of topics (or activities) that a bilingual carries out predominantly in one language (i.e. to an extent of 61–100%), and dividing this total by the total number of topics (or activities) and multiplying by 100, represents an innovative way to assess the degree to which a bilingual's domains of life are language-specific (see Grosjean 2016: 72).

Finally, it is recommendable that the validity of global LDIs be checked and corroborated by running correlations both between the different internal items and modules it is composed of and with independent measures, e.g., of lexical or grammatical proficiency, which were not part of the dominance scale (Birdsong 2016: 104; Montrul 2016; see also Treffers-Daller/Korybski 2016; Montrul/Ionin 2010; Dun/Fox Tree 2009). A good ILD should be able to predict a bilingual's performance on other (linguistic) measures.

To bring this section to a close, it can be assumed that future measures of dominance will become more and more sophisticated and will ever better take into account the many underlying phenomena that characterize the bilingual experience (Grosjean 2016: 84).

CHAPTER 4

Methodology, speakers, and data

This chapter introduces the methods, participants, and linguistic data used in the current study. In Section 4.1, I describe how I assessed the language dominance of the bilinguals whose data I used. In Section 4.2, I provide detailed background information on these speakers, placing special focus on their language history, uses, proficiency, and attitudes. The ensuing section (4.3), finally, presents the speech material that was recorded from the participants and explains how it was processed, outlining the criteria for the data segmentation and analysis.

4.1 Assessing language dominance

Since one of the major goals of the study in this book is to investigate the effects of language dominance (LD) on the speech production of Spanish–Catalan bilinguals, assessing the participants' LD was one of the major prerequisites for this enterprise. In Section 3.3, it was shown that this can be achieved in a large variety of ways — no standard procedure being established yet — and that indices of language dominance (ILD) should ideally be gradient and take into account at least the two major dimensions language use and proficiency.

To assess their LD, a language background questionnaire (LBQ) was thus administered to the 31 participants of the present study. It represented a slightly adapted version of the *Bilingual Language Profile* (BLP, Birdsong et al. 2012), which has gained increasing popularity in recent years (see also Section 3.3.2), and produced a continuous dominance score as well as a general bilingual profile on the basis of self-reports. It contained an introductory section for collecting biographical information about the testees in addition to the four modules designed to assess different dimensions of LD. The modules comprise a total of 18 questions, most of which were directly taken from the BLP:

I. Biographical information
    - Name(s) and surname(s)
    - Year of birth/age
    - Place of birth, place of residence, length of residence, time spent in other places
    - Highest level of formal education

- Current occupation
- Foreign languages
- Place of birth, places of residence, occupations and highest level of formal education, native languages of the mother, of the father, and — if they had one — of the partner

II. Module 1: Language history
- 1. Age of acquisition
- 2. Age of comfort (i.e. age at which the testee started feeling comfortable using each language)
- 3. Home language(s) in childhood (see Simonet 2008: 88)

III. Module 2: Language use
- 4.–6. Percentage of use in an average week with family, friends, and at school or work
- 7. Percentage of use in an average week while shopping (see Simonet 2008: 88)
- 8. Percentage of use in an average week with strangers (see Simonet 2008: 88)
- 9. Percentage of use in thinking
- 10. Percentage of use when counting

IV. Module 3: Language proficiency
- 11. Assessment of speaking proficiency in each language
- 12. Assessment of aural comprehension proficiency in each language
- 13. Assessment of reading proficiency in each language
- 14. Assessment of writing proficiency in each language

V. Module 4: Language attitudes
- 15. Degree to which the testees 'feel like themselves' when speaking each language
- 16. Importance of using each language like a native speaker
- 17. Importance of being mistaken for a native speaker
- 18. Language(s) considered as native language(s) (see Simonet 2008: 88)

Whereas the bibliographical data needed to be filled in, in the four modules, participants were simply asked to tick boxes. In Module 2, on language use, these represented percentage scales (with increments of 10 percent), and in Module 3 and 4, mostly 6-point Lickert scales, expressing different degrees of proficiency or consent to a series of attitudinal statements. Figure 4.1 shows an example question taken from Module 2.

Figure 4.1 Extract from the Spanish-language version of the questionnaire

En una semana normal, ¿qué porcentaje de tiempo usas las siguientes lenguas con tu familia?											
Castellano	☐	☐	☐	☐	☐	☐	☐	☐	☐	☐	☐
	0%	10%	20%	30%	40%	50%	60%	70%	80%	90%	100%
Catalán	☐	☐	☐	☐	☐	☐	☐	☐	☐	☐	☐
	0%	10%	20%	30%	40%	50%	60%	70%	80%	90%	100%
Otras lenguas	☐	☐	☐	☐	☐	☐	☐	☐	☐	☐	☐
	0%	10%	20%	30%	40%	50%	60%	70%	80%	90%	100%

The questionnaire took roughly 10 minutes to complete and was administered in the language of the participant's choice (for the full Catalan and Spanish versions see Appendix).

As for the calculation of the dominance scores, all scalar responses from the modules were associated with a certain point value — typically, the numerical value of the response. Only the items targeting age of acquisition and comfort were scored in the reverse: i.e. a '20' response is worth 0, a '19' response is worth 1, and so on (see "Scoring and interpreting the results" in Birdsong et al. 2012). Furthermore, where responses were non-scalar and either or both of the bilingual's languages had to be indicated (i.e. in question 3, on home language(s) in childhood, and question 18, on the language(s) considered as native), 10 points were added to the score of the ticked language(s). Finally, the language chosen by each participant to complete the questionnaire was integrated in module 2 by adding 10 more points to the score of the respective language, as this choice was interpreted as a proxy for a question like 'Which language do you prefer or use more frequently to fill in forms or, more generally, for reading information boards or flyers, if you have a choice?'.

To calculate global scores, point totals were tallied separately for each language within each module. These language totals were then multiplied by different factors so as to ensure that each module received equal weighting in the global dominance score. The new module totals were summed up to obtain a global score for each language, total points possible being 100.[139] Then, three different composite dominance indices were calculated from these language totals.

---

139. In the BLP, total points possible in the global score for each language (and hence also in the composite dominance index) is 218. As there seems to be no practical reason for this number, a basis of 100 was chosen in the current work, given that this permits for scores to be interpreted as percentages (i.e. 0% dominant meaning 'perfectly balanced' and 100% dominant describing a total monolingual).

The first and most important one for the present work was obtained according to the method proposed in the BLP: i.e. subtracting one language total from the other one (here Catalan from Spanish) yielded a dominance score ranging from −100 to +100. This score will henceforth be referred to as dominance score A. A score near 0 indicates balanced bilingualism, and more positive or negative values reflect LD in Spanish or Catalan, respectively. A numerical score of 100 would theoretically indicate a full monolingual.

Additionally, two ratio-based ILDs were calculated. In ILD B, the global score of the weaker language (i.e. the numerically lower total) was divided by the global score of the stronger one and multiplied by 100 (see Birdsong 2016 and Section 3.3). This method allows to express the degree of dominance of each participant, i.e. the proportional relationship between their languages, which cannot be captured by subtraction. It describes the performance in the non-dominant language as a percentage of performance in the dominant one. Thus, a type-B score approaching 100 (percent) indicates that the bilingual approaches balanced bilingualism. The third score (type C) was calculated using the "Edinburgh subtraction-then-division formula" proposed in Birdsong (2016). In this case, balance is indicated by dominance scores (type C) that approach 0, and extreme dominance is represented by scores that approach 100 in absolute value. The index thus shows the directionality of increased dominance in Catalan (negative values) and Spanish (positive values).

Finally, a Complementarity Index (CI) was computed for each participant, roughly following the method proposed by Grosjean (2016: 72). It assesses the degree to which different domains of a bilinguals' life are language specific. In the present work, it was calculated by counting the number of domains of use enquired in Module 2 of the LBQ (i.e. questions 4 to 10) in which the respective bilingual had indicated to use one language 70% of the time or more. This tally was divided by the total number of domains of use (i.e. by 7) and multiplied by 100. In this case, a CI of 0% means that all domains are covered equally by the bilinguals' two languages, and 100% means that all domains are fully language-specific.

The results of the language-dominance assessment will be presented and discussed in the following section.

4.2 Speakers

The linguistic analyses presented in this book draw on speech data from a total of 31 subjects recruited at the University of Girona.[140] All of them were bilingual speakers of Spanish and Catalan[141] and had been raised in the province of Girona, most of them within the city itself or in its direct surroundings. Three informants were born in the province of Barcelona, one in Bilbao, one in Honduras, and one in Bolivia, but all six had moved to Girona with their parents by the age of two (informants born in Spain) or six (informants born in South America). Consequently, all subjects had attended school entirely in Catalonia, which was the only criterion for participation in the recruitment. All were residents of the province of Girona, and no one had passed more than a half year at a stretch outside Catalonia (with the exception of the three informants not born there, of course).

Nevertheless, it warrants mention that many the subjects' parents were born outside of Catalonia and had moved and settled down there as adults. Table 4.1 gives an overview of the origins of the 31 participants' 62 parents. As can be seen, 69% are born Catalans, whereas almost a third qualify as immigrants.[142]

Table 4.1 Origins of the participants' parents

Category	Number	Places of birth
Province of Girona	36	Province of Girona
Catalonia	7	Province of Barcelona
Spain	14	Provinces of Albacete, Badajoz (3), Córdoba (2), Granada (2), Madrid, Málaga, Segovia, Gipuzkoa, Valladolid, Zaragoza
South America	5	Honduras (2), Bolivia (2), Uruguay

---

140. Girona is a city in northern Catalonia, located roughly 100 km northeast of Barcelona. It is the capital of the province of the same name and has a population of 103,000 (IDESCAT 2021a). Catalan is spoken by 87.4% of the province's population and 55.3% use it as their habitual language in daily life (Generalitat de Catalunya 2021: 15, 21). The locality was chosen for three reasons: (1) like Catalonia as a whole, Girona has a high proportion of immigrants (approx. 35%; Generalitat de Catalunya 2021: 11), (2) still, the degree of bilingualism is higher and the presence of Catalan is more stable and consistent in the public arena than in the metropolis of Barcelona, where there are also large differences between individual neighbourhoods (see Boix-Fuster 2015: 154f.), i.e. Girona's population is more homogeneous from a sociolinguistic point of view, (3) the presence of the university provided easy access to a fairly homogeneous and representative experimental group.

141. One speaker had some basic knowledge of the heritage language Quechua.

142. This figure corresponds to the general proportion of foreign-born inhabitants of Catalonia (see Generalitat de Catalunya 2019: 9 and Section 2.1).

The informants' ages range from 18 to 24, except for one 29-year-old speaker. The mean age of all speakers is 20.0 years (median: 19; SD: 2.1). In the Catalan-dominant (CatD) group ages range from 18 to 23 (mean: 19.6, median: 19), in the Spanish-dominant (SpD) group from 18 to 29 (mean: 20.8, median: 20).[143] Concerning sexes, there is a slightly higher proportion of females ($n=18$) as compared to the males ($n=13$). In the CatD group, the ratio is 12 females vs 8 males, and in the SpD group 6 females vs 5 males.[144]

As said before, all participants were recruited at the University of Girona, more precisely at the Faculty of Arts (Cat. *Facultat de Lletres*) or the Faculty of Tourism (Cat. *Facultat de Turisme*), and they were enrolled students in different courses of study. Table 4.2 gives an overview of their subjects.

Table 4.2 Subjects studied by the participants

Subject	Total number	Number of Catalan-dominants	Number of Spanish-dominants
Spanish Philology	10	2	8
Catalan Philology	7	7	
Advertising and Public Relations	4	2	2
Tourism	5	5	
Spanish and Catalan Philologies	2	2	
Not specified[a]	3	2	1

a. Unfortunately, a small number of informants did not indicate the subject they were studying.

Concerning the level of education, the group is rather homogenous as all participants had attended school in Catalonia,[145] obtained the Catalan baccalaureate (Cat. *batxillerat*), taken the *Selectivitat* test for admission to university, and were currently students of a bachelor's degree.

---

143. As shown below, the participants were divided into two groups according to their dominant language for the purpose of the study. The difference between the age-group means is not statistically significant ($W=135$, $p=0.274$).

144. A Fisher exact test showed that there is no significant association between gender and language-dominance group among the participants. The proportion of males and females can thus be considered to be the same in both groups.

145. This obligatorily implies 6 years of primary education in a *col·legi* and 4 years of ESO (Cat. *Educació Secundària Obligatòria*) in an *institut*. In Catalonia, schools with very few exceptions apply the 'language immersion' technique in their bilingual education, which makes Catalan – at least in theory – the vehicular language of public education (Vila 2020b; see also Woolard 2009; Pujolar 2010; and Section 2.1).

Regarding foreign languages, all had learnt English as a foreign language at school. 13 of them also had some knowledge of French, acquired at school or university, and 6 had taken some German courses at university. Whereas they can be expected to be at least independent users regarding English (i.e. B1 or B2 level according to the Common European Framework of Reference for Languages, CEFRL), they self-assessed their levels in French and German as basic (A1 or A2). Besides, two participants stated to have some basic knowledge of Italian, one of Dutch, and one of Arabic.

All subjects were Spanish–Catalan bilinguals, considering that they fell under Grosjean's (2010: 4) definition of bilinguals as "those who use two [...] languages [...] in their everyday lives" (see Section 3.3). Nevertheless, there were notable differences between them, e.g. with regard to language use. This is clearly reflected in their global dominance scores. Figure 4.2 shows the subtraction-derived dominance scores (type A) obtained. They range from −57.8 (i.e. strongly CatD) to 37.8 (SpD).

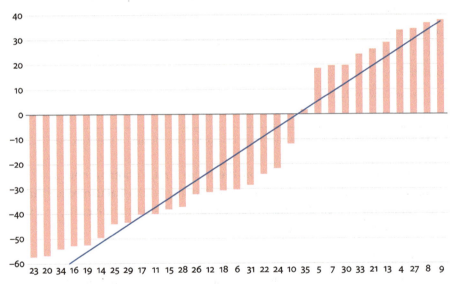

Figure 4.2 Global dominance scores (type A) obtained by the 31 participants (with trendline). Negative values indicate language dominance in Catalan, positive values in Spanish. The numbers on the horizontal axis represent the speaker ID

The distribution of the scores along a continuum shows that there are dominants in either language as well as some few relatively balanced bilinguals among the enquired informants and thereby corroborates the view that LD is a gradient phenomenon (see Section 3.3). However, as it is problematic to set an arbitrary dividing point within this continuum for categorizing bilinguals either as dominant or balanced bilinguals (see Section 3.3.2), a tripartite division (i.e. Catalan-dominant, Spanish-dominant, and balanced bilinguals) was avoided in this book. Instead, only two groups will be distinguished in the presentation of the results: i.e. for the sake of simplicity, all informants having scored numerically negative values of the type A dominance score are labelled as Catalan-dominants (CatD), and all informants with positive values are categorized as Spanish-dominant (SpD). This procedure is also supported by the bimodal distribution of the A-type dominance scores (see Figure 4.3): participants tend to be dominant in either of their languages and balanced bilingualism is rare. Nevertheless, in the interpretation of the results, I shall take into account — whenever it may be necessary — that not all bilinguals within each dominance group are equally dominant in the respective language and that those who have obtained indices in the vicinity of the cusp rather qualify as balanced bilinguals.

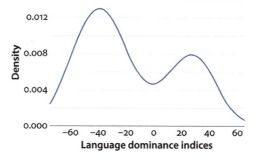

Figure 4.3 Density plot of the distribution of language dominance indices attained by the participants

According to this classification, the current sample thus encompasses 20 CatD and 11 SpD bilingual informants. The following table provides group-specific key measures of central tendency and dispersion of the three dominance scores and the Complementarity Index as calculated following the methodology described in Section 4.1. The participants' individual results can be found in the Appendix.

Interestingly, the CatD are not only more in absolute numbers, but the distribution of their dominance scores (type A) also reveals that their dominance is qualitatively stronger (see also Figures 4.2 and 4.3): the average dominance value of the CatD group is −38.9, and in the SD group it is 25.5. Also, over half of the CatD (11 out of 20) have attained values that exceed the highest score obtained by a Spanish dominant (37.8) in absolute value. This view is corroborated by dominance index B, which evinces that the SD group is closer to balanced bilingualism than the CatD group. Its distribution in both groups is illustrated in Figure 4.4.

Table 4.3 Comparison of the subjects' dominance indices and Complementarity Index (group means and standard deviation)

		Dominance score A	Dominance score B	Dominance score C	Complementarity Index[a]
CatD (n=20)	Mean	−38.9	57	−28	87
	Minimum	−57.3	38	−45	43
	Maximum	−11.9	86	−8	100
	SD	12.3	13	11	16
SpD (n=11)	Mean	25.5	71	18	69
	Minimum	1.7	54	1	43
	Maximum	37.8	98	30	86
	SD	10.1	11	7	12

a. Recall that this index is based on the participants' language use across different domains (viz. speaking with family, friends, or strangers, and when at school/work, shopping, thinking, or counting). The values obtained by the participants will be commented on in Section 4.2.2, on language use.

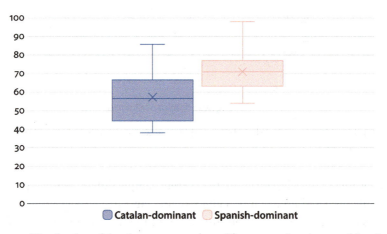

Figure 4.4 Distribution of dominance scores (type B) representing degree of dominance. Values approaching 100 indicate balanced bilingualism. The group means are significantly different ($t_{(23.0)} = 3.1$, $p = 0.005$)

Interestingly, six subjects in the CatD group have scored values (type B) under 50, which could be paraphrased as 'their Spanish is less than half as strong as their Catalan'.

ILD type C, finally, rendered a distribution very similar to that of type A and thus corroborates the classification of the participants in dominance groups. Digressions from the assessments made with ILD A are discernible in Figure 4.5, where participants are arranged according to the size of their type-A dominance score and the height of the columns represents their type-C score. However, the correlation between the two indices is very strong ($r = 0.997$).

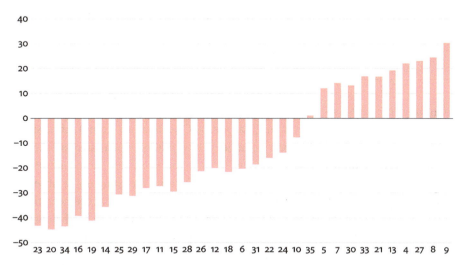

Figure 4.5 Dominance scores (type C) obtained by the 31 participants (arranged by rising type-A dominance scores). Negative values indicate language dominance in Catalan, positive values in Spanish. The numbers on the horizontal axis represent the speaker ID

In what follows, I will further describe the participants' biographical background data as well as their language history, use, self-assessed proficiency, and attitudes by dominance group.[146]

The mother tongues of the participants' parents are shown in Table 4.4. Viewing that all parents were native speakers of Spanish, the presentation is based on whether they have native knowledge of additional languages or not.[147]

Interestingly, there is a strong association between the parents' native languages and the participants' LD:[148] only children whose parents are both native

---

146. The outline of the ensuing part of the current section largely follows the presentation in Grünke (2020), where the results of the questionnaire evaluation were first published and extensively discussed.

147. The formulation of the respective question in the questionnaire was somewhat problematic, since some participants indicated merely Catalan as their parents' mother tongue — something virtually impossible, given that there are no longer any monolingual speakers of Catalan (see Section 2.1). Therefore, all parents described as native speakers of Catalan by their children were considered to be bilingual with Spanish.

Table 4.4 Mother tongue(s) of the parents in addition to Spanish (by LD groups)

Mother tongue(s) of the parents	Both parents native speakers of Catalan	No parent native speaker of Catalan	Mixed	None native speaker of Catalan, but one or both native speakers of third languages
CatD ($n=20$)	15	0	5	0
SpD ($n=11$)	1	8	0	2

monolingual speakers of Spanish or native bilinguals speaking Spanish and a third language (in this case, Aymara, Basque, or Quechua) are dominant in Spanish (10 out of 11 cases). As soon as at least one parent is a native speaker of Catalan ('mixed family'), this language is also the dominant language of the child (see Woolard 2009: 130; Boix-Fuster/Paradís 2015 for comparable observations).[149] Besides, it is worth to point out already at this point that the percentage of Catalan usage is high in 'mixed families' (between 70 and 90%; see below and Boix-Fuster/Paradís 2015). Even so, these participants tend to exhibit numerically rather low dominance indices and are, therefore, more balanced than those of two natively Catalan-speaking parents.

4.2.1 Language history

Concerning age of acquisition (AoA), the participants almost without exception indicated that they started acquiring their dominant language from birth and the second language somewhat later. Table 4.5 shows the average AoA in the two dominance groups.

The apparent difference between the two groups means for the non-dominant language is caused mainly by the fact that the informants born in Latin America started acquiring Catalan only at the age of 6 years: if the two of them are left out, the mean age of acquisition of Catalan in the SpD group drops to 1.3 (SD: 1.9) and is thus very similar to the AoA of Spanish in the CatD group. The same

---

148. This was confirmed by a Fisher's exact test ($p < 0.001$). Note also that the parents' mother tongue(s) were not a variable included in the assessment of the participants' LD. This link thus corroborates the validity of the ILD.

149. There is one exception: curiously, participant No. 7, who is a child of Catalan-speaking parents, is slightly dominant in Spanish (dominance value 19.5). Although both parents were born in Girona and speak Catalan as their mother tongue, the only language in the family is Spanish. Possibly, in this case, the grandparents could be of non-Catalan origin, as suggested by the two Castilian surnames of the informant, and hence Spanish could be his parents' stronger language.

Table 4.5 Age of onset of acquisition of Catalan and Spanish (means of the dominance groups in years and SD)[a]

Age of acquisition	Catalan	Spanish
CatD	0.1 (0.2)	1.5 (1.9)
SpD	2.3 (2.2)	0.1 (0.3)

a. The figures represent group averages and therefore display decimals. For instance, most respondents ticked the box "from birth" for the dominant language but some few marked "1 year", hence the respective average values.

pattern is found with regard to the mean 'distances' between the onset of acquisition of the dominant and the non-dominant language: in the CatD group, the mean size of the gap is 1.4 years (SD: 1.9) and, in the SpD group, it attains 2.2 years (SD: 2.2) when all participants are included, and only 1.3 years (SD: 1.4) without the foreign-born subjects. There are thus no notable differences between the two dominance groups for the subjects born in Catalonia, although the SDs show that there is a fair deal of variance among individuals.

In combination with the biographical background data, the informants' AoA furthermore show that they can be qualified either as simultaneous or successive bilinguals: for the most part, they acquired both Spanish and Catalan either from birth (= simultaneous bilinguals) or the exposure to the second language started at the latest in the third year of life (= simultaneous or successive according to the respective definitions of the terms).[150] Exceptions, i.e. clearly sequential bilinguals, are merely the two SpD participants born in South America as well as two CatD speakers who indicated that they began to learn Spanish only at the age of 4 and 7, respectively.[151]

---

150. According to Silva-Corvalán (2014: 1), there exists no agreement with respect to the age at which bilingual development should be considered sequential. Some researchers propose that bilingualism is successive "when the child's exposure to the second language starts sometime between the first and the third birthday", for others it is still to be considered as simultaneous as long as it begins before the age of 3 (see also Montrul 2013b).

151. Some researchers might consider these cases as examples of early second language acquisition. This particular form of bilingualism occurs when a child already has one established language before starting to hear and learn a second one (De Houwer 2009: 4; Silva-Corvalán 2014: 1). In the cases of the two participants born in South America, it is obvious that they had no contact with Catalan before settling down in Girona with their parents. In the cases of the two Catalan-dominant speakers, on the other hand, it is hard to conceive how the AoA of Spanish could be as late as 7 years (e.g. due to the omnipresence of Spanish-language media in Catalonia). However, this information is congruent with the fact that these two subjects are the least balanced bilinguals of all: their dominance indices are −57.3 and −54.2.

As opposed to AoA, there is a rather clear difference between the two dominance groups concerning age of comfort. In both groups, informants indicated that they started feeling comfortable using their dominant language already in the first years of live, while this goal was attained only much later in the weaker language (see Table 4.6). Despite large inter-subject differences, it is interesting to note that it took the CatD speakers on average more than twice as long as the SpD group to reach this point.

Table 4.6 Age of comfort (averages in years and SD)

Age of comfort	Catalan	Spanish
CatD	1.8 (2.8)	10.6 (5.2)
SpD	4.8 (5.3)	0.6 (1.4)

Whereas the SpD bilinguals generally achieved comfort in Catalan still in their childhood (i.e. with exception of the foreign-born informants before the age of 10), half of the CatD participants stated that they only started feeling comfortable using Spanish during puberty, in early adulthood, or even that they still felt uncomfortable when having to use that language.[152] Little surprisingly, age of comfort correlates moderately with LD, such that the stronger the dominance of one language over the other, the longer it takes the bilingual to achieve comfort in the non-dominant language (CatD: $r = -0.685$; SpD: $r = 0.511$).[153]

A similar relation exists also between the informants' LD and the language(s) spoken at home during their childhood (see Table 4.3).

Table 4.7 Language(s) spoken at home during childhood (absolute numbers of participants)

Family language(s)	Catalan	Spanish	both
CatD ($n = 20$)	20	0	0
SpD ($n = 11$)	0	9	2

---

152. Possibly, this is — at least in part — a merit of the *immersió lingüística* 'linguistic immersion', which makes Catalan the obligatory vehicular language in the Catalan educational system and thereby facilitates its acquisition by children of Spanish-speaking families. On the other hand, the predominance of Catalan in Girona at the societal level reduces the need of using Spanish for children of Catalan-speaking families (see also Chapter 2).

153. In the case of the CatD group, this correlation is statistically significant ($t(18) = -3.991$, $p < 0.001$). However, as age of comfort was one of the variables used to calculate the dominance scores, these variables are not totally independent.

While the CatD group uniformly indicated Catalan as the only home language, among the SpDs, two marked both languages. One of these is speaker 35, who has a dominance index of 1.7 and seems to be a rare case of a perfectly balanced bilingual. His mother is Catalan and his father is from Granada. The second speaker is equally relatively balanced (dominance value: 18.4). However, since her parents stem from the south of the Peninsula, the use of Catalan within the family — which she rates as 40% later in the questionnaire — could only be explained if the parents had learned Catalan as a foreign language or if Catalan were used among the speaker and her siblings.

4.2.2 Language use

Concerning language use, both groups typically use their dominant language most in the seven domains enquired in the LBQ. However, there are some differences across domains, especially regarding the proportions of use of the non-dominant languages.

Within the family, the dominant language is used on average 90% of the time. The rest of the time the second or, in one case, a third language (Quechua) is spoken.

Table 4.8 Mean percentages of language use in an average week within the family (with SD)

With family	Catalan	Spanish
CatD	92 (11)	8 (11)
SpD	9 (15)	88 (15)

With friends, these percentages change considerably. The CatD group use Spanish more often than in familial settings, but Catalan is clearly predominant when talking to friends. Notably, this is true of the SpD group as well. Although the proportions of the two languages are more balanced in their case, this corroborates the predominance of Catalan in Girona at the societal level (see Chapter 2).

Table 4.9 Mean percentages of language use in an average week with friends (with SD)

With friends	Catalan	Spanish
CatD	82 (17)	18 (19)
SpD	54 (24)	45 (23)

Catalan is also the most important language at university or work. While the difference between the two languages is minimal in the SpD group, it reaches 37 percentage points in the CatD group. Finally, to a minor extent, the students also use some other languages, such as German or English, in their language courses (~5%).

Table 4.10 Mean percentages of language use in an average week at university or work (with SD)

At university	Catalan	Spanish
CatD	67 (24)	29 (26)
SpD	47 (24)	48 (24)

For shopping, we observe the same trend: the dominants in Catalan prefer their dominant language, and the SpD group use both languages with similar frequencies.

Table 4.11 Mean percentages of language use in an average week when shopping (with SD)

When shopping	Catalan	Spanish
CatD	75 (19)	26 (19)
SpD	48 (27)	52 (27)

To address strangers, the SpD group equally again both languages in equal measure. In the CatD group, Catalan is somewhat more important, but Spanish has a higher presence in this context than in others. Although it can generally be assumed that Catalan is understood by everyone in Girona, it thus seems that this is not always evident for the surveyed students or that they sometimes have the feeling that Spanish is more appropriate, for example, for reasons of politeness.[154]

Concerning non-communicative language uses, it is not surprising that internal functions such as thoughts are usually covered by the informants' dominant language (see Mackey 2000: 32). Nonetheless, it is noteworthy that the weaker language is somewhat more important in the SpD group than in the other.

---

[154]. On the tendency of Catalan-speakers to use Spanish in formal contexts, in public, and with unknown or Spanish-speaking people, see also Sinner/Wieland (2008: 136–138), Boix-Fuster/Woolard (2020), and the studies cited therein. In its extreme form, such behaviour is known in Catalan sociolinguistics as *auto-odi* 'self-hatred' (see the discussion in Kabatek 1994; Ninyoles 1969: 74–84).

Chapter 4. Methodology, speakers, and data   141

Table 4.12 Mean percentages of language use in an average week with strangers (with SD)

With strangers	Catalan	Spanish
CatD	60 (24)	37 (25)
SpD	50 (19)	49 (19)

Table 4.13 Mean percentages of language use in thoughts (with SD)

Reckoning	Catalan	Spanish
CatD	90 (13)	7 (10)
SpD	16 (17)	84 (17)

This difference between the two groups even increases when it comes to counting. While the CatD group do this almost exclusively in Catalan, the SD group prefer Spanish but also make use of Catalan in over a quarter of the cases.[155]

Table 4.14 Mean percentages of language use in counting (with SD)

Counting	Catalan	Spanish
CatD	96 (8)	4 (8)
SpD	27 (37)	73 (37)

Finally, all participants (except one Catalan-dominant) chose to complete the questionnaire in their dominant language.

With regard to the complementary distribution of the bilinguals' languages over these seven domains of use, the CIs calculated for each participant (see Appendix and Table 4.3) additionally revealed that most are language-specific, i.e. covered mainly (or totally) by only one language. The Complementarity Principle (see Section 3.3) thus applies well in the present sample. However, this tendency is stronger in the CatD bilinguals (group means: 87% vs 69%, see Table 4.3). A closer look into the questionnaires showed their language-specific domains were almost exclusively specific to Catalan (97%).[156] Domains that sometimes were

---

[155]. One possible explanation for this behaviour may be the fact that Catalan schools teach mathematics in Catalan and, consequently, all pupils are well acquainted with Catalan numbers. Moreover, the latter turn out to be more 'practical' as pointed out by some participants, since many have fewer syllables than their Spanish counterparts: *cinc* vs *cinco* 'five', *set* vs *siete* 'seven', *vuit* vs *ocho* 'eight', *nou* vs *nueve* 'nine', *setze* vs *dieciséis* 'sixteen'.

Spanish-specific in CatD bilinguals were merely talking to strangers and, in the CatD students of Spanish philology, university. In the SpD group, on the other hand, language-specific domains were specific to Spanish to an extent of 72% and to Catalan to an extent of 28%. Catalan-specific domains were mostly talking to friends, shopping, and counting.

4.2.3 Language proficiency

The participants generally considered themselves highly proficient in both of their languages (see Table 4.15, below). Especially with regard to receptive skills (reading and listening comprehension), most hardly appreciated any difference between their two languages. The most pronounced differences in proficiency were observed with regard to oral expression in the CatD group, whose average evaluations of competence in two languages reached a difference of 1.1 points on a 6-point Lickert scale (as compared to only 0.5 in the SpD group). Whether this subjective assessment is objectively correct cannot be determined here. However, if it were incorrect, a possible explanation to the participants' erroneous evaluations might be found either in a latent inferiority complex caused by a supposed 'Catalan accent' that would make them underestimate their proficiency (see Montrul 2013a: 54; Sinner 2004: 585–588) or in their language ideology forbidding them to be equally proficient in Spanish — yet, for the time being, this is merely surmise and future studies would be necessary to provide any evidence for it.

Table 4.15 Self-assessment of proficiency in productive and receptive language skills (averages on a 6-point Likert scale[a] and SD)

		Catalan	Spanish
Speaking	CatD	5.9 (0.3)	4.8 (0.8)
	SpD	5.3 (0.9)	5.8 (0.4)
Aural comprehension	CatD	6.0 (0)	5.9 (0.4)
	SpD	5.8 (0.4)	5.9 (0.3)
Reading	CatD	6.0 (0.2)	5.4 (0.9)
	SpD	5.4 (1.1)	5.6 (0.9)
Writing	CatD	5.8 (0.5)	5.3 (0.9)
	SpD	5.2 (0.4)	5.8 (0.4)

a. The Lickert scale ranges from 0 ("not very well at all") to 6 ("very well").

---

156. The percentages are based on the total number of responses per LD group in the LBQ (i.e. 11 SpD participants × 7 domains = 77 and 20 CatD participants × 7 domains = 140).

4.2.4 Language attitudes

Both dominance groups attach somewhat more importance to their dominant language. They feel more like themselves when speaking their dominant language and less so when speaking the second language. In the CatD group, the average evaluation of 3.05 (i.e. in the middle of the scale) clearly indicates that they do not feel like themselves to the same extent when speaking Spanish as when speaking Catalan, although there are notable individual differences.

Table 4.16 Agreement with the statement "I feel like myself when I speak Catalan/Spanish" on a 6-point Likert scale[a] (with SD)

"I feel like myself when I speak …"	Catalan	Spanish
CatD	6.0 (0)	3.05 (2.2)
SpD	4.7 (1.1)	5.9 (0.3)

a. The Lickert scale ranges from 0 ("disagree") to 6 ("agree").

Similarly, it was less important for the CatD group to use Spanish like a native speaker and to be perceived as a native speaker of Spanish, whereas they judged both very important with regard to Catalan (cf. the difference of almost 1.5 and 2.4 points in the average evaluations). Among the SpD, the size of these interlanguage difference was notably smaller (0.45 points for attaining native competence and 1.27 for being perceived as a native speaker).

Table 4.17 Agreement with the statements "It is important to me to use (or eventually use) Catalan/Spanish like a native speaker" and "I want others to think that I am a native speaker of Catalan/Spanish" on a 6-point Likert scale[a] (with SD)

Attainment of native competence	Catalan	Spanish
CatD	6.0 (0.2)	4.5 (1.8)
SpD	5.0 (1.3)	5.5 (1.2)
Perception as native speaker		
CatD	5.8 (0.8)	3.3 (2.1)
SpD	3.7 (1.9)	4.6 (2)

a. The Lickert scale ranges from 0 ("disagree") to 6 ("agree").

Finally, most respondents considered only their dominant language to be their 'mother tongue'. Merely 16% indicated both languages. Their dominance indices show that these were rather balanced bilinguals (average score 17.3). Consequently, when neither language imposes itself strongly on the other, this seems to favour the perception of both languages as mother tongues. A clear dominance, on the other hand, increases the odds of considering only the dominant language as mother tongue.[157]

Table 4.18 Answers to the question "Which language(s) do you consider your mother tongue(s)?"

Language(s) considered mother tongue(s)	Only Catalan	Only Spanish	Both
CatD ($n=20$)	17	0	3
SpD ($n=11$)	0	9	2

4.3 Materials and procedure

The data collection took place in November 2017 in Girona. The corpus was recorded with a Zoom H5 digital recorder and a XYH-5 shock-mounted X/Y microphone capsule in a sound-proof box at the Phonetics Laboratory of the Faculty of Arts of the University of Girona. The participants were naïve to the purpose of the study[158] and interviewed one by one. Before starting the recording sessions, they were asked to fill in the background questionnaire and to sign a declaration of consent. The whole procedure took roughly 40 minutes per participant, after which they had the opportunity to informally comment on and talk about the experiment.

The data used for the intonational analysis of Girona Spanish and Girona Catalan (henceforth GS and GC) consisted predominantly of semi-spontaneous speech (Section 4.3.1). Only for GS, a small additional amount of scripted speech was recorded (Section 4.3.2). The processing, segmentation, and analysis of the data will be dealt with in Section 4.3.3. The recording sessions started with the Catalan version of the discourse-completion task (see 4.3.1). Then, the partici-

---

157. As Pujolar (2011:365) explains Catalans have traditionally constructed language as the main emblem of their identity and in consequence "most native speakers of Catalan identify themselves as such and very rarely as 'bilingual' despite the fact that they have been proficient in Castilian for generations" (see also Woolard 1989).

158. In the recruitment process, the prospective candidates were asked to participate in an experiment that involved listening to short descriptions of a series of situations and uttering a sentence that would fit in that situation as well as reading out loud a text. They were first approached in Catalan, as this language was considered the most neutral choice in the given context. However, in the few cases participants switched to Spanish later on during the recording sessions, the experimenter adapted to their language choice (unless for giving instructions, see below).

pants absolved a series of reading tasks in Spanish. Last, the Spanish-language version of the discourse completion task was recorded. Instructions were given in Catalan or Spanish as a function of the language of the following task.

4.3.1 Semi-spontaneous data

To collect authentic speech data for the investigation of the intonation of Spanish and Catalan as spoken by bilinguals in Girona, a discourse completion task (DCT) was chosen. Originally stemming from research into pragmatics, where it has a long tradition (see Blum-Kulka et al. 1989; Kasper/Dahl 1991; Billmyer/Varghese 2000; Félix-Brasdefer 2010), this method has been first applied to Romance prosody by Prieto (2001). By now, i.e. some two decades later, it has become a popular and wide-spread instrument of data collection (see Vanrell et al. 2018 for an overview of the DCT in Romance prosody research). In its basic version, it can be defined as a questionnaire that comprises descriptions of different scenarios designed to elicit the desired speech act by an informant (Vanrell et al. 2018: 195–196). The inductive method presents some major advantages as it permits the collection of large amounts of (semi-)spontaneous data comparable across speakers and varieties or languages within a short period of time. Furthermore, it allows to control tightly for context (i.e. pragmatic structure and degree of presupposition) and — to a great extent — also for other relevant aspects of the target sentence, such as sentence type or type of subject or verb. At the same time speakers still have the freedom to answer in a natural way, i.e. to utter any response as long as it fits the situation evoked by the prompt, while the researcher interference can be regarded as medium (Vanrell et al. 2018: 195, 199). Even though it is evident that spontaneous speech taken from natural settings represents the most ecologically valid data type, the DCT method of data elicitation was preferred in the present study for a variety of reasons. First, detailed background information on the (necessarily bilingual) speakers was crucially needed to assess their LD patterns. Second, a wide variety of utterances appropriate to different (pragmatic) contexts should be analysed. Third, the analysed utterances needed to be comparable across situations, speakers, and languages. All of these requisites are impossible (or at least extremely difficult) to comply with by using merely corpora of naturalistic speech data.

The DCT questionnaire used in the present study was compiled by and large from the well-tried intonation surveys proposed for Castilian and Cantabrian Spanish by Estebas-Vilaplana/Prieto (2010) and López Bobo/Cuevas Alonso (2010) and a slightly modified version of Prieto and Cabré's (2007–2012) questionnaire for Central Catalan. These surveys were adapted in order to develop two identical questionnaires in both languages (see Appendix for the full questionnaires). They comprise a set of short role-plays based on every-day situations designed to elicit a series of specific speech acts. These scenarios were read to the subjects by the author of this book while they were shown a PowerPoint slide with an image in some way connected to the situation. After each prompt, the informants were asked to respond verbally to the given stimulus. They were explicitly told to react in the most natural way and to phrase their reaction as they wish. Since almost all situations were of the *open item — verbal response only* type, which requires nothing more than a verbal response (Vanrell et al. 2018: 196), the subjects were largely free in choosing their vocabulary and concerning phrasing of their utterances. However, they were told previously to use complete sentences and avoid one-word responses. In some cases, the scenarios contained an indirectly formulated interlocutor initiation, such that responses corresponded to a turn of a hypothetical dialogue. As an illustration, one example taken from the questionnaire is provided in (1) with some possible or expected responses:

(1) Situation 2a1: Information-seeking yes-no question
Catalan: "Entres en una botiga on mai no havies entrat i demanes si tenen mandarines."
'You go into a shop where you've never been before and ask if they have tangerines.'
Possible responses: Hola, teniu mandarines? / Que teniu mandarines? / Venen mandarines?
'Hello, do you have tangerines? / Have you got tangerines? / Do you sell tangerines?'
Spanish: "Entras en una tienda y le preguntas al vendedor si tiene mandarinas."
'You go into a shop and ask the shop assistant if they have got tangerines.'
Possible responses: Hola, ¿tenéis mandarinas? / ¿Tienen mandarinas? / ¿Vende mandarinas?
'Hello, have you got tangerines? / Do you have tangerines? / Do you sell tangerines?'

When a situation was not fully clear to the participant after the first reading, its description was repeated and sometimes explained by the researcher. Yet, this was hardly ever necessary as all scenarios were formulated in a brief and concise manner. Furthermore, it was strenuously avoided to make participants rephrase their responses when these did not correspond to the desired utterance type, since this typically would have implied to make them repeat a sentence pre-phrased by the interviewer, such that their response would no longer represent an instance of (semi-)spontaneous speech. When responses were disfluent, participants were usually asked one time to repeat it. If they did not succeed by the second go, no third intend was made, as such a repetition would no longer be authentically spontaneous and increase the odds of getting rising contours meaning 'Am I doing it well?' or contours expressing obviousness (see Vanrell et al. 2018: 199).

The DCT was carried out in both Catalan (as first task in the recording session) and Spanish (as last task) with each participant. The total number of situations used for the data collection was 30 per language. The elicited utterances correspond to four main sentence types: (1) (neutral and biased) statements, (2) (neutral and biased) questions (i.e. yes–no questions, disjunctive questions, wh-questions, and echo questions), (3) imperatives, and (4) vocatives. In Table 4.19, below, a detailed overview of all sentence types is given. In some cases, more than one scenario was employed to elicit a specific utterance type. This was done to circumvent the common problem of the DCT that it may not portray the variety of language uses found in real situations: since each scenario can only be used once to elicit a verbal reaction by a participant, in communicative contexts where more than one intonational contour would be felicitous, respondents are bound to choose merely one among possible variants (Vanrell et al. 2018: 215; Borràs-Comes et al. 2015: 74–75). By providing the speakers with different situations evoking the same communicative context, one thus increases the chances of observing and capturing possible intonational variation (e.g. in information-seeking yes–no and wh-questions as well as exclamative statements, see Section 3.1.2.2). A full list of all scenarios used for the elicitation can be found in the Appendix.

From the 1860 responses recorded (i.e. 30 situations × 31 speakers × 2 languages), a total of 1602 IPs suitable for an intonational analysis could be extracted (824 for GS and 778 for GC). Roughly 13% of the recorded responses thus needed to be excluded from the analysis. Typically, this was the case when the uttered sentence did not correspond to the desired utterance type or when it contained too strong hesitations or disfluencies to allow a robust analysis (for the exact reasons see the respective subsections in 5.1). Whenever responses contained more than one IP (e.g. when an explanation was added after the direct response to the respective situation), only the IP corresponding to the desired utterance type (i.e. usually the first one) was chosen. The exact number of IPs analysed for each sentence type is given in Table 4.19.

4.3.2 Read data

Alongside the semi-spontaneous data, a short Spanish dialogue was recorded. Its objective was to collect the following two GS utterance types from each participant: yes–no questions headed by the complementizer *que* and statements containing dislocations (see (2), below, and the Appendix). According to the academic literature (see Section 2.3), these two sentence types do either not occur in monolingual Mainstream Spanish at all (viz. *que*-questions in information-

Table 4.19 Sentences analysed with respect to intonation for Girona Spanish and Girona Catalan

Sentence types		Number	Situations (items)	Number of IPs Span	Number of IPs Cat
neutral statements	neutral statements (one unit)	1, 2	1a1, 1a2	58	53
	enumerations	3	1b	31	31
	neutral statements with peripheral elements (dislocations, vocatives, parenthetical elements, appositions)	4, 5, 6, 7	1c1, 1c2, 1c3, 1c4	70	68
biased statements	contrastive-focus statements	8	1d	30	28
	exclamative statements	9, 12	1e1, 1e2	63	55
	contradiction statements	10	1f	30	30
	dubitative statements	11	1g	31	26
neutral polar questions	information-seeking yes-no questions	13, 14, 15	2a1, 2a2, 2a3	93	93
	information-seeking yes-no questions with a peripheral element	16, 17	2b1, 2b2	61	59
	disjunctive questions	18	2c	29	28
biased polar questions	exclamative yes-no questions (with counterexpectational meaning)	19	2d	31	25
	confirmation-seeking yes-no questions	20	2e	30	31
neutral wh-questions	information-seeking wh-questions	21, 22	3a1, 3a2	58	57
biased wh-questions	exclamative wh-questions	23	3b	31	28
	imperative wh-questions	24	3c	29	27
echo questions	echo yes-no questions	25	4a	27	27
	echo wh-question	26	4b	31	30
	exclamative echo yes-no questions (with counterexpectational meaning)	27	4c	29	29
imperatives	commands	28	5a	13	9
	requests	29	5b	18	13
vocatives		30	6	31	31
total				824	778

seeking contexts) or their use is clearly more marked and less frequent than in Catalonian Spanish (*que*-questions in other pragmatic contexts and dislocations). Both sentence types thus contain features whose presence in Catalonian Spanish is normally attributed to the intense language contact with Catalan, where they are common (see Section 2.3). However, given that their intonation in CCS has not yet been thoroughly described, the reading task was administered to guarantee that the corpus would contain such items from each participant. This could not be achieved with semi-spontaneous data only, for the nature of the DCT consists in letting the participants freely chose the phrasing of their sentences and each context allows for only one answer. Considering that the use of *que*-questions and dislocations represents only one possible alternative among many others, it was unlikely that the participants would produce such phrasings in sufficient numbers in the (semi-)spontaneous corpus to permit a sound analysis. Besides, it is likely that at least some bilinguals are aware of the fact that the use of *que* in yes–no questions and of (a large number of) dislocations in CCS is a feature that derives from contact with Catalan. Knowing that these are non-standard variants, they might therefore avoid them in recording situations. A secondary aim of the inclusion of read data into the intonational analysis was to complete the results obtained through the DCT through evidence from additional tasks and thereby increasing the robustness and validity of the present study (a technique known as triangulation of methods, Vanrell et al. 2018: 221).

The dialogue used in the recordings is given in (2); a translation is provided in the Appendix.

(2) *Joan y Mercè están en la oficina trabajando. Son las 12 h.*
Mercè: Joan, voy al bar a tomar un café. ¿Que quieres venir conmigo? (A)

Joan: ¿Que tomas café al mediodía? (B)

Mercè: Sí, claro. Yo bebo muchísimo, de café (D1). Probablemente, demasiado...

Joan: Pues, no lo sabía... Bueno, termino esto y vamos, ¿vale?

Mercè: ¡Que no! Me apetece ir ahora mismo. Ya sabes que tengo muy poca, de paciencia (2).
Salen de la oficina.
Joan: ¿Que llueve? (C)

Mercè: Parece que sí...
Mercè se resbala y se cae al suelo.
Joan: ¡Uy! ¿Que te has hecho daño? (D2)

The dialogue consisted of a total of 62 words of fictional direct speech, embedded in background descriptions of the respective situation (in italics). Catalan person names were used for the fictional characters to situate the scene in Catalonia and to make its Catalan-tinted phrasing more natural. It contained a total of four yes–no questions (marked with capital letters) and two dislocations (D1 and D2). Among the yes–no questions, two were information-seeking (A and D),[159] one was an exclamative echo yes–no question with a counterexpectational meaning (B),[160] and one was confirmation-seeking (C). Question D was taken from Moll (1961: 472) and Wesch (1997: 301), C is a literal translation of Cat. *Que plou?* (Prieto/Rigau 2007: 33). A and B were made up by the author. In A, C, and D, the use of *que* results clearly impossible or unnatural in monolingual varieties of Mainstream Spanish. In B, on the other hand, *que* is natural also in Spanish, since it in this case represents a 'citative' introductory particle marking the yes–no question as 'attributed', i.e. as a question that (partly) cites words actually or supposedly pronounced by the interlocutor and seeks for a confirmation of the meaning expressed by them (Escandell-Vidal 1999: 3965–3967, 3978). The recordings of this question should permit a comparison of the intonation of authentic Spanish *que*-questions with such that are only possible in CCS as an outcome of transfer from Catalan.

Concerning the two dislocations, partitive elements were chosen bearing in mind that they would clearly mark the dislocations as representing a CCS speech style. In both cases (sentence 1 and 2), the dislocated element was the complement of a quantifier (Sp. *muchísimo* and *poca* 'lots of' and 'little', respectively) that was part of the main clause of a declarative statement. The corresponding Catalan quantifiers (Cat. *molt/moltíssim* and *poca*) can be followed either directly by the quantified noun – as in Mainstream Spanish – or a 'partitive' *de* can be intercalated between the quantifier and the noun (Brucart/Rigau 2002: 1543–1545). This use is banned today in (Mainstream) Spanish by prescriptive norms, but it is reportedly found in Spanish varieties that are in contact with Catalan (see Radatz 2008: 123). When the quantified noun phrase is dislocated in Catalan (be it to the right or to the left), it obligatorily needs to be resumed by the adverbial clitic pronoun *en* (Vallduví 2002: 1236). As there is no such pronoun in Modern Spanish, parallel Spanish con-

---

159. Please note that in D a confirmation-seeking interpretation is theoretically possible as well if Joan assumes that Mercè has indeed hurt herself. However, the given context does not favour such an interpretation. In A, an information-seeking interpretation is the only possible interpretation.

160. In theory, this question may also be interpreted either as a simple exclamative yes–no question (with counterexpectational meaning), since *tomas café* 'drink coffee' only partly resumes (i.e. echoes) *tomar un café* 'drink a coffee' from the interlocutor's sentence. However, the presence of *que* as a 'citative' element clearly favours an echo interpretation. Another – but in this context even less probable – interpretation could be one as a simple confirmation-seeking yes–no interrogative.

structions lack it: *¡No quiero más yo, de vino!* (Radatz 2008: 123). While sentence 2 was adapted from Szigetvári (1994: III, 15), who documented it from a radio broadcast, sentence 1 was constructed in a parallel way by the author of this book. Catalan equivalents would be *Jo en prenc/bec moltíssim, de cafè* and *En tinc molt poca, de paciència*. Rather than merely to record dislocations that are common in any other Mainstream Spanish variety by Girona bilinguals, the goal of this way of elicitation and the stimuli just described was to observe how Girona bilinguals intonate dislocations that are common and frequent in Catalan, may occur in CCS, but are ungrammatical in Mainstream Spanish. Considering that such uses typically occur in emphatic or even exclamative constructions (Radatz 2008: 124), similar contexts were chosen in the dialogue as well.

Reading the dialogue was the second task in the experiment and, as such, had to be carried out after the Catalan DCT. The text was presented to the participants on a PowerPoint slide after giving them the necessary instructions: they were first asked to have a look at the text in order to prepare for reading it aloud and then, when they felt ready, to do so playing both parts (i.e. Mercè *and* Joan) and pronouncing each stretch of direct speech as if they were in the described situation.

The dialogues were followed by two further reading tasks consisting of another set of sentences and a text. These should allow an in-depth analysis of prosodic phrasing and of different segmental aspects (especially of the voicing of intervocalic /s/) in the two contact varieties, which are not part of this book. More details on those tasks and the respective results can be found in Grünke (2022).

4.3.3 Data segmentation and labelling

All data recorded in the waveform audio file format (WAV) were transferred to a MacBook Air computer and converted from stereo to mono using the software *Audacity* (version 2.3.3). Subsequently, the files were cut with the same program. All analyses performed on the data were carried out using the software *Praat* (version 6.1, Boersma/Weenink 2020). In what follows, I introduce the criteria for the data segmentation and clarify the methodological choices made.

In a first step, the stretches of speech to be analysed with regard to their intonational properties were extracted from the responses given by the participants in the DCT as well as from the read speech corpus. As laid out in Sections 3.1.1.1 and 3.1.2, it is generally assumed that the IP is the greatest unit relevant for intonation in (Castilian) Spanish and (Central) Catalan and that the ip is the next hierarchically lower level from the IP (see Nibert 2000; Hualde 2002; Estebas-Vilaplana/Prieto 2008, 2010; Hualde/Prieto 2015, among others, for Spanish; Prieto et al. 2015; Benet 2011, Prieto 2014, Prieto et al. 2015 for Catalan). As there is no reason to assume that the varieties studied in this book, GC and GS, behave any differently from the respective reference varieties (see also Grünke 2022), the collected speech material was thus segmented into intonational phrases (IPs), intermediate phrases (ips), and (orthographic) words. Furthermore, stressed syllables were delimited and marked in the corresponding Praat TextGrids.

In this work, I assumed (1) that each IP contains at least one intermediate phrase, (2) that all adjacent intermediate phrases within a root sentence group together within an IP, and (3) that the end of each IP is tonally marked by a nuclear configuration consisting of a combination of a (nuclear) pitch accent (on the last stressed syllable) and an IP boundary tone (i.e. T* T%, where T stands for 'tone'). As for ips, I presupposed that they equally end in a nuclear configuration consisting of a pitch accent and a boundary tone. However, a distinction was made between inner (or non-IP-final) and IP-final ips. In the first case, a (nuclear) pitch accent and an ip boundary tone were labelled (i.e. T* T-). In the latter case, i.e. when the end of the IP-final ip was also the end of the IP, I only labelled the nuclear configuration of the IP (i.e. T* T%).[161]

Concerning the segmentation of utterances into IPs, mainly syntactic criteria were applied. Most importantly, each root sentence of an utterance was assumed to form an IP by its own. Peripheral elements (such as dislocations, parenthetical elements, vocatives, appositions, or tags) were equally analysed as independent IPs in line with, among others, Frota (2014:11), who explains that they form "string[s] not structurally attached to the sentence tree". The same holds for interjections and particles or sentence words such as Cat./Sp. *sí* 'yes' or *no* 'no'.

The criteria applied for the further segmentation of IPs into **ips** were (1) perceptual and (2) theoretical in nature. From a theoretical point of view, ips are defined by the presence of a nuclear pitch accent and a boundary tone (see above and Section 3.1.1.1).[162] With regard to perception, I analysed root sentences as IPs

---

161. This practice is in accordance with the overwhelming majority of recent studies on both Spanish and Catalan carried out within the AM-theoretical framework and represents the Spanish and Catalan ToBI labelling conventions (e.g. Estebas-Vilaplana/Prieto 2010; Hualde/Prieto 2015; Prieto et al. 2015; for further studies see Section 3.1.2.1). Although this way of annotation is not conform with the original AM proposal (nor with the conventions of the ToBI annotation systems for many languages such as English, German, or Greek, see Beckman/Pierrehumbert 1986; Beckman 1996; Beckman et al. 2005; Frota 2012; Grice et al. 2005; Arvaniti/Baltazani 2005), the issue has to my knowledge only been addressed explicitly very rarely in short comments such as "beide Töne werden sozusagen 'in einem' realisiert" 'both tones [i.e. the IP and the ip boundary tone] are realized — so to speak — 'in one' [i.e. merely as an IP boundary tone]' (Gabriel et al. 2013:197).

162. Following Estebas-Vilaplana/Prieto (2008:275) and Prieto et al. (2009:299), among many others, I analyse edge tones of ips as boundary tones rather than as phrase accents (see Section 3.1.1.1).

comprising more than one ip whenever one or more prosodic break(s) were realized within the IP, i.e. when at least one of the following cues was clearly present: a pause, pre-boundary lengthening, a continuation rise, a sustained pitch, a pitch reset, or a drop of the F0 to the base level.[163] In this manner, for example neutral SVO declarative statements with a prosodic break after the subject were analysed as compound IPs consisting of two ips: $((S)_{ip}(VO)_{ip})_{IP}$. I also analysed declarative enumerations (DCT situation 1c; see Appendix) and disjunctive questions (DCT situation 2c) as complex IPs which consist of more than one ip (see Estebas-Vilaplana/Prieto 2010 and Willis 2010 for a similar analysis, but cf. Vizcaíno Ortega et al. 2008). In some few cases, utterances containing (minor) disfluencies due to hesitation, breathing, coughing, laughing, or false starts were retained for the intonational analysis when the researcher was sure that this would not influence the results of the analysis.

The location of **stress** in prosodic words (non-verbs and verbs) was defined on the basis of the stress-assignment rules presented in Oliva/Serra (2002: 348–359), Wheeler (2005: 276–297), and Prieto (2006a) for Catalan, and in Hualde (2005: 222–233), Kubarth (2009: 180, 183–185), and Gabriel et al. (2013: 154–160) for Spanish (see also Section 3.1.2), as well as by taking into account the speakers' individual productions (see below for the annotation of deviant cases).

The segmentation of stressed **syllables** was done following the criteria for syllabification and resyllabification proposed in Lloret (2002: 207–224, 242–246) and Wheeler (2005: 78–123) for Catalan, and those in Hualde (2014: 56–89) for Spanish, as well as by considering the speakers' individual productions (see below for the criteria applied in segmentation of the speech signal).

As for the delimitation of the boundaries between syllables and segments, an acoustic and auditory analysis following standard phonetic criteria was carried out by focusing special attention on the acoustic description of Spanish sounds provided by Hualde (2005: 58–69) and Gabriel et al. (2013: 34–38) and analysing both the oscillogram and the spectrogram. The following criteria were considered: (1) All boundaries were set at the point of zero crossing of the waveform (Peterson/Lehiste 1960; Lang-Rigal 2014; Kireva 2016a). (2) The location of the boundaries between segments was determined considering the formant structure, the amplitude and period of the signal, and the distribution of energy visible in the spectrogram (Peterson/Lehiste 1960; Grabe/Low 2002; White/Mattys 2007). For example, the onset of vowels following a voiced fricative consonant was usually set at the beginning of the vowel's second formant. Sequences of sonorants

---

163. Unclear cases were consulted with at least one, in most cases two further raters, who were familiar with the analysis of prosodic phrasing. An ip boundary was annotated only when at least two raters agreed that it was perceivable.

(especially of combinations of vowels and nasals or laterals as well as diphthongs) were separated by observing their formant transitions and the amplitude of the signal (Grabe/Low 2002). If possible, the beginning of the second segment was placed at the narrowest point of the soundwave. If such a point was not observable, i.e. when the two segments (especially identical vowels or nasals) could not be differentiated, the midpoint of the F2 transition was selected as location of boundary (Lang-Rigal 2014; Henriksen 2014: 94).[164] (3) When a syllable was realized after a silent pause and began with a plosive or an affricate, the beginning of the respective onset consonant was set 0.05 seconds before the burst of the plosive (Mok/Dellwo 2008; Kireva 2016a). (4) When the end of a syllable was followed by a silent pause, the closing boundary was set considering the formant structure (F1 and F2 for final vowels; F2 for final laterals and nasals), the end of the pitch contour, and the amplitude of the signal (Peterson/Lehiste 1960; Grabe/Low 2002; White/Mattys 2007; Kireva 2016a).

In a next step, all pitch accents and boundary tones occurring in the data recorded and judged suitable for the intonational analysis were labelled using the tonal inventory of pitch accents and boundary tones proposed for Castilian Spanish and Central Catalan within the AM model (see Section 3.1.2). To offer a detailed description of the tonal shape of each sentence type and to determine the realization of prenuclear pitch accents that occurred in different positions within the sentence, the prenuclear pitch accents were divided into three groups in the presentation of the results whenever the utterances were long enough to yield a substantial number of items for each group:

- IP-initial prenuclear pitch accents: the first prenuclear accent in an IP (if the IP consists of more than one ip, this is the first prenuclear accent of the first ip)
- phrase-internal prenuclear pitch accents: any prenuclear accent that appears between the first prenuclear accent and the nuclear accent of an ip
- ip-initial prenuclear accents of non-IP-initial ips: the prenuclear pitch accent associated with the stressed syllable of the first prosodic word of an ip which does not occur in the initial position within the IP. For instance, the following IP contains three ips: $((ip)_1(ip)_2(ip)_3)IP$; while $(ip)_1$ is an IP-initial ip, $(ip)_2$ and $(ip)_3$ represent non-IP-initial ips.

Figure 4.7, below, illustrates the intonational analysis by means of an example from GS.[165] The IP *Marina come mandarinas* 'Marina is eating tangerines' con-

---

164. Due to coarticulation effects, i.e. gestural overlap, segments can "ineinander übergehen und sich kontinuierlich verändern" 'merge into each other and change continuously' (Gabriel et al. 2013: 35; Hualde 2005: 233–234, 244; Browman/Goldenstein 1991).

sists of two ips. The first ip is composed only of the prosodic word *Marina*[166] 'Marina', which carries an L+H* pitch on its stressed syllable (*-ri-*). Given that it represents the last (and only) pitch accent of the ip, it is referred to as its nuclear pitch accent. It is followed by a high ip boundary tone (H-). The nuclear configuration of the first (or inner) ip is thus L+H* H-. The second (and IP-final) ip comprises two prosodic words, both of which carry a pitch accent. The first one is the prenuclear pitch accent L+<H*, associated with the stressed syllable *co-* of the prosodic word *come* 'eats'. The second one, L*, is the nuclear pitch accent of this IP-final ip. It associates with the stressed syllable *-ri-* of the prosodic word *mandarinas* 'tangerines'. Together with the boundary tone of the IP, L%, which is aligned with the end of the IP, it forms the nuclear contour of this neutral declarative statement (i.e. L* L%). The nuclear configurations of the inner ip and the final contour of the IP do not merely differ regarding the tones they are composed of (i.e. L+H* H- vs L* L%) but also they express a pragmatic difference: while the nuclear contour of the inner ip conveys that the utterance continues, the final contour indicates its sentence type – here, a neutral statement – as well as the end of the sentence. I will refer to such final contours, composed of the nuclear pitch accent of the IP-final ip and the boundary tone of the IP, as the nuclear contour or nuclear configuration of the IP.

The layout of the figures that illustrate the intonational analysis largely follows the general ToBI conventions (see Section 3.1.1.2), i.e. they consist of the waveform or oscillogram, the spectrogram, and the pitch curve of the respective utterance (upper panel), and usually four annotation levels or 'tiers' (lower level). However, some minor modifications were made with regard to the annotation in the different tiers. In the present study, the lowermost tier provides an orthographic transcription of the whole utterance (followed by a label serving to identify the utterance type). Above, a word tier is represented. In the third tier from below, pitch accents are annotated within the limits of the syllables they associate with. Finally, the uppermost tier, indicates the boundary tones and, if present, disfluencies (marked with 'X-'). The unique ID of each utterance is given at the end of the figure caption. It combines the speaker ID, a letter indicating the language ('S' or 'C' for Spanish and Catalan), and the number of the stimulus used for elicitation (see Table 4.19).

---

165. The figures that illustrate the intonational analysis were made using a Praat script written by Wendy Elvira García (2018), which, in turn, was inspired by a previous script created by Pauline Welby (Aix-Marseille University) in 2003 and subsequently changed by Paolo Roseano (University of Barcelona) in 2011.
166. Stressed syllables are signalled by underlining them.

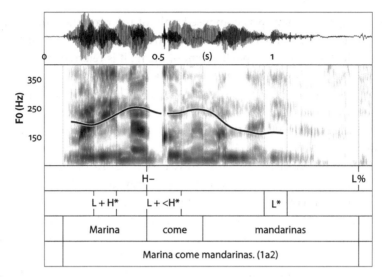

Figure 4.6 Segmentation of a neutral statement for the intonational analysis (Girona Spanish *Ma<u>ri</u>na <u>co</u>me manda<u>ri</u>nas.* 'Marina eats tangerines.'; 5S2)

For reasons of space, no separate break-index tier was included in the representations. The position of the break indices (BI) 0, 1, 3, and 4, proposed within the ToBI frameworks for Spanish and Catalan (see Beckman et al. 2002; Estebas-Vilaplana/Prieto 2008, 2010; Prieto et al. 2009, among others) can be understood from the other tiers included in the representation. BI 0, which marks the separation between orthographic words, is represented by the boundaries in tier 2 (counting from below). BI 1, i.e. the boundaries between prosodic words, can be deduced from tier 2 and 3. Since tier 3 indicates the stressed syllables of each prosodic word, it suffices to take the orthographic word in tier 2 below each stressed syllable in tier 3 and to add the preceding orthographic words which do not have a stressed syllable (or pitch accent) indicated in tier 3 of their own.[167] Break indices 3 and 4, finally, which correspond to intermediate phrase (BI 3) and intonational phrase ends (BI 4), are indicated by the respective boundary-tone labels annotated in the uppermost tier.

As outlined in Sections 3.1.2 and 3.1.2.2, especially IP-internal words can sometimes be pitch-deaccented in both Central Catalan and Castilian Spanish (see also Hualde/Prieto 2015; Prieto et al. 2015). Regarding the analysis of GC and GS, I counted underlyingly stressed syllables of ip-internal prosodic words

---

167. This is possible since in the Spanish and Catalan orthographies proclitics are spelled as orthographic words of their own, whereas enclitics are orthographically attached to their host (either directly, as in Spanish, or using a hyphen or apostrophe, as in Catalan).

as being pitch-deaccented if a high, mid, or low plateau was realized within the temporal boundaries of these syllables (see O'Rourke 2006; Rao 2008b, 2009). However, in view of the fact that such plateaus may be part of a pitch accent such as, e.g., the bitonal L*+H, which is "phonetically realized as an F0 valley on the accented syllable with a subsequent rise on the post-accentual syllable" (Estebas-Vilaplana/Prieto 2010:19), and can appear in prenuclear position in both Castilian Spanish and Central Catalan (Prieto et al. 2015; Estebas-Vilaplana/Prieto 2010), I also checked the tonal movements of the surrounding syllables (i.e. the respective pretonic and the post-tonic syllable) before labelling an underlyingly stressed syllable as pitch-deaccented. Following Hualde/Prieto (2015:364), I used an asterisk ('*') to indicate stressed syllables that show no tonal correlates. For the statement types that were regularly long enough to contain phrase-internal prosodic words, deaccentuation rates were calculated (i.e. for neutral broad-focus declaratives sentences, exclamative and dubitative statements, or information-seeking yes–no questions). When, in individual productions, the underlyingly stressed syllable of a prosodic word was pitch-deaccented but stress was phonetically realized on another syllable of the same prosodic word, the deaccented syllable was equally marked with an asterisk and a pitch accent was labelled on the syllable which actually bore the surface stress.

Concerning further diacritics, the upstep, i.e. '¡', was annotated when the realization of a pitch accent or boundary tone reached a higher pitch level than that of a preceding high target. The downstep diacritic ('!'), on the other hand, was only used when the high target of a pitch accent was realized at a level that was noticeably lower than it would be expected according to regular declination or final-lowering rules (see 3.1.1.1). This is to say, syntagmatic downstep was not indicated in the annotations, since it can be largely considered to be an automatic effect (Hualde/Prieto 2015:362). As for boundary tones, the label '!H-' was used to annotate sustained pitches (see Section 3.1.2). Furthermore, a high boundary tone was occasionally transcribed when an ip ended in a stressed syllable showing a low plateau, i.e. an L* pitch accent, and the following ip began with a high tone, i.e. with a pitch reset (see Frota et al. 2007:134; Benet et al. 2011:109f.).

In the (relatively few) cases where it was impossible to determine the underlying combination of pitch accent and boundary tone by a mere analysis of the surface pitch contour, i.e. typically when the utterance ended in an ultimate-stress word, I usually used the labels of the nuclear configurations found in other items of the same utterance type, which ended in words stressed on the penultimate or antepenultimate. When this was not possible, usually the simplest, i.e. the most parsimonious combination of a pitch accent and a boundary tone was labelled (e.g. L* H% rather than L+H* H% when the respective syllable showed a continuous rise).

After defining the prosodic phrasing patterns and the tonal realization of all sentence types, an inventory of underlying pitch accents and boundary tones was established for both varieties under investigation.

CHAPTER 5

Results

This chapter sets out the results of the intonational analysis of Girona Spanish and Girona Catalan (GS and GC, respectively). Section 5.1 gives the results of the intonational exploration of the contact varieties made (mainly) on the basis of the semi-spontaneous data and offers an overview of the tunes they typically use in the following sentence types: (1) neutral statements (Section 5.1.1); (2) biased statements (Section 5.1.2), (3) neutral polar questions (Section 5.1.3), (4) biased polar questions (Section 5.1.4), (5) neutral wh-questions (Section 5.1.5), (6) biased wh-questions (Section 5.1.6), (7) echo questions (Section 5.1.7), (8) imperatives (Section 5.1.8), and (9), vocatives (Section 5.1.9). Section 5.1.10, finally, completes the observations made with regard to some GS utterance types in the previous sections by means of an intonational analysis of some additional read speech data. In Section 5.2, I then go into the phonological status of the pitch accents and boundary tones attested in the previous sections and establish the inventory of pitch accents and boundary tones for both GS and GC.

5.1 Intonational analysis

5.1.1 Neutral statements

In this section, I present the results of the intonational analysis of neutral declarative statements, enumerations, and four different types of peripheral elements that can be part of a declarative statement (viz. dislocations, vocatives, parenthetical elements, and appositions). In each part, I describe the tunes employed by the participants by presenting the prenuclear pitch accents and nuclear configurations found in the data. Their phonological status will be discussed in Section 5.2, after the description of the tonal realization of all sentence types considered.

5.1.1.1 Neutral declarative statements

From a total of 123 utterances recorded with situation 1a1 and 1a2 (see Appendix), 111 IPs could be included in the analysis (58 for GS and 53 for GC, see also Table 4.19).[168] The prenuclear pitch accents for neutral declaratives gathered with situation 1a1 and 1a2 amounted to 117 for GS and 93 for GC. They were divided into three different groups according to their position: IP-initial prenuclear accents, ip-initial prenuclear accents of non-IP-initial ips, and phrase-internal prenuclear accents.

The following **IP-initial prenuclear pitch accents** were found in the examined data: L+<H* and H* (in both GS and GC), and L+H* (only in GS). Of these, the delayed peak, i.e. L+<H*, occurred by far the most commonly (76% in GC, $n = 31/41$, 63% in GS, $n = 25/40$). An example can be seen in Figure 5.1, below. The three instances of L+H* in the GS data set (accounting for 7.5% of the pitch accents in this position) most probably represent phonetic realizations of L+<H*, since they always occurred in the context of stress clashes or tonal crowding (i.e. on the ultimate-stress word *mujer* 'woman' followed directly by *bebe* 'drinks', stressed on the first syllable, or on *María* directly followed by *come* 'eats') (see also Section 5.2.1).

As concerns the use of H*, which represented 30% ($n = 12$, GS) and 26% ($n = 10$, GC) of the IP-initial prenuclear pitch accents (see Figure 5.2), it was checked whether it can be attributed predominantly to either of the two dominance groups: 9 out of 10 Catalan examples stem from Catalan-dominant speakers (CatD), and in Spanish, this share drops moderately (8 out of 12 items stemming from CatD participants). Even though this distribution suggests that there might be a greater probability for this pitch accent to occur in CatD speakers, Fisher exact tests did not show a significant association between the use of either L+<H* or H* and a particular dominance group in either language (GS: $p = 0.696$; CG: $p = 0.063$, i.e. only marginal significance). However, given that this could be an effect of the small numbers of cases, further research on the topic would be desirable.

As regards ip-initial prenuclear accents of non-IP-initial ips, a somewhat different picture arises. Generally, the pitch accents found in this condition were of the same nature as the IP-initial ones: i.e. H* and L+<H* (see Figures 5.3 and

---

168. While most excluded utterances contained strong disfluencies, six Catalan sentences had to be withdrawn because the participants ended them with a high, question-like intonation, i.e. they were implicitly asking the conductor of the experiment if they were doing well (see Vanrell et al. 2018: 199 on this problem). Since the Catalan neutral declarative statements were the first test items of the DCT, some participants might still have felt some insecurities at this point of the data collection despite the previous training.

Chapter 5. Results   161

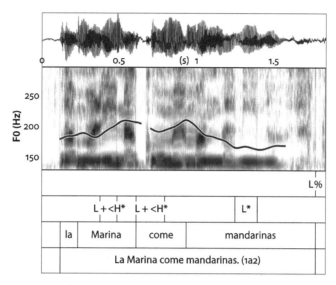

Figure 5.1 Girona Spanish: Waveform, spectrogram, and F0 contour for the neutral statement *La Marina come mandarinas.* 'Marina eats tangerines.' produced by a Catalan-dominant speaker. It represents an IP composed of one ip and is produced with an IP-initial L+<H* prenuclear accent, a phrase-medial L+<H* prenuclear accent, an L* nuclear accent, and an L% boundary tone. The nuclear configuration of the IP is L* L% (24S2)

5.4 for examples). However, H* was more recurrent than in IP-initial position. In Catalan, it accounted for 12 out of 16 items (75%), whereas in Spanish it occurred with the same frequency as L+<H* (7 items of each). Although in Catalan 9 items (i.e. 75%) stemmed from CatD subjects and 5 (71%), in Spanish, no association between the use of H* or L+<H* and language dominance (LD) could be found ($p = 1.0$ for GS and $p = 0.242$ for GC).

Furthermore, it is worth pointing out that the stressed syllable of the first prosodic word of a non-initial ip was sometimes analysed as pitch-deaccented if the fundamental frequency did not show any up- or downwards movement within the limits or in the surroundings of that syllable. Such plateaus occurred four times in each of the languages studied on the auxiliary verbs Sp. *está* or Cat. *està* 'is' which were part of verbs in the present progressive tense. In both varieties, all but one of these instances of deaccentuation were produced by CatD speakers. They were marked with a '*' in both contact varieties (see Figure 5.5).

Finally, one instance of an H+L* pitch accent was registered in Spanish, produced by a Spanish-dominant (SpD) speaker (see Figure 5.6). It is quite clearly conditioned by a lack of space: since it occurs directly after the H- boundary tone of the preceding ip, there is not enough segmental material for the realization of a fall whose end could serve as low prefix to a following rising pitch accent, such

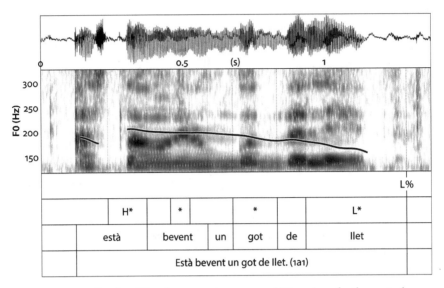

Figure 5.2 Girona Catalan: Waveform, spectrogram, and F0 contour for the neutral statement *Està bevent un got de llet.* 'She is drinking a glass of milk.' produced by a Catalan-dominant speaker. It represents an IP composed of one ip and is produced with an H* prenuclear accent, two pitch-deaccented prosodic words (*bevent* and *got*), an L* nuclear accent, and an L% boundary tone. The nuclear configuration of the IP is L* L% (14C1)

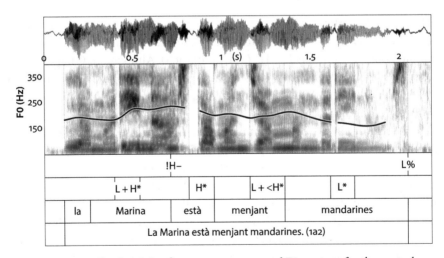

Figure 5.3 Girona Catalan: Waveform, spectrogram, and F0 contour for the neutral statement *La Marina està menjant mandarines.* 'Marina is eating tangerines' produced by a Spanish-dominant speaker. It represents an IP composed of two ips. The first ip is produced with an L+H* nuclear accent and a !H- boundary tone. The second ip consists of an ip-initial H* prenuclear accent, a phrase-internal L+<H* accent, an L* nuclear accent, and an L% boundary tone. The nuclear configuration of the IP is L* L% (8C2)

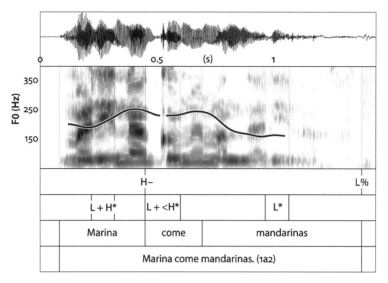

Figure 5.4 Girona Spanish: Waveform, spectrogram, and F0 contour for the neutral statement *Marina come mandarinas*. 'Marina eats tangerines' produced by a Spanish-dominant speaker. It represents an IP composed of two ips. The first ip consists of an L+H* nuclear accent and an H- boundary tone. The second ip is produced with an ip-initial L+<H* prenuclear accent, an L* nuclear accent, and an L% boundary tone. The nuclear configuration of the IP is L* L% (4S2)

as L+<H* (for similar cases see phrase-internal prenuclear accents, below, and Kireva 2016a: 104).

In **phrase-internal** position, pitch deaccentuation was quite common in both varieties (see Section 4.3.3 for the criteria). In the statements collected with situations 1a1 and 1a2, 58% of the Catalan and 52% of the Spanish ip-internal prosodic words did not bear a pitch accent. Figure 5.2, above, and Figure 5.7, below, illustrate the F0 contours of two neutral declaratives realized in GC in which all phrase-internal prosodic words are pitch-deaccented (although the metrically strong syllable may still present other correlates of stress such as a longer duration or higher intensity as opposed to unstressed syllables).

Yet, it is of course also possible for pitch accents to surface in phrase-internal position. If that case, a delayed peak (L+<H*) is clearly the favoured option, appearing on 39% and 30% of the metrically stressed syllables in this position in GS and GC, respectively. For instance, Figures 5.1, 5.3, and 5.4, above, offer examples of neutral SVO declaratives in which each prosodic word is signalled by a pitch accent. Alongside the delayed peaks, the analysed data contained a small number of phrase-medial !H* pitch accents (each 3 per variety) and some single instances of phrase-internal L+H* and H*. Concerning the language dominance

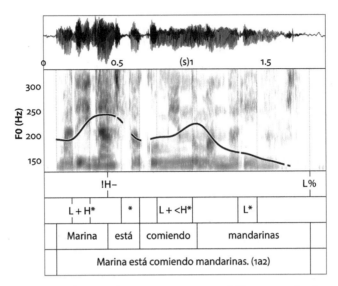

Figure 5.5 Girona Spanish: Waveform, spectrogram, and F0 contour for the neutral statement *Marina está comiendo mandarinas*. 'Marina is eating tangerines' produced by a Spanish-dominant speaker. It represents an IP composed of two ips. The first ip consists of an L+H* nuclear accent and a !H- boundary tone. The second ip is produced with the metrically stressed syllable pitch-deaccented (*), an L+<H* prenuclear accent, an L* nuclear accent, and an L% boundary tone. The nuclear configuration of the IP is L* L% (8S2)

(LD) of the participants, there was again no significant association with the use of pitch deaccentuation (GS: $\chi^2(1) = 0.415$, $p = 0.519$; GC: $\chi^2(1) = 0.0$, $p = 1$).

In summary, both varieties predominantly deploy the same prenuclear pitch accents in IP-initial, in 'ip- but not IP-initial', and in ip-internal position: namely, L+<H* and H*. In phrase medial position, pitch-deaccenting is the most common option. Neither language nor LD seem to have an influence on the choice of the prenuclear pitch accent or on pitch deaccentuation.

With regard to **nuclear** positions, inner ips, such as the first one in an [(S)$_{ip}$ (VO)$_{ip}$]$_{IP}$ pattern, must be distinguished from IP-final ips, such as the second one in that example. According to the intonational analysis, the inner ips of neutral broad-focus statements showed rising nuclear contours (composed of a rising nuclear pitch accent and a high boundary tone). On the contrary, IP-final nuclear contours were almost exclusively realized as low plateaus.

The nuclear configurations of inner ips attested in the data sets gathered with situations 1a1 and 1a2 are displayed in Table 5.1.

In GC, the nuclear configurations of inner ips were predominantly realized as L+H* H- (73%), i.e. as a rise throughout the stressed syllable that continues

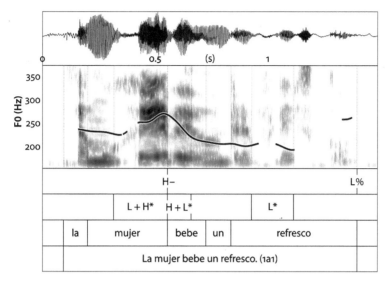

Figure 5.6 Girona Spanish: Waveform, spectrogram, and F0 contour for the neutral statement *La mujer bebe un refresco.* 'The woman is drinking a refreshment.' produced by a Spanish-dominant speaker. It represents an IP composed of two ips. The first ip consists of an L+H* nuclear accent and an H- boundary tone. The second ip is produced with an ip-initial H+L* prenuclear accent, an L* nuclear accent, and an L% boundary tone. The nuclear configuration of the IP is L* L% (5S1)

until the end of the ip, called continuation rise (see, e.g., Prieto 2014: 48; Prieto et al. 2015: 13).[169] This is illustrated in Figure 5.7, above. In 19% of the instances, a pitch plateau, i.e. a (!)H* !H- nuclear configuration, was found (see Figure 5.8 for an example). Furthermore, there were also 9% of other nuclear configurations, such as L+H* !H- (see Figure 5.3, above) or contours ending in L- boundary tones, which I interpret as phonetic surface reflexes of hesitation (see 5.2.2).

---

169. Note that when ip-final words stressed on the penultimate syllable display a rising gesture followed by a continuation rise up to the prosodic break, it cannot be determined whether the underlying pitch accent is L+H* (with the peak in the stressed syllable) or L+<H* (with a delayed peak), as the local maximum is conditioned by the H- boundary tone. Generally, such rises at the end of inner ips have been analysed either as L+H* (e.g. Estebas-Vilaplana/Prieto 2010: 31; Gabriel et al. 2010: 292; López Bobo/Cuevas Alonso 2010: 55; Ortiz et al. 2010: 267; Willis 2010: 140; Kireva 2016a: 105, among others) or, less frequently, as L+<H* (Gabriel et al. 2013: 208; O'Rourke 2010: 232; Hualde/Prieto 2015). In this book, I adopt the first view and posit underlying L+H* pitch accents (for some reasons for this decision see Section 5.2.2). Moreover, there has also been some debate about whether these ip-final contours should be analysed as combinations of prenuclear pitch accents and boundary tones (e.g. in O'Rourke 2010: 232; Gabriel et al. 2013: 196–197) or as nuclear configurations of inner ips (see, e.g., Ortiz et al. 2010: 267; Kireva 2016a: 105).

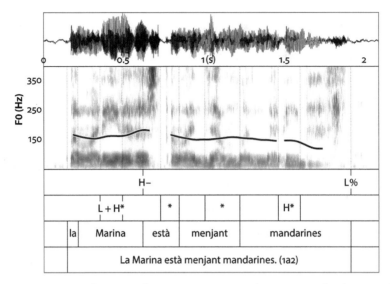

Figure 5.7 Girona Catalan: Waveform, spectrogram, and F0 contour for the neutral statement *La Marina està menjant mandarines*. 'Marina is eating tangerines' produced by a Catalan-dominant speaker. It represents an IP composed of two ips. The first one is produced with an L+H* nuclear accent and an H- boundary tone. The second one contains two metrically strong syllables that are pitch-deaccented and an H* nuclear accent, followed by an L% boundary tone. The nuclear configuration of the IP is H* L% (12C2)

Table 5.1 Percentages and total numbers of nuclear configurations of inner ips of the neutral declarative sentences in Girona Catalan and Girona Spanish

	L+H* H- (continuation rises)	L+H* !H- (sustained pitch)	(!)H* !H- (plateau)	Others
Girona Catalan	73% (34)	2% (1)	19% (9)	7% (3)
Girona Spanish	51% (17)	36% (12)	6% (2)	6% (2)

In GS, too, nuclear configurations of inner ips were predominantly realized as L+H* H- (51% of the items; see Figure 5.6, for an illustration). However, sustained pitches, i.e. the nuclear configuration L+H* !H-, were also observed with a fair degree of regularity (i.e. to an extent of 36%; see Figure 5.5, above, for an example). Finally, a proportion of 6% of (!)H* !H- nuclear contours, i.e. of pitch plateaus, was found (see Figure 5.9, below). The remaining 6% represented other contours ending in a low boundary tone, probably induced by hesitation phenomena (see also Sections 5.2.2).

Chapter 5. Results   167

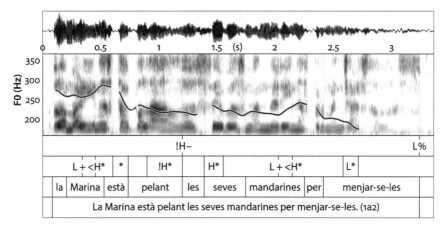

Figure 5.8 Girona Catalan: Waveform, spectrogram, and F0 contour for the neutral statement *La Marina està pelant les seves mandarines per menjar-se-les.* 'Marina is peeling her tangerines to eat them' produced by a Catalan-dominant speaker. It represents an IP composed of two ips. The first one is produced with an L+<H* prenuclear accent and an !H* !H- nuclear configuration. The second one contains an H* and an L+<H* prenuclear accent, an L* nuclear accent, followed by an L% boundary tone. The nuclear configuration of the IP is L* L% (28C2)

In sum, combinations of rising pitch accents and high boundary tones, i.e. continuation rises, were the preferred option for the nuclear configurations of inner ips in both varieties. Nevertheless, they clearly differed with regard to the use of the sustained pitch (see Table 5.1, above). A χ^2-test (performed leaving aside the few contours classified as 'other') confirmed that there exists a significant association between language variety and the choice of nuclear contours of IP-internal ips: $\chi^2(2) = 17.708$, $p < 0.001$. The mosaic plot in Figure 5.10 visually represents the observed frequencies and the corresponding Pearson residuals. It can be seen that the sustained pitch is overrepresented in GS and underrepresented in GC. The realizations were also checked for the LD of the speakers, but the proportions of use of the single boundary cues were very similar in both dominance groups.

Finally, the IP-final nuclear configurations of the neutral declaratives gathered with situation 1a1 and 1a2 need to be taken into account. As expected, in both varieties, the overwhelming majority of the nuclear contours produced in this condition corresponded to the L* L% pattern, i.e. a low pitch tone (L*) followed by a low boundary tone (L%). Its share attained 98% in GC and 91% in GS. Several examples can be seen above in Figures 5.1 to 5.6 and in 5.8. Besides, a minor number of falling nuclear contours were observed: the GS data contained three H+L* L% nuclear contours (5%; see Figure 5.9 for an example). However, these H+L* pitch accents might in fact represent surface variants of L* conditioned by preceding

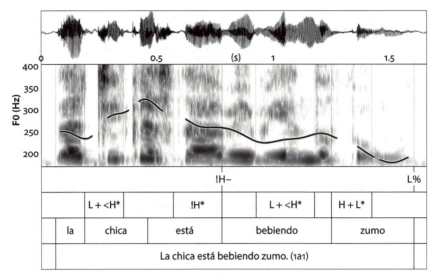

Figure 5.9 Girona Spanish: Waveform, spectrogram, and F0 contour for the neutral statement *La chica está bebiendo zumo*. 'The girl is drinking juice' produced by a Catalan-dominant speaker. It represents an IP composed of two ips. The first ip consists of an L+<H* prenuclear accent and a !H* !H- nuclear configuration. The second ip is produced with an ip-initial L+<H* prenuclear accent, an H+L* nuclear accent, and an L% boundary tone. The nuclear configuration of the IP is H+L* L% (28S1)

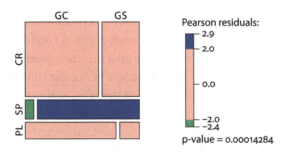

Figure 5.10 Mosaic plot of the uses of L+H* H- ('CR'), L+H* !H- ('SP'), and (!)H* !H- ('PL') in Girona Catalan and Girona Spanish broad-focus declarative statements[170]

high tones, seeing that they appeared when there were not enough unstressed syllables between the high tone and the nuclear stressed syllable that would allow for a falling interpolation. As a consequence, this fall is compressed onto the nuclear syllable, yielding a surface H+L* nuclear pitch accent (see also Section 5.2.3 for

---

170. This mosaic plots was created with the function mosaic( ) from the *vcd* package (Zeileis et al. 2007) in R (R Core Team 2020).

a discussion of the phonological status of this pitch accent). Last, one nuclear contour with a high pitch accent was observed in each variety, viz. H* L% (see Figure 5.7 for an example), and there was also one L+!H* L% nuclear contour in the GS data, produced by a SpD speaker. Both of these nuclear pitch accents could represent surface variants of the L+H* nuclear accent, which is the accent that typically conveys focus and emphasis (see Section 5.2.3). Due to the small numbers of nuclear configurations other than L* L%, no inferences about a possible association between LD and tonal choices could be made.

5.1.1.2 *Enumerations*

A total of 62 enumeration statements (i.e. 31 per variety) were collected with situation 1b, in which participants were asked to enumerate the days of the week. Therefore, all IPs consisted of 7 ips. In most cases, no pauses were made between the elements, even though some speakers did separate some elements by a short pause. Usually, it separated the fifth from the sixth element (i.e. working days from the weekend) or the last element from the preceding ones.

Concerning the intonation of the ips, rising patterns were clearly dominant for all but the last element in both varieties. In GS, this was almost exclusively an L* H- nuclear contour (see Figure 5.11). In quite some cases, the boundary tone was somewhat higher on the first and on the sixth element than on the remaining ones. Other contours present in the GS data set were L* L- (15%) and, more rarely, L+H* H- or L+H* L- (approx. 2% and 6%, respectively). The first one of these was used throughout the first five ips by some speakers, whereas others used it more sporadically. The resulting acoustic impression was that of a grouping of the enumerated elements in units of two or three, which gave the utterance a specific rhythm (see Figure 5.12). In an alternative analysis, such groupings might be regarded as single ips. If that were adequate, the low ip boundary tones could be dispensed with. No associations between the LD of the speaker and the use of a specific tune could be found. The last ip of the IP always showed an L* L% nuclear configuration.

In GC, the same contours and patterns were found, and to similar extents, but it is of note that the nature of the pitch accent underlying the final rising gesture — i.e. whether it corresponded to L* or L+H* — was obscured in many cases as three weekdays are words with ultimate stress in Catalan (Cat. *dilluns* 'Monday', *dimarts* 'Tuesday', *dijous* 'Thursday'). In those cases, the more parsimonious label 'L* H-' was used. Still, L+H* H- contours seem to be somewhat more frequent in GC than in GS, occurring on 19% of the non-final ips ending in a penultimate-stress word (i.e. *dimecres* 'Wednesday', *divendres* 'Friday', and *dissabte* 'Saturday'). Both dominance groups used it to the same degree. An example can be seen in Figure 5.13. The last and IP-final ip always showed an L* L% nuclear contour.

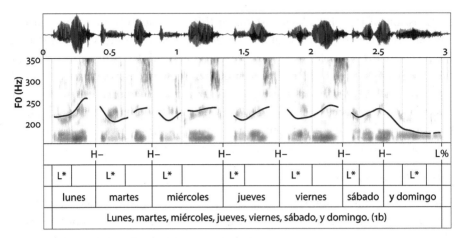

Figure 5.11 Girona Spanish: Waveform, spectrogram, and F0 contour for the enumeration of the days of the week produced by a Catalan-dominant speaker. It consists of an IP containing seven ips. The first six ips show L* H- nuclear contours, whereas the last one is produced with an L* L% nuclear contour. The nuclear configuration of the IP is L* L% (16S3)

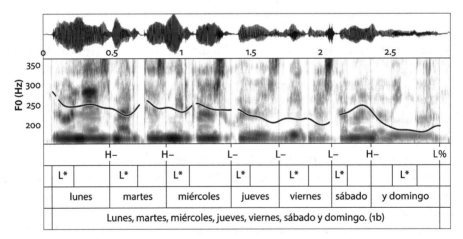

Figure 5.12 Girona Spanish: Waveform, spectrogram, and F0 contour for the enumeration of the days of the week produced by a Spanish-dominant speaker. It consists of an IP containing seven ips. The first six ips show either L* H- or L* L- nuclear contours, the last one is produced with an L* L% nuclear contour. The nuclear configuration of the IP is L* L% (13S3)

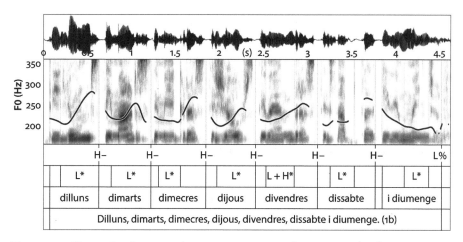

Figure 5.13 Girona Catalan: Waveform, spectrogram, and F0 contour for the enumeration of the days of the week produced by a Catalan-dominant speaker. It consists of an IP containing seven ips. The first six ips show either L* H- or L+H* H- nuclear contours, the last one is produced with an L* L% nuclear contour. The nuclear configuration of the IP is L* L% (25C3)

5.1.1.3 Peripheral elements

Peripheral sentence components — such as dislocations, vocatives, appositions, and other parenthetical elements — usually come along with intonational cues that reflect the fact that they are syntactically independent from the main clause. They form a tonal unit of their own and are separated from the main clause by a tonal inflection, sometimes, together with a pause. In this section, I describe the intonation of different peripheral elements in GS and GC. The phonological status of their nuclear contours will be discussed after the presentation of the intonation of all utterance types in Section 5.2.3.

Dislocations. Even though situation 1c1 of the DCT was originally designed by Prieto and Cabré (2007–2012) for Catalan and by Prieto and Roseano (2009–2013) for Spanish to elicit dislocations, the respondents in this study hardly produced any. Merely 4 GC of their 62 responses contained clear instances of right dislocations. Since all utterances were pragmatically correct responses to the given situation, the interviewer abstained from asking participants to rephrase their answers with a dislocation as this would have implied presenting them with a prephrased sentence and would have been problematical for two reasons: (1) the responses would no longer be spontaneous and (2) their intonation be primed. However, the intonational implementation of GS dislocations will be described in Section 5.1.10.2 on the basis of the corpus of read speech collected for this purpose.

The four GC dislocations recorded as semi-spontaneous responses in the DCT were placed at the right periphery of the sentence. In two cases, a short pause was made between the main clause and the dislocated element. Concerning the intonation of the dislocated element, the nuclear contour of the main sentence was repeated on the dislocated element in all cases (i.e. L* L% or L+H* L%; see Figures 5.14 and 5.15). In the second example, the use of the L+H* L% nuclear contour might add a nuance of exclamativity (see Section 5.1.2.2 for the use of this nuclear configuration in exclamative statements).

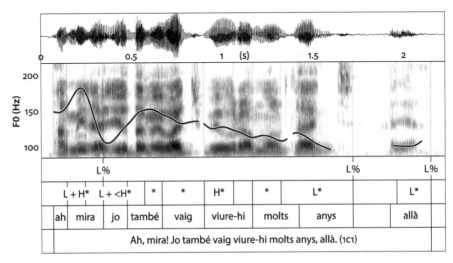

Figure 5.14 Girona Catalan: Waveform, spectrogram, and F0 contour for the statement *Jo també vaig viure-hi molts anys, allà!* 'I have lived there for many years, too' produced by a Spanish-dominant speaker. The dislocated element *allà* is phrased in a separate IP after the main clause. Its nuclear contour repeats the nuclear contour of the main clause, i.e. L* L% (9C4)

Vocatives. From a total of 62 utterances obtained with situation 1c2, 31 GC and 29 GS sentences contained a vocative as a peripheral element, which in all but one cases was placed at the beginning of the utterance. In both varieties, the main clauses were either statements (e.g. Sp. *Salgo un momento a merendar.* 'I'm going out for a snack') or, less frequently, imperatives (e.g. Cat. *Queda't aquí!* 'Stay here') followed by such a statement. The intonation of main clauses corresponded to the ones described for neutral statements (in 5.1.1.1) and imperatives (in 5.1.8), i.e. they showed prenuclear L+<H* pitch accents, followed by nuclear L* L% or H+L* L%, respectively.

The peripheral vocatives were phrased in separate IPs but usually no pause was made between the vocative and the main clause. Similar to vocatives in free

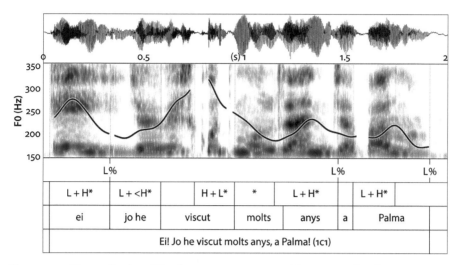

Figure 5.15 Girona Catalan: Waveform, spectrogram, and F0 contour for the statement *Jo he viscut molts anys, a Palma!* 'I have lived in Palma for many years!' produced by a Catalan-dominant speaker. The dislocated element *a Palma* is phrased in a separate IP after the main clause. Its nuclear contour repeats the nuclear contour of the main clause, i.e. L+H* L% (15C4)

vocative sentences (see Section 5.1.9), none presented prenuclear stressed syllables and almost all carried L+H* nuclear pitch accents. The main difference to free vocatives was the absence of lengthening in the post-nuclear, i.e. the phrase-final syllable. This also had an effect on the boundary tones. Whereas HL% is clearly dominant in free vocatives, this boundary tone was only found in roughly a quarter of the peripheral vocatives produced in here (see Figure 5.16 for an example). Instead, the final fall was usually more abrupt: i.e. L+H* L% was clearly the most common nuclear contour in this context (see Figure 5.17 for an example). Finally, some few cases of L+H* H% and of short versions of the 'vocative chant' L+H* !H% were found.

Furthermore, it is interesting to note that peripheral vocatives in opposition to dislocations never copied the tune of the main sentence, nor showed a compressed pitch range as compared to the main clause. An exception to this were two GC utterance-initial vocatives as well as the single instance of a phrase-final peripheral vocative (GS), whose nuclear configurations can best be described as L+!H* L%, if not even as L* L%.

Parenthetical elements. Situation 1c3 of the DCT was originally designed by Prieto and Roseano (2009–2013) for Castilian Spanish (CS) to elicit sentences containing parenthetical elements, i.e. according to Astruc (2003: 16), constituents that are syntactically independent from the main clause and pronounced in a sep-

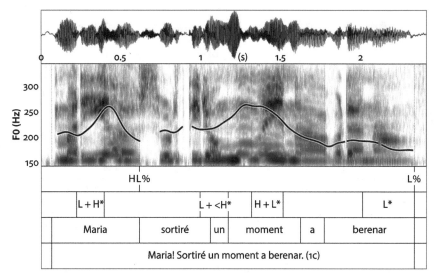

Figure 5.16 Girona Catalan: Waveform, spectrogram, and F0 contour for the peripheral vocative *Maria!* 'Maria!' produced by a Spanish-dominant speaker. It represents an IP consisting of an L+H* nuclear accent, and an HL% boundary tone (8C5)

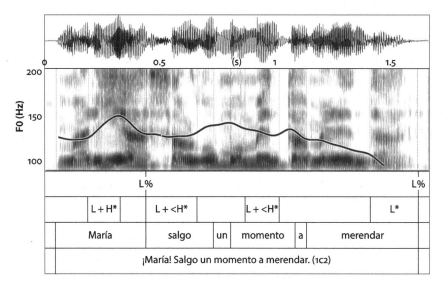

Figure 5.17 Girona Spanish: Waveform, spectrogram, and F0 contour for the peripheral vocative *¡María!* 'María!' produced by a Catalan-dominant speaker. It represents an IP consisting of an L+H* nuclear accent, and an L% boundary tone (18S5)

arate tonal unit, which is detached from the main clause by a pause. The situation is repeated here for convenience (see Appendix for the Catalan-language version).

(1) **Situation 1c3: Parenthetical elements**
Spanish: "Estás enfermo y esta mañana tuviste que ir al médico. Di que has ido a pesar de la lluvia."
'You are ill and this morning you had to go to the doctor. Say that you went despite the rain.'
Possible/expected responses: Esta mañana, a pesar de la lluvia, he ido al médico.
'This morning, despite the rain, I went to the doctor.'

Out of the utterances recorded with this situation, 27 GS and 27 GC utterances contained parenthetical elements. Concessive subordinate clauses (e.g. Sp. *aunque estaba lloviendo* 'although it was raining') and prepositional phrases (e.g. Cat. *tot i la pluja* 'despite the rain') were the most frequent types of parenthetical elements. Only in one case was the response phrased in the same way in the exemplary response in (1) (see Figure 5.18). It was realized with an L+<H* prenuclear pitch accent and an L+H* H- nuclear configuration. The remainder of the recorded utterances did not represent parenthetical elements *strictu sensu*, because they were not inserted into the main clause of the utterance or enclosed by the main clause and another peripheral element as in the example. Rather, they were attached at a peripheral sentence position, i.e. before or after the main clause (each with equal frequency and in both languages considered). Since the position in the sentence has a clear impact on the intonation of parenthetical elements, I shall describe the two cases separately.

When placed before the main clause (15 GS and 11 GC cases), the prenuclei of the parenthetical elements usually displayed either L+<H* pitch accents or were pitch-deaccented. Concerning their nuclear configuration, L+H* H-, with a final continuation rise, was most frequent (53% in GS, $n=8$; 64% in GC, $n=7$). Figure 5.19 provides an example. In some cases, the same pitch accent was combined with a sustained pitch (i.e. L+H* !H-). Furthermore, L* H- was observed to an extent of 40% in GS ($n=6$; see Figure 5.20 for an example), whereas in GC only two cases were registered (18%). This, however, might be an effect of the presence of some ultimate-stress words in nuclear position in the Catalan data (such as *plovent* 'raining' or *molt* 'a lot'), where it could not be decided whether the underlying nuclear contour is L* H- or L+H* H-, and the latter one was labelled due to its higher overall frequency. The corresponding main clauses typically showed the intonation of declarative statements, i.e. prenuclear L+<H* or pitch deaccentuation and an L* L% nuclear configuration.

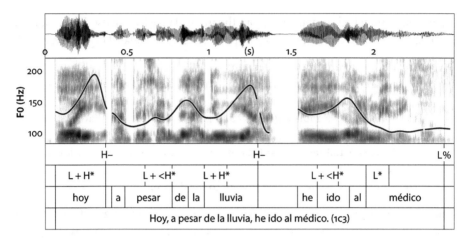

Figure 5.18 Girona Spanish: Waveform, spectrogram, and F0 contour for the parenthetic element *a pesar de la lluvia* 'despite the rain' produced by a Catalan-dominant speaker. It represents an ip consisting of an L+<H* prenuclear accent, an L+H* nuclear accent, and an H- boundary tone (17S6)

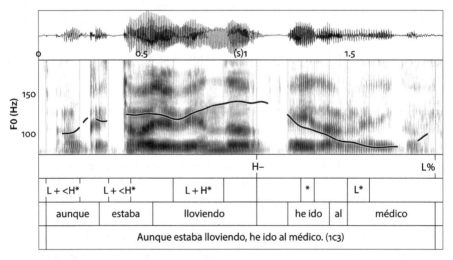

Figure 5.19 Girona Spanish: Waveform, spectrogram, and F0 contour for the parenthetic element *aunque estaba lloviendo* 'although it was raining' produced by a Spanish-dominant speaker. It represents an ip consisting of two L+<H* prenuclear accents, an L+H* nuclear accent, and an H- boundary tone (7S6)

When the parenthetic elements were placed after the main clause (11 GC and 16 GS cases), the distribution of intonation patterns was practically inverse to the aforementioned case: i.e. independently of the variety, the main clause typically ended in nuclear configuration with continuation rise or sustained pitch, whereas

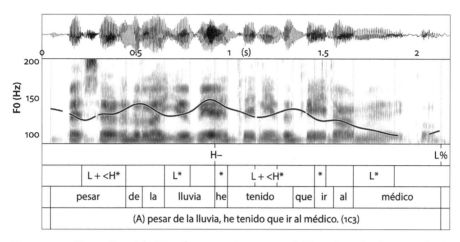

Figure 5.20 Girona Spanish: Waveform, spectrogram, and F0 contour for the parenthetic element *a pesar de la lluvia* 'despite the rain' produced by a Spanish-dominant speaker. It represents an ip consisting of an L+<H* prenuclear accent, an L* nuclear accent, and an H- boundary tone (34S6)

the peripheral elements presented prenuclear deaccentuation and a final L* L% nuclear contour (see Figure 5.21 for an example). Interestingly, here too, the use of the L* pitch accent in the first ip (instead of L+H*) was more common in GS (5 out of 11 instances, i.e. 45%, as opposed to 5 out of 16, i.e. 31%, in GC). In this case, stress patterns had no influence, since all Catalan main clauses ended in the penultimate stress word *metge* 'doctor'.

To sum up, the order of main clause and peripheral elements does not seem to make a big difference for the intonation of the complete utterance. Whereas the first element typically ends in a rising nuclear configuration, the second part always ends in a low nuclear contour. Yet, the chance of encountering pitch deaccentuation in the prenucleus of the second phrase might be higher when it is a peripheral element. Furthermore, the use of L* instead of L+H* as nuclear pitch accent of the first unit seems to be somewhat more common in Spanish (though the difference between the languages does not reach statistical significance: $\chi^2(1) = 0.939$, $p = 0.333$). Finally, the speaker's LD does not seem to have an influence neither on the phrasing of the sentence nor on the choice of pitch accents and boundary tones. All attested types of tunes were produced in very similar proportions by both dominance groups.

Appositions. Similar to the case of dislocations, not all of the 62 utterances elicited with situation 1c4 (31 per variety) contained appositions as was desired (for the scenario see Appendix). Even though all responses were pragmatically adequate, many participants used different strategies to convey the intended

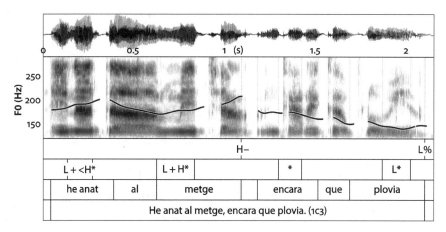

Figure 5.21 Girona Catalan: Waveform, spectrogram, and F0 contour for the parenthetic element *enc*a*ra que plo*v*ia* 'although it was raining' produced by a Catalan-dominant speaker. It represents an ip consisting of an L* nuclear accent and an L% boundary tone (10C6)

meaning (e.g. contrastive-focus accents on the adjective in phrases such as *la Marina morena* 'the dark-haired Marina'). Eventually, 14 appositions could be analysed for GS and 6 for GC. Whereas 9 and 3 of these, respectively, consisted of an article and a specified noun or a (nominalized) adjective (e.g. Sp. *(Marina,) la chica del pelo castaño* '(Marina,) the girl with the brown hair' or Cat. *(Marina,) la morena* 'the dark-haired'), the remainder were appositions in a broader sense, i.e. consisting of the definite article followed directly by a relative clause or a prepositional phrase (e.g. Sp. *(Marina,) la del pelo oscuro* 'the one with dark hair' or Cat. *(Marina,) la que és morena* 'the one who has brown hair'). All appositions were placed at the end of a declarative statement, i.e. at its right periphery.

Concerning their intonation, the appositions replicated the nuclear contour of the main clause of the statement they belonged to, i.e. L* L%, in most cases (see Figure 5.22). Besides that, some sporadic instances of nuclear (L+)H* L% (in GS) and H+L* L% (in GC) were found. These, too, were replications of the nuclear contour of the corresponding main clause. I assume that they express focus, given that these contours typically convey focus in other utterance types (see Section 5.1.2.1). If present, prenuclear stressed syllables were either pitch-deaccented or a compressed version of L+<H* was used (see Figure 5.23). Due to the scarcity of the data and since both languages behave in the same way, no differences related to the LD of the speakers could be established.

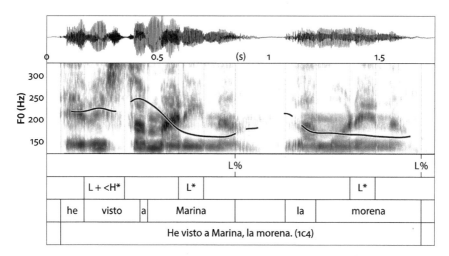

Figure 5.22 Girona Spanish: Waveform, spectrogram, and F0 contour for the apposition *la morena* 'the dark-haired' placed at the end of a declarative statement and produced by a Spanish-dominant speaker. It represents an ip consisting of an L* nuclear accent and an L% boundary tone (19S7)

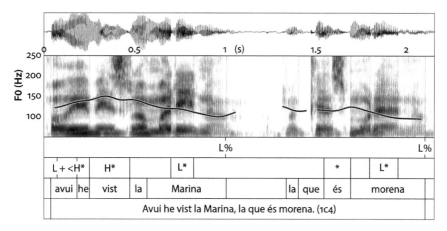

Figure 5.23 Girona Catalan: Waveform, spectrogram, and F0 contour for the apposition *la que és morena* 'the one who is dark-haired' placed at the end of a declarative statement and produced by a Catalan-dominant speaker. It represents an ip consisting of an L* nuclear accent and an L% boundary tone (34C7)

5.1.2 Biased statements

In this section, I describe the intonational properties of the contrastive-focus, exclamative, contradiction, and dubitative statements in my corpus by presenting the phonetic realization of prenuclear pitch accents and nuclear configurations. Their phonological status will be discussed after the description of the tonal realization of all sentence types considered in Sections 5.2.

5.1.2.1 *Contrastive-focus statements*

From the 62 contrastive-focus statements obtained with situation 1d, 30 GS and 28 GC statements could be retained for a tonal analysis (see also Table 4.19; 4 utterances were excluded due to disfluencies and very strong affection by creaky voice). Concerning their phrasing, most contrastive-focus statements were either of the (S)VO type, such as Sp. *Yo quiero naranjas.* 'I want oranges', or formulated as cleft-sentences (e.g. Cat. *El que vull són taronges.* 'It's oranges I want'). In many cases, they were preceded or followed by a further IP containing Sp. *no (quiero) limones* or Cat. *no (vull) llimones* 'not lemons/I don't want lemons'.

As in neutral SVO declarative statements, the most recurrent prenuclear pitch accent was by far L+<H* in both languages (see Figures 5.24). It accounted for 75% of the 28 ip-initial prenuclear pitch accents occurring in GS and for 56% of the 16 GC ones. Additionally, the GC data set contained 6 cases of ip-initial deaccentuation (in cleft sentences). In stress clashes such as *vull taronges*[171] 'I want oranges', L+<H* typically surfaced as L+H* (38%, *n*=6, only in GC; see Figure 5.25). Phrase-medial prenuclear positions equally carried L+<H* or were pitch-deaccented (more rarely).

Nuclear contours of contrastive-focus statements come in two flavours in the two varieties under consideration: L+H* L% (i.e. rising–falling) and L* L% (i.e. low) (see Figures 5.24 and 5.25, above). Each of these tunes was found in roughly half of the utterances in both languages and presented different surface variants. While L* L% can also surface as a fall (i.e. H+L* L%) when it is preceded by a pitch accent with a high target (see Section 5.1.1 for the same pattern in neutral declarative statements), L+H* L% does not always appear as a clear rise, either. Rather, it often surfaces as a kind of 'step' that interrupts the F0 fall between the high target of a prenuclear pitch accent and the final low boundary tone. This can be seen in Figure 5.26, where this nuclear contour is (superficially) labelled as '¡L+H* L%' (following Henriksen/García-Amaya 2012: 122f.; see also Section 5.2.3 for a discussion).

---

[171]. *Vull taronges* is usually pronounced as [ˈbuʎ.ˈtrɔɲ.ʒəs] in Girona, dropping the schwa of what would otherwise be the first syllable of *taronges* (see Veny/Massanell 2015: 143).

Chapter 5. Results 181

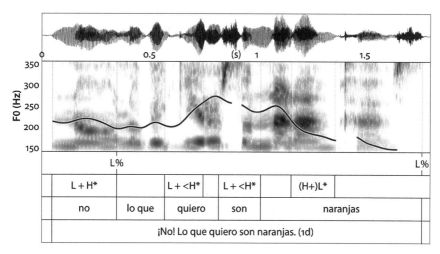

Figure 5.24 Girona Spanish: Waveform, spectrogram, and F0 contour for the contrastive-focus statement *Lo que quiero son naranjas.* 'It is oranges I want.' produced by a Catalan-dominant speaker. It represents an IP composed of one ip and is produced with two L+<H* prenuclear accents, an L* nuclear accent, and an L% boundary tone. The nuclear configuration of the IP is L* L% (14S8)

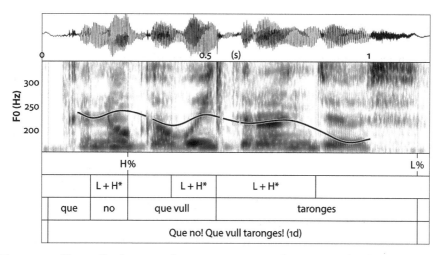

Figure 5.25 Girona Catalan: Waveform, spectrogram, and F0 contour for the contrastive-focus statement *Que vull taronges.* 'I want oranges.' produced by a Catalan-dominant speaker. It represents an IP composed of one ip and is produced with an L+H* prenuclear accent, an L+H* nuclear accent, and an L% boundary tone. The nuclear configuration of the IP is L+H* L% (15C8)

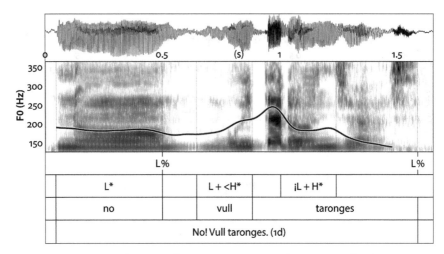

Figure 5.26 Girona Catalan: Waveform, spectrogram, and F0 contour for the contrastive-focus statement _Vull taronges._ 'I want oranges.' produced by a Spanish-dominant speaker. It represents an IP composed of one ip and is produced with an L+<H* prenuclear accent, an H* nuclear accent, and an L% boundary tone. The nuclear configuration of the IP is H* L% (8C8)

While there seems to be no preference for a particular contour by any of the dominance groups, it is likely that the phrasing of the sentence has an influence on pitch accent choice. In GS, for instance, a low nuclear contour is used 16 times, but in 13 of these sentences focus is conveyed morphosyntactically through a cleft structure. As a consequence, there is no need for an additional prosodic marking. Nevertheless, statistical tests did not yield significant associations between the use of cleft structures and pitch-accent choice (GS: $\chi^2(1) = 3.230$, $p = 0.072$; GC: $\chi^2(1) = 0$, $p = 1$). This could, at least in part, be due to the fact that, when rising(–falling) nuclear contours are used, a redundant marking through both syntax and prosody stays perfectly possible: there are 6 GS and 5 GC contrastive-focus statements that contain both a cleft and an (¡)L+H* L% nuclear contour. In total, in 90% of the GS and 71% of the GC contrastive-focus statements, focus is conveyed either through prosodic or syntactic means or both. In the remaining sentences, it needs to be inferred from the contexts. I thus conclude that L+H* L% is the typical prosodic marker of contrastive focus in the varieties of our sample (as opposed to L* L%, which is the typical nuclear contour of neutral declaratives).

5.1.2.2 *Exclamative statements*

A total of 125 utterances were collected with situations 1e1 and 1e2. From these, 63 GS and 55 GC statements could be retained for the intonational analysis. The remainder had to be discarded from the analyses mainly due to hesitation phenomena. As in other statements types, the main prenuclear pitch accent was L+<H* in both languages (see Figure 5.27 for a Spanish example). This accent accounted for 60% of the initial prenuclear accents in GS and for 54% in GC. Two other frequent phrase-initial accents were L*+H and H*, each representing between 13 and 22%. It is worth to point out that H* was usually found on utterance-initial Sp. *qué* and Cat. *quina* 'what (a)' (see Figure 5.28 for an example). Concerning phrase-medial prenuclear positions, L+<H* was equally most common, occurring on roughly 40% of the metrically stressed syllables. Pitch deaccentuation was observed to an extent of approximately 22% in GC and 33% in GS. Other pitch accents, such as L+H*, typically occurred in stress-clash situations, which were frequent (consider, e.g., the Catalan sentence *Mhh, aquest pa fa molt bona olor!* 'This bread smells very good!' with five subsequent underlyingly stressed syllables.

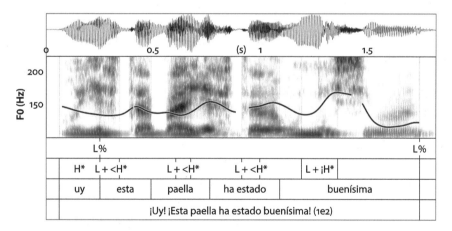

Figure 5.27 Girona Spanish: Waveform, spectrogram, and F0 contour for the exclamative statement *Esta paella ha estado buenísima.* 'This paella has been delicious!' produced by a Spanish-dominant speaker. It represents an IP composed of one ip and is produced with three L+<H* prenuclear accents, an L+¡H* nuclear accent, and an L% boundary tone. The nuclear configuration of the IP is L+¡H* L% (21S12)

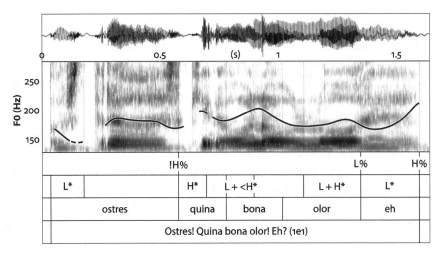

Figure 5.28 Girona Catalan: Waveform, spectrogram, and F0 contour for the exclamative statement *Quina bona olor!* 'What a nice smell!' produced by a Spanish-dominant speaker. It represents an IP composed of one ip and is produced with an ip-initial H* prenuclear accent, a phrase-medial L+<H* prenuclear accent, an L+H* nuclear accent, and an L% boundary tone. The nuclear configuration of the IP is L+H* L% (12C9)

The most typical nuclear configuration in exclamative statements was L+H* L% in both languages, appearing with a proportion of roughly 55%. The pitch accent was occasionally upstepped (yielding L+¡H* L%), which I assume to be a feature reinforcing the exclamatory nature of these sentences. Furthermore, the contour sometimes surfaced as H* L% after preceding high targets. However, the nuclear position of the exclamative statements in the data set evidenced a considerable amount of variation: in 38% of the GC and 28% of the GS utterances, L* L% was used. As this nuclear contour (in combination with prenuclear L+<H*) is also characteristic of neutral declarative statements, it is not immediately clear what additional prosodic cues may be used to distinguish the two pragmatic contexts. One possibility is that a more expanded pitch range in the prenuclear area characterizes the exclamative statements. Examples like the one in Figure 5.29, where all prenuclear pitch accents encompass rises of around 70 Hz or more, suggest that this could be the case. Future work will help to elucidate this issue.

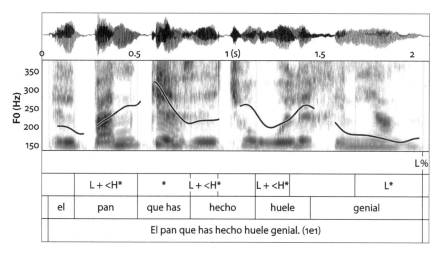

Figure 5.29 Girona Spanish: Waveform, spectrogram, and F0 contour for the exclamative statement *El pan que has hecho huele genial.* 'The bread you have made smells great' produced by a Spanish-dominant speaker. It represents an IP composed of one ip and is produced with an ip-initial L+<H* prenuclear accent, two phrase-medial L+<H* prenuclear accents, an L* nuclear accent, and an L% boundary tone. The nuclear configuration of the IP is L* L% (8S9)

5.1.2.3 *Contradiction statements*

60 contradiction statements (also referred to as 'categorical' or 'contrastive' statements) elicited with situation 1f were included into the intonational analysis (i.e. 30 per variety; see Table 4.19). Concerning prenuclear pitch accents, L+<H* was clearly dominant, both in IP-initial and in phrase-medial positions. It accounted for over two thirds of the prenuclear pitch accents in both varieties (46 out of 56 items in GS, 37 out of 53 in GC; for an example see Figure 5.30, below). The second most common prenuclear pitch accent was L*+H (7 in GS and 9 in GC). Other pitch accent types, such as L+H*, or pitch deaccentuation usually occurred in stress clashes or when there was too little space for the F0 to fall between the high target of a preceding pitch accent and the next stressed syllable.

The nuclear contours registered in the two varieties showed quite a lot of variation, but they can be classified as belonging to the same categories in both languages. First, 20% of the GS and 33% of the GS were realized with the low L* L% nuclear configuration (i.e. the same contour as in neutral broad-focus statements). Given that the contradiction meaning seems to be conveyed only by lexical means in these cases, the respective items will be disregarded in the following calculations of usage rates for the other contours attested. Second, the rising–falling circumflex contour L+H* L%, which occasionally surfaced as H* L% or L+H*

HL%, represented 63% of the GS but only 40% of the GC nuclear contours other than L* L% (see Figure 5.30). In GC, a falling pattern, i.e. H+L* L%, was attested slightly more frequently (45%, see Figure 5.31 for an example), but in GS its share only reached 21% (and it was exclusively produced by CatD speakers, see below). Interestingly, this is in line with the fact that H+L* L% has been documented in Central Catalan (CC) but not in Spanish (see Prieto 2002a: 415f., 2013: 22, and Section 3.1.2.2). Last, the pitch accents H+L* and L* could also be followed by an HL% boundary tone: the nuclear configuration H+L* HL% made up 10% of the contours produced in GC, and 8% of the GS ones (see Figure 5.32 for an example); L* HL% was observed in 5% and 8% of the items, respectively. Although the two pitch accents could theoretically represent different surface variants of a single underlying nuclear configuration (and their appearance be conditioned e.g. by preceding tones or by the used pitch range, increased pitch movements expressing stronger degrees of emphasis), I assume that they correspond to different underlying structures, since it was proposed that L* HL% conveys contradictive meaning in CS (Estebas-Vilaplana/Prieto 2010), whereas H+L* HL% was observed in CC (Prieto 2013: 21–22; Prieto et al. 2015: 21–22).

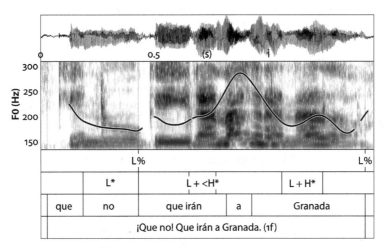

Figure 5.30 Girona Spanish: Waveform, spectrogram, and F0 contour for the contradiction statement *Que irán a Granada.* 'They are going to Granada.' produced by a Catalan-dominant speaker. It represents an IP composed of one ip and is produced with an L+<H* prenuclear accent, an L+H* nuclear accent, and an L% boundary tone. The nuclear configuration of the IP is L+H* L% (15S10)

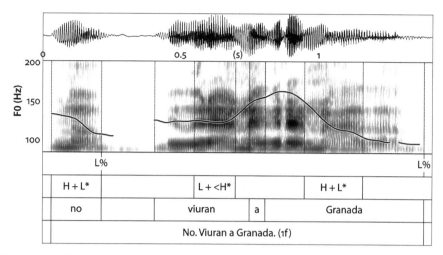

Figure 5.31 Girona Catalan: Waveform, spectrogram, and F0 contour for the contradiction statement *Viuran a Granada*. 'They will be living in Granada.' produced by a Catalan-dominant speaker. It represents an IP composed of one ip and is produced with an L+<H* prenuclear accent, an H+L* nuclear accent, and an L% boundary tone. The nuclear configuration of the IP is H+L* L% (34C10)

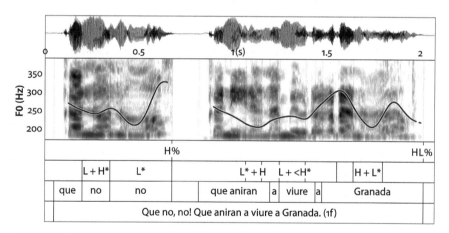

Figure 5.32 Girona Catalan: Waveform, spectrogram, and F0 contour for the contradiction statement *Que aniran a viure a Granada*. 'They are going to live in Granada.' produced by a Spanish-dominant speaker. It represents an IP composed of one ip and is produced with an L*+H and an L+<H* prenuclear accent, an H+L* nuclear accent, and an HL% boundary tone. The nuclear configuration of the IP is H+L* HL% (5C10)

A look into the LD of the producers of all these different patterns is provided in the following table:

Table 5.2 Use of nuclear contours other than L* L% in Girona Spanish and Girona Catalan contrastive statements according to language dominance (percentages and total numbers)

Nuclear contour	Girona Spanish			Girona Catalan		
	CatD	SpD	Total	CatD	SpD	Total
circumflex (L+H* L%)	47% (7)	89% (8)	63% (15)	43% (6)	33% (2)	40% (8)
falling (H+L* L%)	33% (5)	0% (0)	21% (5)	50% (7)	33% (2)	45% (9)
H+L* HL%	13% (2)	0% (0)	8% (2)	7% (1)	17% (1)	10% (2)
L* HL%	7% (1)	11% (1)	8% (2)	0% (0)	17% (1)	5% (1)

It can be seen that the CatD speakers most frequently resorted to the falling pattern in Catalan: H+L* L% accounts for 50% of their productions other than L* L%. As opposed to the SpD speakers, they also used this tune in Spanish (to an extent of 33%). However, in their Spanish production, circumflex contours are somewhat more common, attaining a share of 47%. Furthermore, CatD bilinguals account for 3 out of 4 productions of H+L* HL%. SpD bilinguals, on the other hand, almost exclusively produced circumflex patterns in Spanish (89%) and in Catalan used them with the same frequency as the falling pattern. The other tunes occurred only sporadically in their speech. Although this distribution suggests that falling patterns are more strongly associated with Catalan and/or CatD speakers and that circumflex patterns are more typical of Spanish and/or SpD speakers, statistical tests with respect to this did not reach significance. Even so, considering the fact that shared as well as different tunes were proposed for this utterance type in the literature on Spanish and Catalan intonation (see Table 3.4), it might be no surprise that the Girona bilinguals examined in the present study make use of all of these contours in both of their languages, and it is probable that not all of them have the same inventory of underlying nuclear configurations (in both or either language; see Sections 5.2.3 and 6.4.2 for a more detailed discussion of this topic).

5.1.2.4 Dubitative statements

A total of 63 utterances were recorded with situation 1g, which was designed to elicit dubitative statements. Of these, 1 GS and 5 GC items could not be analysed due to lapsus linguae and hesitation phenomena (see Table 4.19). In both varieties, L+<H* was clearly the dominant prenuclear pitch accent — be it in phrase-initial or phrase-medial position. Yet, in phrase-medial positions pitch deaccentuation attained a higher level in GS (ca 55% vs only 10% in GC).

As concerns nuclear pitch accents, the same inventory was found in both languages: L*, L+H*, and H*. These were followed by low boundary tones (L%) in all but one cases (see below). In GC, the most common nuclear contour, attested in 65% (17 out of 26) of the utterances, was L* L%. It was less common, however, in GS, where it accounted for only 39% of the items (i.e. 12 out of 31; see Figure 5.33). Since the use of this configuration equals the intonation patterns of dubitative statements to those of neutral statements, I assume that the notion of doubt is not expressed by intonation in these cases but by lexical means. Indeed, most of the obtained utterances contained lexical elements expressing doubt or insecurity such as Sp. *quizá(s), a lo major, igual*, Cat. *potser, a lo millor*, all 'maybe' or Cat./Sp. *no sé si* 'I don't know if'. Despite this, the use of rising–falling contours (i.e. L+H* L% or H* L%) seems to be a possibility to differentiate dubitative statements from neutral statements through intonation (see Figures 5.34 and 5.35). Both pitch accents were equally frequent and might represent variants of one common underlying pitch accent (see Section 5.2.3 for a phonological analysis). It is of note, however, that such contours are not unique to dubitative statements but were also observed in contrastive-focus, exclamative, and contradiction statements.

Interestingly enough, no nuclear contours with complex boundary tones of the L+H* LH% type were present in the corpus, even though this is the contour described as typical for this context in Catalan by Prieto (2002a: 416 f.). The only case where a non-low boundary tone was used was a single instance of L+H* HL%, produced in GC.

5.1.3 Neutral polar questions

The following two sections are devoted to the description of the intonational properties of information-seeking yes–no questions with and without peripheral elements and of neutral disjunctive questions. In each case, I will show the realization of prenuclear pitch accents (in both phrase-initial and phrase-medial position) and of nuclear configurations of IPs. Their phonological status will be discussed after depicting the tonal realization of all sentence types considered for the intonational analysis of GS and GC (see Section 5.2).

5.1.3.1 *Information-seeking yes–no questions*

Given that the literature on information-seeking yes–no questions (henceforth IYNQ) in (Castilian) Spanish and (Central) Catalan suggests major intonational and morphosyntactic differences between these two languages, this utterance type represents a site where, in a situation of intense language contact such as the one of Girona, CLI is likely to take place. The most pre-eminent aspect of this cross-

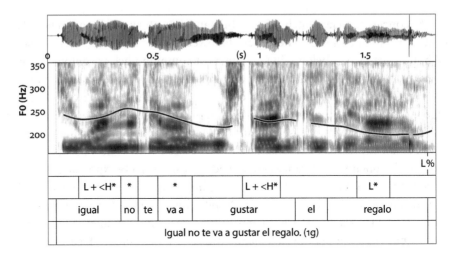

Figure 5.33 Girona Spanish: Waveform, spectrogram, and F0 contour for the dubitative statement *Igual no te va a gustar el regalo.* 'Maybe you won't like the present.' produced by a Catalan-dominant speaker. It represents an IP composed of one ip and is produced with two L+<H* prenuclear accents, two pitch-deaccented prosodic words, an L* nuclear accent, and an L% boundary tone. The nuclear configuration of the IP is L* L% (16S11)

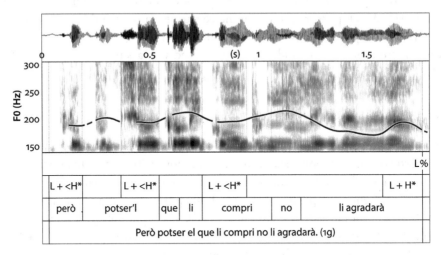

Figure 5.34 Girona Catalan: Waveform, spectrogram, and F0 contour for the dubitative *Però potser el que li compri no li agradarà.* 'Maybe he won't like what I'm going to buy for him' produced by a Catalan-dominant speaker. It represents an IP composed of one ip and is produced with three L+<H* prenuclear accents, an L+H* nuclear accent, and an L% boundary tone. The nuclear configuration of the IP is L+H* L% (24C11)

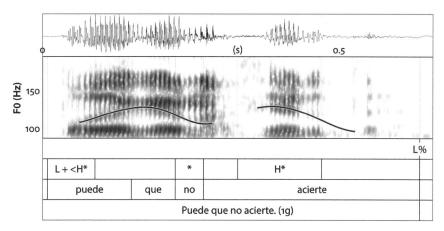

Figure 5.35 Girona Spanish: Waveform, spectrogram, and F0 contour for the dubitative statement *Puede que no acierte*. 'I may not get it right.' produced by a Spanish-dominant speaker. It represents an IP composed of one ip and is produced with an L+<H* prenuclear accent, an H* nuclear accent, and an L% boundary tone. The nuclear configuration of the IP is H* L% (9S11)

linguistic variation concerns the use of the sentence-initial interrogative particle *que*. Optional in Catalan, it is excluded in non-contact varieties of Spanish but has been sporadically documented in CCS (see Section 2.3). While it is known that it appears hand in hand with a high–falling intonation pattern in Catalan, relatively little is known about the intonation of yes–no questions headed by this particle in CCS. Besides, like statements, yes–no questions are known to contain more dislocations in Catalan than in Spanish (see, e.g., Feldhausen/Villalba 2020: 259, and Section 2.3). The present subchapter will therefore draw special attention to the presence and intonation of dislocated elements. A further question that, to my best knowledge, has remained entirely unaddressed to date is whether LD has any influence on the realization of IYNQ in Spanish–Catalan bilinguals (e.g. on the use of the particle *que*, dislocations, or on the choice of intonation patterns). IYNQ are thus of particular interest to the present study. For this reason, their analysis is grounded on a somewhat larger database than that of other utterance types, such that five different DCT scenarios were used for the elicitation of questions of this type.

The current subsection is structured as follows: I will first give an overview of the five scenarios of the DCT and the responses that were obtained with them, focusing, in a first step, primarily on their syntax (i.e. on the presence of the sentence-initial interrogative particle *que* and on peripheral elements; 5.1.3.1.1). I will then provide detailed descriptions of the intonational properties of questions with and without *que* (5.1.3.1.2 and 5.1.3.1.3) and portray the intonation of peripheral elements in yes–no questions consisting of more than one tonal unit (5.1.3.1.4), before discussing, eventually, possible effects of the speakers' LD (5.1.3.1.5). A short résumé will summarize the findings (5.1.3.1.6).

5.1.3.1.1 *Overview of the analysed neutral yes–no questions*
The DCT used in the current study comprised a total of five scenarios designed for the elicitation of IYNQ (2a1–2a3, 2b1, and 2b2, see Appendix). While situation 2a1 was expected to yield rather short questions, consisting of only two prosodic words (and, in consequence, of one prenuclear and one nuclear pitch accent), the responses gathered with situations 2a2 and 2a3 should be somewhat longer and contain at least one phrase-internal prenuclear pitch accent. 2a3 was devised furthermore with the aim of generating questions ending in the antepenultimate-stress word Sp. *filóloga*/Cat. *filòloga* 'philologist'. A greater distance between the last stressed syllable and the end of the phrase allows for a better disentanglement of the nuclear pitch accent and the boundary tone of the respective IP and hence facilitates the concise identification of the underlying tonal representation of the nuclear configurations used in IYNQ. Situations 2b1 and 2b2, finally, should produce IYNQ of more than one tonal unit, i.e. questions containing peripheral elements such as dislocations.

From the 310 IYNQ recorded by means of these DCT situations (i.e. 5 scenarios × 31 speakers × 2 languages), 306 were suitable for an intonational analysis. Although some of these (rather few) contained minor disfluency phenomena such as slight lengthenings, it was not necessary to discard them from the analysis seeing that they nonetheless fit into the picture drawn by the remaining sentences.

As expected, the five DCT scenarios yielded IYNQ of different length and syntactic constituency. Table 5.3 summarizes how many of the responses analysed from each scenario contained the interrogative particle *que* and how many contained peripheral elements. A distinction is made between peripheral elements that must 'obligatorily' be placed outside the root sentence (e.g. appositions and the adverbial adjuncts Sp. *por favor* and Cat. *si us plau* 'please') and those that are 'optionally' placed in a peripheral sentence position such as dislocated subjects, objects, or adverbs. The rationale behind this is that only the number of 'optional' peripheral elements can show whether a particular speaker group, context, or variety is more inclined to divide up the main clause of yes–no questions into more than one tonal unit. By contrast, the use of elements that must (or virtually always do) appear in a separate tonal unit, such as the set phrase Sp. *por favor*, is less telling in this respect.

It can be seen from the table that both *que*-questions and peripheral elements are present only in a minority of the recorded IYNQ. Yet, both phenomena are noticeably more common in GC than in GS, where their occurrence can be con-

Table 5.3 Numbers and proportions of yes–no questions headed by *que* and containing peripheral elements in Girona Spanish and Girona Catalan

Scenario	Girona Spanish			Girona Catalan		
	Total number	Headed by *que*	Peripheral elements || Total number	Headed by *que*	Peripheral elements	
			Optional	Obligatory			Optional	Obligatory
2a1	31	2 (6.5%)	0 (0%)	1 (3%)	31	12 (39%)	3 (10%)	0 (0%)
2a2	32	0 (0%)	1 (3%)	5 (15%)	31	2 (6.5%)	0 (0%)	9 (28%)
2a3	30	0 (0%)	2 (13%)	2 (13%)	30	3 (10%)	4 (13%)	4 (13%)
2b1	30	4 (13%)	1 (3%)	1 (3%)	29	20 (69%)	15 (52%)	1 (3%)
2b2	31	1 (3%)	1 (3%)	0 (0%)	30	8 (26%)	4 (13%)	0 (0%)
total	154	7 (4.5%)	5 (3%)	9 (6%)	152	46 (30%)	26 (17%)	14 (9%)

sidered rather marginal (4.5% for *que*-questions and 3% for optional peripheral elements). Furthermore, neither showed up to the same extent across all contexts, which indicates that some might favour them while others could repel them. For instance, yes–no questions headed by *que* seem to be preferred with rather short questions (scenarios 1a2, 2b1, 2b2), containing only two lexical-stress words. Still, at least in GC, they are not completely impossible with longer sentences (situations 2a2, 2a3). In what follows, I therefore describe the wording of the responses obtained with each scenario in some more detail.

The interrogatives collected with situation **2a1** were often preceded by a greeting (such as Sp. *¡Hola!* 'Hello!') or an excuse (such as Sp. *¡Perdón!* or Cat. *Perdona!* 'Excuse me!') that was considered an apart IP and thus excluded from the intonational analysis of the yes–no question. The interrogatives themselves virtually always combined nothing more than an inflected form of the verb Sp. *tener* or Cat. *tenir* 'to have' and the object Sp. *mandarinas*/Cat. *mandarines* 'tangerines', and hence bore two pitch accents: i.e. one IP-initial prenuclear accent and one nuclear accent. Peripheral elements, phrased in a separate IP after the main clause, were found in one GS and three GC sentences (i.e. the politeness formula Sp. *por favor* 'please' and right-dislocated Cat. *aquí* 'here').

Roughly half of the utterances obtained with situation **2a2** were preceded by vocatives, by imperatives such as Sp. *¡Oye!* 'Listen!' or Sp./Cat. *(¡)Perdona!* 'Excuse me!', or different formulas expressing an apology (e.g. Sp. *¡Perdón!* 'Sorry!'). These elements were considered as separate IPs and excluded from the intonational analyses of IYNQ. The same holds true for some elements following the interrogative clause, such as the politeness formulae Sp. *por favor* and Cat. *si us plau* 'please', as well as for follow-up sentences giving an explanation for the reason of the question (e.g. *Es que tengo prisa y no puedo.* '[It's just that] I am in a hurry and can't [do it]'). The main interrogatives almost exclusively (i.e. to an extent of 94%) consisted of a conjugated form of the modal verb Sp./Cat *poder* 'can' and an infinitive (i.e. Sp. *llevar* and Cat. *portar* or *dur* '(to) take'). Given that they generally continued with Sp. *a mi hermano al campo de fútbol* and Cat. *el meu germà al camp de futbol* 'my brother to the football pitch', the resulting sentences usually contained at least four prosodic words (see Appendix).

The questions from **2a3** generally began with a verb in the perfect tense (e.g. Sp./Cat *has hablado/parlat* 'have you spoken') accompanied by a following (or sometimes preceding) *ya/ja* 'already'. Two thirds of the sentences ended, as desired, with the antepenultimate-stress word *filóloga/filòloga* 'philologist'. In two cases per variety, this nominal constituted an apposition to *vecina/veïna* 'neighbour' and was phrased in a separate IP.

The responses gathered with scenario **2b1** again typically began with a greeting (such as Cat. *Hola!* 'Hello!') or an apology (such as Sp. *¡Perdón!* or Cat. *Perdoneu!* 'Excuse me!'), which were considered as prosodically independent from the IYNQ. The questions themselves were formulated as follows: in Spanish, they for the most part combined the verb form *ha llegado* 'has arrived', preceded or followed by the adverb *ya* 'already', and the subject *María*. As opposed to that, most interrogatives in Catalan were introduced by the particle *que* (69%, see Table 5.3, above) and in the majority of cases used the verb *ésser-hi* or, less frequently, *haver-hi*, both loosely translatable as '(to) be there'. Similar to Spanish, the subject *la Maria* was usually postverbal, but it was frequently phrased in a separate prosodic unit, i.e. as is typical in Catalan *que*-questions (see Section 3.2), it was dislocated from the main clause of the interrogative to a peripheral position at the end of the sentence. In consequence, 55% of the GC interrogatives collected with 2b1 contained the intended peripheral element, whereas this was only the case in 7% of the GS items.

As for the interrogatives obtained via situation **2b2**, only very few contained the desired peripheral elements, although the scenarios were originally devised by Cabré/Prieto (2007–2012) for CC and by Prieto/Roseano (2009–2013) for CS with the purpose of eliciting such. Instead, the responses typically consisted of the verb form Sp./Cat. *has visto/vist* 'have you seen', directly followed by the direct object Sp. *a Maria* and Cat. *(a)*[172] *la Maria*. However, there were four dislocated elements in GC and one in GS. Besides, as in other contexts, many sentences were

---

172. Although the differential marking of the direct object with *a* is proscribed by Catalan prescriptive norms in this context (see Fabra 1918: § 112; Sancho Cremades 2002: 1737; GEIEC 2018: § 14.4.2), it was present in roughly half of the sentences. Interestingly, this was proportionally more often the case in the Spanish-dominant speaker group (5 out of 9 items vs 9 out of 19 in the Catalan-dominant group).

again preceded by greetings or apologies, and some were succeeded by declaratives explaining the reason of the question.

In what follows, I will first describe the intonation of the most common type of interrogative in the corpus, namely of questions without *que* (5.1.3.1.2), and then, in a second step, turn to the scarcer case of questions with *que* (5.1.3.1.3). In both sections, I will initially portray the most representative realizations of prenuclear and nuclear pitch accents and of boundary tones, and then turn to other, less frequent patterns. Finally, I will depict the intonation of peripheral elements, i.e. mainly of dislocations, in questions consisting of more than one tonal unit (5.1.3.1.4). Possible effects of LD on the syntactic and intonational choices will be discussed in a separate section after the presentation of the intonational analysis (5.1.3.1.5).

5.1.3.1.2 *Intonation of information-seeking yes–no questions without que*
The vast majority of the IYNQ without *que* in the corpus show the final rising or 'low–rise' pitch pattern typically described for this question type in much of the literature on (Castilian) Spanish and Catalan intonation (e.g. Hualde/Prieto 2015: 372; Prieto et al. 2015: 23; see also Section 3.1.2.2). In GS, this was the case of 138 out of 147 questions without *que* (i.e. 94%); in GC, 98 out of 106 followed this pattern (i.e. 92%). The present subsection is thus structured in the following way: in a first step, the 'low–rise' intonation pattern will be shortly explained with a few simple examples of (short) yes–no questions. Then, I shall describe the realization of phrase-initial prenuclear pitch accents, phrase-medial pitch accents, and nuclear contours in some more detail. Eventually, I will address some other intonational contours sometimes found in yes–no questions without *que* (representing 6% and 8%, respectively).

The archetypal 'low–rise' pattern consists of an L*+H prenuclear pitch accent and a low–rising nuclear contour. The nuclear pitch accent is L*, i.e. the F0 performs a low plateau during the duration of the nuclear syllable. It is followed by a high boundary tone, for which different labels, such as 'H%', 'HH%', '¡H%', exist in the literature (see Section 3.1.2.2). I will portray the phonetic implementation of this rise in more detail below, but already at this point it is worth pointing out that it was labelled either as 'H%' or as '¡H%' following phonetic criteria. More precisely, the solution with the upstep was adopted whenever the final rise exceeded the hight of a preceding high target present in the prenucleus. The phonological status of the upstep in the nuclear contour of this pattern will be discussed in Section 5.2.3. Figure 5.36. and Figure 5.37 provide two prototypical examples of the contour in GS and GC, respectively.

As advanced above, the first **prenuclear** pitch accent belonging to the 'low–rise' pitch contour in GS and GC IYNQ without *que* used to be of the L*+H type, i.e. a low plateau within the limits of the stressed syllable they are associated with, followed by a pitch rise in the following, unstressed syllable (see

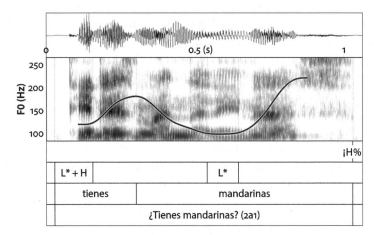

Figure 5.36 Girona Spanish: Waveform, spectrogram, and F0 contour for the neutral information-seeking yes–no question ¿*Tienes mandarinas?* 'Do you have tangerines?' produced by a Catalan-dominant speaker. It represents an IP composed of one ip and is produced with an IP-initial L*+H prenuclear accent, an L* nuclear accent, and an ¡H% boundary tone. The nuclear configuration of the IP is L* ¡H% (17S13)

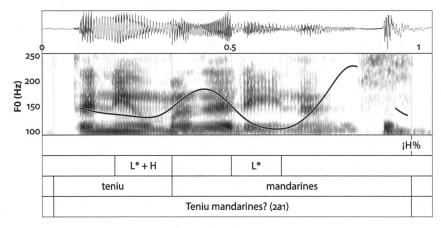

Figure 5.37 Girona Catalan: Waveform, spectrogram, and F0 contour for the neutral information-seeking yes–no question *Teniu mandarines?* 'Do you have tangerines?' produced by a Catalan-dominant speaker. It represents an IP composed of one ip and is produced with an IP-initial L*+H prenuclear accent, an L* nuclear accent, and an ¡H% boundary tone. The nuclear configuration of the IP is L* ¡H% (34C13)

Section 3.1.2.1). The label refers primarily to the overall low–rising shape of the pitch contour in the present data set and does not permit to draw firm conclusions about the absolute surface pitch height, since the initial plateau is often situated clearly over the speaker's baseline and can be considerably higher than the low target of the nuclear L* pitch accent, which is typically the lowest point of the respective IPs. For instance, in the question shown in Figure 5.38, the lowest point of the IP-initial L*+H pitch accent is 27 Hz (4.7 semitones) higher than the lowest point of the nuclear L* pitch accent.

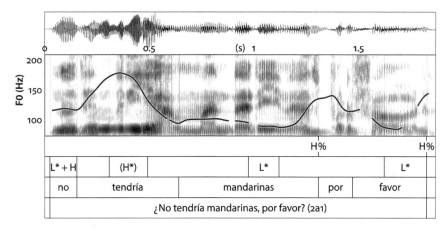

Figure 5.38 Girona Spanish: Waveform, spectrogram, and F0 contour for the neutral information-seeking yes–no question ¿*No tendría mandarinas, por favor?* 'Wouldn't you have some tangerines, please?' produced by a Catalan-dominant speaker. It is composed of two IPs. The first one contains an IP-initial prenuclear L*+H accent, an H* phrase-internal prenuclear accent,[173] an L* nuclear accent, and an H% boundary tone. The nuclear configuration of the IP is L* H%. This nuclear pattern is repeated on the adverbial in the second IP (23S13)

Furthermore, it warrants mention that the low target of the initial L*+H accent did not always surface in form of a level plateau. In some cases, a gentle fall was observed instead. This was frequently the case when the IP began with various unstressed syllables or was preceded by another IP ending in a high boundary tone (for some examples see, e.g., Figures 5.44, 45, 48, or 52, below).

As for the second part of this pitch accent, i.e. the pitch rise originating from the high trailing tone ('+H'), it generally starts right at the beginning of the syllable following the stressed one. Nevertheless, there is some variation as to where it

---

173. Bracketed pitch-accent labels indicate that the F0 contour visible within the limits of a metrically strong syllable is not the surface reflex of an underlying pitch accent carried by that syllable but instead that it results from interpolation between preceding and following tonal targets (and sometimes declination). The bracketed label should therefore be regarded merely as a phonetic description of the surface F0 gesture, while I assume the respective syllable to be underlyingly pitch-deaccented. As will be shown and discussed extensively later on, actually most instances of phrase-medial prenuclear pitch accents are pitch-deaccented in this utterance types.

begins exactly. Sometimes it stars already towards the end of the lexically stressed syllable and sometimes only right at the middle of the following, unstressed syllable. This could be influenced (at least in part) by the segments that appear in the coda and/or in the onset of these syllables. Regarding the peak of this pitch accent, most descriptions and schematic representations (see Section 3.1.2.1) suggest that it is reached within the unstressed syllable following the stressed one. Interestingly, this was the case only in a minority of the items in the present data set. Table 5.4 shows in which of the post-tonic syllables the F0 contour attained the nearest local maximum for all responses from situations 2a1, 2a2, and 2a3 beginning with an L*+H pitch accent.

Table 5.4 Position of the pitch peak of IP-initial L*+H prenuclear pitch accents in information-seeking yes–no questions (percentages and total numbers of items)

Number of post-tonic syllable	1st	2nd	3rd or beyond	Total number
Girona Spanish	22% (18)	63% (50)	14% (11)	79
Girona Catalan	38% (27)	55% (39)	7% (5)	71

As can be seen from the table, the peak is most frequently situated in the second post-tonic syllable rather than in the syllable directly following the stressed one (see, for instance, Figure 5.39 or Figure 5.43, below). Nevertheless, it can also be situated in that syllable or, with a lower probability, as far to the right as in the third post-tonic syllable or beyond (see Figure 5.40, for an example). Sometimes, as e.g. in Figure 5.39, the peak coincides with a subsequent metrically strong syllable of the utterance. In such cases, it would intuitively be considered part of the surface realization of the pitch accent associated with that syllable. This problem will be dealt with below, when the form of the pitch contour in phrase-medial positions is addressed.

Aside from the phrase-initial L*+H pitch accents, the data set contained some cases of phrase-initial underlyingly stressed syllables within the limits of which the F0 already began to rise gently before it followed the typical course of the 'low–rising pattern'. These were labelled as delayed peaks (L+<H*; see Figure 5.41 for an example), but I consider them surface variants of an underlying L*+H pitch accent. In addition, there were some isolated cases of phrase-initial high tones (H*) in contours that otherwise corresponded to the 'low–rise' (see the example in Figure 5.42). I equally interpret these as surface realizations or allotones of the L*+H pitch accent.

As concerns the location of pitch accents, the Autosegmental-Metrical model posits that they associate to stressed syllables (see Section 3.1.1.1). Phrase-initial L*+H prenuclear pitch accents should thus be aligned with the first metrically

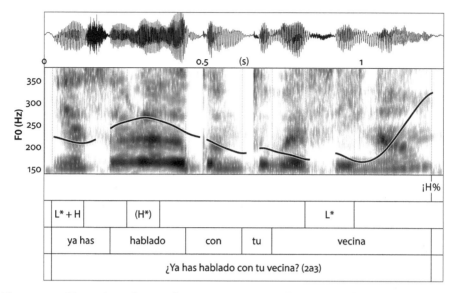

Figure 5.39 Girona Spanish: Waveform, spectrogram, and F0 contour for the neutral information-seeking yes–no question ¿*Ya has hablado con tu vecina?* 'Have you already spoken to your neighbour?' produced by a Catalan-dominant speaker. It represents an IP composed of one ip and is produced with an IP-initial L*+H prenuclear accent, associated to the adverb *ya* 'already' that is merged into one syllable with the following auxiliary (*has* 'you have'), a phrase-medial pitch-deaccented syllable (see Fn. 173), an L* nuclear accent, and a high boundary tone (¡H%). The nuclear configuration is L* ¡H% (14S15)

strong syllable of the ip containing the yes–no interrogative. However, this first stressed syllable was not always the one one might expect at first sight in the present corpus. For instance, while most sentences uttered in context 2a1 and 2a2 began with a simple verb form in the present or conditional tense, the sentences recorded with the contexts 2a3, 2b1, and 2b2 generally began with a compound verb form in the present perfect. Such complex verbs, consisting of a monosyllabic auxiliary, such as Sp./Cat. *has* 'you have', in conjunction with a past participle (here mostly *hablado/parlat* 'spoken'), generally tend to be realized as one prosodic word. In consequence, they bear only one pitch accent that is associated with the morphologically stressed syllable of the participle, leaving the auxiliary pitch-deaccented. In some (Central) Catalan dialects, auxiliaries can be even affected by vowel reduction (see Bonet 2002:986; Wheeler 2005:278; GEIEC 2018:§3.2.2). Interestingly, this was not the case in the present set of IYNQ. In the responses to situation 2a3, 2b1, and 2b2, the IP-initial prenuclear L*+H accent regularly associated with the auxiliaries (e.g. Sp./Cat. *has* or Cat. *vas*) whenever they appeared in the first position of the sentence. Figure 5.43 illustrates this.

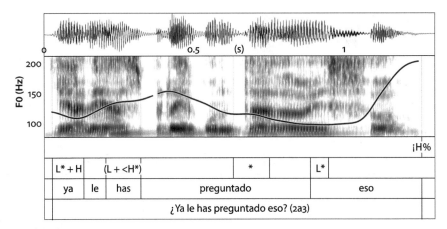

Figure 5.40 Girona Spanish: Waveform, spectrogram, and F0 contour for the neutral information-seeking yes–no question ¿*Ya le has preguntado eso?* 'Have you already asked her about that?' produced by a Catalan-dominant speaker. It represents an IP composed of one ip and is produced with an IP-initial L*+H prenuclear accent, various phrase-medial pitch-deaccented syllables (see Fn. 173), an L* nuclear accent, and a high boundary tone (¡H%). The nuclear configuration is L* ¡H% (18S15)

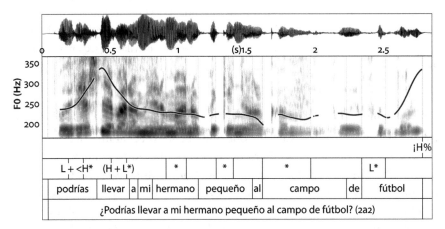

Figure 5.41 Girona Spanish: Waveform, spectrogram, and F0 contour for the neutral information-seeking yes–no question ¿*Podrías llevar a mi hermano pequeño al fútbol?* 'Could you take my little brother to the football (training)?' produced by a Catalan-dominant speaker. It represents an IP composed of one ip and is produced with an IP-initial L+<H* prenuclear accent, several instances of phrase-medial pitch deaccentuation (see Fn. 173), an L* nuclear accent, and a high boundary tone (¡H%). The nuclear configuration is L* ¡H% (16S14)

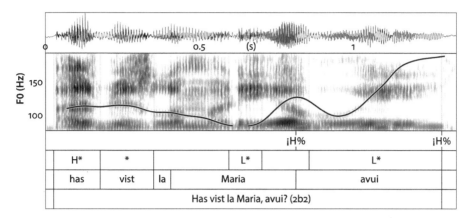

Figure 5.42 Girona Catalan: Waveform, spectrogram, and F0 contour for the neutral information-seeking yes–no question *Has vist la Maria, avui?* 'Have you seen Maria today' produced by a Catalan-dominant speaker. It represents an IP composed of two IPs. The first ip consists of an IP-initial prenuclear H* accent, an L* nuclear accent, and a high boundary tone (¡H%). The second IP shows an L* ¡H% nuclear configuration. The nuclear configuration of the main clause of the question is L* ¡H% (29C17)

When the auxiliary was preceded by an adverb such as Sp. *ya* or Cat. *ja* 'already', it was, of course, the lexically stressed syllable of the adverb that bore the pitch accent. Yet, in many cases, *ya* or *ja* and the following *has* were merged and pronounced as one single syllable (i.e. [ˈjas] in Spanish and [ˈʒas] in Catalan), which then carried the pitch accent (8 cases per variety). This can be seen in Figure 5.39, above, where the initial stressed syllable is only [ja] since the coda /s/ of *(ya) has* is resyllabified into the onset of the following syllable.

Furthermore, in the example in Figure 5.38, L*+H is anchored on the negation particle Sp. *no*. Like auxiliaries, this element can be unstressed (or rather its underlying stress may not be phonetically realized), when it appears in preverbal position, where it can cliticize to the conjugated verb and, in some Catalan dialects, may even suffer vowel reduction (see DCVB, s.v. *no*). As opposed to that, the corpus contains 5 instances (3 in GS, 2 in GC), where it occurs preverbally and bears the phrase-initial L*+H pitch accent. A Catalan example is shown in Figure 5.44.

Finally, the data set contains one case where IP-initial prenuclear L*+H was deployed on a direct object proclitic (13S14). However, this single instance must be treated very carefully since, first, it was produced by a SpD speaker of Honduran origin who — as we shall see — sometimes behaves differently from the rest of the participants and, second, since there are various counterexamples in our

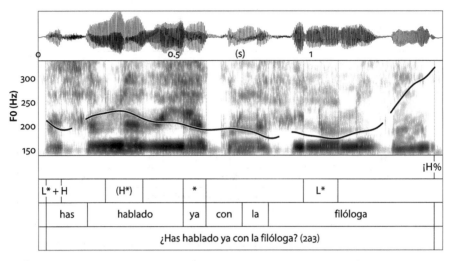

Figure 5.43 Girona Spanish: Waveform, spectrogram, and F0 contour for the neutral information-seeking yes–no question *¿Has hablado ya con la filóloga?* 'Have you already spoken to the philologist?' produced by a Catalan-dominant speaker. It represents an IP composed of one ip and is produced with an IP-initial L*+H prenuclear accent associated to the auxiliary *has* 'you have', various instances of phrase-medial pitch deaccentuation (see Fn. 173), an L* nuclear accent, and a high boundary tone (¡H%). The nuclear configuration is L* ¡H% (24S15)

corpus where IP-initial proclitics are left pitch-unaccented and the L*+H contour associates with the stressed syllable of the ensuing finite verb.

Be that as it may, the present data very strongly suggest that GS and GC IYNQ (without *que*) typically begin with an L*+H pitch accent that associates with the first stressed syllable of the utterance. More precisely, the pitch gesture is anchored as far to the left as possible, which implies that it cannot solely be borne by metrically strong syllables of lexical words but also by grammatical words such as auxiliaries and negation particles, which may appear unstressed in other contexts (e.g. in declarative statements). As discussed below, in Fn. 177, there may be grammatical reasons for this.

Let us now turn to the **phrase-medial** portion of the prenucleus. According to most of the academic literature, this question type should figure L*+H prenuclear pitch accents on all or most metrically stressed syllables of the prenuclear area, even though the possibility of phrase-internal deaccentuation has sometimes beenmentioned (e.g. by Hualde/Prieto 2015; Kireva 2016a: 121). Yet, the present corpus rather suggests that deaccentuation is actually the default case: consistent phrase-medial pitch deaccentuation appeared even in very long questions, and

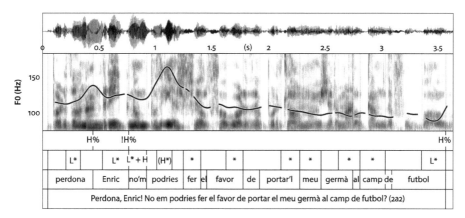

Figure 5.44 Girona Catalan: Waveform, spectrogram, and F0 contour for the neutral information-seeking yes–no question *No em podries fer el favor de portar el meu germà al camp de futbol?* 'Could't you do me the favour of taking my brother to the football pitch?' produced by a Catalan-dominant speaker. It represents an IP composed of one ip and is produced with an IP-initial L*+H prenuclear accent, various instances of phrase-medial pitch deaccentuation (see Fn. 173), an L* nuclear accent, and an H% boundary tone. The nuclear configuration of the IP is L* H% (23C14)

the few sentence-medial pitch accents observed could possibly be associated with some kind of focus or emphasis (see below).

A prototypical realization of the 'long' yes–no questions collected with situations 2a2 and 2a3 is depicted in Figure 5.45. It begins with an IP-initial L*+H pitch accent on *puedes* 'can you', that attains its peak close to the end of the second posttonic syllable (i.e. on the first syllable *llevar* 'take'). After that peak, the F0 drops, showing a falling gesture within the limits of the stressed syllable of *llevar* (which was therefore given the superficial label 'H+L*'). Then, the F0 contour stays low and does not show any further excursions until the last syllable of the sentence where it abruptly rises to its highest point. The phrase-medial part of the utterance is thus clearly pitch-deaccented. The nuclear syllable, finally, is pronounced with a low and flat contour (L*). Some similar Spanish examples can be seen in Figures 5.41 and 5.43, above.

Also in the GC data set, the phrase-initial prenuclear L*+H pitch accent was not repeated on each metrically strong syllable and utterance-internal parts were clearly characterized by pitch deaccentuation in the vast majority of cases. Figure 5.46 provides a typical example: the initial L*+H accent placed on the modal verb *pots* 'can you' attains its peak at the beginning of the second posttonic syllable, i.e. on the metrically strong syllable of *portar* 'take'. This syllable was labelled superficially with an H* pitch accent, but we will later on see that it

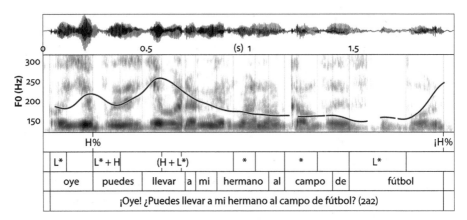

Figure 5.45 Girona Spanish: Waveform, spectrogram, and F0 contour for the neutral information-seeking yes–no question ¿*Puedes llevar a mi hermano al campo de fútbol?* 'Can you take my brother to the football pitch?' produced by a Catalan-dominant speaker. It represents an IP composed of one ip and is produced with an IP-initial L*+H prenuclear accent, several instances of phrase-medial pitch deaccentuation (see Fn. 173), an L* nuclear accent, and an ¡H% boundary tone. The nuclear configuration of the IP is L* ¡H% (12S14)

is actually pitch-deaccented. After that peak, the F0 drops down to the bottom of the speaker's range, stays low and does not show any further excursions until the last syllable of the sentence where it abruptly rises to its highest point. The nuclear syllable is pronounced with a continuous pitch rise that I interpret as an L* ¡H% nuclear contour. A similar example can be appreciated in Figure 5.44, above.

Although pitch deaccentuation is clearly the rule in the prenucleus from the third metrically stressed syllable onwards, it is necessary to have a closer look at the pitch movements that take place within the limits of its **second** metrically stressed syllable, i.e. in the first phrase-internal prenuclear syllable. Always being preceded by the same IP-initial L*+H accent, these syllables presented a surprisingly large amount of tonal variation. At first sight, the array of pitch movements detected in this position encompasses virtually all pitch accents traditionally proposed for the analysis of Spanish and Catalan intonation: i.e. the contours found in the two languages could be (superficially) described as high (H*), falling (H+L*), low (L*), or rising (L+H* or L+<H*). Finally, there were also some instances of L*+H, which, however, are likely to represent a different case (see below). The exact numbers and percentages are given in Table 5.5:

Despite the fact that H* and H+L* represent almost 80% of the instances, there is no clear preference for a particular pitch accent in this position. Instead, the nature of the pitch movement that takes place within or in the proximity of

Chapter 5. Results 205

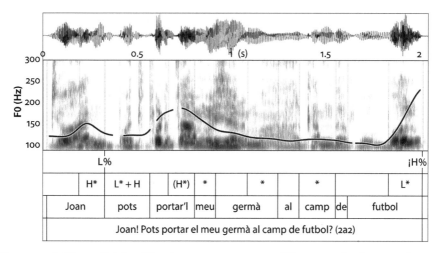

Figure 5.46 Girona Catalan: Waveform, spectrogram, and F0 contour for the neutral information-seeking yes–no question *Pots portar el meu germà al camp de futbol?* 'Can you take my brother to the football pitch?' produced by a Catalan-dominant speaker. It represents an IP composed of one ip and is produced with an IP-initial L*+H prenuclear accent, several instances of phrase-medial pitch deaccentuation (see Fn. 173), an L* nuclear accent, and an ¡H% boundary tone. The nuclear configuration of the IP is L* ¡H% (17C14)

Table 5.5 Shapes of the F0 in the context of the second stressed prenuclear syllable in Girona Spanish and Girona Catalan information-seeking yes–no questions beginning with L*+H

Shape of the F0	H*	H+L*	L*	L+H*	L+<H*	L*+H	Total
Girona Spanish	48% (44)	28% (26)	2% (2)	7% (6)	8% (7)	8% (7)	92
Girona Catalan	37% (22)	40% (24)	2% (1)	7% (4)	7% (4)	8% (5)	60

the second prenuclear stressed syllable seems to depend primarily on the distance between this syllable and the first stressed syllable, which carries the L*+H pitch accent. Seen from the perspective of the rise of this phrase-initial accent, the following cases can be distinguished:

- The IP-initial prenuclear L*+H attains its peak within the limits of the second prenuclear metrically stressed syllable, where the F0 thus takes the form of an H* pitch accent. This is overall the most frequent case (see Figure 5.39, 44, 46, above, and 5.57, below).
- The peak of L*+H is attained already before the beginning of the second prenuclear underlyingly stressed syllable, such that the F0 falls within the limits of this syllable (possibly due to 'common' declination; see 3.1.1.1). The pitch

contour thus looks like an H+L* pitch accent (see Figure 5.45, above, and 5.47, below).[174]
- The pitch has already fallen after the peak of the IP-initial L*+H pitch accent and is low during the second prenuclear underlyingly stressed syllable, i.e. it looks as if this syllable bore an L* pitch accent (see Figures 5.48 and 5.49, below).
- The peak of L*+H is not yet attained, and pitch is still rising within the limits of the second prenuclear metrically stressed syllable, which hence looks as if it were realized with an L+H* or L+<H* pitch accent (see Figure 5.50 and 5.51,[175] below).

As illustrated in the four scenarios above, which pitch movements are realized on the first phrase-internal metrically stressed syllable depends mainly on the position of the peak of the preceding L*+H pitch accents, which can be located within, before, or after this syllable as a function of the distance between the first and the second stressed syllable of the phrase. In consequence, the resulting variety in (superficial) pitch accent labels for the second stressed syllable of the prenucleus (see Table 5.5) should not be explained by positing one specific underlying pitch accent for this position but rather by assuming the absence of such an underlying category, i.e. by positing deaccentuation. This means that any rising or high pitch gestures found within the limits of this syllable are in reality part of the rise of the IP-initial L*+H pitch accent, whose peak extends to the right and can thus cause pitch movements within the limits of other metrically stressed syllables.

Apart from the fact that this would explain the large amount of variation attested, several other arguments further support this analysis. Most importantly, over 80% of the remaining Spanish and even over 90% of the remaining Catalan phrase-internal prenuclear syllables are also clearly pitch-deaccented. This is to say that, from the third stressed syllable until the nuclear syllable, deaccentuation

---

174. Similar-looking contours have sometimes been explained in terms of a conditioned surface variant of an underlying rising prenuclear pitch accent. For instance, Kireva (2016a: 121) argues that the occurrence of H+L* in this position (e.g. in her example in Kireva 2016: 128) is provoked by the preceding rising pitch accent that has its peak in an adjacent syllable and thus by the lack of "sufficient segmental material to realize another rising pitch accent". Although this line of reasoning could be used to account for the example in Figure 5.45, this would not appear very convincing in Figure 5.47, where more segmental material is available between the phrase-initial and the first phrase-medial stressed syllables. Furthermore, the pitch fall on the latter is not particularly steep (which would be expected if there were an underlying high and low target).
175. Although the presence of a stress clash hampers pitch-accent identification in this case, the beginning of the pitch contour in Figure 5.51 could also be interpreted as a surface realization of a phrase-initial L* accent followed by a delayed peak (L+<H*). However, the offered interpretation is in line with the remaining examples of this section.

Chapter 5. Results   207

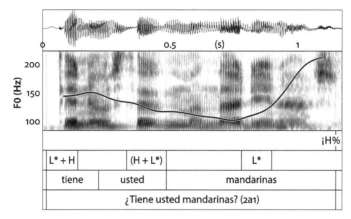

Figure 5.47 Girona Spanish: Waveform, spectrogram, and F0 contour for the neutral information-seeking yes–no question ¿*Tiene usted mandarinas?* 'Do you have tangerines?' produced by a Catalan-dominant speaker. It represents an IP composed of one ip and is produced with an IP-initial L*+H prenuclear accent, a phrase-medial pitch-deaccented syllable (see Fn. 173), an L* nuclear accent, and an ¡H% boundary tone. The nuclear configuration of the IP is L* ¡H% (11S13)

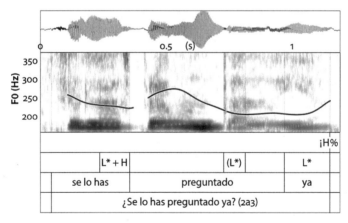

Figure 5.48 Girona Spanish: Waveform, spectrogram, and F0 contour for the neutral information-seeking yes–no question ¿*Se lo has preguntado ya?* 'Have you already asked her?' produced by a Catalan-dominant speaker. It represents an IP composed of one ip and is produced with an IP-initial L*+H prenuclear accent, placed on the auxiliary *has*, a phrase-medial pitch-deaccented syllable (see Fn. 173), an L* nuclear accent, and an H% boundary tone. The nuclear configuration of the IP is L* H% (31S14)

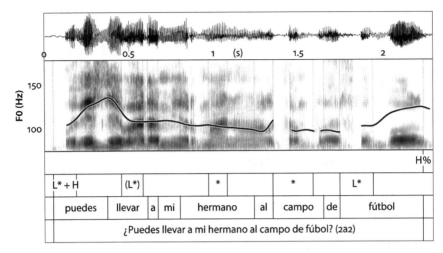

Figure 5.49 Girona Spanish: Waveform, spectrogram, and F0 contour for the neutral information-seeking yes–no question *¿Puedes llevar a mi hermano al campo de fútbol?* 'Can you take my brother to the football pitch?' produced by a Catalan-dominant speaker. It represents an IP composed of one ip and is produced with an IP-initial L*+H prenuclear accent, several instances of phrase-medial pitch deaccentuation (see Fn. 173), an L* nuclear accent, and an H% boundary tone. The nuclear configuration of the IP is L* H% (29S14)

is unmistakeably the norm in this type of GS and GC IYNQ: as can be seen in numerous examples (e.g. in Figures 5.40, 41, 43–46, 49, 50), IP-medial positions are almost invariably realized as low plateaus and do not show any pitch excursions.

Further evidence comes from two examples in which the combination of initial L*+H and the absence of a separate pitch accent on the following stressed syllable make the F0 look (and sound) as if a stress shift had taken place. In Figure 5.52, the strong rise in the first syllable of the word *preguntado* 'asked' and the rather flat pitch movement in its underlyingly stressed syllable give the impression that stress was shifted to the word's first syllable (*preguntado*) that would then bear an L+<H* with a delayed peak (indicated in square brackets). The same holds true for the question shown in Figure 5.48, above. In both cases, however, the pitch contours can be explained more convincingly by assuming not stress shifts but an IP-initial L*+H pitch accent, located on the auxiliary, and subsequent deaccentuation of the following metrically stressed syllable.

A further argument is delivered by a sentence containing a hesitational lengthening of the last syllable of the word *importa* '(it) is important (to)', whose metrically strong syllable bears the initial L*+H accent (see Figure 5.53). In this example, the hesitation causes the pitch drop down almost to the speaker's bottom line. When he goes on with his sentence, no other pitch excursion can be observed

Chapter 5. Results   209

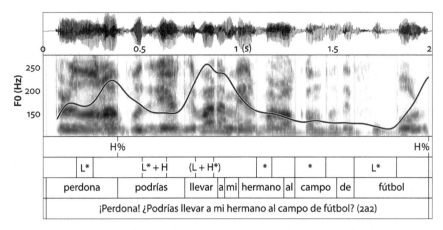

Figure 5.50 Girona Spanish: Waveform, spectrogram, and F0 contour for the neutral information-seeking yes–no question ¿*Podrías llevar a mi hermano al campo de fútbol?* 'Could you take my brother to the football pitch?' produced by a Catalan-dominant speaker. It represents an IP composed of one ip and is produced with an IP-initial L*+ H prenuclear accent, several instances of phrase-medial pitch deaccentuation (see Fn. 173), an L* nuclear accent, and a H% boundary tone. The nuclear configuration of the IP is L* H% (6S14)

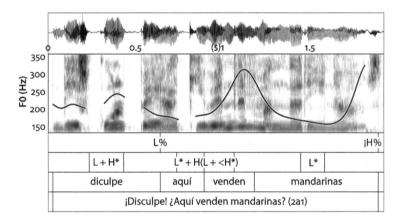

Figure 5.51 Girona Spanish: Waveform, spectrogram, and F0 contour for the neutral information-seeking yes–no question ¿*Aquí venden mandarinas?* 'Do you sell tangerines here?' produced by a Spanish-dominant speaker. It represents an IP composed of one ip and is produced with an IP-initial L*+H prenuclear accent, a phrase-medial pitch-deaccented syllable (see Fn. 173), an L* nuclear accent, and an ¡H% boundary tone. The nuclear configuration of the IP is L* ¡H% (8S13)

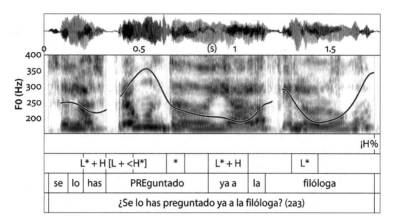

Figure 5.52 Girona Spanish: Waveform, spectrogram, and F0 contour for the neutral information-seeking yes–no question ¿Se lo *has* pregun*ta*do *ya* a la fi*ló*loga? 'Have you already asked the philologist about it?' produced by a Catalan-dominant speaker. It represents an IP composed of one ip and is produced with an IP-initial L*+H prenuclear accent placed on the auxiliary *has*, a pitch-deaccented stressed syllable in *preguntado*, an L*+H phrase-internal prenuclear accent, an L* nuclear accent, and an ¡H% boundary tone. The nuclear configuration of the IP is L* ¡H% (15S15)

until the end of the utterance and all sentence-medial underlyingly stressed syllables are left pitch-deaccented.

To sum up, the previous paragraphs have revealed that GS and GC IYNQ without *que* typically begin with an IP-initial L*+H pitch accent placed on the first 'stressable' syllable of the utterance. As for sentence-medial positions, the data strongly suggest that pitch deaccentuation is the normal case not only from the IP's third stressed syllable onwards but already from its second syllable and that pitch movements within the limits of the latter should be viewed as effects of the phrase-initial pitch accent.

However, before establishing a general model for IYNQ, the few cases in which phrase-internal prenuclear stressed syllables did receive a pitch accent and were not deaccented need to be addressed. In the 'long' questions elicited with situations 2a2 and 2a3, only 9 GC and 17 GS prenuclear pitch accents associated with syllables other than the first or second stressed syllable of the IP were found. Interestingly, the majority of the Catalan items ($n=5$) and a good part of the of the Spanish ones ($n=7$) represented an L*+H contour. The IP-initial pitch accent was thus repeated phrase-internally in these cases. Some Spanish examples can be appreciated in Figure 5.52, above, where L*+H appears on the sentence-medial adverb *ya* 'already', and in Figure 5.54, below, where it surfaces on the stressed overt subject pronoun Sp. *tú* 'you'. A Catalan example, where L*+H equally asso-

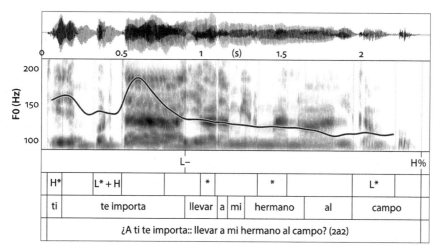

Figure 5.53 Girona Spanish: Waveform, spectrogram, and F0 contour for the neutral information-seeking yes–no question ¿(A) ti te imp_or_ta lle_var_ a mi her_mano_ al c_am_po? 'Do you mind taking my brother to the (football) pitch?' produced by a Spanish-dominant speaker. It represents an IP produced with an IP-initial H* prenuclear accent, a prenuclear L*+H accent, two pitch-deaccented metrically stressed syllables (*), an L* nuclear accent, and an H% boundary tone. The nuclear configuration of the IP is L* H% (21S14)[176]

ciates to the adverb *ja* 'already' is shown in Figure 5.55, below. Since two more among the seven Spanish occurrences of phrase-medial L*+H appeared on *ya* and another one of the Catalan items on Cat. *tu* 'you', the possibility warrants mention that the appearance of this pitch accent in sentence-medial positions of IYNQ may be favoured by elements such as the time adverbs (*ya*) or post-verbal stressed subject pronouns (Sp. *tú*, Cat. *tu*) in the sense that it adds a notion of focus and/or emphasis to them.[177] Nevertheless, such an approach cannot explain why L*+H

---

176. The L- is merely used here to superficially describe to pitch drop that accompanies the hesitational lengthening of the last syllable of *importa*, i.e. it does not indicate a planned prosodic break (see Section 5.2.2). Note furthermore that the high final boundary tone cannot be seen in the graph due to creaky voice.

177. It is worth bringing up at this point that the repetition of the pitch accent could render largely the same function as the morphological marking of such elements with question particles in the languages that possess them (building on the idea that "if a tone has a segmental counterpart in another language, we can conclude that the tone is a morpheme"; Wakefield 2020: 47; see also pp. 202–213 on polar interrogatives). Compare, for instance, Bulgarian ли in Bulg. *Майка ти вече ли иска да бъде баба?* 'Does your mother *already* want to become a grandmother?', where this particle is attached to *вече* 'already', or Turkish *-mİ* in *Merakımı bağışlayın, Yevgeni'm ile çoktan mı tanışıyorsunuz?* 'Excuse my curiosity. Have you already met

was also observed on some nouns and verbs such as Cat. *germà* 'brother' or Sp. *acercar*, since it is rather unlikely that the participants intended to focalize these in their responses. Finally, the remaining pitch accents attested sporadically in this position were mainly (!)H* and H+L*. In most of these cases, the visible F0 contour seemed to be the result of the interaction between the high target of the phrase initial L*+H pitch accent and declination. In accordance with the assumptions made above for phrase-medial positions, they should probably be regarded as pitch-deaccented, too. Having said that, it is evident that the few examples in our data are not enough to make clear inferences about this topic. Therefore, further studies should be carried out in order to investigate the relation between the occurrence of phrase-medial pitch accents and focus in this question type.

The **nucleus** of the IYNQ without *que* that were pronounced with the 'low–rise' intonation pattern — i.e., as shown above, the immense majority of the IYNQ in the present corpus — consistently exhibited a low plateau within the limits of the nuclear-stress syllable (i.e. an L* pitch accent), followed by a pitch rise until the end of the phrase, evoked by a high boundary tone. However, the phonetic realizations of the nuclear contour showed some variation.

Instead of a low plateau, the nuclear syllable sometimes contained a gently falling contour (e.g. in Figures 5.52, above, and 5.55, 5.56, below). Since that solely occurred when the nuclear syllable was located in proximity of a preceding peak (often the one belonging to the initial L*+H pitch accent), it seems to be a conditioned surface variant of L* that is triggered by a preceding high tone and lack of sufficient intervening segmental material for the pitch to descend to a lower level before the beginning of the nuclear syllable (see also Section 5.2.3).

As concerns the final boundary tone, a lot of variation was observed with regard to its height. The realizations were labelled either as ¡H% or as H%. Whereas there has been some controversy about the phonological implications

---

with my Yevgeni?', which makes the adverb *çoktan* 'already' the focus of the question (internet sources; for the use of the particle and information structure in Turkish yes–no questions see Kamali/Büring 2011; Kamali 2015; for Bulgarian see Dukova-Zheleva 2010). L*+H could thus not only represent an intonational means to convey interrogativity in general but constitute a more precise marker of the focus of a polarity question, i.e. it could be the phonological correlate of an abstract interrogative focus operator (see Escandell-Vidal 2017: 237 for a similar proposal). If so, this would explain why it is found on the auxiliary rather than on the lexical verb when the focus of the yes–no question is on the truth value of the full proposition and why, in other cases, it associates with the negation particle (see Escandell-Vidal 1999, 2017 on focus and other semantic and pragmatic aspects of interrogatives in Spanish). The parallel also works in this case: for example, in the Turkish sentence *Bekâr değil misiniz?* 'Are you not single?' the interrogative morpheme *-mİ* follows the negation adverb *değil* 'not'. The same is true for Bulg. *Не ли ти е жално?* 'Are you not sorry?', where the focus of *ли* is on *не* 'not'.

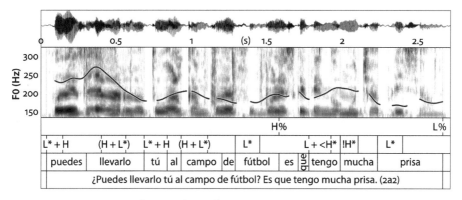

Figure 5.54 Girona Spanish: Waveform, spectrogram, and F0 contour for the neutral information-seeking yes–no question *¿Puedes llevarlo tú al campo de fútbol?* 'Can you take him to the football pitch?' produced by a Catalan-dominant speaker. It represents an IP composed of one ip and is produced with an IP-initial L*+H prenuclear accent, a phrase-medial pitch-deaccented syllable (see Fn. 173), a phrase-internal L*+H prenuclear accent, followed by another case of pitch deaccentuation, an L* nuclear accent, and an H% boundary tone. The nuclear configuration of the IP is L* H% (14S14)

of the scaling of this tone in the literature (see Section 3.1.2.2), I at this point merely aim to describe the realizations found in the corpus at the surface level and will come back to the phonological status of the upstep in Section 5.2.3. The upstepped label '¡H%' was used whenever the height of the IP-final boundary tone exceeded the level of any preceding pitch maximum resulting from a high tonal target within the same ip. According to this criterion, ¡H% was slightly more recurrent than H% in GS, appearing in roughly 57% of the items. On the other hand, ¡H% was observed only in 36% of the GC items.

Several factors may have influenced the height of the final boundary tone. First, there seems to be a connection between the height of the final rise and the stress pattern of the nuclear-stress word. A higher rise, i.e. ¡H%, is favoured with words stressed on the antepenultimate, such as Sp. *filóloga* and Cat. *filòloga* 'philologist', where it can spread over the two post-tonic syllables. In words stressed on the penultimate syllable, such as Sp. *fútbol* 'football', the ascent is generally less acute. Finally, ultimate stress words exhibit the smallest rises, since it needs to be compressed onto the nuclear syllable together with the low L* nuclear pitch accent in that case. In the present data set, this was frequently so with the Catalan ultimate-stress word *futbol* 'football'.[178] In total, ca 80% of

---

178. In three cases, this very word was erroneously mis-stressed and accentuated on the penultimate syllable (like the Spanish cognate *fútbol*). Seeing that these items were produced by Spanish-dominant subjects, this can be interpreted as negative transfer from Spanish.

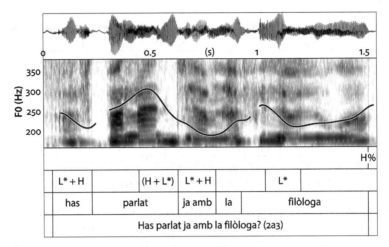

Figure 5.55 Girona Catalan: Waveform, spectrogram, and F0 contour for the neutral information-seeking yes–no question *Has parlat ja amb la filòloga?* 'Have you asked her already?' produced by a Catalan-dominant speaker. It represents an IP composed of one ip and is produced with an IP-initial L*+H prenuclear accent placed on the auxiliary *has*, an instance of phrase-medial pitch deaccentuation (see Fn. 173), an L*+H phrase-internal prenuclear accent on the adverb *ja*, an L* nuclear accent, and an H% boundary tone. The nuclear configuration of the IP is L* H% (31C15)

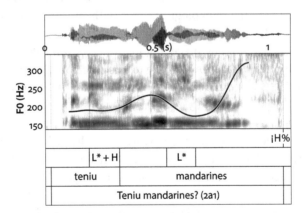

Figure 5.56 Girona Catalan: Waveform, spectrogram, and F0 contour for the neutral information-seeking yes–no question *Teniu mandarines?* 'Do you have tangerines?' produced by a Catalan-dominant speaker. It represents an IP composed of one ip and is produced with an IP-initial L*+H prenuclear accent, an L* nuclear accent, and an ¡H% boundary tone. The nuclear configuration of the IP is L* ¡H% (24C13)

the low–rising nuclear contours on ultimate-stress words in both varieties were labelled as L* H%. In opposition, 75% of the Spanish and 53% of the Catalan antepenultimate-stress words displayed upstepped boundary tones (i.e. ¡H%). In the (most common) case of penultimate stress, both contour types appeared with similar frequencies.

Perhaps even more importantly, the height of the final boundary tone also seems to be influenced by whether the nuclear contour constitutes the end of the utterance or is succeeded by a further IP. The current sample suggests that the presence of a following phrase with no or a very short intervening pause encourages rather low phrasal boundaries. Approximately half of the items labelled as 'L* H%' were followed by another IP (see Figure 5.54), whereas 'L* ¡H%' was found virtually always at the end of the utterance. In the items shown Figures 5.44 and 5.49 following IPs were equally present but could not be included in the graphs for reasons of space. When only utterance-final nuclear contours are taken into account, the abovementioned effects of the stress-patterns become more clear-cut, too. It can thus be concluded that the greater the distance between the low and the high target of the low–rising nuclear contour, the higher the boundary tone.

Finally, utterance length might have an effect on the scaling of the final boundary tone. The longer the IP, the more pitch-deaccented syllables intervene between the IP-initial and the IP-final rises. As the extension of the phrase-medial 'low plateau' — and hence the distance to preceding pitch excursions — increases, the 'need' to produce a high final rise to make it perceptually more salient diminishes. Nonetheless, to determine the exact extent to which each of the mentioned factors (i.e. metrical structure of the prosodic word in nuclear position, total phrase length, and presence of further IPs) influences the scaling of the IP-final boundary tone falls beyond the scope of the present dissertation and must rest a topic for further investigation.

Concerning the alignment and **form of the final rise** in the data set, it generally starts at the left edge of the first post-nuclear syllable and then rises continuously until the end of the phrase — either in a straight or in a slightly sagging way. In words stressed on the antepenultimate syllable, it can occur that the rise does not begin in the first post-tonic but only in the last syllable, or that the slope steepens at the beginning of the last syllable, i.e. that there is a bend or even a jump of the F0 at the onset of the last syllable (see Figure 5.57 for an example). I interpret this finding as an argument in favour of analysing the nuclear contour of this question type underlyingly as a combination of a simple L* nuclear pitch accent followed by a simple high boundary tone and against positing a pitch accent with a high target or a complex boundary tone. If the nuclear pitch accent were, e.g., of the L*+H type, i.e. if it represented a repetition of the pitch accent used in IP-initial position in this sentence type, a steeper rise, beginning immediately after the end of the nuclear syllable, should be expected. Furthermore, the fact that the final rise may start relatively late also speaks against positing a complex boundary tone consisting of two high targets (i.e. HH%), as has been proposed by some authors for CS (see Section 3.1.2.1).

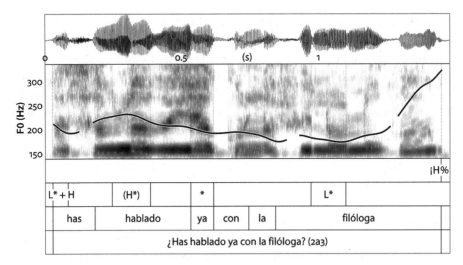

Figure 5.57 Girona Spanish: Waveform, spectrogram, and F0 contour for the neutral information-seeking yes–no question ¿*Has hablado ya con la filóloga?* 'Have you already spoken to the philologist?' produced by a Catalan-dominant speaker. It represents an IP composed of one ip and is produced with an IP-initial L*+H prenuclear accent, various instances of phrase-medial pitch deaccentuation (see Fn. 173), an L* nuclear accent, and a high boundary tone (¡H%). The nuclear configuration is L* ¡H% (24S15)

Although the over 90% of the IYNQ without *que* displayed the 'low–rising contour', described extensively above, there were also some deviating intonational patterns. In what follows, these will be briefly addressed before turning to the IYNQ featuring *que*. In total, 9 GS and 8 GC items (6% and 8%, respectively, of all questions without *que*) are concerned.

Most of these differing items stemmed from the same speaker (No. 13; 4 GS and 2 GC ones). An example is given in Figure 5.58. Whereas one might argue that the initial H* prenuclear pitch accent is triggered by the presence of the immediately preceding high boundary tone, leaving no space for a descent to the low target of the initial L*+H accent, the nuclear configuration of this interrogative is fairly different from the low–rising contour, too. The nuclear stressed syllable is pronounced with a clear fall whose end is attained only at the right edge of this syllable. A low plateau follows in the next, and last, utterance-final syllable whose end is characterized by a LH% boundary tone. For two reasons, this tune cannot convincingly be interpreted as an underlying L* H% contour. First, the preceding pitch accent is three syllables far away. It thus seems very unlikely that it could make a nuclear L* surface as H+L*. Furthermore, the local pitch maximum of the contour is attained only at the beginning of the nuclear syllable. Second, the boundary tone clearly must have a low target, because the first part of the utterance-final syllable contains a well discernible low plateau.

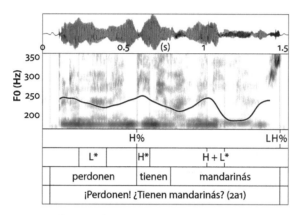

Figure 5.58 Girona Spanish: Waveform, spectrogram, and F0 contour for the neutral information-seeking yes–no question ¿*Tienen mandarinas?* 'Do you have tangerines?' produced by a Spanish-dominant speaker. It represents an IP composed of one ip and is produced with an IP-initial H* prenuclear accent, an H+L* nuclear accent, and an LH% boundary tone. The nuclear configuration of the IP is H+L* LH% (13S13)

The speaker uses this very same nuclear contour, H+L* LH%, in the five other cases again. She typically accompanies it with H+L* prenuclear pitch accents. Figure 5.59 provides a Catalan example.

A possible explanation for the use of this very different contour could be the speaker's origin. Born in Honduras from Honduran parents, she is a clearly SpD speaker and her interrogative intonation might be typical to the variety of Spanish spoken in her country of origin. To my best knowledge, the intonation of Honduran Spanish yes–no questions has not yet been described. However, the same nuclear contour was also observed in other American varieties of Spanish, namely in Paraguayan Spanish (Pešková 2022). Hence, if it were true that it here stems from Honduran Spanish, its use in Catalan would represent a clear case of intonational transfer. Interestingly enough, the speaker employs the same contour again in other types of interrogatives, such as confirmation-seeking and echo yes–no questions, as we shall see further on. Additionally, the same nuclear contour was found two more times in the data set, namely in GC yes–no questions stemming from a slightly CatD speaker (−21.8), whose father comes from Uruguay (see the example in Figure 5.60).

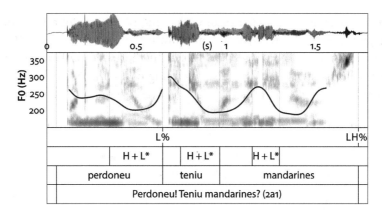

Figure 5.59 Girona Catalan: Waveform, spectrogram, and F0 contour for the neutral information-seeking yes–no question *Teniu mandarines?* 'Do you have tangerines?' produced by a Spanish-dominant speaker. It represents an IP composed of one ip and is produced with an IP-initial H+L* prenuclear accent, an H+L* nuclear accent, and an LH% boundary tone. The nuclear configuration of the IP is H+L* LH% (13C13)

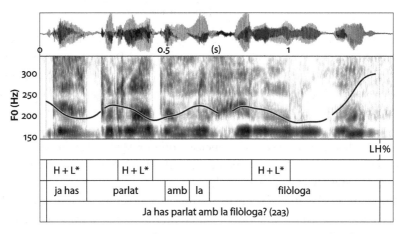

Figure 5.60 Girona Catalan: Waveform, spectrogram, and F0 contour for the neutral information-seeking yes–no question *Ja has parlat amb la filòloga?* 'Do you have tangerines?' produced by a Catalan-dominant speaker. It represents an IP composed of one ip and is produced with two H+L* prenuclear accents, an H+L* nuclear accent, and an LH% boundary tone. The nuclear configuration of the IP is H+L* LH% (24C15)

Another case worth mentioning is that of some items with an L* L% nuclear contour. They pattern with the low–rise contour in showing L*+H in the prenuclear area but lack the utterance-final rise. Since the nuclear contour is identical to the one found in statements, the use of an L*+H prenuclear pitch accent apparently suffices to mark a sentence as a (yes–no) question. The following figures provide some examples.

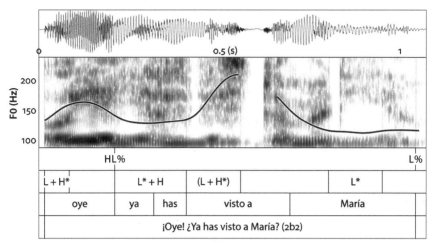

Figure 5.61 Girona Spanish: Waveform, spectrogram, and F0 contour for the neutral information-seeking yes–no question *¿Ya has visto a María?* 'Have you seen María already?' produced by a Spanish-dominant speaker. It represents an IP composed of one ip and is produced with an IP-initial L*+H prenuclear accent, a phrase-medial pitch-deaccented syllable (see Fn. 173), an L* nuclear accent, and an L% boundary tone. The nuclear configuration is L* L% (21S17)

Finally, one further deviating pattern is depicted in Figure 5.63. Here, the pitch contour continually rises from the beginning of the sentence until the last and nuclear syllable. It thus corresponds to a pattern generally referred to as 'high rise contour' in the literature (see Hualde/Prieto 2015: 372 and Fn. 79 in Section 3.1.2.2,), where it is said to be typical to 'quiz questions'.

5.1.3.1.3 *Information-seeking yes–no questions headed by que*

To date, the intonation of *que*-questions has been studied empirically mainly for Catalan. As various studies showed that their intonation follows the so-called 'high–falling' pattern, consisting of a high plateau in the prenuclear area succeeded by a nuclear fall. As for CCS, some authors have impressionistically described this question type as showing the same or similar patterns as the Catalan 'original', which was by and large confirmed by Romera et al. (2007, 2008) on the basis of data from a speaker of Barcelona Spanish (see also Section 2.3). In the present data set, most of the 45 GC and all 7 GS *que*-questions do indeed display this 'high–falling' pattern (see also the overview in Table 5.6, below). However, 13 GC items, i.e. 28% of the *que*-questions recorded in this variety, presented the

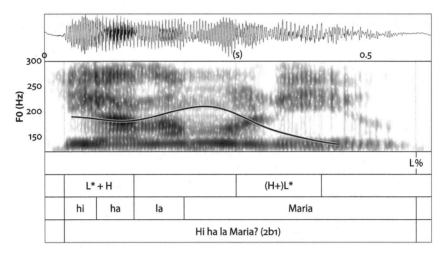

Figure 5.62 Girona Catalan: Waveform, spectrogram, and F0 contour for the neutral information-seeking yes–no question *Hi ha la Maria?* 'Is Maria there?' produced by a Catalan-dominant speaker. It represents an IP composed of one ip and is produced with an IP-initial L*+H prenuclear accent, an L* nuclear accent, and an L% boundary tone. The nuclear configuration is L* L% (10C16)

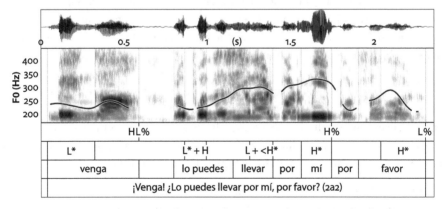

Figure 5.63 Girona Spanish: Waveform, spectrogram, and F0 contour for the neutral information-seeking yes–no question *¿Lo puedes llevar por mí?* 'Can you take him for me?' produced by a Catalan-dominant speaker. It represents an IP composed of one ip and is produced with an IP-initial L*+H prenuclear accent, a phrase-medial L+<H* prenuclear accent, an H* nuclear accent, and an H% boundary tone. The nuclear configuration of the main interrogative is H* H% (28S14)

low–rising contour typical of the questions without *que*. In what follows, I will therefore treat these two cases apart.

In the *que*-questions displaying the iconic 'Catalan' tune, the pitch contour usually began in the highest third of the speakers range and showed a high plateau during the prenucleus. This high and flat contour continued until right before the nuclear syllable within whose limits the pitch fell to the bottom of the speaker's range. Then, the F0 stayed low until the end of the phrase. Two prototypical examples are given in Figure 5.64 (for GC) and Figure 5.65 (for GS). As can be seen, the prenuclear stressed syllable was labelled with an H* pitch accent in both cases and the nuclear contour was characterized as H+L* L%.

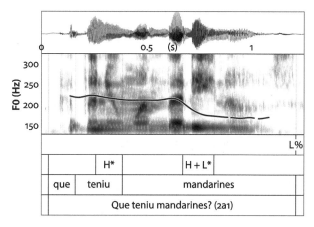

Figure 5.64 Girona Catalan: Waveform, spectrogram, and F0 contour for the neutral information-seeking yes–no question *Que teniu mandarines?* 'Do you have tangerines?' produced by a Catalan-dominant speaker. It represents an IP composed of one ip and is produced with an IP-initial H* prenuclear accent, an H+L* nuclear accent, and an L% boundary tone. The nuclear configuration of the IP is H+L* L% (26C13)

With regard to the beginning of the phrase, it is worth pointing out that the phrase-initial *que* sometimes presented a somewhat deeper pitch as compared to the first stressed syllable, i.e. some questions began with a gentle pitch rise from a mid or mid-to-high level of the speakers range (see Figure 5.66). I take this as an argument for analysing the particle *que* as an underlyingly unstressed proclitic that forms a prosodic unit with the following word. Furthermore, it speaks against assuming a phrase-initial high boundary tone, i.e. %H, as was proposed, e.g., by Romera et al. (2007, 2008).

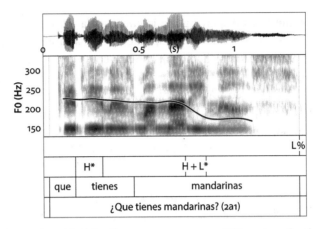

Figure 5.65 Girona Spanish: Waveform, spectrogram, and F0 contour for the neutral information-seeking yes–no question ¿Que *tienes* mandar*i*nas? 'Do you have tangerines?' produced by a Catalan-dominant speaker. It represents an IP composed of one ip and is produced with an IP-initial H* prenuclear accent, an H+L* nuclear accent, and an L% boundary tone. The nuclear configuration of the IP is H+L* L% (19S13)

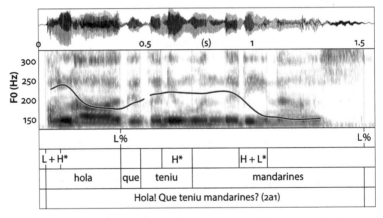

Figure 5.66 Girona Catalan: Waveform, spectrogram, and F0 contour for the neutral information-seeking yes–no question Que te*niu* mandar*i*nes? 'Do you have tangerines?' produced by a Catalan-dominant speaker. It represents an IP composed of one ip and is produced with an IP-initial H* prenuclear accent, an H+L* nuclear accent, and an L% boundary tone. The nuclear configuration of the IP is H+L* L% (12C13)

In 'longer' sentences, i.e. when the prenuclear area consisted of more than one prosodic word, the respective prenuclear stressed syllables usually bore H* pitch accents. The possibility of viewing the absence of any pitch excursions in the phrase-medial part of this question type as an effect of pitch deaccentuation comparable to the one found in questions with the low–rising intonation pattern was discarded: if the respective metrically stressed syllables were pitch-deaccented, there should be an observable effect of regular declination, causing the F0 to display a sagging contour between the phrase-initial prenuclear and the nuclear pitch accent of the IP. Instead, the prenuclear pitch contour stayed continuously at the same level, such that it seems reasonable to assume underlying high targets in this area. Figures 5.67 and 5.68 depicts how this looks like. Note, however, that the sentence in Figure 5.68 consists of two ips.

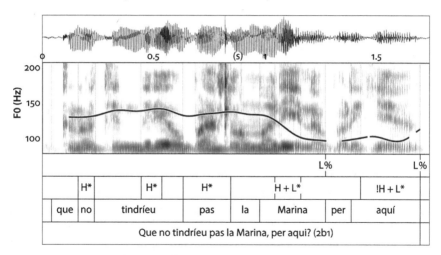

Figure 5.67 Girona Catalan: Waveform, spectrogram, and F0 contour for the neutral information-seeking yes–no question *Que no tindríeu pas la Marina, per aquí?* 'Don't you have Marina here?' produced by a Catalan-dominant speaker. It represents an IP composed of one ip and is produced with an IP-initial H* prenuclear accent, two phrase-internal H* prenuclear accents, an H+L* nuclear accent, and an L% boundary tone. The nuclear configuration of the IP is H+L* L% (28C15)

As mentioned above, the GC data set also contained 13 interrogatives headed by *que* which were pronounced with the intonational pattern typical of yes–no questions without *que*: i.e. the 'low–rising' contour described extensively in Section 5.1.3.1.2, above. Those sentences began with a phrase-initial L*+H prenuclear pitch accent and ended with an L* nuclear pitch accent followed by a high boundary tone (i.e. H% or ¡H%). What comes as a surprise, however, is the fairly consistent placement of the initial prenuclear pitch accent on the metrically

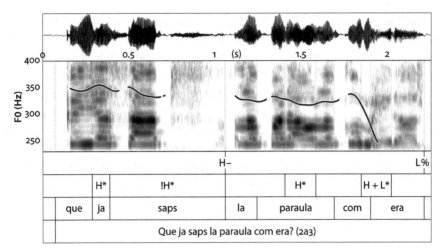

Figure 5.68 Girona Catalan: Waveform, spectrogram, and F0 contour for the neutral information-seeking yes–no question *Que ja saps la paraula com era?* 'Do you already know what the word was?' produced by a Catalan-dominant speaker. It represents an IP composed of two ips. The first one contains an IP-initial H* prenuclear accent, a !H* nuclear accent, and an H- boundary tone. The second one presents an H* prenuclear accent, an H+L* nuclear accent, and an L% boundary tone. The nuclear configuration of the IP is H+L* L% (28C15)

unstressed interrogative particle *que*. I interpret this as a further argument for the assumption made previously that, in questions realized with the low–rising intonational contour, the phrase-initial prenuclear L*+H pitch accent is associated with the leftmost 'stressable' syllable.[179] Figure 5.69 provides an example of these 'mixed' questions, displaying both *que* and the low–rising contour.

As can be seen, the anchoring of the ip-initial L*+H pitch accent on *que* entails that the respective interrogatives contain a phrase-medial metrically stressed syllable on the verb. Like in other questions realized with the low–rising pattern, the pitch movements observed in the context of these phrase-medial prenuclear syllables are different in each sentence, comprising rising movements (L+<H*, L*+H), high peaks (H*), and falling movements (H+L*). I thus assume that they are actually pitch-deaccented and interpret the respective pitch move-

---

179. Following the line of reasoning presented in Fn. 177, it makes perfect sense that L*+H associates with the question-initial interrogative particle, since the focus of these polarity questions covers the whole proposition. In a similar vein, e.g. the Bulgarian interrogative particle *ли* can be attached to *да* (which roughly corresponds to the Sp./Cat. complementizer *que* 'that') yielding the interrogative operator *дали*, which expresses uncertainty, hesitation, and doubt (e.g. *Дали ще я позная?* 'Will I recognize her?').

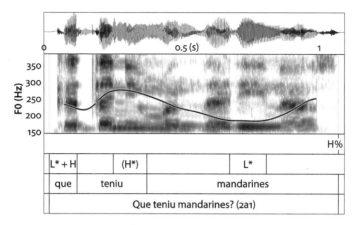

Figure 5.69 Girona Catalan: Waveform, spectrogram, and F0 contour for the neutral information-seeking yes–no question *Que teniu mandarines?* 'Do you have tangerines?' produced by a Spanish-dominant speaker. It represents an IP composed of one ip and is produced with an IP-initial L*+H prenuclear accent, a phrase-medial pitch-deaccented syllable (see Fn. 173), a nuclear L* accent, and an H% boundary tone. The nuclear configuration of the IP is L* H% (4C13)

ments as surface reflexes of the high tonal target belonging to the preceding phrase-initial L*+H pitch accent (see the discussion in Section 5.1.3.1.2). A further example can be seen in Figure 5.70.

5.1.3.1.4 *Peripheral elements in yes–no question of more than one tonal unit*
As displayed in Table 5.2, above, some IYNQ contained dislocated elements. Whereas this was intended in the responses to the situations 2b1 and 2b2, it was a coincidence in the responses to other scenarios. In most cases, the intonation of the peripheral element in some way reflected the intonational contour of the main clause of the interrogative. I will therefore again treat peripheral elements in questions realized with the low–rising contour and in questions with the high–falling pattern apart.

The data set contains a total of 35 peripheral elements attached to IYNQ realized with the low–rising contour ($n = 22$ in GC and $n = 13$ in GS). Among them are dislocated objects, adjuncts (e.g. adverbials such as Cat. *(per) aquí* 'here' or Sp. *por favor* 'please'), and appositions (e.g. Sp. *mi compañera* 'my friend', *la filóloga* 'the philologist'). In these cases, the nuclear configuration of the main interrogative, i.e. L* H%, was usually repeated on the peripheral element. This is to say, both the main clause of the interrogative and the peripheral element) were tonally marked as questions. Typically, the boundary tone was higher in the second ip than in the first one (which again confirms the observation made at the end of Section 5.1.3.1.2 that boundaries are higher when no other IP follows). This

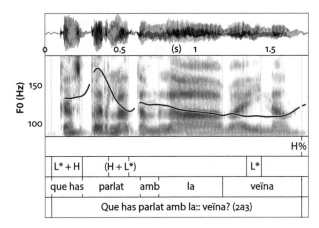

Figure 5.70 Girona Catalan: Waveform, spectrogram, and F0 contour for the neutral information-seeking yes–no question *Que has parlat amb la veïna?* 'Have you talked to the neighbour?' produced by a Spanish-dominant speaker. It represents an IP composed of one ip and is produced with an IP-initial L*+H prenuclear accent placed on the auxiliary *has* that is merged with the interrogative particle *que*, an instance of phrase-internal pitch deaccentuation (see Fn. 173), an L* nuclear accent, and an H% boundary tone. The nuclear configuration of the IP is L* H% (27C15)

can be observed in the example in Figure 5.71, where the nuclear contour on the utterance-final apposition Sp. *la filóloga* 'the philologist' was labelled as L* ¡H%, with an upstepped boundary tone, and the nuclear contour of the main clause of the interrogative, anchored on Sp. *vecina* 'neighbour', as L* H%.

Some more examples can be seen in Figures 5.38 and 5.42, above. When the peripheral element was long enough to contain prenuclear metrically stressed syllables, these were typically pitch-deaccented, i.e. the F0 performed a low plateau.

In the cases in which the main clause of the yes–no question was realized with the high–falling intonational contour, utterance-final peripheral elements typically showed either a low plateau or repeated the nuclear fall of the main contour in a compressed manner. The first case can be seen in Figure 5.72, where the dislocated adjunct Cat. *aquí* 'here' is pronounced with an entirely flat and low contour. Its nuclear configuration was therefore labelled as L* L%. The second case is illustrated in Figure 5.66, above, where, the nuclear contour of the peripheral element was labelled as !H+L* L%.

In the case of *que*-questions pronounced with the high–falling contour, the presence of utterance-final peripheral elements was quite common: such elements were found in 17 out 46 GC *que*-questions (37%). They usually comprised dislocated adverbs or the subject of the sentence. The latter case is illustrated in Figure 5.73.

Chapter 5. Results 227

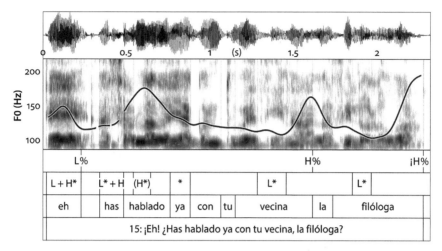

Figure 5.71 Girona Spanish: Waveform, spectrogram, and F0 contour for the neutral information-seeking yes–no question *¿Has hablado ya con tu vecina, la filóloga?* 'Have you already spoken to your neighbour, the philologist?' produced by a Catalan-dominant speaker. It is composed of two IP. The first one, containing the main clause of the yes–no interrogative, consists of an IP-initial L*+H prenuclear accent, various instances of phrase-medial pitch deaccentuation (see Fn. 173), and an L* nuclear accent, followed by an H% boundary tone. The second IP contains an L* nuclear accent followed by an ¡H% boundary tone. The nuclear configuration of the IP containing the main clause of the interrogative is L* H% (17S15)

5.1.3.1.5 *Effects of speaker origin and language dominance*

As shown in the previous sections, the GS and GC IYNQ collected for the present study generally present some variation along two parameters: the first one concerns the presence of the morphosyntactic interrogative marker *que* and the second regards the intonation of the interrogatives. Two main intonational patterns could be established (i.e. the low–rise and the high–falling contour). In this section, I first provide an overview of the interactions between these two factors and then have a closer look at the speakers who actually produced these utterances, estimating the effects of sociolinguistic factors such as the speakers' LD.

As already shown in Table 5.2, yes–no questions headed by *que* were clearly more common in GC than in GS but could be observed in both varieties (30% vs 4.5%). Regarding the intonation of the interrogatives, the 'low–rising' pattern was overall more recurrent than the 'high–falling' one. Table 5.6 shows how these two factors are distributed in the data set.

For GS, the table reveals that questions without *que* and with a low–rising tune are by far the preferred option, accounting for ca 90% of the items analysed

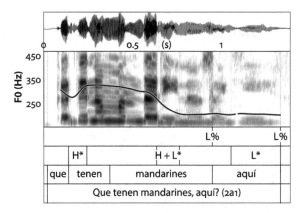

Figure 5.72 Girona Catalan: Waveform, spectrogram, and F0 contour for the neutral information-seeking yes–no question *Que tenen mandarines, aquí?* 'Do you have tangerines here?' produced by a Spanish-dominant speaker. It is composed of two IPs. The first IP contains the main interrogative and consists of an IP-initial H* prenuclear accent, an H+L* nuclear accent, and an L% boundary tone. The nuclear configuration of the IP is H+L* L%. The second IP shows an L* L% nuclear contour (5C13)

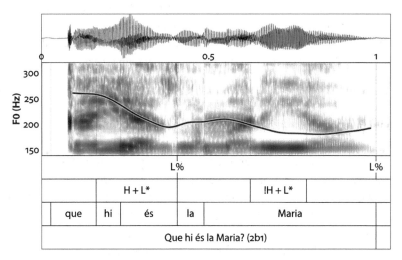

Figure 5.73 Girona Catalan: Waveform, spectrogram, and F0 contour for the neutral information-seeking yes–no question *Que hi és, la Maria?* 'Do you have tangerines here?' produced by a Catalan-dominant speaker. It is composed of two IPs. The first IP contains the main interrogative and consists of an H+L* nuclear accent, and an L% boundary tone. The nuclear configuration of the IP is H+L* L%. The second IP shows a !H+L* L% nuclear contour (19C16)

Table 5.6 Morphosyntactic form (presence of *que*) and intonation of Girona Spanish and Girona Catalan information-seeking yes–no questions (total numbers and percentages per language)

Language	Girona Spanish			Girona Catalan		
Intonation pattern	[– *que*]	[+ *que*]	Total	[– *que*]	[+ *que*]	Total
'low–rising'	138 (90%)		138 (90%)	98 (64%)	13 (8.5%)	111 (73%)
'high–falling'		7 (4.5%)	7 (4.5)		33 (22%)	33 (22%)
other	9 (6%)		9 (6%)	8 (5%)		8 (5%)
total	147 (95.5%)	7 (4.5%)	154 (100%)	106 (69%)	46 (30%)	152 (100%)

in this language. The (relatively few) questions with *que*, on the other hand, always displayed the high–falling pattern. There is thus a clear correspondence between the morphosyntactic form of the question and the intonation pattern used in its phonetic realization. Interestingly, 6 out of the 7 items with *que* and the high–falling pattern stemmed from (five different) clearly CatD bilinguals, whose dominance values are −57.3, −52.6, −37.2, −31.4, and −28.5. The remaining item was produced by a speaker whose dominance value was slightly biased towards Spanish (19.5). However, this value still permits to qualify him as fairly balanced. In sum, *que*-questions were not very common in GS overall and, when they occurred, it was typically in speakers whose dominant language is Catalan.

In GC, questions without *que* and realized with the low–rising intonational contour were the most frequently produced combination, too, accounting for approximately 64% of all items produced in this language. Yet, the presence of *que*-questions was not as marginal as in GS (in 46 out of 152 items, i.e. 30%; see Tables 5.3 and 6). Of these, 61% ($n = 28$) stemmed from CatD and 39% from SpD bilinguals ($n = 18$). However, if the different group sizes or, more precisely, the total number of IYNQ produced by each group is taken into account, the proportion of *que*-questions is of 29% in the CatD and 33% in the SpD group. So, interestingly – and in stark contrast to the GS data set – SpD bilinguals produced roughly the same proportion of *que*-questions in GC as the CatD speakers (the difference being not significant).

Intonationwise, Catalan *que*-questions appeared with two tonal patterns, i.e. on one hand, with the iconic 'high fall' and, on the other, also with the 'low–rising' pattern. While the first case was to be expected (due to the available descriptions of Catalan *que*-questions in the scientific literature), the observation of *que*-questions intonated with the low–rising pattern strongly contrasts with most extant accounts and has, to my best knowledge, only been documented once before (see Fernández-Planas et al. 2007 and the discussion in Section 6.4.3).

However, accounting for 28% of all Catalan IYNQ with *que* (*n*=13), its occurrence was not an exception, even though the high–falling pattern was more typical (*n*=33, i.e. 72% of all *que*-questions).

As for the speakers who produced these questions, Table 5.7 summarizes how many of the Catalan *que*-questions with each intonation pattern were produced by each of the two LD groups.

Table 5.7 Intonation contours used in Girona Catalan information-seeking yes–no questions with *que* by language-dominance group

[+ *que*]	Total	Catalan-dominant	Spanish-dominant
'low–rising'	13 (100%)	3 (23% – 11%)	10 (77% – 55%)
'high–falling'	33 (100%)	25 (76% – 89%)	8 (24% – 44%)
total		28 (100%)	18 (100%)

It can be clearly understood that the CatD speakers overwhelmingly produced their *que*-questions with the iconic high–falling contour (89%). Spanish-dominants, on the other hand, used the low–rising contour in slightly more than half of their items (55%). A chi-squared test showed that there is a statistically highly significant association between the used intonation patterns and the LD of the speaker ($\chi^2(1)=10.459$, $p=0.001$). Finally, concerning the few deviating intonational contours, i.e. contours that followed neither the low–rising nor the high–falling pattern, the previous sections revealed that these can for the most part be attributed to single individuals, who stand out by their Latin American descendance.

The observations made in this section of course raise the question of how all this variation came about. For GS, the answer seems pretty straightforward: (some) CatD speakers transfer both *que* as well as the high–falling intonation pattern from Catalan to Spanish. In GC, the situation is less clear, but the distinct use of intonational tunes in the two dominance groups strongly suggests that the current situation is a result of CLI. Effects of language contact on the intonation of IYNQ will therefore be discussed extensively in Chapter 6 (especially in Section 6.4.3).

5.1.3.1.6 Summary: Information-seeking yes–no questions

IYNQ in GS and GC most commonly come along with rising intonation patterns and are formulated without the particle *que*. Nevertheless, *que* sometimes appears in this question type in both varieties spoken in Girona, which disproves the claims made for Northern CC in the literature that the use of *que* is restricted to confirmation-seeking questions there (Prieto/Rigau 2007: 33, 41; 2011: 35). In

GS, *que*-questions are rather rare (4.5%). They were produced mainly by CatD and with the 'high–falling' intonation pattern. In GC, on the other hand, they accounted for roughly one third of all IYNQ and were produced by both CatD and SpD participants with a similar rate. Most interestingly, however, the LD has a significant effect on their intonation: SpD speakers typically use the 'low–rise' tune in their Catalan *que*-questions, while CatD bilinguals usually do not. Besides, dislocations were more frequent in Catalan than in Spanish IYNQ.

Furthermore, the analysis uncovered some novel details about the 'low–rise' pattern. In both contact varieties, the combination of a low plateau during a stressed syllable and a following rise represents the most important prosodic marker of interrogativity: i.e., for the most part, IYNQ begin with a phrase-initial L*+H pitch accent and end with an L* (¡)H% nuclear contour. The initial pitch accent attaches to the first stressed syllable of the utterance and typically reaches its peak in the second post-tonic syllable (although the peak position can variate). All further metrically stressed syllables of the prenucleus are pitch-deaccented, i.e. pitch movements in IYNQ originate merely from the phrase-initial prenuclear pitch accent and the nuclear configuration. However, the data suggest that additional L*+H accents can be used to convey the information-structure of the question. This is to say, L*+H can be repeated in phrase-medial positions to narrow down the focus of the yes–no question onto the element that bears it. The pitch accent thus seems to work as some sort of 'interrogative toneme', similar to interrogative morphemes in other languages (see Fn. 177, above). This approach would also explain why the phrase-initial accent ordinarily associates with the auxiliary instead of the lexical verb in complex verb forms: the association with the auxiliary indicates that the focus of the yes–no question is on the whole proposition, whereas the position on the lexical verb would narrow it down onto the verb. In the same way, L*+H can be deployed onto the negation particle Sp./Cat. *no* when the focus is on the negative polarity of the proposition. Finally, in the cases in which it was associated with the (otherwise unstressed) interrogative operator *que*, it once more conveys the broad focus of the question.

5.1.3.2 *Disjunctive questions*

As shown in Table 4.19, 57 out of the 62 responses recorded with situation No. 2c (see Appendix) could be used for an intonational analysis (i.e. 29 IPs for GS and 28 IPs for GC).[180] Each of these was made up of two ips, one for each alternative. While the second ip almost exclusively contained only one syllable bearing a pitch accent (i.e. the nuclear one), the first ip could contain up to three stressed

---

180. The remaining five sentences did not correspond to the desired utterance type as they represented simple information-seeking yes–no questions or contained wh-words.

syllables (and thus various pitch accents). This is illustrated by means of some GS examples in (2).

(2) a. ((¿Queréis helado de vainilla)$_{ip}$ (o de avellana)$_{ip}$)$_{IP}$
    b. ((¿Helado de vainilla)$_{ip}$ (o de avellana)$_{ip}$)$_{IP}$
    c. ((¿De vainilla)$_{ip}$ (o de avellana)$_{ip}$)$_{IP}$
    '(Do you want) vanilla (ice cream) or hazelnut [ice cream])?'

The sentences of the type presented in (b) and (c) were usually preceded by a wh-question such as Sp. *¿Qué preferís?* 'What do you prefer?' or Cat. *Què voleu?* 'What do you want?'.

As regards intonation, the same prenuclear pitch accents were found in the first ip of the disjunctive questions in both languages. 25 phrase-initial prenuclear pitch accents were found in GS and 22 in GC. In both languages rising pitch accents were strongly preferred in this position (see Table 5.8).

Table 5.8 Percentages and total numbers phrase-initial prenuclear pitch accents in disjunctive questions

Pitch accent	L+<H*	L*+H	L+H*	Other (H*, H+L*)
Girona Spanish	52% (13)	28% (7)	4% (1)	16% (4)
Girona Catalan	36% (8)	23% (5)	2% (4)	23% (5)

As for phrase-medial prenuclear pitch accents, H+L* was clearly the preferred option among the 13 GS and 11 GC instances found, accounting for 62% and 64% of the items, respectively. I assume that this pitch accent surfaces because of the high target of the preceding phrase-initial prenuclear pitch accent when there is too little space for the pitch to fall before the second stressed syllable. Figures 5.74 and 5.75 contain two examples where the high target of the phrase-initial prenuclear pitch accents L+<H* and L*+H, respectively, is only reached in the syllable directly preceding the phrase-medial metrically stressed syllable.

For the nuclear configurations of the inner ips, one clearly dominant pattern was observed in both languages: a rise within the limits of the nuclear syllable (L+H*), followed by a high boundary tone (H-, see Figure 5.75). When the ip also contained prenuclear pitch accents, the peaks of the nuclear pitch accent were often higher than the preceding ones and therefore labelled with an upstep (i.e. as 'L+¡H*', see Figure 5.74). However, given that the upstep is assumed to be triggered by the high boundary tone, I view such upstepped pitch accents underlyingly as L+H* (see the discussion in 5.2). Concerning the boundary tone, all but two sentences per language displayed a clear continuation rise (i.e. H-) that was usually higher, when a short pause was inserted between the fist and the second ip of the IP. The 4 remaining cases presented sustained pitches (i.e. !H-).

Chapter 5. Results   233

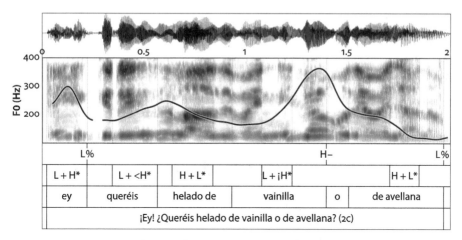

Figure 5.74 Girona Spanish: Waveform, spectrogram, and F0 contour for the disjunctive question *¿Queréis helado de vainilla o de avellana?* 'Do you want vanilla or hazelnut ice cream?' produced by a Catalan-dominant speaker. It represents an IP composed of two ips. The first one consists of an IP-initial L+<H* prenuclear accent, a phrase-internal H+L* prenuclear accent, and an L+¡H* nuclear accent followed by an H- boundary tone. The second ip contains a nuclear H+L* pitch accent followed by an L% boundary tone. The nuclear configuration of the IP is H+L* L% (6S18)

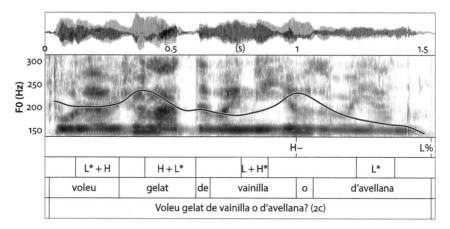

Figure 5.75 Girona Catalan: Waveform, spectrogram, and F0 contour for the disjunctive question *Voleu gelat de vainilla o d'avellana?* 'Do you want vanilla or hazelnut ice cream?' produced by a Catalan-dominant speaker. It represents an IP composed of two ips. The first one consists of an IP-initial L*+H prenuclear accent, a phrase-internal H+L* prenuclear accent, and an L+H* nuclear accent followed by an H- boundary tone. The second ip contains a nuclear L* accent followed by an L% boundary tone. The nuclear configuration of the IP is L* L% (10S18)

Regarding the second ip, the only two prenuclear pitch accents were H* (in the GC data). As for the nuclear configurations of the second ip (and hence of the IP), the same two contours were observed in both varieties: H+L* L% and L* L% (see Figures 5.74 and 5.75, above). While both appeared with the same frequency in Catalan (50% each), H+L* only accounted for 24% of the GS nuclear configurations. A closer look suggests that H+L* could be a 'Catalan' feature and L* more characteristic of Spanish.[181] First, 6 out of 7 occurrences of H+L* in the Spanish data stemmed from CatD speakers and, second, this accent was also preferred over L* by this group in Catalan (used in 11 out of 19 cases, i.e. 58%). The SpD group, on the other hand, produced only four instances of H+L* in both languages combined, two of which came from the same speaker. It thus only appeared in 21% of their sentences. Although these differences between the groups and languages are not big enough to reach statistical significance, they suggest that language contact could have led to a progressive merger of categories stemming originally from different languages, which has now increased the repertoire of variants in both languages (see the discussion in 6.4.2.3).

Finally, one very particular Catalan sentence is worth being presented with some more detail, given it shows a clearly different intonational pattern. The disjunctive question in Figure 5.76 is introduced by the interrogative particle *que* and the fist ip displays a sustained high pitch plateau extending from its beginning until the end (!H-). In the second ip, the pitch drops down drastically during the nuclear syllable (H+L*) and then stays low until the end of the utterance (L%). The sentence was produced by a clearly CatD speaker and its fashioning has no parallel in the Spanish disjunctive questions. However, as shown in the preceding section, the same or a very similar pattern can occur in GC (and GS) IYNQ. Nevertheless, the use of this pattern and of *que* in a disjunctive question is rather peculiar in CC (as opposed to, e.g., Balearic Catalan; see Prieto/Rigau 2007: 42–43).

---

181. The differences cannot be accounted for by factors such as metrical structure in this case, given that all utterances ended in the Catalan-Spanish cognate *avellana* 'hazelnut'.

Chapter 5. Results 235

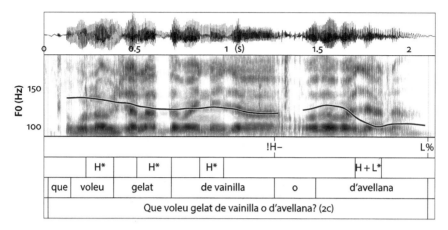

Figure 5.76 Girona Catalan: Waveform, spectrogram, and F0 contour for the disjunctive question *Que vol__eu gel__at de vai__nil__la o d'ave__lla__na?* 'Do you want vanilla or hazelnut ice cream?' produced by a Catalan-dominant speaker. It represents an IP composed of two ips. The first one consists of continuously high and flat plateau, while the second ip contains a nuclear H+L* accent followed by an L% boundary tone. The nuclear configuration of the IP is H+L* L% (11C18)

5.1.4 Biased polar questions

This section offers a description of the intonational properties of exclamative yes–no questions (with counterexpectational meaning) and confirmation-seeking yes–no questions. I here depict the prenuclear pitch accents and nuclear configurations attested in the GS and GC data sets. Their phonological status will be discussed in Section 5.2 after the description of the tonal realization of all sentence types.

5.1.4.1 *Exclamative yes–no questions (with counterexpectational meaning)*

From the 61 responses obtained with situation 2d (see Appendix), six had to be discarded, since they — although being pragmatically correct in the foreseen context — either corresponded to other sentence modalities (e.g. wh-questions such as Cat. *Com pots tenir gana si acabem de dinar?* 'How can you be hungry if we have just had dinner.') or were so strongly affected by creaky voice that a reliable analysis of the F0 was impossible. As shown in Table 4.19, 25 GC and 31 GS IPs were eventually analysed in this context. Regarding their wording, all GC exclamative yes–no questions contained the sequence *tens gana* 'are you hungry' with two adjacent underlyingly stressed syllables, often preceded by adverbs such as *encara* 'still' or *ja* 'already'. The GS data presented more variation but usually included *tienes hambre* 'are you hungry', as well.

Concerning their F0 contours, most (but not all) exclamative yes–no questions displayed patterns similar to those of IYNQ. In both languages, the most common phrase-initial prenuclear accent was L*+H, accounting for slightly more than half of the items. The peak of the high trailing tone was usually attained in one of the three syllables following the stressed one and again was responsible for most phrase-medial pitch movements. In the example shown in Figure 5.77, for example, L*+H is located on the phrase-initial word *aún* 'still', pronounced in one syllable, and the phrase-medial verb *tienes* '(you) have' is pitch-deaccented.

Besides, some instances of other phrase-initial prenuclear accents were registered (e.g. L+<H*, L+H*, or L*). In general, they seem to be surface variants of L*+H, evoked either by an extended pitch range (conveying the exclamatory nature of the utterances; see, e.g., Crespo-Sendra 2011: 111–120) or, in some cases, due to tonal crowding. For instance, in Figure 5.78, the F0 contour can be described with an L* on *todavía* and an H* on *tienes*. However, in a different analysis, the underlying phrase-initial prenuclear L*+H accent could be phonetically rendered as 'split', i.e. the first stressed syllable bears a surface L* accent and the second one an H* accent. Interestingly, such combinations appeared 3 times in the GS and 6 times in the GC data set (all of them on Sp. *todavía tienes* and Cat. *encara tens* 'do you already have').[182] In a similar vein, H* seems to be a truncated or compressed variant of underlying L*+H in stress-clashes such as Cat. *tens gana* 'are you hungry' (see Figure 5.79).

As for the nuclear configurations, the participants overwhelmingly used combinations of an L* pitch accent followed by a high boundary tone (which was very often the highest point of the phrase, labelled '¡H%'). Yet, there was some variation: sometimes, H+L* appeared as a variant of the nuclear L* accent (4 items in GS, 3 in GC). Although it probably surfaced due to tonal crowding in some cases (i.e. when the nuclear syllable was closely preceded by the high target of a previous prenuclear accent), its appearance could also be an effect of the extension of the pitch range due to the exclamative character of the questions and greater speaker involvement (see, e.g., Crespo-Sendra 2011: 91–93, 111–120; Hirschberg/Ward 1992: 241; Lee et al. 2008 for this cross-linguistic trend and Prieto 2002a: 431–432, 2013: 31–33 for similar observations in CC exclamative questions). Likewise, there were three cases in the GS data in which a slight rise, i.e. an 'L+H*'-like pitch gesture, was observed within the limits of the nuclear syllable instead of L*. I equally interpret this as an effect of the expansion of the pitch range.

---

182. In one other case, the combination of L* and L+<H* on *todavía tienes* seems to be a similar case and might equally correspond to an underlying L*+H pitch accent.

Chapter 5. Results   237

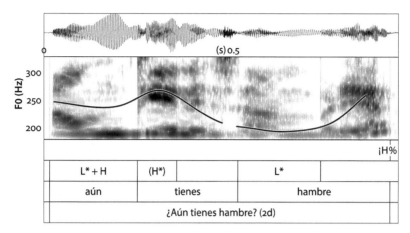

Figure 5.77 Girona Spanish: Waveform, spectrogram, and F0 contour for the exclamative yes–no question *¿Aún tienes hambre?* 'Are you still hungry?' produced by a Spanish-dominant speaker. It represents an IP composed of one ip and is produced with an IP-initial L*+H prenuclear accent, phrase-medial pitch deaccentuation (see Fn. 173), and an L* nuclear accent, followed by an ¡H% boundary tone. The nuclear configuration of the IP is L* ¡H% (5S19)

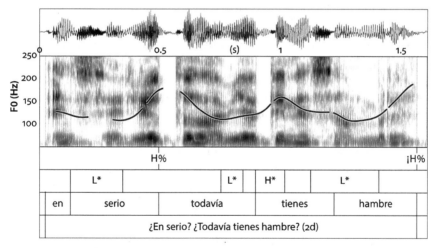

Figure 5.78 Girona Spanish: Waveform, spectrogram, and F0 contour for the exclamative yes–no question *¿Todavía tienes hambre?* 'Are you still hungry?' produced by a Spanish-dominant speaker. It represents an IP composed of one ip and is produced with an IP-initial L* prenuclear accent, a phrase-medial H* accent, and an L* nuclear accent, followed by a ¡H% boundary tone. The nuclear configuration of the IP is L* ¡H% (27S19)

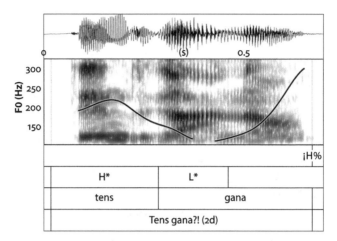

Figure 5.79 Girona Catalan: Waveform, spectrogram, and F0 contour for the exclamative yes–no question *Tens gana?* 'Are you hungry?' produced by a Catalan-dominant speaker. It consists of an IP-initial prenuclear H* accent and an L* nuclear accent, followed by an ¡H% boundary tone. The nuclear configuration of the IP is L* ¡H% (6C19)

Finally, two further combinations of pitch accents and boundary tones are worth mentioning. The first alternative contour is shown in Figure 5.80. It contains two H+L* pitch accents – a prenuclear and a nuclear one – and ends with a high boundary tone. It was observed 4 times in the GS data (13%), produced by three CatD and one SpD speakers.

The other one is, once again, the typically Catalan high–falling pattern that combines with questions introduced by the interrogative particle *que* (see Figure 5.81). It presents high pitch in the prenucleus (H* or ¡H*) followed by a drastic pitch fall during the nuclear syllable (H+L*) and ends in a low boundary tone (L%). This pattern occurred three times in the GC and once in the GS data (12% and 3%, respectively). Interestingly, the last prenuclear syllable was higher than the beginning of the prenuclear area in all cases, which might be, once again, an effect of the use of an extended pitch range conveying incredulity. Lastly, there was one GC exclamative question introduced by the interrogative particle *que* that was pronounced with a nuclear rise (i.e. L* ¡H%). All *que*-questions stemmed from speakers dominant in Catalan.

Chapter 5. Results 239

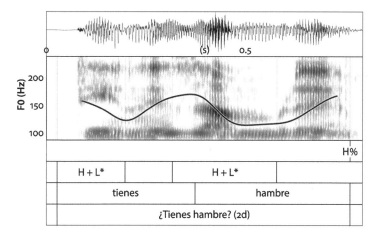

Figure 5.80 Girona Spanish: Waveform, spectrogram, and F0 contour for the exclamative yes–no question *¿Tienes hambre?* 'Are you hungry?' produced by a Catalan-dominant speaker. It represents an IP composed of one ip and is produced with an IP-initial H+L* prenuclear accent and an H+L* nuclear accent, followed by an H% boundary tone. The nuclear configuration of the IP is H+L* H% (6S19)

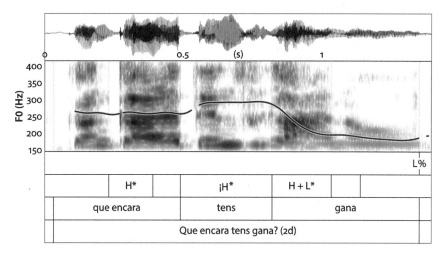

Figure 5.81 Girona Catalan: Waveform, spectrogram, and F0 contour for the exclamative yes–no question *Que encara tens gana?* 'Are you still hungry?' produced by a Catalan-dominant speaker. It represents an IP composed of one ip and is produced with an IP-initial H* prenuclear accent, a phrase-medial ¡H* prenuclear accent, and an H+L* nuclear accent, followed by an L% boundary tone. The nuclear configuration of the IP is H+L* L% (28C19)

5.1.4.2 Confirmation-seeking yes–no questions

As shown in Table 4.19, 31 GC and 30 GS confirmation-seeking yes–no questions were recorded with situation 2e (see Appendix) and subsequently subjected to an intonational analysis. Virtually all questions contained Sp. *vas a venir/vendrás a cenar* 'are you going to come (over) for dinner' or Cat. *vindràs a dinar* 'are you going to come (over) for lunch'. In many cases, this verbal complex was preceded by a vocative (e.g. *¡Juan!* or *Jaume!*) and preceded or followed by the adverbial Sp./Cat. *al final* 'in the end, finally'. Furthermore, some questions contained elements like Sp./Cat. *(¿)o no?* 'or not' or Sp. *¿verdad?* 'right'. Finally, some questions asked explicitly for a confirmation, e.g. Sp. *¿Me puedes confirmar si vienes a cenar?* 'Can you confirm that you're coming over for dinner?' (33S20).

As for intonation, 50 and 64 prenuclear pitch accents were found in the GS and GC data sets, respectively, most of which were IP-initial. Similar to IYNQ, L*+H was by far the most frequent IP-initial prenuclear accent (84% in GC, 80% in GS). Second most common was L+<H*, which might be a surface variant of the first one (6% and 13%). The same is likely for three instances of L+H*. Phrase-medial prenuclear positions showed both parallels and differences with respect to IYNQ. In some few cases, they were pitch-deaccented or displayed falling pitch (i.e. H+L*), which I again interpret as an outcome of tonal crowding after a preceding peak (see Sections 5.1.1.1 and 5.1.3.2). In the majority of cases, however, a second L*+H pitch accent surfaced in this position (see Figure 5.82). This was also the pitch accent that was typically used when there was a second phrase-internal stressed syllable.

Regarding the nuclear configurations of confirmation-seeking yes–no questions, the speakers used the same inventory in both varieties. The most recurrent configuration consisted of an L* pitch accent followed by a high boundary tone that usually represented the highest point in the IP (see Figure 5.82). This 'low-rising' pattern appeared in roughly three quarters of the utterances and is shared with IYNQ. The principal alternative was H+L* L%. However, in most cases, the use of this falling nuclear contour could be related to the wording of the sentence: it usually appeared when the confirmation-seeking question ended with the disjunctive element *o no?* 'or not?' or, in one case, Cat. *o què* 'or what' (5 out of 7 items in GS; 6 out of 8 in GC; see Figure 5.83 for an example).[183] Yet, there were also four cases (2 per language), in which H+L* L% was used by CatD speakers on the main verb (see Figure 5.84). In consequence, despite not being

---

183. In one case, *¿O no?* 'Or not?' was used after a short pause in a separate ip. As in disjunctive questions, the nuclear contour of the first ip was L+H* ¡H- and that of the second one L* L%. In all other items, no phonetic boundary cues (such as pre-boundary lengthening) could be observed whatsoever.

Chapter 5. Results   241

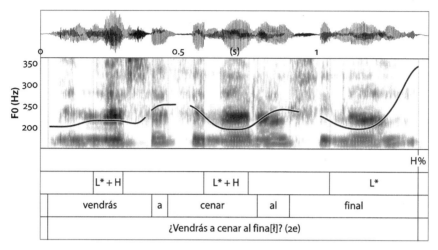

Figure 5.82 Girona Spanish: Waveform, spectrogram, and F0 contour for the confirmation-seeking yes–no question *¿Vendrás a cenar al final?* 'Will you come over for dinner in the end?' produced by a Catalan-dominant speaker. It represents an IP composed of one ip and is produced with an IP-initial L*+H prenuclear accent, a phrase-medial L*+H prenuclear accent, and an L* nuclear accent, followed by an ¡H% boundary tone. The nuclear configuration of the IP is L* ¡H% (19S20)

very frequent (ca 25%), the nuclear fall seems to be an alternative to the low rise for confirmation-seeking questions in both languages. Nevertheless, it is striking that there were no examples without a disjunctive element stemming from SpD speakers (see Section 6.4.3 for further discussion).

While these findings by and large confirm the available intonational descriptions of confirmations-seeking questions for CS, according to which both nuclear contours are possible in this pragmatical context and L*+H is the typical prenuclear pitch accent, this is less so for (Central) Catalan, since there were no instances of high plateaus in the prenuclear region as suggested in the literature (see Section 3.1.2.2). However, our findings endorse Prieto et al.'s (2015: 55) observation that L* H% can be an alternative to the general CC H+L* L% pattern in GC. Furthermore, it is worth pointing out that there were no instances of confirmation-seeking questions introduced by the interrogative particle *que* in neither of the two languages. This is somewhat surprising given that *que*-questions are claimed to be most iconic in this context in GC (see Prieto 2002a: 434–435). However, according to Prieto and Rigau (2007: 43), alternative questions (i.e. questions built as a disjunction of the predicate and the latter negated, e.g. by means of *o no*, forcing the hearer to make a decision) cannot be headed by *que* in Northern CC — which might partly explain the absence of *que* in most questions with the falling contour.

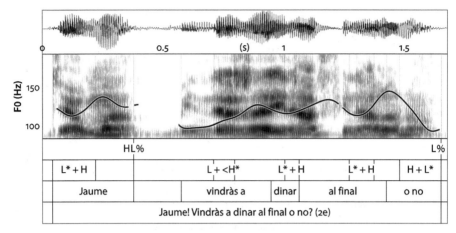

Figure 5.83 Girona Spanish: Waveform, spectrogram, and F0 contour for the confirmation-seeking yes–no question *Vindràs a dinar al final o no?* 'Will you come over for lunch in the end or not?' produced by a Spanish-dominant speaker. It represents an IP composed of one ip and is produced with an IP-initial L+<H* prenuclear accent, two phrase-medial L*+H prenuclear accents, and an H+L* nuclear accent, followed by an L% boundary tone. The nuclear configuration of the IP is H+L* L% (7C20)

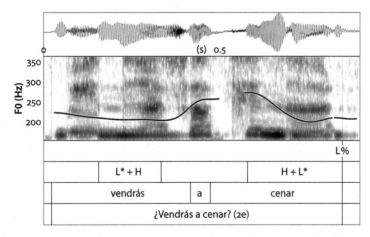

Figure 5.84 Girona Spanish: Waveform, spectrogram, and F0 contour for the confirmation-seeking yes–no question *¿Vendrás a cenar?* 'Are you coming to dinner?' produced by a Catalan-dominant speaker. It represents an IP composed of one ip and is produced with an IP-initial L*+H prenuclear accent and an H+L* nuclear accent, followed by am L% boundary tone. The nuclear configuration of the IP is H+L* L% (31S20)

Finally, one particular item is worth mentioning apart. It was produced by speaker No. 13, of Honduran heritage, and presents two H+L* prenuclear accents and nuclear H+L* LH%[184] (see Figure 5.85). Through the use of this tune, the speaker once more deviates from all others. Yet, her intonation is quite consistent, as she uses the same prenuclear accents and nuclear H+L* LH% also in other question types (see Section 5.1.3.1.2).

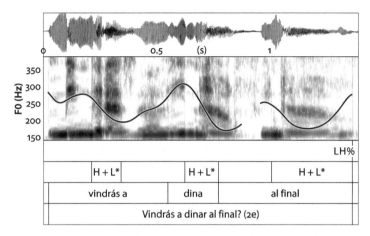

Figure 5.85 Girona Catalan: Waveform, spectrogram, and F0 contour for the confirmation-seeking yes–no question *Vindràs a dinar al final?* 'Are you coming to dinner in the end?' produced by a Spanish-dominant speaker. It represents an IP composed of one ip and is produced with an IP-initial H+L* prenuclear accent, a phrase-medial H+L* prenuclear accent, an H+L* nuclear accent, and an LH% boundary tone. The nuclear configuration of the IP is H+L* LH% (13S20)

5.1.5 Neutral wh-questions

This section offers a description of the intonational properties of the neutral, i.e. information-seeking, wh-questions in the present sample. Each 62 questions were recorded with situation 3a1 and 3a2 per variety. Analysing them was not an easy task, since the subcorpus presented a fair amount of variation. To better understand how neutral wh-questions are intonated by whom, the prenuclear pitch accents and nuclear configurations found will be presented separately for the two recording situations. Given that the sentences elicited with situation 3a1 nearly always contained at least one stress clash — which substantially complicated the

---

184. As the nuclear configuration is realized on an ultimate-stress word, it cannot be decided here whether the underlying boundary tone is actually H% or LH%. The latter representation was chosen in concert with other questions produced by the same speaker.

analysis — the results from situation 3a2 will be discussed first. A summary will be provided at the end of the section.

All but 3 of the 31 sentences gathered for GS with situation 3a2 were direct wh-questions. They contained the wh-word Sp. *qué* 'what' and usually a finite form of either *llevar* 'bring, take' or *comprar* 'buy'. As for the GC counterparts, 27 out of the 31 recorded utterances contained a wh-word (i.e. either Cat. *què* 'what' or — in two cases — Cat. *quin regal* 'which present'). The remaining utterances had to be discarded as they represented IYNQ. Unfortunately, all excluded responses were produced by SpD speakers, which drastically diminished the number of analysable utterances for this group.

When the ip containing the wh-question began directly with the question-word, i.e. Sp./Cat *qué/què* 'what' or Cat. *quin (regal)* 'what present' (18 out 27 GC items, 21 out of 28 GS items), the speakers typically used high pitch, i.e. H*, on the stressed syllable of the interrogative element (see Figures 5.86 and 5.87). In some cases, a rise could be observed instead, which was labelled as L+<H* or L*+H (see Figures 5.88 and 5.89). Such initial rises occurred 7 times in GC and 4 times in GS and were produced by both CatD and SpD bilinguals.

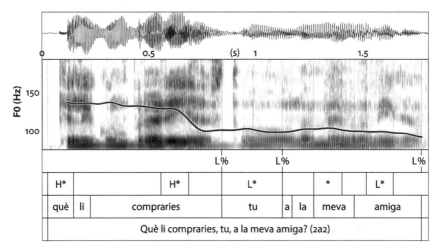

Figure 5.86 Girona Catalan: Waveform, spectrogram, and F0 contour for the information-seeking wh-question *Què li compraries, tu, a la meva amiga?* 'What would you buy for my friend?' produced by a Catalan-dominant speaker. It consists of 3 IPs. The first IP contains the main clause and is produced with an IP-initial H* prenuclear accent and an H* nuclear accent, followed by an L% boundary tone. The nuclear configuration of this IP is H+L* L%. The following two IPs show L* L% nuclear configurations (22C22)

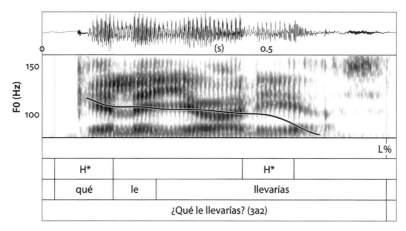

Figure 5.87 Girona Spanish: Waveform, spectrogram, and F0 contour for the information-seeking wh-question ¿*Qué le llevarías?* 'What would you bring him?' produced by a Spanish-dominant speaker. It represents an IP composed of one ip and is produced with an IP-initial H* prenuclear accent and an H* nuclear pitch accent, followed by an L% boundary tone. The nuclear configuration of the IP is H* L% (35C22)

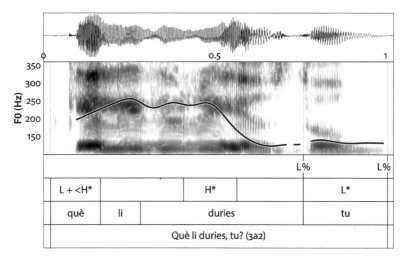

Figure 5.88 Girona Catalan: Waveform, spectrogram, and F0 contour for the information-seeking wh-question *Què li duries, tu?* 'What would you bring him?' produced by a Catalan-dominant speaker. It consists of 2 IPs. The first IP contains the main clause and is produced with an IP-initial L+<H prenuclear accent and an H* nuclear accent, followed by an L% boundary tone. The nuclear configuration of this IP is H* L%. The following IP contains an L* L% nuclear configuration (6C22)

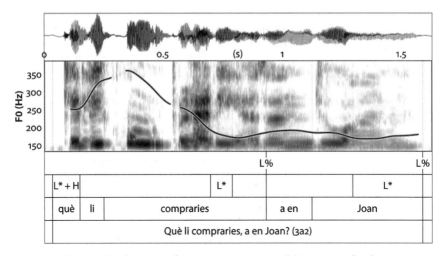

Figure 5.89 Girona Catalan: Waveform, spectrogram, and F0 contour for the information-seeking wh-question *Què li compraries, a en Joan?* 'What would you buy for Joan?' produced by a Catalan-dominant speaker. It consists of 2 IPs. The first IP contains the main clause and is produced with an IP-initial L*+H prenuclear accent, an L* nuclear accent, and an L% boundary tone. The nuclear configuration of this IP is L* L%. The following IP contains an L* L% nuclear configuration (22C22)

A different case seems to be the presence of a phrase-initial low tone when the phrase-initial question-word appeared in a stress clash. For instance, in sequences such as Sp. *qué crees* 'what do you think' or Cat. *què puc* 'what can I', the wh-word itself showed low pitch (L*) while the following syllable presented a high tone (H*; see Figure 5.90 for an example). L* might thus represent a surface variant of the usual H* accent that appears in stress clashes.[185]

Additionally, 6 GS and 9 GC wh-questions that did not begin with the question-word provide further evidence for the analysis just proposed. In all of these items, a personal pronoun, i.e. Sp. *tú* or Cat. *tu* 'you', immediately preceded the interrogative words in a stress clash.[186] These stress clashes were thus resolved

---

185. In an alternative approach, such sequences could be analysed as instances of phrase-initial L*+H pitch accents on *qué* and a subsequent lack of underlying pitch accents. The 'split-up' appearance of the pitch accent would then result from the interruption of the F0 caused by the presence of voiceless plosives. However, this is not in accordance with the acoustical impression of the utterances and would imply pitch-deaccented wh-words in sentences like the one in Figure 5.91, below.

186. There was no prosodic boundary between *tú* and *qué*. Both were pronounced within the same ip in the mentioned cases. This view is also supported by two other utterances in which there actually was a boundary between *(y) tú/(i) tu* and *qué/què*, which was clearly marked by pre-boundary lengthening and a continuation rise (L* H%).

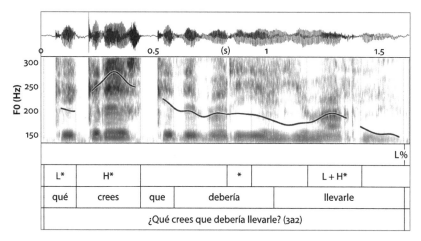

Figure 5.90 Girona Spanish: Waveform, spectrogram, and F0 contour for the information-seeking wh-question *¿Qué crees que debería llevarle?* 'What do you think I should bring for her?' produced by a Spanish-dominant speaker. It represents an IP composed of one ip and is produced with IP-initial L* prenuclear accent, an H* prenuclear accent, and an L+H* nuclear accent, followed by an L% boundary tone. The nuclear configuration of the IP is L+H* L% (12C22)

by pronouncing the personal pronoun with a low tone (L*) and the following wh-word with a high tone (H*). Figure 5.91 provides an example.

In sum, the phrase-initial question-word typically showed a high (or sometimes a rising) pitch accent in the two varieties under concern. When it occurred in a stress clash, the first element was pronounced with a low tone, whereas the second one bore a high tone (independently of the position of the wh-word). This implies that the first pitch accent of neutral wh-questions must not necessarily associate with the wh-word. However, the details of this issue are beyond the scope of this book and must rest a topic for further investigation.

Phrase-medial metrically stressed syllables were quite consistently pitch-deaccented. The few pitch movements produced within their limits can be interpreted as repercussions of high tonal targets belonging to phrase-initial pitch accents. However, seeing that only 5 GS and 7 GC sentences contained more than two phrase-medial prenuclear stressed syllables, deaccentuation could be less consequent in longer sentences. Nevertheless, long main clauses seem to be avoided by the speakers through the use of right-dislocations, especially in Catalan (see below and Section 5.1.3.1.4).

In nuclear position, the speakers exhibited a clear preference for falling or low contours. As can be seen from Table 5.9, H* L% was most common in both languages (see Figures 5.86–88, above, for some examples). Typically, the prenucleus

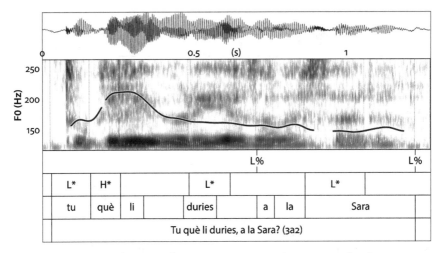

Figure 5.91 Girona Catalan: Waveform, spectrogram, and F0 contour for the information-seeking wh-question ¿*Tu què li duries, a la Sara?* 'What would you bring for Sara?' produced by a Catalan-dominant speaker. It consists of two IPs. The first one contains an IP-initial L*+H prenuclear accent and an L* nuclear accent, followed by an L% boundary tone. The nuclear configuration of the IP is L* L%. The second IP is made up of an L* nuclear accent and an L% boundary tone (12C22)

was characterized by a high plateau when this nuclear configuration was used, and the final F0 fall already set in at the end of the nuclear syllable, attaining its in the post-nuclear stretch.[187] Besides, there were some instances of low, circumflex, and rising nuclear contours. In these cases, the phrase-medial part was usually affected by declination more strongly (see Figures 5.89–91).

Table 5.9 Nuclear contours in Girona Spanish and Girona Catalan neutral wh-questions gathered with situation 3a2 (percentages and total numbers)

Nuclear contour	H* L%	L* L%	L+H* L%	L* H%
GS (*n* = 28)	64% (18)	11% (3)	11% (3)	14% (4)
GC (*n* = 27)	74% (20)	11% (3)	8% (2)	8% (2)

A screening of the nuclear-contour use according to the speakers' LD did not allow to posit a clear influence of this factor: in both languages, virtually all contours were produced by speakers from both dominance groups, making the num-

---

187. As H+L* L% and H* L% cannot be distinguished when the phrase ends in ultimate-stress words, such cases were labelled as H* L% based on the observations made for words stressed on the penultimate and in line with the literature on this question type in CC (see Section 3.1.2.2).

ber of cases of some patterns used by a specific dominance group quite small in many cases. Nevertheless, the most frequent configuration, H* L%, might represent a 'rather Catalan feature' for the following reasons. First, it was slightly more frequent in GC than in GS. Second, CatD speakers used it somewhat more often than SpD bilinguals did (i.e. to an extent of 70% vs 50% in Spanish; and of 75% vs 71% in Catalan). Especially in Spanish, there thus seems to be a relatively high probability for SpD to use different nuclear configurations. Third, H* L% is the configuration typically given for CC in the literature, whereas it does not occur in CS (see Section 3.1.2.2).[188] Yet, this assumption must be treated with great caution owing to the different sampling sizes of the groups and the small numbers of cases.

Finally, it warrants mention that approximately two thirds of the GC ($n=18$) and over one third of the GS wh-questions ($n=10$) contained elements dislocated to the right, among them subjects, objects, adjuncts, subordinate clauses (see Figures 5.86, 5.89 and 5.91 for some examples). These were usually pronounced with entirely flat and low contours, i.e. pitch-deaccenting all metrically stressed syllables independently of the length of the dislocated element (up to 18 syllables). Yet, in two GS and one GC responses, the nuclear contour of the dislocated element was L* H%, and there was one instance of H* L% in GC. In these cases, the nuclear configuration thus repeated the respective nuclear contour of the main clause. Given that dislocations can be seen as a rather typical feature of Catalan in general (see Section 2.3), and of Catalan wh-questions in particular (see, e.g., GEIEC 2018: § 31.3.2), it is interesting to note that 78% of the Catalan and even 90% of the Spanish items were produced by CatD speakers.

As concerns the neutral wh-questions elicited with scenario 3a1 (see Appendix), the 30 responses analysed per language were all phrased in the same way: Sp. *¿Qué hora es?* and Cat. *Quina hora és?* 'What time is it?'. Unfortunately, this wording entails some difficulties for the analysis. In Spanish, it implies a stress clash between the first two syllables: [ˈke.ˈo.ɾa.ˈes]. Furthermore, many speakers reduced one or both of the two hiatuses in this sentence, which again lead to stress clashes: e.g. [ˈke̯o.ˈɾes]. Very similarly, in Catalan, no speakers realized *Quina hora és?* as [ˈki.nə.ˈɔ.ɾə.ˈes], with alternating stressed and unstressed syllables. Instead, most of them removed both of the two hiatuses by dropping the schwa vowels, the result being a triple stress clash: [ˈki.ˈnɔ.ˈres]. Figure 5.92 depicts such an example. Another difficulty sprang from the fact the nuclear accent was always on an ultimate-stress word (i.e. Sp. *es*, Cat. *és* '[it] is'). To perform the intonational analy-

---

188. Note that the contours described by Henriksen (2010, 2014) for Manchego Spanish are not the same. In the variety he studies, the nuclear syllable either contains a clear fall (i.e. H+L*) or a peak whose pitch is higher than that of the preceding prenucleus (transcribed as "¡L+H*" by Henriksen and as "L+¡H*" by Hualde/Prieto 2015: 381).

sis of these utterances, I thus first established the syllable structure on hand, then defined the nuclear contour anchored on the last syllable, and subsequently determined whether any of the other stressed syllables carried a (prenuclear) pitch accent.

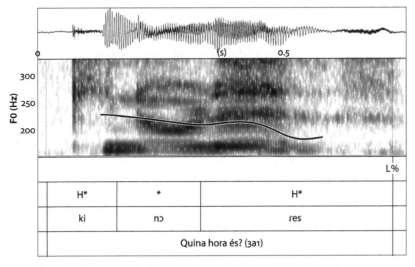

Figure 5.92 Girona Catalan: Waveform, spectrogram, and F0 contour for the information-seeking wh-question ¿*Quina hora és?* 'What time is it' produced by a Catalan-dominant speaker. It represents an IP composed of one ip and is produced with an IP-initial H* prenuclear accent, an H* nuclear accent, and an L% boundary tone. The nuclear configuration of the IP is H* L% (24C21)

In both languages, contours ending in a low tone (i.e. L%) were most common (see Table 5.10, below). However, the most frequent nuclear configuration in GC was H* L%,[189] while L* L% dominated in GS (see Figures 5.92 and 5.93). The association between use of H* or L* in nuclear contours ending in a low boundary tone and Catalan or Spanish, respectively, was statistically significant ($\chi^2(1) = 4.014$, $p = 0.045$). Finally, a rising pattern was registered in roughly one third of the responses (see Figure 5.94 for an example). No significant differences could be detected with regard to the proportions in which the two dominance groups produced the three nuclear configurations.

---

189. As all sentences collected with situation 3a1 ended in ultimate-stress words (i.e. Cat. *és* and Sp. *es* 'is [it]'), it cannot be decided whether the underlying contour is H* L% or H+L* L%. In accordance with the results of the analysis of the wh-questions collected with situation 3a2, the label H* L% was chosen.

Table 5.10 Nuclear configurations in Girona Spanish and Girona Catalan neutral wh-questions gathered with situation 3a1 (percentages and total numbers)

Nuclear contour	H* L%	L* L%	L* H%
GS (n = 30)	30% (9)	40% (12)	30% (9)
GC (n = 30)	50% (15)	13% (4)	37% (11)

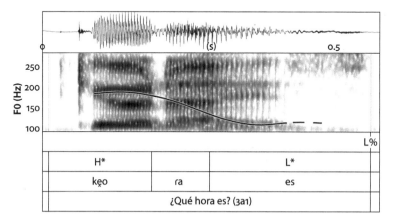

Figure 5.93 Girona Spanish: Waveform, spectrogram, and F0 contour for the information-seeking wh-question ¿Qué hora es? 'What time is it?' produced by a Catalan-dominant speaker. It represents an IP composed of one ip and is produced with an IP-initial H* prenuclear accent and an L* nuclear accent, followed by an L% boundary tone. The nuclear configuration of the IP is L* L% (6S21)

The prenucleus typically contained a high, plateau-like contour in both varieties. Due to the many stress clashes and vowel contractions (i.e. synaloephas), it was not always possible to decide whether the IP-initial prenuclear pitch accent was associated with the first or second syllable of the utterance (i.e. with the wh-word or with Sp./Cat. *hora* 'hour'), especially when the F0 performed a high and flat contour (i.e. H*) within the limits of both stressed syllables. Nevertheless, it is evident that H* was the preferred phrase-initial accent in both varieties (70% in GC, n = 21; 77% in GS, n = 23). It was produced with a proportion of between 60 and 90% by both dominance groups in both varieties. In the remaining cases, the utterances began at a middle or low pitch level (on the wh-word), followed by a gentle rise. Corresponding pitch accents are L+<H* or L*+H (see Figures 5.94 and 5.95, below). Nonetheless, due to the many stress clashes and ultimate-stress words in nuclear position, the intonational analysis of these information-seeking wh-questions is very challenging and some details cannot be definitely decided.

252 Intonation in Language Contact

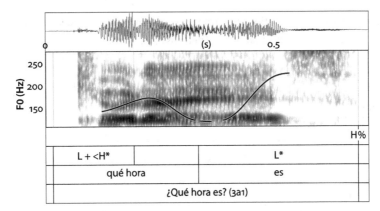

Figure 5.94 Girona Spanish: Waveform, spectrogram, and F0 contour for the information-seeking wh-question *¿Qué hora es?* 'What time is it?' produced by a Catalan-dominant speaker. It represents an IP composed of one ip and is produced with an IP-initial L+<H* prenuclear accent, an L* nuclear accent, and an H% boundary tone. The nuclear configuration of the IP is L* H% (17S21)

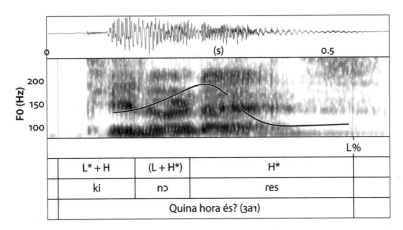

Figure 5.95 GC: Waveform, spectrogram, and F0 contour for the information-seeking wh-question *¿Quina hora és?* 'What time is it' produced by a Catalan-dominant speaker. It represents an IP composed of one ip and is produced with an IP-initial L*+H prenuclear accent, phrase-medial pitch deaccentuation (see Fn. 173), an H* nuclear accent, and an L% boundary tone. The nuclear configuration of the IP is H* L% (17C21)

Summing up, the analysis has revealed that information-seeking wh-questions in both GC and GS typically begin with a phrase-initial H* pitch accent placed on the wh-word. Alternatively, though less frequent, the utterance may begin at a mid or even low level of the speaker's pitch range (i.e. with L+<H* or L*+H pitch accents). Whereas phrase-medial positions tended to be deaccented, a huge gamut

of contours was attested in nuclear position, including falling, low and rising ones. Table 5.11 provides a synopsis (including the utterances recorded with both 3a1 and 3a2).

Table 5.11 Nuclear configurations in Girona Spanish and Girona Catalan neutral wh-questions (percentages and total numbers)

Nuclear contour	H* L%	L* L%	L* H%	Other
GS (n = 58)	47% (27)	26% (15)	22% (13)	5% (3)
GC (n = 57)	61% (35)	12% (7)	23% (13)	4% (2)

As can be seen, falling contours (i.e. H* L%) were overall most common in both varieties, although they were somewhat more recurrent in GC. Interestingly, the literature on CC intonation suggests that falling nuclear contours are most typical in neutral wh-questions, while low contours (i.e. L* L%) are most iconic in CS (see Section 3.1.2.2). Besides, the low–rising contour, i.e. L* H%, is considered a (less frequent) alternative in both languages. It is claimed to express a "nuance of interest and greater speaker involvement in the speech act" (Estebas-Vilaplana/Prieto 2010: 35) or a higher degree of politeness (Sosa 2003b) and was observed to the same extent in both Girona varieties. In the contours ending in a low boundary tone, i.e. L%, the association between the frequencies of H* and L* and language was marginally significant ($\chi^2(1) = 3.018$, $p = 0.082$), which could indicate that a previous difference is currently being lost. Moreover, the different frequencies of H* L% and L* L% cannot be put down to LD either: Table 5.12 shows that both dominance groups behave in the same way.

Table 5.12 Use of H* L% and L* L% in Girona Spanish and Girona Catalan neutral wh-questions according to the speakers' language dominance (percentages and total numbers)

Nuclear contour	Girona Spanish			Girona Catalan		
	CatD	SpD	Total	CatD	SpD	Total
H* L%	67% (20)	58% (7)	47% (27)	83% (24)	85% (11)	61% (35)
L* L%	33% (10)	42% (5)	26% (15)	17% (5)	15% (2)	12% (7)
	100% (30)	100% (12)	100% (42)	100% (29)	100% (13)	100% (42)

Altogether, the results suggest that the bilinguals, independently of their LD and in both languages, make use of contours that probably stem from distinct (i.e. language-specific) repertoires that have largely converged, yielding a new system that allows for a lot of variation (with H* L% being overall dominant). I therefore assume that the present findings are an outcome of bidirectional CLI (see Section 6.4.4 for a detailed discussion).

5.1.6 Biased wh-questions

In this section, I describe the intonational patterns found in GS and GC exclamative (Section 5.1.6.1) and imperative wh-questions (Section 5.1.6.2). The phonological status of the prenuclear pitch accents and nuclear contours found will be discussed in Section 5.2.

5.1.6.1 *Exclamative wh-questions*

Out of the 31 wh-questions gathered for each variety with situation 3b (see Appendix), 31 GS and 28 GC sentences were suitable for an intonational analysis. Concerning their wording, most began with Sp./Cat. *al final* 'in the end', which was pronounced in a separate IP — sometimes detached by a short pause. The main clause of the exclamative wh-question, in turn, always began with the wh-phrase (viz. Sp. *cuánto (dinero)* and Cat. *quant* or *quants diners* 'how much (money)').

L*+H and, less frequently, L+<H* were the typical pitch accents found on the phrase-initial prenuclear syllable (i.e. on the wh-element) in both languages (accounting for 79% and 65% of the items in GC and GS, respectively; see Figure 5.96). H* was used when the main clause was directly preceded by another IP (typically Sp./Cat. *al final* 'in the end' with ultimate stress and thus leading to a stress clash at the phrasal boundary; see Figure 5.97). I interpret these cases as truncated surface variants of L*+H that appear in this particular context. Pitch movements in phrase-medial positions can usually be interpreted as effects of the initial high or rising accents. Otherwise, phrase-medial stressed syllables were generally pitch-deaccented (see also following figures).

In nuclear position, four types of contours were found. Their distribution in the two languages is shown in Table 5.13. It is significantly different across the two varieties ($\chi^2(3) = 10.395$, $p = 0.015$). Concerning LD, all contours were produced by both dominance groups in very similar proportions in both languages, such that no significant differences could be observed (note, however, that this might be an effect of the small numbers of tokens).

In both languages, (¡)H* L% was the most commonly used option (see Figure 5.97, below, for an example). As opposed to neutral wh-questions, this nuclear pitch accent was often upstepped in the exclamative questions, i.e. its peak

Chapter 5. Results 255

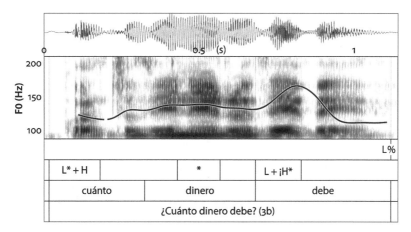

Figure 5.96 Girona Spanish: Waveform, spectrogram, and F0 contour for the exclamative wh-question *¿Cuánto dinero debe?* 'How much money does he owe?' produced by a Catalan-dominant speaker. It represents an IP composed of one ip and is produced with an IP-initial L*+H prenuclear accent, a pitch-deaccented phrase-medial syllable, and an L+¡H* nuclear accent, followed by an L% boundary tone. The nuclear configuration of the IP is L+¡H* L% (34S23)

noticeably exceeded the pitch level of the high plateau in the prenucleus. Furthermore, it frequently represented an overall pitch maximum (see Figure 5.98 for an example). Occasionally, a similar contour was observed (for the most part in GS): L+(¡)H* L%.[190] An example can be seen in Figure 5.96, above. As opposed to (¡)H* L%, this contour showed a clear rise within the nuclear syllable (ending at its right edge) and the respective utterances typically presented more declination in the prenuclear area.

The third nuclear contour, L+H* (¡)H%, seems to be an exclamative variant of the low–rising L* (¡)H% pitch contour used in other question types, such as neutral wh-questions and IYNQ. An example is given in Figure 5.99. In accordance with Prieto (2002a: 446), I assume that the notion of exclamativity is conveyed through the use of increased tonal inflections.

Finally, a low L* L% nuclear contour was sometimes observed in the two varieties (although it was more common in GC). The respective exclamative wh-questions differ from neutral statements in displaying an ip-initial L*+H accent (instead of prenuclear L+<H*), followed by a phrase-medial pitch fall, after which

---

[190]. The pitch accent was labelled as upstepped (i.e. '¡') when it was higher than all preceding pitch peaks and represented the highest point of the utterance. I interpret the upstep as a means of expression of stronger emphasis.

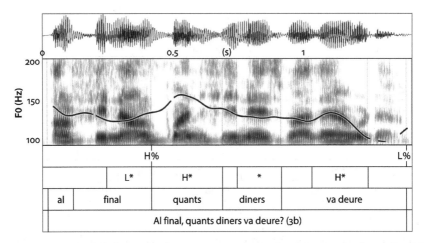

Figure 5.97 Girona Catalan: Waveform, spectrogram, and F0 contour for the exclamative wh-question *Al final, quants diners va deure?* 'How much money did he owe in the end?' produced by a Catalan-dominant speaker. It consists of two IPs. The first one contains an L* H% nuclear configuration. The second one represents the main clause and contains an H* prenuclear accent, a pitch-deaccented phrase-medial stressed syllable, and an H* nuclear pitch accent, followed by an L% boundary tone. The nuclear configuration of this IP is H* L% (18C23)

Table 5.13 Nuclear contours in Girona Spanish and Girona Catalan exclamative wh-questions (percentages and total numbers)

Nuclear contour	(¡)H* L%	L+(¡)H* L%	L+H* (¡)H%	L* L%
GS (*n* = 31)	42% (13)	26% (8)	26% (8)	6% (2)
GC (*n* = 28)	54% (15)	4% (1)	14% (4)	29% (8)

the contour stays low until the end of the utterance. An example is given in Figure 5.100.

In sum, GS and GC exclamative wh-questions present a wide range of intonational contours. They mainly differ from neutral wh-questions through the use of a wider pitch range or, more precisely, though the upstepping of some pitch accents. According to the literature on Spanish and Catalan intonation (see Section 3.1.2.2), some of the nuclear configurations used are rather typical for Catalan (e.g. (¡)H* L%), whereas others appear to me more iconic of Spanish (e.g. L+(¡)H* L%). Nevertheless, if the two languages originally presented different nuclear contours for exclamative wh-questions, the studied bilinguals now mix and use them in both of their languages (see Section 6.4.4 for further discussion).

Chapter 5. Results 257

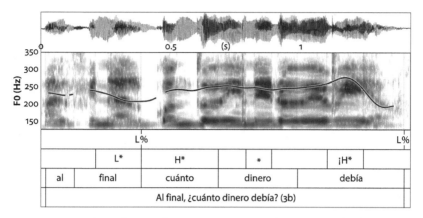

Figure 5.98 Girona Spanish: Waveform, spectrogram, and F0 contour for the exclamative wh-question *Al final, ¿cuánto dinero debía?* 'How much money did he owe in the end?' produced by a Spanish-dominant speaker. It consists of two IPs. The first one contains an L* L% nuclear configuration. The second one represents the main clause and contains an H* prenuclear accent, a pitch-deaccented phrase-medial position, and an ¡H* nuclear accent, followed by an L% boundary tone. The nuclear configuration of the IP is ¡H* L% (5S23)

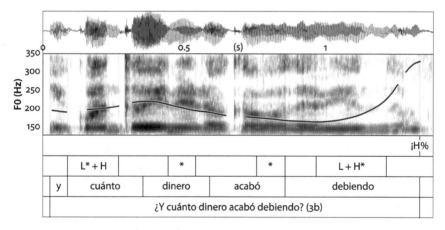

Figure 5.99 Girona Spanish: Waveform, spectrogram, and F0 contour for the exclamative wh-question *¿Y cuánto dinero acabó debiendo?* 'How much money did he end up owing?' produced by a Catalan-dominant speaker. It represents an IP composed of one ip and is produced with an IP-initial L*+H prenuclear accent, two instances of phrase-medial pitch deaccentuation, and an L+H* nuclear accent, followed by an ¡H% boundary tone. The nuclear configuration of the IP is L+H* ¡H% (10S23)

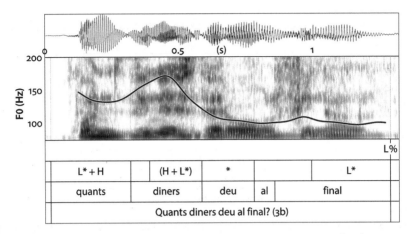

Figure 5.100 Girona Catalan: Waveform, spectrogram, and F0 contour for the exclamative wh-question *Quants diners deu al final?* 'How much money does he owe in the end?' produced by a Catalan-dominant speaker. It represents an IP composed of one ip and is produced with an L*+H prenuclear accent, phrase-medial pitch deaccentuation (see Fn. 173), and an L* nuclear accent, followed by an L% boundary tone. The nuclear configuration is L* L% (22C23)

5.1.6.2 *Imperative wh-questions*

A total of 62 utterances were recorded with situation 3c. Some few had to be discarded due to strong disfluencies or because they did not contain a wh-word, leaving 29 GS and 27 GC items for analysis. The given responses typically began with the question word followed by the verb, which, in turn, was accompanied by an object that could be a clitic, a noun phrase or, in some cases, a relative clause: for instance, Sp. *¿Cuándo lo harás?* 'When are you going to do it?' or Cat. *Quan em faràs allò que et vaig dir?* 'When are you going to do what I asked you to do?'.

As in other question types, L+<H* and L*+H appeared as phrase-initial prenuclear pitch accents in both varieties. However, L+<H* was more common. Phrase-medial prenuclear positions were — for the most part — analysed as pitch-deaccented, since pitch movements found within their limits could be generally interpreted as effects of the initial rising tone.

Various nuclear configurations were used to express imperative wh-questions. The most recurrent one was H+L* L% (see Figure 5.101), but it was only found when the last element in the sentence was the lexical verb (i.e. Sp./Cat *harás/faràs* or Sp. *vas a hacer* 'you are going to do').[191] When the verb was followed by further

---

[191]. As the respective contour exclusively occurred on penultimate-stress words, it could not be decided whether the underlying nuclear configuration was H+L* L% or H* L%. The label H+L L% was chosen in concert with the literature on CC and CS intonation (see Section 3.1.2.2)

elements (e.g. an object), the stressed syllable of the verb displayed a pitch fall and thereafter the intonation continued on a low level until the utterance end (see Figure 5.102). This pattern occurred in 15 GC and 8 GS sentences (i.e. in 56% and 28% of the items, respectively). Technically, the nuclear configuration in these utterances (as defined as anchored on the last metrically strong syllable in an IP) was L* L% at first sight. Yet, given that the pitch fall aligned with verb was clearly more prominent, the possibility needs be considered that the stressed syllable of the verb could actually be a nuclear one. In such an analysis — which I adopt here — the respective interrogatives are viewed as split up into various IPs through a phrasal break at the end of the lexical verb, marked by a low boundary tone, and post-verbal constituents are seen as dislocated to the right. Figure 5.103 illustrates a further case in which this analysis seems pretty straightforward.

In fact, the analysis just presented is very similar to that of other question types such as IYNQ introduced by the particle *que*, where the subject is pronounced in a separate phrase after the verb (see Section 5.1.3.1). Concerning the LD of the speakers, the imperative wh-questions with dislocations attested in the present corpus were produced by speakers of either LD in the same proportion. However, the fact that they occurred with a higher frequency in Catalan once more confirms the stronger propensity of this language to use dislocations.

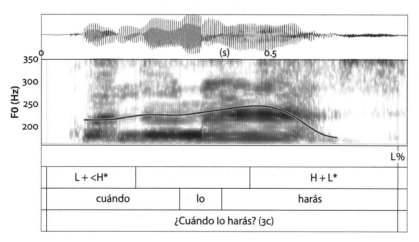

Figure 5.101 Girona Spanish: Waveform, spectrogram, and F0 contour for the imperative wh-question *¿Cuándo lo harás?* 'When are you going to do it?' produced by a Catalan-dominant speaker. It represents an IP composed of one ip and is produced with an IP-initial L+<H* prenuclear accent, and an H+L* nuclear accent, followed by an L% boundary tone. The nuclear configuration of the IP is H+L* L% (24S24)

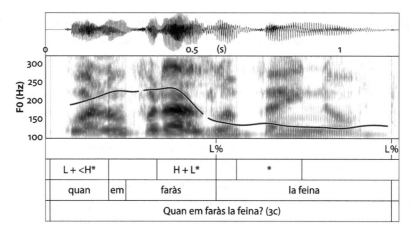

Figure 5.102 Girona Catalan: Waveform, spectrogram, and F0 contour for the imperative wh-question *Quan em faràs la feina?* 'When are you going to do this job for me?' produced by a Catalan-dominant speaker. It consists of two IPs. The first one contains an IP-initial L+<H* prenuclear accent, an H+L* nuclear accent, and an L% boundary tone. The nuclear configuration of the second one is L* L% (6C24)

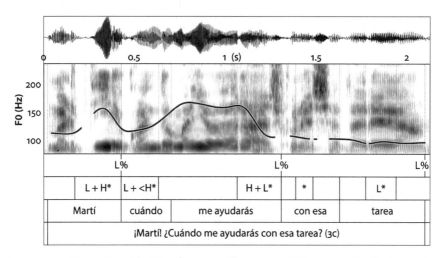

Figure 5.103 Girona Spanish: Waveform, spectrogram, and F0 contour for the imperative wh-question *¿Cuándo me ayudarás con esa tarea?* 'When are you going to help me with that task?' produced by a Catalan-dominant speaker. It consists of two IPs. The first one contains an IP-initial L+<H* prenuclear accent and an H+L* nuclear accent, followed by an L% boundary tone. The second one has an L* L% nuclear configuration (23S24)

Besides H+L* L%, some instances of a low-rising L* H% configuration were observed. Interestingly, they were somewhat more common in GS (29%, n = 8) than in GC (7%, n = 2). In GS, they were produced by speakers of either LD. The GC items stemmed from SpD bilinguals. Bearing in mind that the same contour was also attested in information-seeking yes–no and wh-questions, the questions that arise here are: first, why do some imperative wh-questions show the same nuclear contour? And second, what additional prosodic correlates are used in these cases to convey the imperative meaning?

Finally, the corpus contained 4 GS utterances with a circumflex nuclear configuration, i.e. L+(¡)H* L% (14% of the GS items; see Figure 5.104). According to Estebas-Vilaplana and Prieto (2010: 38), "L+¡H* HL%" can be used in imperative wh-questions with "a nuance of invitation, that is, [when] the speaker offers his/her interlocutor the possibility of doing something". However, in the two cases in which the nuclear syllable was not the last of the IP, there were no signs of an underlying HL% boundary tone. Neither does the upstep seem to be obligatory, since the nuclear peaks exceeded the level of preceding high tones only twice. Furthermore, the mentioned nuance of invitation would be rather unexpected (or even odd) from a pragmatic point of view in the given context. Last, no link between the use of this tune and the bilinguals' LD could be established.

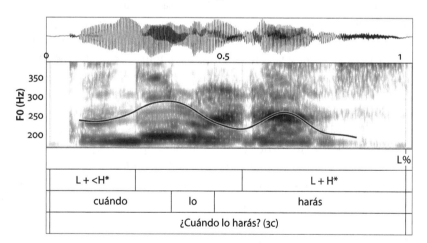

Figure 5.104 Girona Spanish: Waveform, spectrogram, and F0 contour for the imperative wh-question ¿*Cuándo lo harás?* 'When are you going to do it?' produced by a Catalan-dominant speaker. It represents an IP composed of one ip and is produced with an IP-initial L+<H* prenuclear accent, and an L+H* nuclear accent, followed by an L% boundary tone. The nuclear configuration of the IP is L+H* L% (35S24)

5.1.7 Echo questions

In this section, I describe the intonational patterns attested in three different types of echo questions: echo yes–no questions (Section 5.1.7.1), echo wh-questions (Section 5.1.7.2), and echo exclamative yes–no questions with counterexpectational meaning (Section 5.1.7.3). The phonological status of the prenuclear pitch accents and nuclear contours will be discussed in Section 5.2.

5.1.7.1 *Echo yes–no questions*

Each 27 GS and GC IPs collected with situation 4a could be retained for the intonational analysis of echo yes–no questions. 4 utterances per variety had thus to be excluded due to disfluencies or because they did not correspond to the desired sentence type.[192] Most utterances were phrased as Sp. *¿(Has dicho) (que son) las nueve?* or Cat. *(M'has dit) (que eren/són/és) la una?* '(Have you said) (that it is) nine/one o'clock?'.

Similarly to the yes–no questions described in the previous sections, L*+H occurred as the typical ip-initial prenuclear pitch accent in both varieties, accounting for over 83% of the accents in this position. It usually associated with the IP-initial auxiliary (i.e. *has*) and reached the peak corresponding to its high target in one of the two following syllables. Phrase-medial prenuclear positions were usually pitch-deaccented, i.e. they either showed a plateau or the pitch movements found within their limits were caused by the high targets of preceding rising pitch accents (a surface labelling of the F0 contour is given in brackets).

The predominant nuclear configuration used to express echo yes–no questions was L* H% in both varieties. In most cases, the pitch maximum of the utterance was attained at the end of this contour (label: 'L* ¡H%'). Figures 5.105 and 5.106 show typical examples for GC and GS. As in other question types, the nuclear L* accent sometimes surfaced as H+L* (due to the influence of preceding high targets) or as L+H* (as an effect of the following upstepped high boundary tone).

Two other nuclear contours are noteworthy. L+H* L% occurred twice in GC and four times in GS (see Figure 5.107 for an example). It was typically used when the echo question consisted of only one prosodic word. Moreover, speaker 13 — the one of Honduran origin — again used H+L* LH% in both her Catalan and her Spanish sentence. Since the participants overall tended to use L* H%, no inferences can be made about the effect of LD on the choice of intonational patterns in echo yes–no questions.

---

192. This was the case, for instance, when the sentences contained wh-words (e.g. Cat. *Quina hora m'has dit que era?* 'What time did you say it is?') or represented requests rather than echo questions (e.g. Sp. *¿Me puede repetir la hora, por favor?* 'Can you repeat the time for me, please?').

Chapter 5. Results 263

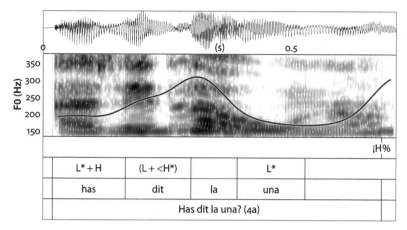

Figure 5.105 Girona Catalan: Waveform, spectrogram, and F0 contour for the echo yes–no question *Has dit la una?* 'Have you said one o'clock?' produced by a Catalan-dominant speaker. It represents an IP composed of one ip and is produced with an L*+H prenuclear accent, phrase-medial pitch deaccentuation (see Fn. 173) and an L* nuclear accent, followed by an ¡H% boundary tone. The nuclear configuration of the IP is L* ¡H% (15C25)

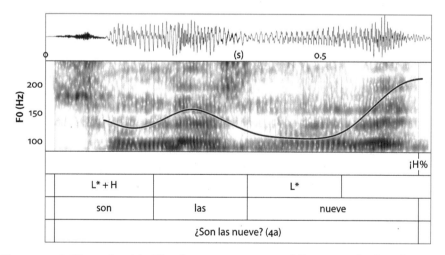

Figure 5.106 Girona Spanish: Waveform, spectrogram, and F0 contour for the echo yes–no question *¿Son las nueve?* 'Is it nine o'clock?' produced by a Catalan-dominant speaker. It represents an IP composed of one ip and is produced with an L*+H prenuclear accent and an L* nuclear accent, followed by an ¡H% boundary tone. The nuclear configuration of the IP is L* ¡H% (22S25)

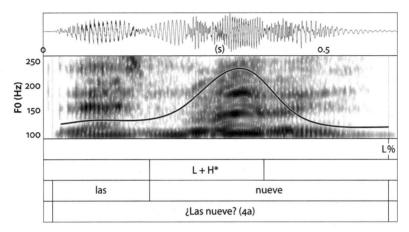

Figure 5.107 Girona Spanish: Waveform, spectrogram, and F0 contour for the echo yes–no question ¿*Las nueve?* 'Nine o'clock?' produced by a Spanish-dominant speaker. It represents an IP composed of one ip and is produced with an L+H* nuclear accent, followed by an L% boundary tone. The nuclear configuration of the IP is L+H* L% (21S25)

The comparison of the echo yes–no questions with the IYNQ described in Section 5.1.3.1 and the exclamative yes–no questions in Section 5.1.4.1 reveals that the bilingual speakers of GC and GC generally use the nuclear configuration L* (¡)H% to mark yes–no questions independently from their pragmatic type. Besides, it showed that L+H* L% appears only in echo yes–no questions, which is interesting, since it is also the typical nuclear contour of biased statements (exclamative, dubitative or with contrastive focus, see Section 5.1.2). Considering that L+H* signals focus and emphasis in both varieties (as opposed to L*, which expresses neutral readings), it can be suggested that the bilinguals can use it in echo yes–no questions to convey narrow focus on the last word. However, further research is needed to confirm this.

5.1.7.2 Echo wh-questions

62 items were collected with situation 4b (see Appendix), of which each 30 GS and 30 GC questions could be studied with regard to their intonation. Like echo yes–no questions, most echo wh-questions began with an element such as Sp. *me has/habéis/han preguntado (que)* or Cat. *m'has/heu dit/demanat/preguntat (que)* 'have you asked me' that preceded the 'echoed' part (for instance, Sp. *(a)dónde voy* or Cat. *on vaig* 'where I am going'). While echo wh-questions are polar questions from a pragmatic point of view – i.e. as opposed to information-seeking wh-questions, they require a 'yes' or 'no' answer – this procedure also marks them 'syntactically' as yes–no questions, since the wh-word becomes indirect when heading a subordinate clause instead of the main clause.

It thus comes as no surprise that most of the utterances in this context display the same intonational patterns as in information-seeking and echo yes–no questions. L*+H accounted for roughly 80% of the phrase-initial prenuclear accents in both varieties and was usually placed on the auxiliary. Phrase-medial positions (including phrase-medial indirect wh-words) were typically pitch-deaccented (see also the IYNQ in Section 5.1.3.1.2). In nuclear position, L* followed by a high boundary tone was used in 80% of the GC (*n* = 24) and 53% of the GS echo questions (*n* = 16). For the most part, the right boundary was the highest point of the utterance (label: '¡H%'). Figure 5.108 provides an example.

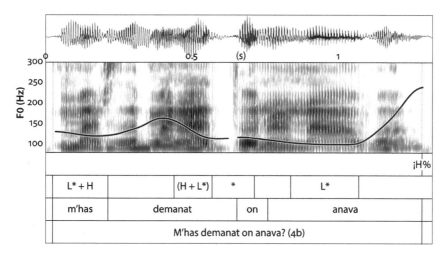

Figure 5.108 Girona Catalan: Waveform, spectrogram, and F0 contour for the echo wh-question *M'has demanat on anava?* 'Did you ask me where I was going?' produced by a Catalan-dominant speaker. It represents an IP composed of one ip and is produced with an initial L*+H prenuclear accent, phrase-medial pitch deaccentuation (see Fn. 173), and an L* nuclear accent, followed by an ¡H% boundary tone. The nuclear configuration of the IP is L* ¡H% (34C26)

Two further nuclear patterns are worth of note. First, high–falling nuclear contours were registered four times in GC and eleven in GS (13% and 37% of the items, respectively). They were labelled as H* L% but given that the nuclear contour was almost exclusively found on ultimate-stress words (viz. Sp. *voy*, Cat. *vaig*, both 'I go') H+L* L% would have been possible as well. The contour often appeared on rather short questions consisting merely of the 'echo part', such as Sp. *¿Adónde voy?* or Cat. *Que on vaig?* 'Where I am going?'. Figure 5.109 provides an example. However, considering that a slight rise could be perceived in the nuclear syllable prior to the final fall, three GS items were labelled as L+H* L%. Interestingly, such a circumflex contour is usually presented as the typical realization of echo wh-questions in much of literature on Peninsular Spanish intonation (see

Hualde/Prieto 2015: 382 and Section 3.1.2.2). In CC, it is an alternative to the more common L* H% pattern (Prieto et al. 2015: 32–33, 57). It is thus possible that the H* L% contours mentioned above actually constitute surface variants of an underlying L+H* L% nuclear configuration. This surface variant would then be conditioned by high preceding tones (see Section 5.2.3 for such an interpretation).

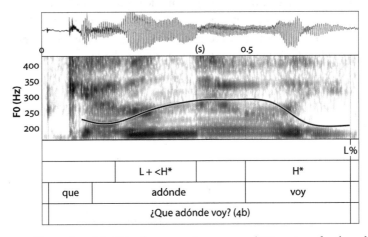

Figure 5.109 Girona Spanish: Waveform, spectrogram, and F0 contour for the echo wh-question ¿Que a*dónde* voy? 'Where I am going?' produced by a Catalan-dominant speaker. It represents an IP composed of one ip and is produced with an initial L+<H* prenuclear accent and an H* nuclear accent, followed by an L% boundary tone. The nuclear configuration of the IP is H* L% (31S26)

Second and last, each two GC and two GS sentences with an (L+)H* LH% nuclear contour were found (see Figure 5.110). They were produced by CatD speakers. Since Prieto et al. (2015: 57) give L+H* LH% as a possible nuclear configuration of CC echo wh-questions, H* LH% might be a surface realization of this underlying contour that appears after high preceding tonal targets (see also Section 5.2.3).

Taken together, these results suggest that echo wh-questions can be intonated the same way as IYNQ, especially when the question is phrased with a main clause representing a yes–no question and the wh-word heads a subordinate clause to this matrix yes–no question. However, when the echo question consists only of the 'echo part', that seems to increase the odds for the sentence to be pronounced with a different nuclear contour, such as (L+)H* L% or (L+)H* LH%. Concerning the LD of the speakers, no clear preferences of either group for a particular intonational pattern could be found in the data due to the relatively small numbers of cases of the more specific contours. Nevertheless, it could be observed that patterns other than the low–rising one were somewhat more frequent in Spanish and produced in a higher proportion by SpD bilinguals.

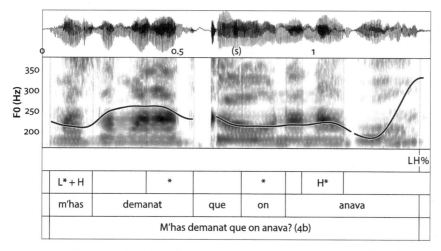

Figure 5.110 Girona Catalan: Waveform, spectrogram, and F0 contour for the echo wh-question *M'has demanat que on anava?* 'Did you ask where I was going?' produced by a Catalan-dominant speaker. It represents an IP composed of one ip and is produced with an initial L*+H prenuclear accent, phrase-medial deaccentuation, and an H* nuclear accent, followed by an LH% boundary tone. The nuclear configuration of the IP is H* HL% (14C26)

5.1.7.3 *Exclamative echo yes–no questions (with counterexpectational meaning)*

From the total of 62 utterances obtained with situation 4c (see Appendix), 29 exclamative echo yes–no questions per variety could be studied with regard to intonation. The remaining utterances either did not correspond to the desired question type or contained too many disfluencies. In respect of their wording, most were formulated as usual yes–no questions, but they generally contained elements expressing surprise such as Cat. *de debò, de veritat* 'really', Sp. *en serio (que)* 'seriously', *¿Dices que...* 'Are you saying that ...', or were preceded by exclamations such as Sp. *¿¡Cómo!?* 'What!?', *¡No me lo creo!* 'I don't believe this!'.

At the intonational level, the gathered exclamative echo yes–no questions generally followed the pattern already established for information-seeking and echo yes–no questions: i.e. roughly 90% of the phrase-initial prenuclear pitch accents corresponded to the L*+H type and, in nuclear position, approximately 90% of the utterances showed an L* (¡)H%[193] nuclear configuration. The few phrase-medial positions contained in the data were usually pitch-deaccented. A GS example is given in Figure 5.111.

---

193. The label '¡H%' was used when the end of the IP represented its highest point.

Nevertheless, the participants often used an extended pitch range and increased pitch movements. It was especially striking that, as opposed to other question types, the syllables preceding the phrase-initial L*+H accent were sometimes noticeably higher than the stressed syllable in exclamative echo yes–no questions. In some cases, even a clear pitch-fall surfaced within the limits of that syllable, as can be seen in Figure 5.112. Whether this phenomenon is only an effect of the use of an expanded pitch range or corresponds to an initial boundary tone (%H) or something like an 'H+L*+H' pitch accent cannot be decided here. Besides, the effects of an extended pitch range also showed up in the fact that the nuclear L* pitch accent sometimes surfaced as H+L*. This is particularly evident in the example in Figure 5.113. Finally, the closing boundary tone was often especially high (i.e. '¡H%'). For instance, in the last two examples the rises were of 269 and 178 Hz (18.6 and 11.5 semitones). The high boundary tones sometimes also affected the nuclear pitch accent, so that it presented a slight rise (i.e. L+H*) instead of a low plateau.

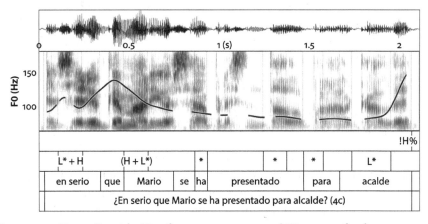

Figure 5.111 Girona Spanish: Waveform, spectrogram, and F0 contour for the exclamative echo yes–no question ¿*En serio que Mario se ha presentado para alcalde?* 'Is Mario seriously running for mayor?' produced by a Spanish-dominant speaker. It represents an IP composed of one ip and is produced with an L*+H prenuclear accent, phrase-medial pitch deaccentuation (see Fn. 173), and an L* nuclear accent, followed by an ¡H% boundary tone. The nuclear configuration of the IP is L* ¡H% (35S27)

Furthermore, six sentences contained clearly different nuclear contours (3 per language, i.e. 10%). Four of these (2 per language) had falling H+L* L% (see Figure 5.114), and two (both from the same SpD speaker) presented L+H* L%, i.e. the typical contour of contrastive-focus and exclamative statements. Given that all nuclear contours occurred in equal proportion in both varieties, no correlation between the use of a particular nuclear contour and language or the speakers' LD could be established.

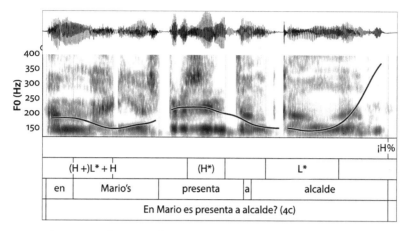

Figure 5.112 Girona Catalan: Waveform, spectrogram, and F0 contour for the exclamative echo yes–no question *En Mario es presenta a alcalde?* 'Mario is going to run for mayor?' produced by a Catalan-dominant speaker. It represents an IP composed of one ip and is produced with an initial (H+)L*+H prenuclear accent, phrase-medial pitch deaccentuation (see Fn. 173), and an L* nuclear pitch accent, followed by an ¡H% boundary tone. The nuclear configuration of the IP is L* ¡H% (19SC67)

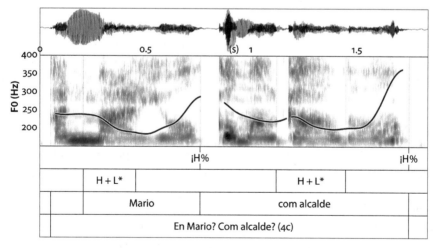

Figure 5.113 Girona Catalan: Waveform, spectrogram, and F0 contour for the exclamative echo yes–no question(s) *En Mario? Com alcalde?* 'Mario? As a mayor?' produced by a Catalan-dominant speaker. It is composed of two IPs. Both are produced with an H+L* nuclear accent, followed by a high boundary tone (¡H%). The nuclear configurations of the IPs are H+L* ¡H% (28SC27)

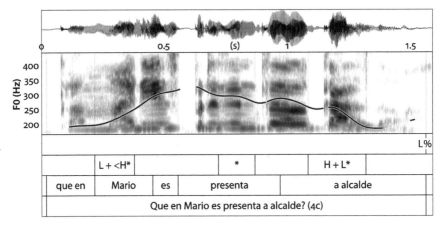

Figure 5.114 Girona Catalan: Waveform, spectrogram, and F0 contour for the exclamative echo yes–no question *Que en Mario es presenta a alcalde?* '(You are saying) that Mario is running for mayor?' produced by a Spanish-dominant speaker. It represents an IP composed of one ip and is produced with a phrase-initial L+<H* prenuclear accent, phrase-medial pitch deaccentuation, and an H+L* nuclear accent, followed by an L% boundary tone. The nuclear configuration of the IP is H+L* L% (5SC27)

5.1.8 Imperatives

In this section, I describe the intonational patterns used in commands and requests in GS and GC. I here present the prenuclear pitch accents and nuclear configurations found in my corpus. Their phonological status will be discussed in Section 5.2.

5.1.8.1 *Commands*

Although all 62 recorded utterances (31 per variety) represented pragmatically felicitous responses to scenario 5a (see Appendix), used in many previous studies to elicit commands containing imperatives, many of them were phrased as interrogatives, such as Sp. *¿Podrían rellenarme este formulario, por favor?* 'Could you fill in this form, please?', or as statements (e.g. Cat. *Heu d'omplir aquest formulari, si us plau.* 'You need to fill in this form, please.'). This seems to be a common problem: for instance, Brehm et al. (2014) report difficulties to make participants utter imperatives because they are considered very impolite in Mexican Spanish (see also Vanrell et al. 2018: 15; Blum-Kulka et al. 1989). Unfortunately, it was not possible to ask participants to reformulate their responses, since explicitly instructing participants to use an imperative would no longer yield spontaneous speech and presenting them with an exemplary response would have influenced their intonation through priming.

Eventually, 7 GS and 6 GC commands involved the desired imperative verb forms (of Sp. *rellenar* and Cat. *emplenar/omplir* all 'fill in'). All consisted of the imperative verb in initial position and an object in nuclear position. In a second step, I additionally analysed 8 further (simple) imperative forms (6 GS and 3 GC items) belonging to the verbs Cat./Sp. *perdonar, disculpar* '(to) excuse' and *mirar* '(to) look' that were used at the beginning of some of the responses formulated as interrogatives or statements.

As concerns the prenucleus, most phrase-initial pitch accents were realized as L+<H* or L*+H in both languages (the former being more frequent), and the few phrase-medial prenuclear positions that occurred in the data were pitch-deaccented. The predominant nuclear contour was H+L* L% (5 instances in GS and 3 in GC, see Figure 5.115 for an example). The flat L* L% contour might be a surface variant (2 items in GC and 1 in GS; see Figure 5.116). The remaining two sentences showed an L+H* L% nuclear contour. Since L+H* conveys focus and emphasis in other sentence types, I suggest that the use of this pitch accent might add emphasis as compared to the other ones.

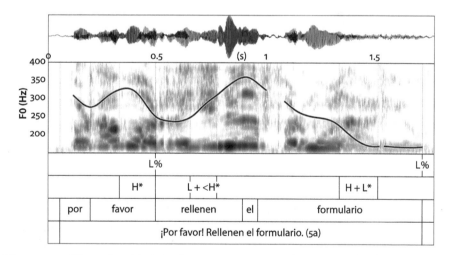

Figure 5.115 Girona Spanish: Waveform, spectrogram, and F0 contour for the command *Rellenen el formulario*. 'Fill in the form' produced by a Catalan-dominant speaker. It represents an IP composed of one ip and is produced with a phrase-initial L+<H* prenuclear accent and an H+L* nuclear accent, followed by an L% boundary tone. The nuclear configuration of the IP is H+L* L% (28S28)

In the one-word ips preceding other sentences, L+H* L% was employed in both varieties — sometimes with its pitch peak slightly delayed into the post-nuclear syllable (see Figure 5.117). However, I assume that imperatives such as *¡Perdona!* 'Excuse me' and *¡Rellenad el formulario!* 'Fill in the form' do not represent

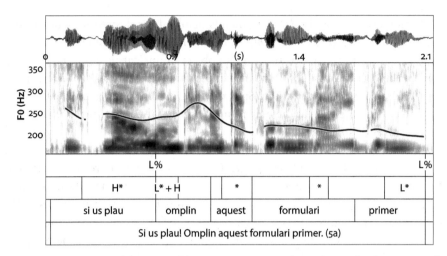

Figure 5.116 Girona Catalan: Waveform, spectrogram, and F0 contour for the command *Omplin aquest formulari primer.* 'Fill in this form first' produced by a Catalan-dominant speaker. It represents an IP composed of one ip and is produced with a phrase-initial L*+H prenuclear accent, phrase-medial pitch deaccentuation, and an L* nuclear accent, followed by an L% boundary tone. The nuclear configuration of the IP is L* L% (31C28)

fully comparable orders with the same imperative force. In the former case, the imperative is rather used to ask for the listener's attention. This type of utterance-initial imperative may thus rather correspond to the requests described in the next section.

5.1.8.2 *Requests*

Although all utterances recorded with situation 5b (i.e. 31 per variety) were pragmatically adequate, some responses were phrased as statements or interrogatives. Only 18 GS and 13 GC were formulated as desired in the imperative mood and could be retained for the intonational analysis. Besides, 16 sentences utterances per variety were introduced with elements such as Sp. *va, venga, vamos* or Cat. *va, vinga*, all 'Come on!'), i.e. by expressions that originally represented imperatives but have become more or less grammaticalized as hortative particles or interjections. Their intonation will be analysed in a second step.

In phrase-initial position, the same two rising pitch accents were observed in both varieties, viz. L+<H* and L*+H, the first one of these being somewhat more frequent. The few phrase-medial prenuclear positions that occurred in the data were either clearly pitch-deaccented or showed a pitch peak (i.e. H*). However, such peaks could also be effects of preceding rising accents. In nuclear position, H+L* L% was most frequent in both GS and GC, appearing in slightly more than half of the utterances (see Figure 5.118).

Chapter 5. Results 273

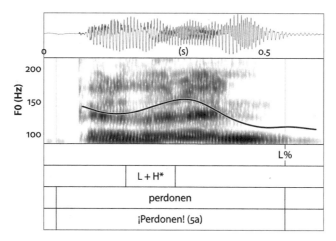

Figure 5.117 Girona Spanish: Waveform, spectrogram, and F0 contour for the command *¡Perdonen!* 'Excuse me!' produced by a Catalan-dominant speaker. It represents an IP composed of one ip and is produced with an L+H* nuclear accent, followed by an L% boundary tone. The nuclear configuration of the IP is L+H* L% (17S28)

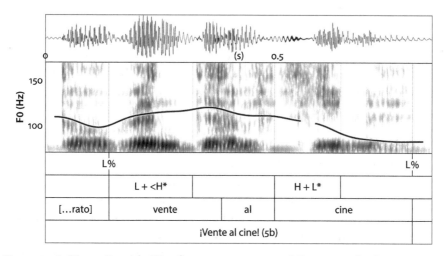

Figure 5.118 Girona Spanish: Waveform, spectrogram, and F0 contour for the request *¡Vente al cine!* 'Come [with me] to the cinema' produced by a Catalan-dominant speaker. It represents an IP composed of one ip and is produced with a phrase-initial L+<H* prenuclear accent and an H+L* nuclear accent, followed by an L% boundary tone. The nuclear configuration of the IP is H+L* L% (18S29)

The remaining sentences had either L+H* L% or L+H* HL%. However, the length of the utterance and/or the position of the imperative verb seem to have an influence on the intonation of the request (see Prieto 2002a: 457–458; Lausecker et al. 2014; Brehm et al. 2014 for similar findings): when it consisted only of the verb in the imperative mood, i.e. when the sentence had only one accented syllable, the nuclear contours used were always L+H* L% or L+H* HL% and never H+L* L% (6 instances in GC, 2 in GS; see Figure 5.119). Regarding the choice of the boundary tone in the 'short' requests (i.e. L% vs HL%), the data do not allow for reliable inferences, but following the literature on CS and CC intonation I assume that HL% conveys more insistence (see Section 3.1.2.2).

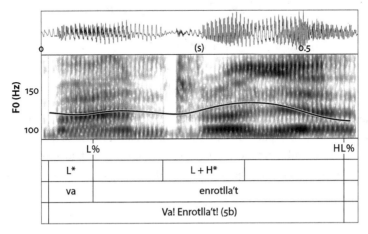

Figure 5.119 Girona Catalan: Waveform, spectrogram, and F0 contour for the request *Enrotlla't!* 'Get involved!' produced by a Catalan-dominant speaker. It represents an IP composed of one ip and is produced with an L+H* nuclear accent, followed by an HL% boundary tone. The nuclear configuration of the IP is L+H* HL% (11C29)

On the other hand, when a request consisted of at least two prosodic words and the imperative verb was in non-final position, H+L* L% was generally used. Whereas no counterexamples to this complementary distribution were found in GC, in GS, L+H* was only less frequent as compared to H+L* in utterances containing a prenucleus (6 vs 9 cases). What conditions the choice of either of these nuclear pitch accents cannot be ultimately answered here. Two lines of thinking could be pursued in further research: first, the length of the utterance and thus the distance between the phrase-initial imperative verb and the nuclear pitch accent could have an impact on pitch-accent choice, viewing that some of the sentences containing nuclear L+H* instead of H+L* were rather long (e.g. Sp. *Deja el trabajo para más adelante.* 'Leave the piece of work for later.'). Second, L+H* could convey emphasis or focus — as in other sentence types — or more insistence (e.g. in Sp. *¡Vente al cine conmigo!* 'Come to the cinema with me!'). This was also suggested by Lausecker et al. (2014). It is worth mentioning that the last syllable was often considerably lengthened independently of the boundary tone used. A check of the speakers' LD did not reveal any correlation with the choice of either nuclear contour.

Concerning the intonation of 'hortative imperative particles' such as Sp./Cat. *va* 'come on!', a large gamut of different pitch contours was attested in both languages. Especially with monosyllables, it could often not be decided which combinations of nuclear pitch accents and boundary tones underlay the realizations. For instance, *va* was found in both languages with low, falling, rising, rising-falling, and falling-rising contours without any clear preference (see Figure 5.120 for a 'low' example). The disyllabic *venga, vaya*, both 'come on', and *vamos* 'let's go', however, were pronounced either with H* L% or L+H* L%, which could be different surface variants of one underlying contour.

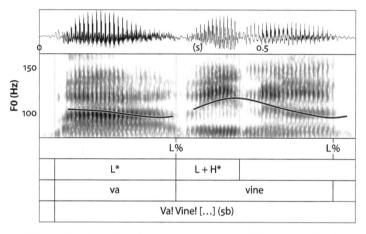

Figure 5.120 Girona Catalan: Waveform, spectrogram, and F0 contour for the request *(Va!) Vine!* '(Come on!) Come (with me)!' produced by a Catalan-dominant speaker. It represents an IP composed of one ip and is produced with an L+H* nuclear accent, followed by an L% boundary tone. The nuclear configuration of the IP is L+H* L% (29C29)

5.1.9 Vocatives

A total of 62 vocatives were recorded with situation 6 (see Appendix). Roughly half of items were followed by a question or an imperative such as Sp. *¿Dónde estás?* 'Where are you?' or Cat. *Vine!* 'Come!', usually with a short pause between the vocative and the following element. Only nuclear contours can be described for these vocatives, since no prenuclear pitch accents were present in the data.

In both varieties, L+H* was used as nuclear pitch accent almost without exceptions. The dominant nuclear configuration was L+H* HL%. In many cases, the final (post-nuclear) syllable was lengthened (350 to 500 ms), in some cases considerably (highest value: 767 ms). Figure 5.121 offers an example with moderate lengthening (362 ms).

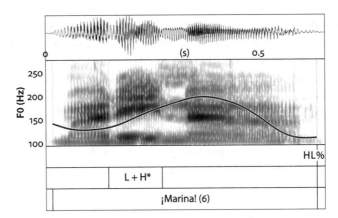

Figure 5.121 Girona Spanish: Waveform, spectrogram, and F0 contour for the vocative ¡Ma*ri*na! 'Marina!' produced by a Catalan-dominant speaker. It represents an IP composed of one ip and is produced with an L+H* nuclear accent, followed by an HL% boundary tone. The post-nuclear syllable is moderately lengthened (362 ms). The nuclear configuration of the IP is L+H* HL% (34S30)

Two further nuclear contours were found. L+H* !H%, the typical 'vocative chant' (see Section 3.1.2.2), was used to an extent of 13% ($n=4$ per variety; see Figure 5.122 for an example). It is of note that this intonational pattern was not very frequent in the present data set, since it is generally described as the most common realization of vocatives in the literature on both languages, whereas L+H* HL% is said to convey more insistence.

Finally, 5 GC (16%) and 6 GS vocatives (19%) were rendered with high boundary tones (i.e. H%). The corresponding nuclear pitch accent were L+H* or, in two cases, L*. An example is given in Figure 5.123. As these combinations of nuclear pitch accents and boundary tones resemble questions, I suggest that vocatives intonated in this way pragmatically convey the same meaning as other vocatives followed by a question such as 'Are you there?' or 'Can you hear me?', i.e. the speaker does not address an interlocutor whom they already know or assume to be present, but they rather check or intend to make sure whether the interlocutor is actually nearby (see also Huttenlauch et al. 2018 for "confirmation-seeking vocatives"). This connotation of the "rising interrogative contour" was also proposed by Borràs-Comes et al. (2015:78), who found it to appear typically "in situations where the speaker had no close relationship with the hearer (i.e. in work situations)".

Chapter 5. Results   277

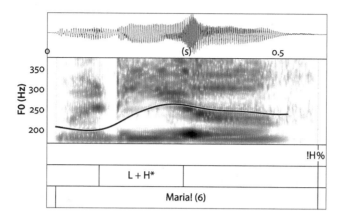

Figure 5.122 Girona Catalan: Waveform, spectrogram, and F0 contour for the vocative *María!* 'Maria!' produced by a Catalan-dominant speaker. It represents an IP composed of one ip and is produced with an L+H* nuclear accent, followed by a !H% boundary tone. The post-nuclear syllable is slightly lengthened (289 ms). The nuclear configuration of the IP is L+H* !HL% (24C30)

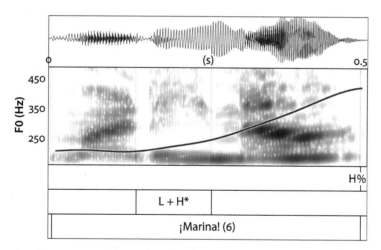

Figure 5.123 Girona Spanish: Waveform, spectrogram, and F0 contour for the vocative *¡Marina!* 'Marina!' produced by a Catalan-dominant speaker. It represents an IP composed of one ip and is produced with an L+H* nuclear accent, followed by an H% boundary tone. The nuclear configuration of the IP is L+H* H% (16S30)

5.1.10 Analysis of Girona Spanish read speech

In this section, I describe the results of the intonational analysis of the GS *que*-questions (5.1.10.1) and dislocations (5.1.10.2) contained in the dialogue that was read aloud by all participants of the experiment as second task (see Section 4.3.2 for a detailed description of the materials and procedure). The phonological status of the pitch accents and boundary tones will be discussed in the following subchapter (Section 5.2).

5.1.10.1 *Girona Spanish* que-*questions*

All 124 yes–no interrogatives recorded could be analysed with respect to their intonation, although five of them contained some minor disfluencies (see below). I will first give an overview of the attested nuclear configurations, then describe who (in terms of LD) used them in which pragmatic question type and finally do the same thing for prenuclear pitch accents.

All but two nuclear configurations clearly corresponded either to the high–falling type, i.e. H+L* L% ($n=77$, 62%), or to the low–rising one, i.e. L* H% ($n=45$, 36%) (see Section 5.1.3.1.3 for extensive descriptions of these patterns). However, the distribution of the two contours was not the same in all question types and there were also slight differences in their use between the two dominance groups. As described in Section 4.3.2, the dialogue comprised two information-seeking yes–no questions (A and D; henceforth IYNQ), one exclamative echo yes–no question with counterexpectational meaning (B), and one confirmation-seeking question (C), all of them introduced by the complementizer *que*.

In the information-seeking yes–no interrogative A (*¿Que quieres venir conmigo?* 'Do you want to come with me?'), the CatD speakers overwhelmingly used the high–falling contour ($n=15$ out of 20, 75%), which is impossible in this context in other Spanish varieties. Figure 5.124 provides an example. In the SpD group, 7 (out of 11) speakers used it (i.e. 64%). As concerns the remaining items, each 4 low–rising contours were found per dominance group (corresponding to 20% in the CatD and 36% in the SpD group, see Figure 5.125). It is of note, however, that 2 CatD and 1 SpD speakers accidentally dropped *que* when reading out the sentence.

Finally, one (CatD) speaker used an H* LH% nuclear configuration, which has been described as typical of echo-questions (see Section 3.1). This is interesting because the context of the utterance in the dialogue actually does not permit such an interpretation. Nevertheless, the participant might have concluded that this must be the case, interpreting *que* as an 'attributive' complementizer.

In the IYNQ D (*¿Que te has hecho daño?* 'Are you hurt?'), the high–falling nuclear configuration, i.e. H+L* L%, was used by all but two speakers (94%). An example is shown in Figure 5.126, below. The other two speakers used the low–ris-

Chapter 5. Results 279

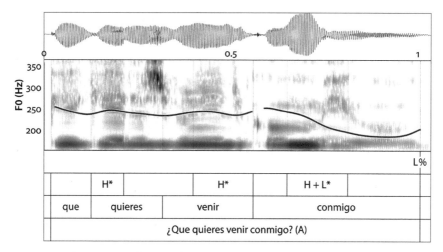

Figure 5.124 Girona Spanish: Waveform, spectrogram, and F0 contour for the information-seeking yes–no question ¿Que *quieres venir conmigo?* 'Do you want to come with me?' produced by a Catalan-dominant speaker. It consists of two prenuclear H* accents and an H+L* nuclear accent, followed by an L% boundary tone. The nuclear configuration of the IP is H+L* L% (16A)

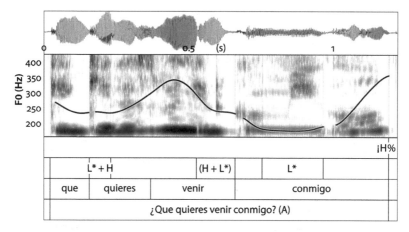

Figure 5.125 Girona Spanish: Waveform, spectrogram, and F0 contour for the information-seeking yes–no question ¿Que *quieres venir conmigo?* 'Do you want to come with me?' produced by a Spanish-dominant speaker. It represents an IP composed of one ip and is produced with an L*+H prenuclear accent, a phrase-medial pitch-deaccented syllable (see Fn. 173), and an L* nuclear accent, followed by an ¡H% boundary tone. The nuclear configuration of the IP is L* ¡H% (13A)

ing contour, but one of them, a CatD, dropped *que* when reading the question, so that the use of the low rise in the reading of the question is not surprising. Still, the stronger predominance of the falling nuclear configuration in D as opposed to A requires an explanation. Therefore, the possibility ought to be considered that at least a part of the participants could have interpreted question D as a confirmation-seeking yes–no interrogative because of the presence of the complementizer *que*, which is grammatical in Mainstream Spanish confirmation-seeking questions (as opposed to information-seeking ones). The context of the question in the dialogue rather favours an information-seeking reading: Joan has seen that Mercè has fallen over and wants to know if she is hurt (see Section 4.3.2). However, albeit less probable, a confirmation-seeking interpretation induced by the presence of *que* cannot be excluded: Joan has seen Mercè falling over and hurting herself and is asking for a confirmation of his observation. This could thus be an explanation for the fact that the H+L* L% was employed noticeably more often in D than in A.

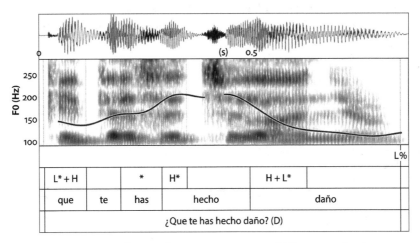

Figure 5.126 Girona Spanish: Waveform, spectrogram, and F0 contour for the information-seeking yes–no question ¿*Que te has hecho daño?* 'Are you hurt?' produced by a Spanish-dominant speaker. It represents an IP composed of one ip and is produced with a phrase-initial L*+H prenuclear accent on the particle *que*, a phrase-medial H* prenuclear accent, and an H+L* nuclear accent, followed by an L% boundary tone. The nuclear configuration of the IP is H+L* L% (27D)

Summing up, I interpret the findings from question A and D as follows: the occurrence of information-seeking *que*-questions intonated with a falling nuclear configuration could indeed be common in GS. Such questions are probably used rather by CatD speakers (see the semi-spontaneous data in Section 5.1.3 and

5.1.4), but (most) SpD speakers will produce them (including the corresponding intonation) when there are obliged to (as was the case in this reading task). Nonetheless, a series of additional findings and observations point towards the possibility that not all speakers find such questions completely natural in Spanish, even though they may be quite common (see also the extensive discussion in Section 6.4.3):

- four bilinguals dropped *que* when reading out the question, which I interpret as an automatic correction;
- all five occurrences of minor disfluencies were found in these two questions of the reading text, which shows that they might have irritated some participants;
- some speakers (most of them SpD bilinguals) used the low–rising nuclear configuration besides the presence of *que*. It cannot be proven here whether the falling contour is also available in their phonological systems, but it is probably not;
- two (CatD) participants commented during the task that the use of *que* in sentence A was incorrect in Spanish, classifying it as a Catalanism, which shows that (at least some) speakers have metalinguistic knowledge about this topic.

The intonational realizations of the exclamative echo yes–no question (B) and the confirmation-seeking question (C) are interesting, as well. In these contexts, *que* is possible in Mainstream Spanish and, regarding intonation, previous research (see Section 3.1) as well as the findings made on basis of the spontaneous data from the DCT (see Sections 5.1.4.1 and 5.1.4.2) suggest that both falling and rising nuclear contours can be used in CS and GS.[194] Interestingly, the participants behaved quite differently in question B and question C.

In interrogative B (*¿Que tomas café al mediodía?* 'You are having coffee at noon?'), all but five (CatD) speakers used the low–rising nuclear configuration, i.e. L* (¡)H%. An example is given in Figure 5.127. In some cases, the rise began already before the end of the nuclear syllable (i.e. the label L+H* ¡H% could be phonetically more adequate). I interpret this as an increase in the pitch movements expressing the nuance of surprise and exclamativity and as an effect of the upstepped boundary tone (see the semi-spontaneous data in Section 5.1.4.1). Furthermore, the fact that 84% of the speakers preferred the low–rising contour in question B, confirms the findings from the DCT, where L* (¡)H% was equally the most common nuclear configuration in this context. Concerning the remaining,

---

194. This is also true for GC, although other CC varieties have been claimed to use exclusively or primarily falling contours in confirmation-seeking yes–no questions (see Section 3.1).

falling realizations, it is striking that in 3 cases (out of 5), the sentence was split into two IPs. In these items, the falling nuclear configuration of the sentence was thus anchored on *café* 'coffee', whereas *al mediodía* 'at noon' was dislocated to the right and pronounced as a low plateau (i.e. L* L%, see Sections 5.1.1.3.1, 5.1.3.1.4, and 5.1.10.2 for dislocations in semi-spontaneous and read data; see Figure 5.128 for an example). Moreover, this finding could be a hint that falling contours are preferred in shorter phrases, whereas longer utterances present a bias towards occurring with rising contours.

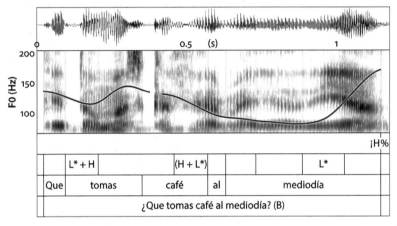

Figure 5.127 Girona Spanish: Waveform, spectrogram, and F0 contour for the exclamative echo yes–no question *¿Que tomas café al mediodía?* 'Do you drink coffee at noon?' produced by a Spanish-dominant speaker. It represents an IP composed of one ip and is produced with an L*+H prenuclear accent, a phrase-medial pitch-deaccented syllable (see Fn. 173), and an L* nuclear accent, followed by an ¡H% boundary tone. The nuclear configuration of the IP is L* ¡H% (7B)

In the confirmation-seeking yes–no interrogative C (*¿Que llueve?* 'Is it raining?'), with a rhetorical nuance, the reverse tendency was observed: the falling contour was the most recurrent overall (20 out of 31 items, 65%; see Figure 5.129 for an example). However, a clear difference in the choices was registered between the two dominance groups. The CatD bilinguals employed the falling configuration in 16 out 20 items (i.e. 80%) and the rising one only 4 times (20%). In the SpD group, on the other hand, the falling one represented merely 36% ($n = 4$), and the rising configuration was used 6 times (i.e. 55%). Adding the realization as H+L* LH% by speaker No. 13, of Honduran descent, rising contours were used to an extent of 64%. Furthermore, it is worth pointing out that the final-rising contours sometimes showed a slight fall in the nuclear syllable, i.e. some nuclear contours were realized phonetically as H+L* H%. In sum, it can be concluded that, in these

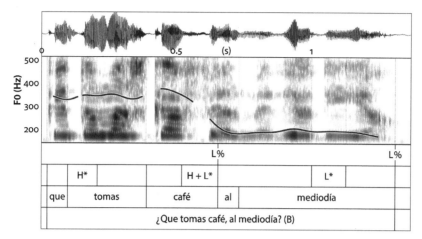

Figure 5.128 Girona Spanish: Waveform, spectrogram, and F0 contour for the exclamative echo yes–no question ¿*Que tomas café, al mediodía?* 'Do you drink coffee at noon?' produced by a Catalan-dominant speaker. It consists of two IPs. The first one contains a prenuclear H* accent, and an H+L* nuclear accent, followed by an L% boundary tone. The nuclear configuration of this IP is H+L* L%. The second IP is produced with an L* L% nuclear configuration. (7B)

rather short confirmation-seeking yes–no interrogative introduced by *que*, CatD speakers preferred the falling configuration, whereas SpD speakers rather opted for rising realizations (according to a Fisher exact test, this difference is significant: $p = 0.023$).

Concerning the prenuclei of the interrogatives A–D, we shall have a quick look only at the phrase-initial prenuclear pitch accents, since (1) not all sentences presented phrase-medial prenuclear pitch accents and (2), if they did, phrase-medial prenuclear accents were typically pitch-deaccented.

With reference to **phrase-initial prenuclear** accents, H* can be generally expected to co-occur with falling nuclear contours and L*+H with rising ones in IYNQ. For other question types, the literature is less explicit, but the tendency seems to be the same. Furthermore, since falling nuclear configurations are said to be more common in (Central) Catalan than in (Castilian) Spanish, prenuclear H* can be considered as being characteristic rather of Catalan and L*+H as more typical of Spanish.

In the IYNQ A, prenuclear H* was used with nuclear H+L* L% and L*+H with nuclear rises without exception. With IYNQ D, the distribution was very similar. However, in the high–falling questions, the pitch level used at the beginning of the sentence (i.e. on *que*) was not always the same: whereas most participants used a high plateau during the whole prenuclear area (i.e. stretching from

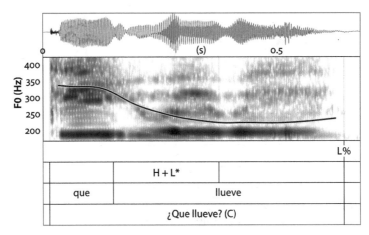

Figure 5.129 Girona Spanish: Waveform, spectrogram, and F0 contour for the confirmation-seeking yes–no question ¿Que *llue*ve? 'Is it raining?' produced by a Catalan-dominant speaker. It represents an IP composed of one ip and is produced with an H+L* nuclear accent, followed by an L% boundary tone. The nuclear configuration of the IP is H+L* L% (28C)

que to the nuclear fall on *daño*), some seemed to deploy an L*+H pitch accent on *que*, i.e. there was a rise from the beginning of the utterance until on the stressed syllable of *he*cho (see Figure 5.126, above). Interestingly, this occurred 5 times in the SpD group (i.e. 45%) but only twice among the CatD (10%). In the confirmation-seeking yes–no question C, all but two SpD speakers began the sentence with high pitch on *que*, which entailed that nuclear L* accents in the following syllable were sometimes phonetically realized as H+L*. The use of *que* thus seems to favour a high onset, here, as well.

In the exclamative echo yes–no question B, finally, most nuclear contours were rising and presented a phrase-initial L*+H accent anchored on the stressed syllable of *to*mas. Yet, there were also some different cases. On the one hand, 4 SpD and 1 CatD bilinguals produced a high tone on *to*mas whereas the preceding *que* was pronounced at a somewhat lower pitch level, i.e. the whole pitch movement roughly corresponded to an L*+H pitch accent placed on *que* instead of *tomas*. On the other hand, there were 3 items in which *que* was the highest syllable in the utterance. I believe that the three CatD participants who produced them were irritated by the phrasing of the sentence with *que*, which once more shows that *que*-questions in GS are not totally natural to all bilinguals.

In sum, the read GS *que*-questions present either high–falling intonation patterns (i.e. prenuclear H* and nuclear H+L*) or low–rising ones (i.e. prenuclear L*+H with nuclear L* H%). Generally, the presence of *que* seems to have favoured the use of the falling contour and a high pitch level at the beginning of the interrogative. However, the results also suggest that *que* is not totally natural to a at least a part of the speakers in some GS question types and could therefore be perceived as a feature transferred from Catalan. When they are obliged to use it – as in the present reading task – not all bilinguals adopt what is supposed to be the 'original' Catalan pattern, consisting of a high plateau in the prenucleus and a falling nucleus, in the same way: some adopt the whole pattern, some adopt the nuclear fall but keep the initial rise, and some others simply stick to the 'normal' low–rising Spanish pattern (i.e. L*+H and L* H%). This, to a certain extent, depends on the question type, but also evinces a fair deal of inter-speaker variation (see Chapter 6, especially Section 6.4.3, for further discussion).

5.1.10.2 *Girona Spanish dislocations*

All 62 readings of the two target sentences could be analysed (see Section 4.2.1.2 for a detailed description of the materials and procedure). In roughly half of the readings, the dislocation was realized in a prosodically independent IP, i.e. there was a clear L% prosodic boundary tone at the end of the main clause that preceded the IP containing the dislocation ($n=30$, 48%). In 56% of these items, there was also a short pause ($n=17$, 27% of all sentences). In these realizations, the quantifiers at the end of the main clause, i.e. *muchísimo* and *poca*, bore either an L* or an L+H* pitch accent, which are the characteristic nuclear accents of neutral and narrow-focus or exclamative statements, respectively. L+H* was especially common in sentence 1, which comes as no surprise as *muchísimo* was clearly the focus of the sentence, whereas the right-dislocated constituent *de café* represented a topic. The dislocated elements themselves were generally pronounced as low plateaus without any notable pitch excursions (i.e. L* L%, see Figure 5.130). However, there were 5 cases (8%) in which a slight peak could be observed on the stressed syllable of the dislocated element. These contours, labelled as 'L+!H* L%', here, represent a pitch-compressed resumption of the nuclear L+H* L% configurations used in the preceding main clause (see Figure 5.131 for an example). The findings pattern with the observations made for GC dislocations in Section 5.1.1.3 on the basis of (semi-)spontaneous speech.

In the remaining sentences, the prepositional phrases *de café* and *de paciencia* were not prosodically independent, i.e. not right-dislocated but integrated prosodically into the main clause. In these cases, the objects *muchísimo de café* 'lots of coffee' and *poca de paciencia* 'little patience' were syntactically simple complements of the verb, consisting of a noun and its quantifier, equivalent to Mainstream Spanish *muchísimo café* and *poca paciencia*. Intonationwise, this translated in the quantifiers carrying the typical prenuclear pitch accent used in statements (i.e. L+<H* or sometimes its surface realization H+L*; see Sections 5.2.1), while the nouns displayed L* L% nuclear configurations. Figures 5.132 and 5.133 provide two examples.

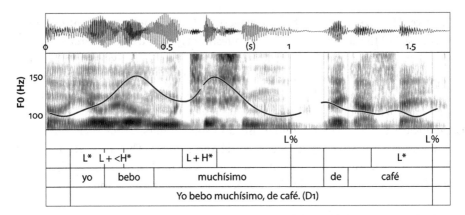

Figure 5.130 Girona Spanish: Waveform, spectrogram, and F0 contour for the statement *Yo bebo muchísimo, de café*. 'I drink a lot of coffee' produced by a Catalan-dominant speaker and composed of two IPs. The first one is produced with an L* and an L+<H* prenuclear accent, an L+H* nuclear accent, and an L% boundary tone. The second IP has an L* L% nuclear configuration (17D1)

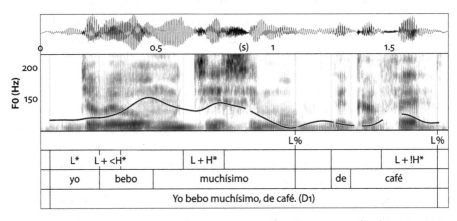

Figure 5.131 Girona Spanish: Waveform, spectrogram, and F0 contour for the statement *Yo bebo muchísimo, de café*. 'I drink a lot of coffee' produced by a Spanish-dominant speaker and composed of two IPs. The first one is produced with an L* and an L+<H* prenuclear accent, an L+H* nuclear accent, and an L% boundary tone. The second IP repeats this nuclear configuration as L+!H* L% (27D1)

In these cases, the presence of an orthographic comma in the text given to the participants does not seem to have influenced their reading pronunciation. Interestingly enough, in one case the speaker accidentally dropped *de*, which yielded a Mainstream Spanish quantifier object construction that she pronounced without dislocating the noun.

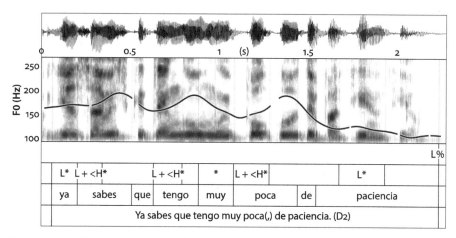

Figure 5.132 Girona Spanish: Waveform, spectrogram, and F0 contour for the statement *Ya sabes que tengo muy poca de paciencia*. 'You know that I have little patience' produced by a Catalan-dominant speaker. It represents an IP composed of one ip and is produced with an L* prenuclear accent, three L+<H* prenuclear accents, and an L* nuclear accent, followed by an L% boundary tone. The nuclear configuration of the IP is L* L% (6D2)

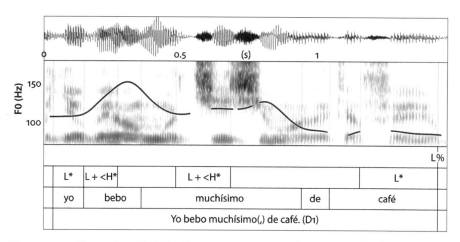

Figure 5.133 Girona Spanish: Waveform, spectrogram, and F0 contour for the statement *Yo bebo muchísimo de café*. 'I drink lots of coffee' produced by a Catalan-dominant speaker. It represents an IP composed of one ip and is produced with an L* prenuclear accent, two L+<H* prenuclear accents, and an L* nuclear accent, followed by an L% boundary tone. The nuclear configuration of the IP is L* L% (23D1)

With respect to the LD, it is hard to make any inferences about whether any dominance group uses a particular realization more frequently than the other one above chance level. Among the CatD bilinguals, prosodically independent dislocations (marked by a boundary tone and/or a pause) were equally frequent as undislocated realizations in both sentences. In the SpD group, the two sentences showed different tendencies. In Sentence 1, 9 out of 11 (i.e. 82%) used the 'integrated' version of the object instead of a dislocation. In Sentence 2, the reverse distribution was found.

5.2 Tonal inventory of Girona Spanish and Girona Catalan

In this subchapter, I discuss the phonological status of the pitch accents and boundary tones found in the intonational analysis of the different GS and GC sentence types (see Section 5.1). I first consider prenuclear pitch accents (Section 5.2.1) and nuclear configurations of inner ips (Section 5.2.2), and then establish an inventory of underlying nuclear configurations of IPs (5.2.3). Finally, I present an inventory of pitch accents and boundary tones for each variety (Section 5.2.4).

5.2.1 Phonological status of the prenuclear pitch accents in Girona Spanish and Girona Catalan

According to the intonational analysis in Section 5.1, the same three pitch accents were used predominantly to mark prenuclear stressed syllables in both Girona varieties: L+<H*, L*+H, and H*. They were attested in various sentence types as IP-initial prenuclear accents, phrase-internal prenuclear pitch accents, and as ip-initial prenuclear accents of non-IP-initial ips. The analysis revealed that they are typically connected with different utterance types. First, L+<H* is the most common prenuclear pitch accent in all types of statements considered in the present study (i.e. neutral broad-focus statements (with and without peripheral elements), contrastive-focus statements, exclamative statements, contradiction, and dubitative statements). In addition, it was found in imperatives (both in commands and requests) and in the prenucleus of non-final ips in disjunctive questions. In exclamative and imperative wh-questions, L+<H* and L*+H were used with a similar frequency.

Second, L*+H is clearly the most recurrent prenuclear pitch accent in most of the examined question types. It appears in information-seeking yes–no questions (with and without peripheral elements), in exclamative and in confirmation-seeking yes–no questions, and in several types of echo questions (echo yes–no, echo wh-, and exclamative echo yes–no questions). What is more, it also occurs in information-seeking, exclamative, and imperative wh-questions. However, it must be mentioned that it mainly appears in phrase-initial position, as phrase-medial syllables present a very strong tendency to be pitch-deaccented in questions (see below).

Prenuclear H*, finally, is also registered primarily in questions. It characterizes information-seeking and exclamative yes–no questions when they are introduced by the complementizer *que* (which happens with a higher frequency in GC than in GS) as well as information-seeking wh-questions. In addition, it is sometimes used in neutral statements – typically at the beginning of the IP or of a non-IP-initial ip (i.e. after a high boundary tone, H- or !H-, of a preceding ip).

Besides L+<H*, L*+H and H*, some further prenuclear pitch accents were occasionally observed in the two varieties under concern here: mainly H+L* and L+H*. Yet, these usually appeared only under specific conditions in both statements and questions. Regarding H+L*, it was noted that the occurrence of a high preceding peak (e.g. L+<H*, L*+H, L+H* or H-, !H-) and lack of space to produce a rising pitch accent contributed to the presence of this falling pitch accent. Similarly, prenuclear L+H* was normally produced due to lack of space when the peak could not be delayed to a following syllable, e.g. in stress clashes (which were more numerous in Catalan, given that oxytone words are more abundant in that language than in Spanish).

As concerns phrase-medial positions, both varieties often showed pitch deaccentuation. Especially in questions, pitch excursions between the phrase-initial prenuclear and the nuclear pitch accent were rare. Depending on the pitch accents at the beginning and at the end of the phrase, the mid part of questions was generally characterized either by declination or by a high plateau and, in consequence, phrase-internal prosodic words were analysed as pitch-deaccented. For instance, in information-seeking yes–no questions, the proportion of phrase-medial deaccented syllables amounted to 87% in GC and 83% in GS. But in statements, too, phrase-internal prenuclear pitch accents were often not realized: for instance, in neutral declaratives, the deaccentuation of phrase-internal lexically stressed syllables reached a share of 26% for GS and of 29% for GC. In exclamative statements, a proportion of 33% and 22% was attained, respectively.

The question that arises after this summary is: are there underlying prenuclear pitch accents in GS and GC and, if any, what is their meaning? The results of the intonational analysis allow for the assumption that the delayed peak (i.e. L+<H*) is an underlying pitch accent used to mark prenuclear stressed syllables in statements in both contact varieties. If this assumption is correct, the remaining pitch accents that appeared occasionally in the prenucleus of statements (i.e. L+H*, H+L*, and also H*) can be seen as surface variants of the underlying L+<H* prenuclear accent that emerge when the conditions described above are met.

As for questions, the intonational analysis suggests that prenuclear L*+H signals interrogativity in both varieties. However, even if this pitch accent was observed on phrase-internal syllables in some few cases, phrase-medial deaccentuation was clearly dominant in questions. The use of phrase-internal pitch accents might thus rather convey information-structural meanings, such as marking the focus of the question (see Section 5.1.3.1.2). Therefore, L*+H should not be viewed in questions as a 'common' underlying prenuclear pitch accent in the traditional sense, i.e. as one whose use is fully comparable to that of L+<H* in statements. Instead, it might be better analysed as a kind of single 'phrase-initial tonal movement'.¹⁹⁵ This view is supported by the fact that, in the analysed data set, phrase-initial L*+H was almost exclusively anchored on the first 'stressable' syllable of the phrase-initial verbal complex, i.e. typically on auxiliaries or negation particles rather than on its lexical part, i.e. on the participle or the conjugated verb, which, in turn, were pitch-deaccented (see Sections 5.1.3–5.1.7). In statements, on the contrary, such grammatical elements usually formed one single prosodic word in conjunction with the (stressed) lexical part of the verb and were thus left pitch unaccented. Furthermore, also the implementation of the rising trailing tone of the initial L*+H tonal movement, which typically reached its peak in the second syllable following the one to which it was associated, is quite particular, as it oftentimes yields tonal movements that extend over at least three syllables irrespective of the position of the next underlyingly, i.e. lexically, stressed syllable (see Section 5.1.3.1). However, in order to determine whether L*+H in questions should be analysed as a common prenuclear pitch-accent in the traditional sense or whether it represents a phrase-initial tonal movement similar to phrase-initial boundary tones but anchored on the first 'stressable' syllable goes beyond the scope of this book and requires further investigation.

Regarding the phonetic implementation of phrase-initial L*+H, it is worth pointing out that it was sometimes realized with a slight pitch fall instead of a low plateau within the limits of the stressed syllable, namely in exclamative yes–no questions and in exclamative echo yes–no questions. Although this pitch movement superficially looks like some sort of 'H+L*+H' pitch accent, I interpret it as an effect of the use of an extended pitch range and of increased tonal movements, as both these features are known to convey exclamativity (see, e.g., Crespo-Sendra 2011: 111–120 and the discussion below). I thus assume that such surface contours underlyingly correspond to L*+H pitch accents and restrain from positing the presence of three tonal targets at an underlying level. Similarly, L*+H may sometimes surface as L+<H* for the same reason (typically also in exclamative questions).

---

195. Similar suggestions were made by Grice/Vella/Bruggeman (2019) for Maltese, where they observed pitch events (viz. a high peak) that regularly associate to the left edge of question words in direct questions instead of being anchored on the question word's stressed syllable (as is the case in indirect questions).

Finally, the phonological status of H* warrants some discussion. In statements, its use is widely conditioned, as we have seen above, and I therefore view it as a surface realization of an underlying L+<H* prenuclear accent. In questions, too, H* can be a surface variant: it emerges for example in stress-clash contexts instead of L*+H when (a) the ip containing the question's main clause begins with a stressed syllable and, at the same time, is preceded by another ip ending in an ultimate stress word, or (b) when the only prenuclear stressed syllable in the ip is directly adjacent to the nuclear syllable of the IP. However, the intonational analysis of different GS and GC question types has revealed that H* prenuclear accents are also common in several distinct types of yes–no questions independently of the phonetic context — namely those headed by the complementizer *que* — as well as in wh-questions, i.e. when the interrogativity of the utterance is already marked by lexical means. I thus assume that H* is a second underlying prenuclear pitch accent that can be used to convey interrogativity besides L*+H. However, these two pitch accents are distributed complementarily, i.e. they occur in different utterance types and combine with different nuclear configurations. Still, there are some issues surrounding prenuclear H* that need to be addressed. In yes–no questions (with *que*), it may 'work' like a 'usual' prenuclear pitch accent, i.e. it is typically repeated on each lexically stressed syllable of the prenucleus, which gives rise to a high plateau spanning from the beginning of the question to the nuclear syllable, i.e. expanding over the whole prenuclear area. This use is clearly more typical of Catalan and CatD bilinguals. Besides that, it can be also found in wh-questions provided that these present a high–falling nuclear contour (which, again, happens more frequently in Catalan and among Catalan dominant speakers; see also the discussion in Section 6.4). Otherwise, in wh-questions with low or rising nuclear contours, H* only occurs once in initial position on the wh-word (similarly to phrase-initial L*+H), whereas phrase-medial positions are mostly pitch-deaccented, i.e. the F0 follows common declination patterns.

Regarding the question of whether prenuclear pitch accents contribute to the identification of a particular sentence type, we can thus expect, based on the suggestions made above, that speakers of GC and GS should in general be able to distinguish neutral statements and information-seeking yes–no questions solely by means of the prenuclear accents.[196] Furthermore, statements produced with L+<H* prenuclear accents and questions produced with initial L*+H followed by

---

196. Note that information-seeking yes–no questions (without the complementizer *que*) and neutral statements usually show the same surface syntactic properties (in both GC and GS). In contrast, other question types or imperatives are normally signalled by syntactic, morphologic, or lexical means in addition to intonation (e.g. the wh-word in wh-questions or the verb form in imperatives).

deaccentuation or with H* followed by a high plateau should be perceived as more natural than other combinations.

Last, it is worth mentioning that L+<H* and L*+H did only appear as prenuclear pitch accents in the contact varieties, whereas H* was used both in nuclear and prenuclear positions. Yet, this is to a certain extent a corollary of the commonly applied ToBI models for Spanish and Catalan (see 3.1.2.1 and 3.1.2.2), in which F0 contours similar to the ones described as L+<H* or L*+H prenuclear pitch accents, are usually classified as combinations of low or rising nuclear pitch accents and high boundary tones when they occur at the right edge of a phrase. For instance, a low plateau that extends within the limits of a stressed syllable and is followed by an F0 rise is ordinarily labelled as L*+H in the prenucleus but as L* H% in nuclear position.

5.2.2 Phonological status of the nuclear configurations of inner ips in Girona Spanish and Girona Catalan

Only some sentence types in the (semi-)spontaneous corpus were phrased in IPs consisting of more than one ip in a proportion that enables sound inferences about the nuclear configurations used in inner ips: neutral statements (without and with peripheral elements),[197] enumerations, and disjunctive questions. The analysis of neutral statements showed that the nuclear configurations of inner ips in both varieties typically present a rise beginning in its nuclear syllable that continues until the end of the phrase, i.e. a rising nuclear pitch accent and a continuation rise. The same is true for the nuclear configurations of inner ips in neutral disjunctive questions. In these cases, it cannot be decided whether the underlying nuclear configuration is L+<H* H- or L+H* H-. However, since the corpus also contained some sustained pitches, i.e. L+H* !H-, which better allow to determine the nature of the nuclear pitch accent, I assume that the underlying nuclear pitch accent is L+H* independently of the boundary tone (H- or !H-). This is also in line with the largest part of the scientific literature (see Section 5.1.1.1). In disjunctive questions, this pitch accent was occasionally upstepped (i.e. L+¡H*) when another rising prenuclear pitch accent was produced before the nuclear pitch

---

197. Dislocations, vocatives, or imperatives were analysed as independent IPs in the current work for the following reasons: (a), they could also be left out without affecting the grammaticality of the sentence, and (b), the nuclear configurations of the main clause were the same in sentences with and without such elements and thus convey completeness of the sentence. Hence, it does not seem reasonable to analyse the main clauses as inner ips and to view the nuclear configurations deployed on the peripheral elements, which are typically intonated with a low plateau, i.e. pitch-deaccented, or repeat the nuclear configuration of the main clause, as the single nuclear configuration of the whole utterance.

accent of the inner ip. I interpret this upstep as an effect of a preceding high target and the high boundary tone and, consequently, analysed such pitch accents as underlying L+H* in all sentence types.[198] Furthermore, there were some instances of non-final ips in neutral statements that were pronounced as high plateaus, in which the nuclear contour was labelled as (!)H* !H-, as well as some rare cases of low boundary tones (i.e. L-). Due to the low frequency of such contours, I suggest that they can be viewed as flat surface realizations of the usual nuclear configuration (see below for a possible pragmatic interpretation).[199] In enumerations, finally, L* H- was more frequent than L+H* H-. Since L* L% is the typical (IP-final) nuclear contour of statements (see also Section 5.2.3, below), L* H-, i.e. the same pitch accent combined with a high boundary tone, H-, which marks incompleteness of the sentence, might signal a greater independence of the ip as compared to L+H* H-. This might be reflected in the fact that L* H- was not found as a nuclear contour of non-final ips separating main clauses into different ips but only in enumerations, i.e. in lists of different independent elements.[200]

Concerning the phonological status of the boundary tones, I assume that the sustained pitched (i.e. !H-) is a surface realization of the continuation rise H-, since it was clearly marginal in GC and, in GS, too, occurred with a noticeably lower frequency than the continuation rise. With reference to the pragmatic meaning of the different boundary tones, I believe that speakers use H-, i.e. a continuation rise, to signal to the hearer that the sentence they are producing is not yet completed, i.e. it expresses (planned) incompleteness of the discourse in both contact varieties. !H-, on the other hand, seems to surface merely as a phonetic realization of H- and, therefore, conveys incompleteness, as well. Yet, it can be suggested, in accordance with Kireva (2016a: 169), that speakers produce it to express a certain degree of uncertainty when they are planning their upcoming thoughts. If so, the pragmatic meaning of the sustained pitch (i.e. !H) would be

---

198. In a slightly different analysis, the boundary tone could be the upstepped tonal target (i.e. L+H* ¡H-). If that were the case, ¡H- could signal a stronger detachment of the ip than H- (see enumerations, in Section 5.1.1.2, for such a use of tonal scaling) as well as interrogativity (see Estebas-Vilaplana/Prieto 2010: 27f. for such an interpretation in CS disjunctive questions).

199. H* !H- was also found in one GC disjunctive question introduced by the complementizer *que*, produced by a strongly CatD bilingual speaker (see Figure 5.76). As it is usual in Catalan questions with *que*, the nuclear contour of the IP was H+L* L%. Although genuinely Catalan, such disjunctive questions can be considered rare in Central Catalan (Maria del Mar Vanrell, p.c.).

200. Some enumerations contained also elements on which the F0 superficially described L* L- nuclear contours. In such cases, the presence of an ip boundary is questionable because it was established mainly on theoretical rather than perceptual grounds. Further investigation will help elucidate this topic.

slightly different from the one of the continuation rise. Furthermore, the whole (!)H* !H- nuclear configuration should then be interpreted in this sense. Similarly, also the very few instances of L- that were observed in the data are most likely to be surface reflexes of hesitation, i.e. they are actually not planned tonal targets but simply result from the pitch fall that accompanies the hesitational lengthening (see Figure 5.53 for an example, see also Section 5.3.3).

5.2.3 Phonological status of the nuclear configurations of IPs in Girona Spanish and Girona Catalan

In this section, I establish an inventory of underlying nuclear configurations of IPs on the basis of the intonational analysis of GS and GC presented in Section 5.1.

For **neutral statements**, I propose L* L% as underlying nuclear contour in both contact varieties. The H+L* nuclear accent, which was sometimes found, should be interpreted as a surface realization of L*, since it typically occurred when it was preceded by a high tone at the end of the prenucleus so that there was too little space for the pitch to fall before the nuclear syllable. Similarly, L* L% was also the nuclear configuration used in enumerations and in the main clauses of neutral statements containing extra-sentential elements, such as (preceding) vocatives, or appositions and dislocations (attached in a separate IP after the main clause at the end of the utterance; see Fn. 197, above). Moreover, L* L% was typically used in the IPs containing the utterance-final appositions and dislocated elements themselves, too.[201] Vocatives preceding the main clause of statements, generally displayed an L+H* L% nuclear configuration, which might be a 'compressed' variant of the contours found in free vocatives (see Section 5.1.9 and below). L* L% furthermore appeared on the last element in neutral statements consisting of a main clause and a subordinate clause or a semantically equivalent element such as a gerund clause or a prepositional phrase (in the complex statements gathered with situation 1c3, see Section 5.1.1.3).

In contrast to L*, which signals neutral/broad-focus readings in statements, L+H* it the typical pitch accent employed to express focus/emphasis in **biased statements** in both varieties under investigation. The nuclear configuration of IPs established for contrastive-focus statements and exclamative statements, and — albeit with some restrictions — for contradiction and dubitative statements is thus L+H* L% in both varieties.[202] In exclamative statements, this pitch contour can

---

201. I interpret the few divergent realizations found besides L* L% (see Section 5.1.1.3) as realizations of an L+H* nuclear accent that expresses focus and/or emphasis (see below).

202. Although the scientific literature on CS and CC posits distinct nuclear contours for the various biased statement types (Section 3.1.2.2), this is in line with the Henriksen and García-

be upstepped (i.e. L+¡H* L%), which I assume to be a means of expressing more emphasis. Furthermore, there is a somewhat 'smoothed' surface realization of this nuclear pitch accent that typically occurs after high tones in the prenucleus when there is little space for the pitch to fall to a lower level before the nuclear syllable. The shape of this surface variant often looks like a sort of step interrupting the pitch fall between the last prenuclear pitch accent and the low final boundary tone, i.e. there is no clearly discernible rise from a low target within the nuclear syllable, which is why the phonetic label '¡L+H*' was employed in these cases.[203] However, the fact that the data contain contours that are so to speak 'intermediate' between L* L% and L+H* L%, also shows that the difference between these two categories is actually a gradual one. Following Feldhausen et al. (2011), it can thus be assumed that high scaling of the nuclear accent will entail biased interpretations, whereas low scaling is more likely to lead to a neutral interpretation.

Still, for all of these **(biased) statement** types, L* L% nuclear configurations were attested, too. Usually, the biased meaning was expressed by other linguistic means in those cases: for instance, by cleft structures in contrastive-focus statements or by lexical means in in dubitative statements (using words such as Cat. *potser* or Sp. *a lo mejor*, both 'maybe'). In exclamative statements, I assume the corresponding reading to be expressed through the use of a wider pitch range and higher scaling of the pitch accents in the prenucleus than in neutral declarative statements, when an L* L% nuclear configuration is used.

In the case of contradiction statements, the underlying nuclear configuration(s) is/are hard to determine, since a large range of contours were attested in the present data set. In GC, falling or low contours, i.e. H+L* L% and L* L%, occurred with the highest frequency. While L* L% has already been established as the underlying nuclear contour of neutral statements (see above), the use of H+L* L% is in accordance with Prieto (2002a: 415f.), who underlines the common falling melodic pattern (H+L* L%) of contradiction statements with orders/commands. Besides, circumflex contours, i.e. L+H* L%, were attested with only a slightly inferior frequency. In GS, on the other hand, L+H* L% was clearly more recurrent than H+L* L% and L* L%. I therefore assume both H+L* L% and L+H* L% to be further underlying nuclear configurations in addition to L* L% in contradiction statements. However, the possibility needs to be considered that individual speak-

---

Amaya (2012:144), who equally establish L+H* L% as single nuclear contour of all biased statement types in Jerezano Spanish (see also the discussion in 6.4.2.2). Similarly, Gabriel et al. (2010:313) establish a common L+H*+L L% nuclear configuration for various biased statement types.

203. The use of this label is inspired by Henriksen and García-Amaya (2012:122f.), who observed a similar nuclear contour in Jerezano Spanish contradiction statements.

ers may have different repertoires depending on factors such as their individual LD and the variety of Spanish they are most exposed to, e.g. through their parents (see the extensive discussion in Section 6.4.2).[204]

A final issue that warrants comment is that in dubitative statements both H* L% and L+H* L% nuclear configurations were observed with the same frequencies. Given that the circumflex contour was used in all biased statement types, I presume that the very similar H* L% is a surface variant of this contour.

The following nuclear configurations can be assumed to express **information-seeking yes–no** questions (with and without peripheral elements) in both GS and GC: L* (¡)H% and H+L* L%. The results of the intonational analysis allow us to posit L* H% and additionally, at least for some speakers, H+L* L% and H+L* LH% (the latter only for one speaker) as underlying nuclear configurations for this question type in both varieties. This decision is motivated as follows: first, in the low–rising L* (¡)H% contour, the occurrence of the H% and the ¡H% boundary tone is widely determined by the space available between the nuclear syllable and the phrase edge, in such a way that this boundary tone is usually higher when no other IP is following directly and when the ip ends in a word with penultimate or antepenultimate stress, which is in line with the observations made for GC by Fernández Planas et al. (2007) and Fernández Planas (2009: 34). Although the final boundary tone usually represents the highest point of the question (i.e. ¡H% is used), the analysed data set does not present any evidence for a phonological contrast between H% and ¡H%. Therefore, I posit L* H% as the underlying nuclear contour. Furthermore, the combination of an H+L* nuclear accent with a high boundary tone seems to be a surface variant of the L* H% nuclear configuration that surfaces due to the lack of space between the peak of a preceding prenuclear accent and the nuclear accent. In total, L* H% (in its respective surface variants) was found with the highest overall frequency in both studied varieties (90% in GS and 73% in GC).

Additionally, H+L* L%, i.e. a high–falling nuclear configuration, was equally used by quite some speakers. As described in the literature (see Section 2.3, 3.1.2.1, and 3.1.2.2), this configuration is typical of Catalan and usually comes along with the complementizer *que* introducing the respective yes–no question. In the present data set, such questions were occasionally observed in Catalan (22%) — especially when they were short — but there were also some instances in GS (4.5%). A

---

204. It is worth noting that a small proportion of nuclear L* and H+L* pitch accents combined with HL% boundary tones was also registered. This is interesting, since L* HL% is one of the typical nuclear contours expressing contradictory force in Castilian Spanish (Estebas-Vilaplana/Prieto 2010: 25; Hualde/Prieto 2015: 369), whereas H+L* HL% is given by Prieto (2013: 21–22) and Prieto et al. (2015: 21) for Catalan.

look at the users' LD patterns in both varieties leads to the conclusion that some bilinguals have this pattern in both languages, while others apparently do not have it at all. More precisely, some (rather strongly) CatD bilinguals use this pattern in both GC (where it originally stems from) and in GS (to which they transfer it) (for an extensive discussion of CLI in this utterance type see Section 6.4.3). As opposed to that, no SpD bilingual used it in Spanish, but some of them chose it in Catalan, i.e. those SpD bilinguals seem to be aware of the naturality of this question type in Catalan. Nevertheless, the fact that the corpus equally contains 13 Catalan questions phrased with *que* but intonated with a low–rising L* H% nuclear contour instead of high falling H+L* L% suggests that some bilinguals most probably do not command this nuclear configuration. Interestingly, such items were mostly produced by rather unbalanced SpD bilinguals.[205] The size of the present corpus does not allow for detailed inferences about individual phonological systems, but the data strongly suggest that there are (a) CatD participants who have both L* H% and H+L* L% as alternative nuclear configurations for information-seeking yes–no questions in both of their varieties, (b) bilinguals belonging to either dominance groups who have both nuclear configurations in Catalan but only L* H% in Spanish, and (c) SpD bilinguals who only have L* H% in the two varieties. This view of differing individual phonological systems in the bilinguals, in which LD might play an important part, is also underpinned by the observation that one SpD speaker, who is of Honduran origin, quite consistently used an H+L* LH% nuclear configuration for her information-seeking yes–no questions in both varieties (see also the discussion of interspeaker variation in Section 6.2).

As for neutral **disjunctive** questions, the underlying nuclear configurations of IPs established for the studied varieties are L* L% and H+L* L%. The distribution of these two configurations in the data (see Section 5.1.3.2) gives reason to assume that H+L* L% originally belonged only to the Catalan system, while L* L% underlies the Spanish system (see Section 6.4.3). However, through the intense contact the languages seem to have converged to a considerable extent. As in the case of the information-seeking questions, I therefore assume that not all bilinguals have the same underlying systems for nuclear configurations of disjunctive questions in either or both of their languages.

---

205. However, 3 cases of Catalan yes–no questions introduced by *que* that were pronounced with an L* H% nuclear configuration and stemmed from CatD bilinguals are attested in the corpus, too. Since this is unexpected and — to my best knowledge — has only been described once before (see Fernández Planas et al. 2007), this topic will be addressed extensively in Section 6.4.3.

The underlying nuclear configurations **exclamative yes–no** questions with counterexpectational meaning are essentially the same as in information-seeking yes–no questions: i.e. L* H% and H+L* L%, the latter one appearing when the question is introduced by *que*. Since such questions were only produced six times by CatD bilinguals (twice in GS and four times in GC), I once more assume that not all participants have it available in their underlying system. However, if there is no difference between the underlying nuclear configurations of neutral and exclamative yes–no questions, how is this semantic difference expressed? I assume that this is achieved by an increase of the pitch movements and an expansion of the pitch range, which, for instance, is apparent from the fact that L* H% frequently surfaced as H+L* H% (both varieties) or L+H* H% (only observed in GS).[206] H+L* and L+H* are thus emphatic realizations of L*, which is in concert with similar findings made for exclamative and other biased statements (as opposed to broad-focus statements), above.

L* H% and H+L* L% are equally the underlying nuclear configurations of **confirmation-seeking yes–no** questions established for the two Girona varieties in the intonational analysis. However, in this case, the falling contour does not come along with a complementizer (*que*) introducing the confirmation-seeking yes–no questions. Rather, it usually — albeit not exclusively — occurs when the question ends with the disjunctive element Sp./Cat. *o no?*. As opposed to CS and to other CC subdialects, the Girona contact varieties thus employ the same nuclear configurations to mark confirmation-seeking and information-seeking yes–no questions. However, this was also observed in other varieties, such as Jerezano or Argentinian Spanish (Henriksen/García-Amaya 2012:144; Gabriel et al. 2010; see also Section 6.4.3).

The bilinguals also used the same types of nuclear configurations in both varieties to express **information-seeking wh**-questions: falling (H* L%, H+L* L%), low (L* L%), rising (L* H%), and circumflex (L+H* L%) ones. As opposed to yes–no questions, which typically display the same surface syntactic properties as statements and therefore require an intonational marking of their interrogativity, in wh-questions, this feature is expressed in the first place by the presence of a lexical marker, i.e. the wh-word. Information-seeking wh-questions may thus be produced with the same nuclear configuration as neutral statements (i.e. L* L%). However, in most cases, the respondents utilized additional intonational cues to reinforce the interrogative meaning. This can be done through the use of the same nuclear configurations as in yes–no questions: i.e. a nuclear rise (L* H%) or, much

---

206. The same effect was also discernible in the prenucleus in this question type, where initial L*+H often surfaced as a 'H+L*+H'-like contour, i.e. as a fall on the stressed syllable, followed by a rise in the post-tonic (see Section 5.2.1).

more frequently, here, a nuclear fall. Nevertheless, in the case of falling nuclear configurations, the contour used in wh-questions was rather H* L% than H+L* L% irrespective of the variety. This is in line with the common descriptions of the intonation of CC (see Section 3.1.2.2), which claim that H* L% is the typical falling nuclear configuration of information-seeking wh-questions. Consequently, the difference between H* L% (in wh-questions) and H+L* L% (in yes–no questions) should be a phonological one (see Prieto 2002a: 440). Interestingly, regarding Spanish, the use of H* L% seems to be a novelty, since falling nuclear contours are usually not part of the Castilian Spanish inventory given for information-seeking wh-questions (see Section 3.1.2.2) — nor do they appear in other Peninsular Spanish varieties (see also Section 6.4.4). The distribution of this nuclear contour in our data set gives some additional hints that it could be a 'rather Catalan' feature: the preference for the falling pattern was stronger in GC across dominance groups. I thus assume that its presence in the GS inventory could be once more the result of an (ongoing) process of convergence between the intonational systems of the two Girona varieties and that individual speakers might (still) have slightly different systems (see Section 6.4.4 for an extensive discussion of CLI in this statement type). Finally, the circumflex contour might simply be a surface variant of H* L%, possibly triggered by phrase length (see Prieto 2002a: 441), or again convey exclamativity as in statements (see above) and in exclamative wh-questions (see the following paragraph). I therefore assume that L+H* L% is not an underlying nuclear contour in neutral wh-questions.

Exclamative wh-questions can be expressed in different ways. In general, the bilinguals resorted to the same nuclear configurations as in information-seeking wh-questions but typically produced them with an extended pitch range and/or upstepped pitch accents. The most common nuclear configuration was thus ¡H* L% (in both varieties). Similarly, the low–rising L* H% contour was typically realized as L+H* ¡H%. Besides, the circumflex contour, i.e. L+(¡)H* L%, can be used, too, to express the notion of exclamativity in a wh-question. This is largely in line with the literature on Catalan intonation (see Prieto 2002a: 446, 2013: 34–36) as well as with the observations made on the basis of the analysis of the biased statements that (a) the L+H* nuclear accent is used to express focus/emphasis and (b) the upstep signals greater emphasis in both GS and GC. Since the distribution of these nuclear contours was significantly different in the two varieties (more falls in Catalan and more circumflex contours in Spanish), it is possible that the intense language contact has led to an (ongoing) merger of two originally different inventories (see Section 6.4.4). Furthermore, different individuals may (still) present somewhat diverse phonological systems.

The underlying nuclear configurations established for **imperative wh**-questions are H+L* L%, L* H%, and L+H* L% (only GS). Whereas the first one was almost exclusive in GC, it was less dominant in GS. However, all these configurations are shared with other question types, such as information-seeking yes–no and wh-questions or exclamative wh-questions. The question of how the contact varieties express the imperative nuance is thus not fully clear: although H+L* L% differs from H* L% (in information-seeking wh-questions) through the earlier alignment of the nuclear fall, no alignment differences could be observed with the two other nuclear configurations. This is thus an issue that remains for further research.

Echo questions (i.e. neutral and exclamative echo yes–no questions as well as echo wh-questions) were expressed for the most part by means of the L* (¡)H% nuclear configuration, i.e. with the same nuclear configuration as in most non-echo yes–no questions and, to a lesser degree, non-echo wh-questions. Here again, the boundary tone usually represented the highest point in the utterance (i.e. ¡H%). However, in some few cases, other configurations were registered. For instance, some occurrences of L+H* L% were attested in all studied echo-question types. It comes as no surprise that the pitch accent typically employed to express focus and emphasis (e.g. in statements) is also utilized in echo yes–no questions, since these have the purpose of checking whether one has understood right what an interlocutor just said — which is achieved by repeating and thus by focusing and emphasizing the respective element. Furthermore, some instances of falling H* L% (or possibly H+L* L%) were found in echo wh-questions, which is also the typical nuclear contour of information-seeking wh-questions. Yet, given that some items presented a slight rise at the beginning of the nuclear syllable, I follow Estebas-Vilaplana and Prieto (2010: 35)[207] and interpret these contours as surface realizations of the circumflex L+H* L% configuration which appear on ultimate-stress words after preceding high targets, i.e. when there is too little space for the F0 to drop down between the high target of a prenuclear pitch accent and the nuclear syllable. In exclamative echo yes–no questions, however, there were also some clear examples of H+L* L% on penultimate-stress words (in both GS and GC), which is thus a contour shared with other types of yes–no questions (viz. information-seeking and exclamative ones).

As we have seen, echo questions do thus not generally show a particular intonation which would oppose them to non-echo questions. Yet, it is worth pointing out that, in the case of echo wh-questions, L* H% was used with a higher frequency than in the respective non-echo information-seeking wh-questions. Since echo wh-questions pragmatically represent yes–no questions which require a polar answer (i.e. 'yes' or 'no') despite the wh-word, this is not surprising. However, an explicit intonational marking is possible: L+H* LH% (or H* LH%), with

---

207. A further reason that speaks in favour of such an interpretation is the fact that L+¡H* L% was also attested sporadically in CC (see Prieto et al. 2015: 32–33, 57).

a complex boundary tone, is a nuclear configuration that was exclusively observed in echo wh-questions (in both varieties but produced solely by CatD speakers). Following the literature on Catalan echo wh-questions and in accordance with the interpretation of H* L% as a surface variant of L+H* L% (see above), I suggest that H* LH% is a surface realization of underlying L+H* LH% that appears due to lack of space. However, it is again likely that not all bilinguals have this configuration at their disposal in their phonological systems.[208] Finally, as concerns the difference between neutral and exclamative echo yes–no question, the main difference seems to consist in the use of a higher pitch range in the latter, which again translates in the appearance of H+L* as a surface variant of L* in both the nucleus and the prenucleus and in the use of particularly high boundary tones (i.e. ¡H%).

H+L* L% and L+H* L% are the two nuclear configurations established for **commands** in both GS and GC. With respect to the first one of these, I suggest that L* L% is a surface realization that might convey a less strong or friendlier command, since it camouflages the command as a statement (see Henriksen/García-Amaya 2012: 139). The same two nuclear configurations may thus be used to express both orders and neutral statements. This is possible since the orders can be easily recognized through the verb in the imperative mood. However, on the basis of the clearly different frequencies of occurrence, I conclude that the underlying forms are distinct: L* L% in statements and H+L* L% in commands. The L+H* L% nuclear configuration, finally, has already been said various times to express emphasis. I assume that this is also the case in orders.

For **requests**, the following nuclear configurations can be proposed on basis of the intonational analysis: L+H* L% and L+H* HL%, as well as H+L* L%. In this case, length of the utterance seems to play a role, since H+L* L% typically appears in sentences with a rising pitch accent in the prenucleus, whereas the other two contours are used to express requests in utterances that only consist of the verb in the imperative mood. I assume that the HL% boundary tone expresses more insistence as opposed to L%. This bitonal boundary tone was also found to express contradiction statements and vocatives in the two contact varieties. However, morphological and lexical cues allow to distinguish these sentence modalities (i.e. the verb in the imperative mood, in requests, and the proper name or noun, in vocatives).

As for **vocatives**, L+H* HL% and L+H* !H% were established as nuclear configurations in both GS and GC. I suggest that the two boundary tones convey

---

208. Such inter-speaker differences are also evident from the fact that the bilingual of Honduran origin once more (and as the only participant) produced an H+L* LH% nuclear contour, which she had already used in other question types, in her echo yes–no questions in both languages.

different degrees of insistence based on their frequency in the data set and in accordance with the literature (see Section 3.1.2.2). Whereas HL% is assumed to convey a neutral vocative ('first call'), !H%, i.e. the so-called 'vocative chant', marks a more insistent vocative ('second call'). L+H* H% (with the surface variant L* H%), finally, is used in 'interrogative vocatives' or 'vocative questions', i.e. when only the name of a person is used to ask implicitly 'Are you there?' or 'Can you hear me?' (see Prieto 2002a: 460; Prieto 2013: 42–43; Prieto et al. 2015: 41; Borràs-Comes et al. 2015: 78).

The reasons why more than one underlying nuclear configuration were established for various sentence types in the two Girona varieties (for instance, in information-seeking yes–no questions) and how single individuals differ with regard to their phonological repertoires will be addressed more extensively in Section 6.4. It will be shown that, in many cases, CLI is responsible for the variable presence of intonational features in the contact population. However, a larger speaker corpus will be necessary to determine the nature of the variation between competing nuclear configurations in all utterance types.

To conclude this section, Table 5.14 summarizes the underlying nuclear configurations of IPs established for the different GC and GS sentence types. When more than one configuration is given, they are arranged according to decreasing frequency of occurrence.

Table 5.14 Inventory of underlying nuclear configurations of IPs in Girona Spanish and Girona Catalan

Sentence types		Girona Catalan	Girona Spanish
neutral statements	neutral statements	L* L%[209]	same
	enumerations[210]	L* L%	same
	peripheral elements in neutral statements[211]		
	dislocations	L* L%	same
	vocatives	L+H* L%	same
	parenthetical elements	L* L%	same
	appositions	L* L%	same

---

209. Surface realizations: H+L* L% (after preceding high tone).
210. This nuclear configuration only refers to the last element in enumerations.
211. The table offers the nuclear configurations of the respective extra-sentential elements, not of the main clause (which behaved like usual neutral statements).

Table 5.14 *(continued)*

Sentence types		Girona Catalan	Girona Spanish
biased statements	contrastive-focus statements	L+H* L%[212]	same
	exclamative statements	L+H* L%[213]	same
	contradiction statements[214]	H+L* L%	same, but L+H* L% is more frequent
		L+H* L%	
		L* HL%	
		H+L* HL%	
	dubitative statements	L+H* L%[215]	same
neutral polar questions	information-seeking yes–no questions[216]	L* H%[217]	same[218]
		H+L* L%[219]	
	disjunctive questions[220]	H+L* L%	L* L%
		L* L%	H+L* L%

---

212. Surface realizations: 'step-like' ¡L+H* L% (after high preceding targets). L* L% can be employed when the contrastive focus is signalled by syntactic means (such as cleft structures).

213. Surface realizations: H* L% and L+¡H* L% (expresses more emphasis). L* L% can be employed when the exclamativity is signalled by increased pitch movements (e.g. higher scaling of pitch accents) in the prenucleus.

214. I assume that not all bilinguals have the same inventory of nuclear configurations as a result of convergence processes between the originally different systems of GC and GS (see Section 6.4.2). For the surface realizations of some of these nuclear configurations see Section 5.1.2.3.

215. Surface realizations: H* L%. L* L% can be employed when the notion of doubt is expressed by lexical means.

216. I assume that not all bilinguals have the same inventory of nuclear configurations as a result of an ongoing but yet uncompleted process of convergence between the originally different systems of GC and Spanish (see Section 6.4.3 for more details). The H+L* LH% nuclear configuration found in only one speaker is not listed here.

217. Usually realized as L* ¡H% in all question types when there is enough post-nuclear material for F0 to rise to the highest point of the utterance.

218. Only used in yes–no questions headed by the complementizer *que*.

219. I assume that only some (typically CatD) bilinguals have H+L* L% in their phonological repertoire for GS.

220. I assume that not all bilinguals have the same inventory of nuclear configurations (see Section 6.4.3).

Table 5.14 *(continued)*

Sentence types		Girona Catalan	Girona Spanish
biased polar questions	exclamative yes–no questions (with counterexpectational meaning)	*nuclear configurations of information-seeking yes–no questions*[221]	
	confirmation-seeking yes–no questions	L* H%	same
		H+L* L%[222]	
neutral wh-questions	information-seeking wh-questions[223]	H* L%	same, although H* L% is less dominant
		L* L%	
		L* H%	
biased wh-questions	exclamative wh-questions[224]	H* L%[225]	same, although L+H* L% is more frequent
		L+H* L%[226]	
		L* H%[227]	
	imperative wh-questions	H+L* L%	H+L* L%
		L* H%	L* H%
			L+H* L%
echo questions	echo yes–no questions	L* H%	same
		L+H* L%[228]	
	echo wh-question	L* H%	same (L+H* L% slightly more frequent)
		L+H* L%[229]	
		L+H* LH%[230]	

---

221. I assume that the notion of exclamativity is expressed by the expansion of the pitch range and an increase of the pitch movements, yielding, e.g., surface realizations of L* H% such as H+L* H%.
222. Typically employed on 'disjunctive elements'.
223. I assume that not all bilinguals have the same inventory of nuclear configurations as a result of convergence processes between the originally different systems of GC and Spanish (see Section 6.4.4).
224. The nuclear configurations found in exclamative wh-questions are virtually the same as in information-seeking wh-questions. However, L+H* L% is clearly more frequent (especially in GS) and a higher pitch range and more tonal movements are typically used to convey the notion of exclamativity. Also, it is probable that not all bilinguals have the same intonational systems for this utterance type.
225. Typical surface realization (in both varieties): ¡H* L% (expresses more emphasis).
226. Alternative surface realization (in both varieties): L+¡H* L% (expresses more emphasis).
227. Typical surface realization (in both varieties): L+H* (¡)H% (expresses more emphasis).
228. Usually found in echo yes–no questions without prenucleus.

Chapter 5. Results 305

Table 5.14 (continued)

Sentence types		Girona Catalan	Girona Spanish
	exclamative echo yes–no questions (with counterexpectational meaning)	L* H%[231]	same
		H+L* L%	
		L+H* L%	
imperatives	commands	H+L* L%[232]	same
		L+H* L%[233]	
	requests	H+L* L%	same
		L+H* L%[234]	
		L+H* HL%[235]	
vocatives		L+H* HL%	same
		L+H* !H%[236]	
		L+H* H%[237]	

5.2.4 Inventory of pitch accents and boundary tones in Girona Spanish and Girona Catalan

The result of the intonational analysis revealed that both GS and GC have an inventory of six pitch accents: L*, H*, L*+H, L+H*, L+<H*, H+L*. Of these, L*+H and L+<H* only occurred in prenuclear position (see Section 5.2.1). Table 5.15 provides a schematic representation and a phonetic description of each pitch

---

229. Surface realizations: H* L% (due to lack of space after a preceding high tone).
230. Surface realizations: H* LH% (due to lack of space after preceding high tone).
231. Surface realizations: L* ¡H% and H+L* (¡)H% (effect of the use of an extended pitch range; expresses more emphasis).
232. Surface realizations: L* L% (less strong command).
233. Typically appears in imperatives consisting of only one prosodic word (i.e. the imperative verb form).
234. Usually appears on short commands consisting of only one prosodic word (i.e. the imperative verb form).
235. I assume that the HL% boundary tone expresses more insistence as opposed to L%.
236. I assume that the !H% boundary tone expresses more insistence as opposed to HL%. The syllables carrying these boundary tones are considerably lengthened.
237. Surface realizations: L* H%. These nuclear configurations are used in 'vocative questions' (see above).

accent. The black line represents the F0, the grey parts illustrate the metrically strong (i.e. stressed) syllable, the white parts correspond to preceding and following unstressed syllables.

Table 5.15 Inventory of pitch accents in Girona Spanish and Girona Catalan[a]

Pitch accents	Phonetic description
Monotonal pitch accents	
L*	L* is phonetically realized as a low plateau during the stressed syllable or can be shaped as a gentle trough valley. Its level typically — though not necessarily — correlates with the minimum of the speaker's range.
H*	H* is phonetically realized as a high plateau during the stressed syllable or as a (rather flat) peak.
Bitonal pitch accents	
L*+H	L*+H is phonetically realized as a flat valley during the stressed syllable followed by a rise in the post-tonic syllable(s). Its level is usually somewhat higher than the minimum of the speaker's range as it appears in prenuclear positions.
L+H*	L+H* is phonetically realized as a rise during the stressed syllable with the peak located at the end of that syllable.
L+<H*	L+<H* is phonetically realized as a rise during the stressed syllable with the peak located in a post-tonic syllable.
H+L*	H+L* is phonetically realized as a fall during the stressed syllable.

a. The pitch accents containing a high target may be upstepped (e.g. H* and L+H* have the surface variants ¡H* and L+¡H*). If so, their peak usually represents the overall F0 maximum of the ip. The illustrations are taken from Aguilar et al. (2009) and (2009–2011).

GS and GC also present the same inventory of boundary tones. It contains three monotonal boundary tones (H-/H%, !H-/!H%, and L-/L%) as well as two bitonal boundary tones (LH% and HL%). Of these, three boundary tones could be found in nuclear configurations of inner ips and in nuclear configurations of IPs (i.e. H-/H%, !H-/!H%, and L-/L%, respectively). The remainder was only attested in nuclear configurations of IPs (L%, LH%, HL%). Table 5.16 provides schematic representations and phonetic descriptions of each boundary tone. The black line represents the F0, the grey parts illustrate the phrase-final syllable on which the boundary tone is realized, the white parts correspond to preceding syllables.

Table 5.16 Inventory of boundary tones in Girona Spanish and Girona Catalan

Boundary tones	Phonetic description
Monotonal boundary tones	
L-/L%	L-/L% is phonetically realized as a sustained low tone or as a falling tone. Its level correlates with the minimum of the speaker's range when it is a sustained low tone. When it is realized as a fall after a preceding high tone it must not attain the minimum of the speaker's range but at least the lower half of it.
H-/H%	H-/H% is phonetically realized as a rising tone. It can be produced after low or rising pitch accents. It has the upstepped surface variant ¡H-/¡H%.
!H-/!H%	!H-/!H% is phonetically realized as a high sustained tone or as a gentle fall to a mid-tone. In principle, it can also be a rise from a low level to a mid-tone.
Bitonal boundary tones	
LH-/LH%	LH-/LH% is phonetically realized as a valley to a mid-level of the speaker's range followed by a rise to a high level of their range. It is realized after high or rising pitch accents.
HL-/HL%	HL-/HL% is phonetically realized as a peak followed by a fall. It occurs after rising and low pitch accents.

The following Table, finally, offers schematic representations of the inventory of nuclear configurations to which the aforementioned pitch accents and boundary tones combined in the GS and GC corpora used for the current study. For convenience, it also repeats the pragmatic utterance types in which each nuclear configuration may appear (see Section 5.2.3, above).

Table 5.17 Inventory of Girona Spanish and Girona Catalan nuclear configurations, their schematic representation, and their use in several sentence types

Nuclear configuration		Sentence type where it is used
	L* L%	Neutral broad-focus statements, enumerations, utterance-final peripheral elements in neutral statements (dislocations, parenthetical elements, appositions), disjunctive questions, information-seeking wh-questions
	L* H%	yes–no questions (information-seeking, exclamative, and confirmation-seeking), wh-questions (information-seeking, exclamative, imperative), echo questions (yes-no, wh-, and exclamative yes–no)
	H* L%	information-seeking and exclamative wh-questions
	H+L* L%	contradiction statements, information-seeking and exclamative yes–no question (with *que*), confirmation-seeking yes–no questions, disjunctive questions, exclamative echo yes–no questions, commands, requests
	L+H* L%	biased statements (i.e. contrastive-focus, exclamative, contradiction, and dubitative statements), exclamative wh-questions, imperative wh-questions (only attested in GS), echo questions (yes-no, wh-, and exclamative yes–no), commands, requests
	L+H* HL%	requests, vocatives
	L+H* LH%	echo wh-questions
	L+H* !H%	vocatives
	H+L* HL%	contradiction statements
	L+H* H%	interrogative vocatives
	L* HL%	contradiction statements

CHAPTER 6

Discussion

The major objective of this book is to provide a comprehensive description of the intonation of Girona Spanish and Girona Catalan as spoken by bilingual speakers. A further aim is to tackle the following research questions:

1. How similar is the intonation of Girona Spanish and Girona Catalan?
2. How uniform is the intonation of the two contact varieties spoken in Girona across speaker groups and individual speakers? Can variation be linked to bilingualism factors such as language dominance?
3. What are the differences and similarities between Girona Spanish and Castilian Spanish intonation? What are the differences and similarities between Girona Catalan and other Central Catalan varieties on the intonational level?
4. How can the similarities and differences between Girona Catalan and the Girona Spanish at the prosodic level be explained in terms of language contact, i.e. how did the current intonational systems emerge?
5. Does the prosodic distance to other Spanish varieties and the level of homogeneity of its intonation across speakers justify that Girona Spanish (or Catalonian Spanish in a wider sense) should be viewed as a variety of Spanish in its own right?
6. How does contact-induced intonational change work? And how is it influenced by the extralinguistic conditions of the contact situation?
7. Which kinds of intonational features can be transferred? And which are most likely to be transferred?

In the course of this chapter, I shall attempt to give answers to these research questions. In Section 6.1, I summarize the similarities and differences between the intonational systems of Girona Spanish (GS) and Girona Catalan (GC) as spoken by bilinguals. In the next section, I address the variation attested in these contact varieties, i.e. I discuss how uniform the they are at the intonational level and whether the variation observed between individual speakers can be linked to extralinguistic factors such as language dominance (LD, see Section 6.2). Section 6.3 is devoted to the comparison between the intonational systems of Girona Spanish and Castilian Spanish (CS) and between GC and other Central Catalan (CC) varieties. In Section 6.4, I strive to uncover the transfer and convergence processes that may have occurred during the development of the two contacting varieties grounded on the comparisons with the reference varieties.

Following next, Section 6.5 examines the status of GS as a distinctive variety within the Spanish diasystem based on the intonational analysis, and Section 6.6 deals with the question of how intonational change works more generally and discusses the role of extralinguistic factors. Finally, Section 6.7 provides the reader with the answers to question 7 presented above, i.e. it approaches the intralinguistic aspects of intonational change from a more theoretical point of view.

6.1 Similarities and differences between the prosodic systems of Girona Spanish and Girona Catalan

The results of the intonational analysis have revealed that the current varieties of GS and GC as spoken by bilinguals with different degrees of LD share numerous intonational features and display few differences. In the ensuing summaries, I briefly outline these similarities and differences.

Similarities between the prosodic systems of Girona Catalan and Girona Spanish

- Both varieties primarily use continuation rises (CR, i.e. the nuclear configuration L+H* H-) to tonally mark the final boundaries of inner ips in neutral broad-focus declaratives, i.e. to convey incompleteness of the discourse. Sustained pitches (SP, i.e. L+H* !H-) are used to a minor extent (more often in GS than in GC).
- L+<H*, i.e. the delayed peak, is the underlying prenuclear pitch accent in statements in both varieties.
- Both prenuclear H+L* and L+H* are surface variants of underlying prenuclear L+<H* in statements in both varieties. Whereas H+L* occurs after preceding high tonal targets, L+H* may surface in stress clashes.
- L*+H was established as underlying phrase-initial prenuclear pitch accent in most question types in both varieties (usually not in *que*-questions and wh-questions).
- Prenuclear H* is the typical prenuclear pitch accent of yes–no questions with *que* and of information-seeking wh-questions in both varieties. However, it can also appear as a surface variant of L+<H* in statements or of L*+H in other question types (e.g. in stress clashes).
- In statements, phrase-internal prosodic words are pitch-deaccented to an extent of roughly 30% in both varieties. In information-seeking yes–no questions this share rises to approximately 80% or more (i.e. the tonal density in this question type questions is very low).

- The nuclear L* pitch accent (attested in numerous IP nuclear configurations) conveys pragmatically neutral broad-focus readings in both varieties, and H+L* is a surface variant that may occur after preceding high tonal targets.
- The nuclear L+(¡)H* pitch accent is used to signal focus and/or emphasis in both varieties (i.e. it is used in biased statements).
- The upstep (¡) as well as an expanded pitch range can be used to indicate emphasis.
- The following shared underlying nuclear configurations were established for both varieties:
  - L* L% for neutral broad-focus statements
  - L+H* L% for contrastive-focus, exclamative, and dubitative statements
  - L+H* L%, H+L* L%, H+L* HL%, and L* HL% for contradiction statements (although with different frequencies and probably not in all speakers)
  - L* H% and H+L* L% in information-seeking, confirmation-seeking, and exclamative yes–no questions
  - H+L* L% and L* L% in disjunctive questions (although with different frequencies)
  - H* L%, L* L%, and L* H% in information-seeking wh-questions (albeit with different frequencies)
  - H* L%, L+H* L%, and L* H% in exclamative wh-questions (although with different frequencies)
  - H+L* L% and L* H% in imperative wh-questions
  - L* H% and L+H* L% in echo yes–no questions
  - L* H%, L+H* L%, L+H* LH% in echo wh-questions
  - L* H%, H+L* L%, and L+H* L%, in exclamative echo yes–no questions (with counterexpectational meaning)
  - H+L* L% and L+H* L% in commands
  - H+L* L%, L+H* L%, L+H* HL% in requests
  - L+H* HL%, L+H* !H%, L+H* H% in vocatives
- In both varieties, L* H% can be used as nuclear contour in all types of yes–no, wh-, and echo questions.

Differences between the prosodic systems of Girona Catalan and Girona Spanish

- Significantly more sustained pitches are used in GS to mark ip-boundaries than in GC.
- H+L* L% is the preferred nuclear contour in contradiction statements in GC. In GS, it was only attested in CatD speakers.
- L+H* L% is the preferred nuclear contour in contradiction statements in GS.

- In information-seeking yes–no questions, the nuclear contour H+L* L% is quite common in GC but quite rare in GS.
- In information-seeking wh-questions, H* L% is less dominant in GS than in GC.
- In exclamative wh-questions, the general preference for H* L% is stronger in GC, as GS uses L+H* L% more frequently than GC.
- In imperative wh-questions, L+H* L% was only attested in GS.
- In disjunctive questions, GC prefers the H+L* L% nuclear contour, while GS prefers L* L%.
- In echo wh-questions, L+H* L% is somewhat more frequent in GS and among SpD bilinguals.

In sum, together with the phonological analysis made in Section 5.2, the comparison of the intonational systems of GS and GC offered in this section demonstrates that the two contacting varieties share their tonal inventories, i.e. they use not only the same pitch accents and boundary tones but also the same nuclear configurations to express identical meanings. The (very few) differences that were registered between the varieties almost invariably arise from distinct frequencies of occurrence of some of the items in this shared inventory (see, e.g., Bulgarian Judaeo-Spanish in Section 3.2.3 for a similar case). The next sections will deal with the question of how this variation can be explained.

6.2 Variation in Girona Spanish and Girona Catalan

The prosodic analysis of GS and GC has revealed that these varieties pattern alike in that they present quite a lot of variation at the intonational level. For most sentence types studied, two or even more distinct underlying nuclear configurations could be established – sometimes appearing with different frequencies in the two languages. This was especially the case of contradiction statements, information-seeking yes–no questions, information-seeking, exclamative, and echo wh-questions, imperatives, and vocatives (see Sections 5.2 and 6.1, above). In contrast, the available descriptions of Spanish and Catalan intonation carried out within the AM model commonly posit only one nuclear configuration per utterance type. This is also the case of the reference varieties CS and CC, to which the contact varieties will be compared in the following section, 6.3. When more than one nuclear contour is offered for a particular type in the literature, these either belong to different diatopical varieties or else the authors usually suggest – and occasionally have demonstrated in follow-up studies – that their use is conditioned by pragmatic factors such as politeness or insistence on part of the speaker (see, e.g., the descriptions of neutral wh-questions in Estebas-Vilaplana/Prieto 2010: 35 or Prieto 2014: 67; see also Table 3.4). The question must thus be posed how the comparatively large variation attested in the Girona contact varieties can be accounted for.

In some cases, pragmatically rooted proposals were made to account for the intonational variation in the current study — though always in accordance with the extant literature on CS and CC intonation, as the size and the composition of the corpus do not allow to explore such factors in a systematic way. For example, in Section 5.2.3, I proposed that the choice between the different nuclear configurations in vocatives depends on the insistence speakers intend to convey in their call. Yet, such pragmatic approaches were not always possible nor did they always seem appropriate. Furthermore, the types of pragmatic distinctions that show categorical phonological differences may vary across different varieties of the same language: this has been observed, e.g., with regard to the intonation of yes–no interrogatives in Spanish, where Jerezano and Argentinian Spanish present a smaller number of pragmatically distinctive contours than CS (see Gabriel et al. 2010; Henriksen/García-Amaya 2012: 145; Hualde/Prieto 2015). More than pragmatic factors, the following two facts seem to be relevant to account for the variation at hand in the present study: (1) A fair deal of the variance documented in the contact varieties is of the diastratic type, i.e. there is no language-internal systemic meaning attached to it, but it can be linked to sociolinguistic parameters such as the speaker's origin and LD. (2) It is likely that the available descriptions of other varieties only reflect a part of the actually existing variation, such that the variation found in the Girona varieties is actually not so much greater. Before I expand on the effects of the speakers' sociolinguistic backgrounds on their linguistic performance (1), the following example will illustrate how conclusion (2) was drawn.

In the present analysis, it is striking that the low–rise nuclear configuration (L* H%) was attested in all interrogative utterance types studied (with the exception of disjunctive questions), i.e. in 10 different, pragmatically neutral or biased question types (see Table 5.1). This clearly shows that the tune merely expresses interrogativity and cannot be used to distinguish different types of pragmatic bias (e.g. the difference between confirmation-seeking or exclamative yes–no questions). When the speakers use it in biased questions, the bias must thus either be conveyed by other linguistic means such as pitch span or lexical choices or it is not expressed explicitly (i.e. it must be inferred from the context or world knowledge). In contrast, L* H% is only reported for 3 CS question types by Estebas-Vilaplana/Prieto (2010) and Prieto (2014) only reports it for neutral yes–no questions. The question thus arises why L* H% is so much more recurrent across different utterance types in the contact varieties spoken in Girona.

There are two plausible answers: (1) the descriptions offered in the literature on the intonation of CS and CC only provide a partial picture of the true variation because they mainly report the tunes that are unique to and hence distinctive of a particular utterance type. Also, they tend to document only the tunes that appear with the highest frequencies (leaving aside less used ones). If this were true, it would explain why the current analysis registered more variants in many cases (e.g. L* H% in all biased question types in addition to the respective utterance-specific nuclear contours that explicitly convey the biased meaning). Regarding the particular example just given, the fact that 'L* H%'-like contours are mentioned for over 8 (biased and non-biased) question types in Prieto's (2002a) theory-neutral description of CC intonation (in opposition to the available AM descriptions) point towards this assumption being correct. (2) On the other hand, it cannot be excluded that the generalization of L* H% to virtually all GS and GC question types could be the result of a simplification process taking place parallelly in both languages due to long-standing language contact (see Blas Arroyo 2011: 386). This is to say, (some) bilinguals could have reduced their tonal repertoires as a strategy of coping with their 'bilingual burden' (see Section 3.2.1 and sources therein). Instead of keeping apart two separate language-specific systems with many context-specific tunes, they could have chosen the 'simplest variant', i.e. the one which in both languages expresses merely the feature [+ interrogative], and generalized it to all question types. Also, as mentioned before, the varieties of a language may differ with regard to the number of pragmatic distinctions expressed through categorical phonological difference. For instance, Henriksen/García-Amaya (2012: 145) suggest that the contrast between rising–falling and falling–rising contours in CS yes–no questions put forth in Escandell-Vidal (1999, 2002, 2017) and taken up, e.g., by Estebas-Vilaplana/Prieto (2010) does not apply to Southern Peninsular varieties of Spanish. The same could be true for GS, as well (and mutatis mutandis also for GC). This is to say, some bilinguals could have given up earlier distinctions, but as the simplification process has not yet spread to the entire speaker community, it synchronically leads to an increase in competing variants.

Be that as it may, the more important factors conditioning the intonational variation observed in the Girona contact varieties are clearly sociolinguistic in nature and hence depend on language-external factors. One such parameter, which was taken into account throughout the analysis, was the bilinguals' **language dominance** (LD). In Section 4.2, it was shown that the linguistic uses and competences of roughly two thirds of the participants of the present study were clearly biased towards Catalan, while the rest were moderately dominant in Spanish, i.e. the sample is representative of the sociolinguistic situation in Girona at the societal level (see Section 2.1 and Fn. 140 in Section 4.2). Almost invariably, the participants' LD correlated with their ethnolinguistic affiliation, viz. with their parents' background (see Section 4.2). Since it was one of the major purposes of this study to gauge the effect of speakers' LD on both their phonetic production and their phonological systems, this factor was given special emphasis in the presentation of the results inasmuch as Spanish- and Catalan-dominant bilingual speaker groups (SpD and CatD) were considered separately whenever it was possible and beneficial. When it made sense, even further shades of the degree of LD (e.g. more balanced vs strong dominance) were brought into play.

In this way, it was shown that SpD and CatD bilinguals do not always behave alike at the intonational level. For instance, in GC information-seeking yes–no questions introduced by *que*, the use of low–rising and high–falling nuclear contours was significantly associated with the speakers' LD (low–rising contours being used almost without exception only by SpD) and, in GS, this question type was almost invariably found in CatD (always coming along with the falling tonal pattern). Clear differences between the two speaker groups were also observed in contradiction statements, exclamative yes–no questions, and, to a minor extent, in echo wh-questions (see Sections 5.1.2.2, 5.1.4.1 and 5.1.7.2). In consequence, it is evident that a substantial amount of the variation we observe in the Girona contact varieties results from CLI between the two languages of their bilingual speakers, i.e. in most cases from the dominant to the non-dominant language (see the analysis of the role of language contact in the development of the contact varieties in Section 6.4).

Nevertheless, in most cases **no clear-cut differences** between the dominance groups could be established. Although frequency-based differences in the use of particular tunes were common, statistical tests rarely reached the conventional significance level of $\alpha = 0.5$. As this may at least in part be a corollary of the smaller number of participants in the SpD group ($n = 11$), and hence of the number of sentences analysed in a specific context, it is fair to point out that there were some cases of marginal significance ($p < 0.1$): e.g. regarding the use of H* as prenuclear pitch accent in neutral statements. Still, the recurrent absence of statistically significant differences first and foremost signals that the ways of speaking of the two dominance groups are quite similar at present. Since we can safely assume that the varieties of Spanish and Catalan spoken in Catalonia by (Catalan-speaking) locals and (Spanish-speaking) settlers were once more distinct (see Section 2.3), this means that they must have very much approached each other in a process of large-scale convergence (see the discussion of the similarities between GS and GC in the light of language contact in Section 6.4).

Besides LD, there must thus be some additional factors. One of these is clearly **inter-subject variability**. This is most evident in the case of participant No. 13, whose interrogative intonation was quite consistently different from that of the other bilinguals. This SpD bilingual (ILD: 28.7) overwhelmingly used an H+L*

LH% nuclear configuration across different types of yes–no questions (typically in connection with H+L* prenuclear pitch accents). In particular, such contours were found in her neutral, confirmation-seeking, and echo yes–no questions as well as in her read data. To my best knowledge, H+L* LH% nuclear contours have not been documented for any other variety of CC or Peninsular Spanish. Given that this bilingual grew up in Girona but was born in Honduras from monolingual Spanish-speaking Honduran parents, it can be presumed that her particular nuclear tune originally derives from Honduran Spanish, of which we unfortunately have no descriptions so far. Interestingly enough, the contour was also produced twice by another, now slightly CatD bilingual (−21.8), whose father stems from Uruguay. Since it was also observed in Paraguayan Spanish by Andrea Pešková (p.c.), it can be surmised that what we are dealing with here are in fact characteristics of American Spanish varieties. Crucially, both participants used the contour not only in Spanish but also in Catalan (i.e. there seems to be prosodic transfer from (Latin American) Spanish to Catalan). Furthermore, these two subjects obiously must have a partially different phonological system compared to the other participants.

However, while this is certainly the most blatant case of inter-speaker variation, it is not the only one. The phonological analysis presented in Section 5.2 repeatedly brought up good reasons to believe that not all of the investigated bilinguals share one and the same intonational system in each language – not even those who have the same dominant language. Instead, the distribution of the attested nuclear contours across speakers and languages in many utterance types (among them, e.g., contradiction statements, information-seeking and exclamative yes–no and wh-questions, disjunctive, and echo questions) strongly suggests that there are different repertoires of nuclear contours among the participants and that most of them only have a selection of the variants found overall.

The reason for this could be that individual speakers differ in their ability to acquire a second language in a target-like manner and that some struggle more than others with keeping their language systems separate, i.e. individual speakers contribute to different degrees to the aforementioned convergence processes between the two languages. For instance, in the present case, some bilinguals – typically those with the strongest bias towards one language – seem to use merely the intonational system of their dominant language (i.e. they fail to acquire the one of the second language), while others (typically more balanced bilinguals) are more successful in partially or fully acquiring the respective target system (see also Section 6.4). This, in turn, leads to a situation in which there are large differences between the phonological systems of the single individuals in the bilingual community as well as within the dominance groups that exist in that society. Still, as we have seen, background factors such as LD play an important role in that they help us predict which tunes a particular bilingual is most likely to use.

In sum, as contact varieties that are virtually always spoken by bilinguals, current GS and GC do present more intonational variation than, e.g., (monolingual) CS does. Yet, this variability can to a substantial degree be linked to the speakers' LD (and hence to their sociolinguistic background) as well as to other bilingualism factors (such as the ability to maintain two separate language systems). In view of the fact that these aspects of bilingualism have traditionally not been paid much attention to when studying this particular but also other language-contact situations involving extensive bilingualism, the results of the present study endorse the recent trend of giving them more importance when accounting for variation in linguistic data stemming from bilinguals. Another conclusion of this subchapter is that the variation observed in Catalan–Spanish bilinguals in 21st-century Catalonia mainly results from language contact between Catalan and Spanish. In the following two sections, I will thus first compare GS and GC to CS and other CC varieties and then use this comparison to show how the language-contact situation has shaped the two Girona varieties, which to a certain extent qualify as mixed varieties that combine both 'Spanish' and 'Catalan' intonational features.

6.3 Prosodic distance between Girona Spanish and Castilian Spanish and between Girona Catalan and other Central Catalan varieties

Before discussing the similarities and differences between the GS and the GC intonational systems in the light of language contact, it is necessary to establish further points of comparison. In this section, I shall therefore contrast the two Girona varieties with the corresponding reference varieties, i.e. with (standard) CS and (standard) CC. This choice will be motivated in the ensuing paragraphs before the actual comparison is made.

As regards GC, this subvariety is actually part of the CC dialect, which — at least in Catalonia — is generally considered the standard (or closest-to-standard) form of Catalan (see, e.g., Prieto 2014: 44). CC is also the variety which Pompeu Fabra took as point of departure for his standardization work (see, e.g., Brumme 2020: 498, 502) and the one which dominates in the Catalan media (see Camps/ Labèrnia 2020, among others). However, this is true especially for the Barcelona variant of CC and less so for other subdialects. In consequence, also most available accounts of (Central) Catalan intonation are based rather on the metropolitan variety than on subdialects such as the one used in Girona, for which only sketchy and fragmentary descriptions are available (see Section 3.1.2). In this work, I shall consider the accessible information on both of these subvarieties, but will mainly have to draw on Barcelona-centred descriptions of CC.

Of course, for obvious reasons, no CC variety can constitute an ideal reference point for the enterprise of uncovering CLI in the Girona speech data analysed in this work, as that preferably ought to be a monolingual non-contact variety of Catalan. Yet, given the fact that all Catalan varieties have been in more or less intense contact with other languages for many decades (e.g. with Spanish, French, or Sardinian) and that all Catalan speakers are (at least) bilingual today (see Section 2.1), such a comparison is no longer possible. Due to its contact with Spanish, CC thus cannot be considered a fully neutral baseline for the comparison with GC in the same way than CS for GS. However, taking it as a landmark is certainly still the best possible practice — as long as this caveat is kept in mind.[238]

As pertains GS, a dialectal classification is still outstanding to date. In Section 2.2, it was outlined that Catalonian Spanish and other Spanish varieties in contact with Catalan in a wider sense have largely been ignored in the traditional Spanish dialectology. While it is common and certainly helpful in many cases to compare varieties to neighbouring varieties spoken in contiguous areas, this does not appear to be an appropriate or even feasible option in case of GS. First, as discussed at some length in Section 2.3, there are not yet any full reports on Catalonian Spanish prosody that could be referred to in such an enterprise. Next, a comparison to the geographically closest monolingual non-contact variety, i.e. the Spanish spoken in most parts of Aragon, was decided against, too, for the following series of reasons: first and most importantly, Spanish in Aragon and in Catalonia originated in utterly different ways and at different times. While Aragonese is usually considered a historic or primary dialect of Spanish (see Zamora Vicente 1960; Coseriu 1980; García Mouton 2007) and the complete language shift to Castilian Spanish in most parts of Aragon occurred quite rapidly after the union with the Crown of Castile (see Tomás Faci 2020: 217), Catalonian Spanish largely arose within the last two centuries (see Section 2.1). Furthermore, Catalonian Spanish first developed as an L2 variety, when native speakers of Catalan began learning (Standard) Castilian Spanish as a foreign language, while the continuous shift from Aragonese to Spanish in Aragon was very probably less conscious (Tomás Faci 2020: 244, 256, 267, and passim).

Second, as the Catalans were becoming bilinguals in their masses, they entered in intense contact with monolingual varieties of Spanish stemming mainly from the South of the Peninsula as well as with the Castilian standard diffused in the mass media (see Ruiz Martínez 2004; Cutillas-Espinosa/Hernández-

---

238. Furthermore, it is worth pointing out that even if the authors of the extant works on Catalan intonation usually do not refer to it directly, it can be assumed that they paid some attention, when selecting their Catalan informants, to choose bilinguals who are clearly dominant in that language and thus approach the ideal of monolingualism as closely as possible.

Campoy 2007). As opposed to these varieties, Aragonese Spanish, though neighbouring, does not seem to have had much of an influence in the genesis of Catalonian Spanish.[239] Hence, a comparison of GS with the direct contact varieties just mentioned appears more natural. Third, there are virtually no data-based descriptions of Aragonese Spanish prosody, which makes a sound comparison impossible in practice.[240] Unfortunately, however, this also widely applies to the Spanish varieties spoken in Southern Spain, where the greatest part of immigrants to Catalonia and, in concert with this, also many of the parents of the participants in the present study stemmed from (see Sections 2.1 and 4.2). To my best knowledge, there are to date no systematic and comprehensive descriptions of the intonation of the Spanish varieties spoken in regions such as Andalusia or Extremadura presented within the AM framework.[241]

For all these reasons, I chose to compare the Girona variety of Spanish studied in the present book first and foremost to CS, which, besides being generally considered the standard variety of Spanish within the Peninsula, has also been the object of the majority of studies into Spanish intonation carried out within the AM framework. In addition to CS being one of the best-known varieties, it is also well-known that regional varieties often converge towards the standard variety (Labov/Harris 1986; Villena Ponsoda 2005, 2008; Morgenthaler García 2008:178–180, 291–322; Cutillas-Espinosa/Hernández-Campoy 2007; Hernández-Campoy 2011; Méndez García de Paredes/Amorós Negre 2016, 2019;

---

239. Although the first immigration wave to Catalonia also encompassed (Spanish-speaking) settlers from Aragon, their numbers stayed comparatively low. In 2020, only about 1% of the inhabitants of Catalonia were born in Aragon (IDESCAT 2021b).

240. The only exception known to me is the work by Castañer et al. (2005), carried out within the AMPER project, who present an overview of the (generally impressionistic) remarks on Aragonese Spanish intonation in the literature and study a little corpus of each 9 declaratives and 9 yes–no interrogatives recorded by a Spanish speaker from Zaragoza. They preliminarily conclude that there exists no fundamental difference between the variety under concern and "Peninsular Standard Spanish".

241. A notable exception is certainly the work of Henriksen/García-Amaya (2012) on Jérez Spanish. Furthermore, the study on Olivenza Spanish prosody by Kireva (2016a) constitutes another exception worth mentioning. However, being itself a contact variety, Olivenza Spanish does not appear to be a suitable variety for Girona Spanish to be compared to. The relatively few other existing studies of Southern Peninsular Spanish varieties for the most part use the AMPER framework (e.g. Congosto Martín et al. 2010; Congosto Martín 2011; Amorós Céspedes 2007, 2011; Pamies Bertrán 2007, 2008, among others). Unfortunately, these studies hardly allow for comparison with the Girona data sets, since the AMPER approach in most cases merely considers two sentence types on the basis of read speech from only one or very few speakers (i.e. neutral declaratives and yes–no questions). What is more, no underlying pitch accents or boundaries are usually established.

Kireva 2016a, among others). CS hence serves as a model to both L1 speakers of Catalan as well as to the L1 speakers of Spanish living in Catalonia (see Sinner 2004: 593–617). In this sense, a comparison between GS and CS enables a discussion about a possible convergence of the current variety of GS towards CS (i.e. towards the standard variety). What is more, in the case of the present study, CS is also one of the direct contact varieties for several bilinguals whose speech was investigated in the present study, because some of the participants' parents stemmed from Madrid, Valladolid, and Segovia (see Section 4.1). Nevertheless, I shall try to consider Southern Peninsular Spanish and the relevant Latin America varieties whenever it is possible and conducive as I discuss the genesis of the current state of the Girona contact varieties following in the next section (6.4).

The intonational analysis of GS with CS has revealed that the two varieties of the same language display a great many similarities but also some differences. Both kinds of features are summarized in the following overview.

Similarities and differences between the prosodic systems of Girona Spanish and Castilian Spanish
- Both varieties tonally mark ip boundaries with continuation rises and use sustained pitches to a minor extent (roughly 10% in both varieties; see Frota et al. 2007: 135 for CS).
- L+<H*, i.e. the delayed peak, is the underlying prenuclear pitch accent in statements in both varieties.
- Both varieties show similar amounts of phrase-internal pitch deaccenting in neutral statements (i.e. approximately 30% of the prosodic words are pitch-deaccented; see Face 2003).[242]
- The nuclear L+(¡)H* pitch accent is used to signal focus and/or emphasis in both varieties (i.e. in biased statements).
- The following underlying nuclear configurations are shared by both varieties:
    - L* L% for neutral broad-focus statements
    - L+H* L% for contrastive-focus and exclamative statements
    - L+H* L% and L* HL% in contradiction statements
    - L* H% in information-seeking and confirmation-seeking yes–no questions[243]

---

242. In the present work a percentage of deaccented phrase-internal prosodic words was calculated. By contrast, in the study of Face (2003: 122), which concludes that "approximately 30% of accentuable words lack a pitch accent" in Castilian Spanish, it is not specified whether this percentage includes only phrase-internal or all prosodic words.

243. Estebas-Vilaplana and Prieto (2010) distinguish between L* ¡H% in information-seeking and L* H% in confirmation-seeking yes–no questions. However, this difference was not retained in Hualde/Prieto (2015) and was not found in the present work, either. The height of the boundary tone seems to depend rather on the metrical structure of the nucleus.

- H+L* L% in confirmation-seeking yes–no questions (although L* H% is much more frequent in GS than in CS, which represents a parallel with Jerezano Spanish; see Henriksen/García-Amaya 2012)
  - L* L% in disjunctive questions
  - L* L% and L* H% in information-seeking wh-questions
  - H+L* L% in imperative wh-questions
  - L+H* L% and L* H% in echo yes–no questions and in echo wh-questions
  - H+L* L% and L+H* L% in requests
  - L+H* HL% and L+H* !H% in vocatives
- The following nuclear contours are not shared by the two varieties:
  - In dubitative statements, GS uses L+H* L%, while CS displays L+H* !H%.[244]
  - In contradiction statements, H+L* L% may occur in GS (only attested in CatD bilinguals)
  - H+L* L% can be used in GS information-seeking yes–no questions introduced with the particle *que* (inexistent in CS)
  - H+L* L% in disjunctive questions (only GS)
  - H* L% in information-seeking wh-questions (only in GS, where it is the most frequent nuclear contour in this question type)
  - L+H* L% and L* H% in GS imperative wh-questions
  - L+H* LH% in GS and L+H* ¡H% in CS echo wh-questions
  - In exclamative echo yes–no questions (with counterexpectational meaning), GS displays L* (¡)H%, H+L* L%, and L+H* L%, whereas in CS L+H* LH% or L+H* ¡H% are used.
  - In commands, GS displays H+L* L% and L+H* L%, while only CS uses L+H* !H%.
  - In requests, GS can show L+H* HL%, whereas CS may present L* HL%.
  - L+H* H% can occur in GS vocatives

Little surprisingly, the comparison of the results of the intonational analysis of GC with other CC varieties has equally revealed a lot of similarities. Yet, there are also some differences, which are summed up in the following overview.

---

244. Other Peninsular varieties of Spanish, such as Cantabrian and Jerezano Spanish, also show L+H* L% in this context (see López Bobo/Cuevas Alonso 2010: 60; Henriksen/García-Amaya 2012: 125)

Differences between the prosodic systems of Girona Catalan and standard Central Catalan
- In contradiction statements, GC may display L+H* L% and L* HL%, whereas these contours are not proposed for CC in the research literature (see Section 3.1.2.2).
- In dubitative statements, GC displays L+H* L%, whereas L+H* !H% is the nuclear contour given for CC in the literature (see Section 3.1.2.2).
- In disjunctive questions, H+L* L% is used only in GC.
- In intonation-seeking yes–no questions with *que*, an L* H% can be found in GC (the two are usually claimed to be incompatible in other Catalan varieties; see Prieto/Rigau 2007: 34f.; Nadeu/Prieto 2011: 845).
- In confirmation-seeking yes–no questions, L* H% rather than H+L* L% is most typical in GC.
- In information-seeking wh-questions, GC as opposed to CC may also display L* H% and L* L%.[245]
- In exclamative echo yes–no questions (with counterexpectational meaning), H+L* L% may be used in GC.
- L+H* LHL% does not seem to be used in GC exclamative echo yes–no questions (with counterexpectational meaning)
- In commands, H+L* L% is usually not indicated for CC but it was attested in GC commands consisting of more than one prosodic word.
- In requests, H+L* L%, L+H* L%, and L+H* HL% were observed in GC, whereas L+H* L!H%, L+H* LHL%, and L* HL% occur in CC.
- 'Interrogative' vocatives are most commonly realized as L+H* H% in GC, whereas CC uses L* H% (see Prieto et al. 2015: 41; Borràs-Comes et al. 2015: 78).

In sum, it can be concluded that the intonational systems of both Girona varieties show traces of language contact. Especially as regards GS, it appears fair to state that its intonational system is best characterized as a mixed system that combines intonational patterns from both Spanish and (Girona) Catalan. This is especially patent in the intonational realization of questions: consider for instance the nuclear configurations of information-seeking yes–no questions, which – as opposed to CS – can be formulated with the interrogative particle *que* and are then intuned with a high-falling H+L* L% nuclear configuration, precisely as it is the case in (Girona) Catalan. The finding that this question type is tonally realized in GS according to the Catalan model supports the observations made by

---

245. It is not fully clear in the available research literature whether these two nuclear configurations can also occasionally occur in CC (see the discussion in 6.4.4).

Romera et al. (2007, 2008) on the basis of read speech for Barcelona Spanish. Furthermore, GS confirmation-seeking yes–no questions are most recurrently pronounced with a low-rising L* H% nuclear configuration (which is equally in accord with GC but contrasts with CS and other CC varieties). In information-seeking wh-questions, the high–falling H* L% contour — which is not found in CS in this context — is the most common nuclear configuration in GS, and also in different types of echo questions the variety shares some of its nuclear contours with GC rather than with CS (e.g. L* (¡)H% and L+(¡)H* L% in exclamative echo yes–no questions with counterexpectational meaning or L+H* LH% in echo wh-questions). Moreover, GS shows pitch patterns that exist in Catalan but not in CS also in other utterance types (e.g. L+(¡)H* L% in commands).[246]

In the case of GC, on the other hand, Spanish influence is less apparent. Yet, there are some features which this variety has in common with Castilian (and Girona) Spanish rather than with other CC varieties. For example, the use of the nuclear configurations L* H% and L* L% in information-seeking wh-questions seems to be rather marginal in other Catalan varieties (see Prieto 2014; Prieto et al. 2015). The same applies to the use of the circumflex pitch pattern (L+H* L%) in requests, which is documented in Estebas-Vilaplana (2010: 41) for CS, but in Catalan only appears in the Northern dialect spoken in France. However, the most blatant and conspicuous trait that sets GC apart from other CC varieties — or, more accurately, from the available descriptions of CC intonation — is certainly the use of the low-rising L* H% nuclear configuration in information-seeking yes–no questions introduced by the particle *que*. In Section 5.1.3.1.5, we have seen that this pitch contour is mostly used by SpD speakers, which suggests that it could be transferred to GC from Spanish. Despite that, the fact that it was also found in some CatD speakers suggests that it has begun to spread across the whole speaker community, without having become (yet) a normative or fully adopted speech variant (see Section 6.4.3 for further discussion).

Whether the two contact-varieties spoken in Girona display overall more CS or more Catalan prosodic features is not an easy question to answer: first, both varieties and, more generally speaking, both languages are prosodically fairly close to one another. Second, the present study revealed that the two Girona varieties present a lot of variation at the intonational level. In sum, there seem to be somewhat more prosodic features that were carried over from (Girona) Catalan to (Girona) Spanish than vice versa. The next subchapter will address the CLI that has taken place between the two varieties in more detail.

---

246. Whether GS should be seen as an independent variety or a self-standing dialect of Peninsular Spanish will be discussed in Section 6.5, below, i.e. after the discussion of the role of language contact in its emergence.

6.4 How can the similarities and differences between the GS and GC intonational systems be explained in terms of language contact?

The preceding sections have made plain that the current varieties of GS and GC display many common features at the prosodic level. It was demonstrated that they are a certain degree 'mixed varieties', given that they combine prosodic features which most likely stem from only one language. On balance, GS seems to present more 'Catalan' prosodic features than GC 'Spanish' ones. In the next subsections, I endeavour to uncover the kinds of mechanisms which are responsible for this present state, drawing mainly on comparisons between the contact varieties and the respective standard or reference varieties of Catalan and Spanish offered in the previous section (6.3), on the mechanisms underlying contact-induced language change outlined in Section 3.2, as well as on the social-historical background of the Catalan-Spanish contact situation (see Section 2.1). I first address prenuclear pitch accents and nuclear configurations in the sentence types studied in the present work (Sections 6.4.1–6.4.7).[247] Then, in Section 6.4.8, I summarize the observations made in the previous sections and propose a schematic model, which represents the linguistic processes involved in the emergence of the current states of the intonational systems of the two Girona contact varieties.

6.4.1 Neutral statements

The results of the intonational analysis allowed us to determine L+<H* as the underlying prenuclear pitch accent in neutral broad-focus statements in both contact varieties spoken in Girona. H+L* and L+H* were analysed as surface realizations of the underlying L+<H* prenuclear accent that typically appear in certain tonally or metrically defined contexts (see Sections 5.1.1.1 and Section 5.2.1). Regarding tonal density, it was shown that roughly 30% of the phrase-internal prosodic words tend to be pitch-deaccented in the Girona varieties, i.e. they bear no pitch accent of their own. Finally, L* L% was established as the underlying nuclear configuration of neutral broad-focus statements and it was proposed that H+L* L% is a surface variant of this nuclear configuration. As far as the scientific literature permits to say, all this equally applies to the two reference varieties, CS and CC (see the comparison in Section 6.2). In consequence, there is no need to

---

247. Some sentence types whose intonation does not give reason to assume any CLI (e.g. when contact and reference varieties show the same intonation) or where possible CLI cannot be established due to the lack of descriptions of the reference varieties (e.g. in the case of enumerations) will not be discussed.

assume that (recent) contact-induced language change has taken place regarding the intonation of neutral statements in either of the two Girona contact varieties. Whether the major similarities between neutral-statement intonation in (Central) Catalan and (Castilian) Spanish could be due to historic language contact is a question that cannot be answered here (on the diachronic reconstruction of intonation patterns in Romance, see, e.g., Hualde 2003b).

6.4.2 Biased statements

Both contact varieties pattern together in marking focus and emphasis first and foremost by means of the rising L+H* pitch accent. The circumflex contour, L+H* L%, is thus the typical nuclear configuration in contrastive-focus and exclamative statements. The use of an upstep (¡) in this contour was assumed to express a higher degree of emphasis (see Section 5.2.3). The same nuclear tune furthermore occurs in other biased statement types, such as contradiction and dubitative statements. In contradiction statements, the nuclear configurations H+L* L%, H+L* HL, and L* HL% were attested in addition to the circumflex contour, albeit with different frequencies in the two contact varieties. I therefore assume that not all bilinguals have the same underlying intonational grammar with regard to this utterance type (see Section 5.2.3 and the discussion below).

The reference varieties CS and CC also use L+(¡)H* to convey focus and emphasis. As shown in Table 3.4 and in Section 6.2, above, L+(¡)H* L% is the nuclear configuration proposed for both contrastive-focus statements (also sometimes referred to as narrow-focus statements) and exclamative statements in these two varieties (see Estebas-Vilaplana/Prieto 2010; Prieto 2014; Prieto et al. 2015).[248] As regards contradiction statements, the nuclear configurations put forward in the literature are mainly L* HL% (for CS)[249] and H+L* L% and H+L* HL% (for CC) (see Hualde/Prieto 2015; Prieto 2002a, 2013; Prieto et al. 2015). A dubitative meaning, finally, is conveyed by the L+H* !H% nuclear configuration in both varieties. Regarding the prenuclear area, the extant literature by and large suggests

---

[248]. The available descriptions of exclamative (or emphatic) statements in Central Catalan do not offer any ToBI descriptions of the nuclear contour, but it can safely be understood that the circumflex contour is meant to be the underlying nuclear configuration in this utterance type (see Prieto 2002, 2013).

[249]. According to Hualde/Prieto (2015: 369), the Spanish dialects which do not have L* HL% use the circumflex contour L+H* L%. In dialects, where both contours are found, L* HL is assumed to carry "a greater emphatic, contradictory force". For the Andalusian variety spoken in Jérez, Henriksen/García-Amaya (2012) give ¡L+H* L%.

that L+<H* is the typical prenuclear pitch accent used in all types of biased statements and the same was found in the Girona contact varieties.

The comparison between the contact and the reference varieties reveals that: first, all varieties pattern together in using the circumflex contour (i.e. L+H* L%) to express focus and emphasis in contrastive-focus and exclamative statements. Second, the contact varieties make use of both 'Spanish' and 'Catalan' nuclear configurations to express contradiction statements. Third, the contact varieties seem to differ from CS and standard CC with regard to the boundary tone used in dubitative statements (i.e. the contact varieties exhibit L%, whereas the reference varieties show !H%). In what follows, I thus strive to show how the intonational patterns used in GS and GC contradiction and dubitative statements can be explained in terms of language contact.

Taking into account the distribution of nuclear configurations in **contradiction statements** across languages and language-dominance groups (see Table 5.2), it can be hypothesized that in a first stage, i.e. before the intensive contact between Catalan and Spanish, H+L* L% and H+L* HL% were the nuclear configurations used to express a strong contradictive meaning in GC statements (i.e. the same as in CC). It is likely that the L1 speakers of Catalan subsequently transferred these combinations of nuclear pitch accents and boundary tones to Spanish in the course of L2 acquisition (substratum transfer). Their presence in modern-day GS can thus be interpreted as an instance of fossilization of a pattern originally belonging to the learning continuum, i.e. to the learners' interlanguage, which took place during the bilingualization of L1 speakers of Catalan. However, the fact that these two configurations were only observed in the Spanish data produced by CatD bilinguals and not among SpD speakers leaves open the possibility that this fossilization could not yet have taken place and that instead we are dealing here with a case of ongoing substratum transfer from the bilinguals' stronger language (i.e. the L1 Catalan) to the weaker one (the L2 Spanish) that only takes place at the performance level, i.e. an 'ephemerous' interference in the sense of Müller et al. (2011: 18; see also Section 3.3.1). On the other hand, the fact that current GS contradiction statements most frequently exhibit circumflex nuclear contours (among both CatD and SpD speakers) and sporadically also the typically 'Spanish' L* HL% nuclear configuration suggests that, in a second stage, the Spanish (learner) variety spoken by those who had by then become CatD bilinguals has converged with its monolingual Spanish contact varieties, i.e. with (a) the Spanish varieties spoken by immigrants from other areas of the Spanish state and their descendants, and (b) with the standard variety used in the media (see Ruiz Martínez 2004; Cutillas-Espinosa/Hernández-Campoy 2007; Méndez García de Paredes/Amorós Negre 2016, among others). The result of these convergence processes is thus a variety that presents a mixed system containing both 'Spanish' and 'Catalan' nuclear configurations.

Nonetheless, in consideration of the distribution of the different nuclear tunes across individual subjects and LD groups, it can be presumed that different intonational grammars exist among the speakers of current GS. While some speakers (i.e. the SpD speakers) only have the 'Spanish' L+H* L% and L* HL% as underlying nuclear contours of contradiction statements, the intonational grammar of some other GS speakers also contains 'Catalan' nuclear contours (i.e. the falling H+L* L% and/or H+L* HL%). Besides, it is possible that the intonational grammar of still some other bilinguals (viz. some CatD speakers) exclusively contains these 'Catalan' nuclear configurations. The examined data set strongly suggests that these interspeaker differences are correlated with LD, as both H+L* L% and H+L* HL% were typically employed in Spanish by bilinguals who showed a rather strong dominance of Catalan (mean LD score: −42), whereas those who employed the 'Spanish' contours tended to be more balanced bilinguals (mean LD score: −27).

As regards GC contradiction statements, a certain degree of CLI was observed, too. Besides the typically 'Catalan' nuclear configurations, the more 'Spanish' L+H* L% was also attested quite frequently, and there was even one item produced with the typically 'Castilian Spanish' L* HL% nuclear tune. While the latter finding can be interpreted as an instance of substratum transfer from Spanish to Catalan by a SpD bilingual, it is more challenging to explain the use of L+H* L%, given that it was quite common among both SpD and CatD bilinguals. However, the CatD speakers who used it in Catalan tended to be somewhat more balanced regarding their LD (mean LD score: −30) than the bilinguals who used the more 'Catalan' contours (mean LD score: −43). Considering this, the following assumptions can be made: (1) as outlined above, H+L* L% and H+L* HL% were the nuclear configurations originally used in GC to express strong contradictory force before the intensive contact with Spanish and the subsequent bilingualization of Catalan natives. (2) In a later stage, i.e. after the recent changes in the composition of Catalonia's population due to massive immigration and the restauration of democracy in 1978, when the L1 speakers of Spanish residing in Catalonia (i.e. almost exceptionally new settlers and their offspring) started to learn Catalan as an L2 in greater numbers,[250] it is likely that they transferred the

---

250. According to the first systematic surveys, carried out in 1986, i.e. roughly a decade after the end of the Francoist dictatorship, only 64% of the inhabitants of Catalonia (older than two) were able to speak Catalan at that time (see Generalitat 2019: 11). For the province of Barcelona, the 1975 census shows that only 10% of those who did not have Catalan as their mother tongue

circumflex contour (as well as L* HL% if their Spanish variety had it) from their L1 Spanish to the TL (substratum transfer). In this way, the circumflex contour increased its presence on the linguistic market: besides serving the purpose of marking emphasis and focus in both Catalan and Spanish, it was now also present in contradiction statements in (a) the Spanish spoken by Spanish- and probably also by CatD bilinguals and (b) in the Catalan of SpD bilinguals. (3) Due to this change in the degree of entrenchment of the tune, it can be assumed that CatD speakers, especially those with a higher (active and passive) use of Spanish, progressively started adopting (or borrowing) the nuclear contour into their Catalan contradiction statements. This is to say, the (Girona) Catalan varieties of speakers of either LD converged. Furthermore, the generalization of the L+H* L% nuclear contour to a larger number of biased statement types (i.e. the same in both languages) can be motivated as a simplification of the bilinguals' intonational system(s) (see López Bobo/Cuevas Alonso 2010 and Henriksen/García-Amaya 2012 for similar findings in two other Peninsular varieties of Spanish).

In consequence, GC, too, can be seen to a certain extent as a mixed variety, considering that it presents some intonational features coming from the contact language Spanish. However, here again, the scrutiny of the bilinguals' production and their LD patterns suggests that different intonational grammars currently exist among the bilingual speakers of GC: while some speakers only have the 'more Catalan' H+L* L% and/or H+L* HL% as underlying nuclear configurations for contradiction statements (probably those with stronger dominance in Catalan), others might additionally or exclusively have the originally 'more Spanish' circumflex contour L+H* L% (the more balanced or SpD bilinguals).

Be that as it may, as a result of the diverse processes of transfer and convergence, both current contact varieties are characterized by the presence of various competing items, which are used to express the same meaning (here: contradictive force). In a further step, it can be expected that the competitors with a lower frequency (i.e. L* HL% and H+L* HL%) disappear from the converged intonational system(s) of the contact varieties over time for the benefit of the more entrenched variants (i.e. L+H* L% and H+L* L%) or that the different nuclear configurations receive a different pragmatic meaning.

Before closing this section, the nuclear configurations of **dubitative statements** are briefly worth being addressed. The comparisons made above have revealed that the contact varieties do not pattern with the respective reference varieties regarding the use of the final boundary tone in this utterance type (L% vs !H%). However, L+H* L% is also attested in other Peninsular varieties of Spanish

---

could speak it (see Arnal 2011: 14 and sources therein). Although far from complete today, the bilingualization of initial speakers of Spanish thus largely took place in the '80s and '90s.

(e.g. Cantabrian and Jerezano Spanish; see López Bobo/Cuevas Alonso 2010: 60; Henriksen/García-Amaya 2012: 125). Different scenarios are theoretically conceivable to account for this situation. The following two variants seem most probable: (1) L+H* L% was the original underlying nuclear contour of dubitative statements in GC (as opposed to L+H* !H% in Barcelona Catalan), from where it spread to GS. Furthermore, its use would have been reinforced through its presence in some of the monolingual varieties of Spanish spoken by migrants. (2) GC originally patterned with Barcelona Catalan and CS in using the L+H* !H nuclear configuration. In this case, it is likely that the complex language contact situation and the resulting CLI between L1 and learner varieties of both Catalan and Spanish lead to a simplification of the prosodic systems of the contact varieties. In that case, the use of the circumflex contour, L+H* L%, which was already recurrent in other biased statement types, would have been extended to cover dubitative statements. Of course, its presence in some of the Spanish migrant varieties would have encouraged this development. Nevertheless, given that the data sets examined in the present study did not contain any occurrences of the L+H* !H nuclear configuration in dubitative statements whatsoever, we can only surmise about the exact provenance of the L+H* L% configuration in this utterance type.

6.4.3 Polar questions

Information-seeking yes–no questions. Two underlying nuclear configurations of IPs were established for information-seeking yes–no questions (henceforth, **IYNQ**) in the two contact varieties: the 'low–rising' L* H% and the 'high–falling' H+L* L% contours. As regards the first (and clearly more frequent) one of these, it was shown that the underlying L* nuclear pitch accent can be phonetically realized as L* or H+L* (after a preceding high target) and that the height of the final boundary tone correlates with the distance between the nuclear syllable and the phrase edge, i.e. the boundary tone tends to be higher (¡H%) the farther away it is from the low nuclear pitch accent. Furthermore, the low–rising nuclear contour usually comes together with (1) an L*+H prenuclear pitch accent, located on the first metrically strong syllable of the ip containing the root clause of the question, and (2) with pitch deaccentuation of phrase-medial prosodic words (deaccentuation rate: ~80%). In GC, this contour was deployed on both IYNQ with and without the initial interrogative particle *que*; in GS, it occurred only in those without *que*. The high–falling nuclear configuration, on the other hand, was realized exclusively on questions that did begin with *que* and most commonly co-occurred with a high tonal plateau in the prenucleus (i.e. it surfaced in combination with prenuclear H* pitch accents). Interestingly, in GS, this combination was almost exclusively produced by CatD.

With regard to the reference varieties, the sole nuclear configuration used to express IYNQ in CS is L* H%[251] (see Estebas-Vilaplana/Prieto 2010; Hualde/Prieto 2015, and Section 3.1.2.1). In CC, both L* H% (in questions without *que*) and H+L* L% (typically in questions with *que*) can be employed (see Prieto 2014; Prieto et al. 2015, and Section 3.1.2.1). Regarding the prenuclear area, low–rising nuclear contours are said to co-occur with prenuclear L*+H and phrase-medial pitch deaccentuation, while high–falling nuclear contours are preceded by a high plateau. In some CC subdialects such as Barcelona Catalan, the use of *que*-questions (realized with the high–falling intonation pattern) has been related to the marking of pragmatic differences corresponding to politeness and proximity relations in discourse: i.e. the selection is sensitive to the pragmatic cost-benefit scale on which the cost or benefit of the proposed action to the hearer is estimated (see Prieto/Rigau 2007, 2011; Prieto 2014: 63; Prieto et al. 2015: 22–23; Astruc et al. 2016). For the Northern CC subdialect, which includes GC, however, these works generally claim that the presence of the interrogative particle *que* is restricted to counterexpectational or confirmatory meanings (Prieto et al. 2015: 22–23), i.e. that *que* (and thus the high–falling nuclear configuration) cannot occur in IYNQ. As opposed to that, Fernández Planas et al. (2007) report having found such questions also in pragmatically neutral contexts in a small corpus of read data recorded from one speaker of GC (see also the cross-dialectal overview of intonation patterns used in Catalan *que*-questions offered by Fernández Planas 2009: 43). Furthermore, it is interesting to note that the GC *que*-questions in their data set were predominantly produced with low–rising nuclear contours, which accounted for roughly 80–90% of the examined items.

Considering the findings presented in this section, it can be concluded that: (1) the low–rising nuclear configuration L* H% can be utilized to mark IYNQ in all varieties under concern here. (2) IYNQ introduced by the interrogative particle *que* and intonated with the high–falling nuclear configuration are used in GS, GC, and 'standard' CC (i.e. in Barcelona Catalan) but not in CS (or any other monolingual variety of Spanish). (3) As opposed to the claim made in great part of the literature that *que*-questions would be restricted to biased question types in Northern CC, the present study confirms the findings made by Fernández Planas et al. (2007), namely that *que*-questions can appear in pragmatically neutral, i.e.

---

251. Although Estebas-Vilaplana and Prieto (2010: 29) proposed a phonological scaling difference between information-seeking (¡H%, there labelled as 'HH%') and confirmation-seeking yes–no questions (H%) in Castilian Spanish, later works such as, among others, Armstrong/Cruz (2014), Hualde/Prieto (2015), or Prieto/Roseano (2018) treat both realizations as belonging to the same underlying category. As explained before, this also seems to be appropriate with regard to the two contact varieties considered here.

information-seeking contexts in GC. Still, contrarily to Barcelona Catalan (see Prieto 2013: 27), IYNQ without *que* and pronounced with the low–rise nuclear configuration were quite clearly the preferred option in the samples examined for GC (73%) and GS (90%) in the present study. (4) GC *que*-questions may sometimes be produced with the low–rising nuclear configuration (i.e. with a prenuclear L*+H pitch accent on the first stressable syllable of the IP and an L* H% nuclear configuration). As mentioned above, this combination was documented before for GC by Fernández Planas et al. (2007), who even found it to be dominant in *que*-questions (accounting for ca 90% of the items in their data). However, in the present study, the low rise accounted for merely 28% of the GC IYNQ featuring *que* (see Section 5.1.3.1.5). Furthermore, the combination was produced for the most part by SpD bilinguals (viz. to an extent of 77%).

Now, how can the distribution of the intonational patterns observed in the IYNQ in the two contact varieties be explained in terms of language contact? Let us first have a look at **GS**, where the situation appears to be somewhat less complex. On the basis of the findings described above, the rather sporadic presence of the high–falling H+L* L% nuclear contour (used in combination with the 'Catalan' interrogative particle *que*) in the prosodic system of current GS can be quite straightforwardly interpreted as a result of CLI from GC. It can be assumed that, for a start, L1 speakers of (Girona) Catalan transferred this particular question type to Spanish (via substratum transfer), when they acquired it as a foreign language (L2) during the large-scale bilingualization of Catalan speakers during the first decades of the 20th century (see Vila 2016; Bernat et al. 2019, 2020).

Following that, it is difficult to decide what happened next, since the current situation can be motivated in (at least) two ways: in one scenario, the interlanguage structure could have fossilized after some time as the learner variety step by step became a native variety, i.e. following generations directly acquired this question type through its presence in the GS input they received. In this way, its steadily increasing entrenchment could have made it a 'stable' feature of this variety. At the same time, it must not be forgotten that the Catalan–Spanish bilinguals were increasingly exposed to (and probably influenced by) other varieties of Spanish, i.e. by the monolingual Spanish of the immigrants as well as by the CS standard variety diffused in broadcasting (Ruiz Martínez 2004; Cutillas-Espinosa/Hernández-Campoy 2007; Méndez García de Paredes/Amorós Negre 2016). The increasing presence of such monolingual models, of course, should have hampered the diffusion of the phenomenon.[252] Furthermore, it can be

---

252. It is also very interesting to note that the SpD speakers (with the exception of one rather balanced one) did not produce any GS questions with the high–falling nuclear contour (and *que*), since Simonet (2008, 2011) and Romera/Elordieta (2013) observed that SpD bilinguals and

expected that the construction was also (and probably continues to be) sanctioned in school education, where the (Castilian-based) standard language as set by instances such as the Royal Spanish Academy is propagated (see Sinner 2004: 602–605, 610–613). In any case, its users do seem to have some metalinguistic awareness about it: e.g., referring to Barcelona Spanish, Sinner (2004: 287) notes that it is "al parecer [un fenómeno] bastante conocido y muy fácil de detectar para los hablantes" ('apparently a well-known phenomenon and very easy for speakers to detect'), and Wesch (1997: 301) emphasizes that the construction has a clear diaphasic mark, i.e. that speakers are cognizant of its status as 'phenomenon of the communicative immediacy' and as 'colloquial'. However, in Hawkey (2014), only a minority of speakers recognized it as a non-normative element. As a consequence, even if *que*-questions had become a fully adopted and hence 'authentic' feature of GS by now, they are certainly not a completely 'neutral' one, given that their diaphasic status is influenced by extra-linguistic factors.

A slightly different view of the current status of the structure should be considered as well: namely, the presence of *que*-questions in current GS could still today be an outcome of ongoing CLI occurring in CatD bilinguals. In that case, it would not be a 'stable' feature of the variety, but instead its appearance would result from continuing substratum transfer occurring during the acquisition and in the use of the non-dominant language Spanish by bilinguals with the initial language Catalan. This point of view would also explain why the construction was much rarer in GS as compared to GC and why it was hardly observed among SpD bilinguals. A further reason why SpD bilinguals do not make use of *que*-questions could be that they typically acquired the L1 Spanish from their immigrant parents and use it mainly in familial settings (see Section 4.2). Outside their home, Catalan is the majority language that they tend to use themselves in most public contexts. It might thus not happen very often that they actually hear CatD speakers using Spanish (and thus producing *que*-questions).

Everything included, the distribution in the present data set as well as the extant literature on the phenomenon suggest that both hypotheses could be accurate to some degree. For one thing, the literature on *que*-questions in CCS describes them as a frequent and very characteristic phenomenon of that variety, such that a certain level of fossilization and following entrenchment can be

---

Spanish-speaking monolinguals in Majorca often did adopt falling nuclear contours into their Spanish IYNQ, i.e. they either borrowed directly from Majorcan Catalan (bilinguals) or accommodated to the Majorcan Spanish spoken by bilinguals (monolinguals). However, an important difference between Majorcan and Central Catalan is that Majorcan Catalan unchangingly uses falling nuclear contours in IYNQ irrespective of the presence of *que*, whose presence is rare in that dialect (see Prieto et al. 2015: 22–25).

expected. The fact that the combination was also used once by a slightly SpD bilingual additionally speaks in favour of such an interpretation as it insinuates that the varieties of GS spoken by CatD and SpD bilinguals are converging. In that case, the structure would be part of the intonational grammars of some bilingual speakers of GS (mostly CatD ones) but not of the intonational grammars of some others. On the other hand, the structure was quite rare in the GS data altogether (being used in only 4.5% of the 154 items analysed), and it was almost exclusively produced by (rather strongly) CatD bilinguals. This makes it appear more likely that we are witnessing instances of in-progress interference (see Müller et al. 2011:18). However, diaphasic factors could be responsible of the low incidence, too. In sum, the investigated sample does not allow for any more secured conclusions to be drawn. An unequivocal definition of the status of IYNQ headed by *que* and realized with a high plateau in the prenuclear area and an H+L* L% nuclear configuration in current GS thus remains a project for future research.

As regards **GC**, how we can explain the current distribution of the two different intonational tunes, L* H% and H+L* L%, in the IYNQ produced in this variety crucially depends on what we assume to be the initial state of its intonational system before the intensive contact with Spanish. Three explanatory scenarios are theoretically conceivable:

1. Initial state: Both L* H% and H+L* L% are underlying nuclear configurations in GC IYNQ, used respectively in questions without and with the interrogative particle *que*. Possibly, the choice between either type depended on pragmatic criteria (see Barcelona Catalan).
   Emergence of current state: In the course of their bilingualization, initial speakers of Spanish acquired the GC *que*-questions only partially, i.e. some learners picked up the (fairly salient and hence easy-to-learn) interrogative particle *que* but failed to grasp its link with the high–falling intonation pattern and hence to reproduce this question type in a target-like manner (imperfect learning). Instead, in the interlanguage of these learners, *que* is combined with the low–rising nuclear configuration and an L*+H prenuclear pitch accent (e.g. via substratum transfer from Spanish), i.e. they preserve their Spanish pronunciation habits in that they deploy a 'melodic construction' from their dominant language onto TL word-forms. Such a course of events is not unlikely from a cross-linguistic point of view: as Dixon (1997:24) points out, speakers tend to think of their languages solely in terms of their lexicon but are usually less aware of functional or grammatical categories. In the case of language-contact situations as the Spanish-Catalan one, this identification means that the principal perceived difference between the two languages is in the form of the words (see Arnal 2011:21), i.e., here, in the absence vs pres-

ence of *que* in yes–no questions. Suprasegmental aspects such as intonation or stress, on the other hand, seem to go unnoticed by many. The fact that SpD bilinguals sometimes stressed this otherwise unstressed particle in their Catalan IYNQ additionally endorses this assumption. Along the same lines, Van Coetsem's (2000: 61, 73f.) model equally suggests that in the learning process of the recipient language (RL), source-language (SL) speakers acquire RL material (i.e. primarily vocabulary, here *que*) but at the same time impose part of the more stable components of their own language upon the RL (e.g. part of the SL phonology, i.e. here intonation).

Building on ideas from Matras's (2011: 150) model of convergence and Torreira and Grice's (2018) 'melodic construction' (see also the considerations made in Section 3.2.2, Fn. 129), this can be interpreted in the following way: unable to deactivate the second language as a wholesale system, the bilingual speakers scan throughout their full (multilingual) repertoire of linguistic structures and identify the *que*-structure as a task-effective morphosyntactic construction. In a next step, the construction is vetted context-appropriate because it belongs to the Catalan subsystem. It can thus be matched with a candidate expression that is licensed in the present interaction context. However, before it comes to phonetically realizing the sentence, a 'melodic construction' needs to be selected.[253] As the only available 'melodic construction' for the task 'IYNQ' in the speaker's multilingual repertoire is the low–rising one, which is 'anchored' in both Spanish and Catalan, it fulfils in the bilingual's view the criterion of being context-appropriate and can be matched with the morphosyntactic construction. Hence, the constraints on the language-specific selection of context-appropriate word-forms appear to be more powerful and adhered to more consistently than the constraints that regulate the selection of constructions. The less secure or less experienced bilingual (but arguably also the fluent bilingual who is more prone to follow a path of conve-nience than adhere to monolingual norms) will continue to respect the constraints on word-form selection but generalize the abstract outline of the construction (Matras 2011: 151).

Next, this amalgam created by the initial speakers of Spanish was also adopted by some initial speakers of Catalan via borrowing or convergence between their variety of GC with the interlanguage spoken by SpD. This later development can be motivated by the fact that the innovative blend must have received some entrenchment in GC: in the present study, it accounted for 55% of the SpD bilinguals' *que*-questions, which they produced with a similar frequency as the CatD group (see 5.1.3.1.5). Recall also that the SpD bilinguals in Girona often speak Catalan in extra-familial settings, e.g. when talking to CatD friends (see Section 4.2; see also Woolard 1992: 240; Pujolar/Gonzàlez

2013) and that the group of Catalan-speakers with the first language Spanish also includes, e.g., teachers, politicians, radio and television announcers, actors, and people interviewed in the media (Arnal 2011: 16). In consequence, besides being perfectly acquainted with the L* H% tune from other contexts in both of their languages, CatD bilinguals also have it in the *que*-questions they are exposed to in the Catalan input they receive. Indeed, as highlighted, e.g., by Arnal (2011), it is normal and common to hear Spanish-accented Catalan now and, as a result, especially younger, urban bilinguals are no longer able "to distinguish between native and non-native speaking styles", i.e. in the light of generalized bilingualism and the genetic proximity of the two languages, new mixed forms are not necessarily perceived as deviant or ill-formed (see Argenter et al. 1998; Arnal 2011; Pujolar/Gonzàlez 2013). Furthermore, language mixing can hardly difficult comprehension and is unlikely to cause misunderstandings in the Catalan context. Besides, the generalization of the 'low rise' contour to *que*-questions among initial speakers of Catalan also represents a simplification of their prosodic systems, which eases their 'bilingual burden' of having to keep different language-specific systems separate (Weinreich 1953: 8; Matras 2009: 151, 235; Kühl/Braunmüller 2014: 18–20).

In a nutshell, these considerations allow for the following suggestions: in the intonational grammar of some GC speakers (mostly CatD bilinguals), H+L* L% is the only underlying nuclear configuration in *que*-questions, while in the intonational grammar of some others, both H+L* L% and L* H% are available. Finally, in the intonational grammar of still some others (SpD bilinguals), L* H% is the only underlying nuclear configuration for information-seeking yes–no questions independently of the presence of *que*.

2. <u>Initial state:</u> Both L* H% and H+L* L% are underlying nuclear configurations in GC IYNQ. In questions with *que*, both nuclear configurations can be used; without *que*, only L* H% is admissible (i.e. the initial state roughly corresponds to the current state; see also Fernández Planas et al. 2007).
<u>Emergence of current state:</u> (Some) initial speakers of Spanish did either not acquire H+L* L% in GC *que*-questions at all (imperfect learning) or they simply prefer the L* H% nuclear configuration in that context because they are more often confronted with it in daily life and know it better from both of their languages (due to its higher degree of entrenchment). Further-

---

253. I view 'melodic constructions' as viable tonal entities in their own right within a speaker's unified repertoire of lexical-grammatical structures. They offer derived meanings that are inferred from a particular combination of tones and are prone to be generalized by bilinguals over their multilingual repertoire owing to the tendency to treat the pragmatic organization of discourse as universal or global rather than language-specific (see Section 3.2.2).

more, the exclusive use of L* H% can be seen as a simplification of the bilinguals' prosodic system(s) (see, e.g., Winford 2003: 217–219 on simplification in SLA). CatD bilinguals, on the other hand, display a very strong tendency to functionally separate the two nuclear contours, i.e. they use them complementarily (H+L* L% in *que*-questions and L* H% in questions without the particle). On the one hand, this makes the initial state of scenario (2) appear less probable, but, on the other, the functional separation of competing variants is a cross-linguistically common procedure. Besides, it is also possible that the use of the high–falling contour may have increased due to pressure from and, hence, convergence with Barcelona Catalan, which is (a) the variety on which the Catalan standard or reference variety is built (see, e.g., Veny 2001; Brumme 2020; Bladas Martí 2020: 540; Camps/Labèrnia 2020: 687)[254] and (b) the predominant variety in media (see Casals/Faura 2010; Ulldemolins-Subirats 2019; Ferrando/Nicolás 2011: 519, 526f.; Camps/Labèrnia 2020) and in school (Ulldemolins-Subirats 2018).[255]

Ultimately, some extralinguistic factors could play a role, as well: considering that *que* and H+L* L% are not licit in CS INYQ, not only the particle but also the tune can be viewed as 'Catalan' features. As I have discussed before, it is likely that many bilinguals are aware of this (see also Section 2.3). In consequence, some bilinguals could consciously choose to use this tune to sound 'more Catalan' – either with the objective of marking their identity as Catalans or to show that they are able to speak 'good' Catalan (which was important to them according to the language-background questionnaire, see Section 4.2).

3. <u>Initial state:</u> GC does not allow for the presence of the interrogative particle *que* in IYNQ, i.e. L* H% is the only underlying nuclear configuration in this question type (see Prieto/Rigau 2007, 2011; Prieto 2014: 63; Prieto et al. 2015: 22–23).

<u>Emergence of current state:</u> The introduction of *que* and of the high–falling nuclear contour H+L* L% in GC in IYNQ can be motivated either as an internal development or through contact with other varieties. If the language change were endogenous to the GC system, that would imply an extension

---

254. On the general tendency of non-standard or regional varieties to converge with the standard variety see, e.g., Labov/Harris (1986); Villena Ponsoda (2005, 2008); Morgenthaler García (2008: 291–322); Cutillas-Espinosa/Hernández-Campoy (2007); Hernández-Campoy (2011); Méndez García de Paredes/Amorós Negre (2016, 2019), among others.

255. It is likely that the influence of the media is less strong in SpD bilinguals, who probably consume more Spanish-language media. They would thus be less exposed to the H+L* L% nuclear tune and, in consequence, use it less than CatD bilinguals.

of the use of the particle in combination with the corresponding tune from confirmation-seeking to information-seeking yes–no questions, i.e. the intonational grammar would have been simplified by eliminating the distinctive tonal marking of these two pragmatic utterance types.[256] A possible cause contributing to such a development could be a relatively higher frequency of confirmation-seeking questions in conversational speech (see, e.g., Torreira/Floyd 2012; Hualde/Prieto 2015: 374, who report this for CS). As regards external sources, the change that must have taken place in the intonational grammar of GC can be related to contact with Barcelona Spanish, i.e. it can be hypothesized that GC converged with the 'standard' variety of Catalan due to normative pressure and the predominant status of this variety in mass media (see Casals/Faura 2010; Ferrando/Nicolás 2011: 519, 526f.; Ulldemolins-Subirats 2019; Camps/Labèrnia 2020; see also Fn. 254).[257] Of course, multiple causation, i.e. the combination of both factors, would be possible, as well.
Either way, the outcome of such developments would be what I have described as the initial stage of scenario 1, above. The further course of evolution would thus be the same as in that scenario, i.e., stated briefly, that the presence of L* H% in present-day GC *que*-questions would be largely attributable to imperfect learning and substratum transfer by initial speakers of Spanish and subsequent convergence between the GC varieties spoken by bilinguals with different dominant languages.

As we have seen in the different scenarios proposed, it is not an easy task to explain how the current distribution of intonational patterns in IYNQ in the two contact varieties has come about. The main reason for this is that we do not know which was the initial state of GC before the onset of the intensive contact with Spanish. Nevertheless, it is plainly evident that some CLI must have taken place since the beginning of the contact and in the course of mass bilingualization, or else we could not explain why bilinguals with different dominant languages behave in distinct ways. Despite the discrepancies, all proposed scenarios involve the same mechanisms of (contact-induced) language change: namely,

---

256. Several Catalan and Spanish varieties employ the same intonational contour to express IYNQ and confirmation-seeking yes–no questions, among them, Argentinian (Gabriel et al. 2010), Canarian (Cabrera Abreu/Vizcaino Ortega 2010), Ecuadorian (O'Rourke 2010), Jerezano Spanish (Henriksen/García-Amaya 2012) and Valencian Catalan (Crespo-Sendra 2013). Furthermore, the dialectal maps in Prieto/Cabré (2013) and Prieto et al. (2015) suggest that L* H% is predominant in both question types in Girona and surroundings.

257. After some 40 years of interruption of the standardization process of Catalan during Franquism, it was incumbent upon the newly emerging Catalan-language media to take part in the creation and diffusion of new language norms (see Casals/Faura 2010: 32, 65).

imperfect learning or substratum transfer (either in SLA or from a dominant to a non-dominant language in bilinguals) as well as convergence (either between the 'bilingual' varieties of speaker groups with different LD or with the standard varieties of the respective languages). As a result, it is highly probable that diverse intonational grammars exist among the bilinguals in the present sample with regard to the prosodic realization of IYNQ in the two contact varieties.

To shed more light on the question, future studies should set out to further explore the realization of IYNQ in prior stages of GC, e.g. by analysing historical speech data (if available) or else data from older speaker groups and speakers who are less influenced by Spanish (i.e. close-to-monolingual speakers). In addition, perception experiments ought to be carried out to tap deeper into the bilinguals' underlying intonational grammars.

Disjunctive questions. The underlying nuclear configurations of IPs established for the two contact varieties based on the analysis of the neutral **disjunctive questions** were H+L* L% and L* L%. Whereas both nuclear configurations occurred with the same frequency in GC, L* L% prevailed in GS.

In CS, L* L% is the IP nuclear configuration proposed for disjunctive questions (Estebas-Vilaplana/Prieto 2010; see also Table 3.4). To my knowledge, this sentence type has not been described within the AM model for CC. However, there is a textual description by Prieto (2002a: 427), in which she mentions a "cadència descendent final" that can be interpreted as H+L* L%. Consequently, it can be assumed that the contact varieties share nuclear contours with both CS (i.e. L* L%) and other CC varieties (i.e. H+L* L%).

On this basis, it can be hypothesized that the H+L* L% contour, when attested in GS, is an outcome of substratum transfer that occurred when the Catalan L1 speakers learned Spanish as an L2. It can be suggested that in a first step, the Spanish spoken by this group showed H+L* L% as a typical nuclear configuration of disjunctive questions. However, the fact that the CatD group most often produced L* L% in GS allows the assumption that the Spanish spoken by initial speakers of Catalan has by now converged with the Spanish spoken by the new settlers who came to Catalonia from the middle of the 20th century onwards. The outcome of this convergence is a mixed system containing the 'Catalan' nuclear configuration H+L* L% in addition to the Spanish L* L%. In turn, regarding GC, it can be presumed that the presence of the L* L% nuclear configuration is the result of (1) substratum transfer that occurred when initial speakers of Spanish learned Catalan as an L2 and (2) convergence between the GC spoken by SpD and CatD bilinguals.

These scenarios lead to the following suggestions: in the intonational grammars of some bilinguals, H+L* L% is the underlying nuclear contour of disjunctive questions and L* L% its surface realization, while in the intonational grammars of other bilinguals, this distribution is inversed, and in the intonational grammars of still some other bilinguals only one nuclear contour is available to convey disjunctive questions (e.g. some SpD bilinguals may only have L* L%).

Exclamative yes–no questions. The underlying nuclear configurations established for **exclamative yes–no questions** (with counterexpectational meaning) in the two contact varieties were the same as those specified for pragmatically neutral, i.e. information-seeking yes–no questions (viz. L* H% and H+L* L%; the latter only in questions headed by the interrogative particle *que*). The notion of exclamativity was expressed through the use of a higher pitch range and more accented pitch movements, which sometimes yielded surface realizations of L* H% such as H+L* ¡H% or L+H* ¡H%. As regards the reference varieties CC and CS, to my knowledge, no accounts of the intonation of this utterance type are available within the AM framework besides one 'L* HH%' label Crespo-Sendra et al. (2010) give in an example of a CC 'incredulity question'.[258] However, the descriptions provided for CC by Prieto (2002a: 431–432, 2013: 31–33) coincide with observations made here. Furthermore, although we do not really know how this question type is tonally realized in CS, what we do know is that phrase-initial *que* is a "citative discourse marker of indirect speech" in Mainstream Spanish questions (Escandell Vidal 1999: 3965) and, hence, that its use should be restricted to echo questions.

Considering this, it can be concluded that the use of *que* and presumably also of the corresponding nuclear contour H+L* L% observed in GS must be an interference from GC. Since only one item of this type was found and given that it was produced by a CatD bilingual, I suggest that substratum transfer is the responsible mechanism for this. Moreover, in consideration of the fact that in GC, too, the combination of particle and high-falling nuclear contour was exclusively produced by CatD bilinguals, I hold the view that SpD bilinguals have either failed to acquire H+L* L% in Catalan or, at minimum, do not put it to use with the due frequency (imperfect learning). In sum, it can be concluded that in the intonational grammars of some bilinguals, L* H% is the only underlying nuclear contour used to express exclamative yes–no questions (SpD bilinguals), whereas the intonational grammars of other bilinguals also contain H+L* L% for Catalan exclamative questions realized with *que* (CatD bilinguals). With regard to future developments, it can be expected that either of these two grammars will impose

---

258. Exclamative yes–no questions (with counterexpectational meaning) should not be confounded with exclamative *echo* yes–no questions (with counterexpectational meaning), of which AM descriptions exist for many varieties.

itself upon the other, i.e. that the varieties spoken by the different groups of bilinguals will converge.

Confirmation-seeking yes–no questions. The underlying nuclear configurations proposed for **confirmation-seeking yes–no** questions (henceforth CYNQ) were equally L* H% and H+L* L% (i.e. the same as in IYNQ). Yet, the latter one of these was clearly less common than the former and typically appeared when the question was formulated as an alternative polar question built with a disjunction of the predicate (i.e. containing, e.g., Sp./Cat. *o no?*; see Prieto/Rigau 2007: 14–15). The underlying prenuclear pitch accent was L*+H in both languages.

As regards CS, the same two nuclear configurations were proposed for this sentence type by Estebas-Vilaplana/Prieto (2010),[259] whereas Hualde/Prieto (2015), in accordance with Escandell-Vidal (1999) and Pérez et al. (2011), rather suggest the circumflex L+¡H* L% contour (see also Table 3.4). Furthermore, it is worth pointing out that other Peninsular Spanish varieties, such as Jerezano Spanish do not tonally distinguish CYNQ from IYNQ and exclusively use L* H% for both (Henriksen/García-Amaya 2012; see also Fn. 256). With respect to Catalan CYNQ, most dialects "typically" exhibit the high–falling H+L* L% contour and introduce them with the interrogative particle *que* (Prieto 2014: 68; Prieto et al. 2015: 28). Partly opposed to that, Vanrell et al. (2010: 87) found that, although falling nuclear contours are more prone to appear in confirmation- than in information-seeking questions in CC, rising ones were still clearly most common in this context (75%). Furthermore, it is worth pointing out that Prieto (2002a: 423, 2013: 27) and Prieto/Rigau (2011: 35) claim that, in GC, the use of the interrogative particle *que* (in combination with the falling H+L* L% nuclear contour) is restricted to CYNQ (i.e. that it cannot appear in GC IYNQ). In stark contrast to this, Prieto (2013: 28–27) and Prieto et al. (2015: 55) report that they exclusively (or at least overwhelmingly) observed the low–rising nuclear configuration L* H% in CYNQ produced by speakers from Girona and its direct surroundings, which is also in opposition to all other CC subdialects.

The comparison between the different varieties thus shows that: (1) all varieties pattern together in exhibiting L* H% as one possible nuclear configuration for CYNQ (albeit with different frequencies of occurrence). (2) With regard to falling patterns, the two Girona varieties pattern with CS (as described by Estebas-Vilaplana/Prieto 2010) in using L*+H prenuclear pitch accents. (3) No CYNQ with *que* were attested in the contact varieties (≠ CC and literature on GC). (4) No circumflex nuclear configurations were attested (≠ CS according to Hualde/

---

259. Estebas-Vilaplana/Prieto (2010) originally claimed that the hight of the final boundary tone in the low–rising nuclear configuration is phonological (viz. ¡H% in IYNQ and H% in CYNQ), while posterior accounts of CS intonation seem to have given up this distinction (e.g. Hualde/Prieto 2015; Prieto/Roseano 2018). No such distribution could be observed in the two contact varieties under concern here.

Prieto 2015). (5) The contact varieties do not make a prosodic distinction between IYNQ and CYNQ (≠ CC and CS but in accordance with various other Spanish and Catalan varieties, see Fn. 256, above).

Based on these observations, it can be inferred that the clear predominance of L* H% characterizes not only the current but also the initial stage of the GC intonational system and that it has had a significant influence in the genesis of the GS system: i.e., more specifically, it can be assumed that CYNQ were predominantly realized with the L* H% nuclear contour in the Spanish spoken by initial speakers of GC when they started to acquire that language, although, as in GC, falling H+L* L% nuclear contours were not completely excluded (substratum transfer). As regards initial speakers of Spanish, it can be suggested that their migrant or heritage varieties, respectively, converged with the GS spoken by CatD bilinguals and, if they did not already use L* H% in the first place, they now borrowed it. Either way, they, too, first and foremost employed the rising contour (no productions of the 'Castilian' nuclear configurations H+L* L% and L+¡H* L% were attested in their data).

Nevertheless, the status of the falling H+L* L% nuclear configuration in the Girona varieties is not fully clear, for a series of reasons: (1) although Prieto (2002a: 423, 2013: 27) and Prieto/Rigau (2011: 35) suggest that the use of the interrogative particle *que* in combination with the falling H+L* L% nuclear contour is only possible in GC in CYNQ and not in neutral yes–no questions, our corpus did not contain any instances of CYNQ headed by *que* whatsoever (instead quite a lot of IYNQ with *que* were found, see previous section). (2) Confirming the observations made for GC CYNQ in Prieto (2013: 28–27) and Prieto et al. (2015: 55), H+L* L% was marginal in the present data set (only 2 cases in non-disjunctive CYNQ). (3) Furthermore, the respective items were produced by two CatD bilinguals in combination with L*+H prenuclear accents, which rather matches the tunes attested for CS in Estebas-Vilaplana/Prieto (2010: 29, 34) than the ones described in the literature on CC intonation. (4) The same combination was also produced twice in GS (albeit by CatD bilinguals). All that being said, it is evident that for the time being the conflicting reports in the extant literature and the few items in the present data set do not allow to determine in how far the (limited) use of the H+L* L% nuclear contour in CYNQ in the two Girona contact varieties is a result of CLI. Furthermore, future research will also be needed to elucidate the status of the interrogative marker *que* in the different types of GC yes–no questions.

6.4.4 Wh-questions

Three underlying nuclear configurations were proposed for information-seeking wh-questions in the contact varieties: H* L% (dominant in both varieties), L* L%, and L* H%. Among these, H* L% is shared with CC, where it seems to be the most recurrent nuclear configuration for this utterance type. L* L% and L* H%, in turn, are both very common in CS and have a somewhat unclear status in CC[260] (see Estebas-Vilaplana/Prieto 2010; Hualde/Prieto 2015; Prieto 2002a, 2014, 2014, Prieto et al. 2015). However, the different contours are usually presumed to convey slightly different pragmatic nuances: while L* L% (CS) and H* L% (CC) are considered the more neutral ones, the low–rising tune (L* H%) typically expresses "a nuance of interest and greater speaker involvement in the speech act" (Estebas-Vilaplana/Prieto 2010: 34) and a "higher degree of curiosity and interest" (Prieto 2002a: 439, translation is mine).

Based on these observations, it can be inferred that prior to the intensive contact with Spanish GC displayed the 'CC tonal marking', i.e. either H* L% or L* H%. Furthermore, it can be hypothesized that L* L% was adopted into GC via convergence with Spanish or with the Catalan spoken by initial speakers of Spanish. More specifically, it can be suggested that L* L% was transferred into GC by this latter speaker group via substratum transfer during the acquisition and that CatD bilinguals later adopted it to some extent through convergence. It is thus likely that, at present, the intonational grammar of some bilingual speakers of GC merely contains H* L%, whereas that of some others solely contains L* L%, and that, thirdly, the two could be surface variants of one another in the intonational grammar of still some other bilinguals.

As for GS, it is probable that the predominant use of H* L% is primarily the outcome of imperfect learning of Spanish by the Catalan monolinguals (i.e. substratum transfer). In other words, this contour was transferred from Catalan to Spanish in the course of the acquisition of Spanish as an L2. If so, it can be expected that it gradually became a steady feature of the Spanish spoken by Catalan–Spanish bilinguals due to fossilization. In a further step, the Spanish of monolingual immigrants — or at least the Spanish spoken by their bilingual descendants — seems to have converged with the Spanish spoken by initial speakers of Catalan.[261] The result of this convergence is an intonational system, in which

---

260. While all sources on CC intonation present H* L% as the main nuclear contour for neutral wh-questions, 'L* H%'-like contours are mentioned merely by Prieto (2002a: 439) and in some older works cited therein. More recently, Prieto (2014) brought up L* L% (or ¡H+L* L% — the account is not fully clear), instead. In Prieto et al. (2015), L* L% was registered only sporadically in some Western Catalan varieties. In Roseano et al. (2016b), it occurred to an extent of merely 3% in CC neutral wh-questions. I therefore assume here that only H* L% and L* H% are the nuclear configurations typically used to convey wh-questions in CC.

261. These observations are consistent with Romera/Elordieta (2013) and Simonet (2008, 2011), who equally observed convergence and accommodation of monolingual Spanish-speakers and SpD bilinguals to the L2-Spanish spoken by CatD bilinguals regarding question

the 'Catalan' nuclear configuration H* L% has become dominant (even among SpD bilinguals), although the 'Spanish' L* L% contour continues to exist. Yet, it is possible that not all bilinguals have identical intonational grammars and that some bilinguals only have one of these two nuclear configurations at their disposal, whereas others may have both (possibly as surface variants of one another).

Exclamative wh-questions. The underlying nuclear contours used to convey **exclamative wh**-questions in the contact varieties are largely the same as the ones used in neutral wh-questions. The notion of exclamativity is mainly expressed through an increased pitch range. More precisely, H* L% usually surfaces as ¡H* L%, and L* H% is typically realized as L+H* ¡H%. Additionally, circumflex contours can be used (i.e. L+(¡)H* L%, attested more often in GS). As concerns CC, the main difference between the contours used in information-seeking and exclamative wh-questions is the "intensified tonicity" in the latter (Prieto 2002a: 446, 2013: 34–36), i.e. the increased hight of the peak of the nuclear pitch accent in high–falling contours (~ ¡H* L%, L+H* L%) and the "amplified tonal inflections" in rising patterns (i.e. L(+H)* (¡)H%; the translations are mine). To my knowledge, there are no further studies which have systematically examined the intonational properties of this utterance type in CC or CS. For this reason, no sound conclusions can be made about the role of language contact in the development of the current intonation of this utterance type in the contact varieties. Nevertheless, the attested distribution (see Section 5.1.6.1) suggests that the circumflex contour could be a 'more Spanish' feature, while the H* L% — as in neutral wh-questions — would originally be rather a 'Catalan feature'. If so, initial speakers of Catalan would have transferred H* L% from GC to GS via substratum transfer and, in a further step, the Spanish varieties spoken by CatD and SpD would have converged.

Imperative wh-questions. Regarding **imperative wh**-questions, the underlying nuclear contours proposed for the two contact varieties are H+L* L%, L* H%. In GS, L+H* L% adds to these. Given that the sparse available accounts of this utterance type in both CS and CC mainly give H+L* L% (see Estebas-Vilaplana/Prieto 2010; Prieto 2002a, 2013) and that the low–rise (L* H%) can appear in virtually all question types in the contact and the reference varieties, no sound inferences

---

intonation in Majorca. In opposition to CS, some other varieties of Peninsular Spanish equally use falling nuclear configurations in information-seeking wh-questions: e.g. H+L* L% (Cantabrian, Manchego, and Jerezano) or ¡L+H* L% (Manchego) (see López Bobo/Cuevas Alonso 2010; Henriksen 2010, 2014; Henriksen/García-Amaya 2012). However, these are not identical to the 'Catalan' H* L% contour, since the alignment of the pitch peak is different. Still, this implies the possibility that some of the speakers of migrant or heritage varieties of monolingual Spanish only needed adapt the alignment of the pitch peak and not learn a wholly new tune in order for their varieties to converge with the Spanish spoken by CatD.

about contact-induced changes can be made in this case. At best, it can be surmised that the circumflex contour found in some (relatively few) cases in our Spanish data set is not exclusive to GS, but that it could be shared with other Spanish varieties as Estebas-Vilaplana and Prieto (2010: 38) bring up a circumflex nuclear configuration (L+¡H* HL%), which can be used in CS with "a nuance of invitation", whereas the sources on Catalan never mention circumflex nuclear tunes.

6.4.5 Echo questions

Due to the strong variation attested with regard to echo questions in all varieties concerned here, uncovering CLI in this utterance type is intricate. Regarding simple **echo yes–no** questions, the Girona contact varieties probably share the nuclear configurations L* H% and L+H* L%[262] with both reference varieties. However, L* H% seems to be more characteristic and predominant in CC (see Prieto 2013; Prieto et al. 2015; Prieto/Borràs-Comes 2018),[263] whereas sources on CS primarily indicate the circumflex L+¡H* L% nuclear configuration (e.g. Estebas-Vilaplana/Prieto 2010; Escandell-Vidal 1999, 2017). L* H% is merely mentioned as an alternative for CS by Hualde/Prieto (2015: 380). If it were true that L* H% is originally 'more Catalan' and L+H* L% 'more Spanish', that would imply that GS has been strongly influenced by GC, since both contact varieties overwhelmingly showed L* H% in the analysed data sets. More specifically, initial speakers of GC would overuse the low–rise contour when speaking Spanish due to substratum transfer and initial speakers of Spanish would have adopted this use via convergence with Catalan and/or the Spanish spoken by CatD.

Second, in the case of **exclamative echo yes–no questions** (with counterexpectational meaning), the Girona contact varieties display the same nuclear configurations as in neutral echo yes–no questions (albeit often with a wider pitch

---

262. The sources on CS and CC usually transcribe this nuclear contour with an upstep, i.e. as L+¡H* L% (see Estebas-Vilaplana/Prieto 2010; Escandell-Vidal 2017; Borràs-Comes et al. 2010; Prieto et al. 2015; Prieto/Borràs-Comes 2018). However, the few GS and GC examples do not allow to postulate such an upstep.

263. In fact, the existing accounts are somewhat inconsistent and in part contradictory: Prieto (2002a: 450–451) mainly describes a 'H* L%'-like nuclear contour but mentions L* H% as an alternative. Prieto (2013) only gives L* H%. Prieto (2014: 68–70) highlights L+¡H* L% as typical nuclear contour of CC echo questions but mentions L* (¡)H% as a variant which conveys incredulity. Prieto et al. (2015) again describe L* H% as the most common contour in CC echo yes–no questions. In Prieto and Borràs-Comes's (2018) perception study, finally, L+H* LH%, L+¡H* L%, and L* H% resulted as valid contours for "understanding echo questions" (i.e. questions in which there is high agreement of the speaker with the addressee").

range): L* (¡)H% and L+H* L%. Additionally, they showed H+L* L% in some few cases. Quite similarly, the available accounts on this utterance type in CC equally suggest L* (¡)H% — with a wider pitch range than in neutral echo questions — and L+¡H* L% (as a little frequent alternative attested in the vicinity of Girona).[264] As concerns CS, the only descriptions known to me propose L+H* LH% and L+H* ¡H% as a less frequent variant (Estebas-Vilaplana/Prieto 2010: 28; Hualde/Prieto: 2015). H+L* L% has thus not been proposed for any of the standard varieties. The comparison of the four varieties suggests that the two contact varieties spoken in Girona mainly display the typically 'Catalan' L* (¡)H% contour in exclamative echo yes–no questions. If it were true that this nuclear configuration is not used in CS (as claimed in the literature), this would point to an interpretation involving CLI. Namely, initial speakers of Catalan would have transferred the L* (¡)H% nuclear contour from GC to GS during acquisition (via substratum transfer) and the varieties of Spanish spoken by initial speakers of Spanish would have converged with their Spanish (and/or with Catalan). However, it cannot be excluded that some of the 'heritage varieties' spoken by the SpD of our sample may already have had it.[265] The origin of the use of H+L* L%, finally, cannot be determined on basis of the available data, but it probably comes from GC, as well, where this nuclear contour is common in many question types (e.g. in IYNQ).

Third, the nuclear configurations established for GS and GC **echo wh-**questions are L* H% (most common, especially in GC), L+H* L% (more frequent in GS), and L+H* LH%. The respective reference varieties, too, display various different nuclear configurations for this sentence type (see Table 3.4). In CC, L* H% is overall most usual, but in Girona and surroundings L+¡H* L% and L+H* LH% may be found as well (Prieto et al. 2015: 57). For CS, L+¡H* L% is claimed to be more natural than L* H% in this context, as the latter "may imply surprise, incredulity, or similar nuances" (Hualde/Prieto 2015: 282).[266] The comparison of

---

264. However, the accounts are not uniform: while Prieto (2002a: 454–455) stresses the wider tonal range but solely gives '¡H* L%'-like contours, Prieto (2013) and Prieto et al. (2015) underscore that CC uses mainly the low rising L* H% nuclear tune (with an extended tonal range) and mention L+¡H* L% as an alternative (attested in Santa Coloma de Farners, a town bordering on Girona). Prieto (2014: 68–70), on the other hand, seems to suggest that L+¡H* L% is most common in CC and that L+H* LH% and L+H* LHL% can be used to express a stronger meaning of surprise and insistence. In a perception study conducted by Prieto/Borràs-Comes (2018), L* H% and L+H* LH% were found to be most felicitous in CC disbelief/incredulity questions (i.e. questions with low agreement between the speaker and the addressee).
265. L* ¡H% appears, e.g., in Canarian Spanish (see Henriksen/García-Amaya 2012: 147; Cabrera Abreu/Vizcaino Ortega 2010).
266. Estebas-Vilaplana/Prieto (2010: 35) find ¡H* L% and L+H* ¡H% in their data but interpret the former as a surface realization of L+¡H* L% (in accordance with Escandell-Vidal 1999). L+H*

the four varieties reveals that: first, both Girona varieties pattern with CC in preferring L* H% as underlying nuclear configuration and using L+H* LH% as a (less frequent) alternative. Second, GS is somewhat closer to CS than GC is, given that it makes more use of the circumflex nuclear configuration L+H* L%. Based on these observations, it can be suggested that CatD bilinguals (1) overuse L* H% in Spanish and (2) sometimes transfer L+H* LH% from GC to GS (substratum transfer). Furthermore, the fact that L+H* L% occurred more frequently in Spanish and among SpD bilinguals speaks to the presence of different intonational grammars in the two dominance groups. More specifically, it is likely that (1) SpD speakers do not have L+H* LH% as underlying nuclear configuration in their intonational grammar and that (2) both L+H* L% and L* H% can be either underlying configuration or surface realization as a function of the speaker's LD. However, it is evident that many opportunities for future research remain with respect to the intonation of echo wh-questions in both Spanish and Catalan.

6.4.6 Imperatives

Commands. The underlying nuclear configurations established for commands were H+L* L% and L+H* L% in both GS and GC. While the first one was attested in IPs containing more than one prosodic word and could surface as L* L%, the second one mainly occurred in short imperatives (consisting only of the verb in the imperative form). Two different nuclear contours for commands are proposed in the literature for CS: L+H* !H% (Estebas-Vilaplana/Prieto 2010: 38) and L+(!)H* L% (Hualde/Prieto 2015: 384; Robles-Puente 2011b; Prieto/Roseano 2018: 230; see also Table 3.4). While the former seems to occur only in short imperatives comprising one prosodic word, the latter is (also) used in longer imperatives. In CC, mainly L+H* L% is used, but L+H* HL% is attested in more insistent calls (see Prieto et al. 2015: 35 and Table 3.4). For target sentences "longer than one word", Prieto et al. (2015: 35) registered L* L%, whereas Prieto (2002a: 456–457) describes a falling, 'H+L* L%'-like nuclear contour.

Taking into account these findings, it can be said that the contact varieties show similarities and dissimilarities in relation to the respective standard varieties: in the longer imperatives, they tend to use H+L* L% (like CC) but sometimes also show L* L% (like CC) or L+H* L% (like CS). In short imperatives, they usually display L+H* L% (thus rather patterning with CC). In sum, it can be suggested that tonal marking of commands in GS and GC can be interpreted as the result of transfer and convergence processes between Catalan and Spanish which took place in the

---

¡H% is also the most typical nuclear configuration used in Jerezano Spanish (Henriksen/García-Amaya 2012).

course of the development of these varieties. However, there seem to be more similarities with CC, which is consistent with the slight societal predominance of Catalan in Girona. It can thus be suggested that initial speakers of Catalan transferred tonal patterns from Catalan to Spanish when acquiring that language (substratum transfer) and that, in a further step, the Spanish spoken by initial speakers of Spanish converged with the variety spoken by the CatD bilinguals.

Requests. The underlying nuclear configurations of IPs proposed for requests were H+L* L% and, in requests consisting of only one prosodic word, L+H* L% and L+H* HL% (the latter conveying more insistence). L* HL% expresses requests in CS (see Table 3.4), but L+H* L% is used, e.g., in Jerezano Spanish (Henriksen/García-Amaya 2012). For IPs encompassing more than one prosodic word, Estebas-Vilaplana/Prieto (2010) equally give L+H* L% and Hualde/Prieto (2015: 385) add H+L* L%. In standard CC, the nuclear configuration which is most commonly proposed for this sentence type is again L* HL% (Prieto et al. 2015: 37), but L+H* LHL% can be utilized to "express a higher degree of insistence on part of the speaker".[267] For larger sequences consisting of "more than two accents", Prieto (2002a: 458) describes contours ending in low nuclear configurations (i.e. L* L%).

Considering this, it can be concluded that: first, GC and GS pattern with CS in showing the H+L* L% nuclear configuration in 'long' requests. Second, regarding 'short' requests, the contact varieties are also closer to CS, since L+H* L% is attested in requests in this language but does not seem to appear in CC. The comparison of the varieties thus allows for the assumption that GC has adopted some 'Spanish' features via convergence with GS.

Still and all, it is necessary to point out that the data sets analysed for orders and requests were too small and presented too strong variation to make safe conclusions about the emergence of their intonation. Also, the available descriptions of the reference varieties are still too unclear and too little comparable as they are based on different imperative-sentence types. Further investigation into all four varieties is thus needed to enable researchers to uncover the type and direction of CLI affecting this sort of utterance in a more structured and principled way.

6.4.7 Vocatives

The nuclear configurations suggested for vocatives on basis of the intonational analysis of GC and GS are L+H* HL%, the so-called 'vocative chant' L+H* !H%, and L+H* H%. While the two former probably convey different degrees of insistence, the last appears in 'interrogative vocatives' or 'vocative questions' (see

---

[267]. In opposition to all other available studies, Prieto (2014: 72) also mentions L+H* L!H for soft requests (i.e. the same contour as in statements of the obvious).

Section 5.1.9 and 5.2.3). L+H* !H% and L+H* HL% are also the nuclear configurations offered in intonational descriptions of CS and CC (see Table 3.4). While the boundary tone HL% is claimed to convey more insistence in CS, the studies on CC are not unanimous and some diatopic variation is reported (see Prieto 2014; Prieto et al. 2015). However, it seems that the vocative chant with the !H% boundary tone is altogether more common in second or more insistent calls in CC (i.e. the other way round as in CS). Furthermore, 'interrogative rising contours' (mainly L* H%) were sporadically observed in CC (Prieto 2002a: 460; Prieto 2013: 42–43; Prieto et al. 2015: 41), whereas they are not mentioned in the accounts on CS (but see Huttenlauch et al. 2018 for rising contours in Columbian Spanish "confirmation-seeking vocatives"). From this, it can be concluded that the findings for the two Girona contact varieties rather pattern with the descriptions of CC. Nevertheless, only further and more detailed investigation into all four varieties would allow to determine whether CLI has played any role in the genesis of the vocative intonation in the contact varieties.

6.4.8 Summary: The prosodic systems of current GS and current GC

Considering the findings of the intonational analysis and the discussion presented in this subchapter (6.4), it can be inferred that:

1. The intonation of the current variety of GS can be interpreted as the result of substratum transfer (that occurred when the monolingual speakers of GC learned Spanish as an L2) and of wholesale convergence (see Matras 2009: 232) or at least strong converging tendencies between the Spanish spoken by CatD bilinguals and the Spanish spoken by the hispanophone settlers (who came to Catalonia during the 20th century and at the beginning of the 21st) and their descendants, as well as with the standard variety of CS propagated in the media and schools. In the SpD bilinguals, these convergence processes can be attributed to first language attrition and accommodation under the pressure of the predominant surrounding language Catalan and of the Spanish variety spoken by CatD bilinguals. As a result of these different processes, numerous 'Spanish' prosodic features have been replaced by (Girona) Catalan ones in current GS. However, on the individual level, some differences – for the most part concerning frequencies of use – continue to exist between speakers as a function of their LD. GS is thus not (yet) a particularly uniform or homogeneous variety (see also Section 6.2 on interspeaker variation).
2. The prosody of the current variety of GC can be equally interpreted as the result of both convergence processes (first only with Spanish and later on also between the varieties of Catalan spoken by CatD and SpD bilinguals) and

substratum transfer (occurring when the monolingual speakers of Spanish learned Catalan as an L2). However, in this case, too, some minor differences (mostly referring to different usage frequencies) persist between individual speakers with different initial languages (see also Section 6.2).

The scheme in Figure 6.1 illustrates these assumptions. In a first step, the (Girona) Catalan monolinguals (who form the initial stage) learn Spanish as an L2 (because it has become the only official state and educational language and intermittently — i.e. under the Franco regime — even the only language allowed to be used in public).[268] The next generations step by step become consecutive (or sometimes simultaneous) bilinguals. Later on, the Spanish (and indirectly also the Catalan) spoken by the Catalan–Spanish bilinguals begins to converge with the Spanish spoken by the ever more numerous Spanish-speaking immigrants (arriving from the 1930s) and by their descendants as well as with the close-to-standard varieties of Spanish diffused in the media. After the restoration of democracy in 1978 and the (partial) recovery of Catalonian self-government in 1979, adult monolingual speakers of Spanish increasingly start learning Catalan as an L2 and their children and subsequent generations grow up as consecutive (or simultaneous) bilinguals (primarily due to the Catalan-medium educational system). In recent years, significant converging tendencies can be observed between the varieties of Catalan spoken by CatD and SpD bilinguals (see Argenter et al. 1998; Arnal 2011). In sum, there is a strong tendency towards wholesale prosodic convergence between the two contact varieties in Girona, although they display altogether more 'Catalan' than 'Spanish' prosodic features. This latter finding is in line with the observation that in today's Catalonia Catalan has high social prestige and that, in Girona, Catalan is slightly predominant at the societal level (i.e. there is a greater number of CatD bilinguals and its public use is greater than that of Spanish;[269] see Sections 2.1 and 4.2).

---

268. As shown in Section 2.1, this process of SLA was rather slow: although Spanish had been more or less the only official language from the 15th century (see Section 2.1), until the turn of the 20th century only very limited sectors of Catalan society had any knowledge of Spanish (as a foreign language) (Bernat et al. 2019, 2020). The acquisition of Spanish largely took place in educational settings, i.e. at school, before the arrival of Spanish-speaking immigrants, which enabled SLA in natural and unstructured contexts. Crucially, however, there were no foreign-language classes in the common sense of the word but Spanish was simply used as the medium of instruction.

269. As Arnal (2011: 16) points out the relative sizes of the speaker groups in contact, e.g. the number of natives and learners, crucially determines which results of contact-induced changes become fixed in a recipient language: "[i]f the group promoting the change is relatively numerous compared to [...] [the other one], it is much more likely that any innovations introduced become fixed."

350 Intonation in Language Contact

Figure 6.1 Schematic representation of the development of (current) Girona Catalan and Girona Spanish[a]

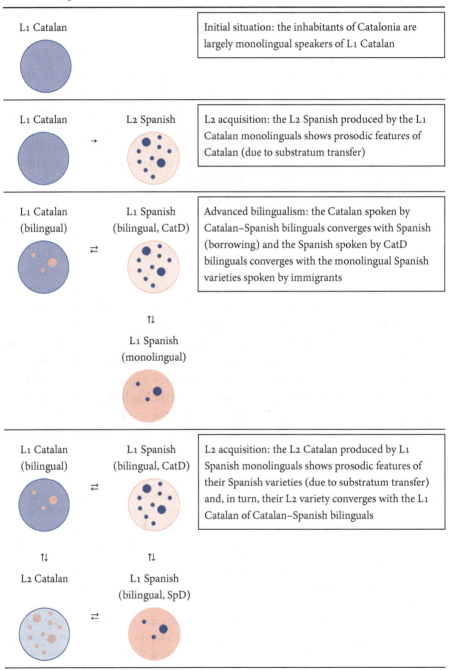

Figure 6.1 *(continued)*

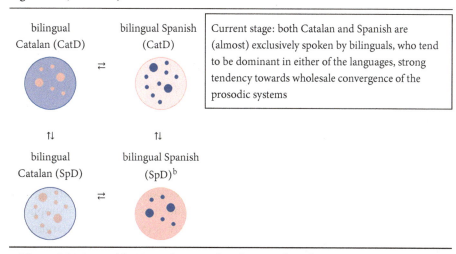

a. The model is inspired by Kireva (2016a: 243). It does not show the continuing influence exerted on the contact situation during all stages by Standard Spanish (e.g. via the media or the educational system) nor are migrant languages incorporated.
b. Contrary to monolingual Catalan, monolingual Spanish has not yet fully disappeared in Catalonia as roughly one in five residents is still unable to speak Catalan (see Section 2.1).

6.5 The status of Girona Spanish (and Catalonian Spanish) as a distinctive variety within the Spanish diasystem

The present study has revealed that the intonation of GS as a subvariety of CCS considerably differs from that of other, monolingual Peninsular varieties of Spanish. It thus provides further evidence from the prosodic level for the observations made by many authors based on other linguistic domains (see Section 2.3). The question must thus be asked whether GS, or Catalonian Spanish in a wider sense, should be regarded as a distinctive variety or dialect of Peninsular Spanish in its own right.

As explained in Chapter 2, the traditional Hispanic dialectology has denied this — often implicitly in that it simply ignored Spanish spoken in Catalan-speaking territories. If addressed at all, CCS was often treated from a puristic point of view and branded as 'accent' or sometimes as 'adstrate variety' (see Section 2.2). Only sporadically was it qualified as a tertiary dialect in the sense of Coseriu (1980) (e.g. by Kailuweit 1996). In more recent years, it has increasingly been referred to as 'contact variety', as is also done here. Apart from the sociolinguistic situation in which GS finds itself, the main reason for this is that the features which set it apart from other Spanish varieties are first of all a result of the intense language contact with Catalan, or more precisely of substratum transfer during SLA and of convergence processes between the varieties of Catalan and Spanish spoken by different social groups (see Sections 6.1–6.3, and especially 6.4). However, while it may be true that GS first developed as a learner variety or interlanguage of Catalan natives, characterized by strong interference from Catalan, this is no longer the case today. Rather the bilingualization of initial speakers of Catalan was completed in the second half of the last century and heavily Catalan-accented speech has become socially secondary (Vila 2016: 152) or has even fully disappeared in the youngest, fully bilingual generations (Arnal 2011: 16). Instead, 'Catalan' features are also observed in SpD speakers who have grown up in Catalonia (i.e. typically descendants of Spanish-speaking immigrants). The varieties of Spanish spoken by locals and immigrants and their offspring have thus converged. This clearly supports the findings of Simonet (2008, 2011) and Romera/Elordieta (2013) for Majorca, who observed comparable converging tendencies regarding the intonation of SpD locals and monolingual hispanophone immigrants. The results furthermore sustain Matras's (2009: 232–233) argument that prosody (and specifically intonation) is 'volatile' and that prosodic systems are susceptible to undergo convergence processes in language contact. From a more sociolinguistic angle, the present work shows that a certain degree of linguistic levelling has taken place across different collectives of Spanish speakers in Catalonia (see Moyer 1991; Corona et al. 2013; Vila 2016: 152).

On the other hand, while these findings point to the emergence of a 'new', 'independent' variety of Spanish, the present study has also revealed that GS displays a great deal of intonational variation. In Section 6.2, I have argued that this variation partly correlates with LD and that individual bilinguals may not have the same intonational systems (see also Section 6.4). Even though levelling tendencies between speaker groups of diverse ethnolinguistic or dialectal origins are doubtlessly perceivable, this process is not yet completed, such that, for the time being, GS cannot (yet) be viewed as a particularly clear-cut or uniform variety. As righteously pointed out by Vila (2016: 152), it is not clear neither that such a distinctive variety of 'Catalonian Spanish' is currently developing or that CCS is moving towards a single form. Consider, for instance, the fact that there are strong geographical discrepancies with regard to the sociolinguistic situation across Catalonia (see Section 2.1) and that the present study is based exclusively on the Spanish spoken in Girona by a sample of young university students raised there. It is thus quite likely that (somewhat) different results would have been obtained using speech data from other areas of Catalonia (e.g. Barcelona) or from other speaker types (e.g. older[270] or less educated bilinguals).

---

270. As Helms (2021: 160) underscores, age is a particularly important factor in the Catalan context due to the "generational divide [...] between those who have and have not had access to prescriptive Catalan norms through schooling".

In sum, the further development of GS can be expected to depend on the sociolinguistic conditions of the contact situation in the future in the same way as did the development of its current state. Extralinguistic factors, like the demographic and political developments or subjective psycho-social factors (e.g. language attitudes or prestige) will thus continue to be pivotal. For instance, an ongoing influx of Spanish-speaking migrants would contribute to enhance variation, whereas its cease would rather advance uniformization, as the locals' gradual loss of the possibility of contrasting their bilingual Catalonian Spanish with the monolingual Spanish spoken by immigrants or relatives from other regions would necessarily lead to the loss of notions like, for example, that certain phenomena could be 'more Catalan', 'more Castilian', or 'more typical of southern Spain' (see Sinner 2004: 595). Furthermore, future language policies or political upheavals such as the possible independence of Catalonia could of course anew bring along significant changes regarding the language status of Catalan and Spanish, which, in turn, would have indirect repercussions on the way the two languages influence each other. The direction of future evolutions thus remains to be seen.

6.6 How does contact-induced intonational change work?

The results of the present study suggest that contact-induced prosodic change is crucially conditioned by extralinguistic factors such as the pressure resulting from the social and political status of the languages involved (e.g. in terms of prestige or demographics). In the case of the Spanish–Catalan contact in Catalonia in general and in Girona in particular, these factors have pushed into opposite directions over the course of time,[271] but they eventually led to a sociolinguistic situation characterized by extensive individual and societal bilingualism (roughly 87% of the inhabitants of the Girona region are at least bilingual; see Section 2.2). The traces of the long-standing intense and course-changing language contact can clearly be seen in both current GC and GS. In the development of both varieties,

---

271. The prestige status as well as the proportional ratio of speakers of Catalan and Spanish practically reversed over time: i.e. during centuries Catalan used to be the 'low variety' in a diglossic situation although it was the only spoken language of the lion's share of society. Then, the social history of the 20th century successively led to the bilingualization of all Catalan speakers, the end of diglossia, and the bilingualization of (most) Spanish-speakers, in such a way that, today, both languages have a similar legal status and Catalan tends to have slightly more social prestige, although Spanish is more widely spoken (see also Section 2.1). Spanish has thus equally become an *agent* language in the present language-contact situation (i.e. initial Spanish speakers now ever more frequently impose features of their L1 onto the recipient language Catalan in the sense of Van Coetsem 2000: 49), whereas in the past this part used to be largely reserved to Catalan (see also Arnal 2011: 18).

the present work has identified interacting processes of convergence and substratum transfer. In what follows, I shall thus depict the different steps I assume the two contacting varieties to have gone through and attempt, in doing so, to describe how contact-induced prosodic change resulting from these mechanisms generally works and how it is determined by language-external factors.[272]

In GS, where substratum transfer precedes convergence processes, the following developmental steps can be proposed:

1. A monolingual speaker group with variety A as a first language is required to learn variety B as a foreign language (e.g. because language B has become the variety used in administration, education, and church and hence holds a high (overt) social prestige, while variety A is increasingly banned from public life, i.e. there is a diglossic situation).
2. In a first stage, the L2 variety of variety B, i.e. the learners' interlanguage, will show prosodic features typical of variety A due to substratum transfer (i.e. imperfect learning in the course of SLA). By way of example: the speakers of the L2 variety use a prosodic feature X (e.g. a pitch accent, a nuclear configuration, or a whole melodic construction) which has been transferred from their L1 (i.e. from variety A), whereas the native speakers of variety B use another prosodic feature Y to express the same thing.
3. Next, the children of these L2 speakers, who may already be consecutive bilinguals, will also use feature X instead of feature Y, when communicating in variety B.
4. In a following step, it can be expected that the variety B spoken by the bilinguals will con- verge with the variety B spoken by monolinguals (especially when the direct contact with monolinguals is strong or increases, e.g. due to the immigration of large numbers of monolingual speakers of variety B). The result of this convergence process may be the following: in the grammar of some speakers of variety B, Y is a surface realization of the underlying feature X, while in the grammar of other speakers of variety B, Y is the underlying feature and X its surface realization, and in the grammar of still some other speakers of variety B, Y is the underlying feature and the realization of Y remains unchanged by external influences.
5. In a subsequent phase, the degree of entrenchment of X and Y (which results from the frequency with which these features appear on the linguistic market, i.e. in variety A and B) will determine their further development in variety

---

272. The account is inspired by Kireva's (2016a: 243–245) model of transfer and convergence in Olivenza Spanish and Olivenza Portuguese and the presentation largely follows her example. It merely refers to contact-induced language change and does not include other possible causes of change.

B. Besides overt prestige of variety B, also demographic factors (i.e. the size of the different speaker groups involved) and the (possibly existing) covert prestige of variety A can be expected to affect the entrenchment of X and Y significantly. The same holds true for changes in the extralinguistic conditions shaping the contact situation such as, e.g., a break-up or a reversal of the diglossic situation in consequence of political transformations. Depending on these external factors, it is likely that either X or Y will be realized less and less frequently due to the higher degree of entrenchment the other variant receives under the given sociolinguistic circumstances.
6. Last, the recessive variant will be replaced by the predominant one entirely and disappear from the prosodic system of variety B.

Similar, though not identical steps can be outlined for the complementary variety, i.e. the second language involved in the same contact situation. While the overall sociolinguistic situation is of course identical, the opposite status of the contacting varieties entails that convergence and transfer processes affect their development in a different chronological order. In the following, I present the steps which I assume GC to have gone through and thereby endeavour to shed a light on the mechanisms that generally underlie contact-induced prosodic change, in this case resulting mainly from convergence (under changing external conditions) and only intermittently from substratum transfer.

1. Two varieties A and B enter into intensive contact (e.g. through political transformations). A diglossic situation emerges in which B is the prestige or 'high' variety (and at some point the only one allowed in public life and education). Speakers of A are thus required to learn B as a second language (see above). Bilingualism is widespread (especially among initial speakers of A), but there are also monolingual speakers of B.
2. Variety A adopts a prosodic feature Y from variety B via borrowing (e.g. a pitch accent, a nuclear configuration, or a whole melodic construction). As a consequence, two competing features, Y (the adopted one) and X (the one belonging to the system of A before the incorporation of Y), are found in variety A, both used to express the same function or meaning. In this first stage, it can be supposed that Y will only be a surface realization of the underlying feature X in variety A.[273]

---

273. It merits emphasizing that, as Bullock (2009: 168) points out, borrowing, i.e. the recruitment of prosodic resources from a contact language (or from an L2-variety of the own language) into the native language has a minimal functional effect on the linguistic system as a whole, since it does not — at least not initially or immediately — supplant native resources, which equally remain accessible to the borrowing speakers. Instead, the borrowed items should better be viewed as additional resources available to the bilinguals.

3. In a second stage, the degree of entrenchment of Y (which is defined by the frequency with which Y appears on the linguistic marketplace, i.e. in variety A and variety B) will determine its further development in variety A. Since Y is the feature which receives its degree of entrenchment from its use in both variety A and variety B (the prestige variety), it can be assumed that it will receive a high degree of entrenchment and that, in consequence, in the grammar of some speakers of variety A, Y will become the underlying feature and X its surface realization. This stage can be seen as an intermediate stage of the ongoing change.

4. If all extralinguistic conditions determining the contact situation were to stay stable, it should be expected that over the course of time, Y would become the underlying feature and X its surface realization in the grammar of all speakers of variety A, and possibly, that the predominant variant Y would eventually end up replacing the receding variant X entirely. In that case the two languages would have converged. However, changes of the extralinguistic conditions (e.g. political or social transformations) may accelerate, stop, or reverse such evolutions, since they can have a significant impact on the entrenchment of the two competing variants. By way of example: the arrival of large numbers of monolingual speakers of variety B could shift demolinguistic factors and additionally increase the presence of Y in the linguistic market. By contrast, a break-up or a reversal of the diglossic situation may come along with a change in the degrees of (overt and covert) prestige allocated to variety A and B. While this, on the one hand, can already be expected to favour the stronger entrenchment of X, it could, on the other, also incite monolingual speakers of B to engage in acquiring A as a foreign language. That, in turn, would be likely to cause transfer of Y from B to A (via substratum transfer in SLA). Depending on the socio- and demolinguistic circumstances at hand, it can thus be expected that either X or Y will be realized less and less frequently due to the higher degree of entrenchment conferred to the competing variant.

5. Last, the recessive variant will be replaced by the predominant one entirely and disappear from the prosodic system of variety A.

To cut a long story short, the cases of the two contact varieties spoken in Girona clearly show that contact-induced change, i.e. the linguistic outcome of the different mechanisms observed above, crucially depends on the external factors that shape the sociolinguistic situation in which the contact takes place. Due to several reasons (e.g. the demographic pressure of the CatD majority in Girona, the regained overt prestige of Catalan after the restauration of democracy, the relatively lower prestige allocated to Spanish as the language of the poor immigrants today; see Section 2.1), 'Catalan' variants seem to be overall somewhat more successful on the present-day linguistic market. It can thus be expected that they will also prevail on the long term in Girona, such that a more uniform and relatively stable variety of (Girona) Spanish will eventually emerge unless the sociolinguistic situation changes again (e.g. due to more migration or political changes in the future). Still, one caveat of this study is, of course, that it is based only on the intonational convergence documented in the Catalan-Spanish contact situation in Girona. However, the present findings largely pattern with what has been observed in some other intense language-contact situations: as shown in Section 3.2.3, for instance, the intonation of Bulgarian Judaeo-Spanish has almost completely converged with the intonation of the surrounding language Bulgarian (Andreeva et al. 2017, 2019, 2021) and Algherese Catalan intonation largely patterns with Sardinian (Roseano et al. 2015; Vanrell et al. 2020). Nevertheless, a more extensive cross-linguistic comparison and further studies will be necessary to confirm or reject the mechanisms proposed here.

6.7 Which intonational features are likely to be transferred?

The results of the intonational analysis of GS and GC have revealed that these contact varieties do not only present the same inventory of underlying tonal units (i.e. pitch accents and boundary tones) but also strongly tend to use them in the same combinations and contexts. Some (minor) differences were attested merely with regard to the frequencies with which these intonational features appear in a particular context (see, e.g., Andreeva et al. 2017, 2019, 2021 for virtually identical findings regarding Bulgarian Judaeo-Spanish). The results of the study thus strongly support Matras's (2009: 323) assumption that prosody is highly susceptible to "wholesale convergence" in situations of intense language contact. Indeed, this is what seems to have occurred in Girona, since current GS and GC taken as a whole display virtually identical intonational systems. On the other hand, the systems still allow for plenty of variation and there are clear individual differences among single speakers. These observations as well as the summary of the studies presented in Chapter 3 (see Section 3.2.3 and the references therein) allow us to suggest that all kinds of intonational features may be transferred when two languages are in contact. In other words, any intonational feature can result from transfer and/or convergence processes between two (or more) languages. The considerations made here thus confirm Thomason's (2001: 63) assumption that "anything" can be adopted by one language from another, at least with regard to the intonational level.

The following prosodic features were claimed to be subject to substratum transfer and/or borrowing and convergence processes in the present study:

(1) prenuclear pitch accents (e.g. in information-seeking yes–no questions); (2) boundary tones (in neutral declarative statements); (3) nuclear configurations of IPs (e.g. in information-seeking yes–no and wh-questions, commands, etc.). In some cases, it can be even presumed that whole melodic constructions, i.e. combinations of prenuclear pitch accents and nuclear configurations, were the object of CLI (e.g. in information-seeking yes–no questions). It is likely that some prosodic features are more sensitive to change in language contact than others (as has been suggested e.g. by Matras 2009: 231–233; Kireva 2016a: 246–247, among others). In the present work, most cases of CLI were observed with regard to nuclear configurations. However, the main reason for this is that Catalan and Spanish largely pattern alike regarding prenuclear pitch accents in most utterance types — at least as far as the varieties spoken in Spain are concerned. It cannot be excluded that there once were more prosodic differences between Catalan and Spanish at some point in the past, but since inferences about CLI in the Girona contact varieties can only be made on the basis of the comparison with other varieties (i.e., here, with the reference or standard varieties of CC and Peninsular Spanish, see the discussion in Section 6.3), this kind of research strongly depends on the knowledge available about the intonation of these (see Section 3.1.2). It is thus no surprise that nuclear configurations proved to be the most fruitful locus of CLI in the present study. Nevertheless, it is possible that, e.g., prenuclear pitch accents could be cross-linguistically more susceptible than nuclear configurations to change in language contact. With regard to the Catalan contact situation, it cannot be excluded that contact-induced changes in prenuclear intonation could have occurred long ago, leaving no traces in contemporary prosody. The fact that Algherese and Roussillon Catalan, which are not in contact with Spanish, use earlier prenuclear peaks in declarative statements than the varieties spoken in Spain to a certain extent suggests this (see Prieto et al. 2015). In consequence, the intonation used in historic recordings of Catalan and Spanish would definitely be an issue worth exploring in future analyses.

Besides that, the question may be asked whether, e.g., certain nuclear configurations are transferred more readily than others and, if so, why. In the present study, the intonation of virtually all studied utterance types presented some degree of CLI (as far as could be determined). One reason for this could be that Catalan-speakers originally learned Spanish as a foreign language and usually without a native model, i.e they presumably used Catalan intonation to pronounce Spanish in the first place. However, one might wonder what conditioned the selection of the nuclear contours they would borrow later on, when there was more contact with Spanish natives. Similarly, it may be asked why certain tunes were picked and borrowed from Catalan by L1 speakers of Spanish and not others. It is of note in this respect that those borrowings took place in an already largely bilingual community. One part of the answer could thus be that speakers may simply accommodate to what hear most frequently, i.e. they are most likely to adopt majority variants. Another important aspect, however, is probably the saliency of the tune itself. A particular nuclear configuration can only be borrowed if it is salient enough for the borrower to (consciously or unconsciously) perceive it. In turn, transfer of a nuclear configuration from the L1 into an L2 may happen most readily when the nuclear configuration used in the TL flies under the radar, i.e. when it is not salient enough for the learner to realize that it is actually different from their L1 patterns (see 'similar sounds' in Flege's 1987 Speech Learning Model for the acquisition of segmental phonology). A nuclear contour may thus be either inherently salient (e.g. because it encompasses drastic pitch movements) or salient in opposition to another one that is part of the L1 (i.e. different enough). To give an example, the use of H* L% in wh-questions could be rather salient for Spanish natives as this nuclear configuration does not occur in (Peninsular) Spanish at all. Since they hear it a lot due to its strong entrenchment in the bilingual community, they eventually adopt it (see Section 6.4.4). The use of H+L* L% in IYNQ, on the other hand, would be less salient given that this nuclear configuration is present, e.g., in Spanish imperative and confirmation-seeking yes–no questions, i.e., besides occurring in another context, it is not perceived as 'new' or 'different' because it is already known by the speakers from their L1. In this sense, it can be suggested that whether a nuclear contour is transferred or not in language contact crucially depends on its (relative) saliency.

CHAPTER 7

Conclusion

The present study investigated and described the intonation of the Spanish and Catalan spoken by Catalan–Spanish bilinguals in Girona. Drawing on a corpus of semi-spontaneous and read speech data specifically compiled for this purpose, it has provided a comprehensive description of the intonation of a previously undocumented variety, i.e. Girona Spanish (GS), and first addressed Girona Catalan (GC) intonation under the angle of its speakers' bilingualism. As one of the very few studies considering intonational data from bilinguals in both of their languages, the current work adds knowledge not only to the sphere of intonational dialectology, but also to the growing fields of intonation in language contact and multilingualism. The selected speakers, while being either dominant in Catalan or in Spanish – as is customary in the Catalan context – otherwise formed a fairly homogeneous sample. The results of the intonational analysis revealed that the contact varieties share numerous prosodic features and exhibit only very few differences. It was shown that GS and GC use the same inventories of pitch accents and boundary tones and that they largely pattern alike with regard to the realization of the nuclear configurations in the analysed utterance types (i.e. neutral declarative statements, enumerations, contrastive-focus statements, exclamative statements, contradiction statements, dubitative statements, information-seeking yes–no questions, disjunctive questions, exclamative yes–no questions (with counterexpectational meaning), confirmation-seeking yes–no questions, information-seeking wh-questions, exclamative wh-questions, imperative wh-questions, echo yes–no questions, echo wh-questions, exclamative echo yes–no questions (with counterexpectational meaning), commands, requests, and vocatives; see Table 5.1). The few differences observed between the two varieties related almost without exception to the frequency with which particular nuclear configurations appeared in a specific context in each variety, not to distinct inventories.

However, it was also found that both varieties, as a result of CLI, display a relatively high variability. This is evident, e.g., from the fact that many utterance types allow for various competing tunes. Yet, the bilingual's differential use of these tunes could to a great deal be accounted for by extralinguistic factors such as their backgrounds and language dominance, stressing the importance of such factors (see Sections 6.2 and 6.4). As a case in point, one of the peculiarities of GC and GS lies in the use of information-seeking yes–no questions introduced by the complementizer *que*: while this type of interrogative sentences appeared exclusively with high–falling nuclear contours in GS (and was produced for the most part by Catalan-dominant bilinguals), both high–falling and low–rising contours were attested in the GC realizations. Whereas Catalan-dominants overwhelmingly used the high–falling patterns in their strong language, too, Spanish-dominant bilinguals tended to prefer low–rising nuclear configurations.

The cross-dialectal comparison between the intonational properties of Girona Catalan and Girona Spanish with the 'reference' or 'standard' varieties of Catalan and (Peninsular) Spanish, i.e with Central Catalan (of which Girona Catalan is a part) and Castilian Spanish, revealed that the contact varieties exhibit, on the one hand, many shared features with Castilian Spanish or other Central Catalan varieties and, on the other, only relatively few properties that are not found in these standard varieties. They thus qualify to a certain extent as 'mixed' varieties, which originate from bidirectional influence between Spanish and Catalan. Considering the fact that Spanish and Catalan are closely related languages within the Romance family and that their intonational systems are quite similar, such an amalgamation in an intense contact situation does not come as a big surprise. Nevertheless, it is worth underscoring that the contact varieties spoken in Girona show overall more 'Catalan' than 'Spanish' prosodic features (see Section 6.3), which is consistent with the slightly predominant position Catalan enjoys at the societal level in that area. In addition to that, the comparison evinced that substantial dialectal differences between CCS and the closest documented monolingual non-contact varieties of Spanish exist not only at the segmental level and in other linguistic domains, but also at the prosodic or intonational level. Until now, however, there had been little empirical evidence on which to base such a claim.

Relying on the comparison made in Section 6.4, it was suggested that: first, the intonation of current GS can be interpreted as an outcome of both substratum transfer (that occurred when the formerly monolingual inhabitants of Girona learned Spanish as an L2 on a mass scale) and (ongoing) convergence processes (between the Spanish spoken by the Catalan–Spanish bilinguals and the Spanish spoken by the immigrants, who came to Catalonia mainly in the second half of 20th century, as well as with the Spanish used by their descendants and in the mass media). This wholesale convergence, in turn, can partly be seen as an instance of first language attrition, since numerous '(Girona) Catalan' prosodic features seem to have replaced the 'Spanish' ones not merely in the GS spoken by Catalan-dominant bilinguals but also in the Girona Spanish spoken by the (bilingual) Catalonia-born descendants of monolingual Spanish-speaking immigrants (i.e., so to speak, by heritage speakers of exogenous varieties of Spanish). The Spanish spoken in Catalonia by initial speakers of Catalan and by initial speakers of Spanish have thus widely converged today and GS has become more, though not yet fully, homogeneous (see Section 6.5).

Second, the intonation of current GC can be viewed as an outcome of (ongoing) convergence (1) between GC and the Spanish prosodic system(s) it has been in contact with during the last centuries and (b), after the more recent return to democracy, increasingly with the (L2) GC spoken by L1 speakers of Spanish or by Spanish-dominant bilinguals. As these latter varieties, in turn, are characterized by substratum transfer from Spanish, this mechanism can be taken to have influenced contemporary GC, too — albeit only to a minor extent until now.

Based on the inferences made about the intonational systems of Girona Spanish and Girona Catalan in Section 6.4, I depicted the steps which varieties resulting from language contact or, more specifically, from bidirectional processes of substratum transfer and convergence appear to go through in Section 6.6. Thereby, it was also shown that whether contact-induced language change occurs crucially depends on the extralinguistic conditions of the contact situation.

Finally, the results of this initial attempt to characterize the intonation of 'bilingual' GS and GC, together with the discussion presented in Chapter 6, allowed to identify some issues that go beyond the scope of this book but may be worth pursuing in future research. Regarding the intonation of current GS and GC, namely the following questions provide interesting opportunities for further in-depth study:

1. To what extent can the scaling of prenuclear pitch accents and/or of nuclear configurations (viz. the use of an extended pitch range and intensified tonal movements) be used as the sole prosodic cue to convey notions such as exclamativity in both statements and different question types (i.e. instead of a particular nuclear configuration)?
2. Which factors condition the use of the particle *que* in GC and GS IYNQ (see Sections 5.2.3 and 6.4.2.3) and how is focus expressed in that question type? Can prenuclear L*+H pitch accents work as interrogative focus markers?
3. Must the initial prenuclear pitch accent (i.e. usually H*) in information-seeking wh-questions always occur on the wh-element? What conditions the occurrence of other prenuclear pitch accents (see Section 6.4.4)?
4. How do utterance length and the position of the imperative verb influence the choice of a particular nuclear contour in orders and requests (see Section 5.1.8)?
5. Why were so few complex boundary tones observed in the contact varieties? (Note that in most (though not all) other Catalan and Peninsular Spanish varieties complex boundary tones are more recurrent; see, e.g., Estebas-Vilaplana 2010; Prieto et al. 2015; Henriksen/García-Amaya 2012).

6. How are specific tonal configurations produced under varied degrees of tonal pressure and in different metrical contexts (see, e.g., Prieto 2005a; Arvaniti/Ladd 2009; Henriksen 2014)?

In addition, perception studies ought to be conducted to make clear (1) whether the proposed phonological contrasts are borne out in the mind of the listeners and (2) how conscious speakers of GC and GS are about the blend of 'Spanish' and 'Catalan' prosodic features in their varieties. As a case in point, it would be interesting to find out whether the use L* H% in GC IYNQ with the particle *que* is perceived as natural by Catalan-dominant bilinguals or whether they recognize it as a 'Spanish element'. Likewise, the influence of linguistic attitudes and of their political or identitarian stances on the bilinguals' linguistic production and perception would be worth further exploration (see, e.g., Romera/Elordieta 2013, 2020; Elordieta/Romera 2020).

Besides that, comparisons with the 'bilingual' Catalan and Spanish spoken in other areas of the Spanish state would be valuable, as the present study has revealed a firm link between the sociolinguistic situation at hand and the direction and amount of CLI. For instance, given the substantially greater use of Spanish as well as the numerical predominance of Spanish-dominant bilinguals in Barcelona and its metropolitan area or in València, different outcomes could be expected regarding the intonation of 'bilingual' Spanish and Catalan spoken in those regions. Also, Catalan dialects are known to differ widely on all linguistic levels, such that the concrete features Spanish enters in contact with are diatopically very diverse.

Finally, we may wonder about the future of the two Girona contact varieties: will any of the various competing nuclear configurations proposed for many utterance types end up replacing the other(s) in the varieties of GS and GC spoken by the next generation(s)? Or will some of the competing variants adopt new, different pragmatic meanings? Will GS (and CCS in general) become more homogeneous and, eventually, emerge as a clear-cut independent dialect of Spanish? Will it converge towards the Castilian standard or 'stay closer' to Catalan, i.e. preserve its 'Catalan' features (e.g. to mark local identity)? How will GC evolve in view of the fact that a significant part of its speakers are now L2 speakers or Spanish-dominant bilinguals and that there is no longer any monolingual reference model? Will it converge towards the Barcelona-based standard variety of Catalan? It is clear that these questions will depend, to a substantial extent, on the future of Catalonia's sociolinguistic situation, i.e., above all, on whether the influx of monolingual Spanish speakers stops or continues and how the political situation (and the language policies connected therewith) develops in days to come.

Bibliography

Aguilar, Lourdes, Carme De-la-Mota, and Pilar Prieto (coords). 2009. *Sp_ToBI Training Materials*. http://prosodia.upf.edu/sp_tobi.

Aguilar, Lourdes, Carme De-la-Mota, and Pilar Prieto (coords). 2009–2011. *Cat_ToBI Training Materials*. http://prosodia.upf.edu/cat_tobi.

Aikhenvald, Alexandra Y. 2007. "Grammars in Contact: A Cross-Linguistic Perspective." In *Grammars in Contact: A Cross-Linguistic Typology*, ed. by Alexandra Aikhenvald and Robert M.W. Dixon, 1–66. Oxford: Oxford University Press.

Alarcón, Amado. 2011. "Economía de la lengua." *Treballs de Sociolingüística Catalana* 21: 19–27.

Alfano, Iolanda. 2016. "Sobre la entonación de las interrogativas absolutas del español de Barcelona en función de su organización informativa y morfosintáctica." *Loquens* 3 (1): e027.

Alvar, Manuel, ed. 1996. *Manual de dialectología hispánica: El español de España*. Barcelona: Ariel.

Alvord, Scott M. 2010. "Miami Cuban Spanish Declarative Intonation." *Studies in Hispanic and Lusophone Linguistics* 3 (1): 1–39.

Amengual, Mark. 2016. "The Perception and Production of Language-Specific Mid-Vowel Contrasts: Shifting the Focus to the Bilingual Individual in Early Language Input Conditions." *International Journal of Bilingualism* 20 (2): 133–152.

Amengual, Mark, and Miquel Simonet. 2020. "Language Dominance Does Not Always Predict Cross-Linguistic Interactions in Bilingual Speech Production." *Linguistic Approaches to Bilingualism* 10 (6): 847–872.

Amorós Céspedes, Mari Cruz. 2007. "El tonema en frases declarativas —con y sin expansión— en el habla granadina." In *III Congreso Internacional de Fonética Experimental*, ed. by Manuel González González, Elisa Fernández Rei, and Begoña González Rei, 79–87. Santiago de Compostela: Xunta de Galicia.

Amorós Céspedes, Mari Cruz. 2011. "La entonación declarativa neutra en el habla de Málaga." *Revista Internacional de Lingüística Iberoamericana* 9 (1): 65–73.

Andreeva, Bistra, Snezhina Dimitrova, Christoph Gabriel, Anna Gazdik, and Jonas Grünke. 2017. "Intonation and Convergence: Evidence from Bulgarian Judeo-Spanish." In *Domination and Adaptation. Proceedings of the International Conference of the Faculty of Slavic Studies. Vol. 2: Linguistics*, ed. by Ekaterina Tarpomanova and Krasimira Aleksova, 169–177. Sofia: University of Sofia "St. Kliment Ohridski."

Andreeva, Bistra, Snezhina Dimitrova, Christoph Gabriel, and Jonas Grünke. 2019. "The Intonation of Bulgarian Judeo-Spanish Spontaneous Speech." In *Proceedings of the 19th International Congress of Phonetic Sciences (ICPhS 19)*, ed. by Sasha Calhoun, Paola Escudero, Marija Tabain, and Paul Warren, 3827–3841. Canberra: Australasian Speech Science and Technology Association.

Andreeva, Bistra, Snezhina Dimitrova, Christoph Gabriel, and Jonas Grünke. 2021. "Intonational Convergence in Bulgarian Judeo-Spanish Spontaneous Speech." In *Prosody and Conceptional Variation. Situational Conditions of Communication, Degree of Communicational Planning, and Activity Types as Parameters for Prosodic Design*, ed. by Alexander Teixeira Kalkhoff, Maria Selig, and Christine Mooshammer, 171–190. Frankfurt: Lang.

Antoniou, Mark. 2019. "The Advantages of Bilingualism Debate." *Annual Review of Linguistics* 5: 395–415.

Appel, René, and Pieter Muysken. 1987. *Language Contact and Bilingualism*. London: Edward Arnold.

Argenter, Joan A. 2020. "Languages in Contact: A Sociocultural Approach." In *Manual of Catalan Linguistics*, ed. by Joan A. Argenter and Jens Lüdtke, 597–628. Berlin: De Gruyter.

Argenter, Joan A., Joan Pujolar, and Elisenda Vilardell. 1998. "L'ús de pronoms febles en la llengua oral: Estudi quantitatiu d'una mostra d'adolescents catalans." In *El contacte i la variació lingüístics*, ed. by Emili Boix-Fuster, Núria Alturo, Maria-Rosa Lloret, Mercè Lorente, and Lluís Payrató, 43–73. Barcelona: Universitat de Barcelona.

Armstrong, Lilias E., and Ida C. Ward. 1926. *Handbook of English Intonation*. Leipzig: Teubner.

Armstrong, Meghan E. 2010. "Puerto Rican Spanish Intonation." In *Transcription of Intonation of the Spanish Language*, ed. by Pilar Prieto and Paolo Roseano, 155–189. München: Lincom.

Armstrong, Meghan E., and Mariza Cruz. 2014. "The Intonational Phonology of Peninsular Spanish and European Portuguese." In *Portuguese-Spanish Interfaces: Diachrony, Synchrony, and Contact (Issues in Hispanic and Lusophone Linguistics 1)*, ed. by Patrícia Amaral and Ana Maria Carvalho, 151–174.

Arnal, Antoni. 2011. "Linguistic Changes in the Catalan Spoken in Catalonia Under New Contact Conditions." *Journal of Language Contact* 4: 5–25.

Arvaniti, Amalia. 2011. "The Representation of Intonation." In *The Blackwell Companion to Phonology*, ed. by Marc Van Oostendorp, Colin J. Ewen, Elizabeth V. Hume, and Keren Rice, 757–780. Malden, MA: Wiley-Blackwell.

Arvaniti, Amalia, and Mary Baltazani. 2005. "Intonational Analysis and Prosodic Annotation of Greek Corpora." In *Prosodic Typology: The Phonology of Intonation and Phrasing*, ed. by Sun-Ah Jun, 84–117. Oxford: Oxford University Press.

Arvaniti, Amalia, and Svetlana Godjevac. 2003. "The Origins and Scope of Final Lowering in English and Greek." In *Proceedings of the 15th International Congress of Phonetic Sciences (ICPhS 15)*, ed. by Maria-Josep Solé, Daniel Recasens, and Joaquín Romero, 1077–1080. Barcelona: Casual Productions.

Arvaniti, Amalia, and D. Robert Ladd. 2009. "Greek Wh-Questions and the Phonology of Intonation." *Phonology* 26: 43–74.

Astruc, Lluïsa. 2003. "Sentence External Elements in Catalan." *Catalan Journal of Linguistics* 2: 15–31.

Astruc, Lluïsa. 2005. The Intonation of Extra-Sentential Elements in Catalan and English. PhD dissertation, University of Cambridge.

Astruc, Lluïsa, Elsa Mora, and Simon Rew. 2010. "Venezuelan Spanish Intonation." In *Transcription of Intonation of the Spanish Language*, ed. by Prieto Prieto and Paolo Roseano, 191–226. München: Lincom.

Astruc, Lluïsa, and Francis Nolan. 2007. "Variation in the Intonation of Sentential Adverbs in English and Catalan." In *Tones and Tunes. Vol. 1: Typological Studies in Word and Sentence Prosody*, ed. by Tomas Riad and Carlos Gussenhoven, 233–262. Berlin: Mouton de Gruyter.

Astruc, Lluïsa, Maria del Mar Vanrell, and Pilar Prieto. 2016. "Cost of the Action and Social Distance Affect the Selection of Question Intonation in Catalan." In *Intonational Grammar in Ibero-Romance: Approaches across Linguistic Subfields*, ed. by Meghan E. Armstrong, Nicholas Henriksen, and Maria del Mar Vanrell, 91–114. Amsterdam: Benjamins.

Atienza, Encarnación, and Grupo Interalia. 1998. "Interferencia catalán-castellano en estudiantes universitarios bilingües." In *Actes del III Congrés Internacional sobre Traducció*, ed. by Pilar Orero, 607–626. Barcelona: Universitat Autònoma de Barcelona.

Auer, Peter, and Frans Hinskens. 1996. "Convergence and Divergence of Dialects in Europe: New and Not So New Developments in an Old Area." *Sociolinguistica* 10: 1–30.

Bachman, Lyle F., and Adrian Palmer. 2010. *Language Assessment in Practice*. Oxford: Oxford University Press.

Badia i Margarit, Antoni M[aria]. 1965. "La integració idiomàtica i cultural dels immigrants. Reflexions, fets, plans." *Qüestions de Vida Cristiana* 31: 91–103.

Badia i Margarit, Antoni M[aria]. 1976. *Cap a una sociolingüística catalana*. Lérida: Artis.

Badia i Margarit, Antoni M[aria]. 1979. "Notes sobre el castellà parlat per catalans." In *Llengua i cultura als Països Catalans*, ed. by Antoni M[aria] Badia i Margarit, 145–153. Barcelona: Edicions 62.

Badia i Margarit, Antoni M[aria]. 1981. "Peculiaridades del uso del castellano en las tierras de lengua catalana." In *Actas del I Simposio para Profesores de Lengua y Literatura Españolas*, ed. by Ricardo Velilla Barquero, 11–31. Madrid: Castalia.

Baetens Beardsmore, Hugo. 1986. *Bilingualism: Basic Principles*. Clevedon: Multilingual Matters.

Báez de Aguilar González, Francisco. 1995. "Phonetische Entwicklung des Andalusischen in Katalonien." In *Minderheiten in der Romania*, ed. by Dieter Kattenbusch, 161–186. Wilhelmsfeld: Egert.

Báez de Aguilar González, Francisco. 1997. *El conflicto lingüístico de los inmigrantes castellanohablantes en Barcelona*. Málaga: Universidad de Málaga.

Bahrick, Harry P., Linda K. Hall, Judith P. Goggin, Lorraine E. Bahrick, and Stephanie A. Berger. 1994. "Fifty Years of Language Maintenance and Language Dominance in Bilingual Hispanic Immigrants." *Journal of Experimental Psychology* 123: 264–283.

Balari, Sergio, Joaquim Llisterri, and Dolors Poch. 1988. "La estructuración fonética de la materia sonora en hablantes bilingües." *ELUA* 5: 93–98.

Baqué, Lorraine, and Mònica Estruch. 2003. "Modelo de Aix-en-Provence." In *Teorías de la entonación*, ed. by Pilar Prieto, 123–153. Barcelona: Ariel.

Beckman, Mary E. 1996. "The Parsing of Prosody." *Language and Cognitive Processes* 11: 17–68.

Beckman, Mary E., Manuel Díaz-Campos, Julia T. McGory, and Terrell A. Morgan. 2002. "Intonation across Spanish in the Tones and Break Indices Framework." *Probus* 14: 9–36.

Beckman, Mary E., and Janet B. Pierrehumbert. 1986. "Intonational Structure in Japanese and English." *Phonology Yearbook* 3: 255–309.

Beckman, Mary E., and Jennifer J. Venditti. 2010. "Intonation." In *The Handbook of Phonological Theory*, ed. by John Goldsmith, Jason Riggle, and Alan C. L. Yu, 485–532. Malden, MA: Wiley-Blackwell.

Beckman, Mary E., Julia Hirschberg, and Stefanie Shattuck-Hufnagel. 2005. "The Original ToBI System and the Evaluation of the ToBI Framework." In *Prosodic Typology: The Phonology of Intonation and Phrasing*, ed. by Sun-Ah Jun, 9–54. Oxford: Oxford University Press.

Benet, Ariadna. 2011. El fraseig prosòdic de la parla espontània del català i del castellà. PhD dissertation, Universität Hamburg.

Benet, Ariadna, Conxita Lleó, and Susana Cortés. 2011. "Phrase Boundary Distribution in Catalan: Applying the Prosodic Hierarchy to Spontaneous Speech." In *Intonational Phrasing in Romance and Germanic: Cross-Linguistic and Bilingual Studies*, ed. by Christoph Gabriel and Conxita Lleó, 97–126. Amsterdam: Benjamins.

Benmamoun, Elabbas, Silvana Montrul, and Maria Polinsky. 2013. "Heritage Languages and Their Speakers: Opportunities and Challenges for Linguistics." *Theoretical Linguistics* 39: 129–181.

Bernat, Francesc. 2014. "La història contemporània de la llengua catalana com a paradoxa." *Llengua, Societat i Comunicació* 12: 3–9.

Bernat, Francesc, Mireia Galindo, and Carles de Rosselló. 2019. "Des de quan som bilingües els catalans?" *Apunts de Sociolingüística i Política Lingüística* 7: 1–4.

Bernat, Francesc, Mireia Galindo, and Carles de Rosselló. 2020. "El procés de bilingüització a Catalunya en el segle XX a partir de testimonis orals." *Treballs de Sociolingüística Catalana* 30: 97–111.

Bernhard, Gerald. 1998. *Das Romanesco des ausgehenden 20. Jahrhunderts: Variationslinguistische Untersuchungen*. Tübingen: Niemeyer.

Berruto, Gaetano. 2005. "Dialect/Standard Convergence, Mixing, and Models of Language Contact: The Case of Italy." In *Dialect Change: Convergence and Divergence in European Languages*, ed. by Peter Auer, Frans Hinskens, and Paul Kerswill, 81–95. Cambridge: Cambridge University Press.

Bialystok, Ellen. 2009. "Bilingualism: The Good, the Bad, and the Indifferent." *Bilingualism: Language and Cognition* 12: 3–11.

Billmyer, Kristine, and Manka Varghese. 2000. "Investigating Instrument-Based Pragmatic Variability: Effects of Enhancing Discourse Completion Tests." *Applied Linguistics* 21: 517–552.

Birdsong, David. 2006. "Dominance, Proficiency, and Second Language Grammatical Processing." *Applied Psycholinguistics* 27: 46–49.

Birdsong, David. 2016. "Dominance in Bilingualism: Foundations of Measurement, with Insights from the Study of Handedness." In *Language Dominance in Bilinguals: Issues of Measurement and Operationalization*, ed. by Carmen Silva-Corvalán and Jeanine Treffers-Daller, 85–105. Cambridge: Cambridge University Press.

Birdsong, David, Libby M. Gertken, and Mark Amengual. 2012. *Bilingual Language Profile: An Easy-to-Use Instrument to Assess Bilingualism*. Austin: University of Texas at Austin, COERLL. https://sites.la.utexas.edu/bilingual.

Bishop, Dorothy V. M., Vivian A. Ross, Mark S. Daniels, and Peter Bright. 1996. "The Measurement of Hand Preference: A Validation Study Comparing Three Groups of Right-Handers." *British Journal of Psychology* 87: 269–285.

Bladas Martí, Òscar. 2020. "Dictionaries of Language Difficulties." In *Manual of Standardization in the Romance Languages*, ed. by Franz Lebsanft and Felix Tacke, 535–558. Berlin: De Gruyter.

Blas Arroyo, José Luis. 1991. "Problemas teóricos en el estudio de la interferencia lingüística." *Revista Española de Lingüística* 21 (2): 265–290.

Blas Arroyo, José Luis. 1993. *La interferencia lingüística en Valencia (Dirección: catalán-castellano): Estudio sociolingüístico*. Castellón: Universitat Jaume I.

Blas Arroyo, José Luis. 1994. "Valenciano y castellano: actitudes lingüísticas en la sociedad valenciana. estudios sobre una comunidad urbana." *Hispania* 77 (1): 143–155.

Blas Arroyo, José Luis. 2007. "Spanish and Catalan in the Balearic Islands." *International Journal of the Sociology of Language* 184: 79–93.

Blas Arroyo, José Luis. 2011. "Spanish in Contact with Catalan." In *The Handbook of Hispanic Sociolinguistics*, ed. by Manuel Díaz-Campos, 374–394. Oxford: Blackwell.

Blas Arroyo, José Luis. 2019. "Español a la catalana: variación vernácula e identidad en la Cataluña soberanista." *Oralia* 22 (1): 7–40.

Blas Arroyo, José Luis. 2020. "'Madrit nos roba': contacto de lenguas, variación e ideología en el discurso político catalán." *Spanish in Context* 17 (1): 30–57.

Blas Arroyo, José Luis, Beatriz Navarro Morales, and Juan Carlos Casañ Núñez. 2009. *Corpus sociolingüístico de Castellón de la Plana y su área metropolitana*. Castelló de la Plana: Publicacions de la Universitat Jaume.

Blas Arroyo, José Luis, and Margarita Porcar Miralles. 1997. "Aproximación sociolingüística al fenómeno de la neutralización modal en las comunidades de habla castellonenses: Análisis de algunos contornos sintácticos." *Sintagma* 9: 27–45.

Bloomfield, Leonard. 1933. *Language*. New York: Henry Holt.

Blum-Kulka, Shoshana, Juliane House, and Gabriele Kasper. 1989. "Investigating Crosscultural Pragmatics: An Introductory Overview." In *Cross-Cultural Pragmatics: Requests and Apologies*, ed. by Shoshana Blum-Kulka, Juliane House, and Gabriele Kasper, 1–34. Norwood: Ablex.

Bochmann, Klaus. 2018. "Language Policies in the Romance-Speaking Countries of Europe." In *Manual of Romance Sociolinguistics*, ed. by Wendy Ayres-Bennett and Janice Carruthers, 433–461. Berlin: De Gruyter.

Boersma, Paul, and David Weenink. 2020. *Praat: Doing Phonetics by Computer*. Computer program, version 6.1.10. http://www.praat.org.

Boix-Fuster, Emili. 2015. "Multilingualism in Barcelona: Towards an Asymmetrical Multilingualism." In *Urban Diversities and Language Policies in Medium-Sized Linguistic Communities*, ed. by Emili Boix-Fuster, 143–176. Bristol: Multilingual Matters.

Boix-Fuster, Emili, and Josep Moran. 2014. "La castellanització de la població d'origen autòcton a la Catalunya contemporània." *Llengua, Societat i Comunicació* 12: 43–52.

Boix-Fuster, Emili, and Anna Paradís. 2015. "Ideologies and Trajectories of 'New Speakers' in Bilingual Families in Catalonia." *Revista de Llengua i Dret* 63: 165–185.

Boix-Fuster, Emili, and Cristina Sanz. 2008. "Language and Identity in Catalonia." In *Bilingualism and Identity: Spanish at the Crossroads with Other Languages*, ed. by Mercedes Niño-Murcia and Jason Rothman, 87–106. Amsterdam: Benjamins.

Boix-Fuster, Emili, and Kathryn A. Woolard. 2020. "Language Ideologies in Society." In *Manual of Catalan Linguistics*, ed. by Joan A. Argenter and Jens Lüdtke, 709–721. Berlin: De Gruyter.

Bolinger, Dwight L. 1958. "A Theory of Pitch Accent in English." *Word* 14: 109–149.

Bolinger, Dwight L. 1972. "Accent is Predictable (if You are a Mind-Reader)." *Language* 48: 633–644.

Bolinger, Dwight L. 1978. "Intonation across Languages." In *Universals of Human Language. Vol. 2: Phonology*, ed. by Joseph H. Greenberg, 471–524. Stanford, CA: Stanford University Press.

Bolinger, Dwight L. 1982. "Intonation and Its Parts." *Language* 58: 505–533.

Bondzio, Wilhelm, ed. 1980. *Einführung in die Grundfragen der Sprachwissenschaft*. Leipzig: Bibliographisches Institut.

Bonet, Eulàlia. 2002. "Cliticització." In *Gramàtica del català contemporani*, ed. by Joan Solà, Maria-Rosa Lloret, Joan Mascaró, and Manuel Pérez Saldanya, 933–989. Barcelona: Empúries.

Borràs-Comes, Joan, Rafèu Sichel-Bazin, and Pilar Prieto. 2015. "Vocative Intonation Preferences Are Sensitive to Politeness Factors." *Language and Speech* 58 (1): 68–83.

Borràs-Comes, Joan, Maria del Mar Vanrell, and Pilar Prieto. 2010. "The Role of Pitch Range in Establishing Intonational Contrasts in Catalan." *Proceedings of Speech Prosody 2010*, article 103, 1–4. https://www.isca-speech.org/archive_v0/sp2010/sp10_103.html.

Bossong, Georg. 2008. *Die Romanischen Sprachen*. Hamburg: Buske.

Brehm, Annika, Alina Lausecker, and Ingo Feldhausen. 2014. "The Intonation of Imperatives in Mexican Spanish." In *Proceedings of the 10th International Seminar on Speech Production (ISSP)*, ed. by Susanne Fuchs, Martine Grice, Anne Hermes, Leonardo Lancia, and Doris Mücke, 53–56. Köln: Universität Köln.

Briz, Antonio. 2001. "El castellano en la Comunidad Valenciana." In *II Congreso Internacional de la Lengua Española: El español en la sociedad de la información*, Valladolid, 16–19 October 2001. https://congresosdelalengua.es/valladolid/paneles-ponencias/unidad-diversidad/briz-a.htm.

Browman, Catherine, and Louis Goldstein. 1991. "Gestural Structures: Distinctiveness, Phonological Processes, and Historical Change." In *Modularity and the Motor Theory of Speech Perception: Followings of a Conference to Honor Alvin M. Liberman*, ed. by Ignatius M. Mattingly and Michael Studdert-Kennedy, 313–338. Hillsdale: Lawrence Erlbaum.

Brown, H. Douglas. 1980. *Principles of Language Learning and Teaching*. Englewood Cliffs: Prentice Hall.

Bruce, Gösta. 1977. *Swedish Word Accents in Sentence Perspective*. Lund: CWK Gleerup.

Brucart, Josep M., and Gemma Rigau. 2002. "La quantificació." In *Gramàtica del català contemporani*, ed. by Joan Solà, Maria-Rosa Lloret, Joan Mascaró, and Manuel Pérez Saldanya, 1517–1589. Barcelona: Empúries.

Brumme, Jenny. 2020. "Normative Grammars." In *Manual of Standardization in the Romance Languages*, ed. by Franz Lebsanft and Felix Tacke, 497–518. Berlin: De Gruyter.

Brumme, Jenny, ed. 1998. *Repertori de catalanòfils (Estudis de Llengua i Cultura Catalanes 36).* Vol. 4. Barcelona: Publicacions de l'Abadia de Montserrat.

Bruyninckx, Marielle, Bernard Harmegnies, Joaquim Llisterri, and Dolors Poch. 1990. "Bilinguisme et qualité vocale: Contribution à l'analyse des variations du spectre à long terme sous l'effet du changement de langue." In *Mélanges de phonétique et didactique des langues : Hommage au Professeur Renard*, ed. by Albert Landercy, 43–53. Mons: Presses Universitaires de Mons et Didier Érudition.

Bruyninckx, Marielle, Bernard Harmegnies, Joaquim Llisterri, and Dolors Poch. 1994. "Language-Induced Voice Quality Variability in Bilinguals." *Journal of Phonetics* 22: 19–31.

Bullock, Barbara E. 2009. "Prosody in Contact in French: A Case Study from a Heritage Variety in the USA." *International Journal of Bilingualism* 13 (2): 165–194.

Bullock, Barbara E., and Chip Gerfen. 2004. "Phonological Convergence in a Contracting Language Variety." *Bilingualism: Language and Cognition* 7 (2): 95–104.

Büring, Daniel. 2016. *Intonation and Meaning.* Oxford: Oxford University Press.

Burridge, Kate. 2006. "Language Contact and Convergence in Pennsylvania German." In *Grammars in Contact: A Cross-Linguistic Typology*, ed. by Alexandra Y. Aikhenvald and Robert M. W. Dixon, 179–200. Oxford: Oxford University Press.

Cabrera Abreu, Mercedes, and Francisco Vizcaíno Ortega. 2010. "Canarian Spanish Intonation." In *Transcription of Intonation of the Spanish Language*, ed. by Prieto Prieto and Paolo Roseano, 87–121. München: Lincom.

Calderón Campos, Miguel. 2015. "El antropónimo precedido de artículo en la historia del español." *Hispania* 98 (1): 79–93.

Camps, Oriol, and Aina Labèrnia. 2020. "Catalan in the Mass Media: The Rise of Stylebooks." In *Manual of Catalan Linguistics*, ed. by Joan A. Argenter and Jens Lüdtke, 683–692. Berlin: De Gruyter.

Carbonell, Joan F., and Joaquim Llisterri. 1999. "Catalan." In *Handbook of the International Phonetic Association: A Guide to the Usage of the International Phonetic Alphabet*, ed. by The International Phonetic Association, 61–65. Cambridge: Cambridge University Press.

Carroll, John B. 1972. "Fundamental Considerations in Testing for English Language Proficiency of Foreign Students." In *Teaching English as a Second Language: A Book of Readings*, ed. by Harold B. Allen and Russel N. Campbell, 364–372. New York: McGraw Hill.

Casals, Daniel, and Neus Faura. 2010. *El català als mitjans de comunicació.* Barcelona: UOC.

Casanovas Català, Montse. 1995. "La interferencia fonética en el español de Lleida: Algunos apuntes para su estudio." *Sintagma* 7: 53–59.

Casanovas Català, Montse. 1996a. "Consecuencias de la interferencia lingüística en la morfosintaxis del español hablado en Lleida." *Verba* 23: 405–415.

Casanovas Català, Montse. 1996b. "Algunos rasgos propios del español en las comunidades de habla catalana: Fonética, morfosintaxis y léxico." *Analecta Malacitana* 19 (1): 149–160.

Casanovas Català, Montse. 2000. Análisis cualitativo y cuantitativo de la morfosintaxis de una segunda lengua: El caso del español en contacto con el catalán. PhD dissertation, Universitat de Lleida.

Casesnoves, Raquel. 2010. "Changing Linguistic Attitudes in Valencia: The Effects of Language Planning Measures." *Journal of Sociolinguistics* 14 (4): 477–500.

Castañer Martín, Rosa María, M. Pilar González Olivera, and Javier Simón Casas. 2005. "Aproximación al estudio de la entonación aragonesa." *Estudios de Fonética Experimental* 14: 275–293.

Cerdà Massó, Ramón. 1967. "Apreciaciones generales sobre cast. /x/ → cat. [x] en el campo de Tarragona." *Revista de Filología Española* 50: 57–96.

Cerdà, Ramón. 1984. "Comentarios en torno a la influencia léxica del castellano sobre el catalán actual." *Beiträge zur Romanischen Philologie* 23 (2): 275–281.

Chun, Dorothy. 2002. *Discourse Intonation in L2: From Theory and Research to Practice.* Amsterdam: Benjamins.

Clyne, Michael. 1967. *Transference and Triggering: Observations on the Language Assimilation of Postwar German-Speaking Migrants in Australia.* Den Haag: Nijhoff.

Clyne, Michael. 2003. *Dynamics of Language Contact: English and Immigrant Languages.* Cambridge: Cambridge University Press.

Cohen, Antonie, and Johan 't Hart. 1967. "On the Anatomy of Intonation." *Lingua* 19: 177–192.

Colantoni, Laura. 2011. "Broad-Focus Declarative Sentences in Argentine Spanish Contact and Non-Contact Varieties." In *Intonational Phrasing in Romance and Germanic: Cross-Linguistic and Bilingual Studies*, ed. by Christoph Gabriel and Conxita Lleó, 183–212. Amsterdam: Benjamins.

Colantoni, Laura, and María Cristina Cuervo. 2013. "Clíticos acentuados." In *Perspectivas teóricas y experimentales sobre el español de la Argentina*, ed. by Laura Colantoni and Celeste Rodríguez Louro, 143–157. Frankfurt/Madrid: Vervuert.

Colantoni, Laura, and Jorge Gurlekian. 2004. "Convergence and Intonation: Historical Evidence from Buenos Aires Spanish." *Bilingualism: Language and Cognition* 7 (2): 107–119.

Colomina i Castanyer, Jordi. 2002. "Paradigmes flectius de les altres classes nominals." In *Gramàtica del català contemporani*, ed. by Joan Solà, Maria-Rosa Lloret, Joan Mascaró, and Manuel Pérez Saldanya, 535–580. Barcelona: Empúries.

Colón, Germà. 1993. *El lèxic català dins la Romània.* València: Universitat de València.

Colón, Germán. 1967. "Elementos constitutivos del español: Catalanismos." In *Enciclopedia Lingüística Hispánica.* Vol. 2, ed. by Manuel Alvar et al., 193–238. Madrid: CSIC.

Comellas, Pere. 2016. "Immigration and Linguistic Diversity: A New and Poorly Understood Situation for Catalan." *International Journal of Multilingualism* 13 (2): 149–164.

Congosto Martín, Yolanda. 2011. "Contínuum entonativo: Declarativas e interrogativas absolutas en cuatro variedades del español peninsular y americano." *Revista Internacional de Lingüística Iberoamericana* 17: 75–90.

Congosto Martín, Yolanda, Liliana Díaz Gómez, María Viejo Lucio-Villegas, and Ruth González Rodríguez. 2010. "Estudio Contrastivo de la entonación del castellano de Don Benito y del asturiano de Mieres en el marco del proyecto AMPER." In *Actes du XXVe Congrès International de Linguistique et de Philologie Romanes.* Vol. 2, ed. by Maria Iliescu, Heidi Siller-Runggaldier, and Paul Danler, 53–65. Berlin: De Gruyter.

Connell, Bruce. 2002. "Downdrift, Downstep and Declination." In *Typology of African Prosodic Systems*, ed. by Ulrike Gut and Dafydd Gibbon, 3–12. Bielefeld: Bielefeld Occasional Papers in Typology 1.

Contini, Michel. 2005. "2ᵉ séminaire international du projet AMPER." *Géolinguistique* 3, special issue: Projet AMPER. Grenoble: Université Stendhal Grenoble 3, Centre de Dialectologie, I–XI.

Cook, Vivian. 1991. "The Poverty-of-the-Stimulus Argument and Multi-Competence." *Second Language Research* 7: 103–117.

Corona, Víctor, and David Block. 2020. "Raciolinguistic Micro-Aggressions in the School Stories of Immigrant Adolescents in Barcelona: A Challenge to the Notion of Spanish Exceptionalism?" *International Journal of Bilingual Education and Bilingualism* 23 (7): 778–788.

Corona, Víctor, Luci Nussbaum, and Virginia Unamuno. 2013. "The Emergence of New Linguistic Repertoires among Barcelona's Youth of Latin American Origin." *International Journal of Bilingual Education and Bilingualism* 16 (2): 182–194.

Cortés, Susana, Conxita Lleó, and Ariadna Benet. 2009. "Gradient Merging of Vowels in Barcelona Catalan under the Influence of Spanish." In *Convergence and Divergence in Language Contact Situations (Hamburg Studies on Multilingualism 8)*, ed. by Kurt Braunmüller and Juliane House, 185–204. Amsterdam: Benjamins.

Coseriu, Eugenio. 1980. "'Historische Sprache' und 'Dialekt'." In *Dialekt und Dialektologie: Ergebnisse des Internationalen Symposions Zur Theorie des Dialekts, Marburg/Lahn, 5.–10. September 1977*, ed. by Joachim Göschel, Pavle Ivic, and Kurt Kehr, 106–122. Wiesbaden: Steiner.

Coseriu, Eugenio. 1981. "Los conceptos de 'dialecto', 'nivel' y 'estilo de lengua' y el sentido propio de la dialectología." *Lengua Española Actual* 3: 1–32.

Costa, Albert, Mireia Hernández, Jordi Costa-Faidella, and Núria Sebastián-Gallés. 2009. "On the Bilingual Advantage in Conflict Processing: Now You See It, Now You Don't." *Cognition* 113: 135–149.

Crespo-Sendra, Verònica. 2011. Aspectes de l'entonació del valencià. PhD dissertation, Universitat Pompeu Fabra.

Crespo-Sendra, Verònica. 2013. "València." In *L'entonació dels dialectes catalans*, ed. by Pilar Prieto and Teresa Cabré, 45–73. Barcelona: Publicacions de l'Abadia de Montserrat.

Crespo-Sendra, Verònica, Maria del Mar Vanrell, and Pilar Prieto. 2010. "Information-Seeking Questions and Incredulity Questions: Gradient or Categorical Contrast?" *Proceedings of Speech Prosody* 2010, article 164, 1–4. https://www.isca-speech.org/archive_v0/sp2010/sp10_164.html.

Cruz, Mariza. 2013. Prosodic Variation in European Portuguese: Phrasing, Intonation and Rhythm in Central-Southern Varieties. PhD dissertation, Universidade de Lisboa.

Crystal, David. 1969. *Prosodic Systems and Intonation in English (Cambridge Studies in Linguistics 1)*. Cambridge: Cambridge University Press.

Crystal, David. 2003. *A Dictionary of Linguistics and Phonetics*. Oxford: Blackwell.

Cummins, James. 1976. "The Influence of Bilingualism on Cognitive Growth: Synthesis of Research Findings and Explanatory Hypotheses." *Working Papers on Bilingualism* 9: 1–44.

Cutillas-Espinosa, Juan Antonio, and Juan Manuel Hernández-Campoy. 2007. "Script Design in the Media: Radio Talk Norms behind a Professional Voice." *Language and Communication* 27: 127–152.

Cutler, Anne, Jacques Mehler, Dennis Norris, and Juan Segui. 1989. "Limits on Bilingualism." *Nature* 340: 229–230.

D'Imperio, Mariapaola, Gorka Elordieta, Sónia Frota, Pilar Prieto, and Marina Vigário. 2005. "Intonational Phrasing in Romance: The Role of Syntactic and Prosodic Structure." In *Prosodies: With Special Reference to Iberian Languages*, ed. by Sónia Frota, Marina Vigário, and Maria João Freitas, 59–97. Berlin: Mouton de Gruyter.

Dalmau, Delfí. 1936. *Poliglotisme passiu*. Barcelona: Publicacions de 'La Revista'.

Davidson, Justin. 2012. "Phonetic Interference of Catalan in Barcelonan Spanish: A Sociolinguistic Approach to Lateral Velarization." In *Selected Proceedings of the 14th Hispanic Linguistics Symposium*, ed. by Kimberly Geeslin and Manuel Díaz-Campos, 319–339. Somerville, MA: Cascadilla Press.

Davidson, Justin. 2014. "A Comparison of Fricative Voicing and Lateral Velarization Phenomena in Barcelona: A Variationist Approach to Spanish in Contact with Catalan." In *Romance Languages and Linguistic Theory 2012: Selected Papers from 'Going Romance' Leuven 2012*, ed. by Karen Lahousse and Stefania Marzo, 223–244. Amsterdam: Benjamins.

Davidson, Justin. 2015a. Social Dynamics of Catalan-Spanish Contact in the Evolution of Catalonian Spanish. PhD dissertation, University of Illinois at Urbana-Champaign.

Davidson, Justin. 2015b. "Intervocalic Fricative Voicing in the Spanish of Barcelona: Considerations for Contact-Induced Sociophonetic Innovation." In *Sociolinguistic Change across the Spanish-Speaking World: Case Studies in Honor of Anna Maria Escobar*, ed. by Kim Potowski and Talia Bugel, 119–146. New York: Peter Lang.

Davidson, Justin. 2020. "Asymmetry and Directionality in Catalan–Spanish Contact: Intervocalic Fricatives in Barcelona and Valencia." *Languages* 5, article 60: 1–22.

DCVB = Alcover, Antoni Maria, and Francesc de Borja Moll. 2020. *Diccionari català-valencià-balear*. Online edition. https://dcvb.iec.cat.

De Houwer, Annick. 2009. *Bilingual First Language Acquisition*. Bristol: Multilingual Matters.

De Houwer, Annick. 2011. "Language Input Environments and Language Development in Bilingual Acquisition." *Applied Linguistics Review* 2: 221–240.

De Houwer, Annick, and Marc H. Bornstein. 2016. "Balance Patterns in Early Bilingual Acquisition: A Longitudinal Study of Word Comprehension and Production." In *Language Dominance in Bilinguals: Issues of Measurement and Operationalization*, ed. by Carmen Silva-Corvalán and Jeanine Treffers-Daller, 134–155. Cambridge: Cambridge University Press.

De Pijper, Jan Roelof. 1983. Modelling British English Intonation: An Analysis by Resynthesis of British English Intonation. PhD dissertation, Rijksuniversiteit te Utrecht.

De-la-Mota, Carme, Pedro Martín Butragueño, and Pilar Prieto. 2010. "Mexican Spanish Intonation." In *Transcription of Intonation of the Spanish Language*, ed. by Prieto Prieto and Paolo Roseano, 319–352. München: Lincom.

Delais-Roussarie, Elisabeth, Brechtje Post, Mathieu Avanzi, Carolin Buthke, Albert di Cristo, Ingo Feldhausen, Sun-Ah Jun, Philippe Martin, Trudel Meisenburg, Annie Rialland, Rafèu Sichel-Bazin, and Hi-Yon Yoo. 2015. "Intonational Phonology of French: Developing a ToBI System for French." In *Intonation in Romance*, ed. by Sónia Frota and Pilar Prieto, 63–100. Oxford: Oxford University Press.

Delattre, Pierre. 1966. "Les dix intonations de base en français." *The French Review* 40: 1–14.

Deuchar, Margaret, and Rachel Muntz. 2003. "Factors Accounting for Code-Mixing in an Early Developing Bilingual." In *(In)vulnerable Domains in Multilingualism*, ed. by Natascha Müller, 161–190. Amsterdam: Benjamins.

Dixon, Robert M. W. 1997. *The Rise and Fall of Languages*. Cambridge: Cambridge University Press.

Dukova-Zheleva, Galina. 2010. Questions and Focus in Bulgarian. PhD dissertation, University of Ottawa.

Dulay, Heidi C., and Marina K. Burt. 1974a. "Natural Sequences in Child Second Language Acquisition." *Language Learning* 24: 37–53.

Dulay, Heidi C., and Marina K. Burt. 1974b. "Errors and Strategies in Child Second Language Acquisition." *TESOL Quarterly* 8: 33–44.

Dunn, Alexandra L., and Jean E. Fox Tree. 2009. "A Quick, Gradient Bilingual Dominance Scale." *Bilingualism: Language and Cognition* 12: 273–289.

Dunn, Lloyd M., and Douglas M. Dunn. 2007. *Peabody Picture Vocabulary Test (PPVT-4)*. Minneapolis: Pearson.

Eckman, Fred R. 1977. "Markedness and the Contrastive Analysis Hypothesis." *Language Learning* 27: 315–330.

Elordieta, Gorka. 2003. "The Spanish Intonation of Speakers of a Basque Pitch-Accent Dialect." *Catalan Journal of Linguistics* 2: 67–95.

Elordieta, Gorka, and Nagore Calleja. 2005. "Microvariation in Accentual Alignment in Basque Spanish." *Language and Speech* 48: 397–439.

Elordieta, Gorka, Sónia Frota, Pilar Prieto, and Marina Vigário. 2003. "Effects of Constituent Length and Syntactic Branching on Intonational Phrasing in Ibero-Romance." In *Proceedings of the 15th International Congress of Phonetic Sciences (ICPhS 15)*, ed. by Maria-Josep Solé, Daniel Recasens, and Joaquín Romero, 487–490. Barcelona: Casual Productions.

Elordieta, Gorka, Sónia Frota, and Marina Vigário. 2005. "Subjects, Objects and Intonational Phrasing in Spanish and Portuguese." *Studia Linguistica* 59: 110–143.

Elordieta, Gorka, and Magdalena Romera. 2020. "The Influence of Social Factors on the Prosody of Spanish in Contact with Basque." *International Journal of Bilingualism*, 1–32.

Elvira García, Wendy. 2018. *Create Pictures with Tiers*. Praat script, version 4.5. http://stel.ub.edu/labfon/en/praat-scripts.

Enrique-Arias, Andrés. 2021. "Vamos en Palma 'We Are Going to Palma': On the Persistence (and Demise) of a Contact Feature in the Spanish of Majorca." In *Spanish Socio-Historical Linguistics: Isolation and Contact*, ed. by Whitney Chappell and Bridget Drinka, 185–203. Amsterdam: Benjamins.

Enrique-Arias, Andrés, and Beatriz Méndez Guerrero. 2020. "On the Effects of Catalan Contact in the Variable Expression of Spanish Future Tense. A Contrastive Study of Alcalá de Henares (Madrid) and Palma (Majorca)." In *Contact in Hispanic Linguistics: Methodological, Theoretical and Empirical Perspectives*, ed. by Luis A. Ortiz López, 315–334. Amsterdam: Benjamins.

Escandell-Vidal, Victoria. 1999. "Los enunciados interrogativos: Aspectos semánticos y pragmáticos." In *Gramática descriptiva de la lengua española*, ed. by Ignacio Bosque and Violeta Demonte, 3929–3991. Madrid: Espasa.

Escandell-Vidal, Victoria. 2002. "Echo-Syntax and Metarepresentation." *Lingua* 112: 871–900.

Escandell-Vidal, Victoria. 2011. "Verum focus y prosodia: cuando la duración (sí que) importa." *Oralia* 14: 181–202.

Escandell-Vidal, Victoria. 2017. "Intonation and Evidentiality in Spanish Polar Interrogatives." *Language and Speech* 60 (2): 224–241.

Escartí, Vincent Josep. 2005. "Nota sobre la decadència." In *Les Lletres hispàniques als segles XVI, XVII i XVIII*, ed. by Tomàs Martínez Romero, 59–70. Castelló de la Plana: Universitat Jaume I/Fundació Germà Colón Domènech.

Escobar, Anna María. 2021. "Variación lingüística en español." In *Introducción a la lingüística hispánica*, ed. by José Ignacio Hualde, Antxon Olarrea, Anna M. Escobar, Catherine E. Travis, and Cristina Sanz, 380–432. Cambridge: Cambridge University Press.

Escudero, David, Lourdes Aguilar, Maria del Mar Vanrell, and Pilar Prieto. 2012. "Analysis of Inter-Transcriber Consistency in the Cat_ToBI Prosodic Labelling System." *Speech Communication* 54: 566–582.

Estebas-Vilaplana, Eva. 2000. The Use and Realisation of Accentual Focus in Central Catalan with a Comparison to English. PhD dissertation, University College London.

Estebas-Vilaplana, Eva. 2003a. "Tonal Structure of Post-Focal L in English and Catalan." *Atlantis* 25: 39–53.

Estebas-Vilaplana, Eva. 2003b. "The Modelling of Prenuclear Accents in Central Catalan Declaratives." *Catalan Journal of Linguistics* 2: 97–114.

Estebas-Vilaplana, Eva. 2006. "Word Edge Tones in Spanish Prenuclear Accents." *Estudios de Fonética Experimental* 15: 11–42.

Estebas-Vilaplana, Eva. 2009. "Cuatro niveles de altura tonal en la frontera de frase en español peninsular." *Onomázein* 2: 11–32.

Estebas-Vilaplana, Eva, and Pilar Prieto. 2008. "La notación prosódica del español: Una revisión del Sp_ToBI." *Estudios de Fonética Experimental* 17: 265–283.

Estebas-Vilaplana, Eva, and Pilar Prieto. 2010. "Castilian Spanish Intonation." In *Transcription of Intonation of the Spanish Language*, ed. by Prieto Prieto and Paolo Roseano, 17–48. München: Lincom.

Fabra, Pompeu. 1918. *Gramàtica catalana*. Barcelona: Institut d'Estudis Catalans.

Fabra, Pompeu. 1925. *Les principals faltes de gramàtica*. Barcelona: Barcino.

Fabra, Pompeyo [Pompeu]. 1912. *Gramática de la lengua catalana*. Barcelona: Tipografia L'Avenç: Massó, Casas & Ca.

Face, Timothy, and Pilar Prieto. 2007. "Rising Accents in Castilian Spanish: A Revision of Sp_ToBI." *Journal of Portuguese Linguistics* 6: 117–146.

Face, Timothy L. 2002a. "Local Intonational Marking of Spanish Contrastive Focus." *Probus* 14: 71–92.

Face, Timothy L. 2002b. "Spanish Evidence for Pitch Accent Structure." *Linguistics* 40: 319–345.

Face, Timothy L. 2002c. *Intonational Marking of Contrastive Focus in Madrid Spanish*. München: Lincom.

Face, Timothy L. 2003. "Intonation in Spanish Declaratives: Differences between Lab Speech and Spontaneous Speech." *Catalan Journal of Linguistics* 2: 115–131.

Favreau, Micheline, and Norman Segalowitz. 1982. "Second Language Reading in Fluent Bilinguals." *Applied Psycholinguistics* 3: 329–341.

Feldhausen, Ingo. 2010. *Sentential Form and Prosodic Structure of Catalan*. Amsterdam: Benjamins.

Feldhausen, Ingo, Andrea Pešková, Elena Kireva, and Christoph Gabriel. 2011. "Categorical Perception of Porteño Nuclear Accents." In *Proceedings of the 17th International Congress of Phonetic Sciences 2011 (ICPhS 17)*, ed. by Wai-Sum Lee and Eric Zee, 116–119. Hong Kong: City University of Hong Kong.

Feldhausen, Ingo, and Xavier Villalba. 2020. "Modality and Information Structure: Focus, Dislocation, Interrogative and Exclamatory Sentences." In *Manual of Catalan Linguistics*, ed. by Joan A. Argenter and Jens Lüdtke, 247–270. Berlin: De Gruyter.

Félix-Brasdefer, J. César. 2010. "Data Collection Methods in Speech Act Performance: DCTs, Role-Plays, and Verbal Reports." In *Speech Act Performance: Theoretical, Empirical, and Methodological Issues*, ed. by Alicia Martínez-Flor and Esther Usó-Juan, 41–56. Amsterdam: Benjamins.

Ferguson, Charles A. 1959. "Diglossia." *Word* 15: 325–340.

Ferguson, Charles A. 1993. "The Language Factor in National Development." *Anthropological Linguistics* 35: 124–129.

Fernández Leborans, María Jesús. 1999. "El nombre propio." In *Gramática descriptiva de la lengua española*, ed. by Ignacio Bosque and Violeta Demonte, 77–128. Madrid: Espasa.

Fernández Planas, Ana María, Eugenio Martínez Celdrán, Lourdes Romera Barrios, Valeria Salcioli Guidi, Josefina Carrera Sabaté, Dorota T. Szmidt, Sabela Labraña Barrero, Lourdes Aguilar Cuevas, and Domingo Román Montes de Oca. 2007. "Estudio de la prosodia de Girona en la modalidad interrogativa encabezada por 'que' en el marco AMPERCAT." In *La prosodia en el ámbito lingüístico románico*, ed. by Josefa Dorta, 155–176. Madrid: La Página Ediciones.

Fernández Planas, Ana María. 2005. "Aspectos generales acerca del proyecto internacional «AMPER» en España." *Estudios de Fonética Experimental* 14: 13–27.

Fernández Planas, Ana María. 2009. "L'estudi de la prosòdia dialectal catalana en el marc AMPER al Laboratori de Fonètica de la Universitat de Barcelona." In *Studi catalani: Suoni e parole*, ed. by Empar Devís and Lídia Carol, 209–224. Bologna: Bononia University Press.

Fernández-Ordóñez, Inés. 2016. "Dialectos del español peninsular." In *Enciclopedia de Lingüística Hispánica*, ed. by Javier Gutiérrez-Rexach, 387–404. London: Routledge.

Fernández-Ordóñez, Inés (coord). 2005–. *Corpus oral y sonoro del español rural (COSER)*. http://www.corpusrural.es.

Ferrando, Antoni. 2020. "The Growth and Expansion of Catalan (1213–1516)." In *Manual of Catalan Linguistics*, ed. by Joan A. Argenter and Jens Lüdtke, 471–484. Berlin: De Gruyter.

Ferrando, Antoni, and Miquel Nicolás. 2011. *Història de la llengua catalana*. Barcelona: Editorial UOC.

Ferrer i Gironés, Francesc. 1985. *La persecució política de la llengua catalana*. Barcelona: Edicions 62.

Féry, Caroline. 2016. *Intonation and Prosodic Structure*. Cambridge: Cambridge University Press.

Fishman, Joshua A. 1967. "Bilingualism with and without Diglossia: Diglossia with and without Bilingualism." *Journal of Social Issues* 23 (2): 29–38.

Fishman, Joshua A. 1971. *Advances in the Sociology of Language*. The Hague: Mouton.

Fishman, Joshua A., Robert L. Cooper, and Roxana Ma. 1971. "Alternative Measures of Bilingualism." In *Bilingualism in the Barrio*, ed. by Joshua A. Fishman, Robert L. Cooper, and Roxana Ma, 483–512. The Hague: Mouton.

Flege, James Emil. 1984. "The Detection of French Accent by American Listeners." *Journal of the Acoustical Society of America* 76 (3): 692–707.

Flege, James Emil. 1987. "The Production of 'New' and 'Similar' Phones in a Foreign Language: Evidence for the Effect of Equivalence Classification." *Journal of Phonetics* 15: 47–65.

Flege, James Emil. 1995. "Second Language Speech Learning: Theory, Findings, and Problems." In *Speech Perception and Linguistic Experience: Issues in Cross-Language Research*, ed. by Winifred Strange, 233–277. Timonium: York Press.

Flege, James Emil, Ian R. A. MacKay, and Thorsten Piske. 2002. "Assessing Bilingual Dominance." *Applied Psycholinguistics* 23: 567–598.

Font Rotchés, Dolors. 2007. *L'entonació del català*. Barcelona: Publicacions de l'Abadia de Montserrat.

Frota, Sónia. 2000. *Prosody and Focus in European Portuguese: Phonological Phrasing and Intonation*. New York: Garland Publishing.

Frota, Sónia. 2012. "Prosodic Structure, Constituents and Their Representations." In *The Oxford Handbook of Laboratory Phonology*, ed. by Abigail C. Cohn, Cécile Fougeron, and Marie K. Huffman, 255–265. Oxford: Oxford University Press.

Frota, Sónia. 2014. "The Intonational Phonology of European Portuguese." In *Prosodic Typology II: The Phonology of Intonation and Phrasing*, ed. by Sun-Ah Jun, 6–42. Oxford: Oxford University Press.

Frota, Sónia, Mariza Cruz, Flaviane Svartman, Gisela Collischonn, Aline Fonseca, Carolina Serra, Pedro Oliveira, and Marina Vigário. 2015. "Intonational Variation in Portuguese: European and Brazilian Varieties." In *Intonation in Romance*, ed. by Sónia Frota and Pilar Prieto, 235–283. Oxford: Oxford University Press.

Frota, Sónia, Mariapaola D'Imperio, Gorka Elordieta, Pilar Prieto, and Marina Vigário. 2007. "The Phonetics and Phonology of Intonational Phrasing in Romance." In *Segmental and Prosodic Issues in Romance Phonology*, ed. by Pilar Prieto, Joan Mascaró, and Maria-Josep Solé, 131–153. Amsterdam: Benjamins.

Frota, Sónia, and Pilar Prieto (eds). 2015. *Intonation in Romance*. Oxford: Oxford University Press.

Gabriel, Christoph. 2006. "Focal Pitch Accents and Subject Positions in Spanish: Comparing Close-to-Standard Varieties and Argentinean Porteño." In *Proceedings of Speech Prosody 2006 (Studientexte zur Sprachkommunikation 40)*, ed. by Rüdiger Hoffmann and Hansjörg Mixdorff. Dresden: TUDpress Verlag der Wissenschaften.

Gabriel, Christoph. 2007. *Fokus im Spannungsfeld von Phonologie und Syntax: Eine Studie zum Spanischen*. Frankfurt: Vervuert.

Gabriel, Christoph, Ingo Feldhausen, and Andrea Pešková. 2011. "Prosodic Phrasing in Porteño Spanish." In *Intonational Phrasing in Romance and Germanic: Cross-Linguistic and Bilingual Studies*, ed. by Christoph Gabriel and Conxita Lleó, 153–182. Amsterdam: Benjamins.

Gabriel, Christoph, Ingo Feldhausen, Andrea Pešková, Laura Colantoni, Su-Ar Lee, Valeria Arana, and Leopoldo Labastía. 2010. "Argentinian Spanish Intonation." In *Transcription of Intonation of the Spanish Language*, ed. by Pilar Prieto and Paolo Roseano, 285–317. München: Lincom.

Gabriel, Christoph, and Jonas Grünke. 2021. "L'intonation en français L3 chez des apprenant·e·s bilingues allemand-turc : Production et perception." In *La prononciation du français langue étrangère : Perspectives linguistiques et didactiques*, ed. by Elissa Pustka. Tübingen: Narr.

Gabriel, Christoph, and Jonas Grünke. 2022. "Acquiring French Intonation against the Backdrop of Heritage Bilingualism: The Case of German-Turkish Learners." *Languages* 7 (1): 68.

Gabriel, Christoph, Jonas Grünke, and Nils Karsten. 2022a. "Production and Perception of L3 French Prosody: Approaching German-Turkish Heritage Bilingualism." In *Language Development in Diverse Settings: Interdisziplinäre Ergebnisse aus dem Projekt „Mehrsprachigkeitsentwicklung im Zeitverlauf" (MEZ)*, ed. by Hanne Brandt, Marion Krause, and Irina Usanova, 333–358. Berlin: Springer.

Gabriel, Christoph, Jonas Grünke, and Elena Kireva. 2020. "Portuguese remnants in the Spanish of Olivenza (Extremadura): Exploring vowel raising, global speech rhythm, and intonation." In *Spanish phonetics and phonology in contact: Studies from Africa, the Americas, and Spain* (Issues in Hispanic and Lusophone Linguistics 28), ed. by Rajiv Rao, 421–450. Amsterdam: Benjamins.

Gabriel, Christoph, Jonas Grünke, and Aldina Quintana. 2024. "Vocalic Alternations in İstanbul Judeo-Spanish: A Pilot Study on Semi-Spontaneous Speech Data." In *Proceedings of the XXII Biennial Conference of the German Society of Hispanic Studies*, ed. by Laura Minervini and Frank Savelsberg, 256–281. Leiden: Brill.

Gabriel, Christoph, Jonas Grünke, and Claudia Schlaak. 2022b. "Unterstützt die Herkunftssprache Türkisch den Erwerb der Französischen Prosodie? Eine Pilotstudie zur Förderung mit Digitalen Aussprachetools." In *Unterricht der Romanischen Sprachen & Inklusion: Rekonstruktion oder Erneuerung?*, ed. by Frank Schöpp and Aline Willems. Stuttgart: ibidem.

Gabriel, Christoph, and Elena Kireva. 2012. "Intonation und Rhythmus im spanisch-italienischen Kontakt: Der Fall des Porteño-Spanischen." In *Testo e Ritmi: Zum Rhythmus in der italienischen Sprache (Studia Romanica et Linguistica 35)*, ed. by Maria Selig and Elmar Schafroth, 131–149. Frankfurt: Lang.

Gabriel, Christoph, and Elena Kireva. 2014. "Prosodic Transfer in Learner and Contact Varieties: Speech Rhythm and Intonation of Buenos Aires Spanish and L2 Castilian Spanish Produced by Italian Native Speakers." *Studies in Second Language Acquisition* 36 (2): 257–281.

Gabriel, Christoph, Trudel Meisenburg, and Maria Selig. 2013. *Spanisch: Phonetik und Phonologie. Eine Einführung*. Tübingen: Narr.

Gabriel, Christoph, and Uli Reich. 2022. "The Phonology of Romance Contact Varieties." In *Manual of Romance Phonetics and Phonology*, ed. by Christoph Gabriel, Randall Gess, and Trudel Meisenburg, 462–502. Berlin: De Gruyter.

Garachana, Mar. 2021. "La evolución de *ir a* + INF en zonas de contacto lingüístico: El caso del español de Barcelona." In *Dinámicas lingüísticas de las situaciones de contacto*, ed. by Azucena Palacios and María Sánchez Paraíso, 321–343. Berlin: De Gruyter.

García Mouton, Pilar. 2007. *Lenguas y dialectos de España*. Madrid: Arco Libros.

García-Lecumberri, María Luisa. 1995. Intonational Signalling of Information Structure in English and Spanish: A Comparative Study. PhD dissertation, University of London.

García-Lecumberri, María Luisa. 2003. "Análisis por configuraciones: La escuela británica." In *Teorías de la entonación*, ed. by Pilar Prieto, 35–61. Barcelona: Ariel.

Garrido, Juan María. 2003. "La escuela holandesa: El modelo IPO." In *Teorías de la entonación*, ed. by Pilar Prieto, 97–122. Barcelona: Ariel.

GEIEC = Institut d'Estudis Catalans. 2018. *Gramàtica essencial de la llengua catalana*. Barcelona: Institut d'Estudis Catalans. https://geiec.iec.cat

Generalitat de Catalunya. 2019. *Informe de política lingüística* 2018. Barcelona: Generalitat de Catalunya, Departament de Cultura. https://llengua.gencat.cat/IPL

Generalitat de Catalunya. 2021. *Informe de política lingüística* 2019. Barcelona: Generalitat de Catalunya, Departament de Cultura. https://llengua.gencat.cat/IPL

Gertken, Libby M., Mark Amengual, and David Birdsong. 2014. "Assessing Language Dominance with the Bilingual Language Profile." In *Measuring L2 Proficiency: Perspectives from SLA*, ed. by Pascale Leclercq, Amanda Edmonds, and Heather Hilton, 208–225. Bristol: Multilingual Matters.

GIEC = Institut d'Estudis Catalans. 2016. *Gramàtica de la llengua catalana*. Barcelona: Institut d'Estudis Catalans. https://giec.iec.cat

Gilbers, Dicky, John Nerbonne, and Jos Schaeken (eds). 2000. *Languages in Contact*. Amsterdam: Rodopi.

Giles, Howard, Richard Y. Bourhis, and Donald M. Taylor. 1977. "Towards a Theory of Language in Ethnic Group Relations." In *Language Ethnicity and Intergroup Relations*, ed. by Howard Giles, 307–349. London: Academic Press.

Giles, Howard, Justine Coupland, and Nikolas Coupland. 1991. "Accommodation Theory: Communication, Context, and Consequence." In *Contexts of Accommodation*, ed. by Howard Giles, Justine Coupland, and Nikolas Coupland. New York: Cambridge University Press.

Goldrick, Matthew, Elin Runnqvist, and Albert Costa. 2014. "Language Switching Makes Pronunciation Less Nativelike." *Psychological Science* 25: 1031–1036.

Goldsmith, John. 1976. Autosegmental Phonology. PhD dissertation, MIT. New York: Garland.

Gómez Molina, José Ramón. 1986. *Estudio sociolingüístico de la comunidad de habla de Sagunto (Valencia)*. Valencia: IAM Investigación.

Gonçalves, Perpétua. 2005. "O português de Moçambique: Problemas e limites da padronização de uma variedade não-nativa." In *Norm und Normkonflikte in der Romania*, ed. by Carsten Sinner, 184–196. München: Peniope.

Grabe, Esther, Greg Kochanski, and John Coleman. 2003. "Quantitative Modelling of Intonational Variation." In *Proceedings of Speech Analysis and Recognition in Technology, Linguistics, and Medicine* 2003. http://www.phon.ox.ac.uk/files/apps/oxigen/publications.php

Grabe, Esther, and Ee Ling Low. 2002. "Durational Variability in Speech and the Rhythm Class Hypothesis." In *Papers in Laboratory Phonology 7*, ed. by Carlos Gussenhoven and Natasha Warner, 515–546. Berlin: De Gruyter Mouton.

Grice, Martine, Stefan Baumann, and Ralf Benzmüller. 2005. "German Intonation in Autosegmental-Metrical Phonology." In *Prosodic Typology: The Phonology of Intonation and Phrasing*, ed. by Sun-Ah Jun, 55–83. Oxford: Oxford University Press.

Grice, Martine, Alexandra Vella, and Anna Bruggeman. 2019. "Stress, Pitch Accent, and Beyond: Intonation in Maltese Questions." *Journal of Phonetics* 76.

Grosjean, François. 1997. "The Bilingual Individual." *Interpreting* 2: 163–187.

Grosjean, François. 1998. "Studying Bilinguals: Methodological and Conceptual Issues." *Bilingualism: Language and Cognition* 1: 131–149.

Grosjean, François. 2008. *Studying Bilinguals*. Oxford: Oxford University Press.

Grosjean, François. 2010. *Bilingual: Life and Reality*. Cambridge, MA: Harvard University Press.

Grosjean, François. 2015. *Parler plusieurs langues*. Paris: Albin Michel.

Grosjean, François. 2016. "The Complementarity Principle and Its Impact on Processing, Acquisition, and Dominance." In *Language Dominance in Bilinguals: Issues of Measurement and Operationalization*, ed. by Carmen Silva-Corvalán and Jeanine Treffers-Daller, 66–84. Cambridge: Cambridge University Press.

Grosjean, François. 2019. *A Journey in Languages and Cultures: The Life of a Bicultural Bilingual*. Oxford: Oxford University Press.

Grünke, Jonas. 2020. "Dominancia y usos lingüísticos entre estudiantes de Gerona." In *Contact, Variation, and Change: Studies in Honor of Trudel Meisenburg (Studienreihe Romania 35)*, ed. by Christoph Gabriel, Andrea Pešková, and Maria Selig, 461–478. Berlin: Erich Schmidt.

Grünke, Jonas. 2022. Intonation in Language Contact: The Case of Spanish in Catalonia. PhD dissertation, Johannes-Gutenberg-Universität Mainz.

Grünke, Jonas, Bistra Andreeva, Christoph Gabriel, and Mitko Sabev. 2023. "Vocative Intonation in Language Contact: The Case of Bulgarian Judeo-Spanish." *Languages* 8: 284.

Guion, Susan G., James E. Flege, and Jonathan D. Loftin. 2000. "The Effect of L1 Use on Pronunciation in Quichua–Spanish Bilinguals." *Journal of Phonetics* 28: 27–42.

Gussenhoven, Carlos. 1984. *On the Grammar and Semantics of Sentence Accents*. Dordrecht: Foris.

Gussenhoven, Carlos. 2004. *The Phonology of Tone and Intonation*. Cambridge: Cambridge University Press.

Hamers, Josiane F., and Michel H.A. Blanc. 2000. *Bilinguality and Bilingualism*. Cambridge: Cambridge University Press.

Harmegnies, Bernard, Marielle Bruyninckx, Joaquim Llisterri, and Dolors Poch. 1989. "Effects of Language Change on Voice Quality: An Experimental Contribution to the Study of the Catalan-Castilian Case." In *Proceedings of the 1st European Conference on Speech Communication and Technology (Eurospeech 1989)*. Vol. 2: 489–492.

Harris, Catherine L., Jean B. Gleason, and Ayşe Ayçiçeği. 2006. "When Is a First Language More Emotional? Psychophysiological Evidence from Bilingual Speakers." In *Bilingual Minds: Emotional Experience, Expression, and Representation*, ed. by Aneta Pavlenko, 257–283. Clevedon: Multilingual Matters.

Hatch, Evelyn. 1977. "An Historical Overview of Second Language Acquisition Research." In *Proceedings of the Los Angeles Second Language Research Forum*, ed. by Carol A. Henning, 1–14. Los Angeles: UCLA.

Haugen, Einar. 1953. *The Norwegian Language in America: A Study in Bilingual Behavior*, Vol. 1: The Bilingual Community. Vol. 2: The American Dialects of Norwegian. Bloomington: Indiana University Press.

Hawkey, James. 2014. "«Ai que em faig un lio». Desenvolupaments recents del coneixement de les normatives lingüístiques catalana i castellana." *Treballs de Sociolingüística Catalana* 2: 389–408.

Heath, Jeffrey. 1984. "Language Contact and Language Change." *Annual Review of Anthropology* 13: 367–384.

Heine, Bernd, and Tania Kuteva. 2013. "Contact and Grammaticalization." In *The Handbook of Language Contact*, ed. by Raymond Hickey, 86–105. West Sussex: Wiley-Blackwell.

Heinemann, Ute. 1996. *Novel·la entre dues llengües: El dilema català o castellà*. Kassel: Reichenberger.

Helms, Annie. 2021. "Bidirectionality of Language Contact: Spanish and Catalan Vowels." *Proceedings of the LSA* 6 (1): 159–172.

Henriksen, Nicholas. 2010. Question Intonation in Manchego Peninsular Spanish. PhD dissertation, Indiana University.

Henriksen, Nicholas. 2014. "Initial Peaks and Final Falls in the Intonation of Wh-Questions in Manchego Peninsular Spanish." *Probus* 26: 83–133.

Henriksen, Nicholas, and Lorenzo García-Amaya. 2012. "Transcription of Intonation of Jerezano Andalusian Spanish." *Estudios de Fonética Experimental* 21: 109–162.

Hernández García, Carmen. 1998. "Algunas propuestas didácticas para trabajar la interferencia catalán-español en el ámbito universitario (a partir del análisis de errores)." In *Didáctica de la lengua y la literatura para una sociedad plurilingüe del siglo XXI. Actas del IV Congreso Internacional de la Sociedad Española de Didáctica de la Lengua y la Literatura; 27–29 de noviembre de 1996*, ed. by Francisco José Cantero, Antonio Mendoza, and Celia Romea, 633–639. Barcelona: Universitat de Barcelona.

Hernández-Campoy, Juan Manuel. 2011. "Variation and Identity in Spain." In *The Handbook of Hispanic Sociolinguistics*, ed. by Manuel Díaz-Campos, 704–727. Malden, MA: Wiley-Blackwell.

Heye, Jürgen. 1979. "Bilingualism and Language Maintenance in Two Communities in Santa Catarina, Brazil." In *Language and Society*, ed. by William McCormack and Stephen Wurm, 401–422. The Hague: Mouton.

Hickey, Raymond. 2013. "Language Contact: Reconsideration and Reassessment." In *The Handbook of Language Contact*, ed. by Raymond Hickey, 1–28. West Sussex: Wiley-Blackwell.

Hinskens, Frans, Peter Auer, and Paul Kerswill. 2005. "The Study of Dialect Convergence and Divergence. Conceptual and Methodological Considerations." In *Dialect Change: Convergence and Divergence in European Languages*, ed. by Peter Auer, Frans Hinskens, and Paul Kerswill, 1–48. Cambridge: Cambridge University Press.

Hirschberg, Julia, and Gregory Ward. 1992. "The Influence of Pitch Range, Duration, Amplitude and Spectral Features on the Interpretation of the Rise-Fall-Rise Intonation Contour in English." *Journal of Phonetics* 20 (2): 241–251.

Hirst, Daniel, and Albert Di Cristo (eds). 1998. *Intonation Systems: A Survey of Twenty Languages*. Cambridge: Cambridge University Press.

Hirst, Daniel, Albert Di Cristo, and Robert Espesser. 2000. "Levels of Representation and Levels of Analysis for the Description of Intonation Systems." In *Prosody: Theory and Experiment*, ed. by Merle Horne, 51–87. Dordrecht: Kluwer Academic Press.

Höder, Steffen. 2014. "Convergence vs. Divergence from a Diasystematic Perspective." In *Stability and Divergence in Language Contact: Factors and Mechanisms*, ed. by Kurt Braunmüller, Steffen Höder, and Karoline Kühl, 39–60. Amsterdam: Benjamins.

Hoffman, Gerard. 1971. "Puerto Ricans in New York: A Language-Related Ethnographic Summary." In *Bilingualism in the Barrio*, ed. by Joshua Fishman, Robert Cooper, and Roxana Ma, 13–42. Bloomington: Indiana University Press.

Hualde, José Ignacio. 2002. "Intonation in Spanish and the Other Ibero-Romance Languages." In *Romance Phonology and Variation: Selected Papers from the 30th Linguistic Symposium on Romance Languages*, ed. by Caroline R. Wiltshire and Joaquim Camps, 101–115. Amsterdam: Benjamins.

Hualde, José Ignacio. 2003a. "El modelo métrico y autosegmental." In *Teorías de la entonación*, ed. by Pilar Prieto, 155–184. Barcelona: Ariel.

Hualde, José Ignacio. 2003b. "Remarks on the Diachronic Reconstruction of Intonational Patterns in Romance with Special Attention to Occitan as a Bridge Language." *Catalan Journal of Linguistics* 2: 181–205.

Hualde, José Ignacio. 2005. *The Sounds of Spanish*. Cambridge: Cambridge University Press.

Hualde, José Ignacio. 2007. "Stress Removal and Stress Addition in Spanish." *Journal of Portuguese Linguistics* 5: 59–89.

Hualde, José Ignacio. 2009. "Unstressed Words in Spanish." *Language Sciences* 31: 199–212.

Hualde, José Ignacio. 2010. "Secondary Stress and Stress Clash in Spanish." In *Selected Proceedings of the 4th Conference on Laboratory Approaches to Spanish Phonology*, ed. by Marta Ortega-Llebaria, 11–19. Somerville, MA: Cascadilla Proceedings Project.

Hualde, José Ignacio. 2014. *Los Sonidos del Español*. Cambridge: Cambridge University Press.

Hualde, José Ignacio, and Christopher D. Eager. 2016. "Final Devoicing and Deletion of /-d/ in Castilian Spanish." *Studies in Hispanic and Lusophone Linguistics* 9: 329–353.

Hualde, José Ignacio, and Marianna Nadeu. 2014. "Rhetorical Stress in Spanish." In *Word Stress: Theoretical and Typological Issues*, ed. by Harry van der Hulst, 228–252. Cambridge: Cambridge University Press.

Hualde, José Ignacio, and Marianna Nadeu. 2020. "Oclusives finals en català i en castellà de Catalunya." In *Contact, Variation and Change: Studies in Honor of Trudel Meisenburg (Studienreihe Romania 35)*, ed. by Christoph Gabriel, Andrea Pešková, and Maria Selig, 23–38. Berlin: Erich Schmidt.

Hualde, José Ignacio, Antxon Olarrea, Anna M. Escobar, and Catherine E. Travis. 2010. *Introducción a la lingüística hispánica*. Cambridge: Cambridge University Press.

Hualde, José Ignacio, and Pilar Prieto. 2015. "Intonational Variation in Spanish: European and American Varieties." In *Intonation in Romance*, ed. by Sónia Frota and Pilar Prieto, 350–391. Oxford: Oxford University Press.

Hualde, José Ignacio, and Pilar Prieto. 2016. "Towards an International Prosodic Alphabet (IPrA)." *Laboratory Phonology* 7 (1): 1–25. https://www.journal-labphon.org/article/id/6173.

Hualde, José Ignacio, and Mahir Şaul. 2011. "Istanbul Judeo-Spanish." *Journal of the International Phonetic Association* 41: 89–110.

Hulstijn, Jan H. (2012). "The Construct of Language Proficiency in the Study of Bilingualism from a Cognitive Perspective." *Bilingualism: Language and Cognition* 15: 422–433.

Huttenlauch, Clara, Ingo Feldhausen, and Bettina Braun. 2018. "The Purpose Shapes the Vocative: Prosodic Realisation of Colombian Spanish Vocatives." *Journal of the International Phonetic Association* 48 (1): 33–56.

IDESCAT. 2021a. "El municipi en xifres. Girona." Barcelona: Generalitat de Catalunya, Institut d'Estadística de Catalunya. https://www.idescat.cat/emex/?id=170792.

IDESCAT. 2021b. "Padró municipal d'habitants." Barcelona: Generalitat de Catalunya, Institut d'Estadística de Catalunya. https://www.idescat.cat/pub/?id=pmh.

Igarreta Fernández, Alba. 2019. "El acento catalán en algunos comunicadores: El caso de los late night." In *El español de Cataluña en los medios de comunicación*, ed. by Dolors Poch Olivé, 105–124. Frankfurt: Vervuert.

Illamola, Cristina. 2003. "De la oralidad a la escritura: Niveles de interferencia en la creación literaria de autores catalanes." *Anuari de Filologia 25–26* (Secció F: Estudios de lengua y literatura españolas): 81–94.

Jakobovits, Leon A. 1969. "Second Language Learning and Transfer Theory: A Theoretical Assessment." *Language Learning* 19: 55–56.

Johanson, Lars. 2002. *Structural Factors in Turkic Language Contacts*. London: Curzon.

Jilka, Matthias. 2000. "Identifizierung verschiedener Aspekte intonatorischen fremdsprachlichen Akzents." *Sprache und Datenverarbeitung* 24 (1): 51–71.

Jones, Daniel. 1918. *An Outline of English Phonetics*. Leipzig: Teubner.

Jorba, Manuel. 1979. "Sobre la literatura catalana al final de l'Antic Règim: el 'Diario de Barcelona' (1792–1808)." *Els Marges* 17: 27–52.

Jordana, Cèsar August. 1968. *El català i el castellà comparats*. Barcelona: Barcino.

Jun, Sun-Ah, ed. 2005. *Prosodic Typology: The Phonology of Intonation and Phrasing*. Oxford: Oxford University Press.

Jun, Sun-Ah, ed. 2014. *Prosodic Typology II: The Phonology of Intonation and Phrasing*. Oxford: Oxford University Press.

Jungbluth, Konstanze. 1996. *Die Tradition der Familienbücher: Das Katalanische während der Decadència*. Tübingen: Niemeyer.

Kabatek, Johannes. 1994. "Auto-odi. Geschichte und Bedeutung Eines Begriffs der Katalanischen Soziolinguistik." In *Akten des 2. Gemeinsamen Kolloquiums der deutschsprachigen Lusitanistik und Katalanistik*, ed. by Axel Schönberger, 159–173. Frankfurt: Domus Editoria Europaea.

Kager, René. 1995. "The Metrical Theory of Word Stress." In *The Handbook of Phonological Theory*, ed. by John A. Goldsmith, 367–402. Oxford: Blackwell.

Kailuweit, Rolf. 1996. "El castellano de Barcelona en torno a 1800. La formación de un dialecto terciario." In *Actas del III Congreso Internacional de Historia de la Lengua Española, Salamanca, 22–27 de noviembre de 1993*, ed. by Alegría Alonso González et al.., 737–746. Madrid: Arco Libros.

Kailuweit, Rolf. 1997. *Vom eigenen Sprechen: Eine Geschichte der spanisch-katalanischen Diglossie in Katalonien (1759–1859)*. Frankfurt am Main: Lang.

Kamali, Beste. 2015. "Information Structure in Turkish Yes/No Questions." In *Ankara Papers in Turkish and Turkic Linguistics*, ed. by Deniz Zeyrek, Çiğdem Sağın Şimşek, Ufuk Ataş, and Jochen Rehbein. Wiesbaden: Harrassowitz.

Kamali, Beste, and Daniel Büring. 2011. "Topics in Questions." Paper presented at *Generative Linguistics in the Old World 34* ("Workshop on the Phonological Marking of Topic and Focus"), Vienna, 28–30 April 2011. https://www.academia.edu/559835/Topics_in _Questions.

Kasper, Gabriele, and Merete Dahl. 1991. "Research Methods in Interlanguage Pragmatics." *Studies in Second Language Acquisition* 13 (2): 215–247.

Kaufmann, Göz. 2010. "Non-Convergence Despite Language Contact." In *Language and Space: An International Handbook of Linguistic Variation. Vol. 1: Theories and Methods*, ed. by Peter Auer and Jürgen Erich Schmidt, 478–493. Berlin: De Gruyter Mouton.

Kimura, Takuya. 2006. "Mismatch of Stress and Accent in Spoken Spanish." In *Prosody and Syntax: Cross-Linguistic Perspectives*, ed. by Yuji Kawaguchi, Ivan Fonágy, and Tsunekazu Moriguchi, 141–155. Amsterdam: Benjamins.

Kireva, Elena. 2016a. Prosody in Spanish-Portuguese Contact. PhD dissertation, University of Hamburg.

Kireva, Elena. 2016b. "El español hablado en Olivenza: ¿una variedad en vías de asimilación al estándar?" *Estudios de Lingüística del Español* 37: 235–262.

Kireva, Elena, and Christoph Gabriel. 2015. "Rhythmic Properties of a Contact Variety: Comparing Read and Semi-Spontaneous Speech in Argentinean Porteño Spanish." In *Prosody and Languages in Contact. L2 Acquisition, Attrition, Languages in Multilingual Situations*, ed. by Elisabeth Delais-Roussarie, Mathieu Avanzi, and Sophie Herment, 149–168. Berlin: Springer.

Kireva, Elena, and Christoph Gabriel. 2016. "Intonational Convergence in Information-Seeking Yes-No Questions: The Case of Olivenza Portuguese and Olivenza Spanish." In *Proceedings of Speech Prosody 2016*, ed. by Jon Barnes, Alejna Brugos, Stefanie Shattuck-Hufnagel, and Nanette Veilleux, 390–394. Boston: Boston University.

Klinger, Thorsten, Irina Usanova, and Ingrid Gogolin. 2019. "Entwicklung rezeptiver und produktiver schriftsprachlicher Fähigkeiten im Deutschen." *Zeitschrift für Erziehungswissenschaften* 22: 75–103.

Kloss, Heinz. 1978 [1952]. *Die Entwicklung neuerer germanischer Kultursprachen seit 1800*. Düsseldorf: Schwann.

Kohler, Klaus J. 1991. "A Model of German Intonation." In *Studies in German Intonation*, ed. by Klaus J. Kohler, 295–360. Kiel: Arbeitsberichte des Instituts für Phonetik und digitale Sprachverarbeitung der Universität Kiel 25.

Kohler, Klaus J. 1997. "Modelling Prosody in Spontaneous Speech." In *Computing Prosody: Computational Models for Processing Spontaneous Speech*, ed. by Yoshinori Sagisaka, Nick Campbell, and Norio Higuchi, 187–210. New York: Springer.

Krefeld, Thomas. 2011. "«Primäre», «sekundäre», «tertiäre» Dialekte – und die Geschichte des italienischen Sprachraums." In *Lexikon, Varietät, Philologie: Romanistische Studien. Günter Holtus zum 65. Geburtstag*, ed. by Anja Overbeck, Wolfgang Schweickard, and Harald Völker, 137–147. Berlin: De Gruyter.

Kremnitz, Georg. 2015. "Sprachenpolitische Folgen des Spanischen Bürgerkrieges." *Europa Ethnica* 72: 4–10.

Kremnitz, Georg. 2018. *Katalanische und okzitanische Renaissance: Ein Vergleich von 1800 bis heute (Romanistische Arbeitshefte 67)*. Berlin: De Gruyter.

Kristensen, Kjeld, and Mats Thelander. 1984. "On Dialect Levelling in Denmark and Sweden." *Folia Linguistica* 18 (1–2): 223–246.

Kubarth, Hugo. 2009. *Spanische Phonetik und Phonologie: Segmente, Silben, Satzmelodien*. Frankfurt am Main: Peter Lang.

Kügler, Frank, and Stefan Baumann. 2020. *Annotationsrichtlinien DIMA 4.0*. http://dima.uni-koeln.de/?page_id=32.

Kühl, Karoline, and Kurt Braunmüller. 2014. "Linguistic stability and divergence: An extended perspective on language contact." In *Stability and Divergence in Language Contact: Factors and Mechanisms*, ed. by Kurt Braunmüller, Steffen Höder, and Karoline Kühl, 13–38. Amsterdam: Benjamins.

Kühn, Jane. 2016. Functionally-Driven Language Change: Prosodic Focus and Sentence Type Marking in German-Turkish Bilingual Yes/No Questions. PhD dissertation, University of Potsdam.

Kupisch, Tanja, and Joost Van de Weijer. 2016. "The Role of Childhood Environment for Language Dominance: A Study of Adult Simultaneous Bilingual Speakers of German and French." In *Language Dominance in Bilinguals: Issues of Measurement and Operationalization*, ed. by Carmen Silva-Corvalán and Jeanine Treffers-Daller, 174–194. Cambridge: Cambridge University Press.

La Morgia, Francesca. 2016. "Assessing the Relationship Between Input and Strength of Language Development: A Study on Italian–English Bilingual Children." In *Language Dominance in Bilinguals: Issues of Measurement and Operationalization*, ed. by Carmen Silva-Corvalán and Jeanine Treffers-Daller, 195–218. Cambridge: Cambridge University Press.

Labov, William, and Wendell A. Harris. 1986. "De Facto Segregation of Black and White Vernaculars." In *Diversity and Diachrony*, ed. by David Sankoff, 1–24. Amsterdam: Benjamins.

Ladd, D. Robert. 1980. *The Structure of Intonational Meaning: Evidence from English*. Bloomington: Indiana University Press.

Ladd, D. Robert. 2008 [1996]. *Intonational Phonology*. Cambridge: Cambridge University Press.

Lang-Rigal, Jennifer. 2014. A Perceptual and Experimental Phonetic Approach to Dialect Stereotypes. The 'Tonada Cordobesa' of Argentina. PhD dissertation, University of Texas at Austin.

Lanza, Elizabeth. 2004. *Language Mixing in Infant Bilingualism: A Sociolinguistic Perspective*. Oxford: Oxford University Press.

Lapesa, Rafael. 1996. "Unidad y variedad de la lengua española." In *El español moderno y contemporáneo. Estudios lingüísticos*, 317–340. Barcelona: Crítica.

Lausecker, Alina, Annika Brehm, and Ingo Feldhausen. 2014. "Intonational Aspects of Imperatives in Mexican Spanish." In *Proceedings of Speech Prosody 2014*, ed. by Nick Campbell, Dafydd Gibbon, and Daniel Hirst, 683–687. Dublin: Trinity College.

Leben, William. 1973 [1978]. Suprasegmental Phonology. PhD dissertation, MIT. [New York: Garland].

Leben, William. 1976. "The Tones of English Intonation." *Linguistic Analysis* 2: 69–107.

Lee, Su Ar, Fernando Martínez-Gil, and Mary E. Beckman. 2008. "The Intonational Expression of Incredulity in Absolute Interrogatives in Buenos Aires Spanish." In *4th Conference on Laboratory Approaches to Spanish Phonology*, ed. by Marta Ortega-Llebaria, 47–56. Somerville, MA: Cascadilla.

Leech, Geoffrey N. 1983. *Principles of Pragmatics*. London: Longman.

Leonetti, Manuel. 2017. "Basic Constituent Orders." In *Manual of Romance Morphosyntax and Syntax*, ed. by Andreas Dufter and Elisabeth Stark, 887–932. Berlin: De Gruyter.

Levis, John M. 2018. *Intelligibility, Oral Communication, and the Teaching of Pronunciation*. Cambridge: Cambridge University Press.

Li, Ping, Fan Zhang, Erlfang Tsai, and Brendan Puls. 2014. "Language History Questionnaire (LHQ 2.0): A New Dynamic Web-Based Research Tool." *Bilingualism: Language and Cognition* 17 (3): 673–680.

Li, Wei. 2000. "Dimensions of Bilingualism." In *The Bilingualism Reader*, ed. by Wei Li, 1–21. London: Routledge.

Liberman, Mark. 1975 [1978]. The Intonational System of English. PhD dissertation, MIT. [New York: Garland].

Liberman, Mark, and Janet B. Pierrehumbert. 1984. "Intonational Invariance under Changes in Pitch Range and Length." In *Language Sound Structure*, ed. by Mark Aronoff and Richard T. Oerhle, 157–233. Cambridge, MA: MIT Press.

Lleó, Conxita, Ariadna Benet, and Susana Cortés. 2009. "Límits de la normalització lingüística: Vocals vulnerables en el català de Barcelona." In *Variació, poliglòssia i estàndard (Biblioteca Catalànica Germànica 7)*, ed. by Johannes Kabatek and Claus D. Pusch, 157–180. Aachen: Shaker.

Llisterri, Joaquim, Dolors Poch, Bernard Harmegnies, and Marielle Bruyninckx. 1992. "Bilingüismo y calidad de voz." In *Bilingüismo y adquisición de lenguas: Actas del IX Congreso Nacional de AESLA*, ed. by Feli Etxeberria and Jesús Arzamendi, 409–416. Bilbao: Universidad del País Vasco.

Lloret, Maria-Rosa. 2002. "Estructura sil·làbica." In *Gramàtica del català contemporani*, ed. by Joan Solà, Maria-Rosa Lloret, Joan Mascaró, and Manuel Pérez Saldanya, 195–249. Barcelona: Empúries.

Long, Michael H. 2003. "Stabilization and Fossilization in Interlanguage Development." In *The Handbook of Second Language Acquisition*, ed. by Catherine J. Doughty and Michael H. Long, 487–535. Oxford: Blackwell.

López Bobo, María Jesús, and Miguel Cuevas Alonso. 2010. "Cantabrian Spanish Intonation." In *Transcription of Intonation of the Spanish Language*, ed. by Prieto Prieto and Paolo Roseano, 49–85. München: Lincom.

Loveday, Leo. 1996. *Language Contact in Japan: A Sociolinguistic History*. Oxford: Clarendon Press.

Lüdi, Georges. 1996. "Mehrsprachigkeit." In *Contact Linguistics: An International Handbook of Contemporary Research*. Vol. 1, ed. by Hans Goebl, Peter H. Nelde, Zdenek Stary, and Wolfgang Wölck, 233–245. Berlin: De Gruyter.

Lüdtke, Jens. 1998. "Español colonial y español peninsular. El problema de su historia común en los siglos XVI y XVII." In *Competencia escrita, tradiciones discursivas y variedades lingüísticas: Aspectos del español europeo y americano en los siglos XVI y XVII*, ed. by Wulf Oesterreicher, Eva Stoll, and Andreas Wesch, 13–36. Tübingen: Narr.

Luk, Gigi, and Ellen Bialystok. 2013. "Bilingualism is Not a Categorical Variable: Interaction Between Proficiency and Usage." *Journal of Cognitive Psychology* 25: 605–621.

Machuca Ayuso, María J. 2016. "Estructura silábica y bilingüismo." In *El español en contacto con otras lenguas peninsulares*, ed. by Dolors Poch Olivé, 299–314. Frankfurt: Vervuert.

Machuca, María J., and Dolors Poch. 2016. "Dinámica de las vocales del español en contacto con el catalán." *Oralia. Análisis del Discurso Oral* 19: 153–175.

Mackey, William F. 1976. *Bilinguisme et contact des langues*. Paris: Klincksieck.

Mackey, William F. 2000 [1962]. "The Description of Bilingualism." In *The Bilingualism Reader*, ed. by Wei Li, 22–50. [Canadian Journal of Linguistics 7: 51–85.] London: Routledge.

Macnamara, John. 1967. "The Bilingual's Linguistic Performance: A Psychological Overview." *Journal of Social Issues* 23: 58–77.

Marian, Viorica, Henrike K. Blumenfeld, and Margarita Kaushanskaya. 2007. "The Language Experience and Proficiency Questionnaire (LEAP-Q): Assessing Language Profiles in Bilinguals and Multilinguals." *Journal of Speech, Language, and Hearing Research* 50: 940–967.

Marsá, Francisco. 1986. "Sobre concurrencia lingüística en Cataluña." In *El castellano actual en las comunidades bilingües de España*, ed. by Víctor García de la Concha et al.., 93–104. Salamanca: Junta de Castilla y León, Consejería de Educación y Cultura.

Martin, Philippe. 2015. *The Structure of Spoken Language*. Cambridge: Cambridge University Press.

Martínez Celdrán, Eugenio. 2003. "Análisis por niveles: La escuela americana." In *Teorías de la entonación*, ed. by Pilar Prieto, 63–95. Barcelona: Ariel.

Martínez Celdrán, Eugenio, Ana María Fernández Planas, Lourdes Romera Barrios, and Paolo Roseano, coords. 2003–2020. *Atlas multimèdia de la prosòdia de l'espai romànic*. http://stel.ub.edu/labfon/amper/cast/index_ampercat.html.

Martínez Celdrán, Eugenio, Ana María Fernández Planas, and Lourdes Romera Barrios. 2011. "Influencia del bilingüismo en la entonación del castellano de Lleida." *Revista Internacional de Lingüística Iberoamericana* 17: 27–38.

Martínez Celdrán, Eugenio, and Paolo Roseano. 2019. "Stress Clash in Spanish, Catalan, and Friulian from a Prosodic Perspective." *Spanish in Context* 16 (3): 475–522.

Mascaró, Ignasi, and Paolo Roseano. 2020. "Intonational Variation in Minorcan: Towards a Prosodic Change?" *Lingua* 243: article 102871.

Massanell i Messalles, Mar. 2012. *«Feve temps que no diva tants verbs!». Manteniment i transformació de paradigmes verbals en el català nord-occidental del tombant de segle*. Barcelona: Publicacions de l'Abadia de Montserrat.

Matisoff, James A. 2001. "Genetic Versus Contact Relationship: Prosodic Diffusibility in South-East Asian Languages." In *Areal Diffusion and Genetic Inheritance*, ed. by Alexandra Y. Aikhenvald and Robert M. W. Dixon, 291–327. Oxford: Oxford University Press.

Matras, Yaron. 2002. *Romani: A Linguistic Introduction*. Cambridge: Cambridge University Press.

Matras, Yaron. 2009. *Language Contact*. Cambridge: Cambridge University Press.

Matras, Yaron. 2010. "Contact, Convergence, and Typology." In *The Handbook of Language Contact*, ed. by Raymond Hickey, 66–85. West Sussex: Wiley-Blackwell.

Matras, Yaron. 2011. "Explaining Convergence and the Formation of Linguistic Areas." In *Geographical Typology and Linguistic Areas: With Special Reference to Africa*, ed. by Osamu Hieda, Christa König, and Hiroshi Nakagawa, 143–160. Amsterdam: Benjamins.

Matras, Yaron, and Jeanette Sakel (eds). 2007. *Grammatical Borrowing in Cross-Linguistic Perspective*. Berlin: Mouton de Gruyter.

Mattheier, Klaus J. 1996. "Varietätenkonvergenz: Überlegungen zu einem Baustein einer Theorie der Sprachvariation." *Sociolinguistica* 10: 31–52.

McKinnon, Sean. 2012. "Intervocalic /s/ Voicing in Catalonian Spanish." Senior honors thesis, Ohio State University.

McMahon, April. 2004. "Prosodic Change and Language Contact." *Bilingualism: Language and Cognition* 7: 121–123.

Meisel, Jürgen. 2007. "The Weaker Language in Early Child Bilingualism: Acquiring a First Language as a Second Language?" *Applied Psycholinguistics* 28: 495–514.

Meisenburg, Trudel. 1999. "Überlegungen zum Diglossiebegriff." In *Dialektgenerationen, Dialektfunktionen, Sprachwandel (Tübinger Beiträge zur Linguistik 411)*, ed. by Thomas Stehl, 19–35. Tübingen: Narr.

Meisenburg, Trudel. 2011. "Prosodic Phrasing in the Spontaneous Speech of an Occitan/French Bilingual." In *Intonational Phrasing in Romance and Germanic*, ed. by Christoph Gabriel and Conxita Lleó, 127–151. Amsterdam: Benjamins.

Méndez García de Paredes, Elena, and Carla Amorós Negre. 2016. "Second Level Pluricentrism in European Spanish: Convergence-Divergence in Andalusian Spanish." In *Pluricentric Languages and Non-Dominant Varieties Worldwide: Pluricentric Languages Across Continents — Features and Usage*, ed. by Rudolf Muhr, Eugênia Duarte, Amália Mendes, Carla Amorós Negre, and Juan Thomas, 243–258. Bern: Peter Lang.

Méndez García de Paredes, Elena, and Carla Amorós Negre. 2019. "The Status of Andalusian in the Spanish-Speaking World: Is it Currently Possible for Andalusia to Have its Own Linguistic Standardization Process?" *Current Issues in Language Planning* 20: 179–198.

Mennen, Ineke. 2004. "Bi-Directional Interference in the Intonation of Dutch Speakers of Greek." *Journal of Phonetics* 32: 543–563.

Mennen, Ineke. 2007. "Phonological and Phonetic Influences in Non-Native Intonation." In *Non-Native Prosody: Phonetic Description and Teaching Practice*, ed. by Jürgen Trouvain and Ulrike Gut, 53–76. Berlin: De Gruyter.

Mennen, Ineke. 2015. "Beyond Segments: Towards a L2 Intonation Learning Theory." In *Prosody and Languages in Contact: L2 Acquisition, Attrition, Languages in Multilingual Situations*, ed. by Elisabeth Delais-Roussarie, Mathieu Avanzi, and Sophie Herment, 171–188. Berlin: Springer.

Mennen, Ineke, and Esther de Leeuw. 2014. "Beyond Segments. Prosody in SLA." *Studies in Second Language Acquisition* 36: 183–194.

Milroy, James, and Lesley Milroy. 1985. *Authority in Language: Investigating Language Prescription and Standardisation*. London: Routledge & Kegan Paul.

Mok, Peggy, and Volker Dellwo. 2008. "Comparing Native and Non-Native Speech Rhythm Using Acoustic Rhythmic Measures: Cantonese, Beijing Mandarin and English." In *Proceedings of Speech Prosody 2008*, ed. by Plínio Barbosa, Sandra Madureira, and César Reis, 423–426. Campinas, Brazil: Editora RG/CNPq.

Moll, Francesc de B[orja]. 1974. *L'home per la paraula*. Palma de Mallorca: Moll.

Moll, Francesc de B[orja]. 1986. *Gramàtica catalana referida especialment a les Illes Balears*. Palma de Mallorca: Moll.

Moll, Francisco [sic] de B[orja]. 1961. "El castellano en Mallorca." In *Studia Philologica. Homenaje ofrecido a Dámaso Alonso por sus amigos y discípulos con ocasión de su 60.º aniversario*. Vol. 2: 469–474. Madrid: Gredos.

Montolío, Estrella, and M. Rosa Vila Pujol. 1993. "La enseñanza del español lengua extranjera (E/LE) en una ciudad bilingüe: Barcelona." *Anuari de Filologia* 16 (Secció F: Estudios de lengua y literatura españolas): 89–105.

Montrul, Silvina. 2013a. *El bilingüismo en el mundo hispanohablante*. Chichester: Wiley-Blackwell.

Montrul, Silvina. 2013b. "Bilingualism and the Heritage Language Speaker." In *The Handbook of Bilingualism and Multilingualism*, ed. by Tej K. Bhatia and William C. Ritchie, 167–189. Chichester: Blackwell.

Montrul, Silvina. 2016. "Dominance and Proficiency in Early and Late Bilingualism." In *Language Dominance in Bilinguals: Issues of Measurement and Operationalization*, ed. by Carmen Silva-Corvalán and Jeanine Treffers-Daller, 15–35. Cambridge: Cambridge University Press.

Montrul, Silvina, and Tania Ionin. 2010. "Transfer Effects in the Interpretation of Definite Articles by Spanish Heritage Speakers." Bilingualism: Language and Cognition 13: 449–473.

Morgenthaler García, Laura. 2008. *Identidad y pluricentrismo lingüístico: Hablantes canarios frente a la estandarización*. Frankfurt am Main: Vervuert.

Moulton, William. 1962. "Toward a Classification of Pronunciation Errors." *Modern Language Journal* 46: 101–109.

Moyer, Melissa G. 1991. "La parla dels immigrats andalusos al barri de Sant Andreu." *Treballs de Sociolingüística Catalana* 9: 83–104.

Moyna, María Irene. 1999. "Pronominal Clitic Stress in Río de la Plata Spanish: An Optimality Account." *The SECOL Review* 23: 15–44.

Müller, Max Friedrich. 1875. *Lectures on Science of Language*. Vol. 1. New York: Scribner/Armstrong.

Müller, Natascha, Tanja Kupisch, Karin Schmitz, and Katja Cantone. 2011. *Einführung in die Mehrsprachigkeitsforschung*. Tübingen: Narr.

Muñoz, Carmen. 2005. "Trilingualism in the Catalan Educational System." *International Journal of the Sociology of Language* 171: 75–93.

Muntendam, Antje. 2012. "Information Structure and Intonation in Andean Spanish." *LSA Annual Meeting Extended Abstracts 2012* (3): 10, 1–5.

Muysken, Pieter. 2013. "Language Contact Outcomes as the Result of Bilingual Optimization Strategies." *Bilingual Language and Cognition* 16 (4): 709-730.

Myers-Scotton, Carol. 2002. *Contact Linguistics: Bilingual Encounters and Grammatical Outcomes*. Oxford: Oxford University Press.

Myers-Scotton, Carol and Janice L. Jake 2000. "Four Types of Morpheme: Evidence from Aphasia, Codeswitching, and Second Language Acquisition." *Linguistics* 38: 1053–1100.

Nadeu, Marianna, and José Ignacio Hualde. 2012. "Acoustic Correlates of Emphatic Stress in Central Catalan." *Language and Speech* 55 (4): 517–42.

Nadeu, Marianna, and Pilar Prieto. 2011. "Pitch Range, Gestural Information, and Perceived Politeness in Catalan." *Journal of Pragmatics* 43: 841–854.

Nation, Paul, and David Beglar. 2007. "A Vocabulary Size Test." *The Language Teacher* 31 (7): 9–12.

Navarro Tomás, Tomás. 1935. *Impresiones sobre el acento* (Manuscrito autógrafo [UCM, BH MSS 302 N.o 4]).

Navarro Tomás, Tomás. 1971. *Manual de pronunciación española*. Madrid: Raycar Impresores.

Navarro Tomás, Tomás. 1974 [1944]. *Manual de entonación española*. Madrid: Guadarrama.

Nespor, Marina, and Irene Vogel. 2007 [1986]. *Prosodic Phonology*. Berlin: De Gruyter. [Dordrecht: Foris.]

Newman, Michael, Adriana Patiño-Santos, and Mireia Trenchs-Parera. 2013. "Linguistic Reception of Latin American Students in Catalonia and Their Responses to Educational Language Policies." *International Journal of Bilingual Education and Bilingualism* 16 (2): 195–209.

NGRAE (Real Academia Española and Asociación de Academias de la Lengua Española). 2011. *Nueva gramática de la lengua española: Fonética y fonología*. Madrid: Espasa Libros.

Nibert, Holly Joy. 2000. Phonetic and Phonological Evidence for Intermediate Phrasing in Spanish Intonation. PhD dissertation, University of Illinois at Urbana-Champaign.

Nicolás, Miquel. 2020. "The Origins of Modern Catalan: Cultural and Linguistic Evolution." In *Manual of Catalan Linguistics*, ed. by Joan A. Argenter and Jens Lüdtke, 487–495. Berlin: De Gruyter.

Ninyoles, Rafael Lluís. 1969. *Conflicte lingüístic valencià*. València: Tres i Quatre.

O'Connor, Joseph Desmond, and Gordon Frederick Arnold. 1973 [1961]. *Intonation of Colloquial English*. London: Longman.

O'Rourke, Erin. 2004. "Peak Placement in Two Regional Varieties of Peruvian Spanish Intonation." In *Contemporary Approaches to Romance Linguistics: Selected Papers from the 33rd Linguistic Symposium on Romance Languages (LSRL), Bloomington, Indiana, April 2003*, ed. by Julie Auger, J. Clancy Clements, and Barbara Vance, 321–341. Amsterdam: Benjamins.

O'Rourke, Erin. 2005. Intonation and Language Contact: A Case Study of Two Varieties of Peruvian Spanish. PhD dissertation, University of Illinois at Urbana-Champaign.

O'Rourke, Erin. 2006. "The Direction of Inflection: Downtrends and Uptrends in Peruvian Spanish Broad Focus Declaratives." In *Selected Proceedings of the 2nd Conference on Laboratory Approaches to Spanish Phonetics and Phonology*, ed. by Manuel Díaz-Campos, 62–74. Somerville, MA: Cascadilla Proceedings Project.

O'Rourke, Erin. 2010. "Ecuadorian-Andean Spanish Intonation." In *Transcription of Intonation of the Spanish Language*, ed. by Prieto Prieto and Paolo Roseano, 227–253. München: Lincom.

Observatori Català de Justícia. 2012. *La llengua catalana a la Justícia*. Barcelona: Generalitat de Catalunya (Departament de Justícia). https://repositori.justicia.gencat.cat/bitstream/handle/20.500.14226/804/llengua_catalana_justicia.pdf.

Odlin, Terence. 1989. *Language Transfer*. Cambridge: Cambridge University Press.

Oliva, Salvador. 1992. *La mètrica i el ritme de la prosa*. Barcelona: Quaderns Crema.

Oliva, Salvador, and Pep Serra. 2002. "Accent." In *Gramàtica del català contemporani*, ed. by Joan Solà, Maria-Rosa Lloret, Joan Mascaró, and Manuel Pérez Saldanya, 345–391. Barcelona: Empúries.

Ortega-Llebaria, Marta, and Pilar Prieto. 2007. "Disentangling Stress from Accent in Spanish: Production Patterns of the Stress Contrast in Deaccented Syllables." In *Segmental and Prosodic Issues in Romance Phonology*, ed. by Pilar Prieto, Joan Mascaró, and Maria-Josep Solé, 155–176. Amsterdam: Benjamins.

Ortega-Llebaria, Marta, and Pilar Prieto. 2010. "Acoustic Correlates of Stress in Central Catalan and Castilian Spanish." *Language and Speech* 54: 1–25.

Ortiz, Héctor, Marcela Fuentes, and Lluïsa Astruc. 2010. "Chilean Spanish Intonation." In *Transcription of Intonation of the Spanish Language*, ed. by Prieto Prieto and Paolo Roseano, 225–283. München: Lincom.

Palmada, Blanca. 2002. "Fenòmens assimilatoris." In *Gramàtica del català contemporani*, ed. by Joan Solà, Maria-Rosa Lloret, Joan Mascaró, and Manuel Pérez Saldanya, 251–270. Barcelona: Empúries.

Palmer, Harold E. 1922. *English Intonation with Systematic Exercises*. Cambridge: Heffer.

Pamies Bertrán, Antonio, Mari Cruz Amorós Céspedes, and Paul O'Neil. 2007. "Esquemas entonativos declarativos en el habla de Almería." In *La prosodia en el ámbito lingüístico románico*, ed. by Josefa Dorta, 299–311. Santa Cruz de Tenerife: La Página.

Pamies Bertrán, Antonio, Mari Cruz Amorós Céspedes, and Paul O'Neil. 2008. "Esquemas entonativos de frase declarativa en el habla de Jaén." *Language Design, Special Issue 2: Experimental Prosody*, 191–201.

Paradis, Johanne, and Elena Nicoladis. 2007. "The Influence of Dominance and Sociolinguistic Context in Bilingual Preschoolers' Language Choice." *The International Journal of Bilingual Education and Bilingualism* 10: 277–297.

Paradis, Michel. 2007. "L1 Attrition Features Predicted by a Neurolinguistic Theory of Bilingualism." In *Language Attrition: Theoretical Perspectives*, ed. by Barbara Köpke, Monika S. Schmid, Merel Keijzer, and Susan Dostert, 121–133. Amsterdam: Benjamins.

Parlament de Catalunya. 2012. *Statute of Autonomy of Catalonia – Consolidated Text*. https://www.parlament.cat/document/cataleg/150259.pdf.

Pavlenko, Aneta. 2004. "L2 Influence and L1 Attrition in Adult Bilingualism." In *First Language Attrition: Interdisciplinary Perspectives on Methodological Issues*, ed. by Barbara Köpke, Monika S. Schmid, Merel Keijzer, and Lina Weilemar, 47–59. Amsterdam: Benjamins.

Pavlenko, Aneta. 2014. *The Bilingual Mind: And What It Tells Us About Language and Thought.* Cambridge: Cambridge University Press.

Payrató, Lluís. 1985. *La interferència lingüística: Comentaris i exemples català-castellà.* Barcelona: Curial/Publicacions de l'Abadia de Montserrat.

Payrató, Lluís. 2002. "L'enunciació i la modalitat oracional." In *Gramàtica del català contemporani,* ed. by Joan Solà, Maria-Rosa Lloret, Joan Mascaró, and Manuel Pérez Saldanya, 1151–1222. Barcelona: Empúries.

Pelegrina, Manuel. 1996. "Interferencia escrita entre L1 y L2 en un proceso de inmersión lingüística: Aplicación de la TDS." *Diálogos Hispánicos* 18: 313–326.

Penny, Ralph. 2000. *Variation and Change in Spanish.* Cambridge: Cambridge University Press.

Perea, Maria Pilar. 2002. "Flexió verbal regular." In *Gramàtica del català contemporani,* ed. by Joan Solà, Maria-Rosa Lloret, Joan Mascaró, and Manuel Pérez Saldanya, 583–646. Barcelona: Empúries.

Pérez Castillejo, Susanna, and Mónica de la Fuente Iglesias. 2024. "Basic Intonation Patterns of Galician Spanish." *Languages* 9: 57.

Pérez, Olimpia, Pilar Prieto, Eva Estebas, and Maria del Mar Vanrell. 2011. "La expresión del grado de confianza en las preguntas: Análisis de un corpus de map tasks." In *El estudio de la prosodia en españa en el siglo XXI, perspectivas y ámbitos,* ed. by Antonio Hidalgo Navarro, Yolanda Congosto Martín, and Mercedes Quilis Merín, 31–60. València: Universitat de València.

Pešková, Andrea. 2019. "L2 Italian and L2 Spanish Vocatives Produced by L1 Czech Learners: Transfer and Prosodic Overgeneralization." In *Proceedings of the 19th International Congress of Phonetic Sciences (ICPhS 19),* ed. by Sasha Calhoun, Paola Escudero, Marija Tabain, and Paul Warren, 1932–1936. Canberra, Australia: Australasian Speech Science and Technology Association.

Pešková, Andrea. 2021. "Gibt es Melodische Konstruktionen? Erwerb von W-Fragen im L2-Italienischen und L2-Spanischen." In *Konstruktionsgrammatische Zugänge zu romanischen Sprachen (Strukturelle Dynamik und Sprachkontakt in der Romania),* ed. by Hans-Jörg Döhla and Anja Hennemann, 241–271. Berlin: Frank & Timme.

Pešková, Andrea. 2022. "Intonational and Syntactic Innovations in a Language Contact Situation: An Explorative Study of Yes/No Questions in Paraguayan Guarani-Spanish Bilinguals." *Language and Speech Journal,* special issue, ed. by Cinzia Avesani, Barbara Gili Fivela, and Michelina Savino.

Pešková, Andrea. 2023. *L2 Spanish and Italian Intonation: Accounting for the Different Patterns Displayed by L1 Czech and German Learners (Open Romance Linguistics).* Berlin: Language Science Press.

Pešková, Andrea, Ingo Feldhausen, Elena Kireva, and Christoph Gabriel. 2012. "Diachronic Prosody of a Contact Variety: Analyzing Porteño Spanish Spontaneous Speech." In *Multilingual Individuals and Multilingual Societies (Hamburg Studies on Multilingualism 13),* ed. by Kurt Braunmüller and Christoph Gabriel, 365–389. Amsterdam: Benjamins.

Peterson, Gordon E., and Ilse Lehiste. 1960. "Duration of Syllable Nuclei in English." *Journal of the Acoustical Society of America* 32: 693–703.

Pierrehumbert, Janet B. 1980. The Phonology and Phonetics of English Intonation. PhD dissertation, MIT.

Pierrehumbert, Janet B. 2000. "Tonal Elements and Their Alignment." In *Prosody: Theory and Experiment*, ed. by Merle Horne, 11–36. Dordrecht: Kluwer Academic Publishers.

Pierrehumbert, Janet B., and Mary E. Beckman. 1988. *Japanese Tone Structure*. Cambridge: MIT Press.

Pierrehumbert, Janet B., and Julia Hirschberg. 1990. "The Meaning of Intonational Contours in the Interpretation of Discourse." In *Intentions in Communication*, ed. by Philip Cohen, Jerry Morgan, and Martha Pollack, 271–311. Cambridge, MA: MIT Press.

Pike, Kenneth L. 1945. *The Intonation of American English*. Ann Arbor: University of Michigan Press.

Piqueres Gilabert, Rosa María, and Matthew Fuss. 2018. "Attitudes Toward Morphosyntactic Variation in the Spanish of Valencian Speakers." In *Language Variation and Contact-Induced Change: Spanish Across Space and Time*, ed. by Jeremy King and Sandro Sessarego, Amsterdam: Benjamins.

Pla Boix, Anna M. 2005. "L'ordenació de la qüestió lingüística a Catalunya de 1892 a 1936: El procés de reconeixement de l'estatut d'oficialitat del català." *Revista de Llengua i Dret* 43: 179–211.

Poch Olivé, Dolors. 2016. "El 'acento catalán': Particularidades fonéticas del español de Cataluña." In *El español en contacto con otras lenguas peninsulares*, ed. by Dolors Poch Olivé, 315–340. Frankfurt: Vervuert.

Poch Olivé, Dolors, and Bernard Harmegnies. 1994. "Dinámica de los sistemas vocálicos y bilingüismo." *Contextos* 12 (23–24): 7–39.

Pompino-Marschall, Bernd. 2003. *Einführung in die Phonetik*. Berlin: De Gruyter.

Pons Bordería, Salvador. 2021. *Corpus Val.Es.Co 2.1*. http://www.valesco.es/.

Pons, Eva. 2013. "The Effects of Constitutional Court Ruling 31/2010 Dated 20 June 2010 on the Linguistic Regime of the Statute of Catalonia." *Catalan Social Sciences Review* 3: 67-92.

Pons, Eva. 2020. "Language Law and Language Policies." In *Manual of Catalan Linguistics*, ed. by Joan A. Argenter and Jens Lüdtke, 648–668. Berlin: De Gruyter.

Portes, Cristel, and Claire Beyssade. 2015. "Is Intonational Meaning Compositional?" *Verbum* 37 (2): 207–233.

Pradilla Cardona, Miquel Àngel. 2016. "El model lingüístic educatiu a Catalunya: Crònica glotopolítica d'una involució." *Estudis Romànics* 38: 295–310.

Prats, Modest, August Rafanell, and Albert Rossich. 1990. *El futur de la llengua catalana*. Barcelona: Empúries.

PRESEEA. 2014– . *Corpus del Proyecto para el Estudio Sociolingüístico del Español de España y de América*. Alcalá de Henares: Universidad de Alcalá. http://preseea.linguas.net.

Prieto, Pilar. 1997. "Prosodic Manifestation of Syntactic Structure in Catalan." In *Issues in the Phonology of the Iberian Languages*, ed. by Fernando Martínez-Gil and Alfonso Morales-Front, 179–199. Washington D.C.: Georgetown University Press.

Prieto, Pilar. 2001. "L'entonació dialectal del català: El cas de les frases interrogatives absolutes." In *Actes del Novè Col·loqui d'Estudis Catalans a Nord-Amèrica*, ed. by August Bover, Maria-Rosa Lloret, and Mercè Vidal-Tibbits, 347–377. Barcelona: Publicacions de l'Abadia de Montserrat.

Prieto, Pilar. 2002a. "Entonació." In *Gramàtica del català contemporani*, ed. by Joan Solà, Maria-Rosa Lloret, Joan Mascaró, and Manuel Pérez Saldanya, 395–462. Barcelona: Edicions 62.

Prieto, Pilar. 2002b. "Tune-Text Association Patterns in Catalan: An Argument for a Hierarchical Structure of Tunes." *Probus* 14: 173–204.

Prieto, Pilar. 2003. "Teorías lingüísticas de la entonación." In *Teorías de la entonación*, ed. by Pilar Prieto, 13–33. Barcelona: Ariel.

Prieto, Pilar. 2005a. "Stability Effects in Tonal Clash Contexts in Catalan." *Journal of Phonetics* 33 (2): 215–242.

Prieto, Pilar. 2005b. "Syntactic and Eurhythmic Constraints on Phrasing Decisions in Catalan." *Studia Linguistica* 59 (2/3): 194–222.

Prieto, Pilar. 2006a. "The Relevance of Metrical Information in Early Prosodic Word Acquisition: A Comparison of Catalan and Spanish." *Language and Speech* 49 (2): 231–259.

Prieto, Pilar. 2006b. "Phonological Phrasing in Spanish." In *Optimality-Theoretic Studies in Spanish Phonology*, ed. by Sonia Colina and Fernando Martínez-Gil, 39–60. Amsterdam: Benjamins.

Prieto, Pilar. 2009. "Tonal Alignment Patterns in Catalan Nuclear Falls." *Lingua* 119: 865–880.

Prieto, Pilar. 2011. "Efectes mètrics sobre l'agrupació prosòdica. El Cas de la resolució de xocs accentuals en català." In *Miscel·lània dedicada a Max Wheeler*, ed. by Maria-Rosa Lloret and Clàudia Pons, Alacant: Institut Interuniversitari de Filologia Valenciana.

Prieto, Pilar. 2013. "Català central." In *L'entonació dels dialectes catalans*, ed. by Pilar Prieto and Teresa Cabré, 15–44. Barcelona: Publicacions de l'Abadia de Montserrat.

Prieto, Pilar. 2014. "The Intonational Phonology of Catalan." In *Prosodic Typology II: The Phonology of Intonation and Phrasing*, ed. by Sun-Ah Jun, 43–80. Oxford: Oxford University Press.

Prieto, Pilar. 2015. "Intonational Meaning." *WIREs Cognitive Science* 6: 371–381.

Prieto, Pilar, Lourdes Aguilar Cuevas, Ignasi Mascaró Pons, Francesc Torres-Tamarit, and Maria del Mar Vanrell. 2009. "L'etiquetatge porosòdic Cat_ToBI en català." *Estudios de Fonética Experimental* 18: 287–389.

Prieto, Pilar, and Joan Borràs-Comes. 2018. "Question Intonation Contours as Dynamic Epistemic Operators." *Natural Language & Linguistic Theory* 36: 563–586.

Prieto, Pilar, Joan Borràs-Comes, Teresa Cabré, Verònica Crespo-Sendra, Ignasi Mascaró, Paolo Roseano, Rafèu Sichel-Bazin, and Maria del Mar Vanrell. 2015. "Intonational Phonology of Catalan and Its Dialectal Variation." In *Intonation in Romance*, ed. by Sónia Frota and Pilar Prieto, 9–62. Oxford: Oxford University Press.

Prieto, Pilar, and Teresa Cabré, coords. 2007–2012. *Atles interactiu de l'entonació del català*. http://prosodia.upf.edu/atlesentonacio/.

Prieto, Pilar, and Teresa Cabré (eds). 2013. *L'entonació dels dialectes catalans*. Barcelona: Publicacions de l'Abadia de Montserrat.

Prieto, Pilar, Mariapaola D'Imperio, and Barbara Gili-Fivela. 2006. "Pitch Accent Alignment in Romance: Primary and Secondary Associations with Metrical Structure." *Language and Speech* 48 (4): 359–396.

Prieto, Pilar, Eva Estebas-Vilaplana, and Maria del Mar Vanrell. 2010. "The Relevance of Prosodic Structure in Tonal Articulation: Edge Effects at the Prosodic Word Level in Catalan and Spanish." *Journal of Phonetics* 38: 687–705.

Prieto, Pilar, Salvador Oliva, Blanca Palmada, Pep Serra, Beatriz Blecua, Sílvia Llach, and Victòria Oliva. 2001. "Manifestació acústica de la resolució de xocs accentuals en català." *Estudios de Fonética Experimental* 11: 11–38.

Prieto, Pilar, and Gemma Rigau. 2007. "The Syntax-Prosody Interface: Catalan Interrogative Sentences Headed by *que*." *Journal of Portuguese Linguistics* 6 (2): 29–59.

Prieto, Pilar, and Gemma Rigau. 2011. "Prosody and Pragmatics." In *The Pragmatics of Catalan*, ed. by Lluís Payrató and Josep M. Cots, 17–48. Berlin: De Gruyter.

Prieto, Pilar, and Paolo Roseano. 2018. "Prosody: Stress, Rhythm, and Intonation." In *The Cambridge Handbook of Spanish Linguistics*, ed. by Kimberly L. Geeslin, 211–236. Cambridge: Cambridge University Press.

Prieto, Pilar, and Paolo Roseano, coords. 2009–2013. *Atlas Interactivo de la entonación del español*. http://prosodia.upf.edu/atlasentonacion/.

Prieto, Pilar, and Paolo Roseano (eds). 2010. *Transcription of Intonation of the Spanish Language*. München: Lincom.

Pujolar, Joan. 2008. "Els joves, les llengües i les identitats." *Noves SL*. http://www.gencat.cat/llengua/noves/noves/hemeroteca/hivern08.htm.

Pujolar, Joan. 2010. "Immigration and Language Education in Catalonia: Between National and Social Agendas." *Linguistics and Education* 21: 229–243.

Pujolar, Joan. 2011. "Catalan-Spanish Language Contact in Social Interaction." In *The Pragmatics of Catalan*, ed. by Lluís Payrató and Josep Maria Cots, 361–286. Berlin: De Gruyter.

Pujolar, Joan. 2020. "Migration in Catalonia: Language and Diversity in the Global Era." In *Manual of Catalan Linguistics*, ed. by Joan A. Argenter and Jens Lüdtke, 723–737. Berlin: De Gruyter.

Pujolar, Joan, and Isaac Gonzàlez. 2013. "Linguistic 'Mudes' and the De-Ethnicization of Language Choice in Catalonia." *International Journal of Bilingual Education and Bilingualism* 16 (2): 138–152.

Pustka, Elisa. 2021. "Loanword Phonology in Romance." In *Manual of Romance Phonetics and Phonology*, ed. by Christoph Gabriel, Randall Gess, and Trudel Meisenburg, 503–527. Berlin: De Gruyter.

Queen, Robin M. 2001. "Bilingual Intonation Patterns: Evidence of Language Change from Turkish-German Bilingual Children." *Language in Society* 30: 55–80.

Quilis, Antonio. 1993. *Tratado de fonología y fonética españolas*. Madrid: Gredos.

Quilis, Antonio. 1981. "Las unidades de entonación." *Revista Española Lingüística* 5: 261–279.

R Core Team. 2020. *R: A Language and Environment for Statistical Computing*. Vienna: Foundation for Statistical Computing. https://www.R-project.org/.

Radatz, Hans-Ingo. 2008. "Castellorquín: El castellano hablado por los mallorquines." In *El castellano en tierras de habla catalana*, ed. by Carsten Sinner and Andreas Wesch, 113–132. Frankfurt: Vervuert.

Rafanell, August. 2020. "From Pompeu Fabra to the Present Day: Language Change, Hindrance to Corpus and Status Planning." In *Manual of Catalan Linguistics*, ed. by Joan A. Argenter and Jens Lüdtke, 545–560. Berlin: De Gruyter.

Ramallo, Fernando. 2018. "Linguistic Diversity in Spain." In *Manual of Romance Sociolinguistics*, ed. by Wendy Ayres-Bennett and Janice Carruthers, 462–493. Berlin: De Gruyter.

Ramírez Verdugo, María Dolores. 2005. "Aproximación a la prosodia del habla de Madrid." *Estudios de Fonética Experimental* 14: 309–326.

Ramírez, Marta, and Miquel Simonet. 2017. "Language Dominance and the Perception of the Majorcan Catalan /ʎ/–/ʒ/ Contrast. Asymmetrical Phonological Representations." *International Journal of Bilingualism* 22: 638–652.

Ramus, Franck. 2002. "Language Discrimination by Newborns: Teasing Apart Phonotactic, Rhythmic, and Intonational Cues." *Annual Review of Language Acquisition* 2: 85–115.

Rao, Rajiv. 2007. "Phonological Phrasing in Barcelona Spanish." In *Proceedings of the 34th Western Conference on Linguistics (WECOL)*, ed. by Erin Bainbridge and Brian Agbayani, 345–360. Fresno, CA: California State University, Fresno, Department of Linguistics.

Rao, Rajiv. 2008a. "Observations on the Roles of Prosody and Syntax in the Phonological Phrasing of Barcelona Spanish." *The Linguistics Journal* 3 (3): 85–131.

Rao, Rajiv. 2008b. "Effects on Deaccenting in Two Speech Styles of Barcelona Spanish." In *Proceedings of the 35th Western Conference on Linguistics (WECOL)*, ed. by Rebecca Colavin, Kathryn Cooke, Kathryn Davidson, Shin Fukuda, and Alex Del Guidice, 202–216. San Diego, CA: University of California, San Diego, Linguistics Department.

Rao, Rajiv. 2009. "Deaccenting in Spontaneous Speech in Barcelona Spanish." *Studies in Hispanic and Lusophone Linguistics* 2: 31–75.

Rasier, Laurent, and Phillippe Hiligsmann. 2007. "Prosodic Transfer from L1 to L2: Theoretical and Methodological Issues." *Nouveaux Cahiers de Linguistique Française* 28: 41–66.

Recasens, Daniel. 2014. *Fonètica i fonologia experimentals del català: Vocals i consonants*. Barcelona: Institut d'Estudis Catalans.

Recasens, Daniel, and Aina Espinosa. 2005. "Articulatory, Positional and Coarticulatory Characteristics for Clear /l/ and Dark /l/: Evidence from Two Catalan Dialects." *Journal of the International Phonetic Association* 35 (1): 1–25.

Rigau, Gemma, and Manuel Pérez Saldanya. 2020. "The Simple Sentence." In *Manual of Catalan Linguistics*, ed. by Joan A. Argenter and Jens Lüdtke, 165–210. Berlin: De Gruyter.

Robles-Puente, Sergio. 2011a. "Absolute Questions Do Not Always Have a Rising Pattern: Evidence from Bilbao Spanish." In *Selected Proceedings of the 5th Conference on Laboratory Approaches to Romance Phonology*, ed. by Scott M. Alvord, 98–107. Somerville, MA: Cascadilla Proceedings Project.

Robles-Puente, Sergio. 2011b. "Looking for the Spanish Imperative Intonation: Combination of Global and Pitch-Accent Level Strategies." In *Selected Proceedings of the 5th Conference on Laboratory Approaches to Romance Phonology*, ed. by Scott M. Alvord, 153–164. Somerville, MA: Cascadilla Proceedings Project.

Robles-Puente, Sergio. 2012. "Two Languages, Two Intonations? Statements and Yes/No Questions in Spanish and Basque." *International Journal of Basque Linguistics and Philology* 46 (1): 252–262.

Robles-Puente, Sergio. 2014. Prosody in Contact: Spanish in Los Angeles. PhD dissertation, University of Southern California.
Romaine, Suzanne. 1989. *Bilingualism*. Oxford: Blackwell.
Romano, Antonio, Jean Pierre Lai, and Stefania Roullet. 2005. "La méthodologie AMPER." *Géolinguistique* 3, special issue: Projet AMPER, Grenoble: Université Stendhal Grenoble 3, Centre de Dialectologie, 1–5.
Romera Barrios, Lourdes. 2014. "La entonación de frases espontáneas en hablantes de castellano de Barcelona: Una primera aproximación." In *Fonética experimental, educación superior e investigación*. Vol. 3, ed. by Yolanda Congosto, María Luisa Montero Curiel, and Antonio Salvador, 341–358. Madrid: Arco Libros.
Romera Barrios, Lourdes, Wendy Elvira-García, Ana María Fernández Planas, Paolo Roseano, Josefina Carrera-Sabaté, and Eugenio Martínez Celdrán. 2015. "Habla no formal en zonas bilingües catalán-castellano." In *Estudos em variação geoprosódica*, coords. by Lurdes de Castro Moutinho, Rosa Lídia Coimbra, and Elisa Fernández Rei, 91–110. Aveiro: Universidad de Aveiro.
Romera Barrios, Lourdes, Ana María Fernández Planas, Valeria Salcioli Guidi, Josefina Carrera Sabaté, and Domingo Román Montes de Oca. 2007. "Una muestra del español de Barcelona en el marco AMPER." *Estudios de Fonética Experimental* 16: 147–184.
Romera Barrios, Lourdes, Ana María Fernández Planas, and Valeria Salcioli Guidi. 2009. "Análisis perceptivo de la entonación del castellano de Barcelona y del catalán de Barcelona." *Estudios de Fonética Experimental* 18: 345–366.
Romera Barrios, Lourdes, Valeria Salcioli Guidi, Ana María Fernández Planas, Josefina Carrera Sabaté, and Domingo Román Montes de Oca. 2008. "Prosody of Simple Sentences in the Spanish of Barcelona: A Spanish-Catalan Bilingual Context." In *Selected Proceedings of the 3rd Conference on Laboratory Approaches on Spanish Phonology*, ed. by Laura Colantoni and Jeffrey Steele, 167–181. Somerville, MA: Cascadilla.
Romera, Magdalena. 2003. "La variedad del castellano actual en Baleares." *Moenia* 9: 359–381.
Romera, Magdalena, and Gorka Elordieta. 2013. "Prosodic Accommodation in Language Contact: Spanish Intonation in Majorca." *International Journal of the Sociology of Language* 221: 127–151.
Romera, Magdalena, and Gorka Elordieta. 2020. "Information-Seeking Question Intonation in Basque Spanish and Its Correlation with Degree of Contact and Language Attitudes." *Languages* 50 (4), article 70: 1–21.
Ronjat, Jules. 1913. *Le développement du langage observé chez un enfant bilingue*. Paris: Champion.
Roseano, Paolo, Ana María Fernández Planas, Wendy Elvira-García, and Eugenio Martínez Celdrán. 2015. "Contacto lingüístico y transferencia prosódica bajo una perspectiva diacrónica: El caso del Alguerés." *Dialectologia et Geolinguistica* 23 (1): 95–123.
Roseano, Paolo, Ana María Fernández Planas, Wendy Elvira-García, Ramon Cerdà Massó, and Eugenio Martínez Celdrán. 2016a. "Caracterització acústica dels accents prenuclears de les interrogatives absolutes i les declaratives neutres en català central." *Estudios de Fonética Experimental* 25: 11–38.

Roseano, Paolo, Ana María Fernández Planas, Wendy Elvira-García, Ramon Cerdà Massó, and Eugenio Martínez Celdrán. 2016b. "La entonación de las preguntas parciales en catalán." *Revista Española de Lingüística Aplicada/Spanish Journal of Applied Linguistics* 28 (2): 511–554.

Roseano, Paolo, Ignasi Mascaró, Wendy Elvira-García, and Ana María Fernández Planas. 2019. "La dimensión rural-urbana en un cambio lingüístico en curso en la entonación del catalán de Menorca." *Dialectologia* 23: 173–192.

Ross, John A. 2006. "The Reliability, Validity, and Utility of Self-Assessment." *Practical Assessment* 11, article 10: 1–13.

Ross, Malcolm D. 2001. "Contact-Induced Change in Oceanic Languages in North-West Melanesia." In *Areal Diffusion and Genetic Inheritance*, ed. by Alexandra Y. Aikhenvald and Robert M. W. Dixon, 134–166. Oxford: Oxford University Press.

Rost Bagudanch, Assumpció. 2016. "La percepción de /ʎ/ y de /j/ en catalán y en español: Implicaciones en la explicación del yeísmo." *Estudios de Fonética Experimental* 25: 39–80.

Rost Bagudanch, Assumpció. 2017. "Variation and Phonological Change: The Case of Yeísmo in Spanish." *Folia Linguistica* 51: 169–206.

Rost Bagudanch, Assumpció. 2019. "Yeísmo in Majorcan Spanish: Phonetic Variation in a Bilingual Context." *Zeitschrift für Romanische Philologie* 135: 426–441.

Rost Bagudanch, Assumpció. 2020. "Bilingualism and Sound Change: Perception in the /ʎ/-/j/ Merger Process in Majorcan Spanish." *Zeitschrift für Romanische Philologie* 136: 106–133.

Rost Bagudanch, Assumpció, and Beatriz Blecua Falgueras. 2017. "Variación fonética en el español de Mallorca: El yeísmo en hablantes bilingües." In *Tendencias actuales en fonética experimental. Cruce de disciplinas en el centenario del "Manual de pronunciación española" (Tomás Navarro Tomás)*, coords. by Victoria Marrero Aguiar and Eva Estebas Vilaplana, 183–186. Madrid: Universidad Nacional de Educación a Distancia.

Royo, Jesús. 1991. *Una llengua és un mercat*. Barcelona: Edicions 62.

Ruiz Martínez, Ana María. 2004. "Norma y usos en el español de los medios de comunicación social: El caso concreto de la radio española." In *Medios de comunicación y enseñanza del español como lengua extranjera. Actas del XIV Congreso Internacional de ASELE*, ed. by Hermógenes Perdiguero and Antonio Álvarez, 996–1003. Burgos: Universidad de Burgos.

Sancho Cremades, Pelegrí. 2002. "La preposició i el sintagma preposicional." In *Gramàtica del català contemporani*, ed. by Joan Solà, Maria-Rosa Lloret, Joan Mascaró, and Manuel Pérez Saldanya, 1689–1796. Barcelona: Empúries.

Santiago, Fabián, and Elisabeth Delais-Roussarie. 2012. "Acquiring Phrasing and Intonation in French as Second Language: The Case of Yes-No Questions Produced by Mexican Spanish Learners." In *Proceedings of Speech Prosody 2012*, ed. by Qiuwu Ma, Hongwei Ding, and Daniel Hirst, 338–341. Shanghai: Tongji University Press.

Santiago, Fabián, and Elisabeth Delais-Roussarie. 2015. "The Acquisition of Question Intonation by Mexican Spanish Learners of French." In *Prosody and Languages in Contact: L2 Acquisition, Attrition, Languages in Multilingual Situations*, ed. by Elisabeth Delais-Roussarie, Mathieu Avanzi, and Sophie Herment, 243–270. Berlin: Springer.

Schmeißer, Anika, Malin Hager, Laia Arnaus Gil, Veronika Jansen, Jasmin Geveler, Nadine Eichler, Marisa Patuto, and Natascha Müller. 2016. "Related but Different: The Two Concepts of Language Dominance and Language Proficiency." In *Language Dominance in Bilinguals: Issues of Measurement and Operationalization*, ed. by Carmen Silva-Corvalán and Jeanine Treffers-Daller, 36–65. Cambridge: Cambridge University Press.

Schmid, Monika S. 2011. *Language Attrition*. Cambridge: Cambridge University Press.

Schmid, Monika S., and Barbara Köpke. 2007. "Bilingualism and Attrition." In *Language Attrition: Theoretical Perspectives*, ed. by Barbara Köpke, Monika S. Schmid, Merel Keijzer, and Susan Dostert, 1–8. Amsterdam: Benjamins.

Schneider, Wolfgang, Matthias Schlagmüller, and Marco Ennemoser. 2017. *LGVT 5–12+. Lesegeschwindigkeits- und Verständnistest für die Klassen 5–12+*. Göttingen: Hogrefe.

Schuchardt, Hugo. 1884. *Slawo-deutsches und Slawo-italienisches*. Graz: Leuschner & Lubensky.

Schulte, Kim. 2018. "Romance in Contact with Romance." In *Manual of Romance Sociolinguistics*, ed. by Wendy Ayres-Bennett and Janice Carruthers, 595–626. Berlin: De Gruyter.

Schwartz, Ana María. 2005. "Exploring Differences and Similarities in the Writing Strategies Used by Students in SNS Courses." In *Contactos y contextos: El español en los estados unidos y en contacto con otras lenguas*, ed. by Luis A. Ortiz López and Manel Lacorte. Madrid/Frankfurt: Iberoamericana/Vervuert.

Selinker, Larry. 1972. "Interlanguage." *International Review of Applied Linguistics in Language Teaching* 10 (3): 209–231.

Selkirk, Elisabeth. 1986. "On Derived Domains in Sentence Phonology." *Phonology Yearbook* 3: 371–405.

Serrano Vázquez, María del Carmen. 1996. "Interferencias léxicas y semánticas en una situación de contacto entre dos lenguas, catalán y castellano." *Diálogos Hispánicos* 18: 375–394.

Sharwood Smith, Michael, and Eric Kellerman. 1986. "Crosslinguistic Influence in Second Language Acquisition: An Introduction." In *Crosslinguistic Influence in Second Language Acquisition*, ed. by Michael Sharwood Smith and Eric Kellerman, 1–9. New York: Pergamon Press.

Sichel-Bazin, Rafèu, Caroline Buthke, and Trudel Meisenburg. 2012a. "Language Contact and Prosodic Interference: Nuclear Configurations in Occitan and French Statements of the Obvious." In *Proceedings of Speech Prosody 2012*, ed. by Qiuwu Ma, Hongwei Ding, and Daniel Hirst, 414–417. Shanghai: Tongji University Press.

Sichel-Bazin, Rafèu, Caroline Buthke, and Trudel Meisenburg. 2012b. "The Prosody of Occitan-French Bilinguals." In *Multilingual Individuals and Multilingual Societies (Hamburg Studies on Multilingualism 13)*, ed. by Kurt Braunmüller and Christoph Gabriel, 349–364. Amsterdam: Benjamins.

Sichel-Bazin, Rafèu, Caroline Buthke, and Trudel Meisenburg. 2015. "Prosody in Language Contact: Occitan and French." In *Prosody and Languages in Contact: L2 Acquisition, Attrition, Languages in Multilingual Situations*, ed. by Elisabeth Delais-Roussarie, Mathieu Avanzi, and Sophie Herment, 71–99. Berlin: Springer.

Sichel-Bazin, Rafèu, and Paolo Roseano. 2013. "Català septentrional." In *L'entonació dels dialectes catalans*, ed. by Pilar Prieto and Teresa Cabré, 127–152. Barcelona: Publicacions de l'Abadia de Montserrat.

Silva-Corvalán, Carmen. 2014. *Bilingual Language Acquisition: Spanish and English in the First Six Years*. Cambridge: Cambridge University Press.

Silva-Corvalán, Carmen, and Jeanine Treffers-Daller. 2016. "Digging into Dominance: A Closer Look at Language Dominance in Bilinguals." In *Language Dominance in Bilinguals: Issues of Measurement and Operationalization*, ed. by Carmen Silva-Corvalán and Jeanine Treffers-Daller, 1–14. Cambridge: Cambridge University Press.

Silverman, Wendy K., Wayne Fleisig, Brian Rabian, and Rolf A. Peterson. 1991. "Childhood Anxiety Sensitivity Index." *Journal of Clinical Child Psychology* 20 (2): 162–68.

Silverman, Kim, Mary E. Beckman, John Pitrelli, Mari Ostendorf, Colin Wightman, Patti Price, Janet Pierrehumbert, and Julia Hirschberg. 1992. "TOBI: A Standard for Labeling English Prosody." In *Proceedings from the 2nd International Conference on Spoken Language Processing (ICSLP 1992)*, 867–870. Edmonton: University of Alberta.

Simonet, Miguel. 2008. Language Contact in Majorca: An Experimental Sociophonetic Approach. PhD dissertation, University of Illinois at Urbana-Champaign.

Simonet, Miquel. 2010. "A Contrastive Study of Catalan and Spanish Declarative Intonation: Focus on Majorcan Dialects." *Probus* 22: 117–148.

Simonet, Miquel. 2011. "Intonational Convergence in Language Contact: Utterance-Final F0 Contours in Catalan–Spanish Early Bilinguals." *Journal of the International Phonetic Association* 41 (2): 157–184.

Simonet, Miquel. 2015. "An Acoustic Study of Coarticulatory Resistance in 'Dark' and 'Light' Alveolar Laterals." *Journal of Phonetics* 52: 138–151.

Sinner, Carsten. 1996. *Phonetisch-phonologische, morphosyntaktische und lexikalische Besonderheiten der Varietät des Kastilischen in Katalonien: Interferenz, Frequenz und Akzeptabilität*. Diploma thesis, Berlin: Humboldt-Universität.

Sinner, Carsten. 2001. *Corpus oral de profesionales de la lengua castellana en Barcelona*. http://www.carstensinner.de/castellano/corpusorales/index.html.

Sinner, Carsten. 2004. *El castellano de Cataluña: Estudio empírico de aspectos léxicos, morfosintácticos, pragmáticos y metalingüísticos*. Tübingen: Niemeyer.

Sinner, Carsten. 2008. "La conjugación de los verbos irregulares, entre prejuicio y análisis lingüístico." In *El castellano en tierras de habla catalana*, ed. by Carsten Sinner and Andreas Wesch, Frankfurt: Vervuert.

Sinner, Carsten, and Andreas Wesch. 2008. "El castellano en las tierras de habla catalana: Estado de la cuestión." In *El castellano en tierras de habla catalana*, ed. by Carsten Sinner and Andreas Wesch, 11–55. Frankfurt: Vervuert.

Sinner, Carsten, and Katharina Wieland. 2008. "El catalán hablado y problemas de la normalización de la lengua catalana: Avances y obstáculos en la normalización." In *Lengua, nación e identidad. La regulación del plurilingüismo en España y América latina*, ed. by Kirsten Süselbeck, Ulrike Mühlschlegel, and Peter Masson, 131–164. Frankfurt am Main/Madrid: Vervuert/Iberoamericana.

Solà, Joan. 1980. "Tractats de catalanismes." In *Miscel·lània Aramon i Serra: Estudis de llengua i literatura catalanes oferts a Ramon Aramon i Serra en el seu setantè aniversari*. Vol. 2, ed. by Emilio Alarcos Llorach et al., 559–582. Barcelona: Curial.

Sosa, Juan Manuel. 1991. Fonética y fonología de la entonación del español hispanoamericano. PhD dissertation, University of Massachusetts.

Sosa, Juan Manuel. 1999. *La entonación del español*. Madrid: Cátedra.

Sosa, Juan Manuel. 2003a. "La notación tonal del español en el modelo Sp_ToBI." In *Teorías de la entonación*, ed. by Pilar Prieto, 185–208. Barcelona: Ariel.

Sosa, Juan Manuel. 2003b. "Wh-Questions in Spanish: Meanings and Configuration Variability." *Catalan Journal of Linguistics* 2: 229–247.

Springer, Jane A., Jeffrey R. Binder, Thomas A. Hammeke, Sara J. Swanson, Julie A. Frost, Patrick S. Bellgowan, Cameron C. Brewer, Holly M. Perry, George L. Morris, and Wade M. Mueller. 1999. "Language Dominance in Neurologically Normal and Epilepsy Subjects: A Functional MRI Study." *Brain* 122 (11): 2033–2046.

Steedman, Mark. 2014. "The Surface-Compositional Semantics of English Intonation." *Language* 90 (1): 2–57.

Stockwell, Robert P. 1972. "The Role of Intonation: Reconsiderations and Other Considerations." In *Intonation: Selected Readings*, ed. by Dwight Bolinger, 87–109. Baltimore: Penguin Books.

Szigetvári, Mónika. 1994. Catalanismos en el español actual (Katalán elemek a mai spanyol nyelvben). Licenciate dissertation, Budapest: Eötvös Loránd Tudományegyetem.

Terken, Jacques, and Dik J. Hermes. 2000. "The Perception of Prosodic Prominence." In *Prosody: Theory and Experiment*, ed. by Merle Horne, 89–127. Dordrecht: Kluwer Academic Publishers.

't Hart, Johan, and René Collier. 1975. "Integrating Different Levels of Intonation Analysis." *Journal of Phonetics* 1: 309–327.

Thomason, Sarah Grey. 2001. *Language Contact: An Introduction*. Edinburgh: Edinburgh University Press.

Thomason, Sarah Grey. 2007. "Language Contact and Deliberate Change." *Journal of Language Contact* 1: 41–62.

Thomason, Sarah Grey. 2013. "Contact Explanations in Linguistics." In *The Handbook of Language Contact*, ed. by Raymond Hickey, 31–47. West Sussex: Wiley-Blackwell.

Thomason, Sarah Grey, and Terrence Kaufman. 1988. *Language Contact, Creolization, and Genetic Linguistics*. Berkeley: University of California Press.

Tomás Faci, Guillermo. 2020. *El aragonés medieval: Lengua y estado en el Reino de Aragón*. Zaragoza: PUZ.

Torreira, Francisco, and Simeon Floyd. 2012. "Intonational Meaning in Spanish Conversation: Low-Rising vs. Circumflex Questions." Poster presented at 5th European Conference on Tone and Intonation (TIE 5), Oxford, 6–8 September 2012.

Torreira, Francisco, and Martine Grice. 2018. "Melodic Constructions in Spanish: Metrical Structure Determines the Association Properties of Intonational Tones." *Journal of the International Phonetic Association* 48 (1): 9–32.

Torreira, Francisco, Miquel Simonet, and José Ignacio Hualde. 2014. "Quasi-Neutralization of Stress Contrasts in Spanish." In *Proceedings of Speech Prosody 2014*, ed. by Nick Campbell, Dafydd Gibbon, and Daniel Hirst, 728–732. Dublin: Trinity College.

Torres, Antonio, Ana María Fernández Planas, Esther Blasco, Mar Forment, María Ángeles Pérez, and Cristina Illamola. 2013. "Estudio del yeísmo en el español de Barcelona a partir de materiales de PRESEEA." In *Variación yeísta en el mundo hispano*, ed. by Isabel Molina Martos and Rosario Gómez, 19–37. Madrid/Frankfurt am Main: Iberoamericana/Vervuert.

Trager, George L., and Henry L. Smith Jr. (1975) [1951]. *An Outline of English Structure*. Washington: American Council of Learned Societies.

Treffers-Daller, Jeanine. 2011. "Operationalizing and Measuring Language Dominance." *International Journal of Bilingualism* 15: 147–163.

Treffers-Daller, Jeanine. 2016. "Language Dominance: The Construct, Its Measurement, and Operationalization." In *Language Dominance in Bilinguals: Issues of Measurement and Operationalization*, ed. by Carmen Silva-Corvalán and Jeanine Treffers-Daller, 235–265. Cambridge: Cambridge University Press.

Treffers-Daller, Jeanine, and Tomasz Korybski. 2016. "Using Lexical Diversity Measures to Operationalize Language Dominance in Bilinguals." In *Language Dominance in Bilinguals: Issues of Measurement and Operationalization*, ed. by Carmen Silva-Corvalán and Jeanine Treffers-Daller, 106–133. Cambridge: Cambridge University Press.

Tremblay, Annie. 2011. "Proficiency Assessment Standards in Second Language Acquisition Research: 'Closing' the Gap." *Studies in Second Language Acquisition* 33: 339–372.

Trouvain, Jürgen, and Ulrike Gut (eds). 2007. *Non-Native Prosody: Phonetic Description and Teaching Practice*. Berlin: De Gruyter.

Truckenbrodt, Hubert. 2007. "The Syntax-Phonology Interface." In *The Cambridge Handbook of Phonology*, ed. by Paul De Lacy, 435–456. Cambridge: Cambridge University Press.

Truckenbrodt, Hubert. 2012. "Semantics of Intonation." In *Semantics: An International Handbook of Natural Language Meaning*. Vol. 3, ed. by Claudia Maienborn, Klaus von Heusinger, and Paul Portner, 2039–2969. Berlin: De Gruyter.

Ulldemolins-Subirats, Amanda. 2018. "«Lo color vermell serà lo roig». Ús dels geosinònims en la població escolar d'Alcanar." *Beceroles: Lletres de Llengua i Literatura* 7: 109–121.

Ulldemolins-Subirats, Amanda. 2019. "Integració dels dialectes occidentals a l'estàndard formal televisiu." *Llengua & Literatura* 29: 7–30.

Vallduví, Enric. 2002. "L'oració com a unitat informativa." In *Gramàtica del català contemporani*, ed. by Joan Solà, Maria-Rosa Lloret, Joan Mascaró, and Manuel Pérez Saldanya, 1221–1279. Barcelona: Empúries.

Vallverdú, Francesc. 1979. *Dues llengües, dues funcions? La història contemporània de Catalunya, des d'un punt de vista sociolingüístic*. Barcelona: Laia.

Van Coetsem, Frans. 1988. *Loan Phonology and the Two Transfer Types in Language Contact*. Dordrecht: Foris.

Van Coetsem, Frans. 2000. *A General and Unified Theory of the Transmission Process in Language Contact*. Heidelberg: Winter.

Van der Hulst, Harry, Rob Goedemans, and Keren Rice. 2015. "Word Prominence and Areal Linguistics." In *The Cambridge Handbook of Areal Linguistics*, ed. by Raymond Hickey, 161–203. Cambridge: Cambridge University Press.

Van Oosterzee, Carlos. 2005. "La percepció de l'entonació declarativa i interrogativa per part de parlants bilingües castellà-català i monolingües castellà de Barcelona." *Estudios de Fonética Experimental* 14: 295–307.

Van Rijswijk, Remy, and Antje Muntendam. 2014. "The Prosody of Focus in the Spanish of Quechua-Spanish Bilinguals: A Case Study of Noun Phrases." *International Journal of Bilingualism* 8 (6): 614–632.

Vann, Robert E. 1997. "Constructing Catalanism: Motion Verbs, Demonstratives, and Locatives in the Spanish of Barcelona." *Catalan Review* 9 (2): 253–274.

Vann, Robert E. 1998. "Pragmatic Transfer from Less Developed to More Developed Systems: Spanish Deictic Terms in Barcelona." In *Romance Linguistics: Theoretical Perspectives*, ed. by Armin Schwegler, Bernard Tranel, and Myriam Uribe-Etxebarria, 307–317. Amsterdam: Benjamins.

Vann, Robert E. 2002. "Linguistic Ideology in Spain's Ivory Tower: (Not) Analyzing Catalan Spanish." *Multilingua* 21 (2/3): 227–246.

Vanrell, Maria del Mar. 2007. "A Tonal Scaling Contrast in Majorcan Catalan Interrogatives." *Journal of Portuguese Linguistics* 6: 147–178.

Vanrell, Maria del Mar. 2011. The Phonological Relevance of Tonal Scaling in the Intonational Grammar of Catalan. PhD dissertation, Universitat Autònoma de Barcelona.

Vanrell, Maria del Mar. 2013. "Pitch Accent Types and the Perception of Focus in Majorcan Catalan Wh-Questions." In *Prosody and Iconicity (Iconicity in Language and Literature 13)*, ed. by Sylvie Hancil and Daniel Hirst, 127–148. Amsterdam: Benjamins.

Vanrell, Maria del Mar, Francesc Ballone, Teresa Cabré, Pilar Prieto, Carlo Schirru, and Francesc Torres-Tamarit. 2020. "Contacte lingüístic i entonació a Sardenya." In *Contact, Variation and Change: Studies in Honor of Trudel Meisenburg (Studienreihe Romania 35)*, ed. by Christoph Gabriel, Andrea Pešková, and Maria Selig, 219–242. Berlin: Erich Schmidt.

Vanrell, Maria del Mar, Ingo Feldhausen, and Lluïsa Astruc. 2018. "The Discourse Completion Task in Romance Prosody Research: Status Quo and Outlook." In *Methods in Prosody: A Romance Language Perspective*, ed. by Ingo Feldhausen, Jan Fliessbach, and Maria del Mar Vanrell, 191–227. Berlin: Language Science Press.

Vanrell, Maria del Mar, Ignasi Mascaró, Francesc Torres-Tamarit, and Pilar Prieto. 2013. "Intonation as an Encoder of Speaker Certainty: Information and Confirmation Yes-No Questions in Catalan." *Language and Speech* 56: 163–190.

Vanrell, Maria del Mar, Ignasi Mascaró, Pilar Prieto, and Francesc Torres-Tamarit. 2010. "Preguntar per saber i preguntar per confirmar: L'entonació de les interrogatives absolutes informatives i confirmatòries en català central i balear." *Randa* 64: 77–95.

Veny, Joan. 2001. *Llengua històrica i llengua estàndard*. València: Universitat de València.

Veny, Joan. 2006. *Contacte i contrast de llengües i dialectes*. València: Universitat de València.

Veny, Joan, and Mar Massanell. 2015. *Dialectologia catalana: Aproximació pràctica als parlars catalans*. Barcelona: Publicacions i Edicions de la Universitat de Barcelona.

Vigário, Marina, and Sónia Frota. 2003. "The Intonation of Standard and Northern European Portuguese: A Comparative Intonational Phonology Approach." *Journal of Portuguese Linguistics* 2 (2): 115–137.

Vila Pujol, M. Rosa. 2001. *Corpus del español conversacional de Barcelona y su área metropolitana*. Barcelona: Edicions Universitat de Barcelona.

Vila, F. Xavier. 2016. "¿Quién habla hoy en día el castellano en Cataluña? Una aproximación demolingüística." In *El español en contacto con otras lenguas peninsulares*, ed. by Dolors Poch Olivé, 135–156. Frankfurt: Vervuert.

Vila, F. Xavier. 2020a. "Language Demography." In *Manual of Catalan Linguistics*, ed. by Joan A. Argenter and Jens Lüdtke, 629–648. Berlin: De Gruyter.

Vila, F. Xavier. 2020b. "Teaching and Learning of Catalan." In *Manual of Catalan Linguistics*, ed. by Joan A. Argenter and Jens Lüdtke, 669–682. Berlin: De Gruyter.

Vila, F. Xavier, and Natxo Sorolla. 2019a. "Els usos lingüístics privats." In *Els usos lingüístics als territoris de llengua catalana*, ed. by Direcció General de Política Lingüística i Xarxa CRUSCAT-IEC, 64–74. Barcelona: Generalitat de Catalunya, Direcció General de Política Lingüística.

Vila, F. Xavier, and Natxo Sorolla. 2019b. "Els Usos lingüístics interpersonals en contextos institucionalitzats." In *Els usos lingüístics als territoris de llengua catalana*, ed. by Direcció General de Política Lingüística i Xarxa CRUSCAT-IEC, 75–93. Barcelona: Generalitat de Catalunya, Direcció General de Política Lingüística.

Villalba, Xavier. 2011. "A Quantitative Comparative Study of Right-Dislocation in Catalan and Spanish." *Journal of Pragmatics* 43 (7): 1946–1961.

Villena Ponsoda, Juan Andrés. 2005. "How Similar Are People Who Speak Alike? An Interpretive Way of Using Social Networks in Social Dialectology Research." In *Dialect Change: Convergence and Divergence in European Languages*, ed. by Peter Auer, Frans Hinskens, and Paul Kerswill, 303–334. Cambridge: Cambridge University Press.

Villena Ponsoda, Juan Andrés. 2008. "Divergencia dialectal en el español de Andalucía: el estándar regional y la nueva koiné meridional." In *Lengua en diálogo: El iberorromance y su diversidad lingüística y literaria. Ensayos en homenaje a Georg Bossong*, ed. by Hans-Jörg Döhla, Raquel Montero Muñoz, and Francisco Báez de Aguilar González, 369–392. Madrid/Frankfurt am Main: Iberoamericana/Vervuert.

Vizcaíno Ortega, Francisco, Mercedes Cabrera Abreu, Eva Estebas Vilaplana, and Lluïsa Astruc Aguilera. 2008. "The Phonological Representation of Edge Tones in Spanish Alternative Questions." *Language Design*, special issue 2: Experimental Prosody, 31–38.

Wang, Xin. 2013. "Language Dominance in Translation Priming: Evidence from Balanced and Unbalanced Chinese–English Bilinguals." *The Quarterly Journal of Experimental Psychology* 66: 727–743.

Wakefield, John C. 2020. *Intonational Morphology*. Singapore: Springer.

Weinreich, Uriel. (1953) [1968]. *Languages in Contact: Findings and Problems*. New York: Linguistic Circle of New York [The Hague: Mouton].

Wells, Rulon S. 1945. "The Pitch Phonemes of English." *Language* 21: 27–29.

Wesch, Andreas. 1992. "Grammatische und lexikalische Aspekte des Spanischen von Barcelona." *Iberoromania* 35: 1–14.

Wesch, Andreas. 1994. "Bereicherung und Nivellierung semantischer Strukturen durch Interferenzen am Beispiel Spanisch/Katalanisch." In *Mehrsprachigkeit in Europa – Hindernis oder Chance?*, ed. by Uta Helfrich and Claudia Maria Riehl, 165–178. Wilhelmsfeld: Egert.

Wesch, Andreas. 1997. "El castellano hablado de Barcelona y el influjo del catalán: Esbozo de un programa de investigación." *Verba* 24: 287–312.

Wesch, Andreas. 2002. "La investigación sobre variedades del español hablado en contacto con el catalán (particularmente en Cataluña y Baleares): Estado de la cuestión y perspectivas para el futuro." In *Actas del V Congreso Internacional de Historia de la Lengua Española*. Vol. 2, ed. by María Teresa Echenique Elizondo and Juan Sánchez Méndez, 1857–1872. Madrid: Gredos.

Wheeler, Max W. 2005. *The Phonology of Catalan*. Oxford: Oxford University Press.

White, Laurence, and Sven L. Mattys. 2007. "Calibrating Rhythm: First Language and Second Language Studies." *Journal of Phonetics* 35: 501–522.

Willis, Eric W. 2010. "Dominican Spanish Intonation." In *Transcription of Intonation of the Spanish Language*, ed. by Prieto Prieto and Paolo Roseano, 123–153. München: Lincom.

Winford, Donald. 2003. *An Introduction to Contact Linguistics*. Malden: Blackwell.

Woolard, Kathryn. 1989. *Doubletalk: Bilingualism and the Politics of Ethnicity in Catalonia*. Stanford: Stanford University Press.

Woolard, Kathryn A. 1987. "Codeswitching and Comedy in Catalonia." *IPRA Papers in Pragmatics* 1 (1): 106–122.

Woolard, Kathryn A. 1992. *Identitat i contacte de llengües a Barcelona*. Barcelona: La Magrana.

Woolard, Kathryn. 2009. "Linguistic Consciousness among Adolescents in Catalonia: A Case Study from the Barcelona Urban Area in Longitudinal Perspective." *Zeitschrift für Katalanistik* 22, 125–149.

Woolard, Kathryn A. 2013. "Is the Personal Political? Chronotopes and Changing Stances Toward Catalan Language and Identity." *International Journal of Bilingual Education and Bilingualism* 16: 210–224.

Xu, Yi. 2005. "Speech Melody as Articulatorily Implemented Communicative Functions." *Speech Communication* 46: 220–251.

Yip, Virginia, and Stephen Matthews. 2006. "Assessing Language Dominance in Bilingual Acquisition: A Case for Mean Length Utterance Differentials." *Language Assessment Quarterly* 3: 97–116.

Zamora Vicente, Alonso. 1960. *Dialectología española*. Madrid: Gredos.

Zeileis, Achim, David Meyer, and Kurt Hornik. 2007. "Residual-Based Shadings for Visualizing (Conditional) Independence." *Journal of Computational and Graphical Statistics* 16 (3): 507–525.

Appendix

APPENDIX 1

Participants' dominance scores and Complementarity Index

Participant ID	Dominance score A (subtraction-derived)	Dominance score B (ratio-derived)	Dominance score C (Edinburgh formula)	Complementarity index
23	−57.3	40	−43	100
20	−56.8	38	−45	86
34	−54.2	39	−43	100
16	−52.9	44	−39	86
19	−52.6	42	−41	100
14	−49.7	47	−36	86
25	−44.0	53	−31	86
29	−43.5	52	−31	71
17	−40.3	56	−28	100
11	−40.1	57	−27	100
15	−38.2	54	−29	57
28	−37.2	59	−26	86
26	−32.1	65	−21	100
12	−31.4	67	−20	100
18	−30.7	64	−22	86
6	−30.4	66	−20	100
31	−28.5	69	−18	71
22	−24.2	72	−16	100
24	−21.8	76	−14	43
10	−11.9	86	−8	86
35	1.7	98	1	57
5	18.4	79	12	71
7	19.5	75	14	86

Appendix 1. Participants' dominance scores and Complementarity Index

Participant ID	Dominance score A (subtraction-derived)	Dominance score B (ratio-derived)	Dominance score C (Edinburgh formula)	Complementarity index
30	19.6	77	13	57
33	24.1	71	17	71
21	26.1	71	17	71
13	28.7	68	19	43
4	33.7	64	22	86
27	34.3	63	23	71
8	36.6	61	24	71
9	37.8	54	30	71

APPENDIX 2

Language background questionnaire (Catalan version)

Perfil lingüístic català–castellà

Ens agradaria demanar-te ajuda per respondre les següents preguntes sobre el teu historial lingüístic, ús, actitud i competència. Aquesta enquesta conté 18 preguntes i et portarà menys de 10 minuts completar-la. No es tracta d'una prova, per tant, no hi ha respostes correctes ni incorrectes. Si us plau, contesta cada pregunta i respon amb sinceritat, ja que només així es podrà garantir l'èxit d'aquesta investigació. Moltes gràcies per la teva ajuda!

I. Informació biogràfica

Nom i cognoms _____
Any de naixement _____ Lloc de naixement _____
Resident a _____ des de _____
Temps passat fora de Catalunya _____
Nivell superior d'estudis _____
Professió _____
Correu electrònic _____
Llengües estrangeres _____

Lloc de naixement de la mare _____
Lloc de residència principal _____
Professió/estudis _____
Llengües maternes _____

Lloc de naixement del pare _____
Lloc de residència principal _____
Professió/estudis _____
Llengües maternes _____

Lloc de naixement de la parella _____
Lloc de residència principal _____
Professió/estudis _____
Llengües maternes _____

Appendix 2. Language background questionnaire (Catalan version)

Declaració de conformitat

Expresso que estic d'acord que l'enregistrament i la seva transcripció respectiva, així com les dades que he posat a disposició siguin arxivats, analitzats i publicats de manera anònima i sense ànims de lucre per fins científics.

Aquesta declaració pot ésser revocada enviant un correu a la següent direcció: jgruenke@uni-mainz.de.

(lloc, data) _____ (signatura) _____

II. Historial lingüístic

En aquesta secció, ens agradaria que contestessis algunes preguntes sobre el teu historial lingüístic marcant la casella corresponent.

1. A quina edat **vas començar a aprendre** les següents llengües?

Castellà

☐	☐ ☐ ☐ ☐ ☐ ☐ ☐ ☐ ☐ ☐ ☐ ☐ ☐ ☐ ☐ ☐ ☐ ☐ ☐ ☐
Des del naixement	1 2 3 4 5 6 7 8 9 10 11 12 13 14 15 16 17 18 19 20+

Català

☐	☐ ☐ ☐ ☐ ☐ ☐ ☐ ☐ ☐ ☐ ☐ ☐ ☐ ☐ ☐ ☐ ☐ ☐ ☐ ☐
Des del naixement	1 2 3 4 5 6 7 8 9 10 11 12 13 14 15 16 17 18 19 20+

2. A quina edat **vas començar a sentir-te còmode/a** emprant les següents llengües?

Castellà

☐	☐ ☐ ☐ ☐ ☐ ☐ ☐ ☐ ☐ ☐ ☐ ☐ ☐ ☐ ☐ ☐ ☐ ☐ ☐ ☐	
Des que recordo	1 2 3 4 5 6 7 8 9 10 11 12 13 14 15 16 17 18 19 20+	encara no

Català

☐	☐ ☐ ☐ ☐ ☐ ☐ ☐ ☐ ☐ ☐ ☐ ☐ ☐ ☐ ☐ ☐ ☐ ☐ ☐ ☐	
Des que recordo	1 2 3 4 5 6 7 8 9 10 11 12 13 14 15 16 17 18 19 20+	encara no

3. Quina llengua empràveu a la teva **família** quan eres petit(a)?

☐ castellà ☐ català

III. Ús de llengües

En aquesta secció, ens agradaria que contestessis algunes preguntes sobre el teu ús de llengües marcant la casella corresponent. L'ús total de totes les llengües a cada pregunta ha d'arribar al 100 %.

4. En una setmana normal, quin percentatge de temps fas servir les següents llengües amb **la teva família?**

Castellà	☐	☐	☐	☐	☐	☐	☐	☐	☐	☐	☐
	0%	10%	20%	30%	40%	50%	60%	70%	80%	90%	100%
Català	☐	☐	☐	☐	☐	☐	☐	☐	☐	☐	☐
	0%	10%	20%	30%	40%	50%	60%	70%	80%	90%	100%
Altres llengües	☐	☐	☐	☐	☐	☐	☐	☐	☐	☐	☐
	0%	10%	20%	30%	40%	50%	60%	70%	80%	90%	100%

5. En una setmana normal, quin percentatge de temps fas servir les següents llengües amb **els teus amics?**

Castellà	☐	☐	☐	☐	☐	☐	☐	☐	☐	☐	☐
	0%	10%	20%	30%	40%	50%	60%	70%	80%	90%	100%
Català	☐	☐	☐	☐	☐	☐	☐	☐	☐	☐	☐
	0%	10%	20%	30%	40%	50%	60%	70%	80%	90%	100%
Altres llengües	☐	☐	☐	☐	☐	☐	☐	☐	☐	☐	☐
	0%	10%	20%	30%	40%	50%	60%	70%	80%	90%	100%

6. En una setmana normal, quin percentatge de temps fas servir les següents llengües a **la universitat/la feina?**

Castellà	☐	☐	☐	☐	☐	☐	☐	☐	☐	☐	☐
	0%	10%	20%	30%	40%	50%	60%	70%	80%	90%	100%
Català	☐	☐	☐	☐	☐	☐	☐	☐	☐	☐	☐
	0%	10%	20%	30%	40%	50%	60%	70%	80%	90%	100%
Altres llengües	☐	☐	☐	☐	☐	☐	☐	☐	☐	☐	☐
	0%	10%	20%	30%	40%	50%	60%	70%	80%	90%	100%

7. En una setmana normal, quin percentatge de temps fas servir les següents llengües en **anar de compres**?

Castellà	☐	☐	☐	☐	☐	☐	☐	☐	☐	☐	☐
	0%	10%	20%	30%	40%	50%	60%	70%	80%	90%	100%
Català	☐	☐	☐	☐	☐	☐	☐	☐	☐	☐	☐
	0%	10%	20%	30%	40%	50%	60%	70%	80%	90%	100%
Altres llengües	☐	☐	☐	☐	☐	☐	☐	☐	☐	☐	☐
	0%	10%	20%	30%	40%	50%	60%	70%	80%	90%	100%

8. En una setmana normal, quin percentatge de temps fas servir les següents llengües amb **desconeguts**?

Castellà	☐	☐	☐	☐	☐	☐	☐	☐	☐	☐	☐
	0%	10%	20%	30%	40%	50%	60%	70%	80%	90%	100%
Català	☐	☐	☐	☐	☐	☐	☐	☐	☐	☐	☐
	0%	10%	20%	30%	40%	50%	60%	70%	80%	90%	100%
Altres llengües	☐	☐	☐	☐	☐	☐	☐	☐	☐	☐	☐
	0%	10%	20%	30%	40%	50%	60%	70%	80%	90%	100%

9. Quan estàs a soles, amb quina freqüència **penses** en les següents llengües?

Castellà	☐	☐	☐	☐	☐	☐	☐	☐	☐	☐	☐
	0%	10%	20%	30%	40%	50%	60%	70%	80%	90%	100%
Català	☐	☐	☐	☐	☐	☐	☐	☐	☐	☐	☐
	0%	10%	20%	30%	40%	50%	60%	70%	80%	90%	100%
Altres llengües	☐	☐	☐	☐	☐	☐	☐	☐	☐	☐	☐
	0%	10%	20%	30%	40%	50%	60%	70%	80%	90%	100%

10. Quan fas càlculs, amb quina freqüència **comptes** en les següents llengües?

Castellà	☐	☐	☐	☐	☐	☐	☐	☐	☐	☐	☐
	0%	10%	20%	30%	40%	50%	60%	70%	80%	90%	100%
Català	☐	☐	☐	☐	☐	☐	☐	☐	☐	☐	☐
	0%	10%	20%	30%	40%	50%	60%	70%	80%	90%	100%
Altres llengües	☐	☐	☐	☐	☐	☐	☐	☐	☐	☐	☐
	0%	10%	20%	30%	40%	50%	60%	70%	80%	90%	100%

IV. Competència

En esta secció, ens agradaria que consideressis la teva competència de llengua marcant la casella de 0 (=no massa bé) a 6 (=molt bé).

11.	a. Com parles **castellà**?	□0	□1	□2	□3	□4	□5	□6
	b. Com parles **català**?	□0	□1	□2	□3	□4	□5	□6
12.	a. Com entens el **castellà**?	□0	□1	□2	□3	□4	□5	□6
	b. Com entens el **català**?	□0	□1	□2	□3	□4	□5	□6
13.	a. Com llegeixes en **castellà**?	□0	□1	□2	□3	□4	□5	□6
	b. Com llegeixes en **català**?	□0	□1	□2	□3	□4	□5	□6
14.	a. Com escrius en **castellà**?	□0	□1	□2	□3	□4	□5	□6
	b. Com escrius en **català**?	□0	□1	□2	□3	□4	□5	□6

V. Actituds

En esta secció, ens agradaria que contestessis a les següents afirmacions sobre actituds lingüístiques marcant les caselles de 0 (=no hi estic d'acord) a 6 (=estic d'acord).

15.	a. Em sento "jo mateix(a)" quan parlo en **castellà**.	□0	□1	□2	□3	□4	□5	□6
	b. Em sento "jo mateix(a)" quan parlo en **català**.	□0	□1	□2	□3	□4	□5	□6
16.	a. Per a mi és important usar/arribar a usar el **castellà** com un(a) parlant natiu/va.	□0	□1	□2	□3	□4	□5	□6
	b. Per a mi és important usar/arribar a usar el **català** com un(a) parlant natiu/va.	□0	□1	□2	□3	□4	□5	□6
17.	a. Vull que els altres pensin que sóc un(a) parlant nadiu(a) del **castellà**.	□0	□1	□2	□3	□4	□5	□6
	a. Vull que els altres pensin que sóc un(a) parlant nadiu(a) del **català**.	□0	□1	□2	□3	□4	□5	□6
18.	Quina llengua/Quines llengües consideres la teva **llengua nativa**?	□ castellà	□ català	□ una altra: _____

APPENDIX 3

Language background questionnaire (Spanish version)

Perfil lingüístico español–catalán

Nos gustaría pedirte ayuda para contestar las siguientes preguntas sobre tu historial lingüístico, uso, actitudes y competencia. La encuesta contiene 18 preguntas y te llevará menos de 10 minutos completarla. No se trata de una prueba, por tanto, no hay respuestas correctas ni incorrectas. Por favor, contesta cada pregunta y responde con sinceridad, ya que solamente así se podrá garantizar el éxito de esta investigación. ¡Muchas gracias por tu ayuda!

I. Información biográfica

Nombre y apellidos _____
Año de nacimiento _____ Lugar de nacimiento _____
Residente en _____ desde _____
Tiempo pasado fuera de Cataluña _____
Nivel superior estudios _____
Profesión _____
Correo electrónico _____
Lenguas extranjeras _____

Lugar de nacimiento de la madre _____
Lugar de residencia principal _____
Profesión/estudios _____
Lenguas maternas _____

Lugar de nacimiento del padre _____
Lugar de residencia principal _____
Profesión/estudios _____
Lenguas maternas _____

Lugar de nacimiento de la pareja _____
Lugar de residencia principal _____
Profesión/estudios _____
Lenguas maternas _____

Declaración de conformidad

Por la presente, expreso que estoy de acuerdo con que la grabación y su respectiva transcripción, así como los datos que he puesto a disposición sean archivados, analizados y publicados de manera anónima y sin ánimos de lucro para fines científicos.

Esta declaración puede ser revocada enviando un correo a la siguiente dirección: jgruenke@uni-mainz.de.

(lugar, fecha) _____ (firma) _____

II. Historial lingüístico

En esta sección, nos gustaría que contestaras algunas preguntas sobre tu historial lingüístico marcando la casilla correspondiente.

1. ¿A qué edad **empezaste a aprender** las siguientes lenguas?

   Español

☐	☐	☐	☐	☐	☐	☐	☐	☐	☐	☐	☐	☐	☐	☐	☐	☐	☐	☐	☐	☐
Desde el nacimiento	1	2	3	4	5	6	7	8	9	10	11	12	13	14	15	16	17	18	19	20+

   Catalán

☐	☐	☐	☐	☐	☐	☐	☐	☐	☐	☐	☐	☐	☐	☐	☐	☐	☐	☐	☐	☐
Desde el nacimiento	1	2	3	4	5	6	7	8	9	10	11	12	13	14	15	16	17	18	19	20+

2. ¿A qué edad **empezaste a sentirte cómodo** usando las siguientes lenguas?

   Español

☐	☐	☐	☐	☐	☐	☐	☐	☐	☐	☐	☐	☐	☐	☐	☐	☐	☐	☐	☐	☐	☐
Tan pronto como recuerdo	1	2	3	4	5	6	7	8	9	10	11	12	13	14	15	16	17	18	19	20+	aún no

   Catalán

☐	☐	☐	☐	☐	☐	☐	☐	☐	☐	☐	☐	☐	☐	☐	☐	☐	☐	☐	☐	☐	☐
Tan pronto como recuerdo	1	2	3	4	5	6	7	8	9	10	11	12	13	14	15	16	17	18	19	20+	aún no

3. ¿Qué lengua utilizabais en tu **familia** cuando eras pequeño/a?

   ☐ español   ☐ catalán

III. Uso de lenguas

En esta sección, nos gustaría que contestaras algunas preguntas sobre tu uso de lenguas marcando la casilla apropiada. El uso total de todas las lenguas en cada pregunta debe llegar al 100 %.

4. En una semana normal, ¿qué porcentaje de tiempo usas las siguientes lenguas con **tu familia**?

Español	☐	☐	☐	☐	☐	☐	☐	☐	☐	☐	☐
	0%	10%	20%	30%	40%	50%	60%	70%	80%	90%	100%
Catalán	☐	☐	☐	☐	☐	☐	☐	☐	☐	☐	☐
	0%	10%	20%	30%	40%	50%	60%	70%	80%	90%	100%
Otras lenguas	☐	☐	☐	☐	☐	☐	☐	☐	☐	☐	☐
	0%	10%	20%	30%	40%	50%	60%	70%	80%	90%	100%

5. En una semana normal, ¿qué porcentaje de tiempo usas las siguientes lenguas con **tus amigos**?

Español	☐	☐	☐	☐	☐	☐	☐	☐	☐	☐	☐
	0%	10%	20%	30%	40%	50%	60%	70%	80%	90%	100%
Catalán	☐	☐	☐	☐	☐	☐	☐	☐	☐	☐	☐
	0%	10%	20%	30%	40%	50%	60%	70%	80%	90%	100%
Otras lenguas	☐	☐	☐	☐	☐	☐	☐	☐	☐	☐	☐
	0%	10%	20%	30%	40%	50%	60%	70%	80%	90%	100%

6. En una semana normal, ¿qué porcentaje de tiempo usas las siguientes lenguas en **la universidad/el trabajo**?

Español	☐	☐	☐	☐	☐	☐	☐	☐	☐	☐	☐
	0%	10%	20%	30%	40%	50%	60%	70%	80%	90%	100%
Catalán	☐	☐	☐	☐	☐	☐	☐	☐	☐	☐	☐
	0%	10%	20%	30%	40%	50%	60%	70%	80%	90%	100%
Otras lenguas	☐	☐	☐	☐	☐	☐	☐	☐	☐	☐	☐
	0%	10%	20%	30%	40%	50%	60%	70%	80%	90%	100%

7. En una semana normal, ¿qué porcentaje de tiempo usas las siguientes lenguas al **ir de compras**?

Español	☐ 0%	☐ 10%	☐ 20%	☐ 30%	☐ 40%	☐ 50%	☐ 60%	☐ 70%	☐ 80%	☐ 90%	☐ 100%
Catalán	☐ 0%	☐ 10%	☐ 20%	☐ 30%	☐ 40%	☐ 50%	☐ 60%	☐ 70%	☐ 80%	☐ 90%	☐ 100%
Otras lenguas	☐ 0%	☐ 10%	☐ 20%	☐ 30%	☐ 40%	☐ 50%	☐ 60%	☐ 70%	☐ 80%	☐ 90%	☐ 100%

8. En una semana normal, ¿qué porcentaje de tiempo usas las siguientes lenguas con **desconocidos**?

Español	☐ 0%	☐ 10%	☐ 20%	☐ 30%	☐ 40%	☐ 50%	☐ 60%	☐ 70%	☐ 80%	☐ 90%	☐ 100%
Catalán	☐ 0%	☐ 10%	☐ 20%	☐ 30%	☐ 40%	☐ 50%	☐ 60%	☐ 70%	☐ 80%	☐ 90%	☐ 100%
Otras lenguas	☐ 0%	☐ 10%	☐ 20%	☐ 30%	☐ 40%	☐ 50%	☐ 60%	☐ 70%	☐ 80%	☐ 90%	☐ 100%

9. Cuando estás solo/a, ¿con qué frecuencia **piensas** en las siguientes lenguas?

Español	☐ 0%	☐ 10%	☐ 20%	☐ 30%	☐ 40%	☐ 50%	☐ 60%	☐ 70%	☐ 80%	☐ 90%	☐ 100%
Catalán	☐ 0%	☐ 10%	☐ 20%	☐ 30%	☐ 40%	☐ 50%	☐ 60%	☐ 70%	☐ 80%	☐ 90%	☐ 100%
Otras lenguas	☐ 0%	☐ 10%	☐ 20%	☐ 30%	☐ 40%	☐ 50%	☐ 60%	☐ 70%	☐ 80%	☐ 90%	☐ 100%

10. Cuando haces cálculos, ¿con qué frecuencia **cuentas** en las siguientes lenguas?

Español	☐ 0%	☐ 10%	☐ 20%	☐ 30%	☐ 40%	☐ 50%	☐ 60%	☐ 70%	☐ 80%	☐ 90%	☐ 100%
Catalán	☐ 0%	☐ 10%	☐ 20%	☐ 30%	☐ 40%	☐ 50%	☐ 60%	☐ 70%	☐ 80%	☐ 90%	☐ 100%
Otras lenguas	☐ 0%	☐ 10%	☐ 20%	☐ 30%	☐ 40%	☐ 50%	☐ 60%	☐ 70%	☐ 80%	☐ 90%	☐ 100%

IV. Competencia

En esta sección, nos gustaría que consideraras tu competencia lingüística marcando la casilla de 0 (=no muy bien) a 6 (=muy bien).

11.	a. ¿Cómo hablas en **español**?	☐0	☐1	☐2	☐3	☐4	☐5	☐6
	b. ¿Cómo hablas en **catalán**?	☐0	☐1	☐2	☐3	☐4	☐5	☐6
12.	a. ¿Cómo entiendes el **español**?	☐0	☐1	☐2	☐3	☐4	☐5	☐6
	b. ¿Cómo entiende el **catalán**?	☐0	☐1	☐2	☐3	☐4	☐5	☐6
13.	a. ¿Cómo lees en **español**?	☐0	☐1	☐2	☐3	☐4	☐5	☐6
	b. ¿Cómo lees en **catalán**?	☐0	☐1	☐2	☐3	☐4	☐5	☐6
14.	a. ¿Cómo escribes en **español**?	☐0	☐1	☐2	☐3	☐4	☐5	☐6
	b. ¿Cómo escribes en **catalán**?	☐0	☐1	☐2	☐3	☐4	☐5	☐6

V. Actitudes

En esta sección, nos gustaría que contestara a las siguientes afirmaciones sobre actitudes lingüísticas marcando las casillas de 0 (=no estoy de acuerdo) a 6 (=estoy de acuerdo).

15.	a. Me siento "yo mismo/a" cuando hablo en **español**.	☐0	☐1	☐2	☐3	☐4	☐5	☐6
	b. Me siento "yo mismo/a" cuando hablo en **catalán**.	☐0	☐1	☐2	☐3	☐4	☐5	☐6
16.	a. Para mí es importante usar/llegar a usar el **español** como un(a) hablante nativo/a.	☐0	☐1	☐2	☐3	☐4	☐5	☐6
	b. Para mí es importante usar/llegar a usar el **catalán** como un(a) hablante nativo/a.	☐0	☐1	☐2	☐3	☐4	☐5	☐6
17.	a. Quiero que los demás piensen que soy un(a) hablante nativo(a) del **español**.	☐0	☐1	☐2	☐3	☐4	☐5	☐6
	a. Quiero que los demás piensen que soy un(a) hablante nativo(a) del **catalán**.	☐0	☐1	☐2	☐3	☐4	☐5	☐6
18.	¿Qué lengua(s) consideras tu **lengua materna**?	☐ español		☐ catalán		☐ otra: _____		

APPENDIX 4

Intonation surveys (Spanish and Catalan)

Note: Colum 1 gives the identifier of each scenario, column 3 indicates the order in which the scenarios were presented to the participants in the Spanish and Catalan DCT.

	Utterance type		Spanish	Catalan
1	**Neutral statements**			
1a1	Neutral broad-focus statements (one unit)	1	Mira el dibujo y di lo que hace la mujer.	Mira el dibuix i digues què fa la dona.
			—*Bebe una limonada.*	—*Beu una llimonada.*
1a2		2	Mira el dibujo y di lo que ves. ¡Empieza la frase con «Marina», por favor!	Mira el dibuix i digues què fa la Marina. Comença la frase amb «la Marina», si us plau!
			—*Marina come mandarinas.*	—*La Marina menja mandarines.*
1b	Enumerations	3	Di los días de la semana.	Digues els dies de la setmana.
			—*Lunes, martes, miércoles, jueves, viernes, sábado y domingo.*	—*Dilluns, dimarts, dimecres, dijous, divendres, dissabte i diumenge.*
	Neutral statements with peripheral elements (more than one unit)			
1c1	Dislocations	4	Imagínate que acabas de conocer a alguien de Palma y resulta que tú habías vivido allí muchos años. ¿Cómo se lo dirías?	Imagina't que acabes de conèixer algú de Palma i resulta que tu hi havies viscut molts anys. Com li ho diries?
			—*Yo viví muchos años allí, en Palma.*	—*Jo també hi havia viscut molts anys, a Palma.*
1c2	Vocatives	5	Estás en casa con tu hija, María, que está viendo la tele. Dile que sales un momento a merendar.	Estàs a casa amb teva filla, la Maria, que està mirant la tele. Digues-li que surts un moment a berenar.
			—*María, salgo un momento a merendar.* —*Salgo un momento a merendar, María.*	—*Maria, surto un moment a berenar.*

	Utterance type		Spanish	Catalan
1c3	Parenthetical elements	6	Estás enfermo/a y esta mañana has tenido que ir al médico. Di que has ido a pesar de la lluvia.	Estàs malalt(a) i aquest matí has hagut d'anar al metge. Digues que hi has anat malgrat la pluja.
			—*Esta mañana, a pesar de la lluvia, he ido al médico.*	
1c4	Appositions	7	Conoces a dos chicas que se llaman Marina, una rubia y otra morena. Di que hoy has visto a la morena.	Coneixes dues noies que es diuen Marina, una rossa i l'altra morena. Digues que avui has vist la (Marina) morena.
			—*He visto a Marina, la morena.*	—*Avui he vist la Marina, la morena.*
	Biased statements			
1d	Contrastive-focus statements	8	Entras en una frutería y resulta que la vendedora es un poco sorda. No te oye bien, y, después de decirle que querías naranjas, ella te pregunta si son limones lo que quieres. Dile que no, que lo que quieres son naranjas.	Entres en una botiga on hi ha una dona que és una mica sorda. No t'ha sentit bé, i, després de dir-li que et posi un parell de taronges, et pregunta si són llimones, el que vols. Digues-li que no, que allò que vols són taronges.
			—*¡Señora, no quiero limones, quiero naranjas!*	—*No! TARONGES, vull.*
1e1	Exclamative statements	9	Entras en una panadería y huele muy bien a pan. Díselo a la panadera.	Entres en un forn i sents una oloreta de pa molt bona. Digues-li-ho, a la fornera.
			—*¡Qué olor a pan tan bueno! ¡Qué bien huele a pan!*	—*Quina oloreta més bona!*
1e2		12	Te invitan a una paella y es la más buena que te has comido en tu vida, estás encantado/a. ¿Qué dices?	Et conviden a paella i és la més bona que has menjat mai, quedes encantat/da. Què dius?
			—*¡Está buenísimo! ¡Está divino!*	—*Que n'és, de bona! Que bona que és!*

	Utterance type		Spanish	Catalan
1f	Contradiction statements	10	Una amiga y tú estáis hablando de unos amigos que se van de viaje. Tú sabes seguro/a que irán a Granada, pero tu amiga piensa, también bastante segura, que irán a Córdoba. Dile, convencido/a, que no, que irán a Granada.	Tu i una amiga esteu parlant d'uns amics que volen comprar un pis i no saben segur on aniran a viure. Tu saps que viuran a Granada. La teva amiga et diu que no, que viuran a Còrdova. Digues-li, convençuda, que no, que viuran a Granada.
			—¡Que no, que se van a Granada!	—Que no, que viuran a Granada!
1e	Dubitative statements	11	Te han encargado comprar un regalo para alguien que no conoces mucho y te da un poco de apuro no acertar. Dile a la persona que te lo ha encargado que igual no le gusta el regalo que le compres.	Un amic teu t'encarrega de comprar un regal per a algú que no coneixes gaire i et fa por de no triar-lo bé. Digues-li que potser no li agradarà el que li puguis comprar.
			—Puede que no le guste el regalo que le compre.	—Potser no li agradarà...
2	**Neutral polar questions**			
2a1	Information-seeking yes–no questions	13	Entras en una tienda y le preguntas al vendedor si tiene mandarinas.	Entres en una botiga on mai no havies entrat i demanes si tenen mandarines.
			—¿Tiene mandarinas?	—(Que) teniu mandarines?
2a2		14	Tienes que llevar a tu hermano pequeño al campo de fútbol, pero tienes mucha prisa. Pregúntale a un amigo tuyo si lo puede llevar.	Havies de portar el teu germà petit al camp de futbol, però tens molta pressa. Demana a un amic teu si l'hi duria.
			—¿Lo llevarías? ¿Puedes llevarlo?	—Que l'hi duries?
2a3		15	Una amiga y tu habéis tenido una duda lingüística y te ha prometido preguntárselo a su vecina, que es filóloga. Pregúntale si ha hablado ya con la filóloga.	Una amiga i tu heu tingut un dubte lingüístic i t'ha promès preguntar-li-ho a la seva veïna, que és filòloga. Demana-li si ja ha parlat amb la filòloga.
			—¿Has hablado ya con la filóloga?	—(Que) Ja has parlat amb la filòloga?

	Utterance type		Spanish	Catalan
2b1	Information-seeking yes–no questions (with a peripheral element)	16	Llamas por teléfono a casa de una amiga que se llama María, pero no está. Más tarde llamas de nuevo, pero ella no coge el teléfono. ¿Cómo preguntas si ya ha llegado?	Truques per telèfon a casa d'una companya que es diu Maria i no hi és. Més tard hi tornes a trucar. Demana als seus pares si hi és.
			—¿*Ha llegado ya, María?* ¿*María, ha llegado ya?*	—(*Que*) *ja hi és, la Maria?*
2b2		17	Estás buscando a María, pero no la encuentras. Ves a alguien que la conoce y, después de hablar un poco sobre ella, le preguntas si la ha visto.	Busques la Maria i no la trobes. Veus algú que saps que la coneix i li demanes si l'ha vista.
			—¿*La has visto, a María?*	—(*Que*) *l'has vist, la Maria?*
2c	Disjunctive questions	18	De postre hay helado de vainilla o de avellana. Pregúntales a los invitados si quieren helado de vainilla o de avellana.	Has comprat gelat de vainilla i d'avellana pel teu sant. Demana als convidats si volen gelat de vainilla o d'avellana.
			—¿*Quieren helado de vainilla o de avellana?*	—(*Que*) *voleu gelat de vainilla o d'avellana?*
	Biased polar questions			
2d	Exclamative yes–no questions	19	Acabas de cenar con un amigo y ves que él se para delante de una pastelería. Como acabáis de cenar, pregúntale, muy sorprendida/o, si tiene hambre.	Acabes de dinar amb un amic i veus que s'atura davant una pastisseria. Pregunta-li (tota estranyat/da, perquè acabeu de dinar) si té gana.
			—¿¡*Todavía tienes hambre!?*	—*Tens gana?!*
2e	Confirmation-seeking yes–no questions	20	Juan dijo que venía a cenar. Le pides que te lo confirme.	En Jaume ha dit que vindria a dinar. Li demanes que t'ho confirmi.
			—(*Juan*), ¿*vienes a cenar* (*conmigo*)?	—*Vindràs a dinar, no?*

	Utterance type		Spanish	Catalan
3	**Neutral wh-questions**			
3a1	Information-seeking wh-questions	21	Pregunta qué hora es.	Pregunta quina hora és.
			—¿Qué hora es?	—Quina hora és?
3a2		22	Tienes que hacer un viaje a Lisboa y quieres comprar un regalo a la persona que te va a acoger, a la que apenas conoces y con la que quieres quedar bien. Quieres que un amigo te aconseje y le preguntas qué le llevaría.	Has de viatjar a París i vols comprar un regal a una persona que no coneixes gaire i amb qui vols quedar bé. Vols que un amic teu t'aconselli i li demanes què li duria.
			—¿Qué le comprarías?	—Què li duries?
	Biased wh-questions			
3b	Exclamative wh-questions (with counterexpectational meaning)	23	Un amigo tuyo te habla de un conocido que debía mucho dinero al banco y seguía tomando préstamos. Pregunta (sorprendido/a, porque ya sabías que debía mucho dinero) cuánto dinero acabó debiendo.	Un amic teu et parla d'un conegut que devia molts diners al banc i encara demanava més préstecs. Pregunta (sorprès(a), perquè ja ho sabies, que en devia molts) quants diners va acabar devent.
			—¡¿Cuánto acabó debiendo!?	—Quants diners va acabar devent?!
3c	Imperative wh-question	24	Le pides a tu hijo que te haga arreglos en la casa y no estás seguro/a de que lo vaya a hacer, ya que no es la primera vez que se lo pides. Pregúntale, medio enfadado, cuándo lo hará.	Demanes a un germà que et faci una feina i no estàs gaire segur(a) que la faci, perquè ja li ho has demanat altres vegades i mai no t'ha ajudat. Demana-li, mig enfadat/da, quan t'ho farà.
			—¿Cuándo lo harás?	—Quan m'ho faràs?!
4	**Echo questions**			
4a	Echo yes–no questions	25	Te dan la hora, pero no acabas de entenderla. Piensas que te han dicho que son las nueve. Vuelve a preguntar.	Et diuen l'hora, però no l'has acabat d'entendre. Et penses que t'han dit la una. Torna a demanar si és la una.
			—¿(Qué has dicho que) son las nueve?	—(Què has dit que) és la una?

Appendix 4. Intonation surveys (Spanish and Catalan)

	Utterance type		Spanish	Catalan
4b	Echo wh-questions-questions	26	Te han preguntado adónde vas, pero no sabes si lo has entendido bien. Pregunta qué te han preguntado.	T'han demanat on anaves, però no saps si ho has entès bé. Demana si és això el que t'han demanat.
			—¿(Qué me has pedido) dónde voy?	—(Què m'has demanat) a on anava?
4c	Exclamative echo yes–no questions (with counterexpectational meaning)	27	Te dicen que un compañero tuyo, Mario, se presenta a alcalde. No te lo crees y lo vuelves a preguntar (muy extrañado/a).	Et diuen que un company teu, en Mario, es presenta a alcalde. No t'ho acabes de creure i ho tornes a preguntar (molt estranyat/da).
			—¿¡(Qué dices que) Mario se presenta a alcalde!?	—Què dius que en Mario es presenta a alcalde!?
5	**Imperatives**			
5a	Commands	28	Estás en la recepción de un hotel y entra una pareja que quiere una habitación. Diles que rellenen un formulario.	Imagina't que ets recepcionista en un hotel i entra una parella que vol una habitació. Digues-los que omplin un formulari.
			—Rellenen este formulario.	—Ompliu aquest formulari.
5b	Requests	29	Quieres ir al cine con un amigo. Te dice que tiene trabajo, pero tú sabes que el trabajo lo puede dejar. ¿Cómo lo convencerías?	Vols anar al cinema amb un amic. Et diu que té feina, però tu saps que la pot deixar per a més endavant. Com ho faràs per convèncer-lo?
			—Va, vente al cine… ¡Venga, hombre!	—Va, vine!
6	**Vocatives**			
6	Vocative	30	Entras en la casa de una amiga tuya, Marina, pero al entrar no la ves. Llámala.	Entres a casa d'una amiga teva, la Maria, però quan ets a dins no la veus. Penses que deu ser a la seva habitació. Crida-la.
			—¡Marina!	—Maria!

APPENDIX 5

Dialogue (with translation)

Joan y Mercè están en la oficina trabajando. Son las 12 h.
'Joan and Mercè are working in the office. It's 12 o'clock.'

Mercè: Joan, voy al bar a tomar un café. ¿Que quieres venir conmigo? (A)
'Joan, I'm going to the bar for a coffee. Would you like to come with me?'

Joan: ¿Que tomas café al mediodía? (B)
'Do you drink coffee at noon?'

Mercè: Sí, claro. Yo bebo muchísimo, de café (D1). Probablemente, demasiado...
'Yes, of course. I drink a lot of coffee. Probably too much ...'

Joan: Pues, no lo sabía... Bueno, termino esto y vamos, ¿vale?
'Well, I didn't know that ... Fine, I'll just finish this and we can go, okay?'

Mercè: ¡Que no! Me apetece ir ahora mismo. Ya sabes que tengo muy poca, de paciencia (D2).
'No! I feel like going right now. You know that I have very little pacience, don't you?'

Salen de la oficina.
'They leave the office.'

Joan: ¿Que llueve? (C)
'Is it raining?'

Mercè: Parece que sí...
'It seems so...'

Mercè se resbala y se cae al suelo.
'Mercè slips and falls to the ground.'

Joan: ¡Uy! ¿Que te has hecho daño? (D)
'Oops, did you hurt yourself?'

Index

A
apposition 152, 177f, 294
Aragonese 8, 318f
attrition 95f, 348, 361

B
bilingualism 16, 19, 83, 97, 110–112, 133f, 137, 353
    balanced bilingualism 111f, 115–117, 119, 123f, 132–134
borrowing 24, 82, 85–91, 99f, 355, 358
    borrowing scale 89f, 99

C
Complementarity Principle 111, 115, 129, 134
construction 50, 100, 333f, 354f
convergence 83f, 99, 254, 314, 319, 336, 348, 356f
cross-linguistic influence 80, 82
    see also interference, transfer
deaccentuation 40, 52, 55, 62, 156f, 197, 206–210, 289, 329

D
declaratives see statements
dialect 15–17, 23, 318, 351–353, 363
    dialect levelling 23, 94
diglossia 9, 13, 113, 353–356
discourse-completion task 145–147
dislocation 27, 151, 171f, 249, 285–288
divergence 84f
dominance see language dominance

E
educational system 10–13, 131, 138, 332, 349

F
focus 43, 68, 180–182, 212, 224, 325f

I
imperatives 72, 78, 270–275, 292, 301, 346f
interference 17f, 39, 81, 82, 91–93, 352
interlanguage 94, 331, 354
interrogatives see questions

L
labelling 44, 57, 64f, 151–158, 197, 213, 255
language attitudes 88f, 120f 143f, 353
language dominance 112–125, 126–129, 132–135, 228–230, 314–316
    index of language dominance 118, 120, 124f, 126, 129
language loss 85, 94f, 97f

M
meaning 25, 50–52, 86, 99, 129, 293
migration 11, 14–16, 23, 92, 319, 326f, 349–353
morphology 26, 59, 89f, 177
multilingualism 12, 15, 81, 97, 112

N
normalization 10f, 19, 23

P
phrasing 40, 48f, 60–62, 152f, 180
proficiency 94, 110, 113f, 118–123, 142
purism 17, 20, 351

Q
questions
    yes/no questions 28–31, 38
    information-seeking questions 189–231, 296f, 329–338
    confirmation-seeking questions 240–243, 298, 340f
    questions with *que* 192f, 219–225, 278–285, 329–338
    wh-questions 243–261, 298–300, 341–344
    echo questions 262–270, 300f, 344–346

S
standardization 9f, 15, 97, 317f, 331, 336f
statements 74, 160–169, 294f, 324–329
stress 40, 55, 59f, 99, 109, 153, 290f
substratum interference see interference
syntax 26–31, 55f, 90

T
ToBI 44f, 56–59, 63f, 152, 154–156
tonal density 55, 62, 289, 310, 329
transfer 17, 81, 82, 85f, 91–93, 348f–351, 354

V
variation 2, 22f, 31, 204, 312–317, 352f
vocatives 79, 172f, 275–277, 301f, 347f
vowels 36f, 100, 153f